Mar Caribe

OCÉANO ATLÁNTICO

Barranquilla
Cartagena
Maracaibo
Caracas
Barquisimeto

VENEZUELA

Río Orinoco

Georgetown
Paramaribo
Cayenne

GUYANA
SURINÁM
GUAYANA FRANCESA (Francia)

Medellín
Manizales
Bogotá
Cali

CORDILLERA DE LOS ANDES

COLOMBIA

Salto Angel

Quito

ECUADOR

Ecuador

Guayaquil
Cuenca

Iquitos

Manaus

Río Amazonas

Belém

Islas Galápagos (Ec.)

Fortaleza

Cajamarca

Río Branco

BRASIL

Recife

Trujillo

PERÚ

Lima
Machu Picchu
Ayacucho
Cuzco

Salvador

OCÉANO PACÍFICO

I. Pinta
I. Fernandina
I. Marchena
I. San Salvador
Santa Cruz
I. Santa Cruz
I. Isabela
Puerto Ayora
I. San Cristóbal
Puerto Villamil
Puerto Baquerizo Moreno

ISLAS GALÁPAGOS (ECUADOR)

Arequipa
Arica
Iquique

Lago Titicaca
La Paz

BOLIVIA

Cochabamba
Sucre
Potosí

Santa Cruz

Brasilia

Belo Horizonte

Desierto de Atacama

PARAGUAY

Antofagasta

Salta

Asunción
Salto Iguazú

São Paulo
Santos

Río de Janeiro

Trópico de Capricornio

OCÉANO PACÍFICO

Cabo Norte
Volcán Katiki
Hanga Roa
Cabo Cumming
Mataveri

ISLA de PASCUA (CHILE)

CHILE

San Miguel de Tucumán

CORDILLERA DE LOS ANDES

ARGENTINA

Coquimbo

Córdoba

Pôrto Alegre

Valparaíso
Santiago
Mendoza
Rosario
Rivera

Río Paraná
Río Uruguay

URUGUAY

Buenos Aires
La Plata
Montevideo

Concepción

OCÉANO ATLÁNTICO

Bahía Blanca

Río de la Plata

Puerto Montt

OCÉANO PACÍFICO

Estrecho de Magallanes

Islas Malvinas (Br.)

Punta Arenas

TIERRA DEL FUEGO
Cabo de Hornos

## América del Sur

PEARSON
**myspanishlab** ¡Hola!

Part of the award-winning MyLanguageLabs suite of online learning and assessment systems for basic language courses, MySpanishLab brings together—in one convenient, easily navigable site—a wide array of language-learning tools and resources, including an interactive version of the *¡Anda! Curso elemental* student text, an online Student Activities Manual, and all materials from the audio and video programs. Chapter Practice Tests, tutorials, and English grammar Readiness Checks personalize instruction to meet the unique needs of individual students. Instructors can use the system to make assignments, set grading parameters, listen to student-created audio recordings, and provide feedback on student work. MySpanishLab can be packaged with the text at a substantial savings. For more information, visit us online at http://www.mylanguagelabs.com/books.html.

| A GUIDE TO *¡ANDA! CURSO ELEMENTAL* ICONS | | |
|---|---|---|
| | **Readiness Check for MySpanishLab** | This icon, located in each chapter opener, reminds students to take the Readiness Check in MySpanishLab to test their understanding of the English grammar related to the Spanish grammar concepts in the chapter. |
| | **MySpanishLab** | This icon indicates that additional resources for pronunciation and grammar are available in MySpanishLab. |
| | **Text Audio Program** | This icon indicates that recorded material to accompany *¡Anda! Curso elemental* is available in MySpanishLab (www.mylanguagelabs.com), on audio CD, or on the Companion Website (www.pearsonhighered.com/anda). |
| | **Pair Activity** | This icon indicates that the activity is designed to be done by students working in pairs. |
| | **Group Activity** | This icon indicates that the activity is designed to be done by students working in small groups or as a whole class. |
| | **Web Activity** | This icon indicates that the activity involves use of the Internet. |
| | **Video icon** | This icon indicates that a video episode is available for the *Ambiciones siniestras* video series that accompanies the *¡Anda! Curso elemental* program. The video is available on DVD and in MySpanishLab. |
| | **Student Activities Manual** | This icon indicates that there are practice activities available in the *¡Anda! Curso elemental* Student Activities Manual. The activities may be found either in the printed version of the manual or in the interactive version available through MySpanishLab. Activity numbers are indicated in the text for ease of reference. |
| | **Workbooklet** | This icon indicates that an activity has been reproduced in the *Workbooklet* available as a print supplement or in MySpanishLab. |
| | **Interactive Globe** | This icon indicates that additional cultural resources in the form of videos, web links, interactive maps, and more, relating to particular countries, are organized on an interactive globe in MySpanishLab. |

Curso elemental

¡Anda!

**Second Edition**

**AUDREY L. HEINING-BOYNTON**
**GLYNIS S. COWELL**
University of North Carolina, Chapel Hill

WITH

Jean LeLoup

María del Carmen Caña Jiménez

**PEARSON**

Boston    Columbus    Indianapolis    New York    San Francisco    Upper Saddle River
Amsterdam    Cape Town    Dubai    London    Madrid    Milan    Munich    Paris    Montréal    Toronto
Delhi    Mexico City    São Paulo    Sydney    Hong Kong    Seoul    Singapore    Taipei    Tokyo

Executive Editor, Spanish: Julia Caballero
Editorial Assistant: Samantha Pritchard
Executive Marketing Manager: Kris Ellis-Levy
Senior Marketing Manager: Denise Miller
Marketing Assistant: Michele Marchese
Development Coordinator: Celia Meana
Development Editor, ¡Anda!: Janet García-Levitas
Development Editor, Spanish: Meriel Martínez
Senior Managing Editor for Product Development:
    Mary Rottino
Associate Managing Editor (Production): Janice Stangel
Senior Production Project Manager: Nancy Stevenson
Executive Editor, MyLanguageLabs: Bob Hemmer
Senior Media Editor: Samantha Alducin

Development Editor, MyLanguageLabs: Bill Bliss
Editorial Coordinator, World Languages:
    Regina Rivera
Senior Art Director: Maria Lange
Cover Design: DePinho Design
Operations Manager: Mary Fischer
Operations Specialist: Alan Fischer
Full-Service Project Management: Melissa Sacco,
    PreMediaGlobal
Composition: PreMediaGlobal
Printer/Binder: R.R. Donnelley
Cover Printer: Lehigh - Phoenix Color
Publisher: Phil Miller
Cover Image: Shutterstock Images

This book was set in 10/12 Janson Roman.

Credits and acknowledgments borrowed from other sources and reproduced, with permission, in this textbook appear on appropriate pages within the text (or on page **A47**).

Student Edition, ISBN-10: 0-205-05010-7
Student Edition, ISBN-13: 978-0-205-05010-9
Annotated Instructor's Edition, ISBN-10: 0-205-05011-5
Annotated Instructor's Edition, ISBN-13: 978-0-205-05011-6

10 9 8 7 6 5 4 3 2 1

www.pearsonhighered.com

# Brief Contents

# FIRST

**CAPÍTULO PRELIMINAR A**

This preliminary chapter is meant to jump-start learning. In some cases, students may have studied some Spanish previously and may already be familiar with this material. The vocabulary in this chapter is high frequency, high usage. Encourage students to refer to this chapter if they forget certain words and expressions.

**CAPÍTULO 1**

Verb presentations such as *tener* are done *deductively*, in which students are given the rules/forms and go directly to practice, to streamline presentation time. All grammar presentations in this chapter are deductive.

**CAPÍTULO 2**

We have made the conscious decision to present a very brief introduction to *gustar*. In order to practice vocabulary in complete sentences, we have decided to introduce the *I, you, s/he, it* forms with *gustar*. Indirect object pronouns and a more in-depth explanation of *gustar* will appear in *Capítulo 8*.

(The numbers next to the grammar and vocabulary sections indicate their location within the chapter.)

| | CAPÍTULO PRELIMINAR A<br>Para empezar | CAPÍTULO 1<br>¿Quiénes somos? | CAPÍTULO 2<br>La vida universitaria |
|---|---|---|---|
| **Vocabulary sections** | **1** Saludos, despedidas y presentaciones p. 4<br>**2** Expresiones útiles para la clase p. 8<br>**4** Los cognados p. 10<br>**7** Los adjetivos de nacionalidad p. 14<br>**8** Los números 0–30 p. 16<br>**9** La hora p. 18<br>**10** Los días, los meses y las estaciones p. 20<br>**11** El tiempo p. 23 | **1** La familia p. 32<br>**6** Gente p. 40<br>**9** Los números 31–100 p. 47 | **1** Las materias y las especialidades p. 62<br>**2** La sala de clase p. 65<br>**5** Los números 100–1.000 p. 72<br>**6** En la universidad p. 74<br>**8** Las emociones y los estados p. 79<br>**10** Los deportes y los pasatiempos p. 81 |
| **Grammar sections** | **3** El alfabeto p. 9<br>**5** Los pronombres personales p. 11<br>**6** El verbo **ser** p. 13<br>**12** **Gustar** p. 25 | **2** El verbo **tener** p. 34<br>**3** Sustantivos singulares y plurales p. 36<br>**4** El masculino y el femenino p. 37<br>**5** Los artículos definidos e indefinidos p. 38<br>**7** Los adjetivos posesivos p. 41<br>**8** Los adjetivos descriptivos p. 43 | **3** Presente indicativo de verbos regulares p. 67<br>**4** La formación de preguntas y las palabras interrogativas p. 70<br>**7** El verbo **estar** p. 76<br>**9** El verbo **gustar** p. 80 |
| **Pronunciation** | | Vowels p. 33 | Word stress and accent marks p. 63 |
| **Cultural readings and country focus** | • **Nota cultural** Cómo se saluda la gente p. 7<br>• **Nota cultural** ¿Tú o usted? p. 12<br>• **Nota cultural** Los hispanos p. 16<br>• **Nota cultural** El mundo hispano p. 17 | • **Nota cultural** Los apellidos en el mundo hispano p. 33<br>• **Nota cultural** El español, lengua diversa p. 46 | • **Nota cultural** Las universidades hispanas p. 64<br>• **Nota cultural** Los deportes en el mundo hispano p. 84 |
| **Cultura** | | **LOS ESTADOS UNIDOS** p. 52 | **MÉXICO** p. 88 |
| **Escucha** | | Presentaciones p. 49<br>**Estrategia:** Determining the topic and listening for words you know p. 49 | Una conversación p. 86<br>**Estrategia:** Listening for the gist p. 86 |
| **¡Conversemos!** | | Communicating about people you know p. 50 | Communicating about university life p. 86 |
| **Escribe** | | Un poema p. 50<br>**Estrategia:** Organizing ideas / Preparing to write p. 50 | Una descripción p. 87<br>**Estrategia:** Creating sentences p. 87 |
| **Ambiciones siniestras** | | **Lectura:** *Conexiones* p. 54<br>**Estrategia:** Recognizing cognates p. 54<br>**Video:** *¿Quiénes son?* p. 56 | **Lectura:** *Las solicitudes* p. 90<br>**Estrategia:** Skimming p. 90<br>**Video:** *La aventura comienza* p. 92 |

# SEMESTER

| CAPÍTULO 3 Estamos en casa | CAPÍTULO 4 Nuestra comunidad | CAPÍTULO 5 ¡A divertirse! La música y el cine | CAPÍTULO 6 ¡Sí, lo sé! |
|---|---|---|---|
| **1** La casa p. 98 <br> **3** Los muebles y otros objetos de la casa p. 106 <br> **4** Los quehaceres de la casa p. 109 <br> **5** Los colores p. 111 <br> **7** Los números 1.000–100.000.000 p. 116 | **1** Los lugares p. 134 <br> **3** ¿Qué tienen que hacer? ¿Qué pasa? p. 140 <br> **7** Servicios a la comunidad p. 149 | **1** El mundo de la música p. 172 <br> **6** El mundo del cine p. 184 | **Reviewing strategies** p. 206 |
| **2** Algunos verbos irregulares p. 101 <br> **6** Algunas expresiones con *tener* p. 113 <br> **8** *Hay* p. 119 | **2** *Saber* y *conocer* p. 137 <br> **4** Los verbos con cambio de raíz p. 142 <br> **5** El verbo *ir* p. 146 <br> **6** *Ir* + *a* + infinitivo p. 147 <br> **8** Las expresiones afirmativas y negativas p. 151 <br> **9** Un repaso de *ser* y *estar* p. 154 | **2** Los adjetivos demostrativos p. 175 <br> **3** Los pronombres demostrativos p. 177 <br> **4** Los adverbios p. 179 <br> **5** El presente progresivo p. 180 <br> **7** Los números ordinales p. 187 <br> **8** *Hay que* + infinitivo p. 188 <br> **9** Los pronombres de complemento directo y la "*a*" personal p. 189 | **Comunicación** <br> Recycling of **Capítulo Preliminar A** to **Capítulo 5** |
| The letters *h, j,* and *g* p. 99 | The letters *c* and *z* p. 135 | Diphthongs and linking p. 173 | |
| • **Nota cultural** ¿Dónde viven los españoles? p. 105 <br> • **Nota cultural** Las casas "verdes" p. 119 | • **Nota cultural** Actividades cotidianas: Las compras y el paseo p. 136 <br> • **Nota cultural** La conciencia social p. 151 | • **Nota cultural** La música latina en los Estados Unidos p. 178 <br> • **Nota cultural** La influencia hispana en el cine norteamericano p. 186 | |
| **ESPAÑA** p. 124 | **HONDURAS, GUATEMALA Y EL SALVADOR** p. 161 | **NICARAGUA, COSTA RICA Y PANAMÁ** p. 195 | **Cultura** |
| Una descripción p. 121 <br> **Estrategia:** Listening for specific information p. 121 | El voluntariado p. 157 <br> **Estrategia:** Paraphrasing what you hear p. 157 | Planes para un concierto p. 192 <br> **Estrategia:** Anticipating content p. 192 | |
| Communicating about homes and life at home p. 122 | Communicating about ways to serve the community p. 158 | Communicating about music and film p. 193 | |
| Un anuncio p. 123 <br> **Estrategia:** Noun → adjective agreement p. 123 | Una tarjeta postal p. 159 <br> **Estrategia:** Proofreading p. 159 | Una reseña p. 194 <br> **Estrategia:** Peer review/editing p. 194 | |
| **Lectura:** *El concurso* p. 126 <br> **Estrategia:** Scanning p. 126 <br> **Video:** *¡Tienes una gran oportunidad!* p. 128 | **Lectura:** *Las cosas no son siempre lo que parecen* p. 164 <br> **Estrategia:** Skimming and Scanning (II) p. 164 <br> **Video:** *¿Quiénes son en realidad?* p. 166 | **Lectura:** *La búsqueda de Eduardo* p. 198 <br> **Estrategia:** Anticipating content p. 198 <br> **Video:** *Se conocen* p. 200 | Recap of Episodes 1–5 |

**CAPÍTULO 3**

We have chosen to introduce *conocer* in *Capítulo 3* as an irregular verb and to focus on the meaning "to be acquainted with." In *Capítulo 4* we present *saber* and contrast it with *conocer*.

**CAPÍTULO 4**

We have chosen to briefly introduce the *personal "a"* here in *Capítulo 4* with *conocer*, and then reintroduce/recycle it in *Capítulo 5* with direct object pronouns. The focus in *Capítulo 4* is to make students aware of the concept. In *Capítulo 5* there will be further practice with direct object pronouns as well as recycling of the *personal "a"* with *conocer*.

**CAPÍTULO 5**

Although a complete grammatical explanation of adverbs would include the fact that students can also modify verbs, whole phrases, clauses, or sentences, we have chosen to simplify the presentation. Also note that we have chosen to use the word *describe* rather than *modify* in the presentation. Although both words are grammatically acceptable, *describe* is a bit more casual and user-friendly.

**CAPÍTULO 6**

In this chapter we have synthesized the main points of the first five chapters in a recycled format for students to practice the new skills they are learning. You will note that all of these activities have the students *put it all together*—in other words, *all of the activities in Capítulo 6 are communicative.*

## CAPÍTULO PRELIMINAR B

The intention of *Capítulo Preliminar B* is to methodically *review* and guide all students to begin at a similar point. You will notice that *Capítulo Preliminar B* moves more by small chunks of material than *Capítulo 6* does. *Capítulo Preliminar B* assumes that students need more step-by-step guidance and remediation so they can all arrive at a more common starting point.

## CAPÍTULO 7

We have chosen to present both regular and irregular preterits in the same chapter to allow for greater focus on form and practice. You will note that this is the primary grammatical focus for *Capítulo 7*. In *Capítulos 8–11*, the preterit will be continually recycled (along with the present tense) for additional practice and reinforcement.

## CAPÍTULO 8

Preferences for presenting the preterit and imperfect tenses can be highly personal. *¡Anda!* breaks down the use of the imperfect into four categories; you may prefer to combine them in a different way. The goal is to reach the learning styles of as many students as possible.

# SECOND

(The numbers next to the grammar and vocabulary sections indicate their location within the chapter.)

| | CAPÍTULO PRELIMINAR B Introducciones y repasos | CAPÍTULO 7 ¡A comer! | CAPÍTULO 8 ¿Qué te pones? |
|---|---|---|---|
| **Vocabulary sections** | Capítulo Preliminar A Capítulo 1 Capítulo 2 Capítulo 3 Capítulo 4 Capítulo 5 | **1** La comida p. 256 **5** La preparación de las comidas p. 269 **7** En el restaurante p. 277 | **1** La ropa p. 294 **5** Las telas y los materiales p. 309 |
| **Grammar sections** | Capítulo Preliminar A Capítulo 1 Capítulo 2 Capítulo 3 Capítulo 4 Capítulo 5 | **2** Repaso del complemento directo p. 261 **3** El pretérito (Parte I) p. 263 **4** El pretérito (Parte II) p. 265 **6** Algunos verbos irregulares en el pretérito p. 272 | **2** Los pronombres de complemento indirecto p. 299 **3** *Gustar* y verbos como *gustar* p. 302 **4** Los pronombres de complemento directo e indirecto usados juntos p. 305 **6** Las construcciones reflexivas p. 312 **7** El imperfecto p. 317 |
| **Pronunciation** | | The different pronunciations of *r* and *rr* p. 257 | The letters *ll* and *ñ* p. 295 |
| **Cultural readings and country focus** | | • **Nota cultural** Las comidas en el mundo hispano p. 261 • **Nota cultural** La comida hispana p. 271 | • **Nota cultural** Zara: la moda internacional p. 298 • **Nota cultural** Los centros comerciales en Latinoamérica p. 316 |
| **Cultura** | | **CHILE Y PARAGUAY** p. 284 | **ARGENTINA Y URUGUAY** p. 324 |
| **Escucha** | | Las compras en el mercado p. 281 **Estrategia:** Combining strategies p. 281 | En el centro comercial p. 321 **Estrategia:** Guessing meaning from context p. 321 |
| **¡Conversemos!** | | Communicating about food shopping and party planning p. 282 | Communicating about clothing and fashion p. 322 |
| **Escribe** | | Una descripción p. 283 **Estrategia:** Topic sentence and conclusion p. 283 | Un email p. 323 **Estrategia:** Circumlocution p. 323 |
| **Ambiciones siniestras** | Ambiciones siniestras | **Lectura:** *El rompecabezas* p. 286 **Estrategia:** Predicting p. 286 **Video:** *¡Qué rico está el pisco!* p. 288 | **Lectura:** *¿Quién fue?* p. 326 **Estrategia:** Guessing meaning from context p. 326 **Video:** *El misterio crece* p. 328 |

viii

# SEMESTER

## CAPÍTULO 9

The presentation of pronouns, which began in *Capítulo 6*, concludes in this chapter with a review of all pronouns. Students have learned the difference between the form and functions of all the sets of pronouns and in *Capítulo 9* are able to analyze their uses through comparison and context.

## CAPÍTULO 10

There are several approaches to teaching the commands. In *¡Anda!* we made the conscious decision to chunk the material; the authors have chosen to present the familiar commands first for several reasons. First, they are the commands that students will tend to use the most among themselves. Next, the affirmative commands are very easy to form. Finally, the negative familiar commands prepare the students for the formal commands to follow, and ultimately for the subjunctive.

## CAPÍTULO 11

You will note that, yet again, we are taking a complex concept, the subjunctive, and breaking it down into "bite-size" chunks that make learning the concept possible. Also, you may have taught these fixed expressions as impersonal expressions with *ser*. In *¡Anda!*, we have chosen to simply call them fixed expressions, under the headings of opinion, doubt, probability, wishes, desires, and hopes. This eliminates any confusion between "personal" and "impersonal", because these expressions can be used regardless of the relationship to the speaker.

## CAPÍTULO 12

After giving students strategies on how to conduct an overall review, this chapter is organized by beginning with communicative and engaging activities that focus on grammar and vocabulary from *Capítulo 7*. The recycling continues to move through the chapters, ending with *Capítulo 11*. This is followed by a more comprehensive review, truly *putting all the chapters together*. Finally, there is a recycling of countries, presented in *Capítulos 7–11*.

## Why *¡Anda!* 2e?

We were pleased by the enthusiastic response to the first edition of *¡Anda!*, and we are honored that so many schools have chosen to adopt it for use in their basic Spanish courses. The response confirmed our sense that many schools were feeling a need for a new kind of Spanish textbook program.

We wrote *¡Anda!* originally because Spanish instructors had told us that their courses were changing. In survey after survey, in focus group after focus group, they had said that they were finding it increasingly difficult to accomplish everything they wanted in their elementary Spanish courses. They told us that contact hours were decreasing, that class sizes were increasing, and that more and more courses were being taught partially or totally online. They told us that their lives and their students' lives were busier than ever. And as a result, they told us, there simply wasn't enough time available to do everything they wanted to do. Some reported that they felt compelled to gallop through their text in order to cover all the grammar and vocabulary, omitting important cultural topics and limiting their students' opportunities to develop and practice communication skills. Others said that they had made the awkward choice to use a text designed for first-year Spanish over three or even four semesters. Many instructors were looking for new ways to address the challenges they and their students were facing. We created *¡Anda!* to meet this need.

The challenges we heard about from all these Spanish instructors still exist today, and thus our goals and guiding principles for the second edition of the *¡Anda!* program remain the same as they were in the first edition. But we have made many changes in response to helpful suggestions from users of the earlier edition, and we have sought to make the program even more flexible than its predecessor and even more focused on students' and instructors' needs.

## NEW to This Edition

Among the many changes we have made to the *¡Anda!* program are the following:

▶ New *learning objectives* accompanying each *Vocabulario* and *Gramática* chunk make the learning goal of each chunk transparent to students.

▶ New *¿Cómo andas?* self-assessment boxes align directly to the chapter objectives and are numbered to match with the corresponding *Comunicación* sections, helping students tie the objectives to learning outcomes.

▶ The new *¡Conversemos!* section provides communicative activities that combine vocabulary and grammar from the chapter and recycle content from previous chapters, providing students with the opportunity to "put it all together."

▶ A new *writing strategy* has been added to each *Escribe* box to guide students to think critically about the writing process before they begin to write.

▶ A new *chapter opening organizer* now includes references to the complete *¡Anda!* program, allowing for easier integration of supplements and resources.

▶ Revised headings and design for each *Comunicación* section, now labeled I and II, help students and instructors effectively navigate the parts of the chapter.

- *Pronunciation practice and activities* are now available solely on MySpanishLab and in the Student Activities Manual. Icons in the text guide students to these resources for more detailed information and practice in an interactive setting that allows for more personalized instruction.
- Many new *teacher annotations* have been added to provide additional guidance and options for instructors and to aid in lesson planning and implementation.
- New *21st Century Skills* teacher annotations help instructors develop students' language proficiency around modes of communicative competency reflecting real-life communication.
- Various versions of the text are now available. In addition to the *complete text, split volumes* are now available, each containing a single semester's worth of material. Also available are special versions designed for *high beginner's* courses and *hybrid* courses. Together with the unbound or *"A la carte"* version and a full range of customization options, these versions give instructors the flexibility to adopt the content and format that best meets the needs of their students and program.

# The *¡Anda!* Story

The *¡Anda!* program was developed to provide practical responses to the challenges today's Spanish instructors are facing. Its innovations center around three key areas:

1. Realistic goals with a realistic approach

2. Focus on student motivation

3. Tools to promote success

## Realistic goals with a realistic approach

*¡Anda!* is the first college-level Spanish program conceived from the outset as a four-semester sequence of materials. The *¡Anda!* program is divided into two halves, *¡Anda! Curso elemental* and *¡Anda! Curso intermedio,* each of which can be completed in one academic year.

Each volume's scope and sequence has been carefully designed, based on advice and feedback from hundreds of instructors and users at a wide variety of institutions. Each volume introduces a realistic number of new vocabulary words, and the traditional first-year grammar sequence has been spread over two volumes so that it can be presented in four semesters rather than two. As a result, students have adequate time throughout the course to focus on communication, culture, and skills development, and to master the vocabulary and grammar concepts to which they are introduced.

Each volume of *¡Anda!,* for both ***Curso elemental*** and ***Curso intermedio,*** has been structured to foster preparation, recycling, and review within the context of a multi-semester sequence of courses. The ten regular chapters are complemented by two *preliminary* chapters and two *recycling* chapters.

| | |
|---|---|
| Capítulo Preliminar A | Capítulo Preliminar B |
| Capítulo 1 | Capítulo 7 |
| Capítulo 2 | Capítulo 8 |
| Capítulo 3 | Capítulo 9 |
| Capítulo 4 | Capítulo 10 |
| Capítulo 5 | Capítulo 11 |
| Capítulo 6 (recycling) | Capítulo 12 (recycling) |

■ *Capítulo Preliminar A* is designed with **ample vocabulary** to get students up and running and to give them a **sense of accomplishment** quickly. Many students will already be familiar with some of this vocabulary. It also has students reflect on the question "Why study Spanish?"

■ *Capítulo Preliminar B* is a **review** of Preliminary A through Chapter 5 and allows those who join the class midyear, or those who need a refresher, to get up to speed at the beginning of the second half of the book.

■ *Capítulos 1–5* and *7–11* are **regular** chapters.

■ *Chapters 6 and 12* are **recycling** chapters. No new material is presented. Designed for in-class use, these chapters recycle and recombine previously presented vocabulary, grammar, and culture, giving students more time to practice communication without the burden of learning new grammar or vocabulary. NEW rubrics have been provided in these chapters to assess student performance. They provide clear expectations for students as they review.

Each regular chapter of *¡Anda!* provides a realistic approach for the achievement of realistic goals.

■ New material is presented in manageable amounts, or **chunks,** allowing students to assimilate and practice without feeling overwhelmed.

■ Each chapter contains a **realistic** number of new vocabulary words.

■ Vocabulary and grammar explanations are interspersed, each **introduced at the point of need.**

■ Grammar explanations are clear and concise, utilizing either deductive or inductive presentations, and include many supporting examples followed by practice activities. The inductive presentations provide students with examples of a grammar concept. They then must formulate the rule(s) through the use of guiding questions. The inductive presentations are accompanied by a new *Explícalo tú* heading and an icon that directs them to Appendix 1 where answers to the questions in the presentations may be found.

■ Practice begins with **mechanical** exercises, for which there are correct answers, progresses through more **meaningful,** structured activities in which the student is guided but has some flexibility in determining the appropriate responses, and ends with **communicative** activities in which students are manipulating language to create personalized responses.

## Focus on student motivation

The many innovative features of *¡Anda!* that have made it such a successful program continue in the second edition to help instructors generate and sustain interest on the part of their students, whether they be of traditional college age or adult learners:

- Chapters are organized around themes that reflect **student interests** and tap into students' **real-life experiences.**

- Basic **vocabulary** has been selected and tested through *¡Anda!'s* development for its relevance and support, while additional words and phrases are offered so that **students can personalize** their responses and acquire the vocabulary that is most meaningful to them. Additional vocabulary items are found in *Vocabulario útil* boxes throughout the chapters as well as in Appendix 3 (*También se dice…*).

- Activities have been designed to foster active participation by students. The focus throughout is on giving students opportunities to speak and on allowing instructors to **increase the amount of student "talk time"** in each class period. The majority of activities **elicit students' ideas and opinions,** engaging them to respond to each other on a variety of levels. Abundant pair and group activities encourage students to learn from and support each other, creating a comfortable arena for language learning.

- **No assumptions** are made concerning previous experience with Spanish or with language learning in general.

- Each activity is designed to begin with **what the student already knows.**

- A **high-interest mystery story,** *Ambiciones siniestras,* runs through each chapter. Two episodes are presented in each regular chapter, one as the chapter's reading selection (in the *Lectura* section), the other in a corresponding video segment (in the *Video* section).

- Both **"high" and "popular" culture** are woven throughout the chapters to enable students to learn to recognize and appreciate cultural diversity as they explore behaviors and values of the Spanish-speaking world. They are encouraged to think critically about these cultural practices and gifts to society.

## Tools to promote success

The *¡Anda!* program includes many unique features and components designed to help students succeed at language learning and their instructors at language teaching.

### Student learning support

- A **"walking tour"** of the *¡Anda!* text and supplements helps students navigate their language program materials and understand better the whys and hows of learning Spanish.

- Explicit, systematic **recycling boxes with page references** help students link current learning to previously studied material in earlier chapters or sections.

- **Periodic review and self-assessment** boxes (*¿Cómo andas? I* and *¿Cómo andas? II*) help students gauge their understanding and retention of the material presented. A final assessment in each chapter (*Y por fin, ¿cómo andas?*) offers a comprehensive self-assessment.

- **Student notes** provide additional explanations and guidance in the learning process. Some of these contain cross-references to other student supplements. Others offer learning strategies (*Estrategia*) and additional information (*Fíjate*).

- **MySpanishLab** offers students a wealth of online resources and a supportive environment for completing homework assignments. When enabled by the instructor, a "Need Help" box appears as students are doing online homework activities, providing links to English and Spanish grammar tutorials, e-book sections, and additional practice activities—all directly relevant to the task at hand. Hints, verb charts, a glossary, and many other resources are available as well.

- A **Workbooklet**, available separately, allows students to complete the activities that involve writing without having to write in their copies of the textbook.

## Instructor teaching support

One of the most important keys to student success is instructor success. The *¡Anda!* program has all of the support that you have come to expect and, based on our research, it offers many other enhancements!

- The **Annotated Instructor's Edition** of *¡Anda!* offers a wealth of materials designed to help instructors teach effectively and efficiently. Strategically placed annotations explain the text's methodology and function as **a built-in course in language teaching methods.**

- **Estimated time indicators** for presentational materials and practice activities help instructors create lesson plans.

- Other annotations provide **additional activities** and suggested answers.

- **The annotations are color-coded** and labeled for ready reference and ease of use.

- A treasure trove of supplemental activities, available for download in the **Extra Activities** folder of MySpanishLab, allows instructors to choose additional materials for in-class use.

## Teacher Annotations

The teacher annotations in the *¡Anda!* program fall into several categories:

- **Methodology:** A deep and broad set of methods notes designed for the novice instructor.

- **Section Goals:** Set of student objectives for each section.

- **National Standards:** Information containing the correlation between each section with the National Standards as well as tips for increasing student performance.

- **21st Century Skills:** Interpreting the new Partnership for the 21st Century skills and the National Standards. These skills enumerate what is necessary for successful 21st century citizens.

- **Planning Ahead:** Suggestions for instructors included in the chapter openers to help prepare materials in advance for certain activities in the chapter. Also provided is information regarding which activities to assign to students prior to them coming to class.

- **Warm-up:** Suggestions for setting up an activity or how to activate students' prior knowledge relating to the task at hand.

- **Suggestion:** Teaching tips that provide ideas that will help with the implementation of activities and sections.

- **Note:** Additional information that instructors may wish to share with students beyond what is presented in the text.

- **Expansion:** Ideas for variations of a topic that may serve as wrap-up activities.

- **Follow-up:** Suggestions to aid instructors in assessing student comprehension.

- **Notes:** Information on people, places, and things that aid in the completion of activities and sections by providing background knowledge.

- **Additional Activity:** Independent activities related to the ones in the text that provide further practice than those supplied in the text.

- **Alternate Activity:** Variations of activities provided to suit each individual classroom and preferences.

- **Heritage Language Learners:** Suggestions for the heritage language learners in the classroom that provide alternatives and expansions for sections and activities based on prior knowledge and skills.

- **Audioscript:** Written script of all *Escucha* recordings.

- **Recap of *Ambiciones siniestras:*** A synopsis of both the *Lectura* and *Video* sections for each episode of *Ambiciones siniestras*.

## The authors' approach

Learning a language is an exciting, enriching, and sometimes life-changing experience. The development of the *¡Anda!* program, and now its second edition, is the result of many years of teaching and research that guided the authors independently to make important discoveries about language learning, the most important of which center on the student. Research-based and pedagogically sound, *¡Anda!* is also the product of extensive information gathered firsthand from numerous focus group sessions with students, graduate instructors, adjunct faculty, full-time professors, and administrators in an effort to determine the learning and instructional needs of each of these groups.

### The Importance of the National Foreign Language Standards in *¡Anda!*

The *¡Anda!* program continues to be based on the *National Foreign Language Standards*. The five organizing principles (the 5 Cs) of the Standards for language teaching and learning are at the core of *¡Anda!*: **Communication, Cultures, Connections, Comparisons,** and **Communities.** Each chapter opener identifies for the instructor where and in what capacity each of the 5 Cs are addressed. The **Weave of Curricular Elements** of the *National Foreign Language Standards* provides additional organizational structure for *¡Anda!* Those components of the **Curricular Weave** are: **Language System, Cultural Knowledge, Communication Strategies, Critical Thinking Skills, Learning Strategies, Other Subject Areas,** and **Technology.** Each of the Curricular Weave elements is omnipresent and, like the 5 Cs, permeates all aspects of each chapter of *¡Anda!*

- The *Language System*, which comprises components such as grammar, vocabulary, and phonetics, is at the heart of each chapter.

- The *Comunicación* sections of each chapter present vocabulary, grammar, and pronunciation at the point of need and maximum usage. Streamlined presentations are utilized that allow the learner to be immediately successful in employing the new concepts.

- *Cultural Knowledge* is approached thematically, making use of the chapter's vocabulary and grammar. Many of the grammar and vocabulary activities are presented in cultural contexts. Cultural presentations begin with the two-page chapter openers and always start with what the students already know about the cultural themes/concepts from their home, local, regional, or national cultural perspective. The *Nota cultural* and *Les presento mi país* sections provide rich cultural information about each Hispanic country.

- *Communication and Learning Strategies* are abundant with tips for both students and instructors on how to maximize studying and in-class learning of Spanish, as well as how to utilize the language outside of the classroom.

- *Critical Thinking Skills* take center stage in *¡Anda!* Questions throughout the chapters, in particular tied to the cultural presentations, provide students with the opportunities to answer more than discrete point questions. The answers students are able to provide do indeed require higher-order thinking, but at a linguistic level completely appropriate for a beginning language learner.

- With regard to *Other Subject Areas*, *¡Anda!* is diligent with regard to incorporating **Connections** to other disciplines via vocabulary, discussion topics, and suggested activities. This edition also highlights a **Communities** section, which includes experiential and service learning activities in the Student Activities Manual.

- Finally, *technology* is taken to an entirely new level with **MySpanishLab** and the *Ambiciones siniestras* DVD. The authors and Pearson Education believe that technology is a means to the end, not the end in and of itself, and so the focus is not on the technology per se, but on how that technology can deliver great content in better, more efficient, more interactive, and more meaningful ways.

By embracing the National Foreign Language Standards and as a result of decades of experience teaching Spanish, the authors believe that:

- A **student-centered classroom** is the best learning environment.

- Instruction must **begin where the learner is,** and all students come to the learning experience with prior knowledge that needs to be tapped.

- All students can learn in a **supportive environment** where they are encouraged to take risks when learning another language.

- **Critical thinking** is an important skill that must constantly be encouraged, practiced, and nurtured.

- **Learners** need to **make connections** with other disciplines in the Spanish classroom.

With these beliefs in mind, the authors have developed hundreds of creative and meaningful language-learning activities for the text and supporting components that employ students' imagination and engage the senses. For both students and instructors, they have created an instructional program that is **manageable, motivating,** and **clear.**

xvi

# The Authors

## Audrey Heining-Boynton

Audrey Heining-Boynton received her Ph.D. from Michigan State University and her M.A. from The Ohio State University. Her career spans K-12 through graduate school teaching, most recently as Professor of Education and Spanish at The University of North Carolina at Chapel Hill. She has won many teaching awards, including the prestigious ACTFL Anthony Papalia Award for Excellence in Teacher Education, the Foreign Language Association of North Carolina (FLANC) Teacher of the Year Award, and the UNC ACCESS Award for Excellence in Working with LD and ADHD students. Dr. Heining-Boynton is a frequent presenter at national and international conferences, has published more than one hundred articles, curricula, textbooks, and manuals, and has won nearly $4 million in grants to help create language programs in North and South Carolina. Dr. Heining-Boynton has also held many important positions: President of the American Council on the Teaching of Foreign Languages (ACTFL), President of the National Network for Early Language Learning, Vice President of Michigan Foreign Language Association, board member of the Foreign Language Association of North Carolina, committee chair for Foreign Language in the Elementary School for the American Association of Teachers of Spanish and Portuguese, and elected Executive Council member of ACTFL. She is also an appointed two-term *Foreign Language Annals* Editorial Board member and guest editor of the publication.

## Glynis Cowell

Glynis Cowell is the Director of the Spanish Language Program in the Department of Romance Languages and Literatures and an Assistant Dean in the Academic Advising Program at The University of North Carolina at Chapel Hill. She has taught first-year seminars, honors courses, and numerous face-to-face and hybrid Spanish language courses. She also team-teaches a graduate course on the theories and techniques of teaching foreign languages. Dr. Cowell received her M.A. in Spanish Literature and her Ph.D. in Curriculum and Instruction, with a concentration in Foreign Language Education, from The University of North Carolina at Chapel Hill. Prior to joining the faculty at UNC-CH in August 1994, she coordinated the Spanish Language Program in the Department of Romance Studies at Duke University. She has also taught Spanish at both the high school and community college level. At UNC-CH she has received the Students' Award for Excellence in Undergraduate Teaching as well as the Graduate Student Mentor Award for the Department of Romance Languages and Literatures.

Dr. Cowell has directed teacher workshops on Spanish language and cultures and has presented papers and written articles on the teaching of language and literature, the transition to blended and online courses in language teaching, and teaching across the curriculum. She is the co-author of two other college textbooks.

## Faculty Reviewers

Silvia P. Albanese, *Nassau Community College*
Ángeles Aller, *Whitworth University*
Nuria Alonso García, *Providence College*
Carlos Amaya, *Eastern Illinois University*
Tyler Anderson, *Colorado Mesa University*
Aleta Anderson, *Grand Rapids Community College*
Ines Anido, *Houston Baptist University*
Inés Arribas, *Bryn Mawr College*
Tim Altanero, *Austin Community College*
Bárbara Ávila-Shah, *University at Buffalo*
Ann Baker, *University of Evansville*
Ashlee Balena, *University of North Carolina–Wilmington*
Amy R. Barber, *Grove City College*
Mark Bates, *Simpson College*
Charla Bennaji, *New College of Florida*
Georgia Betcher, *Fayetteville Technical Community College*
Christine Blackshaw, *Mount Saint Mary's University*
Marie Blair, *University of Nebraska*
Kristy Britt, *University of South Alabama*
Isabel Zakrzewski Brown, *University of South Alabama*
Eduardo Cabrera, *Millikin University*
Majel Campbell, *Pikes Peak Community College*
Paul Cankar, *Austin Community College*
Monica Cantero, *Drew University*
Aurora Castillo, *Georgia College & State University*
Tulio Cedillo, *Lynchburg College*
Kerry Chermel, *Northern Illinois University*
Carrie Clay, *Anderson University*
Alyce Cook, *Columbus State University*
Jorge H. Cubillos, *University of Delaware*
Shay Culbertson, *Jefferson State Community College*
Cathleen G. Cuppett, *Coker College*
Addison Dalton, *Virginia Tech*
John B. Davis, *Indiana University, South Bend*
Laura Dennis, *University of the Cumberlands*
Lisa DeWaard, *Clemson University*
Sister Carmen Marie Diaz, *Silver Lake College of the Holy Family*
Joanna Dieckman, *Belhaven University*
Donna Donnelly, *Ohio Wesleyan University*
Kim Dorsey, *Howard College*
Mark A. Dowell, *Randolph Community College*
Dina A. Fabery, *University of Central Florida*
Jenny Faile, *University of South Alabama*
Juliet Falce-Robinson, *University of California, Los Angeles*
Mary Fatora-Tumbaga, *Kauai Community College*
Ronna Feit, *Nassau Community College*
Irene Fernandez, *North Shore Community College*
Erin Fernández Mommer, *Green River Community College*
Rocío Fuentes, *Clark University*

Judith Garcia-Quismondo, *Seton Hill University*
Elaine Gerber, *University of Michigan at Dearborn*
Andrea Giddens, *Salt Lake Community College*
Amy Ginck, *Messiah College*
Kenneth Gordon, *Winthrop University*
Agnieszka Gutthy, *Southeastern Louisiana University*
Shannon Hahn, *Durham Technical Community College*
Nancy Hanway, *Gustavus Adolphus College*
Sarah Harmon, *Cañada College*
Marilyn Harper, *Pellissippi State Community College*
Mark Harpring, *University of Puget Sound*
Dan Hickman, *Maryville College*
Amarilis Hidalgo de Jesus, *Bloomsburg University*
Charles Holloway, *University of Louisiana Monroe*
Anneliese Horst Foerster, *Queens University of Charlotte*
John Incledon, *Albright College*
William Jensen, *Snow College*
Qiu Y. Jimenez, *Bakersfield College*
Roberto Jiménez, *Western Kentucky University (Glasgow Regional Center)*
Valerie Job, *South Plains College*
Michael Jones, *Schenectady County Community College*
Dallas Jurisevic, *Metropolitan Community College*
Hilda M. Kachmar, *St. Catherine University*
Amos Kasperek, *University of Oklahoma*
Melissa Katz, *Albright College*
Lydia Gil Keff, *University of Denver*
Nieves Knapp, *Brigham Young University*
Melissa Knosp, *Johnson C. Smith University*
Pedro Koo, *Missouri State University*
Allison D. Krogstad, *Central College*
Courtney Lanute, *Edison State College*
Rafael Lara-Martinez, *New Mexico Institute of Mining and Technology*
John Lance Lee, *Durham Technical Community College*
Roxana Levin, *St. Petersburg College: Tarpon Springs Campus*
Penny Lovett, *Wake Technical Community College*
Paula Luteran, *Hutchinson Community College*
Katie MacLean, *Kalamazoo College*
Eder F. Maestre, *Western Kentucky University*
William Maisch, *University of North Carolina, Chapel Hill*
H.J. Manzari, *Washington and Jefferson College*
Lynne Flora Margolies, *Manchester College*
Anne Mattrella, *Naugatuck Valley Community College*
Maria R. Matz, *University of Massachusetts, Lowell*
Sandra Delgado Merrill, *University of Central Missouri*
Lisa Mershcel, *Duke University*
Geoff Mitchell, *Maryville College*
Charles H. Molano, *Lehigh Carbon Community College*
Javier Morin, *Del Mar College*
Noemi Esther Morriberon, *Chicago State University*
Gustavo Obeso, *Western Kentucky University*

**xviii**

i

Elizabeth Olvera, *University of Texas at San Antonio*
Michelle Orecchio, *University of Michigan*
Martha T. Oregel, *University of San Diego*
Cristina Pardo-Ballister, *Iowa State University*
Edward Anthony Pasko, *Purdue University, Calumet*
Joyce Pauley, *Moberly Area Community College*
Gilberto A. Pérez, *Cal Baptist University*
Beth Pollack, *New Mexico State University*
Silvia T. Pulido, *Brevard Community College*
JoAnne B. Pumariega, *Penn State Berks*
Lynn C. Purkey, *University of Tennessee at Chattanooga*
Aida Ramos-Sellman, *Goucher College*
Alice S. Reyes, *Marywood University*
Rita Ricaurte, *Nebraska Wesleyan University*
Geoffrey Ridley Barlow, *Purdue University, Calumet*
Daniel Robins, *Cabrillo College*
Sharon D. Robinson, *Lynchburg College*
Ibis Rodriguez, *Metropolitan University, SUAGM*
David Diego Rodríguez, *University of Illinois, Chicago*
Mileta Roe, *Bard College at Simon's Rock*
Donna Boston Ross, *Catawba Valley Community College*
Marc Roth, *St. John's University*
Kristin Routt, *Eastern Illinois University*
Christian Rubio, *University of Louisiana at Monroe*
Claudia Sahagún, *Broward College*
Adán Salinas, *Southwestern Illinois College*
Ruth Sánchez Imizcoz, *The University of the South*
Love Sánchez-Suárez, *York Technical College*
Gabriela Segal, *Arcadia University*
Diana Semmes, *University of Mississippi*
Michele Shaul, *Queens University of Charlotte*
Steve Sheppard, *University of North Texas, Denton*
Roger K. Simpson, *Clemson University*
Carter Smith, *University of Wisconsin–Eau Claire*
Nancy Smith, *Allegheny College*
Ruth Smith, *University of Louisiana at Monroe*
Margaret L. Snyder, *Moravian College*
Wayne Steely, *Saint Joseph's College*
Irena Stefanova, *Santa Clara University*
Benay Stein, *Northwestern University*
Gwen H. Stickney, *North Dakota State University*
Erika M. Sutherland, *Muhlenberg College*
Carla A. Swygert, *University of South Carolina*
Sarah Tahtinen-Pacheco, *Bethel University*
Luz Consuelo Triana-Echeverria, *St. Cloud State University*
Cynthia Trocchio, *Kent State University*
Elaini Tsoukatos, *Mount St. Mary's University*
Robert Turner, *Shorter University*
Ivelisse Urbán, *Tarleton State University*
Maria Vallieres, *Villanova University*

Sharon Van Houte, *Lorain County Community College*
Yertty VanderMolen, *Luther College*
Kristi Velleman, *American University*
Gayle Vierma, *University of Southern California*
Phoebe Vitharana, *Le Moyne College*
Richard L.W. Wallace, *Crowder College*
Martha L. Wallen, *University of Wisconsin–Stout*
Mary H. West, *Des Moines Area Community College*
Michelangelo Zapata, *Western Kentucky University*
Theresa Zmurkewycz, *Saint Joseph's University*

## Faculty Focus Groups

Stephanie Aaron, *University of Central Florida*
María J. Barbosa, *University of Central Florida*
Ileana Bougeois-Serrano, *Valencia Community College*
Samira Chater, *Valencia Community College*
Natalie Cifuentes, *Valencia Community College*
Ana Ma. Diaz, *University of Florida*
Aida E. Diaz, *Valencia Community College*
Dina A. Fabery, *University of Central Florida*
Ana J. Caldero Figueroa, *Valencia Community College*
Pilar Florenz, *University of Central Florida*
Stephanie Gates, *University of Florida*
Antonio Gil, *University of Florida*
José I. González, *University of Central Florida*
Victor Jordan, *University of Florida*
Alice A. Korosy, *University of Central Florida*
Joseph Menig, *Valencia Community College*
Odyscea Moghimi-Kon, *University of Florida*
Kathryn Dwyer Navajas, *University of Florida*
Julie Pomerleau, *University of Central Florida*
Anne Prucha, *University of Central Florida*
Lester E. Sandres Rápalo, *Valencia Community College*
Arcadio Rivera, *University of Central Florida*
Elizabeth Z. Solis, *University of Central Florida*
Dania Varela, *University of Central Florida*
Helena Veenstra, *Valencia Community College*
Hilaurmé Velez-Soto, *University of Central Florida*
Roberto E. Weiss, *University of Florida*
Robert Williams, *University of Central Florida*
Sara Zahler, *University of Florida*

# Acknowledgments

The second edition of *¡Anda! Curso elemental* is the result of careful planning between ourselves and our publisher and ongoing collaboration with students and you, our colleagues. We look forward to continuing this dialogue and sincerely appreciate your input. We owe special thanks to the many members of the Spanish-teaching community whose comments and suggestions helped shape the pages of every chapter—you will see yourselves everywhere. We gratefully acknowledge the reviewers for this second edition, and we thank in particular our *¡Anda! Advisory Board* for their invaluable support, input, and feedback. The Board members are:

Megan Echevarría, *University of Rhode Island*

Luz Font, *Florida State College at Jacksonville*

Yolanda Gonzalez, *Valenica College*

Linda Keown, *University of Missouri*

Jeff Longwell, *New Mexico State University*

Gillian Lord, *University of Florida*

Dawn Meissner, *Anne Arundel Community College*

María Monica Montalvo, *University of Central Florida*

Markus Muller, *Long Beach State University*

Joan Turner, *University of Arkansas – Fayetteville*

Donny Vigil, *University of North Texas, Denton*

Iñigo Yanguas, *San Diego State University*

We are also grateful to those who have collaborated with us in the writing of *¡Anda!*

We owe many thanks to Megan Echevarría for her superb work on the Student Activities Manual. We also owe great thanks to Donny Vigil for his authoring of the Testing Program as well as Anastacia Kohl for her important Testing Program authoring contributions.

Equally important are the contributions of the highly talented individuals at Pearson Education. We wish to express our gratitude and deep appreciation to the many people at Pearson who contributed their ideas, tireless efforts, and publishing experience to this second edition of *¡Anda! Curso elemental.* First, we thank Phil Miller, Publisher, and Julia Caballero, Executive Editor, whose support and guidance have been essential. We are indebted to Janet García-Levitas, Development Editor, for all of her hard work, suggestions, attention to detail, and dedication to the programs. We have also been fortunate to have Celia Meana, Development Coordinator, bring her special talents to the project, helping to create the outstanding final product. We would also like to thank Bob Hemmer and Samantha Alducin for all of the hard work on the integration of technology for the *¡Anda!* program with MySpanishLab.

Our thanks to Meriel Martínez, Development Editor, for her efficient and meticulous work in managing the preparation of the Student Activities Manual and the Testing Program. Thanks to Samantha Pritchard, Editorial Assistant, for attending to many administrative details.

Our thanks also go to Denise Miller, Senior Marketing Manager, for her strong support of *¡Anda!,* creating and coordinating all marketing and promotion for this second edition.

Many thanks are also due to Nancy Stevenson, Senior Production Editor, who guided *¡Anda!* through the many stages of production, and to our Art Manager, Gail Cocker. We continue to be indebted to Andrew Lange for the amazing illustrations that translate our vision.

We would like to sincerely thank Mary Rottino, Senior Managing Editor for Product Development, for her unwavering support and commitment to *¡Anda!* and Janice Stangel, Associate Managing Editor, Production, for her support and commitment to the success of *¡Anda!* We also thank our colleagues and students from across the country who inspire us and from whom we learn.

And finally, our love and deepest appreciation to our families for all of their support during this journey: David; John, Jack, and Kate.

Audrey L. Heining-Boynton

Glynis S. Cowell

# A WALKING TOUR

## ¡Hola!
## ¡Bienvenidos!

I'm Audrey Heining-Boynton

and I'm Glynis Cowell

We are the authors of *¡Anda!* and we were thinking that when you visit a new place, one of the best ways to get to know your new environment quickly is to consult your guidebook before you take the trip! We thought it would be a good idea for you to join us on a "walking tour" of your new Spanish textbook and supplementary materials because we know from experience that language texts have a unique organization that is different from that of other textbooks. . . . They use terminology that you might not be familiar with, and lots of the material is written in the language you don't know yet. So let's get on with the tour!

*Here it is!*

Curso elemental

¡Anda!

Heining-Boynton | Cowell
SECOND EDITION

xxiii

# CHECK OUT THE "MAP" OF YOUR BOOK!

**Scope and Sequence.** You can think of the scope and sequence as the roadmap of the book. The scope tells you what is covered, and the sequence shows you the order of those topics. In other words, the scope and sequence tells you where everything is! It's a very useful tool for navigating *¡Anda!*

## SEMESTER 1

### Preliminary A

This chapter gets you up and running quickly, presenting many easy-to-learn words that will allow you to begin speaking in Spanish very quickly. You should feel good about how much Spanish you can use after studying the preliminary chapter.

### Chapters 1–5

These are the main textbook chapters. Each chapter has an overall theme—like food, for example—and teaches you the words to use (vocabulary) and how to put them together in a sentence (grammar) so that you can talk about that subject. You'll focus on communication (speaking, listening, reading, and writing) as well as culture.

## SEMESTER 2

### Preliminary B

This chapter reviews the basic vocabulary and grammar from the first half of the book. Maybe you need this; maybe you don't. Maybe you are joining this class from another school or from high school and you need a little refresher. That's what this chapter is for!

### Chapters 7–11

These are typical chapters, just like *Chapters 1–5* above.

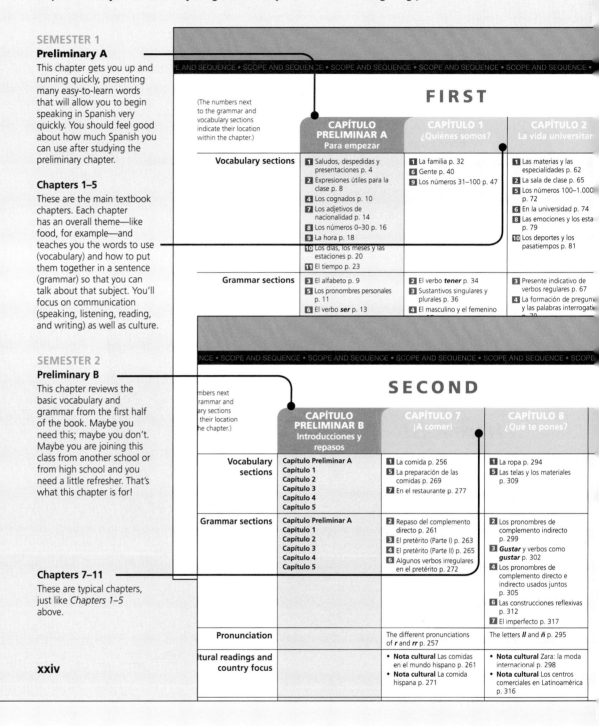

(The numbers next to the grammar and vocabulary sections indicate their location within the chapter.)

### FIRST

| | CAPÍTULO PRELIMINAR A Para empezar | CAPÍTULO 1 ¿Quiénes somos? | CAPÍTULO 2 La vida universitar |
|---|---|---|---|
| **Vocabulary sections** | **1** Saludos, despedidas y presentaciones p. 4 <br> **2** Expresiones útiles para la clase p. 8 <br> **4** Los cognados p. 10 <br> **7** Los adjetivos de nacionalidad p. 14 <br> **8** Los números 0–30 p. 16 <br> **9** La hora p. 18 <br> **10** Los días, los meses y las estaciones p. 20 <br> **11** El tiempo p. 23 | **1** La familia p. 32 <br> **6** Gente p. 40 <br> **9** Los números 31–100 p. 47 | **1** Las materias y las especialidades p. 62 <br> **2** La sala de clase p. 65 <br> **5** Los números 100–1.000 p. 72 <br> **6** En la universidad p. 74 <br> **8** Las emociones y los esta p. 79 <br> **10** Los deportes y los pasatiempos p. 81 |
| **Grammar sections** | **3** El alfabeto p. 9 <br> **5** Los pronombres personales p. 11 <br> **6** El verbo *ser* p. 13 | **2** El verbo *tener* p. 34 <br> **3** Sustantivos singulares y plurales p. 36 <br> **4** El masculino y el femenino | **3** Presente indicativo de verbos regulares p. 67 <br> **4** La formación de pregunt y las palabras interrogati |

### SECOND

| | CAPÍTULO PRELIMINAR B Introducciones y repasos | CAPÍTULO 7 ¡A comer! | CAPÍTULO 8 ¿Qué te pones? |
|---|---|---|---|
| **Vocabulary sections** | Capítulo Preliminar A <br> Capítulo 1 <br> Capítulo 2 <br> Capítulo 3 <br> Capítulo 4 <br> Capítulo 5 | **1** La comida p. 256 <br> **5** La preparación de las comidas p. 269 <br> **7** En el restaurante p. 277 | **1** La ropa p. 294 <br> **5** Las telas y los materiales p. 309 |
| **Grammar sections** | Capítulo Preliminar A <br> Capítulo 1 <br> Capítulo 2 <br> Capítulo 3 <br> Capítulo 4 <br> Capítulo 5 | **2** Repaso del complemento directo p. 261 <br> **3** El pretérito (Parte I) p. 263 <br> **4** El pretérito (Parte II) p. 265 <br> **6** Algunos verbos irregulares en el pretérito p. 272 | **2** Los pronombres de complemento indirecto p. 299 <br> **3** *Gustar* y verbos como *gustar* p. 302 <br> **4** Los pronombres de complemento directo e indirecto usados juntos p. 305 <br> **6** Las construcciones reflexivas p. 312 <br> **7** El imperfecto p. 317 |
| **Pronunciation** | | The different pronunciations of *r* and *rr* p. 257 | The letters *ll* and *ñ* p. 295 |
| **Cultural readings and country focus** | | • **Nota cultural** Las comidas en el mundo hispano p. 261 <br> • **Nota cultural** La comida hispana p. 271 | • **Nota cultural** Zara: la moda internacional p. 298 <br> • **Nota cultural** Los centros comerciales en Latinoamérica p. 316 |

SEQUENCE • SCOPE AND SEQUENCE • SCOPE AND SEQUENCE • SCOPE AND SEQUENCE • SCOPE AND SEQUENCE • SCOPE AN

## SEMESTER

| CAPÍTULO 3 Estamos en casa | CAPÍTULO 4 Nuestra comunidad | CAPÍTULO 5 ¡A divertirse! La música y el cine | CAPÍTULO 6 ¡Sí, lo sé! |
|---|---|---|---|
| La casa p. 98<br>Los muebles y otros objetos de la casa p. 106<br>Los quehaceres de la casa p. 109<br>Los colores p. 111<br>Los números 1.000–100.000.000 p. 116 | **1** Los lugares p. 134<br>**3** ¿Qué tienen que hacer? ¿Qué pasa? p. 140<br>**7** Servicios a la comunidad p. 149 | **1** El mundo de la música p. 172<br>**6** El mundo del cine p. 184 | **Reviewing strategies** p. 206 |
| Algunos verbos irregulares p. 101<br>Algunas expresiones con ***tener*** p. 113 | **2** ***Saber*** y ***conocer*** p. 137<br>**4** Los verbos con cambio de raíz p. 142<br>**5** El verbo ***ir*** p. 146 | **2** Los adjetivos demostrativos p. 175<br>**3** Los pronombres demostrativos p. 177 | **Comunicación**<br>Recycling of **Capítulo Preliminar A** to **Capítulo 5** |

### Chapter 6

We call this a recycling chapter. This means that you will be given the opportunity to reuse everything that you learned from *Preliminary A* through *Chapter 5*. No new information is presented in this chapter so that you can get some time to practice and internalize Spanish. It also helps you prepare for the final exam!

### Chapter 12

This is another recycling chapter, just like *Chapter 6* above.

E AND SEQUENCE • SCOPE AND SEQUENCE • SCOPE AND SEQUENCE • SCOPE AND SEQUENCE • SCOPE AND SEQUENCE • SCOPE AN

## SEMESTER

| CAPÍTULO 9 Estamos en forma | CAPÍTULO 10 ¡Viajemos! | CAPÍTULO 11 El mundo actual | CAPÍTULO 12 Y por fin, ¡lo sé! |
|---|---|---|---|
| **1** El cuerpo humano p. 334<br>**3** Algunas enfermedades y tratamientos médicos p. 341 | **1** Los medios de transporte p. 374<br>**4** El viaje p. 388 | **1** Los animales p. 412<br>**2** El medio ambiente p. 416<br>**4** La política p. 426 | **Reviewing strategies** p. 452 |
| **2** Un resumen de los pronombres de complemento directoe indirecto y reflexivos p. 337<br>**4** **¡Qué!** y **¡cuánto!** p. 346<br>**5** El pretérito y el imperfecto p. 349<br>**6** Expresiones con ***hacer*** p. 356 | **2** Los mandatos informales p. 379<br>**3** Los mandatos formales p. 383<br>**5** Otras formas del posesivo p. 392<br>**6** El comparativo y el superlativo p. 394 | **3** El subjuntivo p. 419<br>**5** ***Por*** y ***para*** p. 429<br>**6** Las preposiciones y los pronombres preposicionales p. 432<br>**7** El infinitivo después de preposiciones p. 436 | **Comunicación**<br>Recycling of **Capítulo Preliminar B** to **Capítulo 11** |
| The letters ***d*** and ***t*** p. 335 | The letters ***b*** and ***v*** p. 375 | Review of Word Stress and Accent Marks p. 413 | |
| • **Nota cultural** El agua y la buena salud p. 346<br>• **Nota cultural** Las farmacias en el mundo hispanohablante p. 356 | • **Nota cultural** ¿Cómo nos movemos? p. 386<br>• **Nota cultural** Venezuela, país de aventuras p. 391 | • **Nota cultural** El Yunque: tesoro tropical p. 419<br>• **Nota cultural** La política en el mundo hispano p. 428 | |

### Appendices

Yes, we know these are at the end of the book, but you might want to look at them now—not at the end of the semester when it's too late! Note that there are five appendices and what each one is for:

**Appendix 1**
Inductive Grammar Answers

**Appendix 2**
Verb Charts

**Appendix 3**
*También se dice…*
*(You can also say . . . )*

**Appendix 4**
Spanish–English Glossary

**Appendix 5**
English–Spanish Glossary

XXV

## ORGANIZATION OF A CHAPTER

 **STOP 1** Have you ever used a Spanish textbook before? Do you know what each section is about? Do you know what you're being asked to read, memorize, and practice, and why? Here's an outline of a typical chapter in *¡Anda!* followed by some actual chapter sections so that you can see what they look like. And we couldn't resist . . . we made lots of notes for you!

### COMUNICACIÓN I

| | |
|---|---|
| **Vocabulary and grammar** | (in manageable chunks, as needed, each numbered consecutively throughout the chapter) |
| **Pronunciation practice** | (after first vocabulary list, located in your Student Activities Manual [SAM] / MySpanishLab) |
| **Nota cultural box** | (brief, contextualized readings, relevant to chapter theme) |
| **¿Cómo andas? I** | (first self-assessment box) |

### COMUNICACIÓN II

| | |
|---|---|
| **Vocabulary and grammar** | (in manageable chunks, as needed, each numbered consecutively throughout the chapter) |
| **Nota cultural box** | (brief, contextualized readings, relevant to chapter theme) |
| **Escucha** | (a focus on listening) |
| **¡Conversemos!** | (fun, contextualized activities where you "put it all together" orally) |
| **Escribe** | (a focus on writing) |
| **¿Cómo andas? II** | (second self-assessment box) |

### CULTURA

(a focus on one or more Spanish-speaking countries—what the people do, what they make, and how they think)

### AMBICIONES SINIESTRAS

(a mystery story told through reading and video)

| | |
|---|---|
| **Y por fin, ¿cómo andas?** | (cumulative self-assessment box) |
| **Vocabulario activo** | (a two-page list of all of the essential vocabulary of the chapter) |

xxvi

**STOP 2**

The chapter title announces the theme of the chapter, which is reflected in the visual on the right.

The questions are designed to get you to think about the topic for the chapter—not to get you to search for THE right answer. Bringing the topic to the forefront of your mind will help you make educated guesses about the meanings of Spanish words. Remember the topic as you work your way through the chapter.

There is a list of goals for the communication, culture, and mystery story sections under *Objetivos*. You will also see other goals such as those for using Spanish outside of your classroom and in the community. Notice how the goals relate to the chapter theme!

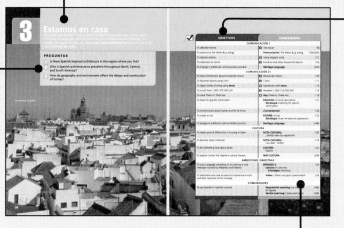

The content related to the goals is listed under *Contenidos,* with page numbers. It's in English so that you can understand it clearly!

# COMUNICACIÓN

**STOP 3**

**Comunicación I and II** are divided into manageable chunks of what you need to learn: vocabulary (the words you need) and grammar (the structures that you use to put the words together). Vocabulary and grammar are two of the most important tools for communication! By the way, we didn't invent this—research indicates that the best presentation of language separates vocabulary and grammar for a manageable progression especially when combined with recycling and reintroduction of previously studied material—more on that later.

The vocabulary sections are numbered consecutively throughout the chapter.

Communicative goals are listed for each vocabulary and grammar section.

The vocabulary chunks introduce new vocabulary through art.

A lot of the vocabulary is presented without translations so that you can try to figure out the meanings of the Spanish words.

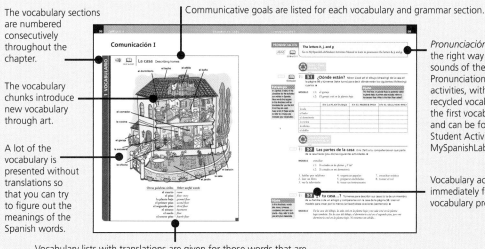

*Pronunciación* indicates the right way to make the sounds of the language. Pronunciation practice and activities, with new and recycled vocabulary, follow the first vocabulary chunk and can be found in your Student Activities Manual / MySpanishLab.

Vocabulary activities immediately follow each vocabulary presentation.

Vocabulary lists with translations are given for those words that are hard to illustrate and, therefore, hard for you to guess the meanings.

# GRAMMAR

The grammar sections introduce new grammar concepts.

**STOP 4**

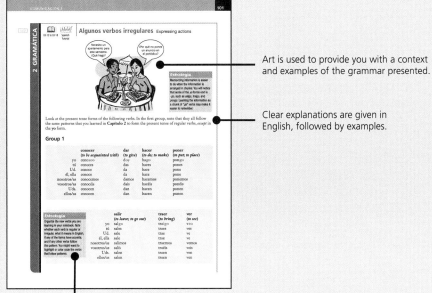

Art is used to provide you with a context and examples of the grammar presented.

Clear explanations are given in English, followed by examples.

Student notes help you with your learning. They provide additional background information, interesting facts, and strategies that help you learn!

Recycling boxes also point out when we have deliberately reused materials from a previous chapter—or from earlier in the same chapter—to help you build upon what you have already studied. Page references are provided so that you can return to that section of the book if you need and/or want to.

Icons indicate when to work in pairs or groups, and also refer you to other resources (e.g., MySpanishLab, audio, corresponding activity numbers in the Student Activities Manual) when you need them.

You'll find a blend of activities that practice individual words and verb forms, as well as activities in which you focus on putting everything together to use the language for purposes of communication.

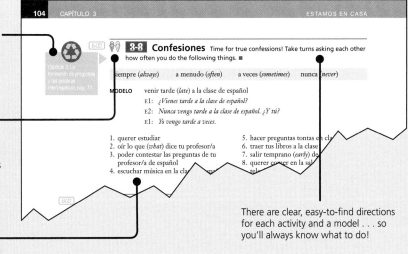

There are clear, easy-to-find directions for each activity and a model . . . so you'll always know what to do!

**STOP 5**

The second **Comunicación** provides listening comprehension (**Escucha**), more interactive oral activities (**¡Conversemos!**), and writing activities (**Escribe**) prior to the self-assessment check (**¿Cómo andas?**).

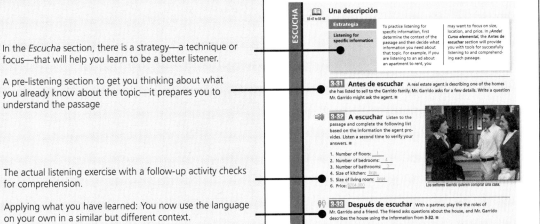

In the *Escucha* section, there is a strategy—a technique or focus—that will help you learn to be a better listener.

A pre-listening section to get you thinking about what you already know about the topic—it prepares you to understand the passage

The actual listening exercise with a follow-up activity checks for comprehension.

Applying what you have learned: You now use the language on your own in a similar but different context.

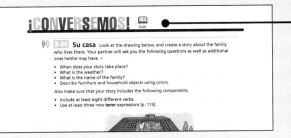

The *¡Conversemos!* section provides you with even more oral practice. In this section you put together all the grammar and vocabulary you have learned in the current chapter along with opportunities to recycle your Spanish knowledge from previous chapters. These are real-life scenarios in which you interact with a classmate or present on your own.

Escribe is also related to the chapter theme, includes a strategy that will help you learn to be a better writer, and walks you through the writing process with pre-writing and post-writing activities.

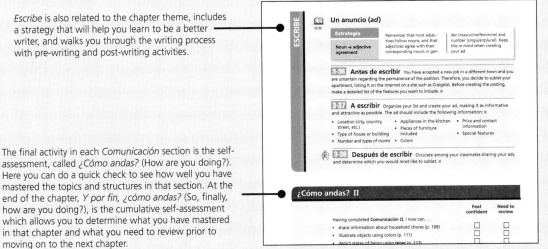

The final activity in each *Comunicación* section is the self-assessment, called *¿Cómo andas?* (How are you doing?). Here you can do a quick check to see how well you have mastered the topics and structures in that section. At the end of the chapter, *Y por fin, ¿cómo andas?* (So, finally, how are you doing?), is the cumulative self-assessment which allows you to determine what you have mastered in that chapter and what you need to review prior to moving on to the next chapter.

xxx

# CULTURE

Time for a break to grab a cup of **café con leche**?

**STOP 6** Between the second **Comunicación** and **Ambiciones siniestras** (the ongoing mystery story) is **Cultura,** designed to provide key facts and high-interest information concerning Spanish-speaking countries and peoples.

You'll find lots of photos with short captions in Spanish.

Read/listen to a native speaker explain a little bit about his or her country . . . what folks do there, what they think, and what they like. We hope you'll want to learn more about these countries and maybe even visit some of them.

An almanac of country statistics is given for each country presented.

Here are some questions to get you thinking about what you've seen and read.

Here's a reminder that there is more information about this country on MySpanishLab.

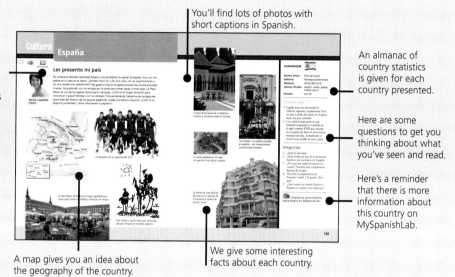

A map gives you an idea about the geography of the country.

We give some interesting facts about each country.

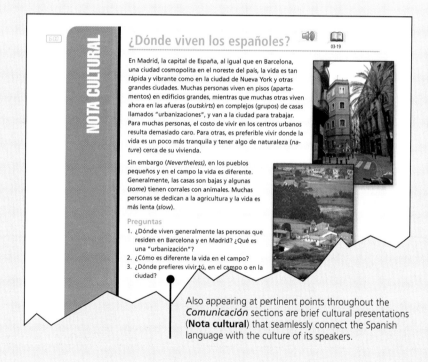

Also appearing at pertinent points throughout the *Comunicación* sections are brief cultural presentations (**Nota cultural**) that seamlessly connect the Spanish language with the culture of its speakers.

xxx

# READING AND VIDEO

**STOP 7**

A mystery story called **Ambiciones siniestras** is presented through readings and videos. It reuses many of the grammar structures and vocabulary words presented in the chapter.

Strategies give you ideas and techniques to help you become a better reader.

The pre-reading activity helps you prepare for what you are about to read. It gets you thinking about topics that will be presented in the story so that the context will help you figure out what is going on.

The reading activity asks you to apply the strategies to the reading.

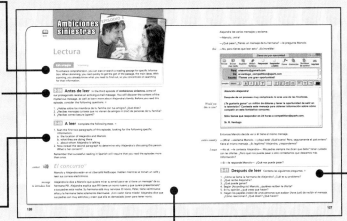

The post-reading activity helps you check your comprehension.

The sequence of activities for the video episode is the same: pre-, during, and post-. The story that was started in the reading is continued in the video. To understand the story, you'll have to read first and then watch the video.

# VOCABULARY SUMMARIES

**STOP 8**

The **Vocabulario activo** section at the end of each chapter is where you have all the new vocabulary from the chapter in one place. The words and phrases are organized by topic, in alphabetical order.

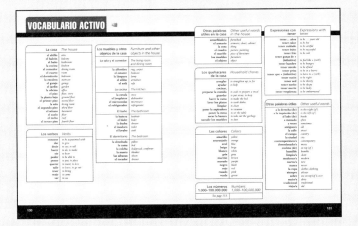

**Meet the cast of the video:**

Alejandra

Cisco

Manolo

Eduardo

Marisol

Lupe

Sr. Verdugo

# SUPPLEMENTARY MATERIALS

 **STOP 9** Before we finish our walking tour, we want to walk through the many supplements that we provide. Your instructor may have selected some of them to be used in your course.

| | |
|---|---|
| **Student Activities Manual (paper)** | The Student Activities Manual (SAM for short) contains practice activities that were designed as homework to reinforce what you learn in class. Your pronunciation activities are also found in the SAM as well as ideas on how to practice Spanish in your community. Additionally, there are activities that can be done by all students and/or those who have a Hispanic heritage. Although instructors may use the SAM in different ways, one thing is constant: the SAM is assigned as homework. So we make no assumptions . . . we know you probably won't have an instructor around to answer any questions when you're doing your homework at 2:00 A.M.! |
| **Answer Key for the Student Activities Manual** | Some instructors want their students to have this answer key; other instructors don't. We'll sell you the answer key only if your instructor requests it. |
| **Workbooklet** | We know that most students don't want to write in their textbooks, but we also know that writing is a great method for helping you to learn Spanish! So, we've created a **Workbooklet,** in which we have reproduced all of the activities in *¡Anda!* where writing is an important part of the activity (e.g., you need to gather information in writing from classmates and then report back to the class orally). |
| **Ambiciones siniestras DVD** | The DVD of **Ambiciones siniestras** allows you to watch or rewatch the video at any point during your busy 24/7 life. This is a great tool for helping you practice your comprehension and listening skills! |
| **Audio CD for the student text** | This audio CD contains the listening passages that correlate with sections of your textbook. A listening icon 🔊 appears in your text with a cross-reference to help you locate the audio. |
| **Audio CDs for the Student Activities Manual** | These audio CDs contain the listening passages you'll need for some of the activities in the SAM. |
| **Vistas culturales DVD** | If you want to listen to native speakers of Spanish and learn more about each of the Spanish-speaking countries, this is the DVD for you! |
| **MySpanishLab** | MySpanishLab contains all of the above supplements and more. It's a state-of-the-art learning management system, designed specifically for language learners and teachers. You'll need an access code to get in, but the price is very reasonable, considering how much you receive. For more information, go to www.myspanishlab.com. |

When traveling, it's always helpful to watch out for the signposts. Here is a list of signposts that we've used in *¡Anda!*

 You will find this first icon in each chapter opener to remind you to take the Readiness Check in MySpanishLab to test your understanding of the English grammar related to the Spanish grammar concepts in the chapter.

 Accompanying the activity instructions, this pair icon indicates that the activity is designed to be completed in groups of two.

 This group icon indicates that the activity is designed to be completed in small groups or as a whole class.

 This icon indicates that an activity involves listening and that the audio is provided for you either on the Companion Website (CW) or, if you are using MySpanishLab, in the eBook.

 Activities that ask you to write have been duplicated in a separate *Workbooklet* so that you don't have to write in your text if you don't want to. This icon indicates that an activity has been reproduced in the *Workbooklet*.

 The activity references below this icon tell you which activities in the Student Activities Manual (SAM) are related to that particular section of the textbook. You may have the printed SAM or the electronic version in MySpanishLab.

 This icon tells you where to find the **Ambiciones siniestras** video: on DVD or in MySpanishLab.

 This icon tells you where to find the **Vistas culturales** video and other cultural resources in MySpanishLab.

 This icon means that the activity that it accompanies requires you to use the Internet.

 This icon indicates that additional resources for pronunciation, practice activities, and Spanish/English tutorials related to the Spanish grammar topic that you are studying are available in MySpanishLab.

## ¡Qué disfruten! Enjoy!

PRELIMINAR

A

---

### NATIONAL STANDARDS

**COMUNICACIÓN**
- To greet, say good-bye, and introduce someone (Communication, Cultures, Comparisons, Communities)
- To understand and respond appropriately to basic classroom expressions and requests (Communication)
- To spell in Spanish (Communication)
- To identify cognates (Communication, Comparisons)
- To express the subject pronouns (Communication)
- To use *to be* (Communication)
- To state nationalities (Communication, Connections)
- To count from 0–30 (Communication)
- To state the time (Communication, Comparisons)
- To elicit the date and season (Communication, Comparisons)
- To report the weather (Communication, Comparisons)
- To share personal likes and dislikes (Communication)
- To engage in additional communication practice (Communication)

**CULTURA**
- To compare and contrast greetings in the Spanish-speaking world and in the United States (Cultures, Comparisons)
- To explain when to use the familiar and formal *you* (Cultures, Comparisons)
- To summarize the diversity of the Spanish-speaking world (Cultures, Comparisons)
- To name the continents and countries where Spanish is spoken (Cultures, Comparisons)
- To explore further the chapter's cultural themes (Cultures)

**COMUNIDADES**
- To use Spanish in real-life contexts (Communities)

**INTRODUCTION to Chapter opener**
Each chapter has a two-page Chapter opener. These pages help to orient your students regarding the content of the chapter and access any prior knowledge they may have regarding the theme. The intention is for the instructor to spend no more than 5 to 7 minutes on these openers.

# Para empezar

You are about to begin the exciting journey of studying the Spanish language and learning about Hispanic culture. Learning a language is a skill much like learning to ski or playing an instrument. Developing these skills takes practice and in the beginning, perfection is not expected. Research has shown that successful language learners are willing to take risks and experiment with the language.

What is essential in learning Spanish is to keep trying and be willing to risk making mistakes, knowing that the practice will garner results. *¡Anda! Curso elemental* will be your guide and provide you with key essentials for becoming a successful language learner.

Why should you study Spanish, or for that matter, any language other than English? For some of you, the answer may be quite frankly, "because it is a graduation requirement!" Bear in mind, however, that Spanish is one of the most widely spoken languages in the world. You may find that knowledge of the Spanish language is a useful professional and personal tool.

If you have never studied Spanish before, this preliminary chapter will provide you with some basic words and expressions you will need to begin to use the language in meaningful ways. If you have already learned or studied some Spanish, this preliminary chapter can serve as a quick review.

**PREGUNTAS**

1. Why is it important to study Spanish?
2. How might Spanish play a role in your future?

2

---

**SECTION GOALS for *Chapter opener***
By the end of the Chapter opener section, students will be able to:
- discuss the importance of speaking Spanish as participants in the global village.
- identify characteristics of a successful language learner.

**NOTE for *Chapter opener***
The specific placement varies according to the source, but Spanish is consistently ranked among the top five most-spoken languages in the world by most reporting agencies. Chinese (Mandarin), English, Hindustani, and Bengali are the other languages most often found on the lists.

**ANSWERS to *Preguntas***
1. *Some of the many reasons to study Spanish (or any language in addition to English) include:* increased awareness and appreciation of others; enhancement for any career choice; learning one's native language more thoroughly by acquiring Spanish grammar and vocabulary; learning more about the culture (art, music, cuisine, etc.) firsthand and in-depth, etc.
2. *Answers may include:* travel to a Spanish-speaking country; volunteering in a hospital or other community setting; job requirements, etc.

| OBJETIVOS | CONTENIDOS | |
|---|---|---|
| **COMUNICACIÓN** | | |
| To greet, say good-bye, and introduce someone | **1** Greetings | 4 |
| To understand and respond appropriately to basic classroom expressions and requests | **2** Useful classroom expressions | 8 |
| To spell in Spanish | **3** Alphabet | 9 |
| To identify cognates | **4** Cognates | 10 |
| To express the subject pronouns | **5** Subject pronouns | 11 |
| To use *to be* | **6** The verb **ser** (*to be*) | 13 |
| To state nationalities | **7** Adjectives of nationality | 14 |
| To count from 0–30 | **8** Numbers 0–30 | 16 |
| To state the time | **9** Telling time | 18 |
| To elicit the date and season | **10** Days, months, and seasons | 20 |
| To report the weather | **11** Weather | 23 |
| To share personal likes and dislikes | **12** The verb **gustar** (*to like*) | 25 |
| To engage in additional communication practice | **Heritage Language** | SAM |
| **CULTURA** | | |
| To compare and contrast greetings in the Spanish-speaking world and in the United States | **NOTA CULTURAL** Cómo se saluda la gente | 7 |
| To explain when to use the familiar and formal *you* | **NOTA CULTURAL** ¿Tú o Ud.? | 12 |
| To summarize the diversity of the Spanish-speaking world | **NOTA CULTURAL** Los hispanos | 16 |
| To name the continents and countries where Spanish is spoken | **NOTA CULTURAL** El mundo hispano | 17 |
| To explore further the chapter's cultural themes | **MÁS CULTURA** | SAM |
| **COMUNIDADES** | | |
| To use Spanish in real-life contexts | **EXPERIENTIAL LEARNING** En un restaurante hispano | SAM |
| | **SERVICE LEARNING** Profesores particulares | SAM |

**NOTE for *Capítulo Preliminar A***
This preliminary chapter is meant to jump-start learning. In some cases, students may have studied some Spanish previously and may be familiar with this material already. The vocabulary in this chapter is high-frequency and high-usage. Encourage students to refer to this chapter if they forget certain words and expressions. The amount of time that you spend on this chapter will depend on the number of true beginners in your class.

**THE NATIONAL STANDARDS**
*National Standards: Standards for Foreign Language Learning in the 21st Century*
*¡Anda! Curso elemental* is committed to and based on the *Standards for Foreign Language Learning in the 21st Century*. These national foreign language standards are sometimes referred to as *the 5 Cs*, and they represent five goal areas: Communication, Cultures, Connections, Comparisons, and Communities. Each goal area has corresponding standards, which in turn promote attainment of the specific goal. The beginning of each chapter will highlight how the standards underlying each of the 5 Cs will be addressed in that chapter of the text, as well as in the *Student Activities Manual*. In particular, the standards and goals highlighted throughout the textbook are taken from the *Standards for Learning Spanish*. These are language-specific standards that reflect the goals as they relate to the teaching and learning of Spanish. Throughout the rest of *¡Anda! Curso elemental*, we will refer to the standards as the National Standards.

**21ST CENTURY SKILLS • DEFINITION**
The Partnership for 21st Century Skills (P21) is a multidisciplinary project. The group, housed in Washington, D.C., has brought together the key national organizations representing the core academic subjects. The American Council on the Teaching of Foreign Languages (ACTFL) collaborated for a year developing the 21st Century Skills Map. The map, created by hundreds of world language educators, reflects the integration of languages and the necessary skills for a successful 21st century citizen.

**INTRODUCTION to *Objetivos***
The chapter objectives are an organizational tool for you and your students. They allow you to see the main points of the chapter at a glance, and they serve as a way for you to assess whether your students have mastered the main ideas and skills from every chapter. You can use the chapter objectives to preview what the students will be learning in a particular chapter and to review what you taught. Encourage your students to preview the chapter by reading the objectives, and to use the objectives from each chapter when they prepare for an assessment. Also encourage your students to use the *¿Cómo andas?* and *Y por fin, ¿cómo andas?* features to help them self-assess their accomplishments and needs.

**EXPANSION for *Preguntas***
Ask your students the following questions:
1. If you could speak fluent Spanish, how would your life change?
2. How could Spanish be relevant for you now?

**SUGGESTION for *Chapter opener***
You may wish to get a paper copy of the ADFL (MLA) brochure *Why Learn Another Language?* or have students download a PDF version from the MLA web site. Lead a discussion of the ways students will use Spanish in their careers, communities, personal growth, and travel.

**INTRODUCTION to**
***Comunicación***

The *Comunicación* section is designed to foster interaction and communication using the target language. Each *Comunicación* section will include objectives that identify what a student will be able to do at the end of the section. Communication is a multifaceted process. There are 3 communicative modes highlighted in the National Standards: interpersonal, interpretive, and presentational. The Communication Goal of the *Standards for Learning Spanish* (*Communicate in Spanish*) has three corresponding standards, and each standard corresponds to a communicative mode. Standard 1.1 (the interpersonal mode) states that "Students engage in conversations, provide and obtain information, express feelings and emotions, and exchange opinions" (p. 434). Standard 1.2 (the interpretive mode) states that "Students understand and interpret written Spanish on a variety of topics" (p. 434). Standard 1.3 (the presentational mode) states that "Students present information, concepts, and ideas in Spanish to an audience of listeners or readers on a variety of topics" (p. 434). *¡Anda! Curso elemental* provides activities that use each communicative mode.

**SECTION GOALS for**
***Comunicación***

By the end of the *Comunicación* section, students will be able to:
• greet others and talk about how they are feeling.
• begin and end conversations politely.
• introduce themselves and others.
• compare how to greet people in the Spanish-speaking world and in the United States.
• understand and respond appropriately to basic classroom expressions and requests.
• spell in Spanish.
• distinguish between the sounds each letter makes and sound out new words.
• recognize cognates.
• understand when to use *tú* and when to use *usted*.
• match the subject pronouns with the appropriate forms of the verb *ser*.
• describe nationalities using *ser*.
• summarize the diversity of the Spanish-speaking world.
• count from 0 to 30.
• name the continents and countries where Spanish is spoken.
• tell time using expressions for A.M. and P.M.
• identify the months and the seasons and describe the weather in a particular month, season, or region.
• express basic likes and dislikes using *gustar*.

# Comunicación

**1 VOCABULARIO**

🔊 A-01 to A-04  📖  **3:00**

## Saludos, despedidas y presentaciones
Greeting, saying good-bye, and introducing someone

(Buenos días.)  (Buenas tardes.)  (Buenas noches.)  (Buenas noches.)

| Los saludos | *Greetings* |
|---|---|
| **¡Hola!** | *Hi! Hello!* |
| **Buenos días.** | *Good morning.* |
| **Buenas tardes.** | *Good afternoon.* |
| **Buenas noches.** | *Good evening; Good night.* |
| **¿Cómo estás?** | *How are you?* (familiar) |
| **¿Cómo está usted?** | *How are you?* (formal) |
| **¿Qué tal?** | *How's it going?* |
| **Más o menos.** | *So-so.* |
| **Regular.** | *Okay.* |
| **Bien, gracias.** | *Fine, thanks.* |
| **Bastante bien.** | *Just fine.* |
| **Muy bien.** | *Really well.* |
| **¿Y tú?** | *And you?* (familiar) |
| **¿Y usted?** | *And you?* (formal) |

| Las despedidas | *Farewells* |
|---|---|
| **Adiós.** | *Good-bye.* |
| **Chao.** | *Bye.* |
| **Hasta luego.** | *See you later.* |
| **Hasta mañana.** | *See you tomorrow.* |
| **Hasta pronto.** | *See you soon.* |

—¿Qué tal?
—Bien.

—¿Cómo estás?
—Bien, gracias.

—Hasta mañana.
—Adiós.

**METHODOLOGY • First Day of Class**

The first day of any class is very important, because it sets the tone for the rest of the term. What follows are a few tips for a successful first day of class:

1. Hand out a detailed syllabus and/or post it on the Internet. This provides the students with a concrete list of your expectations for the course.
2. Go over the syllabus and walk students through the *¡Anda! Curso elemental* text and ancillaries.
3. Leave time at the end of class to begin the first activities of this chapter orally so that students leave class having spoken and practiced Spanish.

It is a guaranteed way to excite students about learning and to motivate them for more!

4. Learn students' names as soon as possible. If you have large classes, you might wish to use one or more of these excellent techniques: create a seating chart on day one, have students make name cards (by folding index cards in half) to place on their desks, or even take digital pictures of your class and label the photos with your students' names.

| Las presentaciones | Introductions |
|---|---|
| ¿Cómo te llamas? | *What is your name?* (familiar) |
| ¿Cómo se llama usted? | *What is your name?* (formal) |
| Me llamo… | *My name is . . .* |
| Soy… | *I am . . .* |
| Mucho gusto. | *Nice to meet you.* |
| Encantado/Encantada. | *Pleased to meet you.* |
| Igualmente. | *Likewise.* |
| Quiero presentarte a… | *I would like to introduce you to . . .* (familiar) |
| Quiero presentarle a… | *I would like to introduce you to . . .* (formal) |

- The expressions **¿Cómo te llamas?** and **¿Cómo se llama usted?** both mean *What is your name?* but the former is used among students and other peers (referred to as *familiar*). You will learn about the differences between these *familiar* and *formal* forms later in this chapter. Note that **Encantado** is said by a male, and **Encantada** is said by a female.
- Spanish uses special punctuation to signal a question or an exclamation. An upside-down question mark begins a question and an upside-down exclamation mark begins an exclamation, as in **¿Cómo te llamas?** and **¡Hola!**

---

 **A-1** **Saludos y despedidas** Match each greeting or farewell with its logical response. Compare your answers with those of a classmate. ■

1. __b__ ¿Qué tal?
2. __d__ Hasta luego.
3. __a__ ¿Cómo te llamas?
4. __c__ Encantada.

a. Me llamo Julia.
b. Bastante bien.
c. Igualmente.
d. Hasta pronto.

---

**SUGGESTION for Los saludos**
You may want to tell students about other types of greetings such as ¿Qué pasó?, ¿Qué pasa?,¿Qué hubo?, and ¿Cómo te va?

**NOTE for Los saludos**
You will find additional greetings in the *También se dice…* section in Appendix 3.

**SUGGESTION for Las presentaciones**
Indirect object pronouns are introduced in *Capítulo 8*. For now, we recommend teaching the expressions lexically. E.g., *Quiero presentarle a…*

**HERITAGE LANGUAGE LEARNERS**
Ask your heritage language learners if there are any other greetings they use at home. See if the greetings vary by country or region.

**NATIONAL STANDARDS**
*Communication*
*Communication* is the first "C" of the National Standards. Communication encompasses all aspects of interaction, including speaking, listening, reading, and writing. Vocabulary is essential to communicating and *¡Anda! Curso elemental* will present high-frequency vocabulary throughout the program.

**INTRODUCTION to**
*Vocabulario Presentations*
Vocabulary is presented in what we refer to as *chunks*. These chunks consist of a highly manageable number of thematically related, high-usage words. The words are always presented via a stimulating and contextualized drawing as a context. The drawings can assist you in the presentation of the vocabulary, and can then be used to review and reinforce the new words. The number of vocabulary presentations varies from chapter to chapter, and they are always related to the chapter theme. All of these drawings are also available in the form of downloadable images from MySpanish Lab or the Instructors Resource Center (IRC). There are also additional activities for each of these sections available in the *Extra Activities* folder under Instructor Resources, as well as audio recordings, to aid with pronunciation.

**NOTE for**
*Heritage Language Learners*
In your classes you will have three main types of students. The first type, true beginners, are students with no background in foreign language learning. You will also have false beginners, who are students with some experience with Spanish or another language, yet they are enrolled in beginning language courses. Lastly, you will have heritage language learners. Unlike bilingual Spanish-English speakers, heritage language learners have a greater command of speaking and listening skills, but since many have not formally studied Spanish in a school setting, their writing and reading skills may not match their level of conversational and listening skills. *¡Anda! Curso elemental* will provide activities and suggestions for the heritage language learners in the *Student Activities Manual*.

**SUGGESTION for Saludos,**
*despedidas y presentaciones*
Pronounce the expressions for students and have them repeat chorally. It is recommended that you pronounce all new vocabulary for your students and allow them to repeat after you.

## METHODOLOGY • Lesson Planning

We have provided suggested amounts of time for you to devote to each activity. These time estimates include: pairing up students, giving your students time to read the directions with their partners, performing the activity, and a brief follow-up. The follow-up should include a spot check of only some pairs and only some of the items. It is not appropriate to redo all of the activities that students have completed with partners. Explain to students that they need to help each other and to self-correct within their small groups.

## METHODOLOGY • Pair Work

The authors of *¡Anda! Curso elemental* strongly believe in the research that says "students learn best from students." Hence, there is an abundance of pair and group activities in *¡Anda! Curso elemental*. For this chapter, simply have students turn to a partner. In subsequent chapters, ideas will be provided so that you can vary partners, preferably on a daily basis.

## METHODOLOGY • Effective Management of Group Activities

To optimize group work, there are specific steps that should be followed:

1. Before beginning an activity, be sure to activate students' schemata (tap into students' prior knowledge and experiences) to prepare them for what they are about to do.
2. Next, give clear directions and model the activity at least once so the assignment is perfectly clear.
3. After modeling, set a time limit for the activity, even if you must adjust it once students are working. This encourages students to get on task immediately and work at a steady pace.
4. Once you have given the time limit, assign groups. It is important that students work with a variety of partners and groups.
5. While students are working together, monitor their work closely. This is a time when students learn both from each other and from you, as you circulate around the room asking and answering questions to keep them on track.
6. End the activity when most students are finished and follow-up by calling on a few groups to share their work. Follow-up is important for several reasons: it validates the work students have completed, it provides students an opportunity to report back using different grammatical forms, and it allows you to make corrections.

---

 **A-2**  **¡Hola! ¿Qué tal?**  Greet five classmates, and ask how each is doing. After you are comfortable with one greeting, try a different one. ∎

MODELO   E1:  *¡Hola! ¿Cómo estás?*
E2:  *Bien, gracias. ¿Y tú?*
E1:  *Muy bien.*

---

 **A-3**  **¿Cómo te llamas?**  Introduce yourself to three classmates. ∎

MODELO   E1:  *¡Hola! Soy… ¿Cómo te llamas?*
E2:  *Me llamo… Mucho gusto.*
E1:  *Encantado/a.*
E2:  *Igualmente.*

---

 **A-4**  **Quiero presentarte a…**  Now, introduce one person you have just met to another classmate. ∎

MODELO   E1:  *John, quiero presentarte a Mike.*
MIKE:  *Mucho gusto.*
JOHN:  *Igualmente.*

---

**A-5**  **Una fiesta**  Imagine that you are at a party. In groups of five, introduce yourselves to each other. Use the model as a guide. ∎

MODELO   AMY:  *Hola, ¿qué tal? Soy Amy.*
ORLANDO:  *Hola, Amy. Soy Orlando. ¿Cómo estás?*
AMY:  *Muy bien, Orlando. ¿Y tú?*
ORLANDO:  *Bien, gracias. Amy, quiero presentarte a Tom.*
TOM:  *Encantado.*
E4:  *…*

---

**SUGGESTION for A-3 to A-5**
Have students stand and circulate around the class. Many students will be shy about introducing themselves to classmates they do not know. Therefore, please encourage them to circulate.

**SUGGESTION for A-5**
If time permits, do this activity several times, changing the groups each time. This gives students an opportunity to get to know others in the class and builds community within the classroom.

## Cómo se saluda la gente

A-05 to A-07

How do you generally greet acquaintances? Do you use different greetings for different people?

When native speakers of Spanish meet, they greet each other, ask each other how they are doing, and respond using phrases like the ones you just learned. In most of the Spanish-speaking world, men usually shake hands when greeting each other, although close male friends may greet each other with an **abrazo** (*hug*). Between female friends, the usual greeting is a **besito** (*little kiss*) on one or both cheeks (depending on the country) and a gentle hug. The **besito** is a gentle air kiss. When men and women greet each other, depending on their ages, how well they know each other, and what country they are in, they either simply shake hands and/or greet with a **besito**. While conversing, Spanish speakers may stand quite close to each other.

### Preguntas

1. How do people in the Spanish-speaking world greet each other?
2. How do your male friends generally greet each other? And your female friends?
3. In general, how much distance is there between you and the person(s) with whom you are speaking?

**METHODOLOGY • Timing Activities**
You will have noted that each activity in the Annotated Instructors' Edition has a time clock. These clocks are suggestions of how long to spend on each activity. These are approximations, as you will have some students progress more quickly and others more slowly. You will also have classes in which you assign group activities to be completed as a whole, and will not need additional time for creating pairs. Nor will all activities necessitate a direct follow-up. Use these as a guide for your lesson planning and classroom activities. They are meant to be helpful, not prescriptive. Also remember never to wait until all students have completed all items of an activity. Rather, consider assigning several activities at once so that partners who finish one activity move on to the next.

**INTRODUCTION to**
*Nota cultural boxes*
Each regular chapter has two *Nota cultural* boxes, one in each *Comunicación* section. They are meant to be brief and are always contextualized and relevant to the theme of the chapter. In this chapter, we have included four *Nota cultural* boxes.

**METHODOLOGY • Planning Ahead**
We recommend assigning *all* culture sections to be read in advance. We also recommend assigning students to read *all* the grammar explanations before class since they are written in a very clear, concise fashion. The instructor's role then becomes that of clarifying or reviewing any points that the students read in advance.

**EXPANSION for *Nota cultural***
Additional questions to ask your students are:
1. How do your male friends greet your female friends?
2. How do your parents greet their friends?
3. How do you greet your family members?

**INTRODUCTION to**
*Chunks / Chunking*

The concept of *chunks* of material and *chunking* of material is a major notion that drove the development of *¡Anda! Curso elemental.* Learning theory and the subsequent research of literally thousands of studies on general learning of any and all subject areas confirm that students learn best when information is grouped into smaller chunks. Giving students *all* of the rules and *all* of the ways to express an idea can be overwhelming. When information is not chunked, learners tend to shut down, since they find the amount of information that needs to be learned overwhelming. Hence, chunking is the best way to insure that students see success and progress and are motivated to learn more.

**METHODOLOGY • Teaching Vocabulary**

We have attempted to streamline the vocabulary, especially when students are just beginning to learn Spanish. A variety of words and expressions can become confusing for some students. For example, at this time, we are only introducing *De nada* rather than including expressions such as *No hay de que*. If you wish to include additional vocabulary, please do so.

**METHODOLOGY • Teaching Commands**

It is intentional that we have introduced lexically only the *usted/ustedes* commands. The similarity in their endings makes it a more streamlined choice since the goal at this stage is to simplify language and to jump start your students, which aids greatly in motivation.

**METHODOLOGY • Use of Commands**

You will note that at this very early point in the learning process only the formal commands are presented lexically. If you prefer to use familiar commands, please do so. A formal presentation of commands will appear in *Capítulo 10*.

## 2 VOCABULARIO

A-08 to A-10

# Expresiones útiles para la clase
Understanding and responding appropriately to basic classroom expressions and requests

The following list provides useful expressions that you and your instructor will use frequently.

| Preguntas y respuestas | *Questions and answers* | Expresiones de cortesía | *Polite expressions* |
|---|---|---|---|
| **¿Cómo?** | *What? How?* | **De nada.** | *You're welcome.* |
| **¿Cómo se dice… en español?** | *How do you say . . . in Spanish?* | **Gracias.** | *Thank you.* |
| **¿Cómo se escribe… en español?** | *How do you write . . . in Spanish?* | **Por favor.** | *Please.* |
| **¿Qué significa?** | *What does it mean?* | | |
| **¿Quién?** | *Who?* | **Mandatos para la clase** | *Classroom instructions (commands)* |
| **¿Qué es esto?** | *What is this?* | **Abra(n) el libro en la página…** | *Open your book to page . . .* |
| **Comprendo.** | *I understand.* | **Cierre(n) el/los libro/s.** | *Close your book/s.* |
| **No comprendo.** | *I don't understand.* | **Conteste(n).** | *Answer.* |
| **Lo sé.** | *I know.* | **Escriba(n).** | *Write.* |
| **No lo sé.** | *I don't know.* | **Escuche(n).** | *Listen.* |
| **Sí.** | *Yes.* | **Lea(n).** | *Read.* |
| **No.** | *No.* | **Repita(n).** | *Repeat.* |
| | | **Vaya(n) a la pizarra.** | *Go to the board.* |

In Spanish, commands can have two forms. The singular form (**abra, cierre, conteste**, etc.) is directed to one person, while the plural form (those ending in **-n: abran, cierren, contesten**, etc.) is used with more than one person.

**A-6 Práctica** Take turns saying which expressions or commands would be used in the following situations. ■

**Estrategia**

When working with a partner, always listen carefully. If your partner gives an incorrect response, help your partner arrive at the correct response.

1. You don't know the Spanish word for something. No lo sé; ¿Cómo se dice/escribe… en español?
2. Your teacher wants everyone to listen. Escuchen.
3. You need your teacher to repeat what he/she has said. Repita por favor.
4. You don't know what something means. ¿Qué significa?
5. Your teacher wants students to turn to a certain page. Abran el libro en la página…
6. You don't understand something. No comprendo.

**A-7 Más práctica** Play the roles of instructor (**I**) and student (**estudiante / E**). The instructor either tells the student to do something or asks a question; the student responds appropriately. Practice with at least **five** sentences or questions, using the expressions that you have just learned; then change roles. ■

MODELO
I: *Abra el libro.*
E: (Student opens the book.)
I: *¿Cómo se dice* "hello"?
E: *Se dice "hola".*

**Estrategia**

To learn Spanish more quickly, you should attempt to speak only Spanish in the classroom.

**3 GRAMÁTICA**

A-11 to A-16

# El alfabeto Spelling in Spanish

The Spanish alphabet is quite similar to the English alphabet except in the ways the letters are pronounced. Learning the proper pronunciation of the individual letters in Spanish will help you pronounce new words and phrases.

| LETTER | LETTER NAME | EXAMPLES | LETTER | LETTER NAME | EXAMPLES |
|--------|-------------|----------|--------|-------------|----------|
| a | a | adiós | ñ | eñe | mañana |
| b | be | buenos | o | o | cómo |
| c | ce | clase | p | pe | por favor |
| d | de | día | q | cu | qué |
| e | e | español | r | ere | señora |
| f | efe | por favor | s | ese | saludos |
| g | ge | luego | t | te | tarde |
| h | hache | hola | u | u | usted |
| i | i | señorita | v | uve | nueve |
| j | jota | julio | w | doble ve o uve doble | Washington |
| k | ka | kilómetro | x | equis | examen |
| l | ele | luego | y | ye o i griega | yo |
| m | eme | madre | z | zeta | pizarra |
| n | ene | noche | | | |

**A-8** **En español** Take turns saying the following abbreviations in Spanish, helping each other with pronunciation if necessary. ■

| | | | | |
|---|---|---|---|---|
| 1. CD-RW | 3. CNN | 5. MCI | 7. WWW | 9. CBS |
| 2. IBM | 4. MTV | 6. UPS | 8. QVC | 10. ABC |

  **A-9** **¿Qué es esto?** Complete the following steps. ■

**Paso 1** Take turns spelling the following words for a partner, who will write what you spell. Then pronounce each word.

1. hola
2. mañana
3. usted
4. igualmente
5. que
6. noches

**Paso 2** Now spell your name for your partner as he/she writes it down. Your partner will pronounce your name, based on your spelling. Use **otra palabra** (*another word*) to indicate the beginning of a new word.

**MODELO** E1: *de, a, uve, i, de, otra palabra, ese, eme, i, te, hache*

E2: (*escribe y repite*) *D-a-v-i-d S-m-i-t-h*

---

**4 VOCABULARIO**

A-17 to A-19

# Los cognados  Identifying cognates

**Cognados,** or *cognates,* are words that are similar in form and meaning to their English equivalents. As you learn Spanish you will discover many cognates. Can you guess the meanings of the following words?

**inteligente**  **septiembre**  **familia**  **universidad**

---

  **A-10** **Práctica** Take turns giving the English equivalents for the following words. ■

| | | | | |
|---|---|---|---|---|
| 1. importante | 3. programa | 5. atractivo | 7. especial | 9. famoso |
| 2. animal | 4. mapa | 6. favorito | 8. fantástico | 10. diferente |

---

  **A-11** **¿Hablas español?**
Read the classified ad and make a list of all of the cognates; then answer the following questions. ■

1. What job is advertised?
2. What are the requirements?
3. How much does it pay?
4. How can you get more information?

**Administrador/a**
Departamento de Servicio Público.
Hospital General de Mesa Grande, AR.
Experiencia necesaria.
Fluidez en inglés y español.
$45,000–$60,000.
Teléfono: 480-555-2347

🔑 **Instructor Resources**
• PPT, Extra Activities

**5 GRAMÁTICA**

A-20 to A-21  Spanish/English Tutorials

# Los pronombres personales
### Expressing the subject pronouns

Can you list the subject pronouns in English? When are they used? The following chart lists the subject pronouns in Spanish and their equivalents in English. As you will note, Spanish has several equivalents for *you*.

| | | | | |
|---|---|---|---|---|
| **yo** | *I* | **nosotros/as** | *we* |
| **tú** | *you* (familiar) | **vosotros/as** | *you* (plural, Spain) |
| **usted** | *you* (formal) | **ustedes** | *you* (plural) |
| **él** | *he* | **ellos** | *they* (masculine) |
| **ella** | *she* | **ellas** | *they* (feminine) |

Tú

Usted

Generally speaking, **tú** (you, singular) is used for people with whom you are on a first-name basis, such as family members and friends.

**Usted,** abbreviated **Ud.,** is used with people you do not know well, or with people with whom you are not on a first-name basis. **Usted** is also used with older people, or with those to whom you want to show respect.

Spanish shows gender more clearly than English. **Nosotros** and **ellos** are used to refer to either all males or to a mixed group of males and females. **Nosotras** and **ellas** refer to an all-female group.

**INTRODUCTION to *Gramática Presentations***

Grammar is introduced, as is vocabulary, in *chunks:* small, manageable amounts of information. The presentations are always in English and employ either deductive or inductive approaches. A very conscious effort has been made to present only the most basic information on each topic and not to burden beginning Spanish students with exceptions to the rules. The more sophisticated nuances of the language are reserved for intermediate levels and beyond. The goal is to build learners' confidence that Spanish is manageable and that they can communicate in the language. English and Spanish tutorials are also available on MySpanishLab to provide students with additional support.

**NOTE for *Los pronombres personales***

*¡Anda! Curso elemental* will present, but not actively practice, the *vosotros* forms. If you wish to practice these forms, please add them to your classroom drills or to any of the exercises in this program.

**METHODOLOGY • Teaching Concepts at the Point of Need**

Our philosophy is to provide students with grammatical information they need to be successful at the moment, and not to overburden them. Hence, we delay the explanation of *it* until gender is introduced and they have noun subjects (in addition to people) to practice. E.g., *El libro es aburrido. No, es interesante.*

**NOTE for *Nota cultural***
You may wish to explain to your students that in some Spanish-speaking countries, parents and children address each other using *usted*. Grandchildren often use *usted* with grandparents, even when grandparents use *tú* with them.

**EXPANSION for *Nota cultural***
Additional questions to ask your students are:
1. What are some regional language differences in the United States? What differences in language occur between the United States and England? What differences in language occur between the United States and Canada? Can the British, Canadians, and Americans understand each other?
2. In the past century, what new words have been added to English?
3. What are some English words that have changed in meaning?

(**Answers:** 1. *soda* vs. *pop* vs. *Coke; lift* vs. *elevator; water fountain* vs. *bubbler*. Yes, the British, Canadians, and Americans can understand each other. 2. Words dealing with transportation, electronics, and household appliances, like *airplane, jet, car, truck, van, television, video recorder, vacuum cleaner, microwave oven*, etc. 3. *cool, gay*, etc.)

**ANSWERS to *Nota cultural***
1. usted
2. *Possible answers include:* technological terms such as virtual reality, cellular, digital, compact disc, etc.
3. *Possible answers include:* groovy, icebox, buggy

**NOTE for *Los pronombres personales***
In this section, usage is mechanical, and students will have ample opportunities to use the pronouns in context in the coming activities.

NOTA CULTURAL

## ¿Tú o usted?

A-22 to A-25

Languages are constantly evolving. Words are added and deleted, they change in meaning, and the use of language in certain situations may change as well. For example, the use of **tú** and **usted (Ud.)** is changing dramatically in Spanish. **Tú** may now be used more freely in situations where **usted** was previously used. In some Spanish-speaking countries, it has become acceptable for a shopper to address a young store clerk

with **tú**. Just a few years ago, only **usted** would have been appropriate in that context. Nevertheless, the traditional use of **tú** and **usted** still exists. Regarding your choice between **tú** and **usted,** a good rule of thumb is: *When in doubt, be more formal.*

There are a few regional differences in the use of pronouns. Spanish speakers in Spain use **vosotros** ("you all") when addressing more than one person with whom they are on a first-name basis. Elsewhere in the Spanish-speaking world, **ustedes,** abbreviated **Uds.,** is used when addressing more than one person on a formal or informal basis. In Costa Rica, Argentina, and other parts of Latin America, **vos** replaces **tú,** but **tú** would be perfectly understood in these countries.

### Preguntas
1. When in doubt, do you use **tú** or **usted**?
2. What new words have been added to the English language in the past twenty years?
3. What are some words and expressions that we do not use in English anymore?

  **A-12** ¿**Cómo se dice?** Take turns expressing the following in Spanish. ■

1. we (all men) nosotros
2. I yo
3. you (speaking to a friend) tú
4. they (just women) ellas
5. we (all women) nosotras

6. you (speaking to a professor) usted
7. they (just men) ellos
8. they (fifty women and one man) ellos
9. we (men and women) nosotros
10. they (men or women) ellos/ellas

  **A-13** ¿**Tú o usted?** Determine whether you would most likely address the following people with **tú** or **usted.** State your reasons, using the categories below. ■

**A** respect
**B** family member

**C** someone with whom you are on a first-name basis
**D** someone you do not know well

1. your sister tú: B
2. your mom tú: B
3. your Spanish professor usted: B
4. your grandfather tú or usted: A/B
5. your best friend's father usted: A/D

6. a clerk in a department store usted: D
7. your doctor usted: A/D
8. someone you've just met who is older usted: A
9. someone you've just met who is your age tú: C
10. a child you've just met tú: C

**Instructor Resources**
• PPT, Extra Activities

A-26 to A-31 Spanish Tutorial

## El verbo *ser* Using *to be*

You have already learned the subject pronouns in Spanish. It is time to put them together with a verb. First, consider the verb *to be* in English. The *to* form of a verb, as in *to be* or *to see*, is called an *infinitive*. Note that *to be* has different forms for different subjects.

**to be**

| I | am | we | are |
|---|---|---|---|
| you | are | you (all) | are |
| he, she, it | is | they | are |

Verbs in Spanish also have different forms for different subjects.

**ser (*to be*)**

| Singular | | | Plural | | |
|---|---|---|---|---|---|
| yo | **soy** | *I am* | nosotros/as | **somos** | *we are* |
| tú | **eres** | *you are* | vosotros/as | **sois** | *you are* |
| Ud. | **es** | *you are* | Uds. | **son** | *you are* |
| él, ella | **es** | *he/she is* | ellos/as | **son** | *they are* |

- In Spanish, subject pronouns are not required, but rather used for clarification or emphasis. Pronouns are indicated by the verb ending. For example:

  **Soy** means *I am*.

  **Es** means either *he is, she is,* or *you* (formal) *are*.

- If you are using a subject pronoun, it will appear first, followed by the form of the verb that corresponds to the subject pronoun, and then the rest of the sentence, as in the examples:

  Yo **soy** Mark.      **Soy** Mark.

  Él **es** inteligente.      **Es** inteligente.

As you continue to progress in *¡Anda! Curso elemental,* you will learn to form and respond to questions, both orally and in writing, and you will have the opportunity to create longer sentences.

---

**A-14** **Vamos a practicar** Take turns saying the forms of the verb **ser** that you would use with the following pronouns. Correct your partner's answers as necessary. ■

1. nosotras somos
2. usted es
3. yo soy
4. él es

5. ellas son
6. tú eres
7. ustedes son
8. ella es

**NOTE for *El verbo ser***
The verb *ser* is the first verb presented in this chapter. Accordingly, the verb *to be* is presented in English with its corresponding subject pronouns. Note that *usted* and *ustedes* have been separated from the other third-person singular and plural subject pronouns. This has been done throughout *¡Anda!* for clarity. You will also note that in the verb chart for *to be*, the authors have used the words *you all* in the translation of *vosotros, vosotras,* and *Uds.* to indicate that this is the plural of the word *you*. At this point in the textbook, you can explain the use of *you all* as a way to express the plural of *you*.

**NOTE for *El verbo ser***
As we instructors know, the pronoun and the concept *it* is not identical in Spanish and English. In many ways, it is an advanced structural concept. The *¡Anda! Curso elemental* recommendation would be the simple approach, which would be to tell beginning students that the subject pronoun *it* does not have an equivalent in Spanish.

**1:00**  **A-15** **"Ser o no ser... "** Take turns changing these forms of **ser** to the plural if they are singular, and vice versa. Listen to your partner for accuracy and help him/her if necessary. ■

MODELO
E1: yo soy
E2: *nosotros somos*

1. usted es   2. nosotros somos   3. ella es   4. ellos son   5. tú eres

**2:00**

## 7 VOCABULARIO

**A-32 to A-34**

## Los adjetivos de nacionalidad  Stating nationalities

| Nacionalidad | Estudiantes | | Nacionalidad | Estudiantes |
|---|---|---|---|---|
| alemán | Hans | | francés | Jean-Paul |
| alemana | Ingrid | | francesa | Brigitte |
| canadiense | Jacques/Alice | | inglés | James |
| chino | Tsong | | inglesa | Diana |
| china | Xue Lan | | japonés | Tabo |
| cubano | Javier | | japonesa | Yasu |
| cubana | Pilar | | mexicano | Manuel |
| español | Rodrigo | | mexicana | Milagros |
| española | Guadalupe | | nigeriano | Yena |
| estadounidense | John/Kate | | nigeriana | Ngidaha |
| (norteamericano/a) | | | puertorriqueño | Ernesto |
| | | | puertorriqueña | Sonia |

In Spanish:

- adjectives of nationality are not capitalized unless one is the first word in a sentence.
- most adjectives of nationality have a form for males, and a slightly different one for females. (You will learn more about this in **Capítulo 1.** For now, simply note the differences.)
- when referring to more than one individual, you make the adjectives plural by adding either an **-s** or an **-es.** (Again, in **Capítulo 1** you will formally learn more about forming plural words.)
- some adjectives of nationality have a written accent mark in the masculine form, but not in the feminine, like **inglés/inglesa** and **francés/francesa.** For example: **Mi papá es** *inglés* **y mi mamá es** *francesa.*

 **A-16** **¿Cuál es tu nacionalidad?**
Describe the nationalities of the students listed on page 14. Form complete sentences using either **es** or **son,** following the model. Then practice spelling the nationalities in Spanish with your partner. ■

MODELO  E1:  china
        E2:  *Xue Lan es china.*
        E1:  chinos
        E2:  *Xue Lan y Tsong son chinos.*

1. francesa  Brigitte es francesa.
2. japonés  Tabo es japonés.
3. estadounidenses  John y Kate son estadounidenses.
4. canadiense  Alice/Jacques es canadiense.
5. mexicanos  Manuel y Milagros son mexicanos.
6. alemán  Hans es alemán.

 **A-17** **¿Qué son?**  Take turns naming the nationalities of the people listed. Make sure you use the correct form of **ser** in each sentence. Follow the model. ■

MODELO  E1:  Yena
        E2:  *Yena es nigeriano.*
        E1:  Yena y Ngidaha
        E2:  *Yena y Ngidaha son nigerianos.*

1. Jacques  Jacques es canadiense.
2. Xue Lan y Tsong  Xue Lan y Tsong son chinos.
3. Ingrid  Ingrid es alemana.
4. Brigitte  Brigitte es francesa.
5. Kate  Kate es estadounidense.
6. Hans  Hans es alemán.
7. Javier y Pilar  Javier y Pilar son cubanos.
8. Jean-Paul  Jean-Paul es francés.
9. yo  Answers will vary.
10. mi familia y yo  Answers will vary.

**EXPANSION for A-17**
If you have a diverse student population, you may wish to practice having students say *Me llamo… Soy* (nationality). *¿Y tú? Yo soy…* or bring in a map of the world and have students mark their countries of origin on the map. The class can take turns guessing: *¿Quién es de…?* and answering _____ *es de…*

### Instructor Resources
• Extra Activities

**CULTURAL BACKGROUND for**
*Nota cultural*
• Regarding the controversy surrounding the terms *Hispanic* and *Latino*, refer to the results of a *Time* magazine survey, cited in the August 13, 2005, article: "The 25 Most Influential Hispanics in America." The results of the poll of Hispanic adults reported 42% said they choose to be called Hispanic, only 17% said Latino and 34% had no particular preference (p. 43).
• *Latino* refers to Latin as an origin: Spanish, French, Portuguese, Italian, and Romanian are Latin-derived languages.

**HERITAGE LANGUAGE LEARNERS**
Most heritage language learners will know the information in this chapter, but they may have interesting comments to share regarding their experiences using the language, such as with *tú* and *usted*.

**SUGGESTION for** *Nota cultural*
Using a map, review the countries that comprise Latin America. Bring in photos of famous Hispanic personalities or use the web to show celebrities' personal fan sites. Find out the origin of each celebrity. Ask the students to determine whether their favorite celebrity is Hispanic or Latino, and why they used the chosen term.

**NOTE for** *Nota cultural*
This *Nota Cultural* is a basic presentation that you may wish to elaborate upon.

**ANSWERS for A-18**
1. uno, tres
2. cuatro, seis
3. siete, nueve
4. diez, doce
5. catorce, dieciséis
6. dieciséis, dieciocho
7. diecinueve, veintiuno
8. veintidós, veinticuatro
9. veintitrés, veinticinco
10. veinticinco, veintisiete

**EXPANSION for A-19**
Create basic math problems so your students can practice *son*, e.g., *Tres más tres son seis.*

---

## NOTA CULTURAL

### Los hispanos
  A-35

Many terms are associated with people from the Spanish-speaking world, most commonly *Hispanic* and *Latino*. While there is some controversy regarding the use of these terms, typically *Hispanic* refers to all people who come from a Spanish-speaking background. *Latino,* on the other hand, implies a specific connection to Latin America. Whichever term is used, the people denoted are far from homogeneous. Some are racially diverse, most are culturally diverse, and some do not even speak Spanish.

**Preguntas**
1. Briefly explain the terms *Latino* and *Hispanic.*
2. Name two people who are of Spanish-speaking heritage, and state how they are similar, and how they are different.

---

## 8 VOCABULARIO

A-36 to A-39

### Los números 0–30 Counting from 0–30

| | | | | | | | | | |
|---|---|---|---|---|---|---|---|---|---|
| 0 | cero | 7 | siete | 13 | trece | 19 | diecinueve | 25 | veinticinco |
| 1 | uno | 8 | ocho | 14 | catorce | 20 | veinte | 26 | veintiséis |
| 2 | dos | 9 | nueve | 15 | quince | 21 | veintiuno | 27 | veintisiete |
| 3 | tres | 10 | diez | 16 | dieciséis | 22 | veintidós | 28 | veintiocho |
| 4 | cuatro | 11 | once | 17 | diecisiete | 23 | veintitrés | 29 | veintinueve |
| 5 | cinco | 12 | doce | 18 | dieciocho | 24 | veinticuatro | 30 | treinta |
| 6 | seis | | | | | | | | |

---

 **A-18** **¿Qué número?** Take turns saying what number comes before and after each of the numbers below. Your partner will check your accuracy. ■

**MODELO** 1 *cero, dos*

| | | | | |
|---|---|---|---|---|
| 1. 2 | 3. 8 | 5. 15 | 7. 20 | 9. 24 |
| 2. 5 | 4. 11 | 6. 17 | 8. 23 | 10. 26 |

  **A-19** **¿Cuál es la secuencia?** Take turns reading the number patterns aloud while filling in the missing numbers. ■

1. 1, 3, 5, __7__, 9, __11__, 13, __15__, __17__
2. 2, 4, __6__, 8, __10__, 12, __14__, 16, __18__, 20, __22__
3. 3, __6__, 9, __12__, 15, __18__, 21, __24__, 27, __30__
4. 1, 3, 6, __10__, 15, __21__, 28

## El mundo hispano

A-40 to A-41

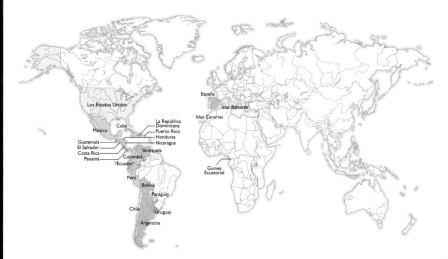

| PAÍS | POBLACIÓN |
|------|-----------|
| ARGENTINA | 41.343.201 |
| BOLIVIA | 9.947.418 |
| CHILE | 16.746.491 |
| COLOMBIA | 44.205.293 |
| COSTA RICA | 4.516.220 |
| CUBA | 11.477.459 |
| ECUADOR | 14.790.608 |
| EL SALVADOR | 6.052.064 |
| ESPAÑA | 46.505.963 |
| GUATEMALA | 13.550.440 |
| GUINEA ECUATORIAL | 650.702 |
| HONDURAS | 7.989.415 |
| MÉXICO | 112.468.855 |
| NICARAGUA | 5.995.928 |
| PANAMÁ | 3.410.676 |
| PARAGUAY | 6.375.830 |
| PERÚ | 29.907.003 |
| PUERTO RICO | 3.978.702 |
| LA REPÚBLICA DOMINICANA | 9.823.821 |
| URUGUAY | 3.510.386 |
| VENEZUELA | 27.223.228 |

*CIA World Fact Book, 2010

**Fíjate**

Spanish uses a period to indicate thousands and millions, rather than the comma used in English.

*(continued)*

**NATIONAL STANDARDS**
*Cultures*
Goal 2 of the *Standards for Foreign Language Learning* is Cultures. The Cultures Goal is to "Gain Knowledge and Understanding of Spanish-Speaking Cultures," and it is defined by 2 standards. Standard 2.1 of the *Standards for Learning Spanish* states that "Students demonstrate an understanding of the relationship between the practices and perspectives of Hispanic cultures." Standard 2.2 states that "Students demonstrate an understanding of the relationship between the products and perspectives of Hispanic cultures." This goal encompasses and embraces the similarities and differences between the many cultures that share a common language.

Note the plural use of the word. It is meant, in the case of Spanish, for us as instructors to guide and encourage our students to learn about and embrace the plurality of the Spanish-speaking world. The goals of the accompanying questions are to have students practice the numbers, and to become familiar with the countries where Spanish is spoken.

**CULTURAL EXPANSION for**
*Nota cultural*
Spanish is an official language in the countries listed in the chart.

Spanish is a major second language, and Spanish speakers are a sizable minority of up to 30% in Andorra, Aruba, Belize, Brazil, Gibraltar (British territory in the Iberian Peninsula), the Netherlands Antilles, Trinidad and Tobago, the United States, and the Virgin Islands.

**EXPANSION for** *Nota cultural*
Additional questions to ask your students are:
1. Where are the majority of the Spanish-speaking countries located?
2. In which country did the Spanish language originate?
3. How did the Spanish language spread to the Americas (North, Central, and South) as well to Africa?

(**Answers:** 1. Sudamérica, 2. España, 3. Exploration by individuals such as Cristobal Colón, Ponce de León, Hernán Cortez, etc.)

**CULTURAL BACKGROUND for**
*Nota cultural*
Through numerous conquests, the Spanish Empire and the Spanish language expanded to various parts of the world, including Equatorial Guinea and the Philippines. The Spaniards named the Philippines after King Phillip II.

**SUGGESTION for** *Nota cultural*
Lead a discussion with your students regarding the number of Spanish-speaking countries across the world with your students. Questions could include: *Why are there so many countries whose official language is Spanish? What are other languages spoken in those countries?* To discover the current numbers of Spanish speakers worldwide, check web sites such as www.actfl. org. Also, to find out other names of indigenous languages spoken in Spanish-speaking countries, search the particular country you are interested in and type "languages." You could also ask a student to research how many Spanish speakers are in the United States.

**ANSWERS to *Nota cultural***

1. América del Norte: 2 (México y Estados Unidos); Centroamérica: 6 (Costa Rica, El Salvador, Guatemala, Honduras, Nicaragua y Panamá); El Caribe: 3 (Cuba, Puerto Rico y La República Dominicana); América del Sur: 9 (Argentina, Bolivia, Chile, Colombia, Ecuador, Paraguay, Perú, Uruguay y Venezuela); Europa: 1 (España); África: 1 (Guinea Ecuatorial); en total, 22 países.
2. 4: América del Norte, América del Sur, Europa y África.
3. 7: Argentina, Colombia, Perú, Venezuela—América del Sur; España—Europa; Estados Unidos, México—América del norte.

**SUGGESTION for *La hora***
You may wish to have a student pretend to be a clock and move the student's "arms" to tell the appropriate time. You may also write different times on the board or overhead and have students give the correct time. This should be done at a quick pace.

**SUGGESTION for *La hora***
You may wish to tell your students that in some countries, a typical way to ask for the time is: *¿Qué hora tienes?* A typical response could be: *Faltan... para las siete.* You may also wish to mention the use of 24-hour time in airports, train and bus stations, and schedules for movie, musical, and theater productions.

**NOTE for *La hora***
You may wish to point out that some Spanish speakers say *un cuarto para,* rather than *menos,* to state the time.

**METHODOLOGY for *La hora***
You may wish to explain to your students that the words in parentheses are optional.

  **Preguntas**

Workbooklet

Use the map and chart of the Spanish-speaking world to answer the following questions in Spanish. Then, compare your answers with your partner's.

1. Fill in the chart with the names of the Spanish-speaking countries in the appropriate columns. How many such countries are there in each of these areas? How many are there in the world?

| AMÉRICA DEL NORTE | CENTROAMÉRICA | EL CARIBE | AMÉRICA DEL SUR | EUROPA | ÁFRICA |
|---|---|---|---|---|---|
| | | | | | |
| | | | | | |

2. How many continents contain Spanish-speaking countries? What are they?
3. How many countries have a Spanish-speaking population of 25,000,000 or more? Name them and their continents.

**9 VOCABULARIO**

🔊 📖  A-42 to A-44

## La hora  Stating the time

Es (la) medianoche.          Es (el) mediodía.          Es la una.          Son las diez y cinco.

Son las tres y cuarto.          Son las seis y media.          Son las nueve menos cuarto.          Son las diez menos veinticinco.

| La hora | *Telling time* | | |
|---|---|---|---|
| **¿Qué hora es?** | *What time is it?* | **...de la noche** | *. . . in the evening, at night* |
| **Es la una. / Son las...** | *It's one o'clock. / It's . . . o'clock.* | **la medianoche** | *midnight* |
| **¿A qué hora... ?** | *At what time . . . ?* | **el mediodía** | *noon* |
| **A la... / A las...** | *At . . . o'clock.* | **menos cinco** | *five minutes to the hour* |
| **...de la mañana** | *. . . in the morning* | **y cinco** | *five minutes after the hour* |
| **...de la tarde** | *. . . in the afternoon, early evening* | | |

When telling time in Spanish:

- use **Es la...** to say times between 1:00 and 1:59.
- use **Son las...** to say times *except* between 1:00 and 1:59.
- use **A la...** or **A las...** to say *at* what time.
- use **la** with **una** (**a la una**) for hours between 1:00 and 1:59.
- use **las** for hours greater than *one* (**a las ocho**).
- use the expressions **mediodía** and **medianoche** to say *noon* and *midnight*.
- **de la tarde** tends to mean from noon until 7:00 or 8:00 P.M.
- **cuarto** and **media** are equivalent to the English expressions *quarter* (fifteen minutes) and *half* (thirty minutes). **Cuarto** and **media** are interchangeable with the numbers **quince** and **treinta**.
- use **y** for times that are before and up to the half-hour mark.
- use **menos** for times that are beyond the half-hour mark.

2:00 🍦🍦 **A-20** **¿Qué hora es?** Look at the clocks, and take turns asking and responding to **¿Qué hora es?** ■

**MODELO** E1: *¿Qué hora es?*

E2: *Son las nueve de la mañana.*

1.
2.
3.
4.

5.
6.
7.
8.

**NOTE for A-21**
Note that we suggest having Student 1 simply ask, *¿A qué hora?* There is no need to translate to English. Student 1's question is used as a prompt for Student 2 and gives your students practice with asking the time.

**METHODOLOGY • Content Taught in *Capítulo Preliminar A***
As mentioned previously, this chapter is meant to jump-start learners. Some students will not be true beginners, and so this vocabulary may be a review for them. For those who are learning this material for the first time, it will be recycled throughout the rest of the program.

**NOTE for *Los días, los meses y las estaciones***
This presentation is based on the northern hemisphere. You may wish to point out to your students that the seasons are reversed in the southern hemisphere.

[2:00]  **A-21 Tu horario** Think about your daily schedule. Then, take turns asking and telling your partner at what times you do the following activities. ■

MODELO   E1: *¿A qué hora?*
         E2: *a la una y media*

1.    2.    3.    4.

5.    6.    7.    8.

[2:00]  **A-22 ¿Y el fin de semana?** What is your schedule for the weekend? Take turns telling your partner at what times you plan to do the activities from **A-21** this coming weekend. ■

[2:00]  **10 VOCABULARIO**  🔊 📖  A-45 to A-51

# Los días, los meses y las estaciones
Eliciting the date and season

**Los meses y las estaciones (*Months and seasons*)**

la primavera                                          el verano

marzo, abril y mayo

junio, julio y agosto

el otoño

septiembre, octubre y noviembre

el invierno

diciembre, enero y febrero

| Los días de la semana | *Days of the week* |
|---|---|
| lunes | *Monday* |
| martes | *Tuesday* |
| miércoles | *Wednesday* |
| jueves | *Thursday* |
| viernes | *Friday* |
| sábado | *Saturday* |
| domingo | *Sunday* |

| Expresiones útiles | *Useful expressions* |
|---|---|
| **¿Qué día es hoy?** | *What day is today?* |
| **¿Cuál es la fecha de hoy?** | *What is today's date?* |
| **Hoy es lunes.** | *Today is Monday.* |
| **Hoy es el 1° (primero) de septiembre.** | *Today is September first.* |
| **Mañana es el 2 (dos) de septiembre.** | *Tomorrow is September second.* |

Unlike in English, the days of the week and the months of the year are not capitalized in Spanish. Also, in the Spanish-speaking world, in some countries, Monday is considered the first day of the week. On calendars the days are listed from Monday through Sunday.

---

 **A-23 Antes y después** Which days come directly before and after the ones listed? Take turns saying the days in Spanish. ■

1. sábado   viernes, domingo
2. lunes   domingo, martes
3. viernes   jueves, sábado
4. domingo   sábado, lunes
5. jueves   miércoles, viernes
6. miércoles   martes, jueves

---

  **A-24 Y los meses** Which months come directly before and after the ones listed? Take turns saying the months in Spanish. ■

1. octubre
2. febrero
3. mayo
4. agosto
5. diciembre
6. junio
7. septiembre
8. enero
9. octubre
10. marzo

**SUGGESTION for A-23 and A-24**
Have students play Ping-Pong with the days and months. This fast-paced game consists of partners taking turns saying the days and months quickly (back and forth) in order.

**MODELO**
E1: *lunes*
E2: *martes*
E1: *miércoles*
E2: *jueves*

**ANSWERS to A-24**
1. septiembre, noviembre
2. enero, marzo
3. abril, junio
4. julio, septiembre
5. noviembre, enero
6. mayo, julio
7. agosto, octubre
8. diciembre, febrero
9. septiembre, noviembre
10. febrero, abril

**EXPANSION for A-25**
Have students determine which activity seems most interesting. Also, using the *Guía del ocio* as a model, have students work together to create one for their own university, town, or a city close by.

**NOTE for ¿Cuándo es?**
The *Guía del ocio* lists the times of the events in the 24-hour clock. You may wish to have your students state the times either in the 24-hour clock or not.

**21ST CENTURY SKILLS •
"THEN" AND "NOW"**
The Partnership for 21st Century Skills identified world languages as a core subject. Along with working with other disciplines, the Partnership identified how classrooms were "then" and how they need to be "now." "Then" the students learned about the language (grammar), and now, students need to be learning how to use the language. Activities like A-25 help students to interact with each other on an interpersonal level which is critical to fostering real communication.

**ANSWERS for A-25**
1. Joe Henderson es a las 21 horas / a las 9 de la noche.
2. El Museo Nacional es de 10 a 21 horas / de las 10 de la mañana a las 9 de la noche; El Museo del Prado es de 9 a 19 horas / de las 9 de la mañana a las 7 de la tarde.
3. Pedro Iturralde es a las 11 menos cuarto de la noche.
4. Alonso y Williams es a las 24 horas / a las doce de la noche / a (la) medianoche.
5. El Museo Nacional es de 10 a 21 horas / de las 10 de la mañana a las 9 de la noche; El Museo del Prado es de 9 a 19 horas / de las 9 de la mañana a las 7 de la tarde.

 **A-25  ¿Cuándo es?**  Look at the activities included in the **Guía del ocio**. Take turns determining what activity takes place and at what time on the following days. ■

**Fíjate**

In Spanish, *h* is the abbreviation for *hora*.

## GUÍA DEL OCIO MADRID

### MÚSICA

**Sábado 4**
• **XVI Festival de Jazz:**
  **Joe Henderson**
  La Riviera. 21 h.
  • **Alonso y Williams**
  La Madriguera. 24 h.

**Domingo 5**
• **Pedro Iturralde**
  Clamores. Pases: 22.45 y 0.45 h. Libre.

**Lunes 6**
• **Moreiras Jazztet**
  Café Central. 22 h.

### CINE

**Las vidas de Celia**
(2005, España)****
**Género:** Drama
**Director:** Antonio Chavarrías
**Interpretación:** Najwa Nimri, Luis Tosar...
*Najwa Nimri da vida a una mujer que intenta suicidarse la misma noche que otra joven es asesinada.*

**Mujeres en el parque**
(2006, España)*****
**Género:** Drama
**Director:** Felipe Vega
**Interpretación:** Adolfo Fernández, Blanca Apilánez...
*Una película llena de pequeños misterios, donde los personajes se enfrentan a lo difícil de las relaciones personales.*

**Volver** (2006, España)*****
**Género:** Comedia dramática
**Director:** Pedro Almodóvar
**Interpretación:** Penélope Cruz, Carmen Maura...
*Se basa en la vida y los recuerdos del director sobre su madre y el lugar donde se crió.*

### EXPOSICIONES

• **Museo Nacional Centro de Arte Reina Sofía**
  Santa Isabel, 52.
  Metro Atocha
  Tel. 91 467 50 62
  Horario: de 10 a 21 h. Domingo de 10 a 14.30 h. Martes cerrado.

*Un recorrido del arte del siglo XX, desde Picasso. Salas dedicadas a los comienzos de la vanguardia. Además, exposiciones temporales.*

• **Museo del Prado**
  Paseo del Prado, s/n. Metro Banco de España.
  Tel. 91 420 36 62 y 91 420 37 68
  Horario: martes a sábado de 9 a 19 h. Domingo de 9 a 14 h. Lunes cerrado.

*Todas las escuelas españolas, desde los frescos románicos hasta el siglo XVIII. Grandes colecciones de Velázquez, Goya, Murillo, etc. Importante representación de las escuelas europeas (Rubens, Tiziano, Durero, etc.). Escultura clásica griega y romana y Tesoro del Delfín.*

**MODELO**    E1:  el lunes por la noche
              E2:  *El Moreiras Jazztet es a las veintidós horas / a las diez.*

1. el sábado por la noche
2. el miércoles por la mañana
3. el domingo
4. el sábado por la noche
5. el martes por la tarde

Instructor Resources
• Textbook images, PPT, Extra Activities

## 11 VOCABULARIO

A-52 to A-56

# El tiempo   Reporting the weather

### ¿Qué tiempo hace? (*What's the weather like?*)

**el sol**
Hace sol.
Hace buen tiempo.

**la lluvia**
Llueve.
Hace mal tiempo.

**la nube**
Está nublado.

**el viento**
Hace viento.

**la nieve**
Nieva.

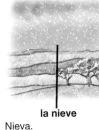

**la temperatura**

99 °F/37 °C

Hace calor.

14 °F/-10 °C

Hace frío.

---

 **A-26** **¿Qué tiempo hace?**   Take turns asking and answering what the most typical weather is during the following seasons where you go to school. ■

**MODELO**   E1:  ¿Qué tiempo hace… en (el) verano?
E2:  *En (el) verano hace sol.*

**¿Qué tiempo hace…?**

1. en (el) otoño
2. en (el) invierno
3. en (la) primavera
4. en (el) verano

**EXPANSION for A-26**
Ask students to create a weather log for where they live for the current week or for the previous week, and then share the log with a partner.

**EXPANSION for A-26**
Ask students to research the current weather of 5 different Spanish-speaking countries on the Internet, and report their findings to the class.

**A-27 España**  Take turns answering the question **¿Qué tiempo hace?** based on the map of Spain. ■

MODELO  E1: ¿Qué tiempo hace en Sevilla?
E2: *Hace calor.*

1. ¿Qué tiempo hace en Mallorca?
2. ¿Qué tiempo hace en Pamplona?
3. ¿Qué tiempo hace en Barcelona?
4. ¿Qué tiempo hace en Madrid?
5. ¿Qué tiempo hace en Córdoba?

1. Hace sol.
2. Hace frío, nieva y hace viento.
3. Está nublado. No hace sol.
4. Está nublado, hace viento y hace frío.
5. Llueve.

**A-28 Y América del Sur**  Take turns making statements about the weather based on the map of South America. You can say what the weather is like, and also what it is not like. Follow the model. ■

MODELO  E1: *Llueve en Bogotá.*
E2: *No hace frío en Venezuela.*

**Fíjate**
To make a negative statement, simply place the word *no* before the verb: *No llueve en Caracas. No nieva en Buenos Aires. No hace calor en Punta Arenas.*

*Possible answers include:* Llueve en Bogotá. Hace sol y hace calor en Caracas. Hace viento en Buenos Aires y está nublado. Nieva en Punta Arenas. Está nublado en Lima.

**Gustar** Sharing personal likes and dislikes

A-57 to A-59

To express likes and dislikes, you say the following:

Me gusta la primavera.

No me gusta el invierno.

Me gustan los viernes.

No me gustan los lunes.

### ¡Explícalo tú!

1. To say you like or dislike one thing, what form of **gustar** do you use?
2. To say you like or dislike more than one thing, what form of **gustar** do you use?

✓ Check your answers to the preceding questions in *Appendix 1*.

**Instructor Resources**
• PPT, Extra Activities

**NOTE for *Gustar***
*Gustar* is introduced here in an abbreviated fashion with the goal of having students state their likes and dislikes. In this chapter, *gustar* is presented lexically. Then, there is an expanded presentation in *Capítulo 2*. Finally, *gustar* is reviewed and then presented in a complete fashion along with verbs like *gustar* in *Capítulo 8*.

**NOTE for *Gramática***
This is an inductive grammar presentation in which the students are given examples of a grammar concept and then guiding questions. By answering the questions, they formulate the rule in their own words. They are then to check their answers in *Appendix 1*. Research indicates that students remember and internalize grammar rules better when they construct their own knowledge.

**SUGGESTION for *Gustar***
Review the months and seasons with the class. Then discuss what the weather is like in your area for each season. Ask the students to describe the pictures in the text. What is the weather like in each picture? Using *gustar*, have students state why they like or dislike the weather in each picture. You might want to include some new verbs in infinitive form such as *tomar el sol, nadar, esquiar,* or *correr en el parque*. That way, students can explain why they like certain weather patterns.

[2:00]  **A-29** **¿Qué te gusta?** Ask your partner whether he/she likes or dislikes the following things. ■

**Estrategia**
Say " ¿Te gusta... ? to ask "Do you like . . . ?"

MODELO    la primavera
      E1:   *¿Te gusta la primavera?*
      E2:   *Sí, me gusta la primavera.*

1. el otoño
2. el invierno
3. el verano
4. los lunes

5. los sábados
6. los domingos
7. los viernes
8. la clase de español

**SUGGESTION for A-30**
You may wish to point out the number of words that look like their English equivalents in this activity to reinforce the presentation on cognates.

[2:00]  **A-30** **¿Qué más te gusta?** Take turns asking your partner about the following places and things. ■

MODELO    E1:   *¿Te gustan las hamburguesas?*
      E2:   *No, no me gustan las hamburguesas.*

1.

Las Vegas, Nevada

2.

las guitarras

3.

las camionetas

4.

la pizza

5.

San Antonio, Texas

6.

los teléfonos celulares

7.

el béisbol

8.

el fútbol

# Y por fin, ¿cómo andas?

Each of the coming chapters of *¡Anda! Curso elemental* will have three self-check sections for you to assess your progress. A **¿Cómo andas? I** (*How are you doing?*) section will appear one third of the way through each chapter, another, **¿Cómo andas? II,** will appear at the two-thirds point, and a third and final one will appear at the end of the chapter called **Y por fin, ¿cómo andas?** (*Finally, how are you doing?*) Use the checklists to measure what you have learned in the chapter. Place a check in the *Feel confident* column of the topics you feel you know, and a check in the *Need to review* column of those that you need to practice more. Be sure to go back and practice because it is the key to your success!

|  | Feel confident | Need to review |
|---|---|---|
| **Having completed this chapter, I now can . . .** | | |
| **Comunicación** | | |
| • greet, say good-bye, and introduce someone (p. 4) | ☐ | ☐ |
| • understand and respond appropriately to basic classroom expressions and requests (p. 8) | ☐ | ☐ |
| • spell in Spanish (p. 9) | ☐ | ☐ |
| • identify cognates (p. 10) | ☐ | ☐ |
| • express the subject pronouns (p. 11) | ☐ | ☐ |
| • use *to be* (p. 13) | ☐ | ☐ |
| • state nationalities (p. 14) | ☐ | ☐ |
| • count from 0 to 30 (p. 16) | ☐ | ☐ |
| • state the time (p. 18) | ☐ | ☐ |
| • elicit the date and season (p. 20) | ☐ | ☐ |
| • report the weather (p. 23) | ☐ | ☐ |
| • share personal likes and dislikes (p. 25) | ☐ | ☐ |
| **Cultura** | | |
| • compare and contrast greetings in the Spanish-speaking world and in the United States (p. 7) | ☐ | ☐ |
| • explain when to use the familiar and formal *you* (p. 12) | ☐ | ☐ |
| • summarize the diversity of the Spanish-speaking world (p. 16) | ☐ | ☐ |
| • name the continents and countries where Spanish is spoken (p. 17) | ☐ | ☐ |
| **Comunidades** | | |
| • use Spanish in real-life contexts (SAM) | ☐ | ☐ |

## Estrategia

The *¿Cómo andas?* and *Por fin, ¿cómo andas?* sections are designed to help you assess your understanding of specific concepts. In *Capítulo Preliminar A*, there is one opportunity for you to reflect on how well you understand the concepts. Beginning with *Capítulo 1* there will be three opportunities per chapter for you to stop and reflect on what you have learned. These checklists help you become accountable for your own learning, and help you determine what you need to review. Use the checklist as a way to communicate with your instructor about any concepts you still need to review. Additionally, you might also use your checklist as a way to study with a peer group or peer tutor. If you need to review a particular concept, more practice is available on MySpanishLab.

**INTRODUCTION to *Y por fin, ¿cómo andas?***
Throughout the textbook, you will encounter three sections per chapter that allow the students to self-assess. The first two sections are titled *¿Cómo andas? I* and *¿Cómo andas? I*, and the last section is titled *Y por fin, ¿cómo andas?* Each section has a chart listing the concepts from the chapter. For each concept, students can check off whether they feel confident about it or whether they need to review it. As students complete the *¿Cómo andas?* section, you can survey the class to see which areas students need to review. If the majority of students are having difficulties, you may want to review the concept in class. As an instructor, you can suggest that students make appointments for extra help on any concepts they need to review. This checklist is especially helpful if students have a peer tutor or study group, because they can keep a record of the concepts that are difficult. Peer tutors will appreciate having a checklist of concepts they should review for each tutoring session. Each chapter will normally have three self-checks, but since *Capítulo Preliminar A* is meant to be a quick introduction to Spanish, there is only one self-check in this chapter. Encourage students to use these self-checks, since they help them become accountable for their own learning and promote self-actualization.

**SUGGESTION for *Y por fin, ¿cómo andas?***
If you have time constraints, we recommend that students complete these self-assessments outside of class. You may want to spot-check some students and ask how they are doing (e.g., "How many of you feel confident with greeting, saying good-bye, and introducing someone?"). For those students who do not raise their hands, remind them that they need to consult the pages listed to review the material. If you have time to do them in class, one approach is to have students write short answers to the topics and then check in their textbooks to verify their answers. Based on this verification, they can rate themselves on the concepts and hand in their ratings to you at the end of class.

**Instructor Resources**
• Testing program information

**INTRODUCTION to**
*Vocabulario activo*
At the end of each chapter is a 2-page spread of the active vocabulary from each chapter. It is organized thematically. Students can use these two pages to organize their study of the core vocabulary for each chapter.

# VOCABULARIO ACTIVO

## Los saludos — *Greetings*

| | |
|---|---|
| Bastante bien. | *Just fine.* |
| Bien, gracias. | *Fine, thanks.* |
| Buenos días. | *Good morning.* |
| Buenas noches. | *Good evening; Good night.* |
| Buenas tardes. | *Good afternoon.* |
| ¿Cómo está usted? | *How are you?* (formal) |
| ¿Cómo estás? | *How are you?* (familiar) |
| ¡Hola! | *Hi! Hello!* |
| Más o menos. | *So-so.* |
| Muy bien. | *Really well.* |
| ¿Qué tal? | *How's it going?* |
| Regular. | *Okay.* |
| ¿Y tú? | *And you?* (familiar) |
| ¿Y usted? | *And you?* (formal) |

## Las despedidas — *Farewells*

| | |
|---|---|
| Adiós. | *Good-bye.* |
| Chao. | *Bye.* |
| Hasta luego. | *See you later.* |
| Hasta mañana. | *See you tomorrow.* |
| Hasta pronto. | *See you soon.* |

## Las presentaciones — *Introductions*

| | |
|---|---|
| ¿Cómo te llamas? | *What is your name?* (familiar) |
| ¿Cómo se llama usted? | *What is your name?* (formal) |
| Encantado/a. | *Pleased to meet you.* |
| Igualmente. | *Likewise.* |
| Me llamo… | *My name is . . .* |
| Mucho gusto. | *Nice to meet you.* |
| Quiero presentarte a… | *I would like to introduce you to . . .* (familiar) |
| Quiero presentarle a… | *I would like to introduce you to . . .* (formal) |
| Soy… | *I am . . .* |

## Expresiones útiles para la clase — *Useful classroom expressions*

| Preguntas y respuestas | *Questions and answers* |
|---|---|
| ¿Cómo? | *What? How?* |
| ¿Cómo se dice… en español? | *How do you say . . . in Spanish?* |
| ¿Cómo se escribe… en español? | *How do you write . . . in Spanish?* |
| Comprendo. | *I understand.* |
| Lo sé. | *I know.* |
| No. | *No.* |
| No comprendo. | *I don't understand.* |
| No lo sé. | *I don't know.* |
| Sí. | *Yes.* |
| ¿Qué es esto? | *What is this?* |
| ¿Qué significa? | *What does it mean?* |
| ¿Quién? | *Who?* |

| Expresiones de cortesía | *Polite expressions* |
|---|---|
| De nada. | *You're welcome.* |
| Gracias. | *Thank you.* |
| Por favor. | *Please.* |

| Mandatos para la clase | *Classroom instructions (commands)* |
|---|---|
| Abra(n) el libro en la página… | *Open your book to page . . .* |
| Cierre(n) el/los libro/s. | *Close your book/s.* |
| Conteste(n). | *Answer.* |
| Escriba(n). | *Write.* |
| Escuche(n). | *Listen.* |
| Lea(n). | *Read.* |
| Repita(n). | *Repeat.* |
| Vaya(n) a la pizarra. | *Go to the board.* |

| Las nacionalidades | Nationalities |
|---|---|
| alemán/alemana | German |
| canadiense | Canadian |
| chino/a | Chinese |
| cubano/a | Cuban |
| español/a | Spanish |
| estadounidense (norteamericano/a) | American |
| francés/francesa | French |
| inglés/inglesa | English |
| japonés/japonesa | Japanese |
| mexicano/a | Mexican |
| nigeriano/a | Nigerian |
| puertorriqueño/a | Puerto Rican |

| Los números 0–30 | Numbers 0–30 |
|---|---|
| See page 16. | |

| La hora | Telling time |
|---|---|
| A la... / A las... | At . . . o'clock. |
| ¿A qué hora... ? | At what time . . . ? |
| ...de la mañana | . . . in the morning |
| ...de la noche | . . . in the evening, at night |
| ...de la tarde | . . . in the afternoon, early evening |
| ¿Cuál es la fecha de hoy? | What is today's date? |
| Es la... / Son las... | It's . . . o'clock. |
| Hoy es... | Today is . . . |
| Mañana es... | Tomorrow is . . . |
| la medianoche | midnight |
| el mediodía | noon |
| menos cinco | five minutes to the hour |
| ¿Qué día es hoy? | What day is today? |
| ¿Qué hora es? | What time is it? |
| y cinco | five minutes after the hour |

| Los días de la semana | Days of the week |
|---|---|
| lunes | Monday |
| martes | Tuesday |
| miércoles | Wednesday |
| jueves | Thursday |
| viernes | Friday |
| sábado | Saturday |
| domingo | Sunday |

| Los meses del año | Months of the year |
|---|---|
| enero | January |
| febrero | February |
| marzo | March |
| abril | April |
| mayo | May |
| junio | June |
| julio | July |
| agosto | August |
| septiembre | September |
| octubre | October |
| noviembre | November |
| diciembre | December |

| Las estaciones | Seasons |
|---|---|
| el invierno | winter |
| la primavera | spring |
| el otoño | autumn; fall |
| el verano | summer |

| Expresiones del tiempo | Weather expressions |
|---|---|
| Está nublado. | It's cloudy. |
| Hace buen tiempo. | The weather is nice. |
| Hace calor. | It's hot. |
| Hace frío. | It's cold. |
| Hace mal tiempo. | The weather is bad. |
| Hace sol. | It's sunny. |
| Hace viento. | It's windy. |
| Llueve. | It's raining. |
| la lluvia | rain |
| Nieva. | It's snowing. |
| la nieve | snow |
| la nube | cloud |
| ¿Qué tiempo hace? | What's the weather like? |
| el sol | sun |
| la temperatura | temperature |
| el viento | wind |

| Algunos verbos | Some verbs |
|---|---|
| gustar | to like |
| ser | to be |

**Instructor Resources**
• IRM: Syllabi and Lesson Plans

---

**NATIONAL STANDARDS**

**COMUNICACIÓN I**
• To describe families (Communication)
• To pronounce vowels (Communication)
• To express what someone has (Communication)
• To use singular and plural nouns (Communication)
• To identify masculine and feminine nouns (Communication)
• To convey *the, a, one,* and *some* (Communication)
• To engage in additional communication practice (Communication)

**COMUNICACIÓN II**
• To give details about yourself and others (Communication)
• To state possession (Communication)
• To supply details about people, places, and things (Communication)
• To count from 31 to 100 (Communication, Cultures)
• To determine the topic and listen for known words (Communication)
• To communicate about people you know (Communication)
• To organize ideas to write a poem (Communication, Cultures)
• To engage in additional communication practice (Communication)

**CULTURA**
• To illustrate formation of Hispanic last names (Cultures, Comparisons, Communities)
• To compare and contrast several regional and national differences in the English and Spanish languages (Communication, Comparisons, Communities)
• To discuss the size, location, and makeup of the Hispanic population in the United States (Cultures, Connections)
• To explore further the chapter's cultural themes (Cultures)

**AMBICIONES SINIESTRAS**
• To recognize cognates when reading and to meet the six protagonists (Communication, Cultures)
• To discover more about the protagonists' classes and their lives (Communication)

**COMUNIDADES**
• To use Spanish in real-life contexts (Communication, Communities)

---

**1**

# ¿Quiénes somos?

What makes us who we are? What makes each of us unique? We may come from different geographical locations and represent different cultures, races, and religions, yet in many respects we are much the same. We have the same basic needs, share common likes and dislikes, and possess similar hopes and dreams.

## PREGUNTAS

**1** List the personal characteristics that make you unique. Which of the characteristics do you share with members of your family? Whom do you resemble most in your family?

**2** How does where people live affect who they are?

**3** What are some different nationalities and cultures you encounter on a regular basis in your community? What do you have in common with them?

30

---

**SECTION GOALS for *Chapter Opener***
By the end of the Chapter opener section, students will be able to:
• list characteristics of themselves and their families.
• compare and contrast various cultures and nationalities.
• discuss what factors contribute to individual differences.
• analyze how the social environment affects the individual.

**METHODOLOGY • The National Foreign Language Standards**
The American Council on the Teaching of Foreign Languages, along with the American Association of Teachers of Spanish and Portuguese and other language organizations, created the National Foreign Language Standards.

*¡Anda! Curso elemental* is based on the National Standards, and the Standards' 5 Cs (*Communication, Cultures, Connections, Comparisons, and Communities*) will always be identified with each chapter's objectives. For more information on the National Foreign Language Standards, please consult www.actfl.org.

**21ST CENTURY SKILLS • INFORMATION AND RESOURCES**
The Partnership for 21st Century Skills (P21) is an organization that has coordinated the core academic subjects, including world languages. On their website, www.P21.org, they provide skills-related information, resources, and community tools. They have also developed a framework.

| OBJETIVOS | CONTENIDOS | |
|---|---|---|

**31**

## NATIONAL STANDARDS
### Communities

Ask students to identify areas in your community where large populations of Spanish speakers live. What do these communities offer? What types of services do these Spanish speakers need? What services could your students provide? Is there an activity that the students and the community members should share? Some ideas of service learning projects in your area might include: collections of food and clothing for shelters; educational services, such as tutoring or after-school enrichment programs; music; reading to those who cannot; and simply keeping someone company. Remind students that everyone shares basic necessities that need to be fulfilled, regardless of nationality or culture.

### NOTE for *Contenidos*

The Heritage Language activities, available in the Student Activities Manual (SAM), are not only for heritage learners, but for all of your students. The activities either require students to reflect on the usage of Spanish, or to use Spanish in ways that encompass all of the 5 Cs. The end product will vary from student to student, which is an expected outcome of performance-based activities.

**METHODOLOGY • Starting Where the Learner Is**
Beginning with what students themselves already know best helps to build interest in the chapter. Answer the questions in *Preguntas* in English in pairs, or as a class activity. The philosophy of *¡Anda! Curso elemental* acknowledges the need to use English briefly at the beginning of each chapter during the first semester in order to access students' prior knowledge. John Dewey's philosophy encourages instructors to start where the learners are, which includes what they already know about the subject. Being able to share about what they already know helps motivate the learners and put them in an anticipatory state for the chapter's content.

**WARM-UP for *Chapter Opener***
Ask students to give their impressions of the photos on this page and the previous one. Have them silently read the chapter objectives. We suggest you spend no more than 5–7 minutes on chapter openers.

**EXPANSION for *Preguntas***
Ask your students: *In what ways will you be a different person in ten years? Why? What social factors have contributed to the development of the person you are today?* These questions should elicit responses based on the socio-anthropological fact that we are all products of our environments and that if in the future students are in a different place, they may find that they too have changed.

**PLANNING AHEAD**
To save time in class, assign **1-2** as homework. Also, assign actividad **1-25** in advance so that students may bring pictures to class. For the *Nota cultural* presentation, *Los apellidos en el mundo hispano* on p. 33, have students bring in wedding announcements for an expansion activity in which they practice formulating names *a la española*.

We recommend assigning *all* culture sections to be read in advance. Also, assign *all* grammar explanations for students to read before class, as they are clear and concise. The instructor's role then is to clarify or review, as necessary, any points students read in advance. Finally, we suggest assigning the *Escribe* sections and the *Ambiciones siniestras* readings and video episodes as homework.

**NOTE on**
***Comunicación I* and *II***

There are two *Comunicación* sections in each chapter of *¡Anda! Curso elemental*. Within each of these sections the new grammar and vocabulary are introduced, and all grammar and vocabulary (both new and recycled from previous chapters) are practiced. There are also *Nota cultural* culture presentations in each *Comunicación* section that reinforce the chapter theme and/or country or countries of focus. You and your students will know that you have reached the end of a *Comunicación* because there is a self-evaluation for your students entitled *¿Cómo andas?*. Each *Comunicación* section is designed to be completed in about one week.

**SECTION GOALS for**
***Comunicación I***

By the end of the *Comunicación I* section, students will be able to:
• describe their family members.
• explain the relationships between members of the family.
• pronounce vowels in Spanish.
• contrast the use of surnames in Spanish and English.
• express possession using the forms of the verb *tener*.
• narrate the characteristics of someone else's family using *tener* and vocabulary from *la familia*.
• form the plural of nouns and adjectives.
• distinguish between masculine and feminine endings of nouns and adjectives.
• practice identifying cognates.
• differentiate between the definite and indefinite articles.

**METHODOLOGY • Introducing New Vocabulary**

For new instructors (and as a reminder for those of us who have been teaching), whenever introducing new vocabulary, say the word, have students repeat after you, then say the word again, having them repeat once again. Even though the words are pronounced in MySpanishLab, the Student Activities Manual, and the *¡Anda! Curso elemental* CD, reinforcement in class helps novice learners. Spend approximately three minutes introducing new vocabulary.

*Note:* Do not repeat in unison with your students since you will be unable to monitor their pronunciation.

# Comunicación I

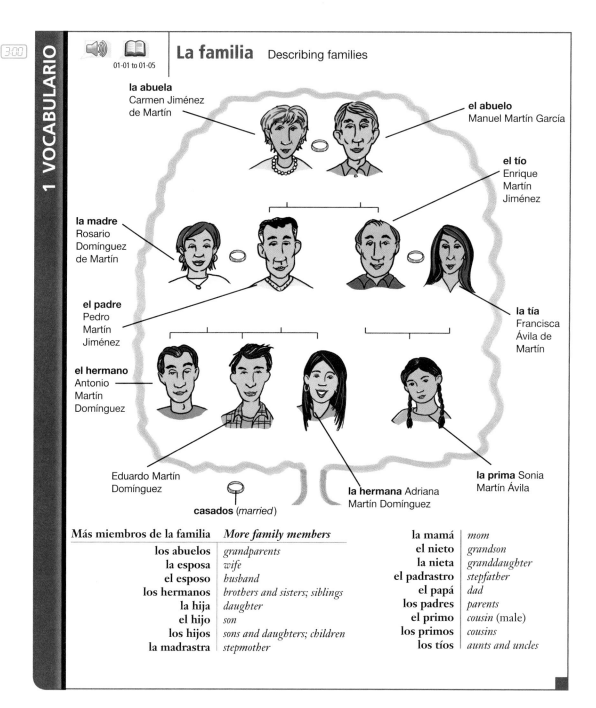

**1 VOCABULARIO**

3:00  🔊 📖  01-01 to 01-05

## La familia  Describing families

**la abuela** Carmen Jiménez de Martín

**el abuelo** Manuel Martín García

**el tío** Enrique Martín Jiménez

**la madre** Rosario Domínguez de Martín

**el padre** Pedro Martín Jiménez

**la tía** Francisca Ávila de Martín

**el hermano** Antonio Martín Domínguez

Eduardo Martín Domínguez

**casados** (*married*)

**la hermana** Adriana Martín Domínguez

**la prima** Sonia Martín Ávila

| Más miembros de la familia | *More family members* | | |
|---|---|---|---|
| los abuelos | *grandparents* | la mamá | *mom* |
| la esposa | *wife* | el nieto | *grandson* |
| el esposo | *husband* | la nieta | *granddaughter* |
| los hermanos | *brothers and sisters; siblings* | el padrastro | *stepfather* |
| la hija | *daughter* | el papá | *dad* |
| el hijo | *son* | los padres | *parents* |
| los hijos | *sons and daughters; children* | el primo | *cousin* (male) |
| la madrastra | *stepmother* | los primos | *cousins* |
| | | los tíos | *aunts and uncles* |

**METHODOLOGY • *También se dice…* Appendix 3**

The *También se dice…* appendix provides additional words that pertain to each topic. Words presented in introductory courses may not be the exact words that students wish to use; even native speakers sometimes search for additional vocabulary. *También se dice…* is meant to serve as an amplification of vocabulary for all students. The list should not be included on chapter assessments.

**NOTE for *La familia***

The terms *madrastra* and *padrastro*, as in English, can sometimes take on negative connotations. Many children would prefer to say "la esposa de mi padre/el esposo de mi madre."

**HERITAGE LANGUAGE LEARNERS**

Encourage your heritage language learners to make family trees, adding additional vocabulary to what is presented in the book. Allow them to use terms of endearment such as *abuelita* or *titi* for their family members.

## PRONUNCIACIÓN

 ¡Hola!

01-06 to 01-08

### Vowels

Go to MySpanishLab / Student Activities Manual to learn about the pronunciation of vowels.

**Fíjate**

You will find this *Pronunciación* section, and accompanying activities, on MySpanishLab and in the Student Activities Manual.

Capítulo Preliminar A.
El verbo *ser*, pág. 13.

**Estrategia**

*¡Anda! Curso elemental* has provided you with recycling references to help guide your continuous review of previously learned material. Make sure to consult the indicated pages if you need to refresh your memory about the topic.

[3:00]    **1-1  La familia de Eduardo**  Look at Eduardo's family tree and state how the following people are related to him. Share your answers with a partner. ■

MODELO    E1:  *¿Quién es* (Who is) *Antonio?*
          E2:  *Es su* (his) *hermano.*

1. Francisca          3. Enrique          5. Pedro          7. Sonia
2. Carmen             4. Manuel           6. Rosario        8. Adriana

**1-2  Mi familia**

[6:00]

**Paso 1**    Draw and label **three** generations of your own family tree, or create a fictitious one. Share your information with a partner, following the model. Please save your drawing! You will need it for **1-6.**

MODELO    E1:  *Mary es mi* (my) *hermana.*
          E2:  *George es mi papá.*

**Paso 2**    Write **five** of the sentences that you shared orally with your partner, or **five** different sentences about your family members. Follow the **modelo** in **Paso 1.**

MODELO    _____ _____ mi _____.  ■
          *(Subject)    (verb)    (family member)*

**Estrategia**

For additional vocabulary choices, consult Appendix 3, *También se dice…*

## NOTA CULTURAL

[5:00]

### Los apellidos en el mundo hispano

01-09 to 01-11

In Spanish-speaking countries, it is customary for people to use both paternal and maternal last names (surnames). For example, Eduardo's father is **Pedro Martín Jiménez** and his mother's maiden name is **Rosario Domínguez Montalvo.** Eduardo's first last name is his father's first last name (**Martín**); Eduardo's second last name is his mother's first last name (**Domínguez**). Therefore, Eduardo's full name is **Eduardo Martín Domínguez.** In most informal situations, though, Eduardo would use only his first last name, so he would call himself **Eduardo Martín.**

In most Spanish-speaking countries, a woman usually retains the surname of her father upon marriage, while giving up her mother's surname. She takes her husband's last name, preceded by the preposition **de** (*of*). For example, when Eduardo's mother married his father, her name became **Rosario Domínguez de Martín.** Therefore, if a woman named **Carmen Torres López** married **Ricardo Colón Montoya,** her name would become **Carmen Torres de Colón.**

*(continued)*

---

**METHODOLOGY • Instructional Delivery**

There are many ways to make instructional delivery more efficient. One way is pairing your students for the day. Put the activities that you want them to do on the board. You suggest the amount of time they may want to spend. Some partners will need more time than others. Give directions in advance for any activities that require additional explanations. Otherwise, the students should be permitted to negotiate meaning together. Finally, always have one or more activities ready for groups that finish early. This may include reviewing the vocabulary from previous chapters, or you may want to list activities from previous chapters that they should go back and redo.

**METHODOLOGY • Process Approach to Writing**

The authors of *¡Anda! Curso elemental* believe in a process approach to writing. Hence, we have provided a step-by-step model for students to create sentences in **1-2**.

---

**INTRODUCTION to** *Pronunciación*

Each chapter has a brief presentation on Spanish pronunciation in MySpanishLab and in the Student Activities Manual after the initial vocabulary section. These presentations are concise, taking examples from vocabulary both just presented and previously learned, as well as from cognates. The presentations are brief so that students can focus on small portions of Spanish pronunciation without feeling overwhelmed. Encourage your students to practice these sections several times.

**SECTION GOALS for** *Pronunciación*

By the end of the *Pronunciación* section, students will be able to:
- pronounce the Spanish vowels *a, e, i, o,* and *u.*
- practice pronouncing cognates and new vocabulary by sounding out each letter.

**ANSWERS to 1-1**
1. Francisca es su tía.
2. Carmen es su abuela.
3. Enrique es su tío.
4. Manuel es su abuelo.
5. Pedro es su padre.
6. Rosario es su madre.
7. Sonia es su prima.
8. Adriana es su hermana.

**METHODOLOGY • Recycling**

We know from thousands of educational research studies that learners need material to be recycled in order to acquire the concepts. The authors of *¡Anda! Curso elemental* firmly believe in recycling previously introduced material and do so frequently throughout every chapter.

**METHODOLOGY • Using English in the Classroom**

The philosophy of *¡Anda! Curso elemental* regarding the use of English is as follows:
1. Grammar explanations are brief and in English.
2. Critical-thinking questions or those tapping students' prior knowledge (such as those in this chapter opener) start in English due to the limited nature of the students' Spanish language capability. As the program progresses, these questions will be in Spanish.
3. Directions for activities are in English until *Capítulo 3,* when students are eased into Spanish and weaned away from English.

The use of Spanish in *¡Anda! Curso elemental* is based on Stephen Krashen's Input Hypothesis (*i* + 1), which states that students acquire more language when exposed to structures that are a little beyond (+1) what they completely comprehend (*i*).

**NATIONAL STANDARDS**
*Cultures, Comparisons, Communities*

In the *Nota cultural* presentation *Los nombres en el mundo hispano*, you will find an explanation of how names and surnames are written in Spanish. This cultural reading addresses Standard 2.1, because it explains the differences between how people are named in Hispanic countries and how people in the United States are named. This cultural difference is important when communicating with Spanish speakers, because students may incorrectly assume that a Hispanic woman is single or divorced if her last name differs from that of her husband. Similarly, Hispanic children and their mothers may use different last names. Standard 4.1 asks students to make comparisons between their own language and Spanish. You can point out that sometimes, for professional or personal reasons, married women in the United States keep their maiden names, while others hyphenate both last names or use both names without a hyphen. When students understand how to address someone correctly, they are more likely to communicate effectively. Standard 5.1 encourages the use of Spanish skills beyond the school setting. Mastering the use of surnames in Spanish allows students to connect with Spanish speakers.

**EXPANSION for *Nota cultural***
Additional questions and projects for your students are:
1. What is your full name in the Spanish style? Write it out, and then write the names of five family members or friends *a la española*. For example, Gail Parker's mother's maiden name is Smith. Her name *a la española* would be *Gail Parker Smith*.
2. Ask students to bring the wedding announcement page of a newspaper to class. Have them work in pairs to decide what the names of five new brides would be *a la española* if they took their new husbands' last names.

**ANSWERS to *Nota cultural***
1. Hyphenated last names, double last names (e.g., Hillary Rodham Clinton).
2. ***Some answers may include***: less confusion in phone books with common names, family last names are not lost as quickly, and potentially easier reconstruction of a family's heritage.

**Preguntas**

1. It may seem unusual to use more than one last name at a time, but this custom is not unique to Spanish-speaking contexts. Are there any equivalents in the United States or in other countries?
2. Can you think of any advantages to using both the mother's and the father's last names?

**Fíjate**

Below are some common Spanish first names and nicknames.

**Hombres**

| | |
|---|---|
| Antonio | Toño, Toni |
| Francisco | Paco, Pancho, Cisco |
| Guillermo | Memo, Guillo, Guille |
| Jesús | Chu, Chuito, Chucho, Chus |
| José | Pepe |
| Manuel | Manolo, Mani |
| Ramón | Moncho, Monchi |

**Mujeres**

| | |
|---|---|
| Antonia | Toñín, Toña, Toñi(ta) |
| Concepción | Concha, Conchita |
| Guadalupe | Lupe, Lupita |
| María Soledad | Marisol |
| María Teresa | Maite, Marité, Maritere |
| Pilar | Pili |
| Rosario | Charo |

**2 GRAMÁTICA**

📖 *¡Hola!* Spanish Tutorial
01-12 to 01-16
1:00

**El verbo *tener*** Expressing what someone has

Tengo una hermana y un hermano.

In **Capítulo Preliminar A** you learned the present tense of **ser.** Another very common verb in Spanish is **tener** (*to have*). The present tense forms of the verb **tener** follow.

**tener** (*to have*)

| Singular | | | Plural | | |
|---|---|---|---|---|---|
| yo | **tengo** | *I have* | nosotros/as | **tenemos** | *we have* |
| tú | **tienes** | *you have* | vosotros/as | **tenéis** | *you all have* |
| Ud. | **tiene** | *you have* | Uds. | **tienen** | *you all have* |
| él, ella | **tiene** | *he/she has* | ellos/as | **tienen** | *they have* |

**METHODOLOGY • Student Accountability**
When students are working in class, either with partners or by themselves, always circulate around the room to ensure they are on task. We suggest giving a daily class participation grade for student accountability. Also, spot-check activity answers not only for comprehension, but also for accountability. It sends a strong message to students that they must stay on task, as does allotting a brief but appropriate time for each activity.

**METHODOLOGY • Grammar Explanations**
Grammar explanations are simple and concise so that students can read them before coming to class. You may wish to review the presentation *briefly* (e.g., pronounce verb forms, etc.), but then move directly into the activities.

**METHODOLOGY • Deductive Presentations of Grammar**
Verb presentations such as the one for *tener* are done *deductively* (give students the rules/forms and go directly to practice) to streamline presentation time. All grammar presentations in this chapter are deductive.

**1-3** **¿Quién tiene familia?** Take turns giving the correct form of the verb **tener** for each subject listed. ■

**MODELO** E1: la prima
E2: *tiene*

1. tú *tienes*
2. los padres *tienen*
3. nosotros *tenemos*
4. Pedro, Carmen y Rosario *tienen*
5. yo *tengo*
6. el tío *tiene*

*Capítulo Preliminar A.*
*El verbo ser, pág. 13.*

**1-4** **¡Apúrate!** One person makes a ball out of a piece of paper, says a subject pronoun, and tosses the ball to someone in the group. That person catches it, gives the corresponding form of **tener**, then says another pronoun and tosses the ball to someone else. After finishing **tener**, repeat the game with **ser**. ■

**MODELO** E1: *yo*
E2: *tengo; ellas*
E3: *tienen; usted*
E4: *tiene;…*

**1-5** **La familia de José** Complete the paragraph with the correct forms of **tener**. Then share your answers with a partner. Finally, based on what you learned in the previous culture presentation regarding last names, what is José's father's last name? What is José's mother's maiden name? ■

Yo soy el primo de José. Él (1) _tiene_ una familia grande. (2) _Tiene_ tres hermanos, Pepe, Alonso y Tina. Su hermano Pepe está casado (*is married*) y (3) _tiene_ dos hijos. También José y sus hermanos (4) _tienen_ muchos tíos, siete en total. La madre de José (5) _tiene_ tres hermanos y dos están casados. El padre de José (6) _tiene_ una hermana y ella está casada con mi padre: ¡es mi madre! Nosotros (7) _tenemos_ una familia grande. ¿Y tú?, ¿(8) _tienes_ una familia grande?

José Olivo Peralta y su familia

**1-6** **De tal palo, tal astilla** Create **three** sentences with **tener** based on the family tree that you sketched for **1-2**, page 33. Tell them to your partner, who will then share what you said with another classmate. ■

**Fíjate**

The word *un* in the *modelo* for **1-6** is the shortened form of the number *uno*. It is used before a masculine noun—a concept that will be explained later in this chapter.

**MODELO** E1 (ALICE): *Tengo un hermano, Scott. Tengo dos tíos, George y David. No tengo abuelos.*

E2 (JEFF): *Alice tiene un hermano, Scott. Tiene dos tíos, George y David. No tiene abuelos.*

**METHODOLOGY • Interpretive, Interpersonal, and Presentation Modes of Communication**
There are three modes of communication: *interpretive, interpersonal,* and *presentational.* The *interpretive* mode of communication includes reading and listening. It is deciphering linguistic code. The *interpersonal* mode of communication is a core concept of *¡Anda!* It is oral communication between two or more individuals. It can also be communicating via writing. Finally, the *presentational* mode of communication is when an individual makes a presentation to an individual or group, usually orally. *¡Anda!* balances all three modes of communication to provide learners with ample opportunities to grow in the language. For example, when students are working in

pairs on the activities in the text, they are employing the interpretive and interpersonal modes of communication. When the activity has students speaking in extended discourse (three or more sentences) to a partner, that is the presentational mode. The *¡Conversemos!* sections of each chapter as well as Chapters 6 and 12 also incorporate extensively all three modes of communication.

**3 GRAMÁTICA**

 01-17 to 01-20 Spanish/English Tutorials

## Sustantivos singulares y plurales
Using singular and plural nouns

Raúl tiene dos primas y Jorge tiene una prima.

To pluralize singular nouns and adjectives in Spanish, follow these simple guidelines.

1. If the word ends in a vowel, add **-s**.

| | | | | | |
|---|---|---|---|---|---|
| hermana | → | hermanas | abuelo | → | abuelos |
| día | → | días | mi | → | mis |

2. If the word ends in a consonant, add **-es**.

| | | | | | |
|---|---|---|---|---|---|
| mes | → | meses | ciudad | → | ciudades |
| televisión | → | televisiones | joven | → | jóvenes |

3. If the word ends in a **-z**, change the **z** to **c**, and add **-es**.

| | | | | | |
|---|---|---|---|---|---|
| lápiz | → | lápices | feliz | → | felices |

> **Fíjate**
> Note that *televisión* loses its accent mark in the plural. Also, note the plural of *joven* is *jóvenes*. You will learn about accent marks in *Capítulo 2.*

---

 **1-7** **Te toca a ti** Take turns making the following singular nouns plural. ▪

**MODELO**    E1: primo
          E2: *primos*

1. padre padres
2. tía tías
3. taxi taxis
4. francés franceses
5. nieto nietos

6. alemán alemanes
7. abuela abuelas
8. sol soles
9. emoción emociones
10. favor favores

---

 **1-8** **De nuevo** Now take turns making the following plural nouns singular. ▪

**MODELO**    E1: primos
          E2: *primo*

1. hijos hijo
2. días día
3. discusiones discusión
4. madres madre
5. lápices lápiz

6. jóvenes joven
7. familias familia
8. libertades libertad
9. nietos nieto
10. meses mes

¡Hola! Spanish Tutorial
01-21 to 01-22

# El masculino y el femenino

Identifying masculine and feminine nouns

El abuelo y las tías.

In Spanish, all nouns (people, places, and things) have gender; they are either masculine or feminine. Use the following rules to help you determine the gender of nouns. If a noun does not belong to any of the following categories, you must memorize the gender as you learn that noun.

1. Most words ending in -a are feminine.
   **la hermana, la hija, la mamá, la tía**
   *Some exceptions: **el día, el papá,** and words of Greek origin ending in -ma, such as **el problema** and **el programa.**

2. Most words ending in -o are masculine.
   **el abuelo, el hermano, el hijo, el nieto**
   *Some exceptions: **la foto** (*photo*), **la mano** (*hand*), **la moto** (*motorcycle*)
   *Note: **la foto** and **la moto** are shortened forms for **la fotografía** and **la motocicleta.**

3. Words ending in -ción and -sión are feminine.
   **la discusión, la recepción, la televisión**
   *Note: The suffix -ción is equivalent to the English *-tion*.

4. Words ending in -dad or -tad are feminine.
   **la ciudad** (*city*), **la libertad, la universidad**
   *Note: these suffixes are equivalent to the English *-ty*.

> **Estrategia**
> Making educated guesses about the meanings of unknown words will help to make you a successful Spanish learner!

As you learned in **Capítulo Preliminar A,** words that look alike and have the same meaning in both English and Spanish, such as **discusión** and **universidad,** are known as *cognates*. Use them to help you decipher meaning and to form words. For example, **prosperidad** looks like what English word? What is its gender?

---

 **1-9** **¿Recuerdas?** Take turns determining which of the following nouns are masculine (**M**) and which are feminine (**F**). ■

1. _F_ hijas    3. _M_ mapa    5. _M_ hermano    7. _F_ mamá
2. _F_ discusión    4. _F_ nacionalidad    6. _F_ manos    8. _M_ abuelos

---

**1-10** **Para practicar** Take turns deciding whether these cognates are masculine or feminine. Can you guess their English equivalents? ■

1. guitarra F / guitar    3. computadora F / computer    5. cafetería F / cafeteria
2. teléfono M / telephone    4. drama M / drama    6. educación F / education

---

**CAPÍTULO 1**

🔑 **Instructor Resources**
• PPT, Extra Activities

**METHODOLOGY • Teaching Written Accent Marks**
Rules for stress and accent marks will be formally presented in the *Capítulo 2 Pronunciación* section in MySpanishLab and in the Student Activities Manual. The philosophy of *¡Anda! Curso elemental* is to present concepts in small chunks. We encourage students to process and master one set of rules first, and then proceed to additional information, such as rules for written accent marks. Therefore, we suggest postponing detailed explanations regarding accent marks and accentuation until *Capítulo 2*.

**METHODOLOGY • False Cognates**
The concept of *false cognates* is presented at the point of need and usage, again, with the goal of streamlining and presenting only essential information at the beginning to help students build confidence.

**METHODOLOGY • Grammar for True Beginners**

Based on decades of experience, the authors of *¡Anda! Curso elemental* believe that the initial presentation of grammar rules needs to be basic. Too many exceptions to the rule may confuse and frustrate true beginners. Hence, additional exceptions, such as *el agua*, are presented at the point of introduction of the vocabulary. If you have heritage language learners or false beginners, you may expand the presentation to suit their needs.

**ADDITIONAL ACTIVITY for**
*Los artículos definidos e indefinidos*

🍦🍦 Use the correct definite article with the following active vocabulary words and cognates, and then repeat the activity with indefinite articles.

1. primavera
2. norteamericanos
3. teléfono
4. sol
5. temperatura
6. nubes
7. domingo
8. viento
9. otoño
10. mañanas

## 5 GRAMÁTICA

[5:00]

 ¡Hola! Spanish/English Tutorials
01-23 to 01-27

# Los artículos definidos e indefinidos
Conveying *the, a, one,* and *some*

Eduardo tiene una hermana. La hermana de Eduardo se llama Adriana.

Like English, Spanish has two kinds of articles, definite and indefinite. The definite article in English is *the;* the indefinite articles are *a, an,* and *some.*

In Spanish, articles and other adjectives mirror the gender (masculine or feminine) and number (singular or plural) of the nouns to which they refer. For example, an article referring to a singular masculine noun must also be singular and masculine. Note the forms of the articles in the following charts.

**Fíjate**
Note that *el* means "the," and *él* means "he."

### Los artículos definidos

| | | | |
|---|---|---|---|
| el hermano | *the brother* | los hermanos | *the brothers/the brothers and sisters* |
| la hermana | *the sister* | las hermanas | *the sisters* |

### Los artículos indefinidos

| | | | |
|---|---|---|---|
| un hermano | *a/one brother* | unos hermanos | *some brothers/some brothers and sisters* |
| una hermana | *a/one sister* | unas hermanas | *some sisters* |

1. **Definite articles** are used to refer to **the** person, place, or thing.
2. **Indefinite articles** are used to refer to **a** or **some** person, place, or thing.

Adriana es **la** hermana de Eduardo y **los** abuelos de él se llaman Carmen y Manuel.
Jorge tiene **una** tía y **unos** tíos.

*Adriana is Eduardo's sister, and his grandparents' names are Carmen and Manuel.*
*Jorge has an aunt and some uncles.*

[3:00]  **1-11** **Vamos a practicar** Complete the following steps. ■

**Paso 1**   Take turns giving the correct form of the *definite* article for each of the following nouns.

**MODELO**   E1: tías
E2: *las tías*

1. tío   el tío
2. padres   los padres
3. mamá   la mamá
4. papá   el papá
5. hermanas   las hermanas
6. hijo   el hijo
7. abuela   la abuela
8. primo   el primo

**Paso 2**   This time provide the correct form of the *indefinite* article.

**MODELO**   E1: tías
E2: *unas tías*

**ANSWERS to 1-11**
Paso 2
1. un tío
2. unos padres
3. una mamá
4. un papá
5. unas hermanas
6. un hijo
7. una abuela
8. un primo

**1-12 Una concordancia** Take turns matching the family members with the corresponding articles. Each family member will have **two** articles: one definite and one indefinite. ■

1. __a/e__ hijo
2. __d/h__ hermanas
3. __b/f__ tía
4. __d/h__ primas
5. __c/g__ abuelos
6. __b/f__ nieta
7. __c/g__ padres
8. __b/f__ madre

a. el
b. la
c. los
d. las
e. un
f. una
g. unos
h. unas

**1-13 ¿Quiénes son?** Fill in the blanks with the correct form of either the definite or indefinite article. Then take turns sharing your answers and explaining your choices. You may want to refer to the family tree on page 32. ■

**MODELO**    Adriana es _la_ hermana de Eduardo.

(1) ___Los (the)___ abuelos se llaman Manuel y Carmen. Eduardo tiene (2) ___un (a)___ tío.

(3) ___El (the)___ tío se llama Enrique. Eduardo tiene (4) ___una (a)___ prima; se llama Sonia.

(5) ___El (the)___ hermano de Eduardo se llama Antonio.

**Estrategia**

To say "Eduardo's sister" or "Eduardo's grandparents," you add _de Eduardo_ to each of your sentences: _Es la hermana de Eduardo. Son los abuelos de Eduardo._

# ¿Cómo andas? I

Each chapter has three places at which you will be asked to assess your progress. This first assessment comes as you have completed approximately one third of the chapter. How confident are you with your progress to date?

| Having completed **Comunicación I,** I now can . . . | Feel confident | Need to review |
|---|---|---|
| • describe families (p. 32) | ☐ | ☐ |
| • pronounce vowels (MSL / SAM) | ☐ | ☐ |
| • illustrate formation of Hispanic last names (p. 33) | ☐ | ☐ |
| • express what someone has (p. 34) | ☐ | ☐ |
| • use singular and plural nouns (p. 36) | ☐ | ☐ |
| • identify masculine and feminine nouns (p. 37) | ☐ | ☐ |
| • convey _the, a, one,_ and _some_ (p. 38) | ☐ | ☐ |

**SECTION GOALS for**
*Comunicación II*

By the end of the *Comunicación II*, section, students will be able to:
• describe themselves and others.
• distinguish between people of different ages and use titles of respect accordingly.
• show possession, using possessive adjectives.
• report characteristics about various family members.
• identify famous people and describe characteristics of each person.
• express the opposites of certain characteristics (e.g., nice, mean).
• make true and false statements.
• understand linguistic variations in vocabulary across regions of the world.
• count from 31 to 100.
• report demographics from Hispanic countries.

**NOTE for *Gente***

The terms "boy/girl" in Spanish can vary from region to region. *El niño/la niña* is often interchangeable with *el chico/la chica. El muchacho/la muchacha* may also be interchanged with *el/la joven.* These terms are not limited to the age depicted in the images presented.

**NATIONAL STANDARDS**
*Communication*

There are many ways to describe yourself and others. If students are in pairs or small groups, sharing information about themselves and asking follow-up questions, the standard this activity addresses is Standard 1.1. You could vary the activity by asking students to create posters of themselves with photos or drawings and captions using simple phrases in Spanish to describe themselves. You could showcase the posters in the classroom to an audience of readers, or students could present the information from the posters orally to the class. Communication Standard 1.3 addresses the presentational mode.

# Comunicación II

**6 VOCABULARIO**

[2:00]

🔊 📖 **Gente** Giving details about yourself and others
01-28 to 1-31

Miguelito/Clarita

**el niño/la niña**

Daniel/Mariela

**el chico, el muchacho/
la chica, la muchacha**

Javier/Ana

**el joven/la joven**

Manuel/Manuela

**el hombre/la mujer**

la Sra. Torres/
la Srta. Sánchez/
el Sr. Martín

**la señora/
la señorita/el señor**

Manolo/Pilar
**el amigo/la amiga**

Roberto/Pepita
**el novio/la novia**

**El hombre** and **la mujer** are terms for *man* and *woman*. **Señor, señora,** and **señorita** are often used as titles of address; in that case, they may also be abbreviated as **Sr., Sra.,** and **Srta.,** respectively.

—Buenos días, **Sr.** Martín.　　*Good morning, Mr. Martín.*
—¿Cómo está Ud., **Sra.** Sánchez?　　*How are you, Mrs. Sánchez?*

> **Fíjate**
> The abbreviations *Sr., Sra.,* and *Srta.* are always capitalized, just like their equivalents in English.

[1:00]

👥 **1-14 Los opuestos** Take turns giving the gender opposites for the following words. Include the appropriate articles. ■

**MODELO**　　E1:　el novio
　　　　　　　E2:　*la novia*

1. el chico  la chica
2. un hombre  una mujer
3. la joven  el joven
4. un señor  una señora /
　　　　　　una señorita
5. una amiga  un amigo
6. la niña  el niño

**Instructor Resources**
• PPT, Extra Activities

**1-15 ¿Cómo se llama?** Take turns answering the following questions, based on the drawings on page 40. ■

MODELO    E1: ¿Cómo se llama el hombre?

         E2: *El hombre se llama Manuel.*

1. ¿Cómo se llama la joven?
2. ¿Cómo se llama el niño?
3. ¿Cómo se llaman los novios?
4. ¿Cómo se llama la señora?

*Capítulo Preliminar A.*
*Saludos, despedidas y*
*presentaciones, pág. 4.*

**ANSWERS to 1-15**
1. La joven se llama Ana.
2. El niño se llama Miguelito.
3. Los novios se llaman Roberto y Pepita.
4. La señora se llama Sra. Torres.

**EXPANSION for 1-15**
Ask your students the following questions:
*¿Cómo se llaman los jóvenes?*
*¿Cómo se llama la niña?*
*¿Cómo se llaman los niños?*
*¿Cómo se llama la señorita?*
*¿Cómo se llaman los amigos?*
*¿Cómo se llaman los chicos?*

# 7 GRAMÁTICA

¡Hola!
01-32 to 01-36 Spanish/English Tutorials

## Los adjetivos posesivos   Stating possession

You have already used the possessive adjective **mi** (*my*). Other forms of possessive adjectives are also useful in conversation.

Look at the following chart to see how to personalize talk about your family (*our* dad, *his* sister, *our* cousins, etc.) using possessive adjectives.

> Mis padres se llaman Juan y María. ¿Cómo se llaman tus padres?

**Fíjate**
*Vuestro/a/os/as* is only used in Spain.

**Fíjate**
Note that *tu* means "your," and *tú* means "you."

### Los adjetivos posesivos

| mi, mis | *my* | nuestro/a/os/as | *our* |
|---|---|---|---|
| tu, tus | *your* | vuestro/a/os/as | *your* |
| su, sus | *your* | su, sus | *your* |
| su, sus | *his, her, its* | su, sus | *their* |

**Note:**

1. Possessive adjectives agree in form with the person, place, or thing possessed, *not with the possessor*.
2. Possessive adjectives agree in number (singular or plural), and in addition, **nuestro** and **vuestro** indicate gender (masculine or feminine).
3. The possessive adjectives **tu/tus** (*your*) refer to someone with whom you are familiar and/or on a first name basis. **Su/sus** (*your*) is used when you are referring to people to whom you refer with *usted* and *ustedes*: that is, more formally and perhaps not on a first-name basis. **Su/sus** (*your* plural or *their*) is used when referring to individuals whom you are addressing with *ustedes* or when expressing possession with *ellos* and *ellas*.

| **mi** hermano | *my brother* | **mis** hermanos | *my brothers/siblings* |
|---|---|---|---|
| **tu** primo | *your cousin* | **tus** primos | *your cousins* |
| **su** tía | *her/his/your/their aunt* | **sus** tías | *her/his/your/their aunts* |
| **nuestra** familia | *our family* | **nuestras** familias | *our families* |
| **vuestra** mamá | *your mom* | **vuestras** mamás | *your moms* |
| **su** hija | *her/his/your/their daughter* | **sus** hijas | *his/her/your/their daughters* |

*(continued)*

**SUGGESTION for *Los adjetivos posesivos***
You may want to physically demonstrate the use of possessive adjectives. For example, bring something unusual to class, like a chocolate bar. Hold it up and say, *¿Es mi chocolate?* Move around the room, repeating the sentence as you look at students, emphasizing the *mi*. Then, stop and present the bar to a student. He/she takes it. Then say to the student, *¿Es tu* (emphasize) *chocolate?* Turn to the other students and say, *X tiene el chocolate. No es mi* (exaggerate) *chocolate, es su* (exaggerate) *chocolate.* Then ask the student, *¿Es tu chocolate?* Guide the student into saying, *Sí, es mi chocolate.* At this point you can take the bar away and say "no" and go through the routine quickly with another student. Now open the bar (or several bars, if you like) and break it into a few pieces, sharing the pieces with your students. Say, *Ahora es nuestro chocolate, ¿no, clase?* Have them respond, *Sí, es nuestro chocolate.*

| | |
|---|---|
| Eduardo tiene una novia. | *Eduardo has a girlfriend.* |
| **Su** novia se llama Julia. | *His girlfriend's name is Julia.* |
| Nuestros padres tienen dos amigos. | *Our parents have two friends.* |
| **Sus** amigos son Jorge y Marta. | *Their friends are Jorge and Marta.* |

 **1-16 ¿De quién es?** Take turns supplying the correct possessive adjectives for the family members listed. ■

MODELO   E1:   *(our)* papás
         E2:   *nuestros papás*

1. *(your/familiar)* novia   tu novia
2. *(my)* hermanos   mis hermanos
3. *(our)* mamá   nuestra mamá
4. *(your/formal)* tío   su tío
5. *(her)* amiga   su amiga
6. *(his)* hermanas   sus hermanas

 **1-17 Relaciones familiares** Take turns completing the paragraph about Eduardo's family relationships, from Sonia's point of view. You may want to refer to the family tree on page 32. ■

Yo soy Sonia. Eduardo es (1) ___mi___ primo. Antonio y Adriana son (2) ___mis___ primos también (*also*). (3) ___Sus___ padres, Pedro y Rosario, son (4) ___mis___ tíos. (5) ___Mis___ padres se llaman Enrique y Francisca. (6) Además (*Furthermore*), ___mi___ amiga Pilar es como (*like*) parte de (7) (*our*) ___nuestra___ familia.

**Estrategia**

Using your own friends and family will help you remember the vocabulary. Write the names of your immediate family or your best friends. Then write a description of how those people are connected to each other. E.g., *Karen es la madre de Brian* or *Brian es el hijo de Karen.*

 **1-18 Tu familia** Using at least **three** different possessive adjectives, talk to your partner about your family. You may want to refer to the family tree you drew for 1-2. ■

MODELO   *En mi familia somos cinco personas. Mi padre se llama John y mi madre es Marie. Sus amigos son Mary y Dennis. Tengo dos hermanos, Clark y Blake. Nuestros tíos son Alice y Ralph y nuestras primas se llaman Gina y Glynis.*

## 8 GRAMÁTICA

 ¡Hola! English Tutorial 01-37 to 01-42

# Los adjetivos descriptivos

Supplying details about people, places, and things

Descriptive adjectives are words that describe people, places, and things.

1. In English, adjectives usually come before the words they describe (e.g., **the** *red* **car**), but in Spanish, they usually follow the words (e.g., **el coche** *rojo*).
2. Adjectives in Spanish agree with the nouns they modify in number (singular or plural) and in gender (masculine or feminine).

| | |
|---|---|
| Carlos es un **chico** simpáti**co**. | *Carlos is a nice boy.* |
| Adela es una **chica** simpáti**ca**. | *Adela is a nice girl.* |
| Carlos y Adela son (unos) **chicos** simpáti**cos**. | *Carlos and Adela are (some) nice children.* |

3. A descriptive adjective can also follow the verb **ser** directly. When it does, it still agrees with the noun to which it refers, which is the subject in this case.

| | |
|---|---|
| Carlos es simpáti**co**. | *Carlos is nice.* |
| Adela es simpáti**ca**. | *Adela is nice.* |
| Carlos y Adela son simpáti**cos**. | *Carlos and Adela are nice.* |

### Las características físicas, la personalidad y otros rasgos

alto   alta   bajo   baja

guapo   guapa

delgado      gordo
delgada      gorda

débil        fuerte

inteligente

joven        mayor

pobre        rico
             rica

*(continued)*

**Instructor Resources**
• PPT, Extra Activities

**SUGGESTION for *Los adjetivos descriptivos***
Bring photos to class to use in illustrating these characteristics and traits. You can also ask students to give examples of famous people who demonstrate them. Doing so will make this presentation more meaningful to your students.

**HERITAGE LANGUAGE LEARNERS**
Bring in photos of famous Hispanics and ask your heritage language learners to describe their characteristics in further detail.

**SUGGESTION for *Los adjetivos descriptivos***
Lead students in playing the association game with this list of new words, using movie and television characters, e.g., *¿Quién es cómico? ¿Homer Simpson?*

**CAPÍTULO 1**

**METHODOLOGY • Actividades**
The sequence of activities **1-19** through **1-25** puts together a wide array of activities using *ser*, which is review, and adjectives. These activities are enjoyable and provide ample practice with the concepts. If your students are false beginners or heritage language learners, pick the most appropriate activities or have students select those they want to do.

| La personalidad | *Personality* |
|---|---|
| aburrido/a | *boring* |
| antipático/a | *unpleasant* |
| bueno/a | *good* |
| cómico/a | *funny; comical* |
| interesante | *interesting* |
| malo/a | *bad* |
| paciente | *patient* |
| perezoso/a | *lazy* |
| responsable | *responsible* |
| simpático/a | *nice* |
| tonto/a | *silly; dumb* |
| trabajador/a | *hard-working* |

| Las características físicas | *Physical characteristics* |
|---|---|
| bonito/a | *pretty* |
| feo/a | *ugly* |
| grande | *big; large* |
| pequeño/a | *small* |

| Otras palabras útiles | *Other useful words* |
|---|---|
| muy | *very* |
| (un) poco | *(a) little* |

Capítulo Preliminar A.
El verbo *ser*, pág. 13.

`1:00` **1-19** **¿Cómo son?** Take turns describing the following people to a classmate. ■

**Estrategia**

Review *Los adjetivos de nacionalidad* in *Capítulo Preliminar A* in order to describe people in more detail.

MODELO     E1:  Jorge
           E2:  *Jorge es débil.*

Jorge

1. Juan
Juan es fuerte.

2. María
Maria es alta y delgada.

3. Lupe y Marco
Lupe y Marco son ricos.

4. Roberto
Roberto es alto y delgado.

5. Beatriz
Beatriz es baja.

6. yo
*Answers will vary.*

**1-20 ¿Cómo los describes?** Circulate among your classmates, asking for descriptions of the following people. Write what each person says, along with his/her name. ∎

Workbooklet

MODELO      E1:  *¿Cómo es Jon Stewart?*

            E2:  *Jon Stewart es cómico, inteligente y muy trabajador.*

            E1:  *¿Cómo te llamas?*

            E2:  *Mi nombre es Rubén.*

| PERSONA(S) | DESCRIPCIÓN | NOMBRE DEL ESTUDIANTE |
|---|---|---|
| Jon Stewart | Es cómico, inteligente y muy trabajador. | Rubén |
| 1. Justin Bieber | | |
| 2. tus padres | | |
| 3. tu mejor (*best*) amigo/a y tú | | |
| 4. Shakira | | |
| 5. los estudiantes en la clase de español | | |

**1-21 Al contrario** Student 1 creates a sentence using the cues provided, and Student 2 expresses the opposite. Pay special attention to adjective agreement. ∎

MODELO      los hermanos González/guapo

            E1:  *Los hermanos González son guapos.*

            E2:  *¡Ay no, son muy feos!*

Capítulo Preliminar
A. El verbo *ser*,
pág. 13.

1. los abuelos / pobre
2. la señora López / muy antipático
3. Jaime / delgado

4. la tía Claudia / mayor
5. Tomás y Antonia / alto
6. nosotros / perezoso

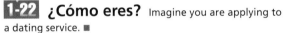

**1-22 ¿Cómo eres?** Imagine you are applying to a dating service. ∎

Paso 1      Describe yourself to your partner using at least **three** adjectives, and then describe your ideal date.

MODELO      *Me llamo Julie. Soy joven, muy inteligente y alta. Mi hombre ideal es inteligente, paciente y cómico.*

Paso 2      How similar are you and your partner and how similar are your ideal mates?

MODELO      *Rebeca y yo somos jóvenes, altas y muy inteligentes. Nuestros hombres ideales son cómicos y pacientes.*

matchideal.com

Soy inteligente, cómico y responsable.

No soy muy rico pero soy trabajador.

¿Eres inteligente, simpática y cómica?

Contacta con matchideal.com/chucho.

NATIONAL STANDARDS
*Communication, Comparisons, Communities*

*El español, lengua diversa* offers insight into the many ways in which communication takes place. Communicating in Spanish is Goal One, and Standard 1.1 encourages students to engage in conversations. The fact that Spanish vocabulary varies by country reinforces the awareness of linguistic variations in English. Students are able to make comparisons, as defined in Standard 4.1, between regional and linguistic differences that occur in English and Spanish. Students can apply this knowledge when interacting with Hispanic people in the United States and abroad. Standard 5.1 encompasses using Spanish within and beyond an academic environment, and taking risks with the language by communicating with Spanish speakers from all over the world is part of being a successful language learner.

   **1-23  ¿Es cierto o falso?**  Describe **five** famous (or infamous!) people or characters. Your partner can react by saying **Es verdad** (*It's true*) or **No es verdad** (*It's not true*). If your partner disagrees with you, he/she must correct your statement. ■

> **Estrategia**
>
> Being an "active listener" is an important skill in any language. *Active listening* means that you hear and understand what someone is saying. Being able to repeat what someone says helps you practice and perfect the skill of active listening.

MODELO        E1:  *Santa Claus es gordo y un poco feo.*
              E2:  *No es verdad. Sí, es gordo pero no es feo. Es guapo.*

 **1-24  ¿Cuáles son sus cualidades?**  Think of the qualities of your best friend and those of someone you do not particularly like (**una persona que no me gusta**). Using adjectives that you know in Spanish, write at least **three** sentences that describe each of these people. Share your list with a partner. ■

MODELO        **MI MEJOR (*BEST*) AMIGO/A**          **UNA PERSONA QUE NO ME GUSTA**
              1. Es trabajador/a.                    1. Es antipático/a.
              2. Es inteligente.                     2. No es paciente.
              3. …                                   3. …

   **1-25  Describe a una familia**  Bring family photos (personal ones or some taken from the Internet or a magazine) to class and describe the family members to a classmate, using at least **five** sentences. ■

MODELO        *Tengo dos hermanas, Kate y Ana. Ellas son simpáticas y bonitas. Mi papá no es aburrido y es muy trabajador. Tengo seis primos…*

## NOTA CULTURAL

# El español, lengua diversa

01-43 to 01-44

The title of this chapter, **¿Quiénes somos?**, suggests that we are all a varied combination of many factors, one of which is language. As you know, the English language is rich in state, regional, and national variations. For example, what word do you use when referring to soft drinks? Some people in the United States say *soda,* others say *pop,* and still others use *Coke* as a generic term for all brands and flavors of soft drinks.

The Spanish language also has many variations. For example, to describe someone as *funny* you could say **cómico/a** in many Latin American countries, but **divertido/a** or **gracioso/a** in Spain. Similarly, there are multiple ways to say the word *bus*: in Mexico,

*(continued)*

**Instructor Resources**
• Textbook images, PPT, Extra Activities

camión; in Puerto Rico and Cuba, **guagua**; in Spain, **autobús**. In *¡Anda! Curso elemental,* such variants will appear in the **También se dice...** section in Appendix 3.

The pronunciation of English also varies in different parts of the United States and throughout the rest of the English-speaking world, and so it is with Spanish across the Spanish-speaking world. Nevertheless, wherever you go you will find that Spanish is still Spanish, despite regional and national differences. You should have little trouble understanding native speakers from different countries or making yourself understood. You may have to attune your ears to local vocabulary or pronunciation, but that's part of the intrigue of communicating in another language.

### Preguntas

1. What are some characteristics of the English spoken in other countries, such as Canada, Great Britain, Australia, and India?
2. What are some English words that are used where you live that are not necessarily used in other parts of the country?

**ANSWERS to *Nota cultural***
1. *Possible answers:* Accents and pronunciation; Different words such as *lift* for *elevator, flat* for *apartment, barbie* for *barbeque,* etc.
2. *Possible answers: Bayou* in Texas and other places in the South; *arroyo* in the Southwest; *put up* versus *put away;* pronunciation differences for words like *roof, creek,* etc.

---

**9 VOCABULARIO**

  01-45 to 01-48

## Los números 31–100   Counting from 31 to 100

The numbers 31–100 function in much the same way as the numbers 0–30. Note how the numbers 30–39 are formed. This pattern will repeat itself up to 100.

| | | | | | |
|---|---|---|---|---|---|
| 31 | **treinta y uno** | 37 | **treinta y siete** | 51 | **cincuenta y uno...** |
| 32 | **treinta y dos** | 38 | **treinta y ocho** | 60 | **sesenta** |
| 33 | **treinta y tres** | 39 | **treinta y nueve** | 70 | **setenta** |
| 34 | **treinta y cuatro** | 40 | **cuarenta** | 80 | **ochenta** |
| 35 | **treinta y cinco** | 41 | **cuarenta y uno...** | 90 | **noventa** |
| 36 | **treinta y seis** | 50 | **cincuenta** | 100 | **cien** |

**Estrategia**

Practice the numbers in Spanish by reading and pronouncing any numbers you see in your daily routine (e.g., highway signs, prices on your shopping receipts, room numbers on campus, phone numbers, etc.).

**SUGGESTION for *Los números 31–100***
Although all vocabulary is pronounced for your students on the accompanying *¡Anda! Curso elemental* MySpanishLab, as well as on CD, it can be helpful to pronounce the numbers in class and have students repeat after you. Additional practice can include having them count by twos or fives or count backwards.

**METHODOLOGY • Teaching Numbers**
An easy way to introduce numbers is to have visuals with numbers that you can then take out of numerical order. Students need practice with numbers out of sequence. Using visuals helps to accommodate different learning styles.

---

 **1-26** ## Examen de matemáticas

Are you ready to test your math skills? Take turns reading and solving the problems aloud. Then create your own math problems to test your partner. ■

**MODELO**   E1: $97 - 53 =$

E2: *Noventa y siete menos cincuenta y tres son cuarenta y cuatro.*

| Vocabulario útil | |
|---|---|
| **más** | *plus* |
| **menos** | *minus* |
| **son** | *equals* |
| **por** | *times; by* |
| **dividido por** | *divided by* |

1. $81 + 13 = 94$    3. $24 + 76 = 100$    5. $12 \times 8 = 96$    7. $65 \div 5 = 13$
2. $65 - 26 = 39$    4. $99 - 52 = 47$    6. $8 \times 7 = 56$    8. $100 \div 2 = 50$

**1-27 ¿Qué número es?** Look at the pages from the telephone book. Say **five** phone numbers and have your partner tell you whose numbers they are. Then switch roles. ■

MODELO    E1:  *Ochenta y ocho, sesenta y ocho, setenta y cinco*

          E2:  *Adelaida Santoyo*

```
SANTOS JAIME-SIERRA 12I 12 SM 3 CP 77500....84-0661
SANTOS JAVIER L1 Y 12 M10 SM43 PEDREGAL CP
77500.................................................80-5138
SANTOS SEGOVIA FREDDY CALLE 45 NTE MANZ 34
LTE 3 COL 77528..................................80-2242
SANTOS SEGURA ALBA ROSA COL LEONA VICARIO
M 8 L SM 74 77500................................80-0861
SANTOS SOLIS FELIPE CALLE 20 OTE NO 181 SM 68
M 12 L 28 CP 77500...............................80-1330
SANTOS VELÁZQUEZ MARÍA JESÚS CALLE 3 NO 181
77537.................................................86-6949
SANTOS VILLANUEVA ARMINDA CALLE 46 PTE
MANZ 20 77510.....................................88-3999
SANTOS JOSÉ E CALLE 33 OTE 171 L 14 M 25 CP
77500.................................................80-1175
SANTOSCOY LAGUNES ELIZABETH CERRADA
FLAMBOYANES                                            2
SM23..................................................87-6204
SANTOYO ADELAIDA CALLE 75 NTE DEPTO 7 EDIF 2
SM 92 CP 77500....................................88-6875
SANTOYO BETANCOURT PEDRO ARIEL HDA NUM 12
NABZ 61 77517.....................................88-7941
SANTOYO CORTEZ LIGIA EDIFICIO QUETZAL DEPTO
C-1 SM 32 77500...................................87-4676
SANTOYO MARTÍN AIDA MARÍA NANCE DEP 4 MZA
12 NUM 13...........................................87-3799
```

**1-28 ¿Quiere dejar un recado?** Imagine that you work in a busy office. You take messages with the following phone numbers. Say the numbers to a partner who will write them down. Then switch roles, mixing the order of the numbers. ■

MODELO    E1:  223-7256

          E2:  *dos, veintitrés, setenta y dos, cincuenta y seis*

1. 962-2136          3. 871-4954          5. 761-7920
2. 615-9563          4. 414-4415          6. 270-2325

**1-29 Los hispanos en los EE.UU.** Use the information from the pie chart to answer the following questions in Spanish. ■

Capítulo Preliminar A.
Los números 0–30,
pág. 16.

**Fíjate**
In most of the Spanish-speaking world, commas are used where the English-speaking world uses decimal points, and vice versa. For example, in English one says "six point four percent," in Spanish, *seis coma cuatro por ciento.*

| Vocabulario útil | |
|---|---|
| **por ciento** | *percent* |

### PORCENTAJE DE POBLACIÓN HISPANA

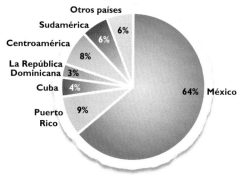

Otros países
Sudamérica 6%
Centroamérica 6%
8%
La República Dominicana 3%
Cuba 4%
64% México
Puerto Rico 9%

Source: US Census Bureau State & County Quick Facts

1. What percentage of U.S. Hispanics is from Cuba?  4%
2. What percentage of U.S. Hispanics is from Puerto Rico?  9%
3. What percentage of U.S. Hispanics is from Mexico?  64%
4. What percentage of U.S. Hispanics is from South America?  6%
5. What percentage of U.S. Hispanics comes from countries other than Mexico?  36%

ESCUCHA

01-49 to 01-50

## Presentaciones

### Estrategia

**Determining the topic and listening for words you know**

The first steps to becoming a successful listener are to determine the topic and then listen for words that you know. If you are in a social situation, you can determine the topic by looking for visual cues (body language, pictures, etc.) or by asking the speaker(s) for clarification.

When listening to passages in *¡Anda! Curso elemental,* look at the activities or questions connected with the passage to help you determine the topic. Remember that words that you know include *cognates* which are words that look and sound like words in English.

Aural comprehension is critical in learning to communicate in Spanish. You are working on developing your listening skills every time your instructor speaks or when you work in pairs or groups in class. You will also practice this skill when you watch the video episodes of *Ambiciones siniestras,* the mystery story that accompanies *¡Anda! Curso elemental.*

In *¡Anda! Curso elemental* you will have the opportunity to learn and practice strategies to assist you in developing listening skills in Spanish. Let's begin with listening for words you know, including cognates.

**1-30** **Antes de escuchar** In the following segment, Alejandra, one of the characters from **Ambiciones siniestras,** introduces her family. Write down two things that you expect to hear. ■

**1-31** **A escuchar** Listen as Alejandra introduces her family. Use the following steps to help you. ■

a. First, look at the incomplete sentences in c. They will give you an idea about the topic of the passage.
b. Listen to the passage, concentrating on the words you know. Make a list of those words.
c. Listen one more time and complete the following sentences.

  1. La familia de Alejandra es _____.
  2. Los nombres de sus padres son _____.
  3. Alejandra tiene _____ hermanos y _____ hermanas.

**1-32** **Después de escuchar** Take turns saying **three** sentences about you and your family to a partner. Your partner will tell you the words he/she knows. ■

---

**METHODOLOGY • Checking for Listening Comprehension in English**
When checking listening comprehension with beginning students, it is always acceptable to check for comprehension in English. At this stage, many students can comprehend more than they can produce. Allowing students to respond to the comprehension questions in English is fine at this point. As they progress, they will be able and expected to respond in Spanish.

---

## CAPÍTULO 1

**INTRODUCTION to** *Escucha*
A listening section entitled *Escucha* appears approximately two thirds of the way through each chapter. These presentations utilize examples from the vocabulary and grammar presented in the current, as well as previous, chapters. The passages are brief to help students focus on and practice one strategy at a time so they will not feel overwhelmed.

**SECTION GOALS for** *Escucha*
By the end of the *Escucha* section, students will be able to:
• identify cognates.
• report about Alejandra's family.
• discuss characteristics of their families.

**NATIONAL STANDARDS**
*Communication*
The strategy *listening for cognates* facilitates communication in the interpretive mode. Standard 1.2 requires that students understand and interpret spoken Spanish on a variety of topics. In *Capítulo 1*, students listen for a description of family members and they focus on cognate recognition. The short conversations that students have about their own families are interpersonal communication: Standard 1.1.

**ANSWERS to 1-30**
*Answers may vary.* Some possibilities include: who her family members are, their names, what they are like.

**ANSWERS to 1-31**
  b. *Possible answers:* grande, hermanos, hermanas, dos.
  1. grande
  2. Raúl y Pilar
  3. tres/dos

**AUDIOSCRIPT for 1-31**
What follows is the audio script that the students will hear when completing the *Escucha* section. The audioscripts will appear in the AIE margins for every *Escucha* section.
    *Hola. Soy Alejandra. Mi familia es muy grande. Mis padres son Raúl y Pilar. Tengo dos hermanas y tres hermanos.*

**METHODOLOGY •** *Escucha*
You may either read these sections aloud or have students listen to them on MySpanishLab or on the CD. This can be done in class or assigned for homework. Encourage students to listen to the *Escucha* sections multiple times outside of class.

# ¡CONVERSEMOS!

01-51

**1-33** **Jefe nuevo** With a partner, imagine that your new boss came to your office today to introduce himself/herself. Call your best friend, and describe your new boss in at least **four** sentences. ◼

**1-34** **Mucho gusto** You have just met a new neighbor. Imagine that your partner is your new neighbor, and describe yourself and your family to him/her. Use at least **six** sentences. In addition to **ser** and **tener,** create sentences using *Me gusta / No me gusta,* etc. ◼

**ESCRIBE**

## Un poema

01-52

| **Estrategia** | Whether you are writing informally or formally, organizing your ideas before you write is important. The advance preparation | will help you express yourself clearly and concisely. Jotting down notes or ideas helps in the organizational process. |
| --- | --- | --- |
| **Organizing ideas / Preparing to Write** | | |

**1-35** **Antes de escribir** Write down all the Spanish nouns and adjectives you can think of that describe you. Start by reviewing the vocabulary lists for **Capítulo 1** and **También se dice...,** Appendix 3. ◼

**1-36** **A escribir** Complete the following steps in order to write your first poem in Spanish. ■

**Paso 1** Using either your first, middle, or last name, match a noun or descriptive adjective with each letter of that name. For example:

"Sarah": **S** = *simpática*, **a** = *alta*, **r** = *responsable*, **a** = *amiga*, **h** = *hermana*

With these words, create what is known as an *acrostic* poem.

**Paso 2** Now build phrases or sentences around your letters, using **tener, ser,** possessive adjectives, and numbers.

| MODELO | *Simpática* | ***SARAH*** |
|---|---|---|
| | *Alta* | *es **S**impática* |
| | *Responsable* | *no es baja; es **A**lta* |
| | *Amiga* | *es **R**esponsable* |
| | *Hermana* | *tiene cien **A**migas* |
| | | *es mi **H**ermana.* |

 **1-37** **Después de escribir** Read your poem to a classmate. ■

## ¿Cómo andas? II

This is your second self-assessment. You have now completed two thirds of the chapter. How confident are you with the following topics and concepts?

| | Feel confident | Need to review |
|---|---|---|
| Having completed **Comunicación II,** I now can . . . | | |
| • give details about myself and others (p. 40) | ☐ | ☐ |
| • state possession (p. 41) | ☐ | ☐ |
| • supply details about people, places, and things (p. 43) | ☐ | ☐ |
| • compare and contrast several regional and national differences in the English and Spanish languages (p. 46) | ☐ | ☐ |
| • count from 31 to 100 (p. 47) | ☐ | ☐ |
| • determine the topic and listen for known words (p. 49) | ☐ | ☐ |
| • communicate about people I know (p. 50) | ☐ | ☐ |
| • organize ideas to write a poem (p. 50) | ☐ | ☐ |

**METHODOLOGY • Teaching Writing**
Writing is a culminating, integrated activity in each chapter of *¡Anda! Curso elemental.* Research suggests that students first focus on speaking, and then on writing, because "if they can say it, they can write it."

**EXPANSION for 1-36**
Have students each create an additional acrostic poem using the name of a friend or family member or a word they have learned, such as *estudiante.*

**NATIONAL STANDARDS**
*Communication*
Activity **1-37** asks students to present their poems. Depending on how you implement the activity, it could satisfy Standard 1.1 or 1.3. Standard 1.1 asks students to express feelings and emotions and share opinions. They are reporting things about themselves to a classmate, and the classmate can offer opinions about the poem. This might include agreement or disagreement with the adjectives used, or what the classmate likes or dislikes about the poem. Implemented in this way, the activity becomes an interpersonal exchange. On the other hand, Standard 1.3 requires students to present to an audience of readers or listeners. Students could write the poems and display them in a collection of class poems, or students could have a poetry reading, where they read their poems aloud to the class. This way of using the poems requires the presentational mode of communication.

**Instructor Resources**
• Text images (map), Video resources

## Cultura

CULTURA • CULTURA • CULTURA • CU

# Los Estados Unidos

Rafael Sánchez Martínez

01-53 to 01-54

## Les presento mi país

Mi nombre es Rafael Sánchez Martínez y soy de San Diego, California. Soy bilingüe: hablo inglés y español. Soy estadounidense y tengo herencia hispana. Mi abuelo es mexicano y mi abuela es puertorriqueña. Hay muchos hispanohablantes (*Spanish speakers*) en los Estados Unidos. **¿Puedes (*Can you*) identificar otras cuatro o cinco ciudades en el mapa con grandes poblaciones hispanohablantes?** Hay hispanohablantes famosos de muchas carreras diferentes, como Soledad O'Brien y Aarón Sánchez. **¿Por qué son famosas estas personas?** También se nota la influencia hispana en los restaurantes y en los supermercados donde se ofrecen productos hispanos de compañías como Goya, Ortega, Corona, Marinela y Tecate. Mi restaurante favorito se llama Café Coyote. **¿Cuál es tu restaurante favorito?**

Los Estados Unidos

Cristina Saralegui es una de las hispanas más influyentes de los Estados Unidos.

Albert Pujols es un famoso beisbolista dominicano.

St. Augustine es la primera ciudad europea en los Estados Unidos, fundada en el año 1565 por los españoles.

Celebrando la herencia puertorriqueña con un desfile en la Quinta Avenida de Nueva York.

**52**

## ESTADO

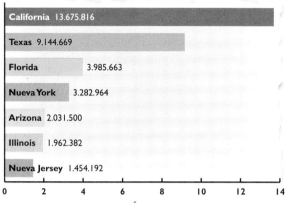

**POBLACIÓN HISPANA**
Source: US Census Bureau State & County Quick Facts

California 13.675.816
Texas 9.144.669
Florida 3.985.663
Nueva York 3.282.964
Arizona 2.031.500
Illinois 1.962.382
Nueva Jersey 1.454.192

## CIUDAD

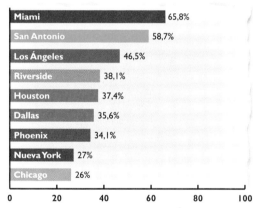

Miami 65,8%
San Antonio 58,7%
Los Ángeles 46,5%
Riverside 38,1%
Houston 37,4%
Dallas 35,6%
Phoenix 34,1%
Nueva York 27%
Chicago 26%

**PORCENTAJE DE POBLACIÓN HISPANA**
Source: Brookings Institution

## ALMANAQUE

| | |
|---|---|
| **Nombre oficial:** | Estados Unidos de América |
| **Gobierno:** | República constitucional y federal |
| **Población:** | 307.006.550 (2010) |
| **Población de origen hispano:** | 15.8% (2010) |
| **Moneda:** | el dólar ($) |

### ¿Sabías que...?

- Para el año 2050, una de cada cuatro personas en los Estados Unidos va a ser de origen hispano.
- En los Estados Unidos se celebra el mes de la herencia hispana entre el 15 de septiembre y el 15 de octubre.

### Preguntas

1. ¿Qué importancia tiene St. Augustine, Florida?
2. ¿Qué estados tienen la mayor (*the largest*) población hispana?
3. ¿Quiénes son algunos (*some*) hispanos famosos en los Estados Unidos? ¿Cuál es tu favorito?

 Learn more about Hispanics in the United States in MySpanishLab.

**CAPÍTULO 1**

**METHODOLOGY • Checking for Reading Comprehension**
As previously mentioned, in the beginning stages of learning Spanish, it is acceptable and even desirable to do a comprehension check in English. For example, ask students to respond in English to the question *¿Por qué son famosas estas personas?* This will demonstrate whether they understand the question and are familiar with the people. If they are unfamiliar with them, have them search for the people on the Internet.

**SUGGESTION for *Cristina Saralegui***
Ask students whether they watch Spanish TV or have ever seen a program in Spanish on TV. You may wish to show a brief segment of Cristina's TV program in class. The theme of this chapter is *¿Quiénes somos?* and Cristina often has her guests talk about personal identity.

**SUGGESTION for *St. Augustine***
Ask students whether any particular cultural or ethnic style of architecture is visible where they live. Point out that even rural American style has been influenced by historic, economic, and cultural factors.

**SUGGESTION for *The Puerto Rican Day Parade***
Draw parallels to other ethnic groups in the United States and how they celebrate their cultural heritage. Ask students to name other parades or celebrations that highlight different cultural groups (e.g., St. Patrick's Day parades, German Oktoberfests, etc.).

**SUGGESTION for *Los productos hispanos***
Ask students what Hispanic products they see in stores or on TV. Ask which they buy; most likely they will mention Hispanic foods.

**HERITAGE LANGUAGE LEARNERS**
Web-based activities that can benefit a variety of students will be provided for each chapter. For example, heritage language learners, false beginners, more advanced students, students who need additional practice, or those who love the Internet can all benefit from the following activities. You may wish to give the directions in Spanish for heritage language learners. Give them in English for the other students.

1. Busca en el Internet cifras que indiquen la participación hispana en la sociedad estadounidense en los siguientes casos:
   a. Número de ciudadanos hispanos que votaron en la última elección presidencial
   b. Número de hispanos que sirven en las fuerzas armadas estadounidenses
   c. Número de negocios con propietarios hispanos

*Palabras clave:* número o porcentaje de hispanos, fuerzas armadas, el voto presidencial, datos de participación, negocios.

2. Trata de encontrar cuál va a ser la población hispana para el año 2050, cuando los hispanos van a constituir el 24 por ciento de la población estadounidense.

*Palabras clave:* población hispana, año 2050.

## INTRODUCTION to
### Ambiciones siniestras

In *Ambiciones siniestras,* you will meet a group of college students. They have become accidentally involved in an international plot. This section will be repeated throughout the chapters, beginning with a reading episode, followed by a video episode that continues the storyline. These episodes contextualize the vocabulary and grammar presented in the chapter.

## SECTION GOALS for
### Ambiciones siniestras

By the end of the *Ambiciones siniestras* reading section, students will be able to:
- highlight cognates in the passage.
- read brief e-mails in Spanish.
- understand the main idea of each e-mail.
- distinguish between the characters.

## NATIONAL STANDARDS
### Communication, Cultures

The reading passage of *Ambiciones siniestras* provides an authentic text in Spanish. The format of this reading uses e-mail messages, a medium familiar to students. This reading highlights Standard 1.2 because the students are required to understand and interpret written Spanish, and the *Ambiciones siniestras* video segment that follows the reading also requires students to understand and interpret spoken Spanish. The reading provides a glimpse into the practices and perspectives of Hispanic cultures (Standard 2.2) because it highlights advertisements written in an e-mail format. Students are able to visualize where this advertisement might be posted in a Hispanic country.

## METHODOLOGY • *Lectura*

The mystery story *Ambiciones siniestras* was created for *¡Anda! Curso elemental* to offer students high-interest reading passages. In doing so, we provide them with the opportunity and motivation to see and use structures that they are acquiring and to develop strategies that will help them become proficient readers of Spanish.

With this in mind, it is important that you do the pre- and post-reading sections with students *in class* for at least the first two chapters. The pre-reading activities serve to activate schemata, alert students to look for cognates, and introduce them to the techniques of skimming, scanning, and questioning meaning from context.

---

# Ambiciones siniestras

01-57

EPISODIO 1

# Lectura

Three students from different universities are writing e-mail messages to friends or family members. What can you learn about the three students from their e-mails? What can you learn about the person to whom or about whom each one is writing?

**Estrategia**    Recognizing Cognates

When you read something for the first time, you are not expected to understand every word. In addition to focusing on the words that you *do* know, look for words similar to those you know in English, *cognates*. Cognates are an excellent way to help you understand what you are reading. Make sure that you complete the **Antes de leer** activities to practice this strategy.

---

**1-38** **Antes de leer** You are about to discover what happens to a group of college students as they unwittingly become involved in a sinister international plot. Before you read the first episode of **Ambiciones siniestras,** answer the following questions. ∎

1. How much time do you spend on the computer composing, reading, and answering e-mails?
2. To whom do you write most frequently? For what purpose(s)?
3. With a partner, list as many reasons as you can for sending e-mails.

---

**1-39** **A leer** Read through the e-mail messages quickly, underlining all cognates. Share your list with a classmate. Then, answer the following questions. ∎

1. How many messages are there?
2. Who wrote each message?
3. To whom or for whom were the messages written?

> **Estrategia**
>
> When writing or reading e-mails, note what parts are common to all of them. Usually you find the following information: who sent the message and the address from where it came, the subject line that indicates what the e-mail is about, a list of other people who might have received it, etc. Use your knowledge of writing and receiving e-mails in English to see whether you can understand the additional information presented in this episode of *Ambiciones siniestras.*

54

---

**METHODOLOGY • Reading Aloud**

We do not recommend having students simply read a passage aloud unless it is to review a portion that you have just completed together or to practice pronunciation. Research suggests that students have difficulty attending to meaning when they read aloud. Time is better spent directing the reading, as explained briefly in the methodology note on page 55 on the teaching of initial reading, or discussing the reading after it has been done silently.

**NATIONAL STANDARDS**
*Comparisons*

The reading from *Ambiciones siniestras* contains many cognates. Students of Spanish should recognize that there are many cognates between English and Spanish. Students use Standard 4.1 when they understand the nature of Spanish by making comparisons between Spanish and their own language. By scanning any reading passage to find cognates, students are focusing on how much they already know in Spanish instead of what they have yet to learn.

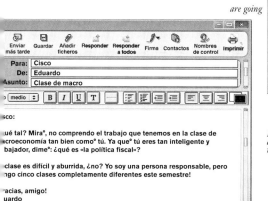

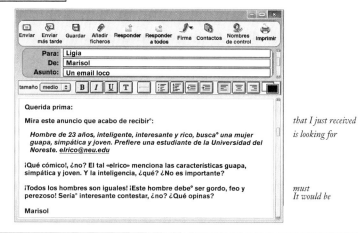

### Conexiones

**Para:** Mamá
**De:** Alejandra
**Asunto:** Un amigo nuevo

Querida mamá:

¿Cómo estás? Yo estoy muy bien. Mis clases van° bien. . . con mucho trabajo, pero son interesantes. Y tengo un amigo nuevo. Se llama Manolo. Tenemos las mismas clases. Es simpático y muy cómico. También es inteligente y guapo. . . ¡como un actor! Tiene dos hermanas como yo.

¿Cómo está papá? ¿Y mis hermanas?
Bueno, es todo por el momento. Mañana te escribo° más.

Besos,
Alejandra

*are going*

*write*

**Para:** Cisco
**De:** Eduardo
**Asunto:** Clase de macro

...sco:

...ué tal? Mira°, no comprendo el trabajo que tenemos en la clase de ...croeconomía tan bien como° tú. Ya que° tú eres tan inteligente y ...bajador, dime°: ¿qué es «la política fiscal»?

...clase es difícil y aburrida, ¿no? Yo soy una persona responsable, pero ...ngo cinco clases completamente diferentes este semestre!

...acias, amigo!
...uardo

*Look*
*as well as / Since*
*tell me*

**Para:** Ligia
**De:** Marisol
**Asunto:** Un email loco

Querida prima:

Mira este anuncio que acabo de recibir°:

*Hombre de 23 años, inteligente, interesante y rico, busca° una mujer guapa, simpática y joven. Prefiere una estudiante de la Universidad del Noreste. elrico@neu.edu*

¡Qué cómico!, ¿no? El tal «elrico» menciona las características guapa, simpática y joven. Y la inteligencia, ¿qué? ¿No es importante?

¡Todos los hombres son iguales! ¡Este hombre debe° ser gordo, feo y perezoso! Sería° interesante contestar, ¿no? ¿Qué opinas?

Marisol

*that I just received*

*is looking for*

*must*
*It would be*

---

**1-40** **Después de leer** Answer the following questions. ■

1. What was the purpose of each message? Was it friendly communication? Did the person need something from someone else?
2. Of the senders, recipients, and others mentioned in the messages, which person is most like you? Which one would you most like to meet? Why?

55

### CAPÍTULO 1

**METHODOLOGY • Teaching Reading**

After completing the pre-reading activities, ask students to read the first paragraph of the first e-mail message. Ask whether there are any words they do not understand. If so, other students may know or be able to infer the meanings quickly. Then read the second paragraph together (an overhead transparency works well here). Have students pick out and discuss words they know before talking them through, discovering the meaning of unfamiliar words. Repeat this process for the remainder of the text. Here is an example for guiding students toward discovering meaning from context.

Take a look at the last two sentences of the first e-mail message: *Bueno, es todo por el momento. Mañana te escribo más.*

1. Explain that in addition to "good," *bueno* can mean "Well, . . ."
2. Ask what students think *por el momento* means, pointing out, if necessary, that *momento* is a cognate.
3. Next ask what *es todo* means, especially given its location in the sentence and the message "Well, . . . for the moment . . ." If the meaning is not readily clear, move on to the last sentence, asking them to decipher it.
4. Finally, based on all the other pieces of the puzzle, the meaning for *es todo* should become clear to at least some.
5. After guiding students through the passage, go immediately to the post-reading activities.

**METHODOLOGY • Checking for Reading Comprehension**

Again, for this first reading we recommend checking comprehension in English. This is a non-threatening, confidence-building way for students to demonstrate that they understood. If you have false beginners or heritage language learners, you may ask brief questions in Spanish about the episode.

**EXPANSION for 1-40**

Ask your students the following questions regarding the e-mails they have just read:

- Questions for the first e-mail: What is the name of Alejandra's new friend? Describe him. How many sisters does he have?
- Questions for the second e-mail: What class is Eduardo struggling with? Do you think Eduardo likes the class? Why? How many classes does Eduardo have?
- Questions for the third e-mail: What kind of person is "el rico" looking for? How does Marisol imagine "el rico" to be?

# Video

01-58 to 01-62

In the first reading episode you were introduced briefly to some of the characters of the mystery story **Ambiciones siniestras.** The next episode in video format will provide a further glimpse into the lives of the characters on their respective campuses.

**1-41** **Antes del video** Let's think about you and your campus experiences for a minute. Do you take classes on a traditional college campus? What courses are you currently taking? Are your classes large or small? Are you friends with any of your classmates? What are your professors like? ■

Cisco y Eduardo en su clase de macroeconomía.

La familia de Lupe es hispana y la familia de Marisol es hispana también.

Alejandra y Manolo en su clase de literatura española.

## ¿Quiénes son?

Episodio 1

Relax and watch the video, more than once if you choose; then complete the following activity.

**1-42** **Después del video** Identify the person(s) who fit(s) each description below. ■

Lupe     Cisco     Eduardo     Marisol     Manolo     Alejandra

This character . . .

1. has grandparents who are Hispanic and speaks Spanish with siblings.   Lupe
2. seems to like Phillip Jones and introduces him to her friend.   Marisol
3. likes afternoon classes.   Alejandra
4. helps Eduardo prepare for class.   Cisco
5. are students in a Spanish literature class.   Alejandra and Manolo
6. needs help with his economics class.   Eduardo

56

# Y por fin, ¿cómo andas?

Each chapter will end with a checklist like the one that follows. This is the third time in the chapter that you are given the opportunity to check your progress. Use the checklist to measure what you have learned in the chapter. Place a check in the *Feel confident* column for the topics you feel you know, and a check in the *Need to review* column for the topics that you need to practice more.

|  | Feel confident | Need to review |
|---|:---:|:---:|
| **Having completed this chapter, I now can . . .** | | |
| **Comunicación I** | | |
| • describe families (p. 32) | ☐ | ☐ |
| • pronounce vowels (MSL / SAM) | ☐ | ☐ |
| • express what someone has (p. 34) | ☐ | ☐ |
| • use singular and plural nouns (p. 36) | ☐ | ☐ |
| • identify masculine and feminine nouns (p. 37) | ☐ | ☐ |
| • convey *the, a, one,* and *some* (p. 38) | ☐ | ☐ |
| **Comunicación II** | | |
| • give details about myself and others (p. 40) | ☐ | ☐ |
| • state possession (p. 41) | ☐ | ☐ |
| • supply details about people, places, and things (p. 43) | ☐ | ☐ |
| • count from 31 to 100 (p. 47) | ☐ | ☐ |
| • determine the topic and listen for known words (p. 49) | ☐ | ☐ |
| • communicate about people I know (p. 50) | ☐ | ☐ |
| • organize ideas to write a poem (p. 50) | ☐ | ☐ |
| **Cultura** | | |
| • illustrate formation of Hispanic last names (p. 33) | ☐ | ☐ |
| • compare and contrast several regional and national differences in the English and Spanish languages (p. 46) | ☐ | ☐ |
| • discuss the size, location, and makeup of the Hispanic population in the United States (p. 52) | ☐ | ☐ |
| **Ambiciones siniestras** | | |
| • recognize cognates when reading and meet the six protagonists (p. 54) | ☐ | ☐ |
| • discover more about the protagonists' classes and their lives (p. 55) | ☐ | ☐ |
| **Comunidades** | | |
| • use Spanish in real-life contexts (SAM) | ☐ | ☐ |

**CAPÍTULO 1**

**METHODOLOGY • Student Self-Assessment with *Y por fin, ¿cómo andas?***
This is the chapter's third and final self-assessment. It is cumulative for the entire chapter. These self-assessments help students determine where they are with regard to their learning, and what individual remediation might be needed. Research contends that instructors have to make students ultimately responsible for their own learning, and one of the ways to do this is by having them self-assess. Research also finds that students tend to be overly critical of what they do and do not know, and periodic self-assessments help them to self-evaluate realistically.

**SUGGESTIONS for *Y por fin, ¿cómo andas?***
Spot-check and ask how they are doing (e.g., "How many of you feel confident using singular and plural nouns?"). Remind students who do not raise their hands that they need to review the topics they don't feel confident with on their own by consulting the pages listed. If you have time to do the assessments in class, one approach is to have students write short answers to the topics, then check in their textbooks to verify answers. Based on this verification, they can rate themselves on the concepts and hand in their ratings to you at the end of class. If you have time constraints, students can complete these self-assessments outside of class.

**Instructor Resources**
• Testing program information

# VOCABULARIO ACTIVO

| La familia | Family |
|---|---|
| el/la abuelo/a | grandfather/grandmother |
| los abuelos | grandparents |
| el/la esposo/a | husband/wife |
| el/la hermano/a | brother/sister |
| los hermanos | brothers and sisters; siblings |
| el/la hijo/a | son/daughter |
| los hijos | sons and daughters; children |
| la madrastra | stepmother |
| la madre/la mamá | mother/mom |
| el/la nieto/a | grandson/granddaughter |
| el padrastro | stepfather |
| el padre/el papá | father/dad |
| los padres | parents |
| el/la primo/a | cousin |
| los primos | cousins |
| el/la tío/a | uncle/aunt |
| los tíos | aunts and uncles |

| La gente | People |
|---|---|
| el/la amigo/a | friend |
| el/la chico/a | boy/girl |
| el hombre | man |
| el/la joven | young man/young woman |
| el/la muchacho/a | boy/girl |
| la mujer | woman |
| el/la niño/a | little boy/little girl |
| el/la novio/a | boyfriend/girlfriend |
| el señor (Sr.) | man; gentleman; Mr. |
| la señora (Sra.) | woman; lady; Mrs. |
| la señorita (Srta.) | young woman; Miss |

| Los adjetivos | Adjectives |
|---|---|
| **La personalidad y otros rasgos** | *Personality and other characteristics* |
| aburrido/a | boring |
| antipático/a | unpleasant |
| bueno/a | good |
| cómico/a | funny; comical |
| inteligente | intelligent |
| interesante | interesting |
| malo/a | bad |
| paciente | patient |
| perezoso/a | lazy |
| pobre | poor |
| responsable | responsible |
| rico/a | rich |
| simpático/a | nice |
| tonto/a | silly; dumb |
| trabajador/a | hard-working |

| Las características físicas | Physical characteristics |
|---|---|
| alto/a | tall |
| bajo/a | short |
| bonito/a | pretty |
| débil | weak |
| delgado/a | thin |
| feo/a | ugly |
| fuerte | strong |
| gordo/a | fat |
| grande | big; large |
| guapo/a | handsome/pretty |
| joven | young |
| mayor | old |
| pequeño/a | small |

| Los números 31–100 | Numbers 31–100 |
|---|---|
| treinta y uno | thirty-one |
| treinta y dos | thirty-two |
| treinta y tres | thirty-three |
| treinta y cuatro | thirty-four |
| treinta y cinco | thirty-five |
| treinta y seis | thirty-six |
| treinta y siete | thirty-seven |
| treinta y ocho | thirty-eight |
| treinta y nueve | thirty-nine |
| cuarenta | forty |
| cuarenta y uno | forty-one |
| cincuenta | fifty |
| cincuenta y uno | fifty-one |
| sesenta | sixty |
| setenta | seventy |
| ochenta | eighty |
| noventa | ninety |
| cien | one hundred |

| Un verbo | Verb |
|---|---|
| tener | to have |
| Otras palabras útiles | Other useful words |
| muy | very |
| (un) poco | (a) little |

| Vocabulario útil | Useful vocabulary |
|---|---|
| más | plus |
| menos | minus |
| son | equals |
| por ciento | percent |
| por | times; by |
| dividido por | divided by |

If you are interested in discovering additional vocabulary for the topics studied in each chapter, consult Appendix 3, **También se dice...**, for additional words. It contains expanded vocabulary that you may need for your own personal expression, including regionally used words and slang. Enjoy!

**Instructor Resources**
• IRM: Syllabi and Lesson Plans

## NATIONAL STANDARDS

### COMUNICACIÓN I

- To share information about courses and majors (Communication)
- To indicate the stressed syllables in words (Communication)
- To describe your classroom and classmates (Communication)
- To relate daily activities (Communication)
- To create and answer questions (Communication)
- To count from 100–1,000 (Communication)
- To engage in additional communication practice (Communication)

### COMUNICACIÓN II

- To elaborate on university places and objects (Communication)
- To express *to be* (Communication)
- To articulate emotions and states of being (Communication)
- To convey likes and dislikes (Communication)
- To offer opinions on sports and pastimes (Communication)
- To glean the main idea (Communication)
- To communicate about university life (Communication)
- To craft a personal description (Communication)
- To engage in additional communication practice (Communication)

### CULTURA

- To examine Hispanic university life (Cultures, Comparisons)
- To compare and contrast sports (Cultures, Comparisons)
- To exchange information regarding Mexico (Cultures, Comparisons)
- To explore further the chapter's cultural themes (Cultures)

### AMBICIONES SINIESTRAS

- To skim a reading and note facts about the protagonists' lives (Comparisons)
- To discover more about the protagonists (Communication, Cultures)

### COMUNIDADES

- To use Spanish in real-life contexts (Communities)

# 2 La vida universitaria

The majority of universities throughout the Spanish-speaking world tend to be public, with vast student enrollments. They usually charge minimal tuition, if any, and students must pass rigorous admission exams in order to attend. In many countries, the exams they take, or the scores they receive, determine the careers they may choose. In their first year, college students begin to take courses in their major area.

## PREGUNTAS

**1** How large is your college or university? What are the advantages of studying at a college or university of this size? Are there any disadvantages?

**2** What are some possible advantages and disadvantages of the large universities of some Spanish-speaking countries?

**3** Why do many colleges and universities require general education courses prior to entering courses for majors? Why do many colleges and universities have language requirements?

**La universidad de Guanajuato, México**

60

---

### SECTION GOALS for *Chapter opener*

By the end of the Chapter opener section, students will be able to:

- summarize how universities in the United States compare to those in other parts of the Spanish-speaking world.
- discuss the advantages and disadvantages of school size and programs.
- consider how the selection of a major differs among schools and countries.

### NATIONAL STANDARDS
*Communities*

College students can be a valuable resource in the community. Consider asking students from different disciplines and majors to make presentations to local high schools and middle schools. This presentation could be bilingual in nature, and they can talk about the number of hours they take at the university, what types of classes are required, how many hours they spend studying per week, and the kind of jobs (and salaries) they anticipate upon graduation. They might spend a semester mentoring a student group from a high school or middle school that shares the same future career plans. Standard 5.1 encourages students to use their Spanish in and beyond the school setting.

### WARM-UP for *Chapter opener*

As in *Capítulo 1,* ask your students to give their impressions regarding the photo on page 60. Also have the students read the objectives for the chapter silently. We suggest you spend no more than 5 to 7 minutes on chapter openers.

61

**METHODOLOGY • Meaningful Learning**

One purpose of the discussion questions is to begin a topic with what your students already know so they can see how major themes of the chapter relate to their lives more clearly. This facilitates learning by encouraging active mental participation in relating new material to existing knowledge, the basic tenet of Ausubel's "meaningful learning." (Ausubel, D. *Educational Psychology: A cognitive view.* New York: Holt, Rinehart & Winston, 1968.) Initially, these questions are in English. As the program progresses, the questions will be in Spanish.

**ANSWERS to** *Preguntas*

1. *Possible advantages of a larger university:* greater number of course offerings, more potential majors/specialties, more extracurricular opportunities, including sporting events; *Possible disadvantages:* less personal attention from administration and faculty. *Possible advantages of a smaller university:* smaller classes, more interaction among students and faculty; *Possible disadvantages:* fewer course offerings, fewer extracurricular opportunities.

2. *Possible advantages:* larger number of course offerings, more possible majors, more students have the opportunity to attend, more economical to maintain. *Possible disadvantages:* large class size, less personal attention.

3. *Possible answers:* General education courses provide a basic knowledge base on which to build, and many entering students have not yet chosen a major/profession. Knowing a second (or multiple) language(s) better prepares individuals for an increasingly global community and may be necessary for some professions.

**EXPANSION for** *Preguntas*

You may want to also discuss other academic settings: junior colleges, community colleges, technical schools, etc. Consider posing the following question for your students: In most Spanish-speaking countries, students take English as a required course in earlier levels of school. Should students in the United States study foreign languages throughout their school years rather than waiting until high school or college?

**PLANNING AHEAD**

For **2-15** you will want to have current exchange rates taken from the newspaper or the Internet. Also, for **2-16,** students should each bring at least five ads of items with prices between $100 and $1,000. They can be items related to this chapter, but it is not necessary. You may want to have extras in case some students forget.

## Instructor Resources
• Textbook images, Extra Activities

### SECTION GOALS for *Comunicación I*

By the end of the *Comunicación I* section, students will be able to:
• report about their courses of study and their daily academic schedules.
• accent words using the rules for word stress.
• differentiate between words spelled the same that change meaning when accented.
• pronounce words correctly to indicate the stressed syllables.
• discuss common stereotypes.
• list classroom objects using *hay*.
• form regular verbs that end in *-ar*, *-er*, and *-ir*.
• ask questions using interrogative words and question marks.
• answer questions affirmatively and negatively.
• count from 100–1,000.

### NATIONAL STANDARDS
*Connections*

What is obvious to us as instructors is not always obvious to students. It is important to help students realize the importance of studying Spanish and other languages as well. As you discuss the vocabulary for majors, have students share how they could use Spanish in their future careers. If they are uncertain of the connection, encourage other students to help them brainstorm how they will be able to do so.

The information presented in *Capítulo 2* is about university life. The cultural readings, vocabulary, and grammar (e.g., *gustar*) provide a starting point from which students can make connections between their courses of study and Spanish (Standard 3.1). This chapter also introduces rules for accents, stereotypes, and sports, which allow students to connect different viewpoints through the lens of a Spanish speaker (Standard 3.2). Some of the grammar presentations, such as *gustar* and regular verbs in the present, also promote making comparisons between English and Spanish (Standard 4.1).

### 21ST CENTURY SKILLS • CORE SUBJECTS

There are nine core subjects that are required for a learner to be prepared for work and life in the 21st century. The core subjects are *English, reading or language arts, world language, the arts, mathematics, economics, science, geography, history, government and civics*. It is important to note that world languages are listed as #2 in the list of nine core subjects. This fact can be shared with your students to help support their decision to study Spanish.

# Comunicación I

**1 VOCABULARIO**

`3:00`   02-01 to 02-05

## Las materias y las especialidades
Sharing information about courses and majors

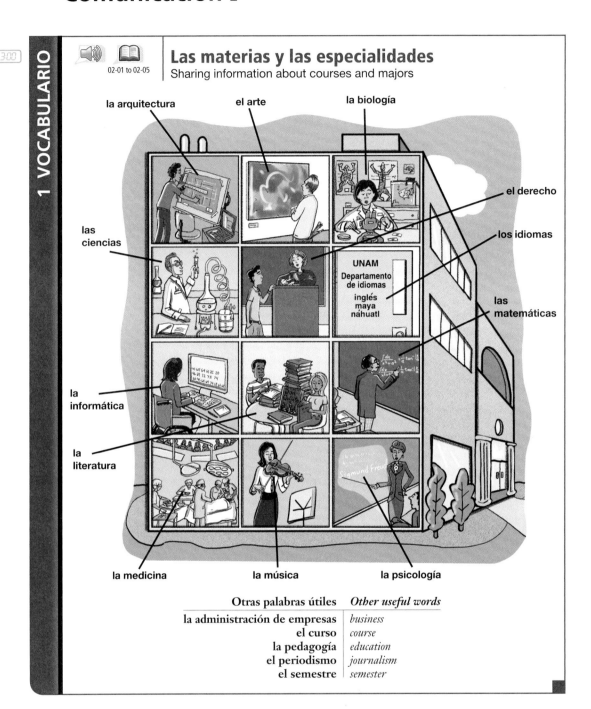

la arquitectura • el arte • la biología • el derecho • los idiomas • las matemáticas • las ciencias • la informática • la literatura • la medicina • la música • la psicología

UNAM
Departamento de idiomas
inglés
maya
náhuatl

| Otras palabras útiles | *Other useful words* |
|---|---|
| la administración de empresas | *business* |
| el curso | *course* |
| la pedagogía | *education* |
| el periodismo | *journalism* |
| el semestre | *semester* |

### NOTE for *Las materias y las especialidades*

There is a great deal of variety in vocabulary throughout the Spanish-speaking world. We have attempted to use the most common words in the text, and variations appear in the *También se dice...* section in Appendix 3. For example, the Spanish equivalent of "business" could be *la administración de empresas* or *los negocios*, and "computer science" could be *la computación* or *la informática*. Feel free to use the words that are most familiar to you.

### METHODOLOGY • Teaching Vocabulary

If you have a local "rival" university, start out by making comparisons in Spanish between that university and yours. For example, *Universidad X es*

*muy pequeña, pero nuestra universidad es grande*. Then ask students to recall certain adjectives by asking whether *grande* refers to your university or the rival university. Brainstorm to see how they think their university differs from universities in Latin America or Spain.

### SUGGESTION for *Las materias y las especialidades*

Sometimes students take required interdisciplinary courses with special names like Western Humanities. When they talk about what they study, they want to translate the exact name of the course. Instead, ask them to think about what subject that course belongs to.

## PRONUNCIACIÓN

### Word stress and accent marks

  ¡Hola!

02-06 to 02-08

Go to MySpanishLab / Student Activities Manual to learn about word stress and accent marks.

---

[2:00]  **2-1** **¿Cuál es su especialidad?** Complete the following steps. ■

**Paso 1** Take turns matching the following famous people with the majors they may have studied in college.

1. __b__ Pablo Picasso
2. __e__ Maya Angelou
3. __f__ Marie Curie
4. __c__ Sigmund Freud
5. __h__ el presidente de Coca-Cola
6. __g__ Supreme Court Justice Sonia Sotomayor
7. __a__ Taylor Swift
8. __d__ Bill Gates

a. la música
b. el arte
c. la psicología
d. la informática
e. la literatura
f. las ciencias
g. el derecho
h. la administración de empresas

**Paso 2** Now, can you name the majors the following famous Hispanics may have studied in college?

1. Ellen Ochoa (astronauta) ciencias
2. Jorge Ramos (periodista *[journalist]*) periodismo
3. Isabel Allende (autora) literatura
4. Carlos Santana (músico) música

---

[5:00]  Workbooklet

Capítulo Preliminar A. La hora, pág. 18; Los días de la semana, pág. 20.

   **2-2** **¿Qué clases tienes?** Complete the following chart, then share your schedule with a partner. ■

**HORARIO DE CLASES**

| CLASES | DÍAS DE LA SEMANA | HORA |
|---|---|---|
| matemáticas | martes y jueves | 1:30 |
| | | |

**MODELO** *Este semestre tengo cinco cursos. Tengo la clase de matemáticas los martes y jueves a la una y media… ¿Y tú?*

> ### Estrategia
> If the meaning of any of the vocabulary words is not clear, verify the definition in the *Vocabulario activo* at the end of this chapter.

---

**NATIONAL STANDARDS**
*Communication*

Activities **2-1** through **2-3** promote communication in the interpersonal mode. Students pair up, engage in conversation, provide and obtain information, and exchange opinions (Standard 1.1). Activity **2-1**, *Paso 1*, also provides a way for students to activate their background information about famous people and their specialties (Standard 3.1). Based on the information the students share about their schedules, including number of hours in class, required courses, and number of credits, they can discuss generalizations about students from each major (Standard 1.1). Using **2-2** as a starting point, students can create their schedules to present to the class and explain how they spend their days (Standard 1.3).

**ADDITIONAL ACTIVITY for Las materias y las especialidades**

The following activity will help students practice with creating memory devices. Group the students in pairs and have them create two lists based on the vocabulary for *Las materias y las especialidades*. Under List 1, have them write all the cognates they find in the new vocabulary words. Under List 2, have them write the remaining words. Students should create a memory device for each word in List 2. For example: *la informática:* "I save a lot of information on my computer." Other sample memory devices:

*Dere cho*se to study law. ⟶ *derecho*
I would be an *idio*t not to study languages. ⟶ *idioma*
*Periodi*cally I dabble in journalism. ⟶ *periodismo*

---

**SUGGESTION for Pronunciación**
Students should be encouraged to practice pronunciation both in and out of the classroom. In class, the most effective way to practice is for the instructor to say the sound, word, or phrase, and then have the students repeat it. Then say the sound, word, or phrase again and have students repeat it once again. Not repeating with the students allows you to hear how well they are imitating the sounds of the words.

**SUGGESTION for Las materias y las especialidades**
Always have a map of your campus available, as a hard copy or bookmarked on the Internet. Ask students to identify where on campus one studies each major. By personalizing the instruction to their campus, they are more likely to remember the information. This promotes learning about what majors other people study, instead of only what each student studies.

**SUGGESTION for Las materias y las especialidades**
Get to know the students in your class. If the class is composed of mostly first-year students, secondary (high school) students, part-time students, or community members taking the course for fun, recognize that they might not have majors or they might not have declared a major yet. Ask them to report about which classes they are currently taking, and ask them to identify to what majors those classes belong.

**SECTION GOALS for Pronunciación**
By the end of the *Pronunciación* section, students will be able to:
- distinguish the differences in pronunciation between accented and non-accented words.
- emphasize the accented syllable.
- pronounce question words and emphasize the stress on the proper syllable.

**WARM-UP for 2-1**
Prepare students for **2-1** by first asking them, *¿Cuál es tu especialidad?*

**SUGGESTION for 2-1**
Have one student match the even items while his or her partner matches the odd ones.

CAPÍTULO 2

Capítulo 1. El verbo *tener*, pág. 34; Los adjetivos descriptivos, pág. 43.

## Estrategia

Go to Appendix 3, *También se dice…*, for an expanded list of college majors. *También se dice…* includes additional vocabulary and regional expressions for all chapters. Although not exhaustive, the list will give you an idea of the variety and richness of the Spanish language.

**2-3** **Unos estereotipos** Do you think stereotypes exist just at your university? In your opinion, the following characteristics are stereotypically associated with students majoring in which fields? Share your responses with your group of three or four students, then report the group findings to the class. ■

**MODELO** Los estudiantes de _____ son ricos.

E1: *Tengo "Los estudiantes de administración de empresas son ricos". ¿Qué tienes tú?*

E2: *También tengo "Los estudiantes de administración de empresas son ricos".*

E3: *Tengo "Los estudiantes de informática son ricos".*

GRUPO: *Tenemos "Los estudiantes de administración de empresas y los estudiantes de informática son ricos".*

**Los estudiantes de…**

1. _____ son ricos.
2. _____ son simpáticos.
3. _____ son trabajadores.
4. _____ son cómicos.

5. _____ son responsables.
6. _____ son pacientes.
7. _____ son interesantes.
8. _____ son muy inteligentes.

## NOTA CULTURAL

# Las universidades hispanas

02-09

There are many similarities and differences between the system of higher education in the United States and that of the Spanish-speaking world. For example, students in universities across the Spanish-speaking world usually begin their career courses immediately, as opposed to having several years of liberal arts courses. Also, although many universities have student housing, it is common for students to live at home or rent apartments with other students.

La Universidad Nacional Autónoma de México (UNAM)

With regard to collegiate sports and pastimes, there are usually varieties of extracurricular activities available in the form of clubs. For example, clubs can be sports-related, or they can be centered around other organized activities such as socially conscious volunteerism groups.

Technology permeates Hispanic universities. As in the United States, it is not uncommon for students to take online courses or have opportunities for some type of distance learning.

**Preguntas**
1. What are similarities between your life as a college student and that of a student in the Spanish-speaking world?
2. Where in the Spanish-speaking world would you like to study? Find the university's web site and share with the class the programs and opportunities that the school has to offer.

## 2 VOCABULARIO

### La sala de clase
Describing your classroom and classmates

02-10 to 02-13

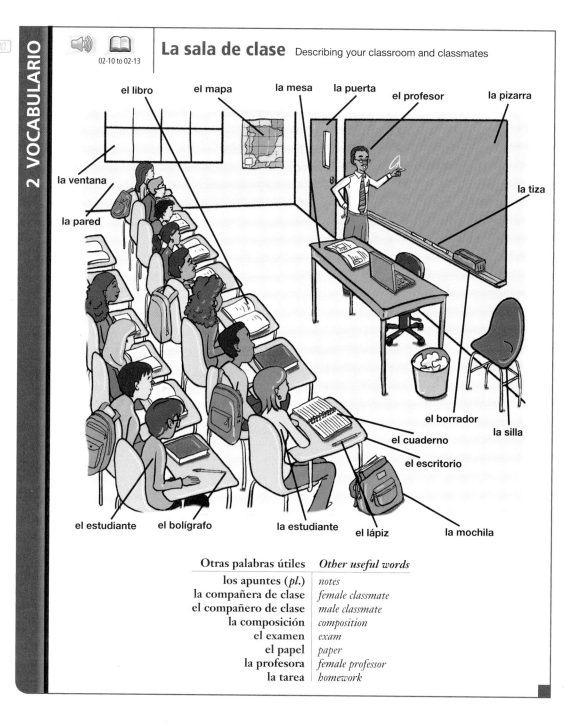

el libro · el mapa · la mesa · la puerta · el profesor · la pizarra · la ventana · la pared · la tiza · el borrador · la silla · el cuaderno · el escritorio · el estudiante · el bolígrafo · la estudiante · el lápiz · la mochila

| Otras palabras útiles | Other useful words |
|---|---|
| los apuntes (*pl.*) | *notes* |
| la compañera de clase | *female classmate* |
| el compañero de clase | *male classmate* |
| la composición | *composition* |
| el examen | *exam* |
| el papel | *paper* |
| la profesora | *female professor* |
| la tarea | *homework* |

**Instructor Resources**

• Textbook images, Extra Activities

**SUGGESTION for *La sala de clase***

You may want to bring a shopping bag to class with some of the items from the vocabulary presentation inside. Practice the words by having students name the items you take out, one by one; or ask students each to reach in, draw an item, and then name it (or call on another student to name it).

**ADDITIONAL ACTIVITY for *La sala de clase***

**Asociación libre**

The following is a list of words associated with school. Take turns calling out the words from the list and naming your associations.

MODELO
E1: *la mochila*
E2: *los libros*

1. los apuntes
2. el lápiz
3. la pizarra
4. la silla
5. la composición
6. la literatura
7. la tarea
8. el/la estudiante
9. la tiza
10. el cuaderno

*Capítulo Preliminar A: Los números 0–30, pág. 16.*

**2-4** **¿Cómo es tu sala de clase?** Using the numbers 0–30, take turns indicating how many there are in your classroom of each of the items presented in **La sala de clase.** You and your partner should each create at least **five** sentences following the model. ■

**MODELO**    E1:   *Hay veinticinco mochilas y tres ventanas.*

           E2:   *Sí, y también hay diecinueve cuadernos.*

**Fíjate**

*Hay* is a little word that carries a lot of meaning. It can be both singular and plural, and it means both "there is" and "there are."

| Vocabulario útil | |
|---|---|
| **hay** | *there is; there are* |
| **pero** | *but* |
| **también** | *too; also* |
| **y** | *and* |

*Capítulo 1, El verbo tener, pág. 34.*

**Fíjate**

To make a negative statement, simply place the word *no* before the verb: *Chucho tiene los apuntes. Chucho no tiene los apuntes.*

**2-5** **¿Qué tiene Chucho?** Chucho is running late for class again. He has remembered some things and forgotten others. Make a list of **five** things he possibly has and does not have for class, using the verb **tener.** Share your list with a classmate. ■

**MODELO**    *Chucho tiene los apuntes, pero no tiene el libro de matemáticas. También tiene…*

**EXPANSION for 2-5**
In groups of 3 or 4, students should brainstorm a list of 4 things that each person in the group has brought to class and at least one thing no one brought.

**Instructor Resources**
• PPT, Extra Activities

Workbooklet

**2-6** **¿Qué tienen tus compañeros?** Randomly choose three students and complete the chart below. Then take turns having your partner identify the classmates as you state **five** things each one has or does not have for class. ■

**NOTE for 2-6**
Activities like **2-6** require students to write. *¡Anda! Curso elemental* offers various writing activities per chapter. Some require recording personal information that will be shared; others require gathering information from others. Students do not need to write in their books. These activities are available in the Workbooklet, or they may write on separate sheets of paper.

### Fíjate

As in English, when listing a series of things, the word *y* (*and*) is placed just before the last item. In Spanish, however, note that you do not place a comma before *y*.

MODELO
    E1: *La estudiante 1 tiene dos cuadernos, un libro, un bolígrafo y dos lápices. ¡No tiene la tarea!*
    E2: *¿Es Sarah?*
    E1: *Sí, es Sarah. / No, no es Sarah.*

| ESTUDIANTE 1 _____ | ESTUDIANTE 2 _____ | ESTUDIANTE 3 _____ |
|---|---|---|
| (NO) TIENE... | (NO) TIENE... | (NO) TIENE... |
| 1. | 1. | 1. |
| 2. | 2. | 2. |
| 3. | 3. | 3. |
| 4. | 4. | 4. |
| 5. | 5. | 5. |

**NATIONAL STANDARDS**
*Comparisons*
Most grammar explanations in *¡Anda! Curso elemental* will encourage students to consider English grammar as the point of departure for understanding Spanish grammar.

## 3 GRAMÁTICA

 02-14 to 02-18   ¡Hola! Spanish/English Tutorials

# Presente indicativo de verbos regulares
### Relating daily activities

**NOTE for *Presente indicativo de verbos regulares***
Preferences vary regarding the presentation of *-ar*, *-er*, and *-ir* verbs separately or together. We believe that presenting them at the same time, but in progression (first *-ar*, then *-er*, then *-ir*), allows students to learn the *-ar* conjugation and then build on that knowledge, substituting the changes for *-er* and then *-ir* conjugations.

**Mario es un estudiante de derecho. ¿Qué hace (*does he do*) todos los días?**

**Llega** a la clase a las nueve de la mañana.

**Lee** en la biblioteca.

**Habla** con sus compañeros.

**Trabaja** dos horas como tutor.

**Come** en la cafetería con amigos.

A las 6:30 **espera** el autobús y **regresa** a su apartamento.

*(continued)*

**SUGGESTION for *Presente indicativo de verbos regulares***
You may want to use these drawings after you have reviewed the present tense conjugations. Have students describe Mario's schedule in more detail. You can also return to these drawings to practice question formation.

Spanish has three groups of verbs which are categorized by the ending of the infinitive. Remember that an infinitive is expressed in English by the word *to: to have, to be,* and *to speak* are all infinitive forms of English verbs. Spanish infinitives end in **-ar, -er,** or **-ir.** Look at the following infinitives.

### Verbos que terminan en *-ar*

| | | | |
|---|---|---|---|
| **comprar** | *to buy* | **preguntar** | *to ask (a question)* |
| **contestar** | *to answer* | **preparar** | *to prepare; to get ready* |
| **enseñar** | *to teach; to show* | **regresar** | *to return* |
| **esperar** | *to wait for; to hope* | **terminar** | *to finish; to end* |
| **estudiar** | *to study* | **tomar** | *to take; to drink* |
| **hablar** | *to speak* | **trabajar** | *to work* |
| **llegar** | *to arrive* | **usar** | *to use* |
| **necesitar** | *to need* | | |

### Verbos que terminan en *-er*

| | | | |
|---|---|---|---|
| **aprender** | *to learn* | **correr** | *to run* |
| **comer** | *to eat* | **creer** | *to believe* |
| **comprender** | *to understand* | **leer** | *to read* |

### Verbos que terminan en *-ir*

| | | | |
|---|---|---|---|
| **abrir** | *to open* | **recibir** | *to receive* |
| **escribir** | *to write* | **vivir** | *to live* |

To talk about daily or ongoing activities or actions, you need to use the present tense. You can also use the present tense to express future events.

Mario **lee** en la biblioteca.

Mario **lee** en la biblioteca mañana.

{ *Mario reads in the library.*
*Mario is reading in the library.*
*Mario will read in the library tomorrow.*

To form the present indicative, drop the **-ar, -er,** or **-ir** ending from the infinitive, and add the appropriate ending. The endings are in blue in the following chart. Follow this simple pattern with all regular verbs.

| **Estrategia** | | **hablar (*to speak*)** | **comer (*to eat*)** | **vivir (*to live*)** |
|---|---|---|---|---|
| If you would like to review the difference between the formal "you" and the informal "you," return to the cultural reading *¿Tú o usted?* on page 12 of *Capítulo Preliminar A.* | yo | hablo | como | vivo |
| | tú | hablas | comes | vives |
| | Ud. | habla | come | vive |
| | él, ella | habla | come | vive |
| | nosotros/as | hablamos | comemos | vivimos |
| | vosotros/as | habláis | coméis | vivís |
| | Uds. | hablan | comen | viven |
| | ellos/as | hablan | comen | viven |

**2-7** **Vamos a practicar** Take ten small pieces of paper and write a different noun or pronoun (**yo, tú, él,** etc.) on each one. On another five small pieces of paper write five infinitives, one on each piece of paper. Take turns drawing a paper from each pile. Give the correct form of the verb you selected to match the noun or pronoun you picked from the pile. Each person should say at least **five** verbs in a row correctly. ■

| MODELO | INFINITIVE: | *preguntar* |
|---|---|---|
| | PRONOUN OR NOUN: | *mi madre* |
| | E1: | *mi madre pregunta* |

**2-8** **El email de Carlos** Complete Carlos's e-mail message to his mother using the correct form of the verbs in parentheses. ■

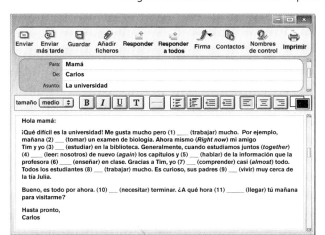

Hola mamá:

¡Qué difícil es la universidad! Me gusta mucho pero (1) ___ (trabajar) mucho. Por ejemplo, mañana (2) ___ (tomar) un examen de biología. Ahora mismo (*Right now*) mi amigo Tim y yo (3) ___ (estudiar) en la biblioteca. Generalmente, cuando estudiamos juntos (*together*) (4) ___ (leer: nosotros) de nuevo (*again*) los capítulos y (5) ___ (hablar) de la información que la profesora (6) ___ (enseñar) en clase. Gracias a Tim, yo (7) ___ (comprender) casi (*almost*) todo. Todos los estudiantes (8) ___ (trabajar) mucho. Es curioso, sus padres (9) ___ (vivir) muy cerca de la tía Julia.

Bueno, es todo por ahora. (10) ___ (necesitar) terminar. ¿A qué hora (11) ___ (llegar) tú mañana para visitarme?

Hasta pronto,
Carlos

Carlos es estudiante de la UNAM. ¿Qué escribe?

 Workbooklet

 **2-9** **Dime quién, dónde y cuándo** Look at the three columns below. Then, connect a pronoun to an activity, and then to a class, to create **five** sentences. Share your answers with a classmate. ■

| MODELO | E1: | *nosotros / usar un microscopio / clase de ciencias* |
|---|---|---|
| | E2: | Usamos un microscopio en la clase de ciencias. |

| PRONOMBRE | ACTIVIDAD | CLASE |
|---|---|---|
| yo | preparar una presentación | matemáticas |
| nosotros/as | leer mucho | literatura |
| ellos/as | necesitar una calculadora | español |
| ella | estudiar leyes (*laws*) | periodismo |
| tú | escribir muchas composiciones | historia |
| Uds. | contestar muchas preguntas | derecho |
| él | aprender mucho | arquitectura |

**Fíjate**

Remember that subject pronouns (*yo, tú, él, ella,* etc.) are used for emphasis or clarification, and therefore do not always need to be expressed.

**NOTE for 2-7**
Remind students that when they are working in pairs, there will sometimes be an odd number of students. Instead of using the *tú* form, they could ask the same questions of the other two students in a group in the *ustedes* form.

**SUGGESTION for 2-7**
Encourage your students to select verbs that they need to practice more.

**ANSWERS to 2-8**
1. trabajo
2. tomo
3. estudiamos
4. leemos
5. hablamos
6. enseña
7. comprendo
8. trabajan
9. viven
10. Necesito
11. llegas

**EXPANSION for 2-9**
This can be expanded into a listening activity. Students take turns reading their sentences to a partner. While one student reads, the other student listens carefully and connects the items mentioned. Then they can check each other's work to see whether the lines match what was read.

**HERITAGE LANGUAGE LEARNERS**
Feel free to modify the directions of an activity for heritage language learners in order for them to practice their writing and reading skills. In particular, the mechanical practice of writing out each question will alert them to the punctuation and accent marks used in questions.

**Instructor Resources**
• PPT, Extra Activities

[8:00]  **2-10** ¿A quién conoces que...? Who do you know who displays the following characteristics? Complete the following questions. Then, take turns asking and answering in complete sentences to practice the new verbs. ∎

MODELO      ¿Quién _____ (hablar) mucho?

         E1: *¿Quién habla mucho?*

         E2: *Mi hermano Tom habla mucho. También mis hermanas hablan mucho.*

1. ¿Quién ___corre___ (correr) mucho?
2. ¿Quién ___estudia___ (estudiar) muy poco (*very little*)?
3. ¿Quién ___escribe___ (escribir) muchos emails?
4. ¿Quién ___llega___ (llegar) siempre tarde a la clase?
5. ¿Quién ___abre___ (abrir) su mochila?
6. ¿Quién ___usa___ (usar) los apuntes de sus amigos?
7. ¿Quién ___comprende___ (comprender) todo (*everything*) cuando el/la profesor/a habla español?
8. ¿Quién ___cree___ (creer) en Santa Claus?

**NOTE for *Las palabras interrogativas***
As students are not familiar with the personal *a*, "whom" is not introduced at this point.

**METHODOLOGY • The Natural Approach**
This sequence of activities is a good example of the *Natural Approach* for language acquisition, taking students from simple yes/no questions to slightly longer sentence utterances.

[5:00]

## 4 GRAMÁTICA

02-19 to 02-23   Spanish/English Tutorials   ¡Hola!

# La formación de preguntas y las palabras interrogativas   Creating and answering questions

### Asking yes/no questions

Yes/no questions in Spanish are formed in two different ways:

1. Adding question marks to the statement.

    Antonio habla español.  →  ¿Antonio habla español?

    *Antonio speaks Spanish.*     *Does Antonio speak Spanish?*
                                  *or Antonio speaks Spanish?*

    As in English, your voice goes up at the end of the sentence. Remember that written Spanish has an upside-down question mark at the beginning of a question.

2. Inverting the order of the subject and the verb.

    Antonio habla español.  →  ¿Habla Antonio español?

    SUBJECT + VERB            VERB + SUBJECT

    *Antonio speaks Spanish.*     *Does Antonio speak Spanish?*

### Answering yes/no questions

Answering questions is also like it is in English.

¿Habla Antonio español?     *Does Antonio speak Spanish?*
**Sí,** habla español.         *Yes, he speaks Spanish.*
**No, no** habla español.      *No, he does not speak Spanish.*

Notice that in the negative response to the question above, both English and Spanish have two negative words.

**Antonio:** ¿Cuántos idiomas hablas?
**Silvia:** Hablo dos, español y francés. ¿Y tú?
**Antonio:** Solo hablo español, pero mi loro habla cinco idiomas.

# Information questions

Information questions begin with interrogative words. Study the list of question words below and remember, accents are used on all interrogative words and also on exclamatory words: **¡Qué bueno!** (*That's great!*)

## Las palabras interrogativas

| | | | |
|---|---|---|---|
| **¿Qué?** | *What?* | **¿Qué** idioma habla Antonio? | *What language does Antonio speak?* |
| **¿Por qué?** | *Why?* | **¿Por qué** no trabaja Antonio? | *Why doesn't Antonio work?* |
| **¿Cómo?** | *How?* | **¿Cómo** está Antonio? | *How is Antonio?* |
| **¿Cuándo?** | *When?* | **¿Cuándo** es la clase? | *When is the class?* |
| **¿Adónde?** | *To where?* | **¿Adónde** va Antonio? | *(To) Where is Antonio going?* |
| **¿Dónde?** | *Where?* | **¿Dónde** vive Antonio? | *Where does Antonio live?* |
| **¿De dónde?** | *From where?* | **¿De dónde** regresa Antonio? | *Where is Antonio coming back from?* |
| **¿Cuánto/a?** | *How much?* | **¿Cuánto** estudia Antonio para la clase? | *How much does Antonio study for the class?* |
| **¿Cuántos/as?** | *How many?* | **¿Cuántos** idiomas habla Antonio? | *How many languages does he speak?* |
| **¿Cuál?** | *Which (one)?* | **¿Cuál** es su clase favorita? | *Which is his favorite class?* |
| **¿Cuáles?** | *Which (ones)?* | **¿Cuáles** son sus clases favoritas? | *Which are his favorite classes?* |
| **¿Quién?** | *Who?* | **¿Quién** habla cinco idiomas? | *Who speaks five languages?* |
| **¿Quiénes?** | *Who? (pl.)* | **¿Quiénes** hablan cinco idiomas? | *Who speaks five languages?* |

Note that, although the subject is not always necessary, when it is included in the sentence it follows the verb.

---

`1:00`  **2-11** **¿Sí o no?** Take turns asking and answering the following yes/no questions in complete sentences. ■

**MODELO**  E1: ¿Estudias francés?

E2: *Sí, estudio francés. / No, no estudio francés.*

1. ¿Hablas español?
2. ¿Estudias mucho?
3. ¿Aprendes mucho?
4. ¿Escribes mucho en clase?
5. ¿De dónde es tu profesor/a?
6. ¿Trabajas?
7. ¿Vives con tus padres?
8. ¿Lees muchas novelas?

---

`1:00`  **2-12** **Preguntas, más preguntas** With a partner, determine which interrogative word would elicit each of the following responses and create a question that would elicit each statement. ■

**MODELO**  E1: Estudio **matemáticas.**

E2: *¿Qué estudias?*

1. Martín estudia **en la sala de clase.**
2. Estudiamos español **porque es interesante.**
3. **Susana y Julia** estudian.
4. Estudian **entre las 7:00 y las 10:00 de la noche.**
5. Leen **rápidamente.**
6. Leo **tres libros.**

**Fíjate**

*Porque* written as one word and without an accent mark means "because."

**2-13** **¿Y tú?** Interview your classmates using the following questions about Spanish class. ∎

MODELO   E1:   ¿Cuántas sillas hay en la clase?

E2:   *Hay veinte sillas.*

1. ¿Quién enseña la clase?
2. ¿Dónde enseña la clase?
3. ¿Quiénes hablan en la clase generalmente?
4. ¿Cuántos estudiantes hay en la clase?
5. ¿Qué libro(s) usas en la clase?
6. ¿Tomas muchos apuntes en la clase?
7. ¿Es la clase fácil o difícil?
8. ¿Trabajas mucho en la clase de español?

| Vocabulario útil | |
| --- | --- |
| **difícil** | *difficult* |
| **fácil** | *easy* |

**2-14** **¿Y tu familia o amigos?** Write **five** questions you could ask classmates about their families or friends, then move around the room asking those questions of as many people as possible. ∎

Capítulo 1. La familia, pág. 32; El verbo *tener*, pág. 34; Los adjetivos descriptivos, pág. 43.

MODELO   E1:   *¿Cómo se llaman tus padres? ¿Dónde viven tus abuelos?*

E2:   *¿Cuántos hermanos tienes?...*

## 5 VOCABULARIO

02-24 to 02-27

## Los números 100–1.000 Counting from 100–1,000

| | | | | | |
| --- | --- | --- | --- | --- | --- |
| 100 | **cien** | 200 | **doscientos** | 600 | **seiscientos** |
| 101 | **ciento uno** | 201 | **doscientos uno** | 700 | **setecientos** |
| 102 | **ciento dos** | 300 | **trescientos** | 800 | **ochocientos** |
| 116 | **ciento dieciséis** | 400 | **cuatrocientos** | 900 | **novecientos** |
| 120 | **ciento veinte** | 500 | **quinientos** | 1.000 | **mil** |

1. The conjuction **y** is used to connect only 31–39, 41–49, 51–59, 61–69, 71–79, 81–89, and 91–99.

32 = treinta **y** dos, 101 = ciento uno, 151 = ciento cincuenta **y** uno

2. **Ciento** is shortened to **cien** before any noun.

**cien** hombres          **cien** mujeres

3. Multiples of **cientos** agree in number and gender with nouns they modify.

**doscientos** estudiantes      **trescientas** jóvenes

4. Note the use of a decimal instead of a comma in **1.000.**

[4:00]  👥  **2-15** **¡Dinero!** Take turns saying the following amounts of money aloud, in the currencies listed below. ■

U.S. dollar (dólares) = USD

Euro (euros) = EUR

Mexican peso (pesos) = MXN

Honduran lempira (lempiras) = HNL

**MODELO**  E1:  325 USD

E2:  *trescientos veinticinco dólares*

| | | | |
|---|---|---|---|
| 1. 110 USD | 3. 376 HNL | 5. 638 MXN | 7. 763 HNL |
| 2. 415 MXN | 4. 822 EUR | 6. 544 USD | 8. 999 EUR |

[8:00]  👥  **2-16** **Vamos a adivinar** On a popular TV show, *The Price is Right,* contestants must guess the prices of different items. Bring in **five** ads of items priced between $100 and $1,000 and cover the prices. In groups of three or four, take turns guessing the prices in U.S. dollars. The person who comes closest without going over the price wins each item! ■

**Fíjate**

If the item you are pricing is plural, the verb form will be *cuestan.*

**MODELO**  E1:  *¿Cuesta (It costs) ciento cincuenta y cinco dólares?*

E2:  *No.*

E1:  *Cuesta ciento ochenta dólares.*

E2:  *Sí.*

## ¿Cómo andas? I

| Having completed **Comunicación I**, I now can . . . | Feel confident | Need to review |
|---|:---:|:---:|
| • share information about courses and majors (p. 62) | ☐ | ☐ |
| • indicate the stressed syllables in words (MSL/SAM) | ☐ | ☐ |
| • examine Hispanic university life (p. 64) | ☐ | ☐ |
| • describe my classroom and classmates (p. 65) | ☐ | ☐ |
| • relate daily activities (p. 67) | ☐ | ☐ |
| • create and answer questions (p. 70) | ☐ | ☐ |
| • count from 100–1,000 (p. 72) | ☐ | ☐ |

**SUGGESTION for 2-15**

Bring in a newspaper, or printout from a web site, with the current values of currency from different Spanish-speaking countries in comparison to that of the U.S. dollar. Then help students convert some of the amounts given into the foreign currencies of your choice.

**ANSWERS to 2-15**

1. ciento diez dólares
2. cuatrocientos quince pesos
3. trescientos setenta y seis lempiras
4. ochocientos veintidós euros
5. seiscientos treinta y ocho pesos
6. quinientos cuarenta y cuatro dólares
7. setecientos sesenta y tres lempiras
8. novecientos noventa y nueve euros

**PLANNING AHEAD**

For **2-16,** the students each need to bring in at least five ads with prices up to $1,000 for their classmates to guess. They can be items related to this chapter, but it is not necessary. You may want to bring extras in case some students forget.

**SECTION GOALS for**
*Comunicación II*

By the end of the *Comunicación II*
section, students will be able to:

• describe common places and
  buildings on a campus.
• state the forms of *estar*.
• use *estar* for location, description of
  feelings, and changes from the norm.
• explain where certain cities are
  located.
• express how they and others are
  feeling.
• give opinions about their likes and
  dislikes using *gustar*.
• report about the sports and leisure
  activities they enjoy.

**NATIONAL STANDARDS**
*Communication*

The activities describing the university,
daily routine, location, and feelings all
require communication. The pair activities
foster interpersonal communication
(Standard 1.1), as students exchange
information, opinions, and feelings about
school. You can modify **2-18** by asking
students to draw, photograph, cut out
pictures, or use clip art to show the items
in their rooms and label those items in
Spanish. If they prepare their inventories
for an audience of readers and/or present
them to an audience, they can satisfy
Communication Standard 1.3.

**SUGGESTION for *En la
universidad***

Have students give actual names for
these places found on your campus: 1. el
estadio, 2. la biblioteca, 3. una residencia
estudiantil, 4. una tienda, 5. el centro
estudiantil, 6. la cafetería, 7. un edificio,
8. una librería. E.g., el estadio: "John F.
Kenan Memorial Stadium."

# Comunicación II

**6 VOCABULARIO**

5:00 | 02-28 to 02-32

## En la universidad  Elaborating on university places and objects

### Los lugares

el cuarto

| Otras palabras útiles | *Other useful words* |
|---|---|
| el apartamento | *apartment* |
| el edificio | *building* |
| el laboratorio | *laboratory* |
| la tienda | *store* |

## La residencia

el radio/la radio

el despertador

la compañera de cuarto

el reloj

la televisión

la computadora

los discos compactos (los CD)

la calculadora

el dinero

el DVD

| Otras palabras útiles | *Other useful words* |
| --- | --- |
| el compañero de cuarto | *male roommate* |
| el horario (de clases) | *schedule (of classes)* |
| el reproductor de CD/DVD | *CD/DVD player* |

**NOTE for *Television***
The RAE accepts the use of both *televisor* and *televisión* to mean "television set." The authors of *¡Anda! Curso elemental* have elected to use only *televisión*.

**NOTE for *Radio***
Please note that the radio can be feminine or masculine (la radio/el radio) depending of the country. Some Spanish-speaking students may say "la radio". The broadcast is always feminine.

**SUGGESTION for *En la universidad***
Have students state the names of the buildings on your campus, e.g., *el gimnasio Woolen*, etc.

**SUGGESTION for *En la universidad***
Have students tell their partners which of the items they have and do not have in their rooms/apartments, e.g., *Tengo una computadora; no tengo un radio*.

2:00    **2-17 ¡Lo sé!**  Take turns choosing the word from the vocabulary list, **Los lugares,** that is associated with each of the following words. ■

MODELO   E1:  leer libros, estudiar
         E2:  *la biblioteca*

1. comer pasta y tomar café
2. comprar libros
3. jugar al básquetbol
4. hacer experimentos científicos
5. jugar al fútbol
6. Hancock Building, Chicago, IL
7. leer libros y estudiar
8. hablar con amigos

3:00    **2-18 En mi cuarto...**  Take turns telling your partner which items from the list **La residencia** you have in your room or where you live. Then say which items you do not have. ■

MODELO   E1:  *Tengo una calculadora, una computadora, un despertador...*
         E2:  *No tengo un radio, un reproductor de DVD...*

10:00   **2-19 Datos personales**  You are a foreign exchange student in Mexico, living with a family. Your Mexican little "brother" wants to know all about you! Answer his questions, which follow, then ask a classmate the same questions. ■

1. ¿De dónde eres?
2. ¿Qué estudias?
3. ¿Dónde estudias?
4. ¿Dónde comes?
5. ¿Dónde compras tus libros?
6. ¿Dónde vives?
7. ¿Qué necesitas para tu clase de español?
8. ¿Qué necesitas para una clase de matemáticas?
9. ¿Qué tienes en tu mochila?

3:00   **7 GRAMÁTICA**

02-33 to 02-37   Spanish Tutorial   ¡Hola!

**El verbo *estar***  Expressing *to be*

¿Dónde está mi hijita?

Estoy aquí, papi, ¡en el armario!

Another verb that expresses *to be* in Spanish is **estar.** Like **tener** and **ser, estar** is not a regular verb; that is, you cannot simply drop the infinitive ending and add the usual **-ar** endings.

|  | estar (*to be*) |  |  |
|---|---|---|---|
| **Singular** |  | **Plural** |  |
| yo | **estoy** | nosotros/as | **estamos** |
| tú | **estás** | vosotros/as | **estáis** |
| Ud. | **está** | Uds. | **están** |
| él, ella | **está** | ellos/as | **están** |

**Ser** and **estar** are not interchangeable because they are used differently. Two uses of **estar** are:

1. To describe the location of someone or something.

| | |
|---|---|
| Manuel **está** en la sala de clase. | *Manuel is in the classroom.* |
| Nuestros padres **están** en México. | *Our parents are in Mexico.* |

2. To describe how someone is feeling or to express a change from the norm.

| | |
|---|---|
| **Estoy** bien. ¿Y tú? | *I'm fine. And you?* |
| **Estamos** tristes hoy. | *We are sad today. (Normally we are upbeat and happy.)* |

---

 **2-20** **¿Cuál es la palabra?** Take turns giving the correct form of **estar** for each subject. ■

1. nosotras estamos
2. el estudiante está
3. tú estás
4. la pizarra está
5. yo estoy
6. los profesores están

---

 **2-21** **Busco...** You are on campus and you want to know where you can find the following items, people, and places. Take turns creating questions to determine the location of each person or thing. Your partner provides a response using the correct form of **estar + en** (*in, on,* or *at*). ■

**MODELO**    el mapa / libro

> E1:  *¿Dónde está el mapa?*
>
> E2:  *El mapa está en el libro.*

1. las calculadoras / la mochila
2. los apuntes / el cuaderno
3. tú / el laboratorio
4. el despertador / la mesa
5. yo / la residencia
6. mi amigo y yo / el centro estudiantil

### Estrategia
You have noted that the majority of the classroom activities are with a partner. So that each person has equal opportunities, one of you should do the even-numbered items in an activity, the other do the odd-numbered items.

---

 **2-22** **¡Ahora mismo!** With a partner, determine what the following people may be doing, using the following verbs. ■

| | | | | |
|---|---|---|---|---|
| aprender | comprar | comer | escribir | estudiar |
| hablar | leer | preparar | tomar | trabajar |

**MODELO**    E1:  Marta está en la sala de clase.

> E2:  *Toma apuntes.*

1. Juan y Pepa están en la biblioteca.
2. Mi hermana está en la librería.
3. El profesor está en su casa.
4. Los estudiantes están en la cafetería.
5. María está en su apartamento.
6. Patricia está en el centro estudiantil.
7. Tú estás en el laboratorio.
8. Mi amiga y yo estamos en la clase de español.

**ADDITIONAL ACTIVITY for**
*El verbo* **estar**

**¿Dónde están?**
Determine together where the following people are based on the statements given. Give as many possibilities as you can.

**MODELO**
La profesora Salgado contesta las preguntas de los estudiantes.
E1:  *La profesora Salgado está en la sala de clase.*
E2:  *La profesora Salgado está en el laboratorio.*

1. Cristina y Nico comen y ven la televisión.
2. Selma necesita comprar un libro para la clase de inglés.
3. Gregorio y David necesitan una calculadora.
4. Pedro termina la tarea.
5. Nosotros tenemos una reunión (*meeting*) con otros estudiantes.

**METHODOLOGY • Pair Work**
For **2-20** through **2-23**, you may want Student 1 to do the even-numbered items while Student 2 does the odd items. It is important for you to overtly tell students to take turns when working in pairs. If not, one student may monopolize the pair work.

**ADDITIONAL ACTIVITY for**
*El verbo* **estar**

Working in pairs, have students say whether the following places are *cerca* or *lejos*. For example: destination vs. where the student is now: *la biblioteca/la sala de clase de español; La biblioteca está lejos.*

1. la biblioteca/la cafetería
2. la residencia estudiantil (o apartamento/casa)/la librería de la universidad
3. un laboratorio de computadoras/el centro estudiantil
4. el gimnasio/el estadio
5. un laboratorio de ciencias/la biblioteca
6. la casa de tu familia/tu residencia estudiantil (o el lugar donde vives)
7. el centro estudiantil/el estadio

**SUGGESTION for 2-23**
If you have not yet modeled the pronunciation of the Spanish-speaking countries and capitals, this is a good opportunity to do so. You may wish to refer to the map on p. 18 of *Capítulo Preliminar A*.

**EXPANSION for 2-23**
You will notice that not all of the Hispanic countries are listed in **2-23.** You can use a classroom map, project a map from the Internet, ask students to turn to the map in *Capítulo Preliminar A*, or project a transparency of a map to include other Hispanic countries such as Venezuela, Ecuador, Uruguay, Paraguay, Colombia, Guatemala, El Salvador, Nicaragua, Costa Rica, and Panama.

 **2-23 La clase de geografía** Take turns asking a partner in which countries the following capitals are located. ■

MODELO  E1: *¿Dónde está Washington, D.C.?*
E2: *Washington, D.C., está en los Estados Unidos.*

> **Fíjate**
> Knowledge of geography is increasingly important in our global community. Activity **2-23** presents an opportunity to review the countries and capitals of the Spanish-speaking world.

1. Madrid
2. México, D.F.
3. Lima
4. San Juan
5. La Paz

6. Buenos Aires
7. Santiago
8. Tegucigalpa
9. Santo Domingo
10. La Habana

## 8 VOCABULARIO

02-38 to 02-41

# Las emociones y los estados
Articulating emotions and states of being

Chema/Gloria    Roberto/Mayra    Samuel/Tina    Ruy/Carmen    Memo/Eva

**aburrido/a**    **cansado/a**    **contento/a**    **enfermo/a**    **enojado/a**

Carlos/Patricia    Ramón/Raquel    Fernando/Silvia    Carlos/Rebeca

**nervioso/a**    **preocupado/a**    **triste**    **feliz**

---

 **2-24** **¿Cómo están?**  Look at the drawings from *Las emociones y los estados* and take turns answering the following questions. ■

**MODELO**    E1:  ¿Cómo está Silvia?
              E2:  *Silvia está triste.*

1. ¿Cómo están Ruy y Carmen? Están enfermos
2. ¿Cómo está Roberto? Está cansado
3. ¿Quién está preocupada? Raquel está preocupada
4. ¿Quiénes están nerviosos? Carlos y Patricia están nerviosos
5. ¿Cómo están Chema y Gloria? Están aburridos
6. ¿Cómo estás tú? Estoy…

---

**2-25** **¿Qué pasa?**  Which adjectives from the drawings above best describe how you might feel in each of the following situations? Share your responses with a partner. ■

**MODELO**    E1:  recibes $1.000
              E2:  *Estoy contento/a.*

1. Estás en el hospital. Estoy enfermo/a
2. Tienes un examen muy difícil hoy. Estoy nervioso/a
3. Corres quince millas (*miles*). Estoy cansado/a
4. Tu profesor de historia lee un libro por (*for*) una hora y quince minutos. Estoy aburrido/a
5. Esperas y esperas pero tu amigo no llega. (¡Y no te llama por teléfono!) Estoy enojado/a / preocupado/a
6. Sacas una "A" en tu examen de español. Estoy contento/a

**Instructor Resources**
• PPT, Extra Activities

**ANSWERS to 2-26**
1. Tomás está en la biblioteca. Estudia/Lee. Está aburrido.
2. Tina está en su cuarto. Está enferma.
3. Ana y Mirta están en una tienda. Compran un disco compacto (CD). Están contentas.
4. Están en la clase. Aprenden matemáticas/Tienen un examen. Están nerviosos.

**METHODOLOGY • Lexical Presentations at the Point of Need**
In *¡Anda! Curso elemental*, we have made the conscious decision to teach *gustar* in a very brief introduction. Educational psychologists inform us that all humans like to talk about themselves. We love to express our likes and dislikes early on in conversation. In order for your students to express their personal feelings and those of their friends or family members, it is important for them to be able to say at the very least *I like . . .* in order to practice vocabulary in complete sentences. In *¡Anda! Curso elemental*, we have decided to introduce the pronouns *I, you, he/she,* and *it* with *gustar*. Indirect object pronouns and a more in-depth explanation of *gustar* will appear in *Capítulo 8*. You may also choose to present "to please" as a possible equivalent to *gustar*.

**NOTE for *Gramática***
This is an inductive grammar presentation in which the students are given examples of a grammar concept and, through the use of guiding questions, they formulate the rule in their own words. Research indicates that students remember and internalize grammar rules better when they construct their own knowledge.

---

**2-26 ¿Dónde y cómo?** Together, look at the following drawings and determine where the people are, what they are doing, and how they might be feeling. ■

Tomás          Tina          Ana y Mirta          El profesor Martín y sus estudiantes

MODELO  E1: El profesor Martín
         E2: *El profesor Martín está en la clase. Enseña matemáticas. Está contento.*

1. Tomás                3. Ana y Mirta
2. Tina                 4. Los estudiantes del profesor Martín

---

**9 GRAMÁTICA**

 ¡Hola!
02-42 to 02-46   Spanish Tutorial

**El verbo *gustar*** Conveying likes and dislikes

¿Te gusta el arte abstracto?

**Fíjate**
You can go back to page 25 in *Capítulo Preliminar A* for more information on *gustar*.

To express likes and dislikes you say the following:

**Me gusta** la profesora.                     *I like the professor.*
**Me gustan** las clases de idiomas.           *I like language classes.*
¿**Te gustan** las novelas de Sandra Cisneros? *Do you like Sandra Cisneros's novels?*
**Te gusta** el arte abstracto.                *You like abstract art.*
No **le gusta** estudiar.                       *He does not like to study.*

**Estrategia**
You may have noticed that there are two types of grammar presentations in *¡Anda! Curso elemental*:
1. You are given the grammar rule.
2. You are given guiding questions to help *you* construct the grammar rule, and to state the rule in your own words.

No matter which type of presentation, educational researchers have found it is *always* important for you to state the rules orally. Accurately stating the rules demonstrates that you are on the road to using the grammar concept(s) correctly in your speaking and writing.

**¡Explícalo tú!**
1. To say you like or dislike one thing, what form of **gustar** do you use?
2. To say you like or dislike more than one thing, what form of **gustar** do you use?
3. Which words in the examples mean *I? You? He/she?*
4. If a verb is needed after **gusta/gustan**, what form of the verb do you use?

✔ **To check your answers to the preceding questions, see Appendix 1.**

**2-27 ¿Qué te gusta?** Decide whether or not you like the following items, and share your opinions with a classmate. ■

MODELO    E1:   las clases difíciles

           E2:   *(No) Me gustan las clases difíciles.*

1. el centro estudiantil
2. los sábados
3. vivir en un apartamento
4. la informática

5. aprender idiomas
6. la cafetería
7. correr
8. los libros de Harry Potter

**2-28 Te toca a ti** Now change the cues from **2-27** into questions, and ask a different classmate to answer. ■

**Estrategia**

Remember, if you answer negatively, you will need to say *no* twice. If you need to review, check *La formación de preguntas* on page 70 of this chapter.

MODELO    E1:   *¿Te gustan las clases difíciles?*

           E2:   *No, no me gustan las clases difíciles.*

## 10 VOCABULARIO

# Los deportes y los pasatiempos
Offering opinions on sports and pastimes

02-47 to 02-50

**bailar**

**caminar**

**escuchar música**

**ir de compras**

**jugar al básquetbol**

**jugar al béisbol**

*(continued)*

**Instructor Resources**
• Textbook images, Extra Activities

**METHODOLOGY •**
**Presentation and Practive of Infinitives**
To reinforce the presentation of *gustar*, the students will practice with the infinitives of *los deportes y los pasatiempos*. Feel free to practice the regular verbs with directed questions such as: *¿Bailas bien?, ¿Cuándo nadas?, ¿Quiénes montan en bicicleta?*, etc.

**ANSWERS to 2-28**
1. ¿Te gusta el centro estudiantil?
2. ¿Te gustan los sábados?
3. ¿Te gusta vivir en un apartamento?
4. ¿Te gustan la informática?
5. ¿Te gusta aprender idiomas?
6. ¿Te gusta la cafetería?
7. ¿Te gusta correr?
8. ¿Te gustan los libros de Harry Potter?

**NOTE for *Los deportes y los pasatiempos***
Remind students that they have already learned several *deportes y pasatiempos* such as *correr* and *leer*.

jugar al fútbol

jugar al fútbol americano

jugar al golf

montar en bicicleta

jugar al tenis

nadar

ver la televisión

patinar

tocar un instrumento

tomar el sol

| Otras palabras útiles | *Other useful words* |
|---|---|
| el equipo | *team* |
| hacer ejercicio | *to exercise* |
| la pelota | *ball* |

Capítulo Preliminar A. Los días, los meses y las estaciones, pág. 20.

**2-29** **¿En qué mes te gusta...?** For a fan or a participant, sports and pastimes can be seasonal. ■

**Paso 1** Make a list of the top **three** sports or pastimes you enjoy in the months listed below.

| enero | mayo | julio | octubre |

**MODELO** enero
*1. patinar, 2. bailar, 3. tocar un instrumento*

**Paso 2** Circulate around the classroom and compare your preferences with those of your classmates. Do you see any trends?

**MODELO** E1: *¿Qué deportes y pasatiempos te gusta practicar más en enero?*

E2: *Me gusta patinar, bailar y tocar un instrumento.*

 Workbooklet

**2-30** **¿Cuánto te gusta?** What activities do you enjoy in your spare time? Write **ten** activities in the chart and rank the sports and pastimes by placing a mark in the column that best describes your feeling toward the sport or pastime. What do you suppose **¡Lo odio!** means? Share your answers with your partner, following the model. ■

**Fíjate**
Remember that *gustar* is formed differently from regular verbs.

**MODELO** E1: *Me gusta mucho el fútbol.*

E2: *No me gusta patinar.*

| | ME GUSTA MUCHO | ME GUSTA | NO ME GUSTA | ¡LO ODIO! |
|---|---|---|---|---|
| 1. el fútbol | X | | | |
| 2. patinar | | | X | |
| 3. ... | | | | |

**METHODOLOGY • Small Group Work**
*¡Anda! Curso elemental* is based on research. One important area of research deals with pair work and cooperative learning. The research states that students learn best from other students. Hence, this program has numerous pair and small group activities. Vary groups and partners on a regular basis. You can group students in numerous ways: the same birth months, physical characteristics, likes and dislikes, colors of clothing, simply by having students count off, etc.

**NATIONAL STANDARDS**
*Communication*
The activities that require students to engage in conversation (**2-30, 2-31**), provide and obtain information (**2-30, 2-31, 2-32**), express feelings and emotions (**2-32**), and exchange opinions (**2-32**) satisfy Standard 1.1. Standard 1.1 is the interpersonal mode, but you could easily transform these activities into the presentational mode (Standard 1.3) by asking the students to create documents with pictures of their favorite activities and making a space for the documents to be displayed, or by having the students present the information from their documents to the class.

## NOTA CULTURAL

4:00

# Los deportes en el mundo hispano

02-51

El fútbol es el deporte más popular en el mundo hispanohablante. Sin embargo (*Nevertheless*), los hispanos participan en una gran variedad de actividades físicas y deportivas como el béisbol, el boxeo, el básquetbol (o baloncesto), el tenis, el vóleibol y el atletismo (*track and field*). España y los países latinoamericanos participan en los Juegos Olímpicos. Además (*Furthermore*), los países latinoamericanos, junto con Canadá y los Estados Unidos, participan en los Juegos Panamericanos que ocurren cada cuatro años, siempre un año antes de los Juegos Olímpicos.

Los deportes forman una parte importante de la vida universitaria, especialmente en la Universidad Nacional Autónoma de México (la UNAM). Además de contar con el equipo de fútbol Club Universidad Nacional, ofrecen (*they offer*) unas treinta y nueve disciplinas deportivas que incluyen los deportes mencionados y también el fútbol americano, el judo, el karate, el ciclismo, la natación, la lucha libre (*wrestling*) y más. Hay varios gimnasios,

Los Juegos Panamericanos ocurren cada cuatro años.

dos estadios, siete piscinas y muchas otras áreas para practicar estos deportes.

## Preguntas
1. What is the most important sport in the Spanish-speaking world?
2. Does your college/university offer the same sports as the UNAM? What are some differences?

### Estrategia
Remember to use your reading strategy *"Recognizing cognates"* from *Capítulo 1* to assist you with this and all future reading passages.

Workbooklet

 **2-31** **¿Eres activo/a?** Just how active are you? Complete the chart with activities that should, or do, occupy your time. Share your results with a partner. So . . . are you leading a well-balanced life? ▪

### Vocabulario útil

| | |
|---|---|
| **a menudo** | *often* |
| **a veces** | *sometimes; from time to time* |
| **nunca** | *never* |

| A MENUDO | A VECES | NUNCA | NECESITO HACERLO (*DO IT*) MÁS |
|---|---|---|---|
| 1. | 1. | 1. | 1. |
| 2. | 2. | 2. | 2. |
| 3. | 3. | 3. | 3. |
| 4. | 4. | 4. | 4. |
| 5. | 5. | 5. | 5. |

Workbooklet

**2-32** **Tus preferencias** Select your **three** favorite sports and/or pastimes (**que más me gustan**) and then select your **three** least favorite (**que menos me gustan**) from **2-31.** ▪

**Paso 1** Write your choices in the chart. Then, create **two** sentences summarizing your choices.

| LOS DEPORTES/PASATIEMPOS QUE MÁS ME GUSTAN | LOS DEPORTES/PASATIEMPOS QUE MENOS ME GUSTAN |
|---|---|
| 1. patinar | 1. |
| 2. bailar | 2. |
| 3. leer | 3. |

**MODELO** *Los deportes o pasatiempos que más me gustan son patinar, bailar y leer. Los deportes o pasatiempos que menos me gustan son…*

**Paso 2** Circulate around the classroom to find classmates with the same likes and dislikes as you. Follow the model. When you find someone with the same likes or dislikes, write his/her name in the chart that follows.

**MODELO** E1: *¿Qué deporte o pasatiempo te gusta más?*

E2: *El deporte que me gusta más es el tenis.*

E1: *¿Qué deporte o pasatiempo te gusta menos?*

E2: *El pasatiempo que me gusta menos es ir de compras.*

| LOS/LAS COMPAÑEROS/AS | EL DEPORTE/PASATIEMPO QUE MÁS LES GUSTA |
|---|---|
| 1. | |
| 2. | |
| 3. | |
| LOS/LAS COMPAÑEROS/AS | EL DEPORTE/PASATIEMPO QUE MENOS LES GUSTA |
| 1. | |
| 2. | |
| 3. | |

**EXPANSION for 2-32**
As a follow-up to **2-32,** determine the top three most popular and three least popular sports and pastimes of the class.

**ADDITIONAL ACTIVITY for** *Los deportes y los pasatiempos*
Instruct students, working in pairs, to make three lists, referring to the vocabulary for *Los deportes y los pasatiempos.* In the first list, they should write the names of activities that are normally done in teams. In the second list, they write the names of the activities that can be done alone, and in the third list, the names of the activities that work best with partners. Have students determine which activities appear on more than one list.

## Una conversación
02-52 to 02-53

| **Estrategia** | When *listening for the gist,* you listen for the main idea(s). You do not focus on each word, but | rather on the overall meaning. Practice summarizing the gist in several words or a sentence. |
|---|---|---|
| **Listening for the gist** | | |

**2-33   Antes de escuchar**   In the following segment Eduardo, a university student and one of the characters from **Ambiciones siniestras**, is talking on the phone with his mother. Write a question you might possibly hear in their conversation. ■

 **2-34   A escuchar**   Listen as Eduardo and his mother converse. ■

1. The first time you listen, concentrate on the questions she asks, noting key words and ideas.
2. In the second listening, focus on Eduardo's answers, again noting key words and ideas.
3. During the third listening determine whether these sentences are true (**T**) or false (**F**).
   a. Eduardo's mother calls Eduardo to see how he is doing.  F
   b. Eduardo does not have classes on Tuesday.  F
   c. Eduardo's mother ends the conversation abruptly.  T

La mamá de Eduardo escucha a su hijo.

 **2-35   Después de escuchar**   In one sentence, what is the gist of their conversation? Share your sentence with a partner. ■

# ¡CONVERSEMOS!
02-54

**2-36   La vida universitaria**   Imagine that you are at a gathering on campus for exchange students from Mexico. Introduce yourself. ■

**Paso 1**   Create at least **five sentences** about you. Then create at least **five questions** to ask the person you are meeting. Include the following information:

- Introductions from *Capítulo Preliminar A* (p. 4)
- Vocabulary including majors, courses, professions, campus places, emotions and states of being, and sports and pastimes
- New **–ar, -er,** and **-ir** verbs from this chapter.

**Paso 2**   Take turns playing the roles of the student on your campus and the visiting Mexican student.

**ESCRIBE**

## Una descripción

02-55

| **Estrategia** | You have been practicing speaking in sentences. Remember: | 3. To make a sentence negative, place **no** before the verb, e.g., *No nadamos.* |
| **Creating sentences** | 1. Basic sentences need: (subj.) + verb + (rest of the sent.) | 4. Make sure that your intended subject and verb ending agree, e.g., **yo** = **-o**, etc. *Yo corro.* |
| | 2. A sentence can express a complete idea with just a verb form, e.g., *Corren.* Subjects clarify, e.g., *Ellos corren* or *Juan y Marta corren.* | 5. Make sure that adjectives agree with their corresponding nouns, e.g., *amigos inteligentes.* |

**2-37** **Antes de escribir** Imagine that you are applying for a job on campus—either to work in the library, the student center, or the athletic department. Make a list in Spanish of what makes you a viable applicant.

MODELO    (athletic department)

Lista:    ✔ Me gustan los deportes; nado y corro muy bien.
✔ Soy buena estudiante, inteligente, creativa, organizada y trabajadora.
✔ Me gustan las cosas nuevas/las personas nuevas..

**2-38** **A escribir** Using your list, create a personal description using the model.

MODELO    Tengo veinte años y soy buena estudiante. Soy organizada y trabajadora. Me gustan mucho...

 **2-39** **Después de escribir** Your instructor will collect the descriptions, and read some of them to the class. He/She may ask you to guess who wrote each one.

# ¿Cómo andas? II

| Having completed **Comunicación II**, I now can . . . | Feel confident | Need to review |
|---|---|---|
| • elaborate on university places and objects (pp. 74–75) | ☐ | ☐ |
| • express *to be* (p. 76) | ☐ | ☐ |
| • articulate emotions and states of being (p. 79) | ☐ | ☐ |
| • convey likes and dislikes (p. 80) | ☐ | ☐ |
| • offer opinions on sports and pastimes (p. 81) | ☐ | ☐ |
| • compare and contrast sports (p. 84) | ☐ | ☐ |
| • glean the main idea (p. 86) | ☐ | ☐ |
| • communicate about university life (p. 86) | ☐ | ☐ |
| • craft a personal description (p. 87) | ☐ | ☐ |
| • engage in additional communication practice (SAM) | ☐ | ☐ |

**METHODOLOGY • Building and Creating Sentences**
We are committed to helping students work toward building and creating sentences. These kinds of descriptions and activities help to move them in that direction.

**SECTION GOALS for *Escribe***
By the end of the *Escribe* section, students will be able to:
• organize their pre-writing thoughts by creating sentences.
• create a description of themselves and their likes/dislikes.
• write a brief summary using complete sentences to form a paragraph.

**NATIONAL STANDARDS**
*Communication, Communities*
The activities in **2-37** and **2-38** facilitate communication in Spanish (Standard 1.3) because students are presenting information and ideas in Spanish to an audience of readers. You can modify **2-39** by asking half the class to be employers and the other half to be potential student workers. The student employees can present their paragraphs to the employers (Standard 1.3) and instead of using the presentational mode for an audience of readers (as in **2-38**), the employers become an audience of listeners.

**Instructor Resources**
• Text images (map), Video resources

**SECTION GOALS for *Cultura***
By the end of the *Cultura* section, students will be able to:
• scan the reading for important information about Mexico.
• compare the UNAM and Oaxaca with where they attend school.
• list several popular forms of *artesanía*.
• comprehend brief background information from the *almanaque*.

**NATIONAL STANDARDS**
*Cultures, Comparisons*
The information about Mexico in the cultural reading addresses the Cultures and Comparisons goals. Standard 2.2 is about understanding the relationship between the practices and perspectives of Hispanic cultures. Students learn that, in Mexico, unlike in the United States, there are fewer student residences on campus; therefore, many students live with their immediate family or with other family members. This is very different from American universities, where students who live on campus live in residence halls, town houses, or apartments. The reading also describes some of the common regional *artesanía* and the organic ingredients for chewing gum and some pharmaceuticals. The Mexican products differ from those produced in the United States because Mexico has different natural resources. Students can make comparisons between university housing options and products in the United States and Mexico (Standard 4.2).

**METHODOLOGY • Contrasting and Comparing**
When possible, every effort will be made to give students an opportunity to compare the culture of their own home/university communities with those they are learning about. Additionally, as appropriate, the students will be asked to compare what they are currently learning with previous chapters. Comparing cultures will be reinforced in *Capítulo 6* and *Capítulo 12* as well.

# Cultura

# México

CULTURA • CULTURA • CULTURA • CU

02-56 to 02-57

## Les presento mi país

Gabriela García
Cordera

Mi nombre es Gabriela García Cordera y soy de Monte Albán, México. Soy una estudiante de la Universidad Nacional Autónoma de México (la UNAM) que está en la Ciudad de México. Vivo cerca de (*near*) la universidad con la familia de mi tía porque normalmente hay pocas residencias estudiantiles en las universidades y muchos estudiantes viven con sus parientes (*relatives*). La UNAM es la universidad más grande de México y de América Latina. **¿Cuántos estudiantes hay en tu universidad?** En la UNAM, tenemos un equipo de fútbol, los "Pumas". El fútbol es muy popular en mi país: es el pasatiempo nacional. **¿Qué deporte es muy popular en tu país?** Monte Albán está en el estado de Oaxaca, un centro famoso de artesanía. En particular, hay hojalatería (*tin work*), cerámicas de barro negro (*black clay*), cestería (*basket making*), fabricación de textiles y de alebrijes (*painted wooden animals*) y mucho más. **¿Qué tipo de artesanía hay en tu región?**

La biblioteca de la Universidad Nacional Autónoma de México. La fachada tiene un mosaico de la historia de México.

En Oaxaca, un centro famoso de artesanía, venden alebrijes. Estas figuras de madera son una forma de arte popular.

El fútbol es el pasatiempo nacional del país.

El Palacio Nacional de Bellas Artes es un centro cultural muy importante de México.

El tianguis de Tepotzlán en Morelia se instala los sábados y domingos con una variedad de artículos como comida y ropa.

## ALMANAQUE

| | |
|---|---|
| **Nombre oficial:** | Estados Unidos Mexicanos |
| **Gobierno:** | República federal |
| **Población:** | 111.211.789 (2010) |
| **Idiomas:** | español (oficial); maya, náhuatl |
| **Moneda:** | peso mexicano ($) |

### ¿Sabías que…?

- El origen del chicle (*gum*) es el látex del chicozapote (*sapodilla tree* en inglés), un árbol tropical de la península de Yucatán. Los mayas, tribu antigua y muy importante de Yucatán, usaban (*used*) el látex como chicle.
- La planta "cabeza de negro", del estado mexicano de Veracruz, forma la base del proceso para crear la cortisona y "la píldora", el contraceptivo oral.

### Preguntas

1. What is the most popular sport in Mexico?
2. What is a "tianguis"? What do we have in the United States that is similar?
3. What are the origins of cortisone and the birth control pill?
4. What are some of the handcrafted items from Mexico? What are similar handcrafted items made in your region?
5. What are some differences between the UNAM and your school?

 Amplía tus conocimientos sobre México en MySpanishLab.

89

**CULTURAL BACKGROUND for** *Almanaque*

The Mexican flag is a vertical tricolor flag with bands of green, white, and red (from left to right). In the center is a coat of arms, with a well-known emblem. The emblem contains an eagle holding a serpent in its talon, perched on top of a prickly pear cactus. The cactus is situated on a rock that rises above a lake. This coat of arms evolved from an Aztec legend. In the legend, the Aztec supreme deity, Huitzilopochtli, instructed the Aztec people to seek a place where they would find an eagle sitting on a prickly pear cactus eating a snake. In that place, they were to construct their city. After many years of wandering, they found this "sign" in Lake Texcoco, a swampy place. They established the city of Tenochtitlán (Place of the Prickly Pear Cactus), and it remained an important Aztec city until these people suffered defeat at the hands of the Spaniards in 1521. Mexico City is built on the ruins of this site.

**HERITAGE LANGUAGE LEARNERS**

Your heritage language learners, false beginners, advanced students, students who need additional practice (as well asstudents who love the Internet) can benefit from the following activities. For heritage language learners, you may wish to give the directions provided in Spanish. For the rest of your students, these directions should be in English.

1. *Busca en el Internet más información acerca de la UNAM. Trata de encontrar el lema de la universidad. Luego compara este lema con el de tu universidad. ¿Qué tienen en común? ¿Por qué piensas que las universidades tienen lemas? Suggested Keywords: la UNAM, lema*
2. *Tu universidad probablemente tiene muchos equipos deportivos. El público que asiste a los partidos grita para animar a los deportistas. Muchas veces estos gritos o "porras" tienen palabras sin sentido. ¿Cuál es un grito o "porra" tradicional en tu universidad? Busca en el Internet la porra de la UNAM. Suggested Keywords: la UNAM, porra, "Goya," cachún*

**ANSWERS to** *Preguntas*

1. Soccer is the most important sport in Mexico.
2. It is a market. In the United States we have flea markets.
3. It comes from a plant from the state of Veracruz.
4. *Possible answers include:* woven blankets, hand carved objects, handmade furniture, handmade baskets, etc.
5. *Possible answers include:* entrance requirements and size.

**SECTION GOALS for *Lectura***
By the end of the *Lectura* section, students will be able to:

- summarize information about each character.
- distinguish between when the narrator gives background information and when Sr. Verdugo is speaking.
- read a text that includes cognates, new vocabulary, and unfamiliar words.
- organize the information they have read into a chart.

**NATIONAL STANDARDS**
*Communication*
The *Ambiciones siniestras* reading provides more in-depth information about the characters and their backgrounds. By reading information about the essays of the characters in Spanish, students understand written Spanish (Standard 1.2).

**RECAP OF *AMBICIONES SINIESTRAS* Episodio 1**
**Lectura:** In the first episode of *Ambiciones siniestras*, there were three e-mail messages from some of the characters to various people. The first message was from Alejandra, and she wrote to her mother about a new friend, Manolo. In the e-mail, she described how handsome Manolo was, and she asked about her other family members. In the second e-mail, Eduardo wrote to Cisco about a *macroeconomía* assignment he didn't understand. Eduardo needed help, and he wrote to Cisco since Cisco has a better grasp of the material. The last e-mail was forwarded from Marisol to her cousin, Ligia. Marisol received a personal ad from another student looking for a girlfriend, and she wanted to know if Ligia thought she should respond.
**Video:** In the video episode for *Capítulo 1*, the main characters (Marisol, Lupe, Alejandra, Manolo, Cisco, and Eduardo) of *Ambiciones siniestras* were introduced. The students attend 3 different universities in the Midwest, the Northeast, and the West. At the northeastern university, Cisco and Eduardo discussed the macroeconomics homework; at the midwestern university, Marisol introduced Phillip (not a recurring character) to Lupe; and at the western university, Alejandra talked to Manolo.

**ANSWERS to 2-41**
1. a. Reading e-mails.
   b. *Answers may vary.*
   c. Three students.
2. and
3. *Answers may vary.*

# Ambiciones siniestras

EPISODIO 2

02-60

# Lectura

**Estrategia**   Skimming

When you skim, or read quickly, you generally do so to capture the gist of the passage. Practice with skimming helps you learn to focus on main ideas in your reading.

**2-40   Antes de leer**   In this episode you will discover more information about three of the university students who are among the six protagonists of the story, specifically Alejandra, Manolo, and Cisco. You will learn their complete names, where they are from, and some of their interests. ■

1. Note that there are a few key words in the reading passage you may not know. They are written below with their English equivalents and are listed in order of appearance. They are also boldfaced in the body of the reading.

| | |
|---|---|
| **la seguridad (-dad = -*ty*)** | *security* |
| **las solicitudes** | *applications* |
| **mientras** | *while* |
| **los ensayos** | *essays* |
| **el oeste** | *west* |
| **el noreste** | *northeast* |

Based on this list of words, can you begin to guess what the context of the reading will be?

**2-41   A leer**   To boost your comprehension, it is helpful to skim the passage for the first reading and then ask yourself what key information you have learned. ■

1. Skim the first three paragraphs of this episode, then answer the following questions.
   a. What is the person doing?
   b. Do you think what he is doing is part of his job?
   c. How many students has he located so far?
2. Now skim the remaining paragraphs and write down key points for each paragraph.
3. Then, reread the entire episode, this time more carefully, to add details to those main ideas. Do not forget to take advantage of cognates like **prestigiosa** and **paciencia** to boost your comprehension.

90

**SUGGESTION for reviewing *Episodio 1***
In both the reading and the video, the main characters were introduced: Alejandra, Manolo, Cisco, Eduardo, Marisol, and Lupe.
**Reading:** 1. Which three characters wrote e-mails and to whom? (Alejandra to her mother, Eduardo to Cisco and Marisol to Ligia); 2. What were the e-mails about? (Alejandra wrote her mom to say hello; she asks about the family and tells her about her new friend, Manolo. Eduardo wrote about the tough time he is having in their macroeconomics class and to ask a question. Marisol sent Ligia an interesting personal ad she found.)

**Video:** 1. Is Cisco and Eduardo's macroeconomic class large or small? (*small*) Do they sit together in class? (*yes*); 2. Lupe and Marisol are in psychology class. How large is it? (*around 30–40 students*) What is the professor like? (*He is young, disheveled, late, disorganized*); 3. With whom do the young women converse before class begins? (*Phillip*); What do they speak about? (*their families, and that the three of them speak Spanish*); 4. What is the class Manolo and Alejandra have together? (*Spanish literature*) Do they sit together in class? (*yes*)

## *Las solicitudes*

*in front of*
*at his side*

Un hombre joven está enfrente de° su computadora. Trabaja impacientemente y con rapidez. A su lado° tiene unos papeles con unos códigos misteriosos.

*Let's see*

—A ver°. ¿Cómo paso por **la seguridad** de esta prestigiosa universidad? Ahhhh… sí. Paciencia. Ahora… para encontrar la lista de los estudiantes y sus **solicitudes**… Excelente. Es fácil dar con° jóvenes inteligentes, creativos e inocentes.

*to find*

El hombre lee **los ensayos** de las solicitudes de varios estudiantes, dos de una universidad del **oeste** y uno de una universidad del **noreste**. **Mientras** lee, habla.

—De la universidad del **oeste**:

*far from*

Alejandra Sánchez Torres. Es de San Antonio, Texas; está lejos de° su casa. Aquí habla mucho de su familia. Tiene muchos hermanos. Hmmm… le gusta pintar y escribir poesía. También le gusta viajar. ¡Perfecto! Y espera estudiar arte…

Manuel Rodríguez Ángulo. Manolo. Es de California, San Diego. Tiene cuatro hermanos… sus padres están divorciados. Le gustan todos los deportes, especialmente el fútbol americano. Es excelente estudiante también… desea especializarse en medicina.

De la universidad del **noreste**:

*what a name!*
*so many / such*

Francisco Quiroga Godoy, Cisco, es de familia hispana y vive en West Palm Beach. Cuando no estudia, trabaja en restaurantes, cafés y, ¡qué nombre!°, "El Golden Gal Day Spa". Con tantos° trabajos y tan° buenas notas debe ser un joven muy disciplinado. Especialidad: informática. Muy bien.

*...icious / to be interested in*
*does he want*

A este hombre tan sospechoso°… ¿por qué le interesan° estos estudiantes? ¿Qué quiere° de ellos?

---

**2-42** **Después de leer** Answer the following questions. ■

1. How many applications does the man review in this episode? Who are the students about whom he reads?
2. Complete the following chart:

| PERSONAJE | ¿DE DÓNDE ES? | ¿FAMILIA? | ¿POSIBLE ESPECIALIDAD? | ¿ACTIVIDADES? |
|-----------|---------------|-----------|------------------------|---------------|
| Alejandra |  |  |  |  |
| Manolo |  |  |  |  |
| Cisco |  |  |  |  |

3. According to the information in the previous chart, create sentences about the similarities and differences between Alejandra, Manolo, and Cisco.

**Instructor Resources**
• Video script

**SECTION GOALS for** *Video*
By the end of the video section, students will be able to:
• describe the characters in more detail.
• recap the events in chronological order.
• make predictions about the next episode.

**ANSWERS to 2-44**
1. *Possible answers:* joven, alto, fuerte, impaciente, guapo, curioso
2. An Internet café; No
3. *Possible facts about Eduardo:* third-year student; major is Economics; speaks Spanish, English, and Portuguese; likes to play tennis and swim; volunteers to help poor children; spends time with his family
   *Possible facts about Lupe:* 25 years old; history and journalism major; spent 3 months in Brazil; speaks Spanish, English, German, and Portuguese; likes to write; family is important to her
   *Possible facts about Marisol:* born in New York; psychology major; junior; only child; likes to play golf and read detective novels; works as a volunteer in a hospital and in an elementary school
4. He reads it and thinks about it.
5. He is writing and sending an e-mail message.

# Video

02-61 to 02-63

**2-43** **Antes del video** In **Las solicitudes,** a suspicious man is reading information off the computer about three of our protagonists. In the second part of this episode you will watch him in video format as he continues to discover information about our characters. Before watching the episode, think about the possible answers to these questions: ■

1. Who is this person and why is he interested in Lupe, Cisco, Eduardo, Marisol, Manolo, and Alejandra?
2. What information could this man discover on the Internet about you?
3. What web sites could provide him with information about you?
4. What do you have in common with the characters so far?

Otras actividades: trabajar como voluntario en una organización de ayuda para niños.

Especialidad: periodismo e historia. Aficiones: jugar al básquetbol, nadar y correr.

¡Aquí comienza la aventura!

Episodio 2

## «La aventura comienza»

Relax and watch the video, more than once if you choose; then answer the following questions.

**2-44** **Después del video** Answer the following questions. ■

1. What Spanish adjectives best describe the man at the computer?
2. Where might he be? Is he alone?
3. Which characters is he investigating now? List two facts he discovers about each one.
4. What does he do with the information he gets?
5. What is he doing as the episode ends?

92

## Y por fin, ¿cómo andas?

| | Feel confident | Need to review |
|---|---|---|

Having completed this chapter, I now can . . .

**Comunicación I**

- share information about courses and majors (p. 62) ☐ ☐
- indicate the stressed syllables in words (MSL/SAM) ☐ ☐
- describe my classroom and classmates (p. 65) ☐ ☐
- relate daily activities (p. 67) ☐ ☐
- create and answer questions (p. 70) ☐ ☐
- count from 100–1,000 (p. 72) ☐ ☐

**Comunicación II**

- elaborate on university places and objects (pp. 74–75) ☐ ☐
- express *to be* (p. 76) ☐ ☐
- articulate emotions and states of being (p. 79) ☐ ☐
- convey likes and dislikes (p. 80) ☐ ☐
- offer opinions on sports and pastimes (p. 81) ☐ ☐
- glean the main idea (p. 86) ☐ ☐
- communicate about university life (p. 86) ☐ ☐
- craft a personal description (p. 87) ☐ ☐

**Cultura**

- examine Hispanic university life (p. 64) ☐ ☐
- compare and contrast sports (p. 84) ☐ ☐
- exchange information regarding Mexico (p. 88) ☐ ☐

**Ambiciones siniestras**

- skim a reading and note facts about the protagonists' lives (p. 90) ☐ ☐
- discover more about the protagonists (p. 92) ☐ ☐

**Comunidades**

- use Spanish in real-life contexts (SAM) ☐ ☐

**Instructor Resources**
• Testing program information

# VOCABULARIO ACTIVO

| Las materias y las especialidades | Subjects and majors |
|---|---|
| la administración de empresas | business |
| la arquitectura | architecture |
| el arte | art |
| la biología | biology |
| las ciencias (pl.) | science |
| el curso | course |
| el derecho | law |
| los idiomas (pl.) | languages |
| la informática | computer science |
| la literatura | literature |
| las matemáticas (pl.) | mathematics |
| la medicina | medicine |
| la música | music |
| la pedagogía | education |
| el periodismo | journalism |
| la psicología | psychology |
| el semestre | semester |

| En la sala de clase | In the classroom |
|---|---|
| los apuntes (pl.) | notes |
| el bolígrafo | ballpoint pen |
| el borrador | eraser |
| el/la compañero/a de clase | classmate |
| la composición | composition |
| el cuaderno | notebook |
| el escritorio | desk |
| el/la estudiante | student |
| el examen | exam |
| el lápiz | pencil |
| el libro | book |
| el mapa | map |
| la mesa | table |
| la mochila | book bag; knapsack |
| el papel | paper |
| la pared | wall |
| la pizarra | chalkboard |
| el/la profesor/a | professor |

| | |
|---|---|
| la puerta | door |
| la sala de clase | classroom |
| la silla | chair |
| la tarea | homework |
| la tiza | chalk |
| la ventana | window |

| Los verbos | Verbs |
|---|---|
| abrir | to open |
| aprender | to learn |
| comer | to eat |
| comprar | to buy |
| comprender | to understand |
| contestar | to answer |
| correr | to run |
| creer | to believe |
| enseñar | to teach; to show |
| escribir | to write |
| esperar | to wait for; to hope |
| estar | to be |
| estudiar | to study |
| hablar | to speak |
| leer | to read |
| llegar | to arrive |
| necesitar | to need |
| preguntar | to ask (a question) |
| preparar | to prepare; to get ready |
| recibir | to receive |
| regresar | to return |
| terminar | to finish; to end |
| tomar | to take; to drink |
| trabajar | to work |
| usar | to use |
| vivir | to live |

| Las palabras interrogativas | Interrogative words |
|---|---|
| *See page 70.* | |

| Los números 100–1.000 | Numbers 100–1,000 |
|---|---|
| See page 72. | |

| Los lugares | Places |
|---|---|
| el apartamento | apartment |
| la biblioteca | library |
| la cafetería | cafeteria |
| el centro estudiantil | student center; student union |
| el cuarto | room |
| el edificio | building |
| el estadio | stadium |
| el gimnasio | gymnasium |
| el laboratorio | laboratory |
| la librería | bookstore |
| la residencia estudiantil | dormitory |
| la tienda | store |

| La residencia | The dorm |
|---|---|
| la calculadora | calculator |
| el/la compañero/a de cuarto | roommate |
| la computadora | computer |
| el despertador | alarm clock |
| el dinero | money |
| el disco compacto (el CD) | compact disk |
| el DVD | DVD |
| el horario (de clases) | schedule (of classes) |
| el radio/la radio | radio |
| el reloj | clock; watch |
| el reproductor de CD/DVD | CD/DVD player |
| la televisión | television |

| Los deportes y los pasatiempos | Sports and pastimes |
|---|---|
| bailar | to dance |
| caminar | to walk |
| el equipo | team |
| escuchar música | to listen to music |
| hacer ejercicio | to exercise |
| ir de compras | to go shopping |
| jugar al básquetbol | to play basketball |
| jugar al béisbol | to play baseball |
| jugar al fútbol | to play soccer |
| jugar al fútbol americano | to play football |
| jugar al golf | to play golf |
| jugar al tenis | to play tennis |
| montar en bicicleta | to ride a bike |
| nadar | to swim |
| patinar | to skate |
| la pelota | ball |
| tocar un instrumento | to play an instrument |
| tomar el sol | to sunbathe |
| ver la televisión | to watch television |

| Otras palabras útiles | Other useful words |
|---|---|
| a menudo | often |
| a veces | sometimes; from time to time |
| difícil | difficult |
| fácil | easy |
| hay | there is; there are |
| nunca | never |
| pero | but |
| también | too; also |
| y | and |

| Emociones y estados | Emotions and states of being |
|---|---|
| aburrido/a | bored (with estar) |
| cansado/a | tired |
| contento/a | content; happy |
| enfermo/a | ill; sick |
| enojado/a | angry |
| feliz | happy |
| nervioso/a | upset; nervous |
| preocupado/a | worried |
| triste | sad |

**Instructor Resources**
• IRM: Syllabi and Lesson Plans

## NATIONAL STANDARDS

### COMUNICACIÓN I
- To describe homes (Communication, Cultures, Comparisons)
- To pronounce the letters *h, j,* and *g* (Communication)
- To express actions (Communication, Comparisons)
- To elaborate on rooms (Communication, Cultures)
- To engage in additional communication practice (Communication)

### COMUNICACIÓN II
- To share information about household chores (Communication)
- To illustrate objects using colors (Communication)
- To depict states of being using *tener* (Communication)
- To count from 1,000–100,000,000 (Communication, Cultures, Connections)
- To state *There is / There are* (Communication)
- To listen for specific information (Communication)
- To communicate about homes and life at home (Communication)
- To create an ad (Communication)
- To engage in additional communication practice (Communication)

### CULTURA
- To relate general differences in housing in Spain (Communication, Cultures, Comparisons)
- To discover green initiatives (Communication, Cultures, Connections, Comparisons)
- To list interesting facts about Spain (Cultures, Comparisons)
- To explore further the chapter's cultural themes (Cultures)

### AMBICIONES SINIESTRAS
- To investigate a passage consisting of an enticing e-mail message received by Alejandra and Manolo (Communication, Comparisons)
- To discover who else receives the mysterious e-mail and their reactions to the message (Communication)

### COMUNIDADES
- To use Spanish in real-life contexts. (Communication, Communities)

# 3 Estamos en casa

From the most modern of skyscrapers, to Spanish colonial styles, to the variety of homes of indigenous populations, Hispanic architecture is as varied as the people who speak Spanish. **En los países hispanohablantes** (*Spanish-speaking countries*) **hay de todo.**

## PREGUNTAS

**1** Is there Spanish-inspired architecture in the region where you live?

**2** Why is Spanish architecture so prevalent throughout North, Central, and South America?

**3** How do geography and environment affect the design and construction of homes?

Carmona, España

96

### SECTION GOALS for *Chapter opener*

By the end of the Chapter opener section, students will be able to:
- identify common elements of Spanish architecture.
- compare and contrast housing options in the Spanish-speaking world.
- identify how geographical and environmental variables affect construction.

### NATIONAL STANDARDS
*Communities*

Use the community in which you teach as a resource for your students. Standard 5.1 states that students use Spanish both within and beyond the school setting. If students have not learned the appropriate vocabulary for these ideas, you will need to provide them a list of vocabulary for situations they might encounter. If your institution or community has a branch of Habitat for Humanity or another service organization, consider giving credit for volunteering for building projects for Spanish-speaking residents.

Another idea would be to consider assisting senior citizens who might need help with a seasonal cleaning of their houses, with moving from residences to assisted-living facilities, or with getting ready to market and sell their property.

Ask students to find a Spanish-speaking realtor, skilled laborer, architect, construction manager, housekeeper, building superintendent, etc., who lives and works in the community. Have the students shadow that person on the job and see how that job impacts the community.

**97**

### PLANNING AHEAD
For this chapter it is helpful if students bring in a die for **3-5,** and pictures of rooms from magazines for **3-18.** You may want to have extras in case some students forget.

### NOTE for *Chapter opener*
In **3-4,** as well as in other activities throughout the chapter, students will view additional photos that provide a variety of housing possibilities predominantly in Spain, the chapter's theme country, but also from other countries in the Spanish-speaking world. You may wish to share housing images from additional places in the Spanish-speaking world.

### WARM-UP for *Chapter opener*
As in previous chapters, ask students to give their impressions of the photo, and to describe different types of housing options available where they live. Also, have students read the chapter objectives silently. Spend no more than 5 to 7 minutes on chapter openers.

### SUGGESTION for *Chapter opener*
Take digital photos of the most recognizable buildings on campus or in your community. Ask students to identify the buildings, and, using drawings and cognates, ask them whether the buildings are *apartamentos, residencias, grandes, modernos,* and how many *pisos* they have. You could also take several pictures of housing options in the area and ask students to predict where you live and why.

### EXPANSION for *Preguntas*
Discuss with students the wide range of housing types that exists, from humble dwellings to mansions in the city, urban vs. rural housing, etc.

### NATIONAL STANDARDS
*Connections*
Question #3 of *Preguntas* connects the chapter theme to the disciplines of architecture, design, and construction as well as other disciplines such as geography, environmentalism, and anthropology.

---

**ANSWERS to *Preguntas***
1. *Answers may vary.*
2. Spanish explorers carried that influence with them when they explored the Americas. The French also intervened in Mexico and Emperor Maximilian ruled there from 1864 to 1867.
3. Dwellings are built to withstand the elements and are made out of materials that are readily available.

**21ST CENTURY SKILLS • DEFINITION**
The Partnership for 21st Century Skills (P21) is a multidisciplinary project. The group, housed in Washington, D.C., has brought together the key national organizations representing the core academic subjects. The American Council on the Teaching of Foreign Languages (ACTFL) collaborated for a year developing the 21st Century Skills Map. The map, created by hundreds of world language educators, reflects the integration of languages and the necessary skills for a successful 21st century citizen.

**SECTION GOALS for**
*Comunicación I*

By the end of the *Comunicación* section, students will be able to:

• compare the features of their houses with the houses of others.

• explain how floors or stories of buildings are numbered in other countries.

• form the irregular verbs *dar, conocer, hacer, poner, salir, traer,* and *ver*.

• recognize patterns in the verbs with irregular *yo* forms.

• conjugate the stem-changing verbs *decir, oír, poder, venir,* and *querer*.

• express preferences using *querer*.

• combine *poder* with other infinitives.

• report on the activities of classmates.

• talk about the housing options available in Spain.

• describe the interior and exterior spaces of a house.

**NATIONAL STANDARDS**
*Comunicación I*

The activities in this *Comunicación* section address Standard 1.1. Students can partner with classmates and engage in conversations about their houses. A simple summary sheet containing the vocabulary related to a house, the number of rooms, and/or its square footage can provide the basis for giving and obtaining information and exchanging opinions. Students can draw diagrams or write inventories of the things in their houses and present short narrations to the class using the new vocabulary (Standard 1.3). The students in their seats can listen to the presenter and compare their summary sheets with the information given by the speaker (Standard 1.2).

**NOTE for *La casa***

Remind students that across the Spanish-speaking world there are many variations in vocabulary depending on where you are and with whom you are speaking. For example, the English word "bedroom" can mean *el dormitorio, la alcoba, la habitación, la recámara,* etc.

# Comunicación I

**1 VOCABULARIO**

4:00    03-01 to 03-07

## La casa  Describing homes

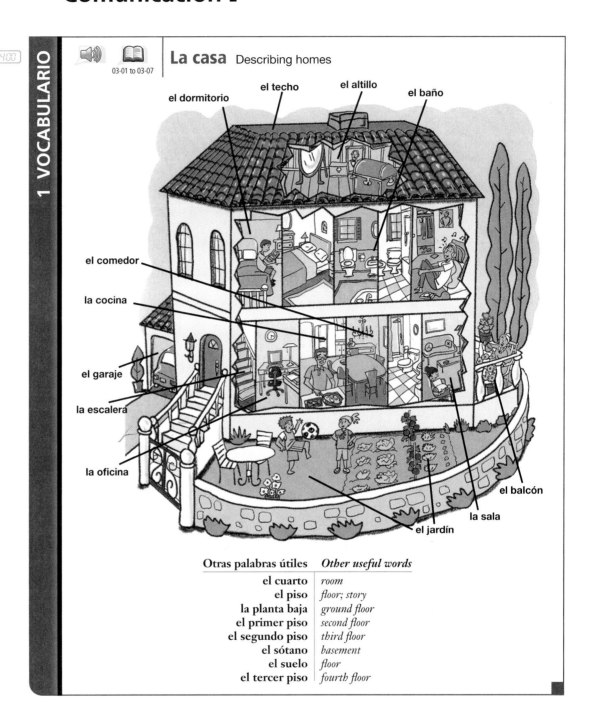

el dormitorio — el techo — el altillo — el baño

el comedor

la cocina

el garaje

la escalera

la oficina

el jardín

el balcón

la sala

| Otras palabras útiles | *Other useful words* |
|---|---|
| el cuarto | *room* |
| el piso | *floor; story* |
| la planta baja | *ground floor* |
| el primer piso | *second floor* |
| el segundo piso | *third floor* |
| el sótano | *basement* |
| el suelo | *floor* |
| el tercer piso | *fourth floor* |

**METHODOLOGY • Teaching Vocabulary**

With beginning language students, we believe in presenting vocabulary that is the most commonly used, and giving few, if any, country/regional variations. Presenting several ways to say the same thing becomes too complicated for the novice learner. Having said that, as Spanish language instructors, we all know it is difficult to determine exactly which words have the highest frequency of usage among Spanish-speakers in the world. In *¡Anda! Curso elemental,* we have attempted to select what appear to be the most commonly used words, but please feel free to use whatever words you may prefer. We encourage you to direct students to the *También se dice…* section in *Appendix 3,* for variations and additional vocabulary to enrich the basic *Vocabulario activo*.

PRONUNCIACIÓN

## PRONUNCIACIÓN

### The letters *h*, *j*, and *g*

 ¡Hola!

03-08 to 03-11

Go to MySpanishLab/Student Activities Manual to learn to pronounce the letters **h**, **j**, and **g**.

*Capítulo 2. El verbo estar, pág. 76.*

### Estrategia

In *Capítulo 3* many of the directions for the activities are written in Spanish. New words that appear in the directions will be translated for you the first time they are used. Keep a list of those words to refer to; it helps you increase your vocabulary.

Workbooklet

 **3-1** **¿Dónde están?** Miren (*Look at*) el dibujo (*drawing*) de la casa en la página 98 y túrnense (*take turns*) para decir dónde están los siguientes (*following*) cuartos. ■

**MODELO** E1: el garaje

E2: *El garaje está en la planta baja.*

#### Fíjate

The first floor, or ground floor, is generally called *la planta baja; el primer piso* actually refers to the second floor. What is the third floor called?

| | EN LA PLANTA BAJA | EN EL PRIMER PISO | EN EL SEGUNDO PISO |
|---|---|---|---|
| la sala | X | | |
| el baño | X | X | |
| el dormitorio | | X | |
| la cocina | X | | |
| la oficina | X | | |
| el altillo | | | X |

*Capítulo 2. Los deportes y los pasatiempos, pág. 81.*

 **3-2** **Las partes de la casa** Dile (*Tell*) a tu compañero/a en qué parte de la casa haces (*you do*) las siguientes actividades. ■

**MODELO** estudiar

E1: *Yo estudio en la oficina. ¿Y tú?*

E2: *Yo estudio en mi dormitorio.*

1. hablar por teléfono
2. leer un libro
3. ver la televisión
4. organizar papeles
5. preparar enchiladas
6. tocar un instrumento
7. escuchar música
8. tomar el sol

### Fíjate

In the directions, words like *miren, túrnense, comparen,* and *usen* are plural—they refer to both you and your classmate.

**3-3** **¿Y tu casa…?** Túrnense para describir sus casas (o la de un miembro de su familia o de un amigo) y compararlas con la casa de la página 98. Usen el modelo para crear por lo menos (*at least*) **cinco** oraciones (*sentences*). ■

**MODELO** *En la casa del dibujo, la sala está en la planta baja y mi sala está en la planta baja también. En la casa del dibujo, el dormitorio está en el segundo piso, pero mi dormitorio está en la planta baja. No tenemos un altillo…*

**METHODOLOGY • Writing**

Research strongly supports our belief that class time should be spent engaging students almost exclusively in meaningful *oral* activities. Virtually all of the activities in *¡Anda! Curso elemental* are meant to be done orally in pairs or groups. This maximizes students' opportunities to speak and use Spanish in confidence-building *i + 1* settings. Research confirms that strong oral skills translate into better writing skills. Therefore, students need a controlled environment to practice speaking so that outside of class, they will be more successful and confident writers. For more mechanical writing activities, please refer your students to the Student Activities Manual, Extra Activities, and MySpanishLab.

**SECTION GOALS for**
*Pronunciación*

By the end of the *Pronunciación* section, students will be able to:
- distinguish between the English *h* sound and the silent Spanish *h*.
- pronounce the Spanish letter *j*.
- distinguish between the hard *g* and soft *g* sounds.
- use *refranes* as a way to integrate culture and pronunciation practice.

**NOTE for *La casa***

Remind students that when communicating with native speakers from different Spanish-speaking areas of the world, they can combine words that they may have learned already with new vocabulary to express their ideas. You can use the word *el cuarto* to describe a room in general and then tell what function the room has. For example, you can refer to a bedroom as *un cuarto de dormir,* etc.

**HERITAGE LANGUAGE LEARNERS**

You might explain that for the true beginners in the class, you have been using more cognates, gestures, pictures, and speaking slightly slower than a native speaker would typically speak in order to facilitate their learning. You can tell the heritage language learners that the pace of your speech and your word choice will change as students acquire more Spanish.

**HERITAGE LANGUAGE LEARNERS**

Ask your heritage language learners if they have any words related to the house that they use on a regular basis. Add those words to your vocabulary list so other students are familiar with them.

**HERITAGE LANGUAGE LEARNERS**

Your heritage language learners may have a different concept of housing if they have spent time abroad with their families. Some families in Spain and Mexico, for example, are not considered wealthy by American standards, yet they have a summer chalet or a house in another part of the country where the family goes to spend time together. In many Spanish-speaking countries, even families of limited resources, have *empleadas domésticas* to help with the daily chores, but they are not the same type of personnel that we think of in the United States for those who are very wealthy (e.g., butlers, nannies, chauffeurs, cooks, gardeners, etc.).

## NOTE for 3-4

This activity exposes students to more variety on the subject of housing in the Spanish-speaking world. Further discussion may include housing in other parts of the Spanish-speaking world that are not represented here, the typical organization around the centralized urban state vs. provinces, economic disparity in Latin America, urban immigration and ghettos, etc.

## SUGGESTION for 3-4

Remind of students, or help them brainstorm, useful vocabulary they already know in addition to the *Vocabulario útil* listed, e.g., *alto, bajo, grande, pequeño, pobre, rico, bueno, malo, fuerte, débil, el edificio,* etc.

## EXPANSION for 3-4

Bring in a photo of a recognizable house or building, such as the White House, Trump Towers, or some other famous example of architecture in your area. Ask students to compare these buildings with the photos, or with the places in which they live.

## SUGGESTION for *La casa*

Encourage students to use this location strategy to learn the parts of a house: Imagine that you are in your house, or a house that is familiar to you, and you learn the vocabulary by arranging the list in the order that you see the rooms. You might enter through *la puerta,* then see *la sala,* then *el comedor, la cocina,* and *el baño.* If you can, walk through the house and pronounce the vocabulary as you enter each room or hang a sign in each room with the corresponding vocabulary word. When it is time to take your test, close your eyes and remember the order in which you learned the rooms, just as they appear when you walk through them.

## ADDITIONAL ACTIVITY for *La casa*

Have your students create architectural diagrams or floor plans of the houses or apartments in which they grew up. Have them label the rooms in Spanish, using the correct definite articles. Along with labeling the rooms, they can write to whom the room belongs.

---

`5:00` 👥👥 **3-4 Es una casa interesante...** Look at the following photos and together, create a short description of one of the houses. Imagine the interior, and the person(s) who may live there. Share your description with the class. ■

**MODELO**    *La casa está en México y es grande y muy moderna. Tiene seis dormitorios, cuatro baños, una cocina grande y moderna, una sala grande y un balcón. Gastón y Patricia viven allí. Tienen tres hijos. Ellos trabajan en la ciudad...*

### Vocabulario útil

| | | | |
|---|---|---|---|
| **antiguo/a** | *old* | **humilde** | *humble* |
| **la calle** | *street* | **moderno/a** | *modern* |
| **el campo** | *country* | **nuevo/a** | *new* |
| **la ciudad** | *city* | **tradicional** | *traditional* |
| **contemporáneo/a** | *contemporary* | **viejo/a** | *old* |

1.

Oviedo, España

2.

México

3.

Guanajuato, México

4.

Cartagena, Colombia

5.

Las islas flotantes de los Uros, Perú

6.

Luarca, España

---

## ADDITIONAL ACTIVITY for *La casa*

Give students the following list of "words" to unscramble.

| **MODELO** | sipo |
| | *piso* |
| 1. louse | (suelo) |
| 2. reascale | (escalera) |
| 3. oñba | (baño) |
| 4. alas | (sala) |
| 5. naiciof | (oficina) |
| 6. mocored | (comedor) |

## ADDITIONAL ACTIVITY for *La casa*

Play Twenty Questions with the parts of the house and the furniture. Hide a picture or a flashcard of the vocabulary word. Students can only ask questions that have "yes" or "no" answers. Model questions using the verb *Hay,* such as ¿*Hay agua?,* ¿*Hay mesas?,* ¿*Hay una cama?,* etc.

03-12 to 03-18   Spanish Tutorial

## Algunos verbos irregulares  Expressing actions

Necesito un apartamento para este semestre. ¿Qué hago?

¿Por qué no pones un anuncio en el periódico?

### Estrategia

Memorizing information is easier to do when the information is arranged in chunks. You will notice that some of the *yo* forms end in *-go*, such as *salgo*, *traigo*, and *pongo*. Learning the information as a chunk of "*go*" verbs may make it easier to remember.

Look at the present tense forms of the following verbs. In the first group, note that they all follow the same patterns that you learned in **Capítulo 2** to form the present tense of regular verbs, *except* in the **yo** form.

### Group 1

|  | conocer (to be acquainted with) | dar (to give) | hacer (to do; to make) | poner (to put; to place) |
|---|---|---|---|---|
| yo | conozco | doy | hago | pongo |
| tú | conoces | das | haces | pones |
| Ud. | conoce | da | hace | pone |
| él, ella | conoce | da | hace | pone |
| nosotros/as | conocemos | damos | hacemos | ponemos |
| vosotros/as | conocéis | dais | hacéis | ponéis |
| Uds. | conocen | dan | hacen | ponen |
| ellos/as | conocen | dan | hacen | ponen |

### Estrategia

Organize the new verbs you are learning in your notebook. Note whether each verb is regular or irregular, what it means in English, if any of the forms have accents, and if any other verbs follow this pattern. You might want to highlight or color code the verbs that follow patterns.

|  | salir (to leave; to go out) | traer (to bring) | ver (to see) |
|---|---|---|---|
| yo | salgo | traigo | veo |
| tú | sales | traes | ves |
| Ud. | sale | trae | ve |
| él, ella | sale | trae | ve |
| nosotros/as | salimos | traemos | vemos |
| vosotros/as | salís | traéis | veis |
| Uds. | salen | traen | ven |
| ellos/as | salen | traen | ven |

### Instructor Resources
• PPT, Extra Activities

**NOTE for *Algunos verbos irregulares***

These common irregular verbs have been grouped by similarities—irregular *yo* forms, verbs with first-person *-go* endings, and four stem-changing verbs. *Poder* and *querer* are included here because they are useful in practicing chapter vocabulary. They will also serve as a point of reference when stem-changing verbs are presented in *Capítulo 4*.

**NOTE for *Algunos verbos irregulares***

The students who studied Spanish in high school might have learned about "shoe verbs" or "boot verbs." If you use the *vosotros/as* forms in your teaching, you might want to arrange the verb charts in two columns, with the singular forms on the left and the plural forms on the right. Then, you can draw a circle around the forms that change (excluding *nosotros/as* and *vosotros/as*) to form a boot or shoe. This helps students to remember which forms change and which do not.

If you use the *vosotros/as* forms in your class, point out that the verbs *dar* and *ver* have no accent in the *vosotros/as* forms.

**NOTE for *Conocer***

We have chosen to introduce *conocer* in *Capítulo 3* as an irregular verb, and to focus on the meaning "to be acquainted with." In *Capítulo 4*, *saber* is presented and contrasted with *conocer*.

**METHODOLOGY • Teacher Talk**
Although we simplify our spoken language in class, in order to stay within the range of *i + 1*, we should strive to speak at a speed as close to natural as possible. Gradually increase speed as the semester progresses.

**HERITAGE LANGUAGE LEARNERS**
Remind students that *salir* is generally used with prepositions. A few common examples are:

| | |
|---|---|
| *salir de* | to leave from |
| *salir con* | to go out with |
| *salir por* | to leave for an errand; to leave through (e.g., a window or door) |
| *salir para* | to leave for (a destination) |

In the second group, note that **venir** is formed similarly to **tener,** which you learned about in **Capítulo 1,** on p. 34.

## Group 2

|  | venir (*to come*) |
|---|---|
| yo | vengo |
| tú | vienes |
| Ud. | viene |
| él, ella | viene |
| nosotros/as | venimos |
| vosotros/as | venís |
| Uds. | vienen |
| ellos/as | vienen |

In the third group of verbs, note that all of the verb forms have a spelling change except in the **nosotros** and **vosotros** forms.

## Group 3

|  | decir (*to say; to tell*) | oír (*to hear*) | poder (*to be able to*) | querer (*to want; to love*) |
|---|---|---|---|---|
| yo | digo | oigo | puedo | quiero |
| tú | dices | oyes | puedes | quieres |
| Ud. | dice | oye | puede | quiere |
| él, ella | dice | oye | puede | quiere |
| nosotros/as | decimos | oímos | podemos | queremos |
| vosotros/as | decís | oís | podéis | queréis |
| Uds. | dicen | oyen | pueden | quieren |
| ellos/as | dicen | oyen | pueden | quieren |

Capítulo Preliminar A. El verbo *ser*, pág. 13; Capítulo 1. El verbo *tener*, pág. 34; Capítulo 2. El verbo *estar*, pág. 76.

 **3-5** **La ruleta** How competitive are you? Listen as your instructor explains how to play this fast-paced game designed to practice the new verb forms. When you finish with this list, repeat the activity with different verbs and include **estar, ser,** and **tener.** ■

1. traer
2. hacer
3. oír
4. querer
5. conocer
6. dar
7. decir
8. venir
9. poder
10. poner
11. ver
12. salir

 **3-6** **Combinaciones** Forma oraciones lógicas combinando los elementos de las dos columnas. Compara tus oraciones con las de tu compañero/a (*with those of your partner*). ■

1. __f__ Hoy mis hermanos…
2. __d__ Mis amigos y yo…
3. __a__ Mi abuelo…
4. __g__ Quiero…
5. __h__ Mi perro (*dog*)…
6. __b__ Mi profesor/a…
7. __c__ Yo…
8. __e__ Tú…

a. pone sus recuerdos (*mementos*) en el altillo.
b. conoce bien la arquitectura de España.
c. oigo música en la sala.
d. hacemos fiestas en el jardín.
e. ves la televisión en tu dormitorio.
f. no pueden salir de casa.
g. una casa con dos pisos, tres baños y un garaje.
h. siempre viene a la cocina para comer.

 **3-7** **Otras combinaciones** Completa los siguientes pasos. ■

**Paso 1** Escribe una oración lógica con cada (*each*) verbo, combinando elementos de las tres columnas.

**MODELO** (A) nosotros, (B) hacer, (C) la tarea en el dormitorio

*Nosotros hacemos la tarea en el dormitorio.*

| COLUMNA A | COLUMNA B | COLUMNA C |
|---|---|---|
| Uds. | (no) hacer | estudiar en el balcón |
| mamá y papá | (no) ver | programas interesantes en la |
| yo | (no) conocer | televisión los domingos |
| tú | (no) oír | de la casa |
| el profesor | (no) querer | la tarea en el dormitorio |
| nosotros/as | (no) salir | los libros al segundo piso |
| ellos/ellas | (no) traer | ruidos (*noises*) en el altillo por la noche |
|  |  | bien el arte de España |

**Paso 2** En grupos de tres, lean las oraciones y corrijan (*correct*) los errores.

**Paso 3** Escriban juntos (*together*) **dos** oraciones nuevas y compártanlas (*share them*) con la clase.

---

**INSTRUCTIONS FOR 3-5:**
*La ruleta*
Form groups of 2 to 4 students. Each group will need either a die or six small pieces of paper on which the numbers 1 through 6 have been written. Number 1 = *yo;* 2 = *tú;* 3 = *él, ella;* 4 = *Ud.;* 5 = *nosotros, nosotras;* 6 = *ellos, ellas.* The first person in the group rolls the die (or selects a numbered piece of paper) and gives the correct verb form, matching the number rolled. Other group members must verify the answer. After the correct verb form is given, the player passes the die to the next person. Players continue until the forms come quickly and automatically.

You may wish to keep 10 dice on hand to provide to students for activities like **3-5.**

**SUGGESTION for 3-5**
Repeat the activity and include *tocar, mirar, trabajar, comprender,* etc.

**ADDITIONAL ACTIVITY for**
*Algunos verbos irregulares*
*Jugar a la pelota*
Use a softball or make one out of paper. Say an infinitive and a subject, then toss the ball to a student. The student must give the correct form of the verb. At this point, you can either remain in control of the ball by having the student toss it back to you so that you can continue as before, or students can take over the game. If students take control, then the one who catches the ball and gives the correct answer (sometimes with some coaching by the teacher or other students) then says another infinitive and subject and tosses the ball to a different student, who must give the correct verb form.

Be sure to say the infinitive and subject before tossing the ball, so that all students formulate the answer instead of only the one who catches the ball.

**NOTE for 3-5**
Activities like *La ruleta* and *Jugar a la pelota* can be used regularly in class. The first time you give directions, a more detailed explanation may be required, but thereafter, set-up for the activity is minimal.

**SUGGESTION for 3-7**
*Paso 3* could also be used to follow up and summarize group work.

---

**METHODOLOGY • Direction Lines**
Beginning in this chapter, direction lines will be in Spanish if they are *i + 1.* The nomenclature *i + 1* comes from research by Stephen Krashen known as the Input Hypothesis. (See Krashen, Stephen. *Principles and Practice in Second Language Acquisition.* New York: Pergamon Press, 1982, pp. 9–32.) The Input Hypothesis states that learners can comprehend input (language) based on words they already know plus a few additional words they may not know, but can intuit from context. A level higher than *i + 1* is not comprehensible; it causes confusion and frustrates many learners, causing them to shut down to a point where they cannot comprehend anything. By the end of the first semester, virtually all direction lines will be in Spanish.

**METHODOLOGY • Teaching Techniques**
Most of the vocabulary and grammar activities are designed to be completed either in pairs or small groups. Krashen's Affective Filter Hypothesis states that students need a non-threatening environment, and having students work with each other provides just such an environment.

**SUGGESTION for 3-8**
Remind students that for **3-8,** they can confess what other people do. Sometimes shy students are more willing to participate if they can talk about other people, instead of themselves. They could say: *Yo no vengo tarde, pero mi hermana siempre viene tarde.* That way, they also practice the other verb forms.

**SUGGESTION for 3-9**
As a follow-up, instead of just asking questions such as: *¿Quién ve la televisión todas las noches?* also ask *¿Quiénes ven la televisión todas las noches?* Or, after gathering some answers, check to make sure students are listening by asking questions like *¿Tom ve la televisión todas las noches? ¿Shirley y Steve ven la televisión todas las noches?*

Capítulo 2. La formación de preguntas y las palabras interrogativas, pág. 70.

## 3-8 Confesiones
Time for true confessions! Take turns asking each other how often you do the following things. ▪

siempre (*always*)   a menudo (*often*)   a veces (*sometimes*)   nunca (*never*)

**MODELO**   venir tarde (*late*) a la clase de español
   E1:   *¿Vienes tarde a la clase de español?*
   E2:   *Nunca vengo tarde a la clase de español. ¿Y tú?*
   E1:   *Yo vengo tarde a veces.*

1. querer estudiar
2. oír lo que (*what*) dice tu profesor/a
3. poder contestar las preguntas de tu profesor/a de español
4. escuchar música en la clase de español
5. hacer preguntas tontas en clase
6. traer tus libros a la clase
7. salir temprano (*early*) de tus clases
8. querer comer en la sala para ver la televisión

Workbooklet

## 3-9 Firma aquí
Complete the following steps. ▪

**Paso 1**   Circulate around the room, asking your classmates appropriate questions using the cues provided. Ask those who answer **sí** to sign on the corresponding line in the chart.

**MODELO**   venir a clase todos los días
   E1:   *Roberto, ¿vienes a clase todos los días?*
   E2:   *No, no vengo a clase todos los días.*
   E1:   *Amanda, ¿vienes a clase todos los días?*
   E3:   *Sí, vengo a clase todos los días.*
   E1:   *Muy bien. Firma aquí, por favor.*   *Amanda*

> **Fijate**
> Part of the enjoyment of learning another language is getting to know other people. Your instructor structures your class so that you have many opportunities to work with different classmates.

| ¿QUIÉN... ? | |
|---|---|
| 1. ver la televisión todas las noches | _____ |
| 2. hacer la tarea siempre | _____ |
| 3. salir con los amigos los jueves por la noche | _____ |
| 4. estar enfermo/a hoy | _____ |
| 5. conocer Madrid | _____ |
| 6. poder estudiar con música fuerte (*loud*) | _____ |
| 7. querer ser arquitecto | _____ |
| 8. tener una nota muy buena en la clase de español | _____ |

**Paso 2**   Report some of your findings to the class.

**MODELO**   *Joe ve la televisión todas las noches. Toni siempre hace la tarea. Chad está enfermo hoy...*

**3-10** **Entrevista** Complete the following steps. ■

**Paso 1** Ask a classmate you do not know the following questions. Then change roles.

1. ¿Haces ejercicio? ¿Con quién? ¿Dónde?
2. ¿Cuándo ves la televisión? ¿Cuál es tu programa favorito?
3. ¿Con quién(es) sales los fines de semana (*weekends*)? ¿Qué hacen ustedes?
4. ¿Qué días vienes a la clase de español? ¿A qué hora?
5. ¿Dónde pones tus libros?
6. ¿Siempre dices la verdad?

**Paso 2** Share a few of the things you have learned about your classmate with the class.

**MODELO** *Mi compañero sale los fines de semana con sus amigos y no hace ejercicio.*

## NOTA CULTURAL

## ¿Dónde viven los españoles?

03-19

En Madrid, la capital de España, al igual que en Barcelona, una ciudad cosmopolita en el noreste del país, la vida es tan rápida y vibrante como en la ciudad de Nueva York y otras grandes ciudades. Muchas personas viven en pisos (apartamentos) en edificios grandes, mientras que muchas otras viven ahora en las afueras (*outskirts*) en complejos (grupos) de casas llamados "urbanizaciones", y van a la ciudad para trabajar. Para muchas personas, el costo de vivir en los centros urbanos resulta demasiado caro. Para otras, es preferible vivir donde la vida es un poco más tranquila y tener algo de naturaleza (*nature*) cerca de su vivienda.

Sin embargo (*Nevertheless*), en los pueblos pequeños y en el campo la vida es diferente. Generalmente, las casas son bajas y algunas (*some*) tienen corrales con animales. Muchas personas se dedican a la agricultura y la vida es más lenta (*slow*).

### Preguntas

1. ¿Dónde viven generalmente las personas que residen en Barcelona y en Madrid? ¿Qué es una "urbanización"?
2. ¿Cómo es diferente la vida en el campo?
3. ¿Dónde prefieres vivir tú, en el campo o en la ciudad?

**NATIONAL STANDARDS**
*Communication, Cultures, Comparisons*
By reading texts in Spanish (Standard 1.2), students are exposed to the culture of the people whose language they study. An article on Spanish housing provides a glimpse into one important aspect of the culture (Standard 2.1) while simultaneously reinforcing the reading comprehension and communication skills of the learners. The reading is short, it includes definitions for unfamiliar vocabulary, and it includes appropriate cognates. University students are familiar with different types of housing, and they can make comparisons between typical housing arrangements in the United States and abroad (Standard 4.2). They understand the cost of housing as part of their room and board at school or by paying rent in an off-campus apartment. This background knowledge helps them compare the cultural differences.

**METHODOLOGY • Students Taking Responsibility**
We recommend assigning *all* culture sections to be read in advance. Additionally, we recommend assigning students to read *all* the grammar explanations before class since they are written in a very clear, concise fashion. The instructor's role then becomes that of clarifying or reviewing any points that the students read in advance.

Finally, we suggest assigning the *Escribe* sections as homework, as well as the *Ambiciones siniestras* text and video episodes. You may also want to assign pages from the book for students to study for homework. Remind them to read through the activities, including direction lines, so that less class time is spent setting up activities and more time can be spent with students actively engaged.

**METHODOLOGY • Reading**
Prior to assigning a reading, always activate students' schemata, e.g., tap into their pre-existing knowledge. For example, prepare students for this reading by asking:
1. where most people live in New York City (or a large city near your university).
2. what types of dwellings are found out in the country.

You can also brainstorm with them words they know that relate to housing. You may want to pick out a few key words from the reading and ask what they mean.

**Instructor Resources**
• Textbook images, PPT, Extra Activities

**METHODOLOGY • Vocabulario**
Pronounce the new vocabulary words, and then have students repeat after you, both chorally and individually. You may also ask them to point to the part of the drawing in their books that represents each new word. Remember that overhead transparencies of art for ¡Anda! Curso elemental are available in hardcopy form and on MySpanishLab. Also, computer slides are another way to verify meaning and practice pronunciation, by pointing to different items and having students say the Spanish word that corresponds to each illustration.

**SUGGESTION for Los muebles**
You may want to explain that with faucets "C" does not mean "cold" but rather "hot" (caliente) and "F" means "cold" (fría).

**ADDITIONAL ACTIVITY for Los muebles**
Form groups of at least 4 students. Student 1 says Vivo en una casa que tiene... and inserts something relevant. Student 2 says the phrase, inserting what his or her own house has, and then repeats what Student 1 has.

**MODELO**

E1: *Vivo en una casa que tiene un jardín grande.*

E2: *Vivo en una casa que tiene una estufa y un jardín grande.*

E3: *Vivo en una casa que tiene tres camas, una estufa y un jardín grande.*

Have students continue to see how many rooms or things in a house they can add.

## 3 VOCABULARIO

**4:00**   03-20 to 03-25

# Los muebles y otros objetos de la casa
Elaborating on rooms

| Otras palabras útiles | Other useful words |
|---|---|
| amueblado/a | *furnished* |
| el armario | *armoire; closet; cabinet* |
| la cosa | *thing* |
| el cuadro | *picture; painting* |
| el mueble | *piece of furniture* |
| los muebles | *furniture* |
| el objeto | *object* |

Capítulo 1. El verbo *tener*, pág. 34.

  **3-11  En mi casa**  Túrnense para describir qué muebles y objetos tienen en sus casas. ■

MODELO      E1:  *Yo tengo una cama y dos sillas en mi dormitorio. ¿Qué tienes tú?*

E2:  *Yo tengo una cama, un cuadro, una lámpara y una televisión. ¿Qué tienes en tu cocina?*

 **3-12  El dormitorio de Cecilia**  Mira (*Look at*) la foto y con un/a compañero/a determina dónde está cada objeto. ■

### Fíjate

The preposition *de* combines with the masculine definite article *el* to form the contraction *del*. The feminine article *la* does not contract. Note the following examples.

| | |
|---|---|
| El tocador está a la derecha **de la** puerta. | *The dresser is to the right of the door.* |
| El tocador está a la derecha **del** armario. | *The dresser is to the right right of the closet.* |

MODELO      E1:  ¿Dónde están los cuadros?

E2:  *Los cuadros están en las paredes; uno está sobre la cama y otro está sobre un mueble.*

**¿Dónde está(n)...?**

1. la cama
2. el armario
3. las lámparas
4. la alfombra
5. la puerta

### Vocabulario útil

| | |
|---|---|
| **a la derecha (de)** | *to the right (of)* |
| **a la izquierda (de)** | *to the left (of)* |
| **al lado (de)** | *beside* |
| **encima (de)** | *on top (of)* |
| **sobre** | *on; on top (of); over* |

Capítulo 2. El verbo *gustar*, pág. 80.

**3-13** **¿Quieres una casa estupenda?** You have received a grant to study abroad in Sevilla, Spain! Now you need to find a place to live. Look at the three apartment ads below, and select one of them. Give your partner at least **three** reasons for your choice. Use expressions like **Me gusta(n)…** or **Tiene un/una…** Be creative! ■

**MODELO** *Me gusta el edificio nuevo y tiene muebles. No me gustan…*

---

Piso. Plaza de Cuba, Los Remedios. Edificio nuevo: dos dormitorios, baño, cocina, sala grande y balcón. Amueblado. 750€ al mes. Tel. 95 446 04 55.

Piso. Colonia San Luis. Sala, cocina, dormitorio y baño. Sin muebles. 400€ al mes. Tel. 95 448 85 32.

Alquilo piso de lujo en casa patio rehabilitada del siglo XVIII. Dos plantas, sala, cocina con zona de comedor, baño y dormitorio. Totalmente amueblado (junto a la Plaza Nueva, a dos minutos de la Catedral, Alcázar). Para más información por favor ponte en contacto con Teresa Rivas. Tel. 95 422 47 03.

---

## ¿Cómo andas? I

| | Feel confident | Need to review |
|---|:---:|:---:|
| Having completed **Comunicación I,** I now can . . . | | |
| • describe homes (p. 98) | ☐ | ☐ |
| • pronounce the letters **h, j,** and **g** (MSL /SAM) | ☐ | ☐ |
| • express actions (p. 101) | ☐ | ☐ |
| • relate general differences in housing in Spain (p. 105) | ☐ | ☐ |
| • elaborate on rooms (p. 106) | ☐ | ☐ |

# Comunicación II

**4 VOCABULARIO**

## Los quehaceres de la casa
### Sharing information about household chores

03-26 to 03-29

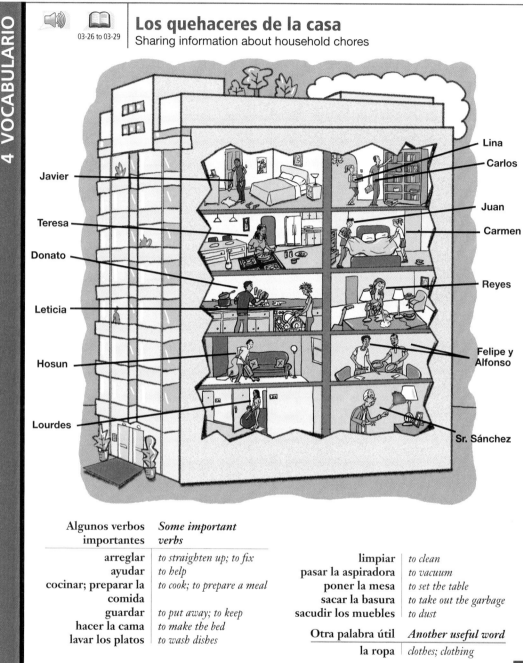

Javier
Teresa
Donato
Leticia
Hosun
Lourdes

Lina
Carlos
Juan
Carmen
Reyes
Felipe y Alfonso
Sr. Sánchez

| Algunos verbos importantes | Some important verbs | | |
|---|---|---|---|
| arreglar | to straighten up; to fix | limpiar | to clean |
| ayudar | to help | pasar la aspiradora | to vacuum |
| cocinar; preparar la comida | to cook; to prepare a meal | poner la mesa | to set the table |
| | | sacar la basura | to take out the garbage |
| guardar | to put away; to keep | sacudir los muebles | to dust |
| hacer la cama | to make the bed | | |
| lavar los platos | to wash dishes | **Otra palabra útil** | *Another useful word* |
| | | la ropa | clothes; clothing |

**SECTION GOALS for**
*Comunicación II*
By the end of the *Comunicación* section, students will be able to:
• share information about household chores.
• discuss responsibilities and obligations using *tener que* + infinitive.
• summarize daily activities related to running a household.
• compare their household chores with the chores of other students.
• discover environmental initiatives in the Spanish-speaking world.
• identify colors and use adjectives to modify nouns.
• inventory the contents of a house, including appliances and accessories.
• compare aspects of their houses with the houses of classmates.
• experience a Spaniard's house by taking a virtual tour.
• use idiomatic expressions with *tener* to express feelings.
• write the numbers 1,000–100,000,000.
• review the numbers 0–999.
• report the price and features of a property for sale.
• analyze the population data of Spanish cities.
• budget euros and use the budget to furnish a house.
• recognize the meaning and uses of *hay*.
• listen for specific details about the rooms of a house.
• communicate on chapter's themes.
• create an ad.

**NATIONAL STANDARDS**
*Comunicación II*
Students can use household chores and everyday activities such as cleaning as a starting point for conversation. They engage in conversations comparing what types of chores they do, what responsibilities they have, how often they do specific chores, and their likes and dislikes (Standard 1.1). This topic lends itself well to exchanging opinions and providing and obtaining information, through interviews, signature activities, presentations or TPR modeling in front of the class, and role plays. One effective way of using role plays in this situation to elicit communication is to pair students and have one student be the parent and the other student be the child. The division of household labor and the equities or inequities involved are familiar situations in most families.

**SUGGESTION for 3-14 and 3-15**
Pair students by the household chore they like the least, or by the appliance they could least/most live without.

**3-14** **¡Mucho trabajo!** Mira el dibujo en la página 109 y con un/a compañero/a determina qué hacen las siguientes personas. ■

MODELO     E1:  *Carmen*
           E2:  *Carmen hace la cama.*

1. El Sr. Sánchez  El Sr. Sánchez sacude los muebles.
2. Hosun  Hosun pasa la aspiradora.
3. Javier  Javier arregla su dormitorio.
4. Reyes  Reyes sacude los muebles y limpia la casa.
5. Donato y Leticia  Donato y Leticia lavan los platos.
6. Lourdes  Lourdes saca la basura.
7. Lina y Carlos  Lina y Carlos guardan los libros.
8. Teresa  Teresa cocina/prepara la comida.
9. Felipe y Alfonso  Felipe y Alfonso ponen la mesa.
10. Juan y Carmen  Juan y Carmen hacen la cama.

**NOTE for 3-15**
Explain that days of the week are plural when talking in general, e.g., *los lunes* for "on Mondays," or *Limpio el apartamento los sábados.*

**METHODOLOGY • *Tener que* + infinitive**
*Tener que* + infinitive is introduced lexically in **3-15** and then introduced on page 115, *Algunas expresiones con* tener.

**NOTE for 3-15**
A more in-depth presentation of *tener que* + infinitive comes later in this chapter. The use here of *tener que* + infinitive is to introduce the new vocabulary. Thus the expression is used lexically.

Workbooklet

**3-15** **Responsabilidades** ¿Cuáles son tus responsabilidades? ¿Cuánto tiempo dedicas a (*do you devote to*) estas tareas? ¿Cuándo? Completa el cuadro y comparte (*share*) oralmente tu información con un/a compañero/a. ■

**Fíjate**
The expression *tener que* + infinitive means "to have to do" something. *¿Qué tienes que hacer?* means "What do you have to do?" Later in this chapter you will learn more expressions with *tener*.

| Vocabulario útil | |
|---|---|
| **desordenado/a** | *messy* |
| **limpio/a** | *clean* |
| **sucio/a** | *dirty* |
| **tener que +** (*infinitive*) | *to have to +* (*verb*) |

MODELO     *Tengo que limpiar mi dormitorio y sacar la basura los lunes. Dedico dos horas porque está muy sucio y tengo mucha basura.*

| LUGAR | ¿QUÉ TIENES QUE HACER? | ¿CUÁNDO? | ¿CUÁNTO TIEMPO DEDICAS? |
|---|---|---|---|
| 1. mi dormitorio | limpiar mi dormitorio y sacar la basura | el lunes | dos horas |
| 2. el baño | | | |
| 3. la cocina | | | |
| 4. la sala | | | |
| 5. el garaje | | | |
| 6. el comedor | | | |

# 5 VOCABULARIO

🔊 📖 03-30 to 03-33

## Los colores  Illustrating objects using colors

**amarillo**   **marrón**

una casa sevillana

**gris**

la catedral en Bilbao

**verde**

las botellas para la sidra

**anaranjado**

el puerto de Ribadeo

**beige**

una casa urbana española

Un viñedo en La Rioja

**morado**

**rojo**   un autobús

**blanco**

**negro**

Los Picos de Europa

**azul**

el mar al lado de Baiona

**rosado**

una casa privada

🔑 **Instructor Resources**
• Textbook images, PPT, Extra Activities

**SUGGESTION for *Los colores***
Ask students to identify any additional colors they see in the photos.

**NOTE for *Los colores***
Although "beige" is spelled the same in both English and Spanish, reinforce the proper Spanish pronunciation.

**EXPANSION for *Los colores***
For further practice with colors, use the photos *El dormitorio de Cecilia,* from **3-12,** and *¿Cómo son?* **3-17.** Ask specific questions like *¿Qué colores ves en la foto? ¿De qué color es la alfombra? ¿De qué color es la lámpara?* or ask students to describe the two rooms orally and/or in writing.
    Additional questions include: *¿De qué color es tu dormitorio? ¿De qué color es tu silla favorita? ¿Qué color te gusta más? ¿Qué color no te gusta?* etc.

Colors are descriptive adjectives, and as such, they must agree with the nouns they describe in number and gender.

- Adjectives ending in **-o** have four forms.

  rojo      roja      rojos      rojas

- Adjectives ending in a vowel other than **-o,** or in a consonant, have two forms.

  verde      verdes

  azul      azules

> **Fíjate**
>
> You learned in *Capítulo 1* (p. 30) that adjectives normally follow nouns in Spanish: e.g., el coche *rojo*.

| ¿De qué color es...? | What color is . . . ? |
|---|---|
| La casa es blanca y tiene un techo rojo. | *The house is white and has a red roof.* |
| Las casas son blancas y tienen techos rojos. | *The houses are white and have red roofs.* |
| Tengo un armario marrón. | *I have a brown armoire.* |
| Tengo una alfombra marrón. | *I have a brown rug.* |
| Tengo dos sillones marrones. | *I have two brown armchairs.* |

How would you say "a black refrigerator," "a white sofa," "a green kitchen," and "some yellow chairs?"

---

[5:00]  **3-16 La casa ideal** Termina (*Finish*) las siguientes oraciones para describir tu casa ideal, incluyendo los colores. Comparte tus respuestas con un/a compañero/a. ■

**MODELO**    E1: *Quiero una casa con…    una cocina…*

              E2: *Quiero una casa con una cocina amarilla.*

**Quiero una casa con…**

1. una alfombra…
2. una bañera…
3. un inodoro y un lavabo…
4. un refrigerador…
5. un comedor…
6. unos sillones…
7. un techo…
8. ¿?

Capítulo Preliminar A. El verbo *ser*, pág. 13; Capítulo 1. El verbo *tener*, pág. 34

---

[5:00]  **3-17 ¿Cómo son?** Túrnense para comparar la sala de Luis con la tuya (*yours*) o la sala de un/a amigo/a. Usen los verbos **ser** y **tener.** ■

**MODELO**    E1: *Luis tiene una sala grande, pero yo tengo una sala pequeña.*

              E2: *La sala de Luis es grande y mi sala es grande también.*

La sala de Luis

**3-18 Buena memoria** Bring in colorful pictures of a house or rooms in a house. Select one picture and take a minute to study it carefully. Turn it over and relate to a partner as much detail as you can remember about the picture, especially pertaining to colors. Then listen to your partner talk about his or her picture. Who remembers more? ■

 **3-19 En la casa de Dalí** Go to the Internet to take a virtual tour of the home of a famous Spaniard, such as the house of the famous artist Salvador Dalí, the Castillo Gala Dalí in Púbol, Spain. While you are exploring his house, or the house of another Spaniard, answer the following questions. Then compare your answers with those of a classmate. ■

El Castillo Gala Dalí

1. ¿Qué ves en el jardín?
2. ¿Qué muebles ves o imaginas en cada cuarto?
3. ¿Cuáles son los colores principales de cada cuarto?
4. ¿Qué te gusta más de esta casa? ¿Qué te gusta menos?

## 6 GRAMÁTICA

03-34 to 03-37

### Algunas expresiones con *tener*
Depicting states of being using *tener*

The verb **tener,** besides meaning *to have,* is used in a variety of expressions.

Susana tiene 19 años.

| | |
|---|---|
| **tener... años** | *to be . . . years old* |
| **tener calor** | *to feel hot* |
| **tener cuidado** | *to be careful* |
| **tener éxito** | *to be successful* |
| **tener frío** | *to be cold* |
| **tener ganas de + (*infinitive*)** | *to feel like + (verb)* |
| **tener hambre** | *to be hungry* |
| **tener miedo** | *to be afraid* |
| **tener prisa** | *to be in a hurry* |
| **tener que + (*infinitive*)** | *to have to + (verb)* |
| **tener razón** | *to be right* |
| **tener sed** | *to be thirsty* |
| **tener sueño** | *to be sleepy* |
| **tener suerte** | *to be lucky* |
| **tener vergüenza** | *to be embarrassed* |

**Fíjate**

You have learned that adjectives in Spanish, like the color *amarillo,* have four forms (masculine singular, feminine singular, masculine plural, feminine plural). When you use expressions like *tener frío* or *tener éxito,* you do not change the *o* of *frío* or *éxito* to make it feminine or plural.

—Mamá, **tengo hambre.** ¿Cuándo comemos?
—**Tienes suerte,** hijo. Salimos para el restaurante Tío Tapas en diez minutos.

*Mom, I'm hungry. When are we eating?*
*You are lucky, son. We are leaving for Tío Tapas Restaurant in ten minutes.*

---

**SUGGESTION for 3-18**
This activity can be assigned as homework. Ask students to bring in photos from magazines, etc. Bring extra photos of your own in case some students forget theirs.
    For additional practice, repeat the activity with other photos students bring in or have students pass their photos to someone else.

**SUGGESTION for 3-19**
Assign **3-19** for homework. Students should bring answers to class to compare them with classmates' answers.

**ADDITIONAL ACTIVITY for *Los colores***
    Assign students to work in groups of three. *Estudiante 1* selects a color and identifies something in the classroom with that color. *Estudiante 2* names something else that is the same color. *Estudiante 3* does the same. A student who cannot respond is "out." The last person left chooses the color for the next round.

**MODELO**
E1: *Veo una mochila roja.*
E2: *Veo un cuaderno rojo.*
E3: *Veo unos libros rojos.*
E1: *...*

**SUGGESTION for *Algunas expresiones con* tener**
Practice expressions with directed questions, such as *¿Qué no tienes ganas de hacer los lunes? ¿Cuándo tienes hambre? ¿Cuándo tienes sueño? ¿Cuántos años tienes? ¿En qué meses tienes frío? ¿En qué meses tienes calor?* etc.

**NOTE for *Algunas expresiones con* tener**
Remind students that they learned *frío* and *calor* in *Capítulo Preliminar A,* when the words were used with *Hace...*

**NOTE for *Algunas expresiones con* tener**
To practice the *tener* expressions, you may wish to pair students as follows:
    Create slips of paper with half of a sentence that needs to be matched by another half, e.g., *Cuando no como...* [One slip of paper]
    *... tengo hambre.* [One slip of paper that matches the previous sentence]
    Create enough clauses for your class.
    Have students circulate to find the match to their clause and hence their partner. To save you time, collect the strips after the students have found their partners so that you can reuse them in another class. The slips can be used in subsequent chapters, as they act as review.

**114** CAPÍTULO 3

 **3-20 ¿Qué pasa?** Mira los dibujos y, con un/a compañero/a, crea una oración para cada persona. Usa expresiones con **tener.** ∎

MODELO

*Susana tiene 19 años.*

Rosario   Alicia       Beatriz   Julián          Pilar

Jorge   Ramón   Roberto       Carmen      David

**3-21 ¿Qué haces cuando…?** ¿Qué haces en casa en las siguientes situaciones? Contesta combinando los elementos de las dos columnas de la forma más lógica. Compara tus respuestas con las de un/a compañero/a. ∎

MODELO    E1: tener ganas de descansar    ver la televisión
           E2: *Cuando tengo ganas de descansar, veo la televisión.*

**Cuando…**

1. __b__ tener hambre            a. estar muy feliz
2. __d__ tener suerte             b. preparar comida en la cocina
3. __g__ tener cuidado           c. hacer una limonada
4. __f__ tener prisa              d. no tener que limpiar la casa
5. __h__ tener frío               e. ver la televisión
6. __a__ tener éxito             f. salir rápidamente en mi carro
7. __c__ tener sed               g. no hacer errores
8. __e__ tener ganas de descansar    h. tomar el sol en el jardín

**3-22** **¿Qué tengo yo?** Expresa cómo te sientes (*you feel*) en las siguientes ocasiones usando (*using*) expresiones con **tener**. Compara tus respuestas con las de un/a compañero/a. ■

**MODELO**   E1:   antes de comer

E2:   *Antes de comer tengo hambre.*

1. temprano en la mañana
2. los viernes por la tarde
3. después de correr mucho
4. en el verano
5. en el invierno

6. cuando tienes tres minutos para llegar a clase
7. cuando sacas una "A" en un examen
8. cuando lees un libro de Stephen King o ves una película (*movie*) de terror

---

**3-23** **Pobre Pablo** Poor Pablo, our friend from Madrid, is having one of those days! With a partner, retell his story using **tener** expressions. ■

**MODELO**

El despertador de Pablo no funciona (*does not work*). Tiene una clase a las 8:00 y es tarde. Sale de casa a las 8:10.

*Pablo tiene prisa.*

1. Es invierno y Pablo no tiene abrigo (*coat*).
Pablo tiene frío.

2. Pablo tiene un insuficiente (60% en los Estados Unidos) en un examen.
Pablo no tiene éxito. / Pablo tiene que estudiar.

3. Pablo recibe una oferta (*offer*) de trabajo increíble.
Pablo tiene suerte.

4. Pablo ve que no tiene dinero para comer.
Pablo tiene vergüenza. / Pablo tiene hambre.

5. Pablo está en casa y quiere una botella de agua. En el refrigerador no hay ninguna (*none*).
Pablo tiene sed.

**3-24 Datos personales** Túrnense para hacerse esta entrevista (*interview*). ■

1. ¿Cuántos años tienes?
2. ¿Qué tienes que hacer hoy?
3. ¿Tienes ganas de hacer algo diferente? ¿Qué?
4. ¿En qué clase tienes sueño?
5. ¿En qué clase tienes mucha suerte?
6. ¿Siempre tienes razón?
7. ¿Cuándo tienes hambre?
8. ¿Cuándo tienes sueño?
9. Cuando tienes sed, ¿qué tomas?
10. ¿En qué tienes éxito?

**7 VOCABULARIO**

03-38 to 03-42

# Los números 1.000–100.000.000
Counting from 1,000 to 100,000,000

| | | | |
|---|---|---|---|
| **1.000** | mil | **100.000** | cien mil |
| **1.001** | mil uno | **400.000** | cuatrocientos mil |
| **1.010** | mil diez | **1.000.000** | un millón |
| **2.000** | dos mil | **2.000.000** | dos millones |
| **30.000** | treinta mil | **100.000.000** | cien millones |

1. **Mil** is never used in the plural form when counting.

   mil      dos mil      tres mil

   > **Fíjate**
   > To express "a/one thousand," use *mil*. Do not use the word *un* with *mil*.

2. To state numbers in the thousands (such as the following dates), use mil, followed by hundreds in the masculine form (if needed).

   1492      mil cuatrocientos noventa y dos
   1950      mil novecientos cincuenta
   2012      dos mil doce

3. The plural of **millón** is **millones** and when followed by a noun, both take the preposition **de.**

   un millón de autos      cinco millones de personas

   > **Fíjate**
   > Note that *millón* has an accent mark in the singular form but loses the accent mark in the plural form, *millones.*

4. **Cien** is used before **mil** and **millones (de).**

   cien mil euros      cien millones de euros

5. Decimals are used instead of commas in some Hispanic countries to group three digits together, and commas are used to replace decimals.

   1.000.000 (un millón)      $2.000,00 (dos mil dólares)

🍦🍦 **3-25** **¿Cuánto cuesta?** Look at the ads for houses in Spain. Take turns asking for the price and other details for each of the houses. ■

**MODELO**
E1: *¿Cuánto cuesta la casa en Carmona?*
E2: *Cuesta ochocientos noventa y cinco mil euros.*
E1: *¿Cuántos dormitorios tiene?*
E2: *Tiene dos dormitorios.*

### Casa en venta

2 dormitorios,
2 baños,
calefacción,
aire acondicionado.

Cerca de la calle
Santa Ana.

**Carmona, España.**

Precio: 895.000€          Tel: (+34) 954 190 576

### Casa independiente en venta

6 dormitorios, 3 baños, cocina amueblada,
terrazas, piscina.

**Los Gigantes, Tenerife, España.**
Precio: 2.620.000€     Tel: (+34) 922 787 718

### Casa independiente en venta

3 dormitorios, 2 baños, cocina amueblada,
calefacción, terrazas, chimenea. Jardín grande.
Posibilidad de ampliación de dormitorios.

**Costa Brava, España.**
Precio: 960.607€          Tel: (+34) 972 212 315

### Casa unifamiliar en venta

Casa señorial de
cuatro plantas.

La construcción
data del año 1800.

En buen estado
de conservación.

5 dormitorios,
2 baños, chimenea,
terrazas, jardín
grande.
**Oviedo, España.**

Precio: 620.000€          Tel: (+34) 984 223 591

**NATIONAL STANDARDS**
*Communication, Connections*
**Activity 3-25** asks students to engage in conversations about real estate advertisements. They look at the advertisements, and then they take turns providing and obtaining information about each property. The open-ended format of the activity also allows students to exchange opinions about the properties by using familiar expressions (*me gusta, es caro, es feo, es bonito,* etc.) (Standard 1.1).

This activity also reinforces their knowledge of other disciplines such as geography, math, international business, and political science. The prices listed are in euros, so that students can convert the prices to U.S. dollars and decide whether the properties are reasonably priced and how they compare to property values in their area. Students can use their knowledge of Spanish geography to make predictions about the climate, the locations of the properties relative to other Spanish cities, and how the locations affect the value of the properties. They can use their political science studies to examine what type of local government each city or community has, what types of property taxes a buyer might pay, and how owning real estate in a particular community impacts the local economy (Standard 3.1).

**SUGGESTION for 3-25**
For up-to-date exchange rates, please consult the Internet.

**SUGGESTION for 3-25**
Have students describe the houses, determine which one they would prefer to live in, imagine what they are like inside, etc.

**3-26 ¿Cuál es su población?** Lee las poblaciones de las siguientes ciudades de España mientras (*while*) tu compañero/a te escucha y corrige. Después, cambien de papel (*change roles*). ■

1. Madrid      2.824.000
2. Barcelona   1.454.000
3. Valencia    736.000
4. Sevilla     695.000
5. Granada     242.000

**3-27 ¿Qué compras?** Your rich uncle left you an inheritance with the stipulation that you use the money to furnish your house. Refer to the pictures on page 108 to spend 3.500€ on your house. Make a list of what you want to buy, assigning prices to any items without tags. Then share your list with your partner, who will keep track of your spending. Did you overspend? ■

MODELO    *Quiero comprar una televisión por ( for) ochocientos noventa y nueve euros.*

**Fíjate**

The sentence in the model includes two verbs; the second verb is an infinitive (*-ar, -er, -ir*).

| Quiero compr**ar** | I want to buy |
| un televisor. | a television. |

## NOTA CULTURAL

### Las casas "verdes"

03-46

El norte de España (Galicia, Asturias, Cantabria y el País Vasco) se llama "la España verde" a causa del color verde del paisaje (*countryside*). Hay suficiente lluvia y los árboles y la otra vegetación responden bien a la madre naturaleza.

Pero verde significa otra cosa también. España y otros países hispanohablantes tratan de (*try to*) vivir una vida verde. "Vivir una vida verde" significa valorar, cuidar (*care for*) y preservar los recursos naturales. Por ejemplo, usan el viento para producir energía. España produce entre 30 y 50 por ciento de su electricidad del viento. También hay casas con paneles solares.

En el sur de España, muchas casas son de color blanco. Es una tradición muy vieja. El color blanco refleja los rayos del sol y conserva la casa más fresca. Es aún otra manera para vivir una vida verde.

#### Preguntas

1. Explica los dos sentidos (*meanings*) de la palabra "verde".
2. ¿Dónde hay edificios o casas verdes en los Estados Unidos?

## 8 GRAMÁTICA

03-43 to 03-45

### Hay   Stating *There is / There are*

In **Capítulo 2,** you became familiar with **hay** when you described your classroom. To say *there is* or *there are* in Spanish you use **hay.** The irregular form **hay** comes from the verb **haber.**

| | |
|---|---|
| **Hay** un baño en mi casa. | *There is one bathroom in my house.* |
| **Hay** cuatro dormitorios también. | *There are also four bedrooms.* |
| —¿**Hay** tres baños en tu casa? | *Are there three bathrooms in your house?* |
| —No, no **hay** tres baños. | *No, there aren't three bathrooms.* |

¿Qué hay en ese cuarto?

 **Instructor Resources**
• PPT, Extra Activities

**NATIONAL STANDARDS**
*Communication, Cultures, Comparisons*
The reading offers students examples of living "green" in Spain. The summary allows students to understand and interpret written Spanish (Standard 1.2) while describing some of the steps the country is taking toward being environmentally conscious.

**METHODOLOGY • Reading**
You can introduce the reading in class and have students complete it at home, along with *Preguntas*. Then in class, you can emphasize points and discuss the answers to *Preguntas*.

**ANSWERS to *Nota cultural***
1. "Verde" significa el color y también significa valorar, cuidar y preservar la madre naturaleza.
2. Hay edificios y casas verdes por todas partes de los Estados Unidos.

**NOTE for *Hay***
*Hay* was introduced lexically in *Capítulo 2*, **2-4**, when students were asked to describe their classroom. The authors believe that structures should be introduced when needed. *Hay* is treated formally here.

**METHODOLOGY • *Hay***
*Hay* has been introduced more in depth in *Capítulo 3* and not earlier since the grammatical syllabus has allowed students a variety of ways to express themselves using other structures. *Hay* was used lexically in *Capítulo 2*. Most students benefit from this type of chunking of material.
   If you feel your students would benefit from an earlier or more in-depth presentation, please do so.

**NOTE for *Hay***
*¡Anda!* introduces compound tenses using *haber* in *¡Anda! Curso intermedio*. A discussion of *haber* is left for that time, which is at the point of need.

NOTE for 3-29
Time will vary for **3-29,** depending on how thorough your students are. Encourage them to give complete descriptions. To discourage students from getting off-task and chatting, monitor them closely and end the activity when a third to half of your students have finished.

 **3-28** **¡Escucha bien!** Descríbele un cuarto de tu casa (real o imaginaria) a un/a compañero/a en **tres** oraciones. Él/Ella tiene que repetir las oraciones. Después, cambien de papel. ∎

MODELO     E1:  *En mi dormitorio hay una cama, una lámpara y un tocador. También hay dos ventanas. No hay una alfombra.*

E2:  *En tu dormitorio hay una cama, una lámpara y un tocador…*

 **3-29** **¿Qué hay en tu casa?** Descríbele tu casa a un/a compañero/a. Usen todas las palabras que puedan (*you can*) del vocabulario de **La casa**, p. 98, y **Los muebles y otros objetos de la casa**, p. 106. ∎

MODELO     E1:  *En mi casa hay un garaje. ¿Hay un garaje en tu casa?*

E2:  *No, en mi casa no hay un garaje.*

E2:  *En mi baño hay una bañera y una ducha. ¿Qué hay en tu baño?*

E1:  *Hay una ducha, un inodoro y un lavabo grande.*

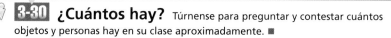 Capítulo Preliminar A. Los números 0–30, pág. 16; Capítulo 2. La formación de preguntas y las palabras interrogativas, pág. 70.

 **3-30** **¿Cuántos hay?** Túrnense para preguntar y contestar cuántos objetos y personas hay en su clase aproximadamente. ∎

MODELO     libros de español

E1:  *¿Cuántos libros de español hay?*

E2:  *Hay treinta libros de español.*

1. puertas
2. escritorios
3. mochilas azules
4. cuadernos negros
5. estudiantes contentos
6. estudiantes cansados
7. computadoras
8. estudiantes a quienes les gusta jugar al fútbol
9. estudiantes a quienes les gusta ir a fiestas (*parties*)
10. estudiantes a quienes les gusta estudiar

**ESCUCHA**

03-47 to 03-48

## Una descripción

| Estrategia | | |
|---|---|---|
| **Listening for specific information** | To practice listening for specific information, first determine the context of the passage and then decide what information you need about that topic. For example, if you are listening to an ad about an apartment to rent, you | may want to focus on size, location, and price. In *¡Anda! Curso elemental,* the **Antes de escuchar** section will provide you with tools for successfully listening to and comprehending each passage. |

**3-31** **Antes de escuchar**   A real estate agent is describing one of the homes she has listed to sell to the Garrido family. Mr. Garrido asks for a few details. Write a question Mr. Garrido might ask the agent. ■

 **3-32** **A escuchar**   Listen to the passage and complete the following list based on the information the agent provides. Listen a second time to verify your answers. ■

1. Number of floors: _1_
2. Number of bedrooms: _4_
3. Number of bathrooms: _3_
4. Size of kitchen: large
5. Size of living room: large
6. Price: $204,000

Los señores Garrido quieren comprar una casa.

**3-33** **Después de escuchar**   With a partner, play the the roles of Mr. Garrido and a friend. The friend asks questions about the house, and Mr. Garrido describes the house using the information from **3-32**. ■

---

**SECTION GOALS for**
*Escucha*

By the end of the *Escucha* section, students will be able to:
- practice pre-listening strategies.
- prepare questions they might ask a real estate agent.
- complete checklists of features of houses.
- listen for specific details.
- use the information from a listening passage to relay information to others.

**NATIONAL STANDARDS**
*Communication*

Once students are able to listen for cognates and the main idea, the next strategy they can apply is listening for specific information. The communicative mode is interpretive (Standard 1.2) as they understand and interpret spoken Spanish. The *Después de escuchar* activity allows students to practice role-playing, and the communication is interpersonal (Standard 1.1). If the students describe the house in front of an audience of listeners, they are also communicating in the presentational mode (Standard 1.3).

**AUDIOSCRIPT for 3-32**

| | |
|---|---|
| AGENTE | Tengo la casa perfecta para usted y su familia. Es una casa bella de un solo piso. Tiene cuatro dormitorios —uno grande y los otros tres más pequeños— y tres baños. La cocina es enorme y muy moderna. |
| SR. GARRIDO | ¿Y la sala? Siempre tenemos muchos amigos en casa. |
| AGENTE | La sala es grande y está al lado de la cocina. Hay mucho espacio para su familia y sus amigos. |
| SR. GARRIDO | ¿Cuál es el precio de la casa? |
| AGENTE | Es muy razonable. Solo 204.000 dólares. |

**METHODOLOGY • *Escucha***

Students can complete this section at home or in class. Encourage them to practice and apply the listening strategy, rather than racing through the exercise. Follow up by checking answers.

# ¡CONVERSEMOS!

03-49

 **3-34** **Su casa** Look at the drawing below, and create a story about the family who lives there. Your partner will ask you the following questions as well as additional ones he/she may have. ■

- When does your story take place?
- What is the weather?
- What is the name of the family?
- Describe furniture and household objects using colors.

Also make sure that your story includes the following components.

- Include at least *eight* different verbs.
- Use at least *three* new **tener** expressions (p. 113).

**3-35** **Mi casa ideal** Describe tu casa ideal. Di por lo menos (*at least*) **diez** oraciones, usando palabras descriptivas (adjetivos) en cada oración. Tu compañero/a de clase va a hacer por lo menos **tres** preguntas sobre tu descripción. ■

## ESCRIBE

03-50

### Un anuncio (ad)

**Estrategia**

**Noun → adjective agreement**

Remember that most adjectives follow nouns, and that adjectives agree with their corresponding nouns in gender (*masculine/feminine*) and number (*singular/plural*). Keep this in mind when creating your ad.

**3-36 Antes de escribir** You have accepted a new job in a different town and you are uncertain regarding the permanence of the position. Therefore, you decide to sublet your apartment, listing it on the Internet on a site such as Craigslist. Before creating the posting, make a detailed list of the features you want to include. ■

**3-37 A escribir** Organize your list and create your ad, making it as informative and attractive as possible. The ad should include the following information: ■

- Location (city, country, street, etc.)
- Type of house or building
- Number and types of rooms
- Appliances in the kitchen
- Pieces of furniture included
- Colors
- Price and contact information
- Special features

**3-38 Después de escribir** Circulate among your classmates sharing your ads, and determine which you would most like to sublet. ■

## ¿Cómo andas? II

Having completed **Comunicación II**, I now can . . .

| | Feel confident | Need to review |
|---|---|---|
| • share information about household chores (p. 109) | ☐ | ☐ |
| • illustrate objects using colors (p. 111) | ☐ | ☐ |
| • depict states of being using **tener** (p. 113) | ☐ | ☐ |
| • count from 1,000–100,000,000 (p. 116) | ☐ | ☐ |
| • discover green initiatives (p. 119) | ☐ | ☐ |
| • state *There is / There are* (p. 119) | ☐ | ☐ |
| • listen for specific information (p. 121) | ☐ | ☐ |
| • communicate about homes and life at home (p. 122) | ☐ | ☐ |
| • create an ad (p. 123) | ☐ | ☐ |

**EXPANSION for Escribe**
Here is an additional idea for a writing task:
Have students be realtors/clients in search of a home or apartment home. Students would organize a "tour of homes" where realtors have to list all the pros of their houses and clients have to ask follow-up questions about information not listed on the brochure.

**CAPÍTULO 3**

**SECTION GOALS for Escribe**
By the end of the *Escribe* section, students will be able to:
- brainstorm and edit a list of the features of an apartment.
- create an ad to post on the Internet.
- organize the contents of the ad into appropriate categories.
- compare their ad to those of their classmates.
- express their likes and dislikes about the ads.
- choose the most enticing ad.

**NATIONAL STANDARDS**
*Communication, Connections*
Creating an ad as is done in **3-37** provides real-life experiences for students.
The listening and writing activities give students the opportunity to engage in conversations about renting, buying, or selling property. They must provide and obtain information about the house they wish to sell, or the property they want to buy. The listening activity (**3-32**) requires students to understand and interpret spoken Spanish. The Internet ad/posting made in **3-37** uses written Spanish, but depending on how you implement the activity, the students could also present their ads to the class; **3-38** combines written Spanish with the presentational mode of the classroom discussion about the ads.
Students make connections between their real world experiences and what they are learning in school. The types of skills they practice while making ads, taking inventories, listening for specific information, and preparing to relocate are practical skills they are learning in college. They use applications from the visual arts for the ads, marketing for preparing their property, economics for calculating where they can afford to live, and life skills they will utilize upon their graduation. Students may also use these skills for making lodging arrangements while traveling or working abroad.

**SUGGESTION for 3-38**
You may want to use the ads in a different way. For example, put students in groups of 4 or 5 and have them determine which ad is the most interesting, will be the easiest to sublet, etc.

**EXPANSION for 3-38**
Ask students to print an ad or spec sheet of a house from a real estate web site such as http://www.realtor.com. Have them pretend they are realtors, and explain the features or selling points of the house to the class in Spanish. Have classmates guess the actual price of the home using the numbers they have just learned.

**Instructor Resources**
- Text images (of map)

**SECTION GOALS**
for *Cultura*
By the end of the *Cultura* section, students will be able to:
- compare housing options in Spain.
- learn about the nightlife in the Plaza Mayor.
- recognize the *tortilla*.
- discover the importance of *el fútbol*.
- discuss pastimes.
- understand the history and symbolism of Don Quijote.
- identify La Alhambra and some of its architectural influences.
- identify Gaudí's architecture.
- summarize the statistics about Spain and its government.
- identify *los castillos*.

**NATIONAL STANDARDS**
*Cultures, Comparisons*
These 2-page culture presentations encourage students to compare and contrast the featured country or region with their own.

The cultural information about *la tortilla*, *La Alhambra*, Gaudí, *los castillos*, and the *Almanaque* section provide an excellent resource for making comparisons between the English language and Spanish (Standard 4.1). You could discuss the *influencia árabe* and the inclusion of words beginning with *al* into the Spanish language, the linguistic diversity within Spain's autonomous communities, the difference between the Mexican *tortilla* and the Spanish *tortilla* (Standard 4.2), and the frequency of "borrowed" words between the languages. The topics of *tapas*, nightlife, and soccer lend themselves well to comparing other cultural differences such as the hours for eating, the size of portions, the drinking age, the *discotecas*, the way Spaniards socialize, and their zeal for soccer (Standard 2.1).

**METHODOLOGY • Cultura**
These 2-page culture spreads in every chapter provide points of departure for future student exploration. *¡Anda! Curso elemental* acknowledges multiple intelligences, different learning styles, and the need for differentiated instruction. For example, the photos and map will appeal to visual learners (visual intelligence), while students who have the ability to relate to and understand others (interpersonal intelligence) will enjoy learning about the cultural aspects of Spain, and students with verbal/linguistic intelligence will enjoy reading and discussing the information. Check MySpanishLab for additional information your students can explore regarding Spain.

# Cultura

# España

CULTURA • CULTURA • CULTURA • C

03-51 to 03-53

## Les presento mi país

Mariela Castañeda Ropero

Mi nombre es Mariela Castañeda Ropero y soy de Madrid, la capital de España. Vivo con mis padres en un piso en el centro. **¿Dónde vives tú? ¿En una casa, en un apartamento o en una residencia estudiantil?** Me gusta la vida en la capital porque hay mucha actividad. A veces, me gusta salir con mis amigos por la tarde para comer tapas y tomar algo. La Plaza Mayor es uno de los lugares típicos para ir de tapas. **¿Cuál es tu lugar favorito para conversar y pasar tiempo con tus amigos?** Frecuentemente, hablamos de los deportes, sobre todo del fútbol y de los equipos españoles. ¡Cada uno tiene su favorito! **¿Cuál es tu deporte preferido? ¿Eres aficionado o jugador?**

Los ganadores de la Copa Mundial 2010

La Plaza Mayor de Madrid es un lugar agradable para comer tapas, tomar una bebida y conversar con amigos.

Don Quijote y Sancho Panza son personajes del autor Miguel de Cervantes Saavedra.

**SUGGESTION for *Don Quijote y Sancho Panza***
Ask students whether they have heard of *Don Quijote de la Mancha*, of the musical *Man of La Mancha*, and of the popular song "The Impossible Dream." The musical and song are takeoffs on the themes of the novel.

El patio de los leones de La Alhambra muestra la influencia árabe en Granada.

La tortilla española es una tapa (un aperitivo) muy típica y popular.

Los *castells* —o castillos (*castles*) en español— son impresionantes construcciones humanas.

La Pedrera (la Casa Milà) en Barcelona es un ejemplo de la arquitectura creativa de Antonio Gaudí.

**ALMANAQUE**

| | |
|---|---|
| **Nombre oficial:** | Reino de España |
| **Gobierno:** | Monarquía parlamentaria |
| **Población:** | 46.505.963 (2010) |
| **Idiomas oficiales:** | español, catalán, gallego, euskera (vasco) |
| **Moneda:** | euro (€) |

## ¿Sabías que...?

- España tiene una diversidad de culturas, regiones y arquitectura. Para un país el doble del estado de Oregon, tiene una gran variedad.
- Los *castells* forman parte de una tradición empezada en Cataluña en el siglo (*century*) XVIII que consiste en competir por hacer la torre (*tower*) humana más alta. ¡Actualmente el récord es un castillo de nueve pisos!

## Preguntas

1. ¿Qué es una tapa?
2. ¿Qué evidencia hay de la presencia histórica de los árabes en España?
3. ¿Por qué son impresionantes los *castells*? Nombra una competencia famosa de tu país.
4. Describe la arquitectura de Antonio Gaudí. ¿Te gusta? ¿Por qué?
5. ¿Qué tienen en común México y España en cuanto a los deportes?

Amplía tus conocimientos sobre España en MySpanishLab.

**NOTE for *La tortilla española***
You may wish to point out to your students the different types of *tortilla*, e.g., Spain's *tortilla* made with eggs and potatoes, and the corn or wheat *tortilla* of Latin America.

**SUGGESTION for *La Alhambra***
Ask students whether they can identify any particular kind of architecture from their area. What influenced it? What makes it unique?

**SUGGESTION for *Gaudí***
Show students photos of *La Sagrada Familia* and ask them to compare this to churches in the United States. Do they like this structure by Gaudí? Why? Students can learn more about Guadí in the Interactive Globes folder in MySpanishLab.

**SUGGESTION for *Los castells***
Ask students whether we have unusual contests involving physical activity in the United States (e.g., log rolling, ice sculpture, lumberjack sports). Ask why they think people participate in such activities. Ask whether *they* would like to participate and, if so, in which activity?

**METHODOLOGY • *¿Sabías que...?***
As with any country, there is an abundance of fascinating information. At this point in each chapter, you may wish to have students explore additional areas of interest, or you may wish to guide your students. For example, students who plan to pursue a career in architecture may wish to further research Spanish architects such as Gaudí or Calatrava. Those majoring in history or government may wish to explore information regarding Franco and the Spanish Civil War.

**ANSWERS to *Preguntas***
1. Es un aperitivo.
2. La Alhambra en Granada es evidencia de la presencia histórica de los árabes.
3. Los *castells* son torres humanas. *Answers may vary.*
4. La arquitectura de Gaudí es muy creativa y modernista. *Answers may vary.*
5. El deporte más popular de México y de España es el fútbol.

**125**

# Ambiciones siniestras

EPISODIO 3

03-57

# Lectura

**Estrategia** .......... Scanning

To enhance comprehension, you can scan or search a reading passage for specific information. When skimming, you read quickly to get the gist of the passage, the main ideas. With scanning, you already know what you need to find out, so you concentrate on searching for that information.

**3-39** **Antes de leer** In the third episode of **Ambiciones siniestras,** some of our protagonists receive an enticing e-mail message. You will discover the content of the mysterious message, as well as learn more about Alejandra's family. Before you read this episode, consider the following questions. ■

1. ¿Hablas sobre los miembros de tu familia con tus amigos? ¿Qué dices?
2. ¿Recibes mensajes curiosos que no vienen de amigos ni (*nor*) de personas de tu familia?
3. ¿Recibes correo basura (*spam*)?

**3-40** **A leer** Complete the following steps. ■

1. Scan the first two paragraphs of this episode, looking for the following specific information:
   a. the location of Alejandra and Manolo
   b. what they are doing there
   c. about whom Alejandra is talking
2. Now reread the second paragraph to determine why Alejandra is discussing this person. What is her concern?

Remember that successful reading in Spanish will require that you read the episodes more than once.

*contest*  ## El concurso°

Manolo y Alejandra están en el cibercafé NetEscape. Hablan mientras se toman un café y leen sus correos electrónicos.

*message*
*to introduce him*

Alejandra le dice a Manolo que quiere mirar su email para ver si tiene un mensaje° de su hermana Pili. Alejandra explica que Pili tiene un novio nuevo y que quiere presentárselo° a sus padres esta noche. Su hermana está muy nerviosa. El novio, Peter, tiene veintinueve años y la hermana tiene solamente diecinueve. ¡Con razón tiene miedo! Alejandra dice que sus padres son muy estrictos y creen que ella es demasiado joven para tener novio.

126

Alejandra lee varios mensajes y exclama:

—Manolo, ¡mira!

—¿Qué pasa? ¿Tienes un mensaje de tu hermana? —le pregunta Manolo.

*this* —No, pero tienes que leer esto°. ¡Es increíble!

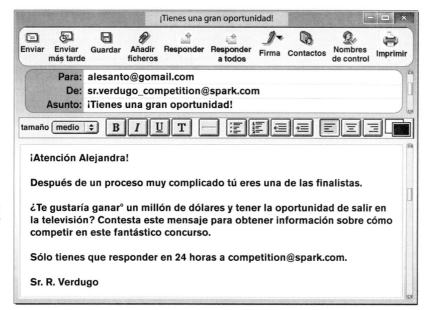

**¡Tienes una gran oportunidad!**

Enviar    Enviar    Guardar    Añadir    Responder    Responder    Firma    Contactos    Nombres    Imprimir
          más tarde            ficheros                 a todos                                de control

**Para:** alesanto@gomail.com
**De:** sr.verdugo_competition@spark.com
**Asunto:** ¡Tienes una gran oportunidad!

tamaño [ medio ÷ ]    B  I  U  T

**¡Atención Alejandra!**

**Después de un proceso muy complicado tú eres una de las finalistas.**

*Would you like to win?* **¿Te gustaría ganar° un millón de dólares y tener la oportunidad de salir en la televisión? Contesta este mensaje para obtener información sobre cómo competir en este fantástico concurso.**

**Sólo tienes que responder en 24 horas a competition@spark.com.**

**Sr. R. Verdugo**

Entonces Manolo decide ver si él tiene el mismo mensaje.

*entire country* —¡Mira! —exclama Manolo. —¡Aquí está! ¡Qué bueno! Pero, seguramente el país entero° tiene el mismo mensaje. ¿Es legítimo? Alejandra, ¿respondemos?

*I must* —No sé. —le contesta Alejandra—. Mis padres siempre me dicen que debo° tener cuidado con las ofertas. ¿Pero qué nos puede pasar si sólo contestamos que deseamos más información?

—Sí —le responde Manolo—. ¿Qué nos puede pasar?

---

**3-41** **Después de leer** Contesta las siguientes preguntas. ■

1. ¿Cómo se llama la hermana de Alejandra? ¿Cuál es su problema?
2. ¿Qué recibe Alejandra?
3. ¿Qué puede ganar?
4. Según (*According to*) Manolo, ¿quiénes reciben la oferta?
5. En tu opinión, ¿qué crees que hacen?
6. Hagan los papeles (*roles*) de unas personas que acaban (*have just*) de recibir el mensaje. ¿Cómo reaccionan? ¿Qué dicen? ¿Qué hacen?

127

## Instructor Resources

• IRM: Video script.

**SECTION GOALS for *Video***

By the end of the *Video* section, students will be able to:

• recognize the living space of Lupe.
• listen for specific pieces of information, such as the phrase *tal vez*.
• describe the homes and/or rooms of Eduardo and Cisco.
• narrate the characters' activities.
• summarize the messages the characters receive.
• arrange the events of the video in chronological order.

**METHODOLOGY • Video**

The video episode in each chapter, as well as the reading episode in the text, contextualizes new vocabulary and grammatical structures. This feature is a critical part of the *¡Anda! Curso elemental* program, as each episode (reading and video) ends in a mini-cliffhanger that is continued or resolved in the subsequent episode. If either the reading or the video is omitted, students will not be able to follow the story and a wonderful learning opportunity will be missed.

**SUGGESTION for 3-43**

You may want students to watch the video once for general comprehension, then a second time for specific information required to answer the questions.

**ANSWERS to 3-43**

1. *Possible answers may include:* Es bonito y grande. Su dormitorio tiene una ventana, etc.
2. Un email sobre un concurso. También recibe el mismo email.
3. En la biblioteca. Estudian matemáticas (*or whatever your students reply that would have mathematical problems*).
4. *Possible answers may include:* Es bastante grande con una cama grande, un armario, un sillón y una mesa para su computadora.
5. *Possible answers may include:* Es muy grande con una piscina grande. Es impresionante.
6. Eduardo y Cisco reciben el mismo email que reciben Marisol, Lupe, Alejandra y Manolo.

# Video

03-58 to 03-61

**3-42** **Antes del video** Take a minute to think back to the first time you visited a friend in his or her dorm room, apartment, or house. Were you interested in seeing what the new living space was like? Did he/she take time to show you around and elaborate on some of the furnishings? In this video episode you will see Lupe's apartment as well as Eduardo's and Cisco's families' homes. They are also checking e-mail. Listen for the phrase **Seguro que es una broma.** (*It's got to be a joke.*) Who says it? Also listen for **Tal vez** (*Perhaps*) **sea un mensaje en cadena. Cadena** means "chain." Can you guess what the sentence means? ■

¡Es una gran oportunidad! ¿No crees?   Tal vez sea un mensaje en cadena.   No lo puedo creer. ¡Qué piscina! ¡Es impresionante!

### «¡Tienes una gran oportunidad!»

Episodio 3 Relax and watch the video, more than once if you choose; then answer the following questions.

**3-43** **Después del video** Contesta las siguientes preguntas. ■

1. ¿Cómo es el apartamento de Lupe?
2. ¿Qué mensaje recibe Marisol? ¿Y Lupe?
3. ¿Dónde están Cisco y Eduardo? ¿Qué estudian?
4. ¿Cómo es el dormitorio nuevo de Eduardo?
5. ¿Cómo es la casa de los padres de Cisco?
6. ¿Qué ocurre al final del episodio?

128

# Y por fin, ¿cómo andas?

| | Feel confident | Need to review |
|---|:---:|:---:|
| Having completed this chapter, I now can . . . | | |

**Comunicación I**

- describe homes (p. 98) ☐ ☐
- pronounce the letters **h**, **j**, and **g** (MSL/SAM) ☐ ☐
- express actions (p. 101) ☐ ☐
- elaborate on rooms (p. 106) ☐ ☐

**Comunicación II**

- share information about household chores (p. 109) ☐ ☐
- illustrate objects using colors (p. 111) ☐ ☐
- depict states of being using **tener** (p. 113) ☐ ☐
- count from 1,000–100,000,000 (p. 116) ☐ ☐
- state *There is / There are* (p. 119) ☐ ☐
- listen for specific information (p. 121) ☐ ☐
- communicate about homes and life at home (p. 122) ☐ ☐
- create an ad (p. 123) ☐ ☐

**Cultura**

- describe general differences in housing in Spain (p. 105) ☐ ☐
- discover green initiatives (p. 119) ☐ ☐
- list interesting facts about Spain (p. 124) ☐ ☐

**Ambiciones siniestras**

- scan a passage consisting of an enticing e-mail message received by Alejandra and Manolo (pp. 126–127) ☐ ☐
- determine who else receives the mysterious e-mail and their reactions to the message (p. 128) ☐ ☐

**Comunidades**

- use Spanish in real-life contexts (SAM) ☐ ☐

# VOCABULARIO ACTIVO

| La casa | The house |
|---|---|
| el altillo | attic |
| el balcón | balcony |
| el baño | bathroom |
| la cocina | kitchen |
| el comedor | dining room |
| el cuarto | room |
| el dormitorio | bedroom |
| la escalera | staircase |
| el garaje | garage |
| el jardín | garden |
| la oficina | office |
| el piso | floor; story |
| la planta baja | ground floor |
| el primer piso | second floor |
| la sala | living room |
| el segundo piso | third floor |
| el sótano | basement |
| el suelo | floor |
| el techo | roof |
| el tercer piso | fourth floor |

| Los verbos | Verbs |
|---|---|
| conocer | to be acquainted with |
| dar | to give |
| decir | to say; to tell |
| hacer | to do; to make |
| oír | to hear |
| poder | to be able to |
| poner | to put; to place |
| querer | to want; to love |
| salir | to leave; to go out |
| traer | to bring |
| venir | to come |
| ver | to see |

| Los muebles y otros objetos de la casa | Furniture and other objects in the house |
|---|---|
| **La sala y el comedor** | The living room and dining room |
| la alfombra | rug; carpet |
| el estante | bookcase |
| la lámpara | lamp |
| el sillón | armchair |
| el sofá | sofa |
| **La cocina** | The kitchen |
| la estufa | stove |
| el lavaplatos | dishwasher |
| el microondas | microwave |
| el refrigerador | refrigerator |
| **El baño** | The bathroom |
| la bañera | bathtub |
| el bidet | bidet |
| la ducha | shower |
| el inodoro | toilet |
| el lavabo | sink |
| **El dormitorio** | The bedroom |
| la almohada | pillow |
| la cama | bed |
| la colcha | bedspread; comforter |
| la manta | blanket |
| las sábanas | sheets |
| el tocador | dresser |

| Otras palabras útiles en la casa | Other useful words in the house |
|---|---|
| amueblado/a | furnished |
| el armario | armoire; closet; cabinet |
| la cosa | thing |
| el cuadro | picture; painting |
| el mueble | piece of furniture |
| los muebles | furniture |
| el objeto | object |

| Los quehaceres de la casa | Household chores |
|---|---|
| arreglar | to straighten up; to fix |
| ayudar | to help |
| cocinar, preparar la comida | to cook; to prepare a meal |
| guardar | to put away; to keep |
| hacer la cama | to make the bed |
| lavar los platos | to wash dishes |
| limpiar | to clean |
| pasar la aspiradora | to vacuum |
| poner la mesa | to set the table |
| sacar la basura | to take out the garbage |
| sacudir los muebles | to dust |

| Los colores | Colors |
|---|---|
| amarillo | yellow |
| anaranjado | orange |
| azul | blue |
| beige | beige |
| blanco | white |
| gris | gray |
| marrón | brown |
| morado | purple |
| negro | black |
| rojo | red |
| rosado | pink |
| verde | green |

| Los números 1.000–100.000.000 | Numbers 1,000–100,000,000 |
|---|---|
| See page 118. | |

| Expresiones con *tener* | Expressions with tener |
|---|---|
| tener… años | to be … years old |
| tener calor | to be hot |
| tener cuidado | to be careful |
| tener éxito | to be successful |
| tener frío | to be cold |
| tener ganas de + (infinitive) | to feel like + (verb) |
| tener hambre | to be hungry |
| tener miedo | to be afraid |
| tener prisa | to be in a hurry |
| tener que + (infinitive) | to have to + (verb) |
| tener razón | to be right |
| tener sed | to be thirsty |
| tener sueño | to be sleepy |
| tener suerte | to be lucky |
| tener vergüenza | to be embarrassed |

| Otras palabras útiles | Other useful words |
|---|---|
| a la derecha (de) | to the right (of) |
| a la izquierda (de) | to the left (of) |
| al lado (de) | beside |
| a menudo | often |
| a veces | sometimes |
| antiguo/a | old |
| la calle | street |
| el campo | country |
| la ciudad | city |
| contemporáneo/a | contemporary |
| desordenado/a | messy |
| encima (de) | on top (of) |
| humilde | humble |
| limpio/a | clean |
| moderno/a | modern |
| nuevo/a | new |
| nunca | never |
| la ropa | clothes; clothing |
| siempre | always |
| sobre | on; on top (of); over |
| sucio/a | dirty |
| tradicional | traditional |
| viejo/a | old |

**Instructor Resources**
• IRM: Syllabi and Lesson Plans

## NATIONAL STANDARDS

### COMUNICACIÓN I
• To identify places in and around town (Communication, Cultures, Connections, Comparisons, Communities)
• To pronounce the letters *c* and *z* (Communication, Cultures)
• To state whom and what is known (Communication)
• To relate common obligations and activities (Communication)
• To express actions (Communication)
• To engage in additional communication practice (Communication)

### COMUNICACIÓN II
• To share where you and others are going (Communication)
• To convey what will happen in the future (Communication)
• To impart information about service opportunities (Communication, Cultures, Connections, Comparisons, Communities)
• To articulate concepts and ideas both affirmatively and negatively (Communication, Comparisons)
• To describe states of being, characteristics, and location (Communication)
• To paraphrase what you hear (Communication)
• To communicate about ways to serve the community (Communication, Connections)
• To write a postcard and proofread it for accuracy (Communication, Comparisons)
• To engage in additional communication practice (Communication)

### CULTURA
• To describe shopping and other daily activities in Spanish-speaking countries (Cultures, Comparisons)
• To discuss the concept of social consciousness (Communication, Connections, Comparisons)
• To list interesting facts about Honduras, Guatemala, and El Salvador (Cultures, Comparisons)
• To explore further the chapter's cultural themes (Cultures)

### AMBICIONES SINIESTRAS
• To practice the reading strategies of skimming and scanning, and learn more about Lupe and Marisol (Communication, Comparisons)
• To discover that Cisco may not be who Eduardo and the others think he is (Communication)

### COMUNIDADES
• To use Spanish in real-life contexts (Connections, Comparisons, Communities)

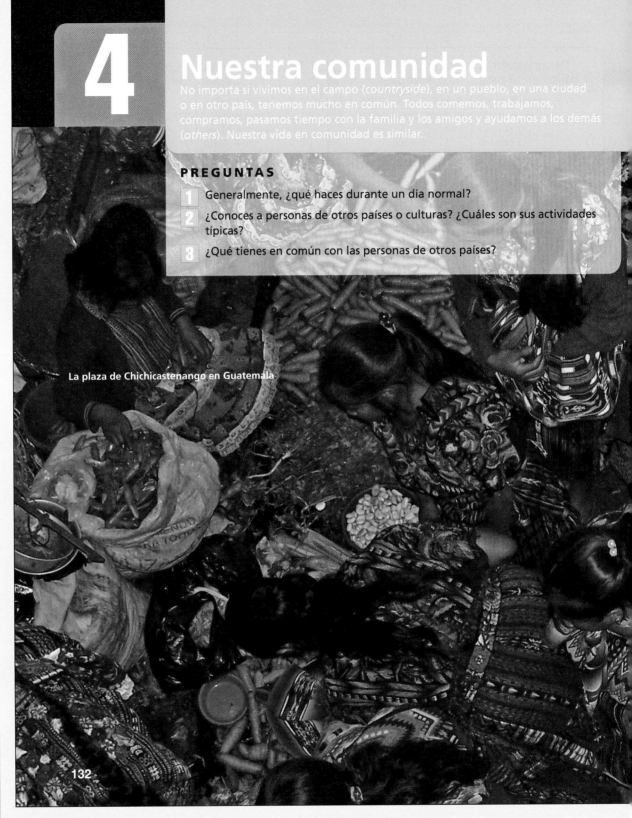

# 4 Nuestra comunidad

No importa si vivimos en el campo (*countryside*), en un pueblo, en una ciudad o en otro país, tenemos mucho en común. Todos comemos, trabajamos, compramos, pasamos tiempo con la familia y los amigos y ayudamos a los demás (*others*). Nuestra vida en comunidad es similar.

### PREGUNTAS

**1** Generalmente, ¿qué haces durante un día normal?

**2** ¿Conoces a personas de otros países o culturas? ¿Cuáles son sus actividades típicas?

**3** ¿Qué tienes en común con las personas de otros países?

La plaza de Chichicastenango en Guatemala

132

**SECTION GOALS for *Chapter opener***
By the end of the Chapter opener section, students will be able to:
• discuss their daily routines.
• reflect about what they have in common with people from other countries.
• identify what it means to be part of a global community.

**SUGGESTION for the *Chapter opener***
Ask students to define *la comunidad*. Write their ideas on the board. Is it the people in the area? Is it the physical location? Is it the architecture and the landmarks? Is it the blending of cultures? Find out what they think the word *community* encompasses and explain that this chapter includes all aspects of community. Ask students to think about what their school community is noted for.

**EXPANSION for *Preguntas***
You may also want to ask your students additional questions regarding the Chapter opener, and we have included a suggestion for a question in Spanish. Remember that they will understand the question in Spanish, but some of your beginning students may need to answer in English. That is pedagogically acceptable, since the goal is for them to demonstrate that they comprehend the question as well as the reading. Additionally, the following question will give you insight into which Spanish-speaking countries interest your students: *¿Qué países quieres conocer? ¿Por qué?*

| OBJETIVOS | CONTENIDOS |
|---|---|

### COMUNICACIÓN I

### COMUNICACIÓN II

### CULTURA

### AMBICIONES SINIESTRAS

### COMUNIDADES

133

**NATIONAL STANDARDS**
*Communities*

The goal of this chapter is for students to learn that although people have different backgrounds and life experiences, each person has similar needs and responsibilities. Volunteerism is a great way to get your students involved in the community, and through doing so they can learn that people are more alike than different. You could start by asking them to brainstorm ideas about what jobs they think are most important to the running of a community (e.g., services such as fire and police, transportation, food, etc.) and then ask them to find a Spanish-speaking person who has each job. You could assign each student to shadow someone with a different job or career so that they may acquire a broader perspective of the jobs that contribute to the success of the community. Depending on the scope and sequence of the assignment, you could also invite community members to class as guest speakers or as members of a panel, or ask that students submit videos of their time on the job which they can post using MediaShare in MySpanishLab.

**PLANNING AHEAD**
You may want to assign **4-3** and **4-14** as homework so that students come prepared to do the tasks in class. For **4-31**, it is useful to have large sheets of newsprint paper and markers for your students, one sheet for every two students. Additionally, as a reminder, it is recommended that you assign the grammar explanations and the culture sections to be read before class. They are written in clear language so that the students will be able to understand them. Then you can maximize use of class time for students to ask for any possible clarification of the grammar and to answer the comprehension and critical-thinking questions that accompany the culture readings.

**METHODOLOGY • Checking for Reading Comprehension**
The text and questions for this chapter opener are completely in Spanish. The reading is at an *i + 1* level for your students. Regarding checking for comprehension, you can use several techniques. If your students are true beginners, allow them to answer in English, since they will be learning new vocabulary in the chapter to help them answer the questions. Some of your beginning students will be able to answer the questions in Spanish, perhaps not as completely as they would like, but they will still be able to communicate. Your heritage language learners will be able to answer the questions in a complete fashion in Spanish.

**SECTION GOALS for**
*Comunicación I*

By the end of the *Comunicación* section, students will be able to:

• identify common buildings and services in a typical city.
• talk about the places they go or errands they run in a city.
• use prepositions to describe where buildings are located in relation to other buildings.
• correctly pronounce the letters *c* and *z*.
• distinguish between *saber* and *conocer*.
• report what chores or tasks they do using *tener* + *que* + infinitive.
• form stem-changing verbs in the present tense.

**NATIONAL STANDARDS**
*Communication*

The activities that follow provide an excellent range that allows students to personalize their new vocabulary. The activities that ask students to name the places in their town, tell where they are located, and explain what services they provide are all communicative in nature. Many of the activities follow Standard 1.1, which asks students to engage in conversations, provide and obtain information, and exchange opinions about various topics. Activity **4-2** can also fulfill Standard 1.3 if you ask students to present the information about "the best of the best." They could each take a photo of their favorite place, create a written document stating why this place is their favorite, and present it to the class. If several students have the same favorite restaurant, you could have them generate an award certificate to the business voted the best by the Spanish class of University X. They might also select their favorite products or services from "the best of the best" and make flyers in Spanish telling why these are their favorite items. This activity is excellent for encouraging discussion and disagreement among your students as they share their opinions.

# Comunicación I

**1 VOCABULARIO**

🔊 📖  04-01 to 04-04

## Los lugares   Identifying places in and around town

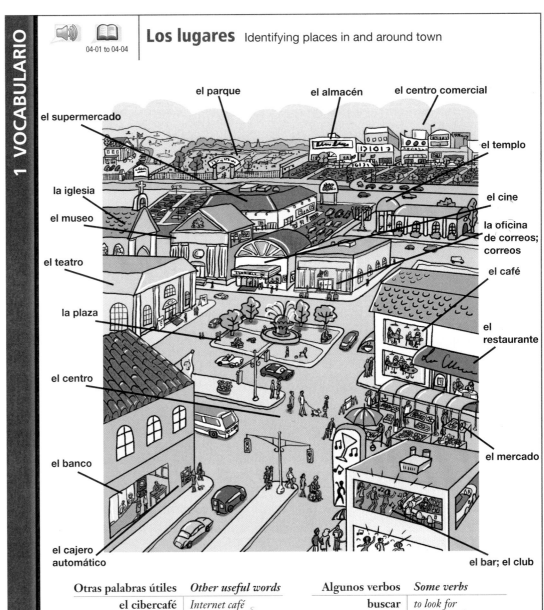

el parque   el almacén   el centro comercial   el supermercado   el templo   la iglesia   el cine   el museo   la oficina de correos; correos   el teatro   el café   la plaza   el restaurante   el centro   el banco   el mercado   el cajero automático   el bar; el club

| Otras palabras útiles | *Other useful words* | Algunos verbos | *Some verbs* |
|---|---|---|---|
| el cibercafé | *Internet café* | buscar | *to look for* |
| la ciudad | *city* | mandar una carta | *to send / mail a letter* |
| la cuenta | *bill; account* | | |
| la película | *movie; film* | | |
| el pueblo | *town; village* | | |

**SECTION GOALS for** *Pronunciación*

By the end of the *Pronunciación* section, students will be able to:

• state the rules of pronunciation for the letter *c*.
• distinguish between the sounds the letters *c* and *z* make.

**NOTE for** *Pronunciación*

MySpanishLab provides pronunciation practice for students with a wide array of native speakers from across the Spanish-speaking world. If your students will have multiple instructors throughout their language coursework, you can also explain that they will hear different accents depending on the instructor.

**METHODOLOGY • Progression of Activities**

In planning your lessons it is important to follow a progression of activities: move from *mechanical* (highly structured, focus on form, one correct answer) to *meaningful* (structured but focus of activity shifts more toward creation of meaning) to *communicative* activities (the learner is afforded the opportunity for true, self-directed communication). In doing so, students are not only better equipped to follow along and succeed, but they also build their confidence.

## PRONUNCIACIÓN

### The letters *c* and *z*

¡Hola!

04-05 to 04-06

Go to MySpanishLab / Student Activites Manual to learn how to pronounce the letters *c* and *z*.

---

Capítulo 2. El verbo
estar, pág. 76.

**4-1** **¿Dónde está?** Tu amigo está muy ocupado. Túrnate con un/a compañero/a para decir dónde está en este momento. ■

**MODELO**   E1:   Quiere mandar una carta.
   E2:   *Está en la oficina de correos.*

1. Quiere ver una película.
2. Necesita dinero para pagar una cuenta.
3. Quiere comer algo (*something*).
4. Quiere ver una exposición de arte.
5. Quiere caminar y hacer ejercicio.
6. Tiene sed y quiere tomar algo.
7. Quiere mandar un email.
8. Tiene que ir a una boda (*wedding*).

**Fíjate**

Note that you use a form of *querer* + *infinitive* to express "to want to _____."
For example:

*Quiero mandar…* = I want to send …

*Queremos ver…* = We want to see …

---

Capítulo Preliminar A.
El verbo *ser*, pág. 13;
Capítulo 2. El verbo
estar, pág. 76.

**4-2** **El mejor de los mejores** ¿Cuáles son, en tu opinión, los mejores lugares en tu comunidad? ■

**Estrategia**

Remember that you learned vocabulary in *Capítulos 2* and *3*, such as *a la derecha, a la izquierda,* and *al lado de* that you can also practice with your new vocabulary.

#### Vocabulario útil

| | |
|---|---|
| **detrás (de)** | *behind* |
| **enfrente (de)** | *in front (of)* |
| **estar de acuerdo** | *to agree* |
| **el/la mejor** | *the best* |
| **el/la peor** | *the worst* |

**Paso 1**   Haz (*Make*) una lista de los mejores lugares de tu pueblo o ciudad según las siguientes categorías.

**MODELO**   E1:   restaurante
   E2:   *El mejor restaurante es* The Lantern.

1. almacén
2. banco
3. centro comercial
4. cine
5. café
6. teatro
7. tienda
8. restaurante
9. supermercado

*(continued)*

---

---

**EXPANSION for *Los lugares***

As your students learn more prepositions of location, have them get copies of your campus map to keep track of the new words. Have them each label the building where they attend most of their classes and the building where they live, work, study, or park their car. Then have students write down how the buildings are related to one another in Spanish (behind, in front of, next to, etc.). This will help them remember the prepositions.

**SUGGESTION for 4-3**

To save class time, ask your students to draw their maps for **4-3** as homework.

**METHODOLOGY • Active Listening**

It is important to provide students with active listening opportunities: hence the progression of **4-3**.

**NATIONAL STANDARDS**
*Cultures, Comparisons, Communities*

The *Nota cultural* reading, *Actividades cotidianas: Las compras y el paseo*, addresses the Goal Areas of Cultures, Comparisons, and Communities. In particular, Standards 2.1 and 2.2 refer to the practices, perspectives, and products of Hispanic cultures. By reading about shopping and daily activities, students learn about where shopping takes place, the types of products or services one can buy, and why for many Hispanic countries *la plaza* is the center of daily life. They also learn about how local businesses or shops are more common in Hispanic cultures than the giant malls and superstores typically found in the United States. Standard 4.2 is about developing insight into the nature of language and culture by making comparisons between Hispanic cultures and the students' cultures. The cultural reading also prepares them to participate in Hispanic communities in the United States and abroad by highlighting the differences in daily activities, illustrating how social the weekends are, and preparing them for shopping in cities.

---

| Paso 2 | Compara tu lista con las listas de los otros estudiantes de la clase. ¿Están de acuerdo? |
| MODELO | E1: *En mi opinión, el mejor restaurante es* The Lantern. *¿Estás de acuerdo?* |
| | E2: *No, no estoy de acuerdo. El mejor restaurante es* The Cricket. |
| Paso 3 | Túrnense para explicar dónde están los mejores lugares. |
| MODELO | E1: *Busco el mejor restaurante.* |
| | E2: *El mejor restaurante es* The Lantern. |
| | E1: *¿Dónde está?* |
| | E2: *Está al lado del Banco Nacional.* |

**Fíjate**

A reminder from *Capítulo 3*: The preposition *de* combines with the masculine singular definite article *el* to form the contraction *del*. The feminine article *la* does not contract.

---

[9:00] 🍦 **4-3** **Chiquimula y mi ciudad...**

Chiquimula es un pueblo de 24.000 personas que está en el este de Guatemala. ■

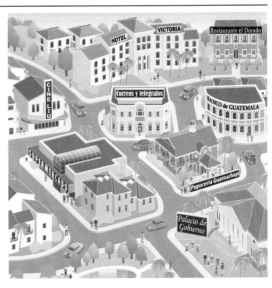

**Paso 1** Túrnense para describir el centro del pueblo. Mencionen dónde están los edificios principales.

**MODELO** *El Hotel Victoria está al lado del Restaurante el Dorado...*

**Paso 2** Ahora dibuja (*draw*) un mapa del centro de tu pueblo o ciudad. El dibujo debe incluir los edificios principales. Después, túrnense para describirlo oralmente.

**Paso 3** Túrnense para describir sus dibujos mientras tu compañero/a dibuja lo que dices.

---

[2:00] **NOTA CULTURAL**

## Actividades cotidianas: Las compras y el paseo 🔊 📖

04-07 to 04-08

En los Estados Unidos, la gente hace gran parte de las compras en los centros comerciales. En los países hispanohablantes, también se hacen las compras en los centros comerciales, especialmente en las ciudades grandes. En Guatemala, Honduras y El Salvador algunos de los más conocidos son Hiper Paiz, Maxi Bodega y Despensa Familiar.

**Instructor Resources**
• PPT, Extra Activities

**ANSWERS to *Nota cultural***

1. En las ciudades grandes hay centros comerciales. En los pueblos pequeños hay tiendas de todo tipo, oficinas de correos, bancos y restaurantes. También hay bullicio, especialmente durante los fines de semana. La gente va de compras, se encuentra para conversar y pasea por las calles y los parques.
2. *Answers may vary.*

En los pueblos pequeños la gente va al centro de la ciudad. En el centro está el mercado y hay muchas tiendas además de la oficina de correos, el banco y los restaurantes. Se puede encontrar gente de todas las clases sociales y muchos vendedores ambulantes (*roving*).

Otro lugar importante en el centro de los pueblos es la plaza. Allí se encuentra la gente (*people meet*) para conversar, pasear, ir de compras o ir a la iglesia. Además, los lugareños (*locals*) pasean a diario por las calles principales y los parques del pueblo. En los pueblos hispanos siempre hay mucho bullicio (*hubbub*) y actividad, especialmente los fines de semana.

### Preguntas

1. En los países hispanohablantes, ¿qué hay en las ciudades grandes? ¿Cómo son los pueblos pequeños? ¿Qué hace la gente todos los días?
2. ¿Dónde prefieres comprar, en las tiendas pequeñas o en los centros comerciales? ¿Por qué?

> **Fíjate**
>
> Note that the word *gente*, unlike the word *people* in English, is singular: *La gente **va** al centro de la ciudad. Gente*, although made up of more than one person, is considered a collective noun like the singular nouns *la clase*, *el equipo*, and *la familia*.

## 2 GRAMÁTICA

04-09 to 04-12

## *Saber y conocer* Stating whom and what is known

¿Sabes dónde hay un cibercafé?

No, no conozco muy bien la ciudad.

In **Capítulo 3**, you learned that **conocer** means *to know*. Another verb, **saber**, also expresses *to know*.

> **Fíjate**
>
> Note that *conocer* and *saber* both have irregular *yo* forms: *conozco* and *sé* respectively.

**saber (*to know*)**

| Singular | | Plural | |
|---|---|---|---|
| yo | **sé** | nosotros/as | **sabemos** |
| tú | **sabes** | vosotros/as | **sabéis** |
| Ud. | **sabe** | Uds. | **saben** |
| él, ella | **sabe** | ellos/as | **saben** |

*(continued)*

**METHODOLOGY • Chunking Information Into Smaller Parts**
You will note that we have "chunked" the presentation of *conocer* and *saber* as follows:
**Step 1:** Introduce *conocer* and its forms in *Capítulo 3*.
**Step 2:** Introduce *saber* and its forms here in *Capítulo 4*, reminding students that they have already learned the forms of *conocer*, and then comparing and contrasting the two verbs. We have chosen to briefly introduce the *personal "a"* here in *Capítulo 4* with *conocer*, and then reintroduce/recycle it in *Capítulo 5* with direct object pronouns. The focus in *Capítulo 4* is to make students aware of the concept. In *Capítulo 5*, there will be further practice with direct object pronouns as well as recycling of the *personal "a"* with *conocer*.

**SUGGESTION for *conocer***
Refer students to *Capítulo 3* to review the forms of *conocer*.

The verbs are not interchangeable. Note when to use each.

## CONOCER

- Use **conocer** to express *being familiar or acquainted with people, places, and things.*

  Ellos **conocen** los mejores restaurantes de la ciudad.    *They know the best restaurants in the city.*

  Yo **conozco** a tu hermano, pero no muy bien.    *I know your brother, but not very well.*

### Note:

1. When expressing that *a person* is known, you must use the personal "a." For example: **Conozco** *a* **tu hermano**…
2. When **a** is followed by **el, a + el = al.** For example: **Conozco** **al** **señor (a + el señor)**…

## SABER

- Use **saber** to express *knowing facts, pieces of information,* or *how to do something.*

  ¿Qué **sabes** sobre la música de Guatemala?    *What do you know about Guatemalan music?*

  Yo **sé** tocar la guitarra.    *I know how to play the guitar.*

> **Fíjate**
>
> A form of *saber* + *infinitive* expresses knowing how to do something. For example:
>
> *Sé nadar.* = I know how to swim.
>
> *Sabemos tocar la guitarra.* = We know how to play the guitar.

---

[2:00]  **4-4** **¿Sabes o conoces?** Completa las siguientes preguntas usando **sabes** o **conoces.** Después, túrnate con un/a compañero/a para hacer y contestar las preguntas. ■

**MODELO**    E1:   *¿Conoces San Salvador?*

         E2:   *Sí, conozco San Salvador. / No, no conozco San Salvador.*

1. ¿__Sabes__ usar una computadora?
2. ¿__Conoces__ al presidente del Banco Central?
3. ¿__Sabes__ dónde hay un cajero automático?
4. ¿__Conoces__ Tegucigalpa, Honduras?
5. ¿__Conoces__ el mejor restaurante mexicano?
6. ¿__Sabes__ llegar a la oficina de correos?
7. ¿__Conoces__ las películas de James Cameron?
8. ¿__Sabes__ cuál es el mejor café de esta ciudad?

**4-5** **¿Qué sabemos de Honduras?** Completen juntos el diálogo con las formas correctas de **saber** y **conocer.** ∎

PROF. DOMÍNGUEZ: ¿Qué (1) ___saben___ ustedes sobre Honduras?

DREW: Yo (2) ___sé___ que la capital de Honduras es Tegucigalpa.

DREW Y TANYA: Nosotros (3) ___sabemos___ mucho sobre el país.

PROF. DOMÍNGUEZ: ¿Y (4) ___saben___ ustedes cómo se llaman las personas de Honduras?

TANYA: Sí, se llaman *hondureños*. (5) ___Conocemos___ la cultura hondureña bastante bien. Nuestra hermana, Gina, es una estudiante de intercambio allí este año y nos manda muchas fotos y cartas. Ella (6) ___conoce___ a mucha gente interesante, incluso al hijo del Presidente.

PROF. DOMÍNGUEZ: ¡No me digan! ¿Estudia allí su hermana? ¿(7) ___Saben___ ustedes que hay dos universidades muy buenas en Tegucigalpa?

TANYA: Sí, el novio de Gina estudia allí, pero yo no (8) ___sé___ en qué universidad. Él es salvadoreño y nuestros padres no lo (9) ___conocen___ todavía. Gina dice que no quiere volver a los Estados Unidos. Yo (10) ___sé___ que mis padres van a estar muy tristes si ella no vuelve.

PROF. DOMÍNGUEZ: Yo (11) ___conozco___ a tu hermana y (12) ___sé___ que es una mujer inteligente. Va a pensarlo bien antes de tomar una decisión.

 **4-6** **¿Me puedes ayudar?**

Sofía acaba de llegar a San Salvador y se siente un poco perdida (*she is feeling a little lost*). Túrnense para hacer y contestar sus preguntas de manera creativa. Luego, creen (*create*) y contesten **dos** preguntas más usando **saber** y **conocer.** ∎

MODELO    SOFÍA: *¿Sabes dónde hay una iglesia?*

TÚ: *Sí, sé que hay una iglesia en la plaza.*

1. ¿Conoces un buen restaurante típico?
2. ¿Sabes dónde está el restaurante?
3. ¿Sabes qué tipo de comida sirven en el restaurante?
4. ¿Conoces al cocinero (*chef*)?
5. ¿?
6. ¿?

**21ST CENTURY SKILLS •
THINKING CREATIVELY**

The Partnership for 21st Century Skills values highly creativity and innovation. Supported are creation techniques such as brainstorming. In *¡Anda!*, students are frequently encouraged to brainstorm with a partner to creatively use new and recycled vocabulary and grammar in recombined, real-life contexts.

**Instructor Resources**
• Textbook images, PPT, Extra Activities

**METHODOLOGY • Chunking**
A common pedagogical technique for breaking up complex tasks is to chunk information into manageable bits. We have done that with stem-changing verbs and the *¿Qué tienen que hacer? ¿Qué pasa?* presentation. These verbs are presented first as vocabulary and then as stem-changing verbs. Practicing them as infinitives first helps students focus on and learn their meanings. The next step will be to introduce them as stem-changing verbs in the following grammar presentation on page 142.

**METHODOLOGY •**
**Constructing Knowledge**
Since the 1940s and 1950s, educational researchers have explored how we learn and what assists in learning. We now know that when learners *construct knowledge,* the knowledge becomes internalized and transfers into long-term memory. On the other hand, memorizing lists, for example, goes into short-term memory but usually does not transfer into long-term memory. There are many learning devices that help students retain information. Mnemonic devices assist in learning. So does connecting vocabulary with visual images. The *"Where's Waldo?"* style visuals for *¿Qué tienen que hacer? ¿Qué pasa?* help students learn the new verbs. Students may need to consult the *Vocabulario activo* pages at the end of the chapter to clarify/negotiate meaning, but that task helps them associate a visual image with a vocabulary word and acquire the word. The same concept is true with the vocabulary in *Servicios a la comunidad* on page 149. These visuals will be excellent to use when you are introducing or practicing new tenses, since the students will have associated these verbs with the images.

**NOTE for *Vocabulario***
Remind students that in *Capítulo 3* they learned some expressions with *tener.* They will recall that *tener + que + infinitive* means "to have to do something."

## 3 VOCABULARIO

04-13 to 04-16

### ¿Qué tienen que hacer? ¿Qué pasa?
Relating common obligations and activities

**4-7 Tic-tac-toe** Escucha mientras tu instructor/a explica el juego del tic-tac-toe. ■

*Capítulo 1. El verbo tener, pág. 34.*

MODELO    E1:  *¿Tienes "volver"?*
            E2:  *Sí, tengo "volver". / No, no tengo "volver".*

**INSTRUCTIONS for 4-7**
While at first glance this activity may seem too simple, it provides excellent practice with the new verbs. Provide these instructions to your students:
    Make a tic-tac-toe grid on a sheet of paper. Write a different verb from the list of new verbs in each of the nine boxes. Do not show your grid to your partner. Take turns guessing the words your partner has selected. Each time you guess correctly, your partner marks an X over the word. The first person to have three "X" in a row, either horizontally, vertically, or diagonally, wins. You may also want to require that students provide the English equivalents of the three infinitives in a row.

**NOTE for 4-8**
This activity works well as review or "filler" activity when you have groups that finish early. They can go back and review verbs or vocabulary words while waiting for other groups to finish.

**NATIONAL STANDARDS**
*Communication*
Note that these stem-changing verbs are first practiced in their infinitive form. Then, in **4-9** and **4-10,** students utilize the *tener que…* grammar point that they learned in the previous chapter. This is an excellent form of recycling, and it is a meaningful exercise for students, since they always have to do something!

Standard 1.1 focuses on an interpersonal exchange for Communication. The stem-changing verbs such as *dormir, preferir, almorzar, entender, pensar,* etc. facilitate communication about things that students are familiar with. They can use the new verbs to exchange their opinions (*pensar*), express feelings and emotions (*preferir, pensar*), and provide and obtain information about each other (*almorzar, dormir, entender, recordar,* etc.) and how these verbs relate to their daily lives.

  **4-8** **¿Y lo opuesto?** Decidan juntos qué verbo expresa lo opuesto (*opposite*) de cada una de las palabras o expresiones de la siguiente lista. ■

**MODELO**    E1:  no comer por la tarde
              E1:  *almorzar*

| repetir | encontrar | volver | entender | pedir |
|---------|-----------|--------|----------|-------|
| perder  | comenzar  | querer | cerrar   | almorzar |

1. salir  volver
2. terminar  comenzar
3. abrir  cerrar
4. perder  encontrar
5. decir una vez  repetir
6. dar  pedir
7. encontrar  perder
8. no comprender  entender

---

**Estrategia**
Make an attempt to work with a different partner in every class. This enables you to help and learn from a variety of your peers, an important and highly effective learning technique.

**Fíjate**
Remember that in *Capítulo 3* you learned that *tener + que + infinitive* means "to have to do something."

  **4-9** **Los quehaceres** Túrnense para expresar qué tienen que hacer ustedes generalmente. ■

**MODELO**    Tengo que encontrar…
              E1:  *Tengo que encontrar mi libro de español.*
              E2:  *Tengo que encontrar los apuntes para la clase de español.*

1. Tengo que comenzar…
2. Tengo que repetir…
3. Tengo que pedir…
4. Tengo que recordar…
5. Tengo que almorzar…
6. Tengo que dormir…

Capítulo 2. La sala de clase, pág. 65; Presente indicativo de verbos regulares, pág. 67.

---

**EXPANSION for 4-10**
You may also want to ask your students the following questions or add them to the list of interview questions in this activity:
*¿Qué tienes que hacer para ayudar a tus amigos?*
*¿Qué tienes que hacer para ayudar a tu familia?*
*¿Qué cosas tienes que buscar con frecuencia?*

**4-10** **Entrevistas** Entrevista a tres compañeros para averiguar si (*to find out whether*) hacen cosas similares. Después, comparte la información con la clase. ¿Qué tienen ustedes en común? ■

1. ¿Qué tienes que hacer para prepararte bien para las clases?
2. ¿Qué tienes que hacer durante la clase de español para sacar buenas notas?
3. Generalmente, ¿qué tienes que hacer cuando terminas con tus clases?

### Instructor Resources
• PPT, Extra Activities

**NOTE for *Los verbos con cambio de raíz***
Remind students that there are two types of grammar presentations in *¡Anda! Curso elemental:*
1. Presentations in which they are given the grammar rule.
2. Presentations in which they are given guiding questions to help *them* construct the grammar rule and state the rule in their own words.

**METHODOLOGY • Inductive Grammar Presentations**
Research reports that students learn best from inductive grammar approaches. So you might ask, why not present *all* grammar inductively? The main reason is that the inductive approach takes more time, and some grammar points do not merit the additional time, e.g., the formation of regular verbs, or when to use *saber* and *conocer.*

**NOTE for *Gramática***
This is an inductive grammar presentation in which the students are given examples of a grammar concept and, through the use of guiding questions, they formulate the rule in their own words. Research indicates that students remember and internalize grammar rules better when they construct their own knowledge.

**NOTE for *Los verbos con cambio de raíz***
True beginners may have difficulty replacing the stem when there are multiple vowels in the verb. In the case of *repetir,* you should highlight that the first *e* stays the same and the second *e* makes the change. Tell students to remember where the change occurs in *seguir* by taking the *-ir* ending off: they are left with *segu.* They are learning that the stem change occurs with *e* and *i,* so that should make it clearer.

**SUGGESTION for *Los verbos con cambio de raíz***
Some Spanish language learners find it helpful to remember these stem-changing verbs by the name *shoe verbs.* Draw a line around the forms of the verb that *do* have the spelling changes. The verb forms that *do not* have the spelling changes (*nosotros / vosotros*) are "outside" the shoe.

---

## 4 GRAMÁTICA

04-17 to 04-24

### Los verbos con cambio de raíz  Expressing actions

> ¡Cierro la ventana, pido una pizza y empiezo a estudiar!

In **Capítulo 3,** you learned a variety of common verbs that are irregular. Two of those verbs were **querer** and **poder,** which are irregular due to some changes in their stems. Look at the following verb groups and answer the questions regarding each group.

### Change e → ie

**cerrar (*to close*)**

| Singular | | Plural | |
|---|---|---|---|
| yo | cierro | nosotros/as | cerramos |
| tú | cierras | vosotros/as | cerráis |
| Ud. | cierra | Uds. | cierran |
| él, ella | cierra | ellos/as | cierran |

### ¡Explícalo tú!
1. Which verb forms look like the infinitive **cerrar**?
2. Which verb forms have a spelling change that differs from the infinitive **cerrar**?

✔ Check your answers to the preceding questions in Appendix 1.

Other verbs like **cerrar** (**e → ie**) are:

| | | | | | |
|---|---|---|---|---|---|
| **comenzar** | *to begin* | **mentir** | *to lie* | **preferir** | *to prefer* |
| **empezar** | *to begin* | **pensar** | *to think* | **recomendar** | *to recommend* |
| **entender** | *to understand* | **perder** | *to lose; to waste* | | |

### Change e → i

**pedir (*to ask for*)**

| Singular | | Plural | |
|---|---|---|---|
| yo | pido | nosotros/as | pedimos |
| tú | pides | vosotros/as | pedís |
| Ud. | pide | Uds. | piden |
| él, ella | pide | ellos/as | piden |

### ¡Explícalo tú!
1. Which verb forms look like the infinitive **pedir**?
2. Which verb forms have a spelling change that differs from the infinitive **pedir**?

✔ Check your answers to the preceding questions in Appendix 1.

Other verbs like **pedir** (**e → i**) are:

**repetir** *to repeat*     **seguir*** *to follow; to continue (doing something)*     **servir** *to serve*

*Note: The **yo** form of **seguir** is **sigo.**

## Change o → ue

### encontrar (*to find*)

|  | Singular |  | Plural |
|---|---|---|---|
| yo | encuentro | nosotros/as | encontramos |
| tú | encuentras | vosotros/as | encontráis |
| Ud. | encuentra | Uds. | encuentran |
| él, ella | encuentra | ellos/as | encuentran |

### ¡Explícalo tú!

1. Which verb forms look like the infinitive **encontrar**?
2. Which verb forms have a spelling change that differs from the infinitive **encontrar**?

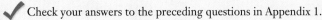 Check your answers to the preceding questions in Appendix 1.

Other verbs like **encontrar** (o → ue) are:

| | | | | | | | |
|---|---|---|---|---|---|---|---|
| **almorzar** | *to have lunch* | **dormir** | *to sleep* | **mostrar** | *to show* | **volver** | *to return* |
| **costar** | *to cost* | **morir** | *to die* | **recordar** | *to remember* | | |

## Change u → ue

### jugar (*to play*)

|  | Singular |  | Plural |
|---|---|---|---|
| yo | juego | nosotros/as | jugamos |
| tú | juegas | vosotros/as | jugáis |
| Ud. | juega | Uds. | juegan |
| él, ella | juega | ellos/as | juegan |

### ¡Explícalo tú!

1. Which verb forms look like the infinitive **jugar**?
2. Which verb forms have a spelling change that differs from the infinitive **jugar**?
3. Why does **jugar** not belong with the verbs like **encontrar**?

 Check your answers to the preceding questions in Appendix 1.

### ¡Explícalo tú!

**To summarize . . .**

1. What rule can you make regarding all four groups of stem-changing verbs and their forms?
2. With what group of stem-changing verbs would you put **querer**?
3. With what group of stem-changing verbs would you put each of the following verbs?

| | | | |
|---|---|---|---|
| **demostrar** | *to demonstrate* | **encerrar** | *to enclose* |
| **devolver** | *to return (an object)* | **perseguir** | *to chase* |

Check your answers to the preceding questions in Appendix 1.

[5:00]  **4-11** Categorías

Paso 1   With a partner, write the stem-changing verbs that were just presented on individual slips of paper. Next, make a chart with four categories: **e → ie, e → i, o → ue,** and **u → ue.**

Paso 2   Join another pair of students. When your instructor says **¡Empieza!,** place each verb under the correct category (**e → ie, e → i, o → ue,** or **u → ue**). Do several rounds of this activity, playing against different doubles partners.

[2:00]  **4-12** Nuestras preferencias  Averigua cuáles son las preferencias de tu compañero/a. Luego, comparte tus respuestas con la clase. ■

MODELO   el cine o el teatro

E1:  ¿Qué prefieres, el cine o el teatro?

E2:  Prefiero el cine.

**¿Qué prefieres,…?**

1. correr en el parque o en el gimnasio
2. comer en un restaurante o en un café
3. visitar un gran almacén o un centro comercial
4. comprar comida (*food*) en un supermercado o en un mercado al aire libre (*open-air*)
5. trabajar en un banco o en una oficina de correos
6. conversar con amigos en un bar o en una plaza

[5:00]  **4-13** ¿Quién hace qué?  Túrnense para decir qué personas que ustedes conocen hacen las siguientes cosas. ■

MODELO   E1:  siempre perder la tarea

E2:  *Mi hermano Tom siempre pierde la tarea.*

1. pensar ser profesor/a
2. almorzar en McDonald's a menudo
3. querer visitar Sudamérica
4. siempre entender al/a la profesor/a de español
5. preferir dormir hasta el mediodía
6. volver tarde a casa a menudo
7. perder dinero
8. pensar que Santa Claus existe
9. nunca mentir
10. comenzar a hacer la tarea de noche

**4-14 ¿Quién eres?** Escribe las respuestas a las siguientes preguntas en forma de párrafos. ■

### Primer párrafo

1. ¿Qué clases tienes este semestre?
2. ¿A qué hora empieza tu clase preferida? ¿Cuándo termina?
3. ¿Qué prefieres hacer si (*if*) tienes tiempo entre (*between*) tus clases?
4. ¿A qué hora vuelves a tu dormitorio/ apartamento/casa?

### Segundo párrafo

1. ¿Qué carro tienes (o quieres tener)? ¿Cuánto cuesta un carro nuevo?
2. ¿Cómo vienes a la universidad? (Por ejemplo, ¿vienes en carro?)
3. ¿Dónde prefieres vivir, en una residencia estudiantil, en un apartamento o en una casa?
4. ¿Dónde quieres vivir después de graduarte?

### Tercer párrafo

1. ¿Qué deporte y/o pasatiempo prefieres?
2. Si es un deporte, ¿juegas a ese deporte? ¿Ves ese deporte en la televisión?
3. Normalmente, ¿cuándo y con quién(es) juegas el deporte / disfrutas (*enjoy*) el pasatiempo?
4. ¿Qué otros deportes y pasatiempos te gustan?

## ¿Cómo andas? I

| | Feel confident | Need to review |
|---|:---:|:---:|
| Having completed **Comunicación I**, I now can . . . | | |
| • identify places in and around town (p. 134) | ☐ | ☐ |
| • pronounce the letters *c* and *z* (MSL/SAM) | ☐ | ☐ |
| • describe shopping and other daily activities in Spanish-speaking countries (p. 136) | ☐ | ☐ |
| • state whom and what is known (p. 137) | ☐ | ☐ |
| • relate common obligations and activities (p. 140) | ☐ | ☐ |
| • express actions (p. 142) | ☐ | ☐ |

**METHODOLOGY • Recycling**
Activity **4-14** is an excellent recycling activity for previously learned grammar structures. Recycling is extremely important, as it helps your students review and recombine vocabulary and structures that help increase their linguistics skills.

**SUGGESTION for 4-14**
Activity **4-14** should be assigned as homework to save time in class.

**SUGGESTION for 4-14**
Select and read as many of the writing samples from **4-14** as time permits. This can also be done during the warm-up segments of several subsequent classes. You may want to have students guess who wrote each one as you read them aloud.

**SUGGESTION for 4-14**
In the second paragraph, question 4, students will have to answer *Quiero vivir… después de graduarme.* Since they do not know about reflexive verbs yet, you can tell them in advance how to answer and explain that this will be presented at a later point. Otherwise you could tell them to say… *después de la graduación.*

**ADDITIONAL ACTIVITY for**
*Los verbos con cambio de raíz*
**¡Preparados, listos, ya!**
A practicar. Escucha mientras tu profesor/a explica esta actividad.
**INSTRUCTIONS:** Form teams of equal size with at least four people, but no more than six. Team members sit in a row, one behind the other, facing the chalkboard. The first team member writes the subject pronouns *out of order* on the left side of a piece of paper, as in the model *tú, nosotros, ella, yo, ustedes, ellos.* You, the instructor, write a stem-changing verb on the board. The first team member in each row writes the *tú* form of the verb next to the pronoun and quickly passes the paper to the team member behind him/ her. The next team member has to write the *nosotros* form and pass the paper to the next team member, and so on. Any team member may correct any of his/ her teammates' previous answers if they are incorrect. The final person in the row brings (or runs!) the team's answers to you. The first group to get all of the verb forms correct gets five points, the second group gets four, and so forth. This activity is extremely successful with all types of students. It is an excellent activity to repeat when reviewing any and all verb tenses.
    A variation is: The first team to finish (Team A) gets five points, but the other team (Team B) has the opportunity to earn some points as well. Team B may ask Team A one form of any three verbs they choose. For any verb form that Team A gets incorrect, Team B gets a point.

## SECTION GOALS for *Comunicación II*

By the end of the *Comunicación* section, students will be able to:

- form the verb *ir* correctly.
- combine what they have to do (*tener + que + infinitive*) with where they go (*ir*) to do it.
- construct sentences in the periphrastic future using *ir + a + infinitive*.
- discuss jobs and volunteer work.
- use negative and affirmative indefinite expressions.
- demonstrate their understanding of how *ser* and *estar* are used.

## METHODOLOGY • Presenting Information as Needed

We instructors love the Spanish language and are eager to share what we know with our students, yet sometimes we share more than students can grasp at a time. Too much information can confuse students and can also cause a raising of what Stephen Krashen calls the *affective filter,* where the students become hesitant to produce language for fear of making a mistake with the vast amount of information they have been given. If you feel that your students will benefit from a more in-depth presentation (e.g., heritage language learners), then please provide it.

## SUGGESTION for *El verbo ir*

After drilling *ir* forms mechanically by giving subjects and having students give the matching verb forms, practice with directed questions, such as *¿Adónde vas mañana? ¿Adónde vas de vacaciones? ¿Adónde van tus amigos este fin de semana?*

## SUGGESTION for *El verbo ir*

Create a substitution drill for students to practice the different forms of *ir*. Highlight the portions of the sentence the students should replace with different information. Encourage them to be creative and create as many versions as possible.

**MODELO**

*Esta mañana Li-Ling va a la biblioteca porque tiene que estudiar. Después de cuatro horas, su compañera de cuarto y ella van al banco. Esta noche Li-Ling y yo vamos a un restaurante para comer con nuestros amigos.*

# Comunicación II

04-25 to 04-27

## 5 GRAMÁTICA

### El verbo *ir*   Sharing where you and others are going

Voy al almacén. ¿Adónde vas tú?

Another important verb in Spanish is **ir**. Note its irregular present tense forms.

**ir (*to go*)**

| Singular | | Plural | |
|---|---|---|---|
| yo | voy | nosotros/as | vamos |
| tú | vas | vosotros/as | vais |
| Ud. | va | Uds. | van |
| él, ella | va | ellos/as | van |

**Voy** al parque. ¿**Van** ustedes también?
No, no **vamos** ahora. Preferimos **ir** más tarde.

*I'm going to the park. Are you all going too?*
*No, we're not going now. We prefer to go later.*

---

**4-15 ¿Adónde vas?** Túrnense para completar la conversación que tienen Memo y Esteban al salir de la clase de música. Usen las formas correctas del verbo **ir**. ■

**Fíjate**

In *Capítulo 2* you learned two words for the question word "Where?" Use *¿Adónde?* with *ir*.

**Fíjate**

Remember that *a + el = al*.

MEMO:   Hola, Esteban. ¿Adónde (1) ___vas___ ahora?

ESTEBAN:   ¿Qué hay? Pues, (2) ___voy___ a la clase de física.

MEMO:   Ah sí. Bueno, mi compañero de cuarto y yo (3) ___vamos___ al gimnasio. Tenemos un torneo *(tournament)* de tenis.

ESTEBAN:   Buena suerte. Oye, ¿tú (4) ___vas___ a la fiesta de Isabel esta noche?

MEMO:   No sé. ¿Quiénes (5) ___van___? Creo que (yo) (6) ___voy___ al cine para ver la película nueva de Steven Spielberg.

ESTEBAN:   ¿Por qué no (7) ___vas___ primero a la fiesta y después al cine?

MEMO:   Buena idea. ¿(8) ___Vamos___ (tú y yo) juntos?

ESTEBAN:   Muy bien. Mi amigo Roberto (9) ___va___ también. Hablamos después del torneo.

MEMO:   Bueno, hasta luego.

---

**4-16 Los "¿por qué?"** Esperanza tiene una sobrina que está en la etapa de los "¿por qué?" Tiene muchas preguntas. Túrnense para darle las respuestas de Esperanza a Rosita. ■

**MODELO**   ROSITA:   ¿Por qué va mi papá al gimnasio?

          ESPERANZA:   *Tu papá va al gimnasio porque quiere hacer ejercicio.*

1. ¿Por qué va mi mamá al mercado?
2. ¿Por qué va mi hermana a la oficina de correos?
3. ¿Por qué van mis hermanos al parque?
4. ¿Por qué vas a la universidad?
5. ¿Por qué no vamos al cine ahora?

---

## ADDITIONAL ACTIVITY for *El verbo ir*

**Hoy es sábado y…** En grupos de 6 a 8 personas, túrnense para decir adónde van. Luego, tienen que repetir lo que dice cada persona.

**MODELO**

E1: *Hoy es sábado y esta mañana voy al gimnasio.*

E2: *Hoy es sábado y Jim va al gimnasio y yo voy a Krispy Kreme para comer donas.*

E3: *Hoy es sábado y Jim va al gimnasio, Carla va a Krispy Kreme y yo voy a la biblioteca…*

🍦🍦 **4-17 ¿Adónde van?** Miren los horarios de las siguientes personas.
Túrnense para decir adónde van, a qué hora y qué hacen en cada (*each*) lugar. ∎

Capítulo Preliminar A:
La hora, pág. 18.

| Mis padres | Mi hermano | Yo |
|---|---|---|

**MODELO**     *A las diez mis padres van a la librería para comprar unos libros. Luego…*

## 6 GRAMÁTICA

📖
04-28 to 04-30

# *Ir + a + infinitivo*  Conveying what will happen in the future

¿Vamos a
almorzar pronto?
¡Tengo hambre!

Sí. Voy a
pedir comida
guatemalteca.

Study the following sentences and then
answer the questions that follow.

—**Voy a mandar** esta carta. ¿Quieres ir?          *I'm going to mail this letter. Do you want to go?*
—Sí. Luego, **¿vas a almorzar?**                    *Yes. Then, are you going to have lunch?*
—Sí, **vamos a comer** comida guatemalteca.         *Yes, we are going to eat Guatemalan food.*
—¡Perfecto! **Voy a pedir** unos tamales.           *Perfect! I am going to order some tamales.*
—Pero, primero, **¡vamos a ir** al banco.           *But first we are going to the bank!*

### ¡Explícalo tú!

1. When do the actions in the previous sentences take place: in the *past*, *present*, or *future*?
2. What is the first bold type verb you see in each sentence?
3. In what form is the second bolded verb?
4. What word comes between the two verbs? Does this word have an equivalent in English?
5. What is your rule, then, for expressing future actions or statements?

✔ Check your answers to the preceding questions in Appendix 1.

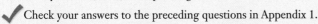

🔑 **Instructor Resources**
• PPT, Extra Activities

**EXPANSION for 4-17**
Have students write out their own
schedules for a particular day, or week,
and share with classmates. Who is
busiest? Who has the most exciting
schedule? Who has more study time?
Who goes to the most places? etc.

**NOTE for *Gramática***
This is an inductive grammar
presentation in which the students
are given examples of a grammar
concept and, through the use of guiding
questions, they formulate the rule in
their own words. Research indicates
that students remember and internalize
grammar rules better when they
construct their own knowledge.

**NATIONAL STANDARDS**
*Communication*
Speaking in the future tense is one of the
main time frames. When an individual
can sustain communication in the
present, future, and past tenses, they are
emerging into the ACTFL Advanced Level
of oral proficiency.
    The new verb *ir* and the *ir + a +
infinitive* construction allow students
a greater range of communication,
because they can talk about where they
are going and what they are doing in
the immediate future. Learning the new
construction provides more opportunities
for communication in the interpersonal
mode (Standard 1.1), as they engage
in conversations about their plans and
provide and obtain information. The *ir
+ a + infinitive* construction works well
with Standard 1.3, because students are
able to present about their future plans
to an audience of listeners or readers.
With the appropriate vocabulary, they can
communicate their weekend plans, what
they want to do after they graduate, how
they will spend the next 5 years, and the
characteristics of their ideal mate. You
could also ask them to predict what their
hometown or university town will be like
in 10 years.

**SUGGESTION for *ir + a +
infinitivo***
After the initial presentation, the following
directed questions can be used to
practice *ir + a + infinitive*. They can also
be used as warm-up questions to begin a
class: ¿*Cuándo vas a almorzar? ¿Cuándo
vas a trabajar? ¿Cuándo vas a hacer tu
tarea? ¿Adónde vas a estudiar? ¿Qué
vas a estudiar? ¿Cuándo vas a limpiar tu
casa? ¿Cuándo vas a lavar los platos?
¿Adónde vas a ir este verano?*

**4-18** **¿Y en el futuro?** Túrnense para contestar las siguientes preguntas sobre el futuro. ■

1. ¿Vas a dedicar más tiempo a tus estudios?
2. Después de terminar con tus estudios, ¿vas a vivir en una ciudad, un pueblo pequeño o en el campo?
3. ¿Vas a vivir en una casa grande?
4. ¿Tus amigos y tú van a visitar Honduras u otro país en Centroamérica?
5. ¿Vamos a encontrar la cura para el cáncer?
6. ¿Vamos a poder acabar con (*end*) el terrorismo?

Capítulo Preliminar A. Los días de la semana, los meses y las estaciones, pág. 20.

**4-19** **Mi agenda** ¿Qué planes tienes para la semana que viene? Termina las siguientes frases sin (*without*) repetir los quehaceres. ■

MODELO       E1:  El lunes…

              E2:  *El lunes voy a pasar la aspiradora.*

1. El lunes…
2. El martes…
3. El miércoles…
4. El jueves…
5. El viernes…
6. El sábado…
7. El domingo…
8. El fin de semana…

**4-20** **Qué será, será…** ¿Qué tiene el futuro para ti, tus amigos y tu familia? Escribe **cinco** predicciones de lo que va a ocurrir en el futuro. ■

MODELO       *Mi primo va a ir a la Universidad Autónoma el año que viene. Mis padres van a limpiar el armario y el altillo este fin de semana. Yo voy a estudiar en Sudamérica…*

**NATIONAL STANDARDS**
*Communication, Connections, Communities*
This vocabulary connects with other disciplines, such as health care professions. It also provides students with ideas of where they can use Spanish in their community. Some of your institutions require or encourage community service projects, and this vocabulary connects directly with many university offerings or initiatives. This vocabulary also ties in well with the chapter title *Nuestra comunidad*.

The vocabulary in the section, *Servicios a la comunidad*, provides a glimpse into the many types of volunteer work and paid work available to students. Ask the career center of your school what types of volunteer jobs are available and bring that information to class. Standards 1.1 and 1.3 apply to volunteer work because students can communicate interpersonally about the types of work they would like to do and they can present about the types of work. To integrate Standard 1.3, ask students each to research a particular volunteer position (or internship) available in their community and make a presentation to the class about their job. You could also invite a local organization in need of Spanish-speaking volunteers to present to students. Standard 3.1 states that students reinforce and further their knowledge of other disciplines through Spanish. Have the students research internships or volunteer positions that tie in with their majors so that they make connections and they are able to work in the community, applying their majors and the skills they have acquired in Spanish (Standard 5.1).

**7 VOCABULARIO**

04-31 to 04-36

# Servicios a la comunidad

Imparting information about service opportunities

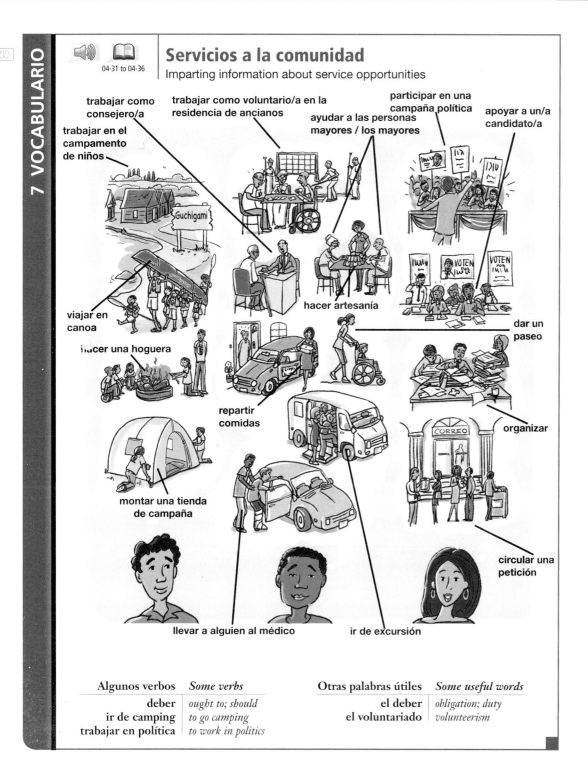

trabajar como consejero/a

trabajar como voluntario/a en la residencia de ancianos

participar en una campaña política

ayudar a las personas mayores / los mayores

apoyar a un/a candidato/a

trabajar en el campamento de niños

viajar en canoa

hacer artesanía

hacer una hoguera

dar un paseo

repartir comidas

organizar

montar una tienda de campaña

circular una petición

llevar a alguien al médico

ir de excursión

| Algunos verbos | *Some verbs* | Otras palabras útiles | *Some useful words* |
|---|---|---|---|
| deber | *ought to; should* | el deber | *obligation; duty* |
| ir de camping | *to go camping* | el voluntariado | *volunteerism* |
| trabajar en política | *to work in politics* | | |

**4-21** **Definiciones** Túrnense para leer las siguientes definiciones y decir cuál de las palabras o expresiones del vocabulario de **Servicios a la comunidad** corresponde a cada una. ■

**MODELO**    E1:  personas que tienen muchos años

              E2:  *las personas mayores*

1. salir en un bote (*boat*) para una o dos personas
2. dar un documento a personas para obtener firmas (*signatures*)
3. "construir" una estructura portátil (no permanente) que se usa para dormir fuera de casa
4. acompañar a una persona a una cita (*appointment*) con el médico
5. trabajar con niños en un campamento
6. servir a las personas sin recibir dinero a cambio (*in exchange*)
7. disfrutar de (*enjoy*) un tipo de arte que puedes crear con materiales diversos
8. un lugar donde van los niños, generalmente en el verano, para hacer muchas actividades diferentes
9. trabajar para un candidato político
10. un lugar donde viven las personas mayores

Capítulo 2. El verbo *gustar*, p. 80.

  **4-22** **En tu opinión...** Termina las siguientes oraciones sobre el voluntariado. Después, comparte tus respuestas con un/a compañero/a. ■

**MODELO**    *Yo soy una consejera perfecta porque me gustan los niños. También sé escuchar muy bien…*

1. Yo (no) soy un/a consejero/a perfecto/a porque…
2. Dos trabajos voluntarios que me gustan son…
3. Hay muchas residencias de ancianos en los Estados Unidos porque…
4. Yo apoyo al candidato _____ porque…
5. Cuando repartes comidas, puedes…

 **4-23** **Elaborando el tema** En grupos de tres o cuatro, discutan las siguientes preguntas. ■

1. ¿Cuáles son las actividades más interesantes en los campamentos de niños?
2. ¿Cuáles son las oportunidades de voluntariado que existen en tu universidad/iglesia/templo?
3. ¿Cuáles son los trabajos voluntarios que se asocian más con apoyar a un candidato?
4. ¿Crees que servir a la comunidad es un deber?

## NOTA CULTURAL

### La conciencia social

04-37

Tanto en los Estados Unidos como en los países hispanohablantes, la gente se interesa cada día más en servir a la comunidad. Su conciencia social se puede manifestar tanto *(as much as)* en un trabajo remunerado *(job with a salary)* como en trabajos voluntarios: por ejemplo, ser entrenadores de deportes, llevar a los ancianos a pasear por los centros comerciales, trabajar para los congresistas, etc. En los Estados Unidos muchos trabajos voluntarios tienen que ver con *(are related to)* las personas mayores o con los jóvenes.

#### Preguntas

1. ¿Cuáles son algunos trabajos voluntarios comunes en los Estados Unidos?
2. ¿Cómo sirves a tu comunidad?

## 8 GRAMÁTICA

  ¡Hola!

04-38 to 04-40 | English Tutorial

### Las expresiones afirmativas y negativas
Articulating concepts and ideas both affirmatively and negatively

Siempre me gusta hacer artesanía con los niños, ¡pero jamás voy a ir en una canoa con ellos!

In the previous chapters, you have seen and used a number of the affirmative and negative expressions listed on the following page. Study the list, and learn the ones that are new to you.

*(continued)*

**NOTE for Gramática**
This is an inductive grammar presentation in which the students are given examples of a grammar concept and, through the use of guiding questions, they formulate the rule in their own words. Research indicates that students remember and internalize grammar rules better when they construct their own knowledge.

**Instructor Resources**
• PPT, Extra Activities

**NATIONAL STANDARDS**
*Communication, Connections, Communities*
The *Nota cultural* reading, *La conciencia social,* provides a starting point for discussing how students can help others in the community. Students can engage in conversations about how they contribute to the community and whether they feel they are doing enough to participate in their community (Standard 1.1). They can also brainstorm with other students to use what they are learning in their programs of study and apply their content knowledge to improving the community (3.1). Lastly, depending upon the size of the Hispanic population in your area, students could think of ways to serve the community now, during their experience as college students (Standard 5.1) or use *ir + a + infinitive* to talk about how they might combine their Spanish skills and their majors to serve the community after they graduate (Standard 5.2).

**NOTE for *Nota cultural***
The concept of volunteerism is expanding throughout the Spanish-speaking world, but still may not exist to the degree that it exists in the United States. In the United States, many schools and communities have highly developed programs for volunteering. In some schools, it is a requirement to volunteer a certain number of hours each year.

**ANSWERS to *Nota cultural***
1. *Answers may include:* participar en una campaña política, ayudar a las personas mayores, repartir comida, llevar a alguien al médico, trabajar como voluntario en un hospital, etc.
2. *Answers will vary.*

**METHODOLOGY • Maximizing Class Time**
None of us ever has enough class time to do what we feel is important and necessary. The authors of *¡Anda! Curso elemental* are committed to helping students spend as much of the class period as possible speaking Spanish. Hence, as was suggested from the beginning, we highly recommend that all of the culture readings are assigned to be read before class, especially as they become longer.

| Expresiones afirmativas | | Expresiones negativas | |
|---|---|---|---|
| **a veces** | *sometimes* | **jamás** | *never; not ever* (emphatic) |
| **algo** | *something; anything* | **nada** | *nothing* |
| **alguien** | *someone* | **nadie** | *no one; nobody* |
| **algún** | *some; any* | **ningún** | *none* |
| **alguno/a/os/as** | *some; any* | **ninguno/a/os/as** | *none* |
| **siempre** | *always* | **nunca** | *never* |
| **o… o** | *either . . . or* | **ni… ni** | *neither . . . nor* |

Look at the following sentences, paying special attention to the position of the negative words, and answer the questions that follow.

—¿Quién llama?               *Who is calling?*
—**Nadie** llama. (**No** llama **nadie.**)    *No one is calling.*
—¿Vas al gimnasio todos los días?    *Do you go to the gym every day?*
—No, **nunca** voy. (No, **no** voy **nunca.**)    *No, I never go.*

> **Fíjate**
> Unlike English, Spanish can have two or more negatives in the same sentence. A double negative is actually quite common. For example, *No tengo nada que hacer* means *I don't have anything to do.*

### ¡Explícalo tú!

1. When you use a negative word (**nadie, nunca,** etc.) in a sentence, does it come before or after the verb?
2. When you use the word **no** and then a negative word in the same sentence, does **no** come before or after the verb? Where does the negative word come in these sentences?
3. Does the meaning change depending on where you put the negative word (e.g., **Nadie llama** *versus* **No llama nadie**)?

 Check your answers to the preceding questions in Appendix 1.

## *Algún* and *ningún*

1. Forms of **algún** and **ningún** need to agree in gender and number with the nouns they modify.
2. **Alguno** and **ninguno** are shortened to **algún** and **ningún** when they are followed by *masculine, singular nouns.*
3. When no noun follows, use **alguno** or **ninguno** when referring to masculine, singular nouns.
4. The plural form **ningunos** is rarely used.

Study the following sentences.

MARÍA:   ¿Tienes **alguna** clase fácil este semestre?
JUAN:   No, no tengo **ninguna.** ¡Y **ningún** profesor es simpático!
MARÍA:   Vaya, ¿y puedes hacer **algún** cambio?
JUAN:   No, no puedo hacer **ninguno.** (No, no puedo tomar **ningún** otro curso.)

Workbooklet

## 4-24 ¿Con qué frecuencia?

Indica con qué frecuencia tus compañeros/as de clase hacen las siguientes actividades. Escribe el nombre de cada compañero/a debajo de la columna apropiada y comparte los resultados con la clase. ■

**MODELO** ir de excursión con niños

*A veces Josefina va de excursión con niños.*

|  | SIEMPRE | A VECES | NUNCA |
|---|---|---|---|
| 1. ir de excursión con niños | | Josefina | |
| 2. participar en una campaña política | | | |
| 3. hacer una hoguera | | | |
| 4. circular una petición | | | |
| 5. firmar una petición | | | |
| 6. repartir comidas a los mayores | | | |
| 7. visitar una residencia de ancianos | | | |
| 8. trabajar en un campamento para niños | | | |
| 9. trabajar como voluntario en un hospital o una clínica | | | |
| 10. dormir en una tienda de campaña | | | |

Capítulo 2. La sala de clase, pág. 65; En la universidad, pág. 74.

## 4-25 El/La profesor/a ideal

Túrnense para decir si las siguientes características son ciertas (*true*) o no en un/a profesor/a ideal. ■

**MODELO**
E1: a veces duerme en su trabajo
E2: *No. Un profesor ideal nunca duerme en su trabajo.*
E1: jamás va a clase sin sus apuntes
E2: *Sí, un profesor ideal jamás va a clase sin sus apuntes.*

**Un/a profesor/a ideal...**

1. siempre está contento/a en su trabajo.
2. a veces llega a clase cinco minutos tarde.
3. prepara algo interesante para cada clase.
4. piensa que sabe más que nadie.
5. falta (*misses*) a algunas clases.
6. nunca pone a los estudiantes en grupos.
7. jamás asigna tarea para la clase.
8. siempre prefiere leer sus apuntes.
9. no pierde nada (la tarea, los exámenes, etc.).
10. no habla con nadie después de la clase.

 **Instructor Resources**
• PPT, Extra Activities

[3:00]  **4-26** **¿Sí o no?** Túrnense para contestar las siguientes preguntas. ∎

MODELO
   E1: *¿Siempre almuerzas a las cuatro de la tarde?*
   E2: *No, nunca almuerzo a las cuatro de la tarde. / No, no almuerzo nunca/jamás a las cuatro de la tarde.*

1. ¿Pierdes algo cuando vas de vacaciones?
2. ¿Siempre encuentras las cosas que pierdes?
3. ¿Siempre montas una tienda de campaña cuando vas de camping?
4. ¿A veces vas de excursión con tus amigos?
5. ¿Siempre almuerzas en restaurantes elegantes?
6. ¿Conoces a alguien de El Salvador?
7. ¿Siempre piensas en el amor (*love*)?
8. ¿Hay algo más importante que el dinero?

[2:00]  **4-27** **No tienes razón** Tu amigo/a es muy idealista. Túrnense para decirle (*tell him/her*) que debe ser más realista, usando expresiones negativas. ∎

MODELO

1. Tengo que buscar una profesión sin estrés.
2. Quiero el carro perfecto, un Lexus.
3. Voy a tener hijos perfectos.
4. Pienso que no voy a estudiar la semana que viene.
5. Voy a encontrar unos muebles muy baratos (*cheap*) y elegantes.

---

[5:00]  **9 GRAMÁTICA** 📖 04-41 to 04-45

## Un repaso de *ser* y *estar*
Describing states of being, characteristics, and location

You have learned two Spanish verbs that mean *to be* in English. These verbs, **ser** and **estar**, are contrasted here.

### SER

**Ser** is used:

• **To describe physical or personality characteristics that remain relatively constant**

| | |
|---|---|
| Gregorio **es** inteligente. | *Gregorio is intelligent.* |
| Yanina **es** guapa. | *Yanina is pretty.* |
| Su tienda de campaña **es** amarilla. | *Their tent is yellow.* |
| Las casas **son** grandes. | *The houses are large.* |

**NOTE for *Gramática***
This is an inductive grammar presentation in which the students are given examples of a grammar concept and, through the use of guiding questions, they formulate the rule in their own words. Research indicates that students remember and internalize grammar rules better when they construct their own knowledge.

**NOTE for reviewing *Ser* and *estar***
Remind students that when using *ser* to say what or who someone or something is, as in the case of professions, they should omit the indefinite article (*un, una, unos, unas*) before the noun: *El Dr. Suárez es profesor de literatura* (Dr. Suárez is a professor of literature).

**HERITAGE LANGUAGE LEARNERS**
Remind heritage language learners that while *¡Anda! Curso elemental* has presented the basic rules about most concepts, there are subtle rules and exceptions that exist, for example, with *ser* and *estar*. The more subtle differences will be explained at a later point, although they may well be aware of those differences now. If you choose to individualize instruction, you may wish to spend a brief amount of time with your heritage language learners discussing some of the additional uses of *ser* and *estar*.

- **To explain what or who someone or something is**

El Dr. Suárez **es** profesor de literatura.          *Dr. Suárez is a literature professor.*
Marisol **es** mi hermana.                            *Marisol is my sister.*

- **To tell time, or to tell when or where an event takes place**

¿Qué hora **es**?                                     *What time is it?*
**Son** las ocho.                                     *It's eight o'clock.*
Mi clase de español **es** a las ocho y              *My Spanish class is at eight o'clock and*
    **es** en Peabody Hall.                               *is in Peabody Hall.*

- **To tell where someone is from and to express nationality**

**Somos** de Honduras.                                *We are from Honduras.*
**Somos** hondureños.                                 *We are Honduran.*
Ellos **son** de Guatemala.                           *They are from Guatemala.*
**Son** guatemaltecos.                                *They are Guatemalan.*

## ESTAR

**Estar** is used:

- **To describe physical or personality characteristics that can change, or to indicate a change in condition**

María **está** enferma hoy.                           *María is sick today.*
Jorge y Julia **están** tristes.                      *Jorge and Julia are sad.*
La cocina **está** sucia.                             *The kitchen is dirty.*

- **To describe the locations of people, places, and things**

El museo **está** en la calle Quiroga.               *The museum is on Quiroga Street.*
**Estamos** en el centro comercial.                   *We're at the mall.*
¿Dónde **estás** tú?                                  *Where are you?*

---

### ¡Explícalo tú!

Compare the following sentences and answer the questions that follow.

Su hermano **es** simpático.
Su hermano **está** enfermo.

1. Why do you use a form of **ser** in the first sentence?
2. Why do you use a form of **estar** in the second sentence?

> **Estrategia**
> Review the forms of *ser* (p. 13) and *estar* (p. 76).

✔ Check your answers to the preceding questions in Appendix 1.

---

You will learn several more uses for **ser** and **estar** by the end of *¡Anda! Curso elemental*.

**ADDITIONAL ACTIVITY for** *Un repaso de* ser y estar

**Pero yo…** Completa los siguientes pasos.

**Paso 1** Escribe una oración (verdadera para ti) para los siguientes usos de *ser* y *estar*.

1. your origin
2. what you are (student, brother, relationship to another person, etc.)
3. time of your first class (*primera clase*) on Monday
4. location of that class
5. what the professor of that class is like
6. brief description of you
7. brief description of how you feel today
8. location of an upcoming event on or around campus

**Paso 2** Túrnense para compartir sus oraciones.

**MODELO**
E1:  *Soy de Austin, Texas. ¿Y tú?*
E2:  *Yo no soy de Austin. Soy de Little Rock, Arkansas. Soy estudiante. ¿Y tú?*
E1:  *Soy estudiante, pero también soy mecánico. Los lunes tengo clase de biología a las ocho. ¿A qué hora es tu primera clase?…*

**ADDITIONAL ACTIVITY for** *Ser y estar*

**Quiero conocerte mejor**
Túrnense para hacer y contestar las siguientes preguntas.

1. ¿De dónde eres?
2. ¿Cómo eres?
3. ¿Cómo estás hoy?
4. ¿A qué hora son tus clases?
5. ¿Cómo es tu casa?
6. ¿Dónde está tu casa?
7. ¿De qué color es tu casa?
8. ¿Dónde está tu dormitorio?
9. ¿Cómo es tu dormitorio?
10. ¿Cuál es tu color favorito?
11. Describe la persona más importante para ti.
12. ¿Dónde está él/ella ahora (*now*)?

You may wish to tell your students to interpret *casa* in this activity as either *casa*, *apartamento*, or *residencia estudiantil*.

**6:00** **4-28** **¿Y Margarita?** Estér y Margarita son estudiantes de la Universidad Francisco Marroquín en la ciudad de Guatemala. Ellas tienen clase ahora pero Margarita no llega. Completen juntos el siguiente párrafo con las formas correctas de **ser** o **estar** para conocerla mejor. ∎

**Paso 1**

(1) _____Son_____ las siete y media de la mañana. Nuestra clase de física (2) _____es_____ a las ocho y siempre vamos juntas. Bueno, ¿dónde (3) _____está_____ Margarita? Es raro porque ella (4) _____es_____ muy puntual y no le gusta llegar tarde. Yo (5) _____soy_____ su mejor amiga y sé que (6) _____está_____ preocupada por sus abuelos. Ellos (7) _____son_____ mayores y a veces (8) _____están_____ enfermos. Margarita (9) _____es_____ muy responsable y ayuda mucho a sus abuelos. Toda su familia (10) _____es_____ de la ciudad de Antigua y siempre piensa en ellos. Aqui viene Margarita, ¡menos mal!

**Paso 2** Expliquen por qué usaron (*you used*) **ser** o **estar** en **Paso 1.**
**MODELO** 1. (*Son*) telling time

**1:00** **4-29** **Nuestro conocimiento** ¿Qué sabes de Guatemala, Honduras y El Salvador? Túrnense para hacerse y contestar las siguientes preguntas. ∎

1. ¿Dónde están estos países: en Norteamérica, Centroamérica o Sudamérica?
2. ¿Cuál está más cerca de México? ¿Cuál está más cerca de Panamá?
3. ¿Son países grandes o pequeños?
4. ¿Cuáles son sus capitales?

**5:00** **4-30** **¡A jugar!** Vamos a practicar **ser** y **estar**. ∎

**Paso 1** Draw two columns on a piece of paper labeling one **ser** and the other **estar**. Write as many sentences as you can in the three minutes you are given.

**Paso 2** Form groups of four to check your sentences and uses of the verbs.

**10:00** **4-31** **Somos iguales**

**Paso 1** Draw **three** circles, as per the model below, and ask each other questions to find out what things you have in common and what sets you apart. In the center circle write sentences using **ser** and **estar** about things you have in common, and in the side circles write sentences about things that set you apart.

**MODELO** E1: *¿Cuál es tu color favorito?*
E2: *Mi color favorito es el negro.*
E1: *Mi color favorito es el negro también.*
E2: *Hoy estoy nerviosa. ¿Cómo estás tú?*
E1: *Yo estoy cansado.*

**Paso 2** Share your diagrams with the class. What are some of the things that all of your classmates have in common?

Hoy estoy nerviosa. | Nuestro color favorito es el negro. | Hoy estoy cansado.

**ESCUCHA**

## El voluntariado

04-46

| Estrategia | When you know the context and listen carefully, you can repeat or paraphrase what you hear. Start by saying one | or two words about what you hear and work up to complete sentences. |
|---|---|---|
| **Paraphrasing what you hear** | | |

**4-32** **Antes de escuchar** Do you volunteer? What service opportunities exist in your city/town? You are going to hear a conversation between Marisol and Lupe, in which Marisol shares her experiences with volunteering. Think of three Spanish words dealing with volunteering that you might hear. ■

Marisol y Lupe conversan sobre el trabajo voluntario.

**4-33** **A escuchar** After listening to the conversation for the first time, note three main points, words, or topics. After listening a second time, paraphrase their conversation with at least **three** complete sentences. You may use the following questions to guide your listening. ■

1. ¿Quién hace trabajo voluntario?
2. ¿Qué trabajo hace ella en la escuela? ¿Qué más quiere hacer?
3. ¿Adónde va a ir mañana? ¿Con quién?

 **4-34** **Después de escuchar** Form **three** sentences about your volunteering experiences, and tell them to your classmate. Your classmate will paraphrase what you have said. ■

**SECTION GOALS for** *Escucha*

By the end of the *Escucha* section, students will be able to:

- paraphrase what they hear in short sentences.
- practice brainstorming in pre-listening activities for words they might hear.
- narrate how they volunteer and repeat what their classmates say about volunteering.

**NATIONAL STANDARDS**
*Communication*

The listening strategy for *Capítulo 4* is paraphrasing what you hear. This section represents Standard 1.2 as students listen, understand, and interpret what they have heard. Students also use Standard 1.1, the interpersonal mode, when they pair off and discuss volunteerism. The practice in a small group lends itself well to reinforcing the new strategy of paraphrasing.

**AUDIOSCRIPT for 4-33**

LUPE:    Marisol, ¿es verdad que tú haces trabajo voluntario?

MARISOL:    Sí, para mí el voluntariado es muy importante.

LUPE:    ¿Qué tipo de trabajo haces?

MARISOL:    Pues, me gusta trabajar con los niños. Generalmente voy a la escuela y los ayudo con la tarea.

LUPE:    ¿Qué más?

MARISOL:    Quiero trabajar en el hospital. Quiero visitar a los pacientes y llevarles las comidas.

LUPE:    ¿Vas a hacer trabajo voluntario ahora que estás en la universidad?

MARISOL:    Pienso que sí. Mañana voy a ir al hospital. Quiero saber si hay oportunidades. ¿Quieres venir?

LUPE:    ¡Sí! Quiero ir también.

**ANSWERS to 4-33**
*Answers may include:* Marisol hace trabajo voluntario. En la escuela ayuda a los niños con la tarea. Quiere trabajar en el hospital y visitar a los pacientes y llevarles las comidas. Mañana va a ir con Lupe al hospital.

# ¡CONVERSEMOS!
04-47

**4-35  Mi comunidad**  You and a partner are on the planning commission(s) of your town(s). Take turns sharing your ideas with the other commissioners, stating at least **five** positive aspects of your town and **five** areas that could be improved. You should also respond to your partner's ideas, agreeing or disagreeing. Use vocabulary words *Los lugares,* on page 134, and verbs from page 140, *¿Qué tienen que hacer? ¿Qué pasa?*  ▪

**4-36  Servicio a nuestra comunidad**  Your college has a community service component, and you are a coordinator for these services. With a partner, take turns describing the opportunities available to fellow students in your town(s) or school community. Create at least **ten** sentences using the vocabulary *Servicio a la comunidad* on page 149.  ▪

**ESCRIBE**

## Una tarjeta postal (*A postcard*)

04-48

| Estrategia | It is important to always carefully read over what you have written to check for meaning and accuracy. You want to minimally: <br>• verify spelling. <br>• check all verb forms. | • confirm that subjects and verbs, as well as nouns and adjectives, agree in number and gender. <br>• review for appropriate meaning. |
|---|---|---|
| Proofreading | | |

**4-37 Antes de escribir** Escribe una lista de los lugares importantes o interesantes de tu pueblo o ciudad. Luego escribe por qué son importantes o interesantes. Usa el vocabulario de este capítulo y de **También se dice…** en el Apéndice (*Appendix*) 3. ▪

**4-38 A escribir** Organiza tus ideas usando las siguientes preguntas como guía. Escribe por lo menos **cinco** oraciones completas. Puedes consultar el modelo. ▪

> Querido/a_____:
>
> Tienes que conocer mi pueblo, Roxborough. Hay _____. Me gusta(n) _____. Es interesante porque _____. Los fines de semana _____.
>
> Con cariño,
> __(Tu nombre)__

1. ¿Qué lugares hay en tu pueblo o ciudad?
2. ¿Por qué son importantes o interesantes?
3. Normalmente, ¿qué haces allí?
4. ¿Adónde vas los fines de semana?
5. ¿Qué te gusta de tu pueblo?

**4-39 Después de escribir** Tu profesor/a va a recoger las tarjetas y "mandárselas" (*mail them*) a otros miembros de la clase para leerlas. Luego, la clase tiene que escoger los lugares que desean visitar. ▪

## ¿Cómo andas? II

| | Feel confident | Need to review |
|---|---|---|

Having completed **Comunicación II,** I now can . . .

- share where I and others are going (p. 146) ☐ ☐
- convey what will happen in the future (p. 147) ☐ ☐
- impart information about service opportunities (p. 149) ☐ ☐
- discuss the concept of social consciousness (p. 151) ☐ ☐
- articulate concepts and ideas both affirmatively and negatively (p. 151) ☐ ☐
- describe states of being, characteristics, and location (p. 154) ☐ ☐
- paraphrase what I hear (p. 157) ☐ ☐
- communicate about ways to serve the community (p. 158) ☐ ☐
- write a postcard and proofread it for accuracy (p. 159) ☐ ☐

04-49, 04-52

## Honduras

César Alfonso Ávalos

## Les presento mi país

Mi nombre es César Alfonso Ávalos y soy de La Ceiba, Honduras, una ciudad en el Mar Caribe que está cerca de unas islas hondureñas bellas (*beautiful*) y muy interesantes. Mi lugar favorito para visitar es Utila, bien conocido en el mundo por el buceo (*scuba diving*). **¿Te gusta bucear?** Mi país tiene un pasado cultural muy rico, ya que los mayas viven aquí desde la época precolombina. Las ruinas más importantes que tenemos están en Copán. **¿Hay ruinas importantes cerca de tu pueblo?**

La playa de Utila,
Islas de la Bahía

Un charancaco
(*basilisk*) de la
isla Roatán

Las ruinas de Copán

### ALMANAQUE

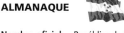

**Nombre oficial:** República de Honduras

**Gobierno:** República democrática constitucional

**Población:** 7.989.415 (2010)

**Idiomas:** español (oficial); miskito, garífuna, otros dialectos amerindios

**Moneda:** Lempira (L)

### ¿Sabías que...?

• El nombre original de esta región es *Higüeras*, que es el nombre de una planta nativa. Al llegar a la costa norteña, Cristóbal Colón renombra la región *Honduras* a causa de la profundidad del agua en la bahía.

### Preguntas

1. ¿Qué significa *Honduras*? ¿De dónde viene el nombre?
2. ¿Quiénes son los habitantes originales de Copán?
3. ¿Qué semejanzas hay entre Honduras y México?

 Amplía tus conocimientos sobre Honduras en MySpanishLab.

**161**

---

**NOTE for *El charancaco***

Honduras is home to a stunning array of animals:

• More than 210 species of mammals including monkeys, jaguars, pumas, anteaters, armadillos, coyotes, deer, foxes, peccaries, pocket gophers, porcupines, and tapirs.

• More than 95 species of amphibians and reptiles such as the bushmaster, coral snake, fer-de-lance, horned viper, rattlesnake, whip snake, caiman, crocodile, and iguana.

• 715 species of tropical birds including the toucan, black robin, hummingbird, macaw, nightingale, thrush, partridge, quail, quetzal, toucanet, and wren.

• Numerous varieties of freshwater and saltwater fish and turtles.

**NOTE for *La playa de Utila, Islas de la Bahía***

The small island of Utila, part of the Honduran Bay Islands, is known for excellent scuba diving and snorkeling. It lies 18 miles off shore the Honduran port town of La Ceiba and is only 11 kilometers long and 4 kilometers wide.

**EXPANSION for *¿Sabías qué...?***

Ask students about names of places in the United States and their meanings. If your students are not native to the United States, ask about their home countries.

---

### Instructor Resources

• Text images (maps), Video Resources

**SECTION GOALS for *Cultura***

By the end of the *Cultura* section, students will be able to:

• identify the ruins of Copán in Honduras.

• describe how Honduras was named.

• identify the Mayan ruins and pyramids of Tikal, Guatemala.

• compare the indigenous populations and languages of Honduras, Guatemala, and El Salvador.

• discuss geographical features of Honduras, Guatemala, and El Salvador including coastal areas, mountains, and volcanoes.

• highlight the similarities and differences between Honduras, Guatemala, and El Salvador.

**NATIONAL STANDARDS**

*Cultures, Comparisons*

This three-page culture spread introduces students to basic information about Honduras, Guatemala, and El Salvador. Encourage students to compare and contrast these three Central American countries to each other as well as to the other feature countries up to this point.

The *Les presento mi país* section compares the cultural information of Honduras, Guatemala, and El Salvador. Goal Two, Cultures, states that students gain knowledge and understanding of the cultures of the world. These readings encompass the practices, perspectives, and products of Hispanic cultures (Standards 2.1, 2.2). They present information about the indigenous people, the local economy, the tourism sector, pastimes, geography, and flora and fauna. Students are able to compare (Standard 4.2) the cultures of Honduras, Guatemala, and El Salvador with their own culture.

**ANSWERS to *Preguntas***

1. Significa *profunda;* de Cristóbal Colón, por la profundidad del agua en la bahía
2. Los mayas en la época precolombina
3. Ruinas, la presencia maya (You may also want to discuss comparisons beyond the scope of the reading to geography, history, food, etc.)

**NOTE for *El charancaco***

A *charancaco* (basilisk), also known as *monkey lala*, is one of most interesting animals on Roatan Island, Honduras. They move like miniature dragons on two legs with their finlike crests expanded. These long-toed relatives of the iguanas can actually hydroplane across water with their forelegs folded and the long tail lifted, creating the appearance of walking on water.

**Instructor Resources**
• Text images (maps), Video Resources

**NOTE for *Tajumulco***
Tajumulco is the highest volcano in Central America and the highest elevation in Guatemala. It is 4,220 meters high, which is 13,845 feet. It is a peak in the Sierra Madre de Chiapas mountain range, which extends from southern Mexico into Guatemala. It is possible to climb this volcano.

**SUGGESTION for *Tajumulco***
Ask students whether they have climbed a mountain or volcano. What was the experience like?

**NOTE for *Tikal***
The Tikal National Park in northern Guatemala is a stunning archeological discovery. Covering an area of 222 square miles, much of the ruins are surrounded by jungle and have yet to be excavated. The University of Pennsylvania assisted in the initial excavation and restoration between 1956 and 1969. Work continued under the Proyecto Nacional Tikal, University of San Carlos in Guatemala, and the Instituto de Antropología e Historia. It is said to be the largest excavated site in the American continent.

**ANSWERS to *Preguntas***
1. Hay muchas montañas y volcanes.
2. Español y 23 idiomas amerindios reconocidos oficialmente. En total, 24 oficialmente.
3. México y Honduras

**NOTE for *Antigua***
A UNESCO World Heritage Site, the city is a gem of Spanish architecture and is full of historic buildings, monuments, fountains and ruins.

# Cultura

## Guatemala

CULTURA • CULTURA • CULTURA • C ... ...A • C

04-50, 04-53

Luis Pedro Aguirre Maldonado

# Les presento mi país

Mi nombre es Luis Pedro Aguirre Maldonado y soy de Antigua, Guatemala. Muchas personas vienen a mi ciudad para estudiar en nuestras excelentes escuelas de lengua española. **¿Visitan muchas personas tu ciudad o pueblo?** Mi país es montañoso (*mountainous*) con muchos volcanes, como el gran Tajumulco, y algunos de ellos son muy activos. También hay ruinas mayas muy antiguas, como las de Tikal y algunas de nuestras pirámides son las más altas de las Américas. **¿En qué otros lugares encuentras pirámides?**

Un templo muy alto de Tikal es El Gran Jaguar.

Tajumulco es el volcán más alto de Centroamérica y la montaña más alta de Guatemala.

Antigua, la primera capital de Guatemala

**ALMANAQUE**

**Nombre oficial:** República de Guatemala
**Gobierno:** República democrática constitucional
**Población:** 13.550.440 (2010)
**Idiomas:** español (oficial); idiomas amerindios (23 reconocidos oficialmente)
**Moneda:** Quetzal (Q)

## ¿Sabías que...?

• Los mayas tienen un calendario civil, *El Haab*. Consiste en 18 "meses" de 20 días cada uno. Los últimos cinco días del año, conocidos como *el Wayeb*, se consideran de muy mala suerte.

## Preguntas

1. Nombra dos cosas que sabes de la geografía guatemalteca.
2. ¿Cuántos idiomas se hablan en Guatemala?
3. ¿Qué otros países tienen herencia maya?

 Amplía tus conocimientos sobre Guatemala en MySpanishLab.

162

# El Salvador

04-51, 04-54

Claudia Figueroa Barrios

## Les presento mi país

Mi nombre es Claudia Figueroa Barrios. Soy de La Libertad, al sur de nuestra capital San Salvador. Mi ciudad está en la costa del Pacífico cerca de la playa El Sunzal, donde mucha gente practica los deportes acuáticos. **¿Te gustan los deportes acuáticos?** El Salvador es el único país de Centroamérica que no tiene costa caribeña. En mi casa viven tres generaciones de mi familia y nos gusta mucho la comida salvadoreña, como las pupusas. **¿Cuál es tu comida favorita?**

Las pupusas son la comida nacional de El Salvador.

La playa El Sunzal es un lugar excelente para el surfing, el snorkeling y el buceo.

En la antigüedad, los mayas usaron (*used*) granos de cacao como dinero.

GUATEMALA

HONDURAS

Lago de Güija
Río Lempa
SIERRA MADRE
Santa Ana
Ilobasco
Lago de Ilopango
San Salvador ★ ▲ **EL SALVADOR**
La Libertad
San Miguel
Golfo de Fonseca
NICARAGUA

OCÉANO PACÍFICO

---

## ALMANAQUE

**Nombre oficial:** República de El Salvador
**Gobierno:** República democrática constitucional
**Población:** 6.052.064 (2010)
**Idioma:** español (oficial)
**Moneda:** Dólar estadounidense

## ¿Sabías que...?

• Algunos salvadoreños, sobre todo los que viven en las partes rurales del país, van a los curanderos (*folk healers*) para buscar ayuda médica.

## Preguntas

1. ¿Qué importancia tiene el cacao en la historia maya?
2. ¿Qué deportes practican en El Salvador?
3. ¿Qué cosas de El Salvador son únicas o diferentes a las de otros países hispanos?

 Amplía tus conocimientos sobre El Salvador en MySpanishLab.

**163**

---

**Instructor Resources**
• Text images (maps), Video Resources

**SUGGESTION for *El Salvador***
Ask students: How are El Salvador and the United States similar? How are they different? What do you have in common with people your age in El Salvador, Guatemala, and Honduras?

**NOTE for *El Sunzal***
The beach at El Sunzal is touted as one of the ten best places in the world for surfing. It is also ideal for other aquatic sports, such as snorkeling and scuba diving.

**SUGGESTION for *El Sunzal***
Ask students what aquatic sports are popular at beaches they may have visited. Also, ask them what factors make some coastal areas better suited than others for specific activities. For example, why are some geographic regions better than others for surfing, snorkeling, and scuba diving?

**NOTE for *Las pupusas***
*Pupusas* are the national food of El Salvador. They are thick corn tortillas stuffed with various fillings, such as refried beans, cheese, pork rinds (*chicharrones*), and *loroco* (the flower from a shrub that grows in Central America). Restaurants that specialize in these are called *pupuserías*.

**SUGGESTION for *Las pupusas***
Ask students: Do we have restaurants that specialize in certain foods?

**NOTE for *El cacao***
Cacao (*Theobroma cacao*), also called cocoa tree, is an evergreen tree native to El Salvador. Cocoa beans, or seeds, are used to make cocoa powder and chocolate and were once used by Salvadoran ancestors, the Mayans, as currency.

**ANSWERS to *Preguntas***
1. Los mayas lo usaron como dinero.
2. Los deportes acuáticos
3. *Possible answers:* Es el único país de Centroamérica que no tiene costa caribeña; es un país pequeño, etc.

## Ambiciones siniestras
### EPISODIO 4

# Lectura

| **Estrategia** | Skimming and Scanning (II) |
| --- | --- |

Continue to practice focusing on main ideas and important information. Remember, when you *skim* a passage you read quickly to get the gist of the passage. When you *scan* a passage you already know what you need to find out, so you concentrate on searching for that particular information.

**4-40** **Antes de leer** Ya (*Already*) sabemos que Manolo, Alejandra, Cisco, Eduardo, Lupe y Marisol son finalistas de un concurso misterioso. En este episodio Marisol y Lupe no lo pueden celebrar porque tienen que trabajar en un proyecto sobre (*about*) sus pueblos. Antes de leer contesta las siguientes preguntas. ■

1. ¿Cómo es tu pueblo? ¿Es un buen lugar donde vivir? ¿Por qué?
2. ¿De dónde son tus mejores amigos? ¿Sabes mucho sobre sus familias y sus pueblos?

**4-41** **A leer** Complete the following steps. ■

1. *Skim* the first paragraph, looking for the answers to the following questions.
   a. About whom is this paragraph?
   b. Which statement best describes where they are?
      They are in sociology class.
      They are at a party.
      They are in an apartment.
2. Now *scan* the second paragraph, looking for the following information:
   a. Where is Lupe's parents' home—in the country or in the middle of town?
   b. Is her parents' home large or small?
   c. What city is next to Lupe's hometown?

This gives you a good start to discovering what happens next in **Ambiciones siniestras.**

## Las cosas no son siempre lo que parecen°

*seem*

Alejandra, Manolo, Cisco, Eduardo, Marisol y Lupe están emocionados al saber que son finalistas del concurso. Muchos van a celebrarlo, pero Marisol y Lupe no pueden. Están ahora en el apartamento de Lupe. Tienen que terminar un proyecto sobre sus pueblos para la clase de sociología.

*countryside*
*Nevertheless*
*outskirts*

Las fotos que tiene Lupe de la casa de sus padres y de su pueblo en general representan un lugar muy tranquilo en el campo°, con una casa pequeña y un jardín muy grande. Sin embargo°, Lupe nunca quiere hablar de su familia ni de su pueblo. Sólo dice que es de un pueblo de las afueras° de Akron, Ohio.

En cambio, a Marisol le gusta hablar de su familia y de su pueblo que está muy cerca de la ciudad de Nueva York. Marisol viene de una familia muy grande. Es hija única pero tiene muchos tíos y primos. Todos viven cerca de Nueva York.

*proud*

Marisol está muy orgullosa° de su pueblo. Siempre le dice a Lupe que tiene de todo cerca de su casa. Por ejemplo, dice que hay un cine donde ponen quince películas diferentes a la vez. Ella vive en un apartamento y enfrente hay un supermercado pequeño, una librería y un restaurante que siempre recibe la distinción de ser el mejor restaurante chino del pueblo. ¡Ella no comprende cómo alguien puede vivir en otro lugar!

*laugh*

Mientras Marisol trabaja de manera muy seria, escucha a Lupe reírse° y hacer comentarios casi inaudibles. De pronto Lupe le dice a Marisol que tiene que salir un momento para hacer una llamada por teléfono. Marisol, muy curiosa, decide mirar lo que Lupe escribe.

*strange*

Se acerca a su computadora y lee allí algo muy extraño°. Lupe no escribe sobre su pueblo en Ohio. ¡Escribe sobre Los Ángeles!

---

**4-42** **Después de leer** Contesta las siguientes preguntas. ■

1. ¿Qué tipo de proyecto hacen Lupe y Marisol?
2. ¿Qué no quiere hacer Lupe?
3. ¿Cómo es la familia de Marisol?
4. ¿Dónde vive Marisol? ¿Cómo es su pueblo?
5. ¿Qué escribe Lupe en su computadora?

**NATIONAL STANDARDS**
*Comparisons*
You may wish to ask students how well they skim and scan in their first language. For those who say they skim and scan well in their first language, you may wish to follow up and have those students describe the techniques they use to the class.

Standard 4.1 promotes making comparisons between Spanish and English. You can encourage students to use reading strategies (like skimming and scanning) from their first language and apply them to learning Spanish. Brainstorm the vocabulary in Spanish (such as question words) that they will need to answer when they skim the passage. Highlight the words that they will be looking for in Spanish as they scan for specific information. When they are finished, ask them whether the strategies they use for reading in Spanish are different from those strategies they use when reading in English.

**ANSWERS to 4-42**
1. Es un proyecto acerca de sus pueblos para la clase de sociología.
2. No quiere hablar de su familia.
3. Es una familia grande con muchos tíos y primos. Es hija única.
4. Vive en un pueblo cerca de Nueva York. Tiene de todo cerca de su casa.
5. Escribe sobre Los Ángeles, no sobre su pueblo en Ohio.

**Instructor Resources**
• Video script

**SECTION GOALS for Video**
By the end of the *Video* section, students will be able to:
• make predictions about the characters' volunteer activities.
• report the main events in chronological order.

**NATIONAL STANDARDS**
*Communication*
The *Ambiciones siniestras* section requires students to understand and interpret spoken (*Video*) and written (*Lectura*) Spanish (Standard 1.2) as they discover more about the characters and the plot. Depending on how you implement the activities that correspond to the reading and video sections, you can also encourage interpersonal communication in small groups or with partners (Standard 1.1). If you assigned the roles of the characters, students could act out a video scene and present their understanding of what happens in the video (Standard 1.3).

**ANSWERS to 4-44**
1. Van a su apartamento.
2. *Answers may include:* Hablan de unos supermercados, de Centroamérica (y de Guatemala) y de sus trabajos como voluntarios.
3. Eduardo trabaja como voluntario. Ayuda a los niños.
4. Porque Eduardo toca sus papeles.
5. Eduardo va a un cibercafé y escribe un email.

---

04-60 to 04-61

# Video

**4-43** **Antes del video** Do you volunteer your time with a group or organization? In the video episode of **Ambiciones siniestras,** you will learn about Cisco's and Eduardo's volunteerism experiences (or lack thereof!). Also listen for "**¡No toques** (*touch*) **mis cosas nunca más! ¿Me oyes?**" Why do you think the character says this? And finally, you will discover that either Cisco or Eduardo is not being totally honest! Who do you think it is? Why? ■

Trabajo como voluntario en una organización que ayuda a los niños.

¡No toques mis cosas nunca más! ¿Me oyes?

Cisco piensa que lo sabe todo…

Episodio 4

## «¿Quiénes son en realidad?»

Relax and watch the video, more than once if you choose. Then answer the questions that follow.

**4-44** **Después del video** Contesta las siguientes preguntas. ■

1. ¿Adónde van Cisco y Eduardo?
2. ¿Qué hacen allí?
3. ¿Quién trabaja como voluntario? ¿A quiénes ayuda?
4. ¿Por qué está enojado Cisco?
5. ¿Qué hace Eduardo al final?

166

## Y por fin, ¿cómo andas?

|  | Feel confident | Need to review |
|---|:---:|:---:|
| Having completed this chapter, I now can . . . | | |

**Comunicación I**

| | | |
|---|:---:|:---:|
| • identify places in and around town (p. 134) | ☐ | ☐ |
| • pronounce the letters *c* and *z* (MSL/SAM) | ☐ | ☐ |
| • state whom and what is known (p. 137) | ☐ | ☐ |
| • relate common obligations and activities (p. 140) | ☐ | ☐ |
| • express actions (p. 142) | ☐ | ☐ |

**Comunicación II**

| | | |
|---|:---:|:---:|
| • share where I and others are going (p. 146) | ☐ | ☐ |
| • convey what will happen in the future (p. 147) | ☐ | ☐ |
| • impart information about service opportunities (p. 149) | ☐ | ☐ |
| • articulate concepts and ideas both affirmatively and negatively (p. 151) | ☐ | ☐ |
| • describe states of being, characteristics, and location (p. 154) | ☐ | ☐ |
| • paraphrase what I hear (p. 157) | ☐ | ☐ |
| • communicate about ways to serve the community (p. 158) | ☐ | ☐ |
| • write a postcard and proofread it for accuracy (p. 159) | ☐ | ☐ |

**Cultura**

| | | |
|---|:---:|:---:|
| • describe shopping and other daily activities (p. 136) | ☐ | ☐ |
| • discuss the concept of social consciousness (p. 151) | ☐ | ☐ |
| • list interesting facts about Honduras, Guatemala, and El Salvador (pp. 161–163) | ☐ | ☐ |

**Ambiciones siniestras**

| | | |
|---|:---:|:---:|
| • practice the reading strategies of skimming and scanning, and learn more about Lupe and Marisol (p. 164) | ☐ | ☐ |
| • discover that Cisco may not be who Eduardo and the others think he is (p. 166) | ☐ | ☐ |

**Comunidades**

| | | |
|---|:---:|:---:|
| • use Spanish in real-life contexts (SAM) | ☐ | ☐ |

**Instructor Resources**
• Testing program information

# VOCABULARIO ACTIVO

| Los lugares | Places |
|---|---|
| el almacén | department store |
| el banco | bank |
| el bar; el club | bar; club |
| el café | café |
| el cajero automático | ATM machine |
| el centro | downtown |
| el centro comercial | mall; business/shopping district |
| el cibercafé | Internet café |
| el cine | movie theater |
| la iglesia | church |
| el mercado | market |
| el museo | museum |
| la oficina de correos; correos | post office |
| el parque | park |
| la plaza | town square |
| el restaurante | restaurant |
| el supermercado | supermarket |
| el teatro | theater |
| el templo | temple |

| Algunos verbos | Some verbs |
|---|---|
| buscar | to look for |
| estar de acuerdo | to agree |
| mandar una carta | to send/mail a letter |

| Otras palabras útiles | Other useful words |
|---|---|
| la ciudad | city |
| la cuenta | bill; account |
| detrás (de) | behind |
| enfrente (de) | in front (of) |
| el/la mejor | the best |
| la película | movie; film |
| el/la peor | the worst |
| el pueblo | town; village |

| Servicios a la comunidad | Community service |
|---|---|
| apoyar a un/a candidato/a | to support a candidate |
| ayudar a las personas mayores/los mayores | to help elderly people |
| circular una petición | to circulate a petition |
| dar un paseo | to go for a walk |
| deber | ought to; should |
| hacer artesanía | to make arts and crafts |
| hacer una hoguera | to light a campfire |
| ir de camping | to go camping |
| ir de excursión | to take a short trip |
| llevar a alguien al médico | to take someone to the doctor |
| montar una tienda de campaña | to put up a tent |
| organizar | to organize |
| participar en una campaña política | to participate in a political campaign |
| repartir comidas | to hand out/deliver food |
| trabajar como consejero/a | to work as a counselor |
| trabajar en el campamento de niños | to work in a summer camp |
| trabajar como voluntario/a en la residencia de ancianos | to volunteer at a nursing home |
| trabajar en política | to work in politics |
| viajar en canoa | to canoe |

| Otras palabras útiles | Other useful words |
|---|---|
| el deber | obligation; duty |
| el voluntariado | volunteerism |

| Otros verbos | Other verbs |
|---|---|
| ir | to go |
| saber | to know |

| ¿Qué tienen que hacer? | What do they have to do? |
|---|---|
| (Verbos con cambio de raíz) | (Stem-changing verbs) |
| almorzar (ue) | to have lunch |
| cerrar (ie) | to close |
| comenzar (ie) | to begin |
| costar (ue) | to cost |
| demostrar (ue) | to demonstrate |
| devolver (ue) | to return (an object) |
| dormir (ue) | to sleep |
| empezar (ie) | to begin |
| encerrar (ie) | to enclose |
| encontrar (ue) | to find |
| entender (ie) | to understand |
| jugar (ue) | to play |
| mentir (ie) | to lie |
| morir (ue) | to die |
| mostrar (ue) | to show |
| pedir (i) | to ask for |
| pensar (ie) | to think |
| perder (ie) | to lose; to waste |
| perseguir (i) | to chase |
| preferir (ie) | to prefer |
| recomendar (ie) | to recommend |
| recordar (ue) | to remember |
| repetir (i) | to repeat |
| seguir (i) | to follow; to continue (doing something) |
| servir (i) | to serve |
| volver (ue) | to return |

| Expresiones afirmativas y negativas | Affirmative and negative expressions |
|---|---|
| a veces | sometimes |
| algo | something; anything |
| alguien | someone |
| algún | some; any |
| alguno/a/os/as | some; any |
| jamás | never; not ever (emphatic) |
| nada | nothing |
| nadie | no one; nobody |
| ni... ni | neither . . . nor |
| ningún | none |
| ninguno/a/os/as | none |
| nunca | never |
| o... o | either . . . or |
| siempre | always |

**Instructor Resources**
• IRM: Syllabi and Lesson Plans

## NATIONAL STANDARDS

### COMUNICACIÓN I

- To discuss music (Communication, Connections, Cultures, Comparisons)
- To practice pronouncing diphthongs and linking words (Communication, Cultures)
- To identify people and things (Part I) (Communication)
- To identify people and things (Part II) (Communication)
- To explain how something is done (Communication)
- To describe what is happening at the moment (Communication)
- To engage in additional communication practice (Communication)

### COMUNICACIÓN II

- To share information about movies and television programs (Communication, Connections, Cultures)
- To rank people and things (Communication, Comparisons)
- To state what needs to be accomplished (Communication)
- To express *what* or *whom* (Communication)
- To anticipate content when listening (Communication)
- To communicate about music and film (Communication)
- To write a movie review and practice peer editing (Communication, Connections, Communities, Cultures)
- To engage in additional communication practice (Communication)

### CULTURA

- To discuss Hispanic music in the United States (Communication, Cultures, Connections, Comparisons)
- To describe Hispanic influences in North American film (Communication, Cultures, Connections, Comparisons)
- To list interesting facts about Nicaragua, Costa Rica, and Panama (Cultures, Comparisons)
- To explore further the chapter's cultural themes (Cultures)

# 5 ¡A divertirse! La música y el cine

En el mundo hispanohablante la gente trabaja pero también sabe divertirse (*enjoy themselves*). La música, el baile y el cine son formas de expresión y de distracción comunes. Estos pasatiempos, además de otros como los deportes o leer un buen libro, nos hacen la vida muy agradable. Sobre todo (*Above all*), es importante buscar maneras de relajarse y aliviar el estrés.

## PREGUNTAS

1 ¿Qué haces cuando no estudias?

2 ¿Qué hacen tus amigos y tú para relajarse y aliviar el estrés?

3 Hay una expresión en español que dice: "Algunas personas viven para trabajar y otras trabajan para vivir". ¿Cuál es tu filosofía de la vida?

**170**

### AMBICIONES SINIESTRAS

- To anticipate content when reading and discover what Cisco does in his search for Eduardo (Communication, Comparisons)
- To find out who is the second student to disappear (Communication)

### COMUNIDADES

- To use Spanish in real-life contexts (Connections, Comparisons, Communities)

### SECTION GOALS for *Chapter opener*

By the end of the *Chapter opener* section, students will be able to:

- name some forms of diversion in Hispanic countries.
- think about ways to alleviate stress.
- reflect on the concept of *trabajar para vivir* or *vivir para trabajar*.

| OBJETIVOS | CONTENIDOS | |
|---|---|---|
| **COMUNICACIÓN I** | | |
| To discuss music | **1** The world of music | 172 |
| To practice pronouncing diphthongs and linking words | **Pronunciación:** Diphthongs and linking | MSL/SAM |
| To identify people and things (Part I) | **2** Demonstrative adjectives (*this, that, these, those*) | 175 |
| To identify people and things (Part II) | **3** Demonstrative pronouns (*this one, that one, these, those*) | 177 |
| To explain how something is done | **4** Adverbs | 179 |
| To describe what is happening at the moment | **5** Present progressive | 180 |
| To engage in additional communication practice | **Heritage Language** | SAM |
| **COMUNICACIÓN II** | | |
| To share information about movies and television programs | **6** The world of cinema and television | 184 |
| To rank people and things | **7** Ordinal numbers | 187 |
| To state what needs to be accomplished | **8** Hay que | 188 |
| To express *what* or *whom* | **9** Direct object pronouns and the personal *a* | 189 |
| To anticipate content when listening | **ESCUCHA:** Concert plans **Estrategia:** Anticipating content | 192 |
| To communicate about music and film | **¡Conversemos!** | 193 |
| To write a movie review and practice peer editing | **ESCRIBE:** A review **Estrategia:** Peer review/editing | 194 |
| To engage in additional communication practice | **Heritage Language** | SAM |
| **CULTURA** | | |
| To discuss Hispanic music in the United States | **NOTA CULTURAL** La música latina en los Estados Unidos | 178 |
| To describe Hispanic influences in North American film | **NOTA CULTURAL** La influencia hispana en el cine norteamericano | 186 |
| To list interesting facts about Nicaragua, Costa Rica, and Panama | **CULTURA** Nicaragua, Costa Rica y Panamá | 195–197 |
| To explore further the chapter's cultural themes | **MÁS CULTURA** | SAM |
| **AMBICIONES SINIESTRAS** | | |
| To anticipate content when reading and discover what Cisco does in his search for Eduardo | **EPISODIO 5** **Lectura:** *La búsqueda de Eduardo* **Estrategia:** Anticipating content | 198 |
| To find out who the second student is to disappear | **Video:** *Se conocen* | 200 |
| **COMUNIDADES** | | |
| To use Spanish in real-life contexts | **Experiential Learning:** El cine y la música **Service Learning:** Un festival de cine | SAM SAM |

171

**NATIONAL STANDARDS**
*Communities*
This chapter focuses on music and movies. Use the resources in your modern language department, the library, or audiovisual services to plan a foreign film festival. If you do not have videos or DVDs, you can rent them from teacher video rental companies, video stores, or from other video rental companies on the web. Compile several titles you feel may be appropriate for the community and its population, and ask students to plan a weekly or monthly movie that students and community members are invited to attend. You may require that students attend a certain number of films or that a certain number of students attend a particular film, to introduce themselves to the community members who attend. Standard 5.1 encourages the use of Spanish both within and beyond the school setting, and watching authentic movies and discussing them with the community members builds bridges between the campus and the community.

**NOTE for *Chapter opener***
Note that the chapter introduction talks about other pastimes such as sports, reading, and ways to alleviate stress, but the main focus of the chapter is music and cinema. You might also want to expand on the importance of theater in Hispanic cultures, such as *El teatro campesino*, whose roots were in the United Farm Workers Union in California. It was started by Luis Valdez and featured Chicano themes. Other classic plays such as *La Celestina* or *La casa de Bernarda Alba* are offered throughout the United States by traveling theater groups. Browse the Internet for Spanish theater groups that might be coming to a city near you.

**SUGGESTION for *Chapter opener***
Bring in a photo of your favorite Hispanic recording artist or group (or an American artist who sings in Spanish) and ask students to identify who they think the artist is. Play a track from your favorite CD or download the song and play a clip of the song. Ask your students to identify characteristics about the song and the artist from the clip. What genre of music do they think it is? Is this artist's music representative of his/her country? What is the tempo? What kinds of instruments do they hear?

**PLANNING AHEAD**
You will want to play music in class for the students to listen to, or ask students to bring in music they want to share. It is helpful to have access to a compact disc player or computer for music files, and blank CDs for students to bring in their music to share. You may also wish to plan on playing music daily in the background while students are working in their groups. Students find this technique adds to the immersion-style atmosphere.

**METHODOLOGY • Making Topics Relevant for Students**
The text and questions for this chapter opener are completely in Spanish, just as in *Capítulo 4*. Note that the questions begin with your learners and their preferences, something that we have learned from educational philosopher John Dewey. Try having your students each turn to a partner and answer the questions in pairs. Then have them share the answers their partners gave. This has them practice listening and paraphrasing.

**PLANNING AHEAD**
Remember that all grammar explanations and culture presentations should be assigned to be read before class. Class time should be spent answering clarification questions for the grammar presentations, or answering the comprehension/critical thinking questions that follow the culture presentations. Activities **5-4** and **5-9** can be assigned to be written at home and then shared in class.

**SECTION GOALS for**
*Comunicación I*

By the end of the *Comunicación* section, students will be able to:

• talk about the world of music, including genres and characteristics of each genre.
• pronounce strong vowels (*a, e, o*), weak vowels (*i, u*), and diphthongs.
• link words and pronounce identical vowels and consonants.
• discuss Hispanic music in the U.S.
• form demonstrative adjectives and demonstrative pronouns.
• review the agreement rules of nouns and adjectives.
• form adverbs from adjectives.
• produce the forms of the present progressive using regular and irregular gerunds.

**NATIONAL STANDARDS**
*Communication, Cultures, Comparisons*

If you have a collection of different types of music from the Spanish-speaking world, this chapter is an excellent opportunity for you to expose your students to a wide variety. Encourage them to compare and contrast the music within the Spanish-speaking world as well as with music from the English-speaking world.

The activities related to music provide you with multiple ways to address the Standards. In particular, you can address the Communication Goal (Standards 1.1, 1.2, and 1.3) by incorporating music into the class. Play your favorite Hispanic artist's music and have your students share their opinions and preferences about the artist and the music (Standard 1.1) in pairs or small groups. Give students a copy of the lyrics in Spanish, and ask them to interpret what the song is about. The combination of hearing the words and following along with the written lyrics facilitates interpretation (Standard 1.2). Ask students to present part of the song (reading aloud or singing in front of the class) or a different song of their choosing (Standard 1.3). They can bring in the Spanish lyrics for others to read along (Standard 1.2) as they present (Standard 1.3). Goal Two, Cultures, is also easily addressed through music. Highlight the different types of music in Spanish-speaking countries, how different cultures incorporate music into daily life, and the types of commercially produced music with which students might be familiar.

# Comunicación I

## 1 VOCABULARIO

05-01 to 05-07

### El mundo de la música  Discussing music

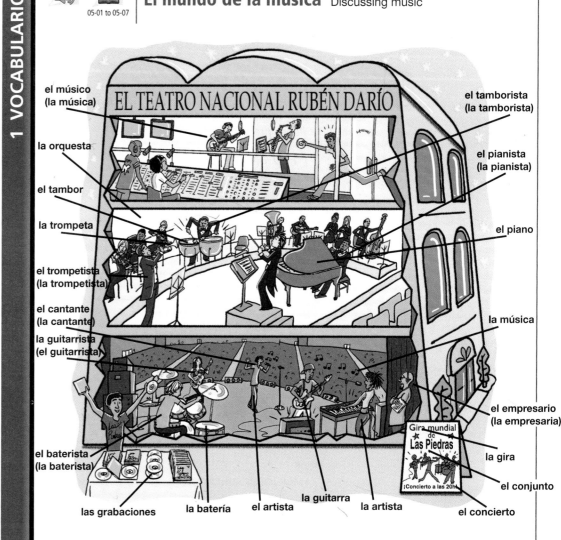

Encourage students to make comparisons (Standard 4.2) between what role music has in the United States and in Spanish-speaking countries, and among the different types of music available. When you analyze the lyrics, you can explain the literal meaning versus the figurative meaning, or how they translate versus what they mean. That allows students to make comparisons between Spanish and English (Standard 4.1).

| Algunos géneros musicales | Some musical genres |
|---|---|
| el jazz | jazz |
| la música clásica | classical music |
| la música folklórica | folk music |
| la música popular | pop music |
| la música rap | rap music |
| la ópera | opera |
| el rock | rock |
| la salsa | salsa |

| Algunos adjetivos | Some adjectives |
|---|---|
| apasionado/a | passionate |
| cuidadoso/a | careful |
| fino/a | fine; delicate |
| lento/a | slow |
| suave | smooth |

| Algunos verbos | Some verbs |
|---|---|
| dar un concierto | to give/perform a concert |
| ensayar | to practice/rehearse |
| grabar | to record |
| hacer una gira | to tour |
| sacar un CD | to release a CD |
| tocar | to play (a musical instrument) |

| Otras palabras útiles | Some useful words |
|---|---|
| el/la aficionado/a | fan |
| la fama | fame |
| el género | genre |
| la habilidad | ability; skill |
| la letra | lyrics |
| el ritmo | rhythm |
| la voz | voice |

**PRONUNCIACIÓN**

### Diphthongs and linking

05-08 to 05-12

Go to MySpanishLab/Student Activities Manual to learn about diphthongs and linking.

---

**7:00** **5-1 Dibujemos** Escuchen mientras su profesor/a les da (*gives you*) las instrucciones de esta actividad. ∎

---

**5-2 Listas** Túrnate con un/a compañero/a para decir y escribir todas las palabras del vocabulario nuevo que recuerden (*you both remember*) de las tres categorías en el modelo. ¿Cuántas palabras pueden recordar? ∎

MODELO

| TIPOS DE MÚSICA | INSTRUMENTOS | OTRAS PALABRAS |
|---|---|---|
| el jazz | la trompeta | el conjunto |

---

**METHODOLOGY • Comprehensive input**
Notice that virtually all of the direction lines in this chapter are in Spanish. For all students, this provides reading practice. You may choose to model some of the activities such as **5-2** to make sure that students understand what they are supposed to do with their partners.

**METHODOLOGY • Visual Organizers**
For **5-2,** you may wish to project the image of the new vocabulary that does not have the words written on it. Students can then use the image as a visual organizer to assist them in remembering the vocabulary they have just learned.

**METHODOLOGY • Working in Pairs**
Remember that it is ideal for students to change partners daily. In this way, students have the opportunity to work with everyone in the class, and you build community within your classroom. At the very least, partners should be changed weekly.

---

**NOTE for *Algunos géneros musicales***
You will notice that the genres listed here are mostly cognates. Students should be able to discuss the instruments and artists most commonly associated with each genre. *Salsa* is the genre that may require the most explanation. You can discuss the roots of *salsa* in the United States during the 1960s and 1970s, stemming from Puerto Rican immigration and Cuban influences. *Salsa* is quite popular in Latin America and is sometimes referred to as *música tropical* or Latin jazz. You may also want to add *el reggaetón, la soca, el norteño, el tejano, la cumbia,* etc. to the vocabulary list. An excellent source of types of popular music and musicians in the Spanish-speaking world is the Latin Grammys web site, http://www.latingrammy.com.

**SECTION GOALS for *Pronunciación***
By the end of the *Pronunciación* section, students will be able to:
- differentiate between strong vowels and weak vowels.
- recognize diphthongs and how they are pronounced.
- link using the 4 rules: consonants to vowels, vowels to vowels, identical consonants, and identical vowels.
- pronounce new vocabulary using the rules for vowels and consonants.

**SUGGESTION for *El mundo de la música***
Have students brainstorm 5 artists/musical groups from each decade and decide what musical genres dominated each decade. Depending on the age and composition of your class, you might start in the 1970s or later. Come prepared with a list of your most influential artists and see whether they match those of your students.

**NOTE for 5-1**
Activity **5-1** continues with the mechanical practice for your students to learn the new vocabulary. This activity can be used in other chapters as well, to either present or review vocabulary. It is also a good activity for pairs who finish early. Please give the following extended directions to your students: if you are familiar with the game *Pictionary,* it is very similar. It is like charades, but they have to draw pictures rather than act the words out.
**INSTRUCTIONS:** Divide your class into groups of 4. Each group of 4 will work as 2 teams of 2 students. "Captains" from each team select the word that they are going to draw. Their teammate needs to try to guess what the word is in Spanish as they draw. The round is over when one of the teams guesses the word. The roles are then switched, and the 2 team members who did the guessing now select the word that each will draw for his/her partner. We suggest doing this activity for at least 4 rounds. It is a motivating way to practice vocabulary.

**5-3 Para conocerte mejor** Hazle las siguientes preguntas a un/a compañero/a. Toma apuntes y luego comparte las respuestas con otros dos compañeros. ■

**Estrategia**
When reporting your information, make complete sentences, and remember to use the *él* or *ella* form of the verb. Also, simply refer to your notes; do not read from them. This technique will help you to speak more fluidly and will help you speak in paragraphs, an important skill to perfect when learning a language.

1. ¿Con qué frecuencia vas a conciertos?
2. ¿Qué género de música prefieres?
3. ¿Cuál es tu grupo favorito?
4. ¿Cuál es tu cantante favorito/a? ¿Cómo es su voz?
5. ¿Qué instrumento te gusta?
6. ¿Cuál es tu canción favorita?
7. ¿Sabes tocar un instrumento? ¿Cuál?
8. ¿Sabes cantar bien? ¿Te gusta cantar? ¿Cuándo y dónde cantas?
9. ¿En qué tienes mucha habilidad o talento?
10. ¿Conoces algún conjunto o cantante hispano? ¿Cuál?

Capítulo 2. La formación de preguntas y las palabras interrogativas, pág. 70.

**5-4 Los famosos** Completa los siguientes pasos. ■

**Fíjate**
Remember that if you are interviewing people whom you don't know, use the *usted/ustedes* form.

**Paso 1** Como reportero/a de la revista *Rolling Stone* tienes la oportunidad de entrevistar a los hermanos Mejía, dos músicos populares de Nicaragua. Escribe por lo menos **cinco** preguntas que vas a hacerles.

**Paso 2** Haz una investigación en el Internet para ver si puedes descubrir las respuestas a tus preguntas y para escuchar la música de Luis y Ramón Mejía. Después, comparte tus resultados y tu opinión con la clase; diles (*tell them*) qué canción te gusta más y por qué.

05-13 to 05-15  ¡Hola! Spanish/English Tutorials

## Los adjetivos demostrativos
### Identifying people and things (Part I)

*Esta mujer toca muy bien. Ese hombre toca bien y aquel hombre toca muy mal.*

When you want to point out a specific person, place, thing, or idea, you use a *demonstrative adjective*. In Spanish, they are:

| DEMONSTRATIVE ADJECTIVES | MEANING | FROM THE PERSPECTIVE OF THE SPEAKER, IT REFERS TO . . . |
|---|---|---|
| **este, esta, estos, estas** | *this, these* | something nearby |
| **ese, esa, esos, esas** | *that, those over there* | something farther away |
| **aquel, aquella, aquellos, aquellas** | *that, those (way) over there* | something even farther away in distance and/or time . . . perhaps not even visible |

Since forms of **este, ese,** and **aquel** are adjectives, they must agree in gender and number with the nouns they modify. Note the following examples.

**Este** conjunto es fantástico.
**Esta** cantante es fenomenal.
**Estos** conjuntos son fantásticos.
**Estas** cantantes son fenomenales.

*This group is fantastic.*
*This singer is phenomenal.*
*These groups are fantastic.*
*These singers are phenomenal.*

**Ese** conjunto es fantástico.
**Esa** cantante es fenomenal.
**Esos** conjuntos son fantásticos.
**Esas** cantantes son fenomenales.

*That group is fantastic.*
*That singer is phenomenal.*
*Those groups are fantastic.*
*Those singers are phenomenal.*

**Aquel** conjunto es fantástico.
**Aquella** cantante es fenomenal.
**Aquellos** conjuntos son fantásticos.
**Aquellas** cantantes son fenomenales.

*That group (over there) is fantastic.*
*That singer (over there) is phenomenal.*
*Those groups (over there) are fantastic.*
*Those singers (over there) are phenomenal.*

### ¡Explícalo tú!

**In summary:**
1. When do you use **este, ese,** and **aquel**?
2. When do you use **esta, esa,** and **aquella**?
3. When do you use **estos, esos,** and **aquellos**?
4. When do you use **estas, esas,** and **aquellas**?

 Check your answers to the preceding questions in Appendix 1.

**SUGGESTION for *Los adjetivos demostrativos***
Use the demonstrative adjectives with classroom objects to indicate the distance from the speaker, using *this, that,* and *that one over there*: *Este lápiz es rojo, ese lápiz es azul y aquel lápiz es amarillo.* You can also use demonstrative adjectives as a way to review possession and possessive adjectives. Borrow various items from your students while the class is watching. Then ask *¿De quién es esta mochila?* and have them answer by using *ser + de* or an appropriate possessive adjective.

**METHODOLOGY • Streamlining the Syllabus**
Based on research, as well as consultation with hundreds of instructors, the decision was made that *¡Anda! Curso elemental* will teach a more streamlined syllabus so that students may learn well (acquire) what is being presented. This is a departure from how it has been done in the past: to introduce everything and have students leave the course with little or nothing that they can do with the language. You have noticed that, when presenting grammar, we have not presented all of the exceptions to the rules or nuances of the language that can be presented at a later time so that students will comprehend the differences. Having said that, if you have heritage language learners or false beginners, feel free to present them. As always, we as instructors must ultimately decide what is best for our students.

**SUGGESTION for *Los adjetivos demostrativos***
You may wish to use the following saying for students who need extra help with demonstratives: *This* and *these* both have *t*'s in Spanish; *that* and *those* do not in Spanish; (e.g., *Este, esta,* and *estos, estas* mean *this* and *these* and have *t*'s. *Ese, esa, esos,* and *esas* mean *that* and *those* and do not have *t*'s).

**5-5** **Amiga, tienes razón** Tu amigo/a te da su opinión y tú respondes con una opinión similar. Cambia la forma de **este/a** a (*to*) **ese/a** y añade (*add*) la palabra **también**. ▪

MODELO TU AMIGO/A: Esta música es muy suave.

TÚ: *Sí, y esa música es suave también.*

1. Este grupo es fenomenal.
2. Estos cantantes son muy jóvenes.
3. Esta gira empieza en enero.
4. Este CD sale ahora.
5. Estas canciones son muy apasionadas.
6. Estos pianistas tocan muy bien.

 **5-6** **En el centro estudiantil** Completen el diálogo de Lola y Tina con las formas correctas de **este, ese** y **aquel**. ▪

LOLA: Tina, mira (1) ___este___ (*this*) grupo de estudiantes que acaba de entrar.

TINA: Sí, creo que conozco a (2) ___este___ (*this*) hombre alto. Es guitarrista del trío de jazz *Ritmos*.

LOLA: Tienes razón. Y (3) ___esta___ (*this*) mujer rubia es pianista en la orquesta de la universidad.

TINA: ¿Quiénes son (4) ___esas___ (*those*) dos mujeres morenas?

LOLA: Están en nuestra clase de química. ¿No las conoces? Y (5) ___aquellos___ (*those over there*) dos hombres de las camisas rojas ¡son muy guapos!

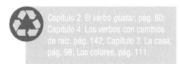
Capítulo 2: El verbo *gustar*, pág. 80;
Capítulo 4: Los verbos con cambios de raíz, pág. 142; Capítulo 3: La casa, pág. 98; Los colores, pág. 111.

 **5-7** **¿Qué opinas?** Miren el dibujo y expresen sus opiniones sobre las casas. Usen las formas apropiadas de **este, ese** y **aquel**. ▪

MODELO *Me gusta esta casa blanca, pero prefiero esa casa beige. Pienso que aquella casa roja es fea. También creo que este jardín de la casa blanca es bonito.*

## 3 GRAMÁTICA

05-16 to 05-17   ¡Hola! Spanish/English Tutorials

# Los pronombres demostrativos
## Identifying people and things (Part II)

**Demonstrative pronouns** take the place of nouns. They are identical in form and meaning to demonstrative adjectives.

¡Esta es muy buena! Ese no me gusta, pero ¡aquel es fenomenal!

| Masculino | Femenino | *Meaning* |
|-----------|----------|-----------|
| este | esta | *this one* |
| estos | estas | *these* |
| ese | esa | *that one* |
| esos | esas | *those* |
| aquel | aquella | *that one (way over there/not visible)* |
| aquellos | aquellas | *those (way over there/not visible)* |

A demonstrative pronoun must agree in gender and number with the noun it replaces. Observe how demonstrative adjectives and demonstrative pronouns are used in the following sentences.

Yo quiero comprar **este CD**, pero mi hermana quiere comprar **ese**.

*I want to buy this CD, but my sister wants to buy that one.*

—¿Te gusta **esa guitarra**?
—No, a mí me gusta **esta**.

*Do you like that guitar?*
*No, I like this one.*

**Estos instrumentos** son interesantes, pero prefiero tocar **esos**.

*These instruments are interesting, but I prefer to play those.*

En **esta** calle hay varios cines. ¿Quieres ir a **aquel**?

*There are several movie theaters on this street. Do you want to go to that one over there?*

---

 2:00

**5-8** **Comparando cosas** Tu compañero/a te propone (*proposes*) una cosa pero tú siempre prefieres otra (*another one*). Responde a sus comentarios usando las formas correctas de **este, ese** y **aquel**. ■

**MODELO**    E1:   ¿Quieres ir a este concierto?
           E2:   *No, quiero ir a ese/aquel.*

1. ¿Quieres escuchar a estos músicos?
2. ¿Vamos a ir a ese teatro?
3. ¿Entiendes la letra de esta canción?
4. ¿Tus amigos tocan en aquel conjunto?
5. ¿Vas a comprar aquellas camisetas (*T-shirts*)?
6. ¿Piensas arreglar este cuarto para la fiesta?

---

**5-9  ¡Vamos a un concierto!**

¡Qué suerte! Tienes dos entradas gratis (*free tickets*)
para ir a un concierto. ∎

**Paso 1**   Haz una investigación en el Internet para escuchar la música de El Gran Combo, Marc Anthony, Juan Luis Guerra y Los Tigres del Norte.

**Paso 2**   Tu compañero/a y tú tienen que decidir a qué concierto quieren ir. Túrnense para describir a quién prefieren escuchar y por qué. Usen **este, ese** y **aquel** en sus descripciones.

**MODELO**   *Prefiero ir al concierto de Marc Anthony. ¡Él canta muy bien! Pero es difícil decidir porque los músicos de Los Tigres del Norte son muy buenos también. Estos saben tocar y cantar muy bien. Y aquellos…*

## NOTA CULTURAL

# La música latina en los Estados Unidos

05-18 to 05-19

La música latina abarca (*encompasses*) muchos géneros, estilos e intérpretes (músicos, cantantes). Entre los géneros más populares en los Estados Unidos se encuentran la salsa, el merengue, el Tex-Mex o norteño y otros. Algunos intérpretes de estos tipos de música son El Gran Combo, Marc Anthony, Juan Luis Guerra y Los Tigres del Norte.

El rock y el jazz son influencias que están presentes en la música latina en los Estados Unidos, aunque esta ha evolucionado (*has evolved*) y producido nuevos géneros como el merenhouse, el rock latino, el rap en español, el jazz latino, el reggaetón y otros.

Néstor Torres

La influencia de los países hispanohablantes del Caribe —Cuba, Puerto Rico y la República Dominicana— y su herencia africana forman parte de los ritmos, las melodías y la instrumentación de la música y los bailes latinos. También les dan vida (*they give life*) a géneros como la plena, la cumbia y la bachata.

Entre los artistas populares de hoy en día se encuentra Néstor Torres, flautista de música de jazz latino. Torres ganó un premio Grammy latino por su interpretación de *This Side of Paradise*.

Marc Anthony

### Preguntas

1. ¿Cuáles son cuatro de los géneros de la música latina? ¿Cuáles conoces tú?
2. ¿Quiénes son los artistas latinos más conocidos en este momento?

Juan Luis Guerra

## 4 GRAMÁTICA

05-20 to 05-23    ¡Hola!
Spanish/
English
Tutorials

## Los adverbios
Explaining how something is done

Este baterista toca horriblemente.

An **adverb** usually describes a verb and **answers the question "how."** Many Spanish adverbs end in **-mente,** which is equivalent to the English *-ly.* These Spanish adverbs are formed as follows:

1. Add **-mente** to the *feminine singular* form of an *adjective.*

| ADJETIVOS | | ADVERBIOS |
|---|---|---|
| **Masculino** | **Femenino** | |
| rápido → | *rápida* + -mente → | **rápidamente** |
| lento → | *lenta* + -mente → | **lentamente** |
| tranquilo → | *tranquila* + -mente → | **tranquilamente** |

2. If an *adjective* ends in a *consonant* or in **-e,** simply add **-mente.**

| ADJETIVOS | | ADVERBIOS |
|---|---|---|
| fácil → | *fácil* + -mente → | **fácilmente** |
| suave → | *suave* + -mente → | **suavemente** |

**NOTE:** If an adjective has a written accent, it is retained when **-mente** is added.

♻ Capítulo 1. Los adjetivos
descriptivos, pág. 43.

1:00        **5-10** **Lógicamente** Túrnense para transformar en adverbios los siguientes adjetivos. ∎

### Estrategia
Remember to first determine the *feminine singular* form of the adjective and then add *-mente.*

MODELO    E1:  normal
              E2:  *normalmente*

1. interesante  interesantemente
2. perezosos  perezosamente
3. feliz  felizmente
4. nervioso  nerviosamente
5. fuertes  fuertemente
6. claro  claramente
7. seguro  seguramente
8. apasionadas  apasionadamente
9. difícil  difícilmente
10. débil  débilmente
11. rápida  rápidamente
12. pacientes  pacientemente

**Instructor Resources**
• PPT, Extra Activities

**NOTE for *Los adverbios***
Although a complete grammatical explanation of adverbs would include the fact that they can also modify adjectives, adverbs, whole phrases, clauses, or sentences, we have chosen to simplify the presentation. Also note that we have chosen to use the word *describe* rather than the word *modify* in the presentation. Although both words are grammatically acceptable, *describe* is a bit more casual and user-friendly.

**NOTE for *Los adverbios***
You may want to remind your students of common adverbs that they already know: *bien, mal, regular, mucho, poco, siempre, nunca, después,* etc.

**SUGGESTION for *Los adverbios***
For students who need additional help or practice with the concepts of adverbs, direct them to MySpanishLab, where they can practice with the English grammar tutorial as well as the Spanish grammar tutorial.

Capítulo 2. Presente indicativo de verbos regulares, pág. 67; Capítulo 4. Los verbos con cambio de raíz, pág. 142.

## 5-11 Para conocerte
Túrnense para hacerse y contestar las siguientes preguntas. Pueden usar los adjetivos de la lista. ■

| | | | | |
|---|---|---|---|---|
| alegre | constante | paciente | difícil | divino |
| fácil | horrible | perfecto | rápido | tranquilo |

**MODELO**    E1: ¿Cómo bailas? (divino)
          E2: *Bailo divinamente.*

1. ¿Cómo cantas?
2. ¿Cómo duermes?
3. ¿Cómo hablas español?
4. ¿Cómo juegas al béisbol?
5. ¿Cómo tocas el piano?
6. ¿Cómo cocinas?
7. ¿Cómo lavas los platos?
8. ¿Cómo manejas (*drive*)?

## 5-12 Di la verdad
Hazle (*Ask*) a tu compañero/a las siguientes preguntas. Después, cambien de papel. ■

**Estrategia**
Answer in complete sentences when working with your partner. Even though it may seem mechanical at times, it leads to increased comfort speaking Spanish.

**MODELO**    E1: ¿Qué haces diariamente (todos los días)?
          E2: *Limpio mi dormitorio, voy a clase, estudio, como, hago ejercicio y duermo.*

1. ¿Qué haces perfectamente?
2. ¿Qué haces horriblemente?
3. ¿Qué haces fácilmente?
4. ¿Qué debes hacer rápidamente?
5. ¿Qué debes hacer lentamente?

## 5 GRAMÁTICA

05-24 to 05-27   Spanish/English Tutorials   ¡Hola!

## El presente progresivo
Describing what is happening at the moment

So far you have been learning and using the present tense to communicate ideas. If you want to emphasize that an action is **occurring at the moment and is in progress,** you can use the *present progressive* tense.
    The English present progressive is made up of a form of the verb *to be* + *present participle* (*-ing*). Look at the following sentences and formulate a rule for creating the present progressive in Spanish. Use the following questions to guide you.

—¿Qué *estás* **haciendo**?     *What are you doing?*
—*Estoy* **ensayando.**     *I'm rehearsing.*

—¿*Está* **escuchando** música tu hermano?     *Is your brother listening to music?*
—No, *está* **tocando** la guitarra.     *No, he is playing the guitar.*

—¿*Están* **viendo** ustedes la televisión?     *Are you watching television?*
—No, les *estamos* **escribiendo** una carta a nuestros padres.     *No, we are writing a letter to our parents.*

> **Fíjate**
>
> The present progressive is *not* used to express the future.
>
> Present progressive: *Estoy ensayando.* I am rehearsing (right now).
>
> Future: *Voy a ensayar mañana.* I am going to rehearse tomorrow.

### ¡Explícalo tú!

1. What is the infinitive of the first verb in each sentence that is in *italics*?
2. What are the infinitives of **haciendo, ensayando, escuchando, tocando, viendo,** and **escribiendo**?
3. How do you form the verb forms in **boldface**?
4. In this new tense, the *present progressive*, do any words come between the two parts of the verb?
5. Therefore, your formula for forming the *present progressive* is:
   **a form of the verb _____ + a verb ending in _____ or _____.**

✓ Check your answers to the preceding questions in Appendix 1.

> **Fíjate**
>
> When the stem of an *-er* or *-ir* verb ends in a vowel, e.g. *creer* and *leer*, the present participle ends in *-yendo* (the *i* changes to *y*).

**NOTE:** The following are some verbs that have irregular forms in this tense.

decir → diciendo
mentir → mintiendo
pedir → pidiendo
preferir → prefiriendo
perseguir → persiguiendo
repetir → repitiendo
seguir → siguiendo
servir → sirviendo

dormir → durmiendo
morir → muriendo

creer → creyendo
leer → leyendo

> **Fíjate**
>
> For the *-ir* stem-changing verbs only, these vowel changes occur in the stem: *e* → *i* (*diciendo*) and *o* → *u* (*durmiendo*).

---

[3·00]  **5-13 Progresando**   Escuchen mientras su instructor/a les da (*gives you*) las instrucciones de esta actividad. ¡Diviértanse! (*Enjoy!*) ■

**MODELO**    E1:   *hablar, yo*
          E2:   *estoy hablando*
          E2:   *comer, nosotros*
          E3:   *estamos comiendo*

**NOTE and INSTRUCTIONS for 5-13**

The authors of *¡Anda! Curso elemental* believe in offering highly creative activities while at the same time keeping the direction lines at an *i + 1* level. There are activities, such as this one, where it is more efficient for you to give the directions in English, unless you have a large number of heritage language learners or false beginners, in which case you may choose to give the following directions in Spanish.

**INSTRUCTIONS:** Work in groups of at least four students. One student makes a ball out of a piece of paper, says an infinitive and a subject (noun or pronoun), and then tosses the ball to someone in the group. The person who catches the ball must give the correct form of the verb in the present progressive. If correct, he or she receives a point. The activity continues until you, the teacher, call "time."

**FOLLOW-UP for 5-14**
If a student is absent, you can ask the class to predict what that student might be doing during the time when the other students are in class. If no one is absent, you might ask them what they think the university administrators are currently doing, or what the students in the other classes are doing.

 Capítulo 2: El verbo *gustar*, pág. 80.

**5-14 ¿Tienes telepatía?** Es sábado. Túrnense para decir qué está haciendo su profesor/a en varios momentos del día. ■

MODELO   E1: Le gusta tomar café por la mañana.

   E2: *Está tomando café en su terraza.*

1. Le gusta hacer ejercicio para comenzar su día.
2. Le gusta la música latina y está en una tienda.
3. Está cansado/a y tiene mucho sueño.
4. Trabaja en la computadora y tiene muchos mensajes de sus estudiantes.
5. Le gusta comer algo ligero (*light*) antes de ir a la fiesta.
6. Está con sus amigos en la fiesta y les gusta mucho la música que están tocando.

**5-15 ¿Qué está ocurriendo?** Túrnense para decir qué están haciendo estas personas. ■

MODELO   E1: Felipe

   E2: *Felipe está preparando su comida y está comiendo también.*

1. Manuel   Manuel está lavando los platos.
2. Sofía   Sofía está sacando la basura.
3. Raúl y Mari Carmen   Raúl y Mari Carmen están tocando música. Raúl está tocando el piano y Mari Carmen la flauta.
4. José   José está viendo la televisión.
5. Mercedes y Guillermo   Mercedes y Guillermo están escuchando música.

Felipe          Manuel          Sofía

Raúl y Mari Carmen          José          Mercedes y Guillermo

EXPANSION for 5-16
Find a photo (or assign students to bring a photo to class) of a group such as Calle 13 or Maxwell performing a concert. Using the present progressive, have students describe the photo.

NOTE for 5-17
Rather than having your students write songs, you may prefer to have them create dialogues.

**5-16**  **No, ¡ahora mismo!** Contesten las siguientes preguntas para indicar que las personas están haciendo las acciones en este momento. ■

MODELO    E1:  ¿Ellos van a ver la nueva película de Javier Bardem mañana?

             E2:  *No, están viendo la película ahora mismo.*

1. ¿Tú vas a comprar el nuevo CD de Calle 13 la semana que viene?
2. ¿Maxwell va a hacer una gira mundial el próximo verano?
3. ¿Nosotros vamos a escuchar música rap esta noche?
4. ¿El conjunto va a vender muchas grabaciones el año que viene?
5. Este festival de música es impresionante. ¿Van a tocar Bebo y Chucho Valdés esta tarde?

**5-17** **¡Qué creativo!** Juntos escriban la letra de una canción popular usando **el presente progresivo** un mínimo de **seis** veces (*times*). Deben usar verbos de la siguiente lista. ■

| | | | | |
|---|---|---|---|---|
| decir | dormir | repetir | creer | morir |
| mentir | leer | ir | seguir | servir |

## ¿Cómo andas? I

|  | Feel confident | Need to review |
|---|---|---|
| Having completed **Comunicación I,** I now can . . . | | |
| • discuss music (p. 172) | ☐ | ☐ |
| • practice pronouncing diphthongs and linking words (MSL/SAM) | ☐ | ☐ |
| • identify people and things (Part I) (p. 175) | ☐ | ☐ |
| • identify people and things (Part II) (p. 177) | ☐ | ☐ |
| • discuss Hispanic music in the United States (p. 178) | ☐ | ☐ |
| • explain how something is done (p. 179) | ☐ | ☐ |
| • describe what is happening at the moment (p. 180) | ☐ | ☐ |

**SECTION GOALS for**
*Comunicación II*
By the end of the *Comunicación* section, students will be able to:
• discuss their favorite films and current releases.
• categorize films by genre.
• identify the Hispanic influence and presence in North American movies.
• rank items using ordinal numbers.
• construct sentences using the expression *hay + que + infinitive*.
• identify direct objects and use direct object pronouns.

**NATIONAL STANDARDS**
*Communication*
This vocabulary is optimal because so many of the words are cognates in English. Also, students enjoy talking about what interests them, and most students enjoy some genre of film. This vocabulary motivates students to share orally, which will then lead to meaningful communication in writing with the guidance that *¡Anda! Curso elemental* provides.

The activities in this *Comunicación* section provide opportunities for communication in the interpersonal and presentational modes. Students are encouraged to share their opinions and observations with others about their favorite movies and actors (Standard 1.1). Activities **5-19** and **5-20** can be adapted to address Standard 1.3 by having students each present a poster for their favorite movie and try to persuade others to see it. They can each vote for the movie they would most like to see, and then write a review of that movie in Spanish, practicing the new chapter vocabulary. If you have a particular movie that you like, you can write a description of the movie in Spanish, and students can practice listening as you present your movie. They could also practice reading if you make a pamphlet or jacket cover that summarizes what you said about the movie (Standard 1.2).

# Comunicación II

**6 VOCABULARIO**

05-28 to 05-31

## El mundo del cine
Sharing information about movies and television programs

- la pantalla
- el actor
- la actriz
- un documental
- una película musical
- una película romántica
- una película de misterio
- una película de ciencia ficción
- una película de acción
- una película de guerra
- la estrella
- la entrada
- una película de terror
- una película dramática
- una película de humor

| Otras palabras útiles | Other useful words |
|---|---|
| el estreno | opening |
| la película | movie |
| una película... | a . . . movie |
| aburrida | boring |
| animada | animated |
| conmovedora | moving |
| creativa | creative |
| deprimente | depressing |
| emocionante | moving |
| entretenida | entertaining |
| épica | epic |

| | |
|---|---|
| de espanto | scary |
| estupenda | stupendous |
| imaginativa | imaginative |
| impresionante | impressive |
| sorprendente | surprising |
| de suspenso | suspenseful |
| trágica | tragic |

| Algunos verbos | Some verbs |
|---|---|
| estrenar una película | to release a film/movie |
| presentar una película | to show a film/movie |

**5-18** **¿Cuál es el género?** Clasifiquen las siguientes películas según su género y usen el mayor (*the largest*) número de palabras posibles para describirlas. ■

**MODELO**    E1:   Avatar

E2:   Avatar *es una película dramática, de acción. Es emocionante, impresionante y entretenida…*

1. *The Social Network (La red social)*
2. *Inception (Origen)*
3. *Black Swan (El cisne negro)*
4. *Tangled (Enredados)*
5. *Ironman II (El hombre de hierro II)*

6. *The Hurt Locker (Zona de miedo)*
7. *The Blind Side (Un sueño posible)*
8. *Sanctum (El santuario)*
9. *Precious (Preciosa)*
10. ¿?

**5-19** **En mi opinión**  Túrnense para completar las siguientes oraciones sobre las películas. ¿Están ustedes de acuerdo? ■

Capítulo Preliminar A.
El verbo *ser*, pág. 13.

**MODELO**    E1:   La mejor película de terror…

E2:   *La mejor película de terror es Saw VI.*

1. Las mejores películas de humor…
2. Una película épica deprimente…
3. Mis actores favoritos de las películas de acción…

4. La película de misterio que más me gusta…
5. Unas películas creativas…
6. El mejor documental…

 **5-20** **Mis preferencias**  Lee las reseñas (*reviews*) de las tres películas. Después, túrnate con un/a compañero/a para describir la película que prefieres ver y por qué. ■

**MODELO**    *Prefiero ver _____. Es una película _____ y _____. Me gusta _____ porque _____ …*

## En el cine

**Invictus** (2010, EE.UU.)
**Género:**            Drama
**Director:**           Clint Eastwood
**Interpretación:**     Morgan Freeman, Matt Damon

Basada en el libro de John Carlin, *The Human Factor: Nelson Mandela and the Game That Changed the World.* Mandela (Morgan Freeman) reconoce la importancia de tener la Copa del Mundo de Rugby en Sudáfrica en el año 1995, después de ser excluidos durante muchos años de las competiciones debido al apartheid.

**El hombre lobo** (2010, EE.UU.)
**Género:**            Terror
**Director:**           Joe Johnston
**Interpretación:**     Benicio del Toro, Anthony Hopkins

Nueva versión del clásico del cine de terror en el que un hombre recibe la maldición del hombre lobo.

**Origen** (2010, EE.UU.)
**Género:**            Ciencia ficción, Acción
**Director:**           Christopher Nolan
**Interpretación:**     Leonardo DiCaprio, Michael Caine

Dom Cobb (Leonardo DiCaprio) es un ladrón que roba secretos del subconsciente durante el estado de sueño en un tipo de espionaje corporativo, pero esto lo hace un fugitivo internacional.

**NATIONAL STANDARDS**
*Communication, Cultures,*
*Connections, Comparisons*
When discussing the National Standards, it is always interesting to note how the 5 Cs overlap. If you have a film festival at your school, you may wish to request either vintage movies or current films with Hispanic actors.

This reading highlights the four goal areas of Communication, Cultures, Connections, and Comparisons. Students are able to communicate about this reading in 1 of 3 ways. First, you can ask them to work in pairs or small groups and have them research one of the profiled actors. You can bring the information to class, they can bring the information to class, or you can take them to the language lab for research. The discussions that they have about the actors satisfy Standard 1.1. The reading they are doing in Spanish contributes to Standard 1.2. If you have them present the information they have read as a group or turn in a report of the information, it addresses Standard 1.3. If you have time to show a film, or film clip, from one of these actors, you can also use that as a starting point for discussion, assignments, and presentations. Students see the products and perspectives (Standard 2.2) through the contributions that Hispanics have made to the film industry. They can connect the new information to what they might have known about the actor(s) or topics discussed in the movie (Standard 3.2) and think about it in the context of learning Spanish. (The films by directors Pedro Almodóvar and Alfonso Cuarón are especially useful for Standard 3.2). Students can make comparisons between Spanish and English (subtitled movies work well to show the difference between translation and interpretation) and the cultural differences they see in the films (Standards 4.1 and 4.2).

**21ST CENTURY SKILLS •**
**COMMUNICATION AND**
**COLLABORATION**
Two core elements of the Partnership for 21st (P21) Century Skills and *¡Anda!* are to communicate clearly and to collaborate with others. P21 lists not only communicating thoughts and ideas effectively, but also listening effectively. *¡Anda!* provides students with strategies on how to become good listeners. Also, *¡Anda!* uses almost exclusively pair and group activities, supporting P21's goal of "demonstrating the ability to work effectively and respectfully with diverse teams, and to assume shared responsibility for collaborative work, valuing the individual contributions made by each team member."

5:00 **5-21** ## En nuestra opinión...

**Paso 1** Habla de algunas películas que conoces con un/a compañero/a, usando las siguientes preguntas como guía (*guide*).

1. ¿Cuáles son las películas que más te gustan? ¿Por qué?
2. ¿Quiénes son tus actores y actrices favoritos?
3. ¿Qué películas que van a estrenar pronto quieres ver?

**Paso 2** Ahora hablen sobre programas de televisión.

**NOTA CULTURAL**

2:00

## La influencia hispana en el cine norteamericano

05-32 to 05-33

Javier Bardem

Cameron Díaz

La influencia hispana en el cine estadounidense empieza a tener importancia en los años 50. Actores como Gilbert Roland, Anthony Quinn y Ricardo Montalbán se destacan (*stand out*) en películas de habla inglesa. Les siguen más tarde estrellas del cine y de la televisión como Raquel Welch y Rita Moreno y continúan hasta el presente con Antonio Banderas, Javier Bardem, Jimmy Smits, Jennifer López, John Leguizamo, Edward James Olmos, Benicio del Toro, America Ferrera, Andy García, Salma Hayek, Zoe Saldana, Cameron Díaz, Diego Luna y Penélope Cruz, entre muchos otros. Su presencia en la industria representa el cambio demográfico de los Estados Unidos.

### Preguntas

1. De los actores mencionados, ¿a cuáles conoces? ¿Qué sabes de ellos?
2. ¿Quiénes son los actores hispanos más populares en este momento?

Benicio del Toro

Jennifer López

¡Hola! Spanish/English Tutorials 05-34 to 05-37

## Los números ordinales Ranking people and things

An ordinal number indicates position in a series or order. The first ten ordinal numbers in Spanish are listed below. Ordinal numbers above *décimo* are rarely used.

*¿Te gusta la primera sinfonía de Beethoven?*

*Sí, pero prefiero la novena.*

| | | | |
|---|---|---|---|
| **primer, primero/a** | *first* | **sexto/a** | *sixth* |
| **segundo/a** | *second* | **séptimo/a** | *seventh* |
| **tercer, tercero/a** | *third* | **octavo/a** | *eighth* |
| **cuarto/a** | *fourth* | **noveno/a** | *ninth* |
| **quinto/a** | *fifth* | **décimo/a** | *tenth* |

1. Ordinal numbers are adjectives and agree in number and gender with the nouns they modify. They usually *precede* nouns.

   el **cuarto** año         *the fourth year*
   la **octava** sinfonía       *the eighth symphony*

2. Before masculine, singular nouns, **primero** and **tercero** are shortened to **primer** and **tercer.**

   el **primer** concierto       *the first concert*
   el **tercer** curso de español    *the third Spanish course*

3. After *décimo*, a cardinal number is used and *follows* the noun.

   el piso **catorce**
   el siglo (*century*) **veintiuno**

---

**5-22** **Orden de preferencia** Asigna un orden de preferencia a las actividades de la lista: desde la más importante (primero) hasta la menos importante (octavo). Después, comparte tu lista con un/a compañero/a usando oraciones completas. ■

**MODELO**   *Primero, me gusta ver una película con mi actor favorito, Colin Firth. Segundo, quiero visitar a mis hermanos. Tercero, prefiero…*

1. ir a un concierto de tu conjunto favorito   _____
2. visitar a tus amigos   _____
3. ver una película con tu actor/actriz favorito/a   _____
4. leer una novela buena   _____
5. ir a un partido de fútbol americano   _____
6. estudiar para un examen   _____
7. visitar Costa Rica   _____
8. conocer al presidente de los Estados Unidos   _____

**ANSWERS to 5-23**
1. *Answers may vary.*
2. *Answers may vary.*
3. El tercer mes del año es marzo y el sexto es junio.
4. El séptimo día de la semana es el domingo (en los países hispanohablantes).
5. El primer presidente de los Estados Unidos se llama George Washington.
6. *Answers may vary.*

**FOLLOW-UP for 5-24**
You may choose to do both *Pasos 2* and *3* as whole-class activities by creating the list of 10 best movies and then ordering the list together.

**METHODOLOGY • Chunking**
You will note that *¡Anda! Curso elemental* presented *tener + que + infinitive* separately from *hay que + infinitive.* Once again, the purpose is to chunk information so that the students focus on smaller bits, giving them one way to express an idea and then providing them with another way to vary their repertoire.

**NOTE for *Hay que + infinitivo***
For a quick drill that reinforces the use of the infinitive after *hay que,* have students make a list of 10 infinitives. Then in pairs, they take turns calling out an infinitive while their partners must quickly make an expression with *hay que,* e.g., *ensayar* ➔ *Hay que ensayar.*

---

  **5-23 Preguntas de trivia** Túrnense para hacerse y contestar las siguientes preguntas. ■

 *Capítulo Preliminar A. Los días, los meses y las estaciones, pág. 20.*

1. ¿En qué piso está tu clase de español?
2. ¿A qué hora es tu primera clase los lunes? ¿Y la segunda?
3. ¿Cuál es el tercer mes del año? ¿Y el sexto?
4. ¿Cuál es el séptimo día de la semana?
5. ¿Cómo se llama el primer presidente de los Estados Unidos?
6. ¿Cómo se llama la cuarta persona de la tercera fila (*row*) en la clase de español?

**Estrategia**
Remember that when asked a question with *tu/tus,* you need to answer *mi/mis.*

---

 **5-24 La lista de los mejores** ¿Cuáles son las mejores películas para los estudiantes de tu clase? ■

*Workbooklet*

**Paso 1** Entrevista a cinco estudiantes y pregúntales cuáles son sus opiniones sobre las tres películas mejores. Usa las palabras **primera, segunda** y **tercera.**

**Paso 2** Con el/la profesor/a, haz una lista de las **diez** películas más populares de la clase.

**Paso 3** Organiza por orden de preferencia la lista de las películas más populares de la clase. Escribe el número ordinal apropiado para cada película.

| PELÍCULAS FAVORITAS | ESTUDIANTE 1 | ESTUDIANTE 2 | ESTUDIANTE 3 | ESTUDIANTE 4 | ESTUDIANTE 5 |
|---|---|---|---|---|---|
| PRIMERA | | | | | |
| SEGUNDA | | | | | |
| TERCERA | | | | | |

---

**8 GRAMÁTICA**

05-38 to 05-40

## *Hay que* + infinitivo
Stating what needs to be accomplished

So far when you have wanted to talk about what someone should do, needs to do, or has to do, you have used the expressions **debe, necesita,** or **tiene que.** The expression **hay que** + *infinitive* is another way to communicate responsibility, obligation, or the importance of something. **Hay que** + *infinitive* means:

*It is necessary to . . .*
*You must . . .*
*One must/should . . .*

Para ser un músico bueno **hay que** ensayar mucho.
**Hay que terminar** nuestro trabajo antes de ir al cine.
**Hay que ver** la nueva película de Almodóvar.

*To be a good musician it is necessary to rehearse a lot.*
*We must finish our work before we go to the movies.*
*You must see the new Almodóvar film.*

Hay que trabajar. ¡No hay que ser perezoso!

**5-25  Para generalizar** Túrnense para sustituir **tener que** por **hay que** en las siguientes oraciones. Sigan el modelo. ∎

MODELO  E1:  Tenemos que consultar al empresario.

 E2:  *Hay que consultar al empresario.*

1. Ustedes tienen que sacar un CD con estas canciones nuevas.
2. Marisol, tú tienes que ser más paciente si quieres conseguir buenas entradas para ese concierto.
3. Mamá, ¡tienes que conocer la música de este conjunto nuevo!
4. Jorge y Catrina, ustedes tienen que hacer una gira con su grupo de jazz.
5. Rafael, tienes que visitar a tu hermana porque ella quiere ensayar contigo.
6. Enrique, tú tienes que leer los mensajes que escriben tus aficionados.

**5-26  ¿Obligaciones?** ¿Qué hay que hacer para llegar a tener las siguientes características? Túrnense para completar las frases dando por lo menos **dos** ideas. ∎

MODELO  E1:  Para ser un pintor excelente…

 E2:  Para ser un pintor excelente *hay que pintar mucho y hay que ser muy creativo.*

**Para ser…**
1. un músico impresionante…
2. un político honesto…
3. un cantante estupendo…
4. un director de cine sorprendente…
5. una actriz conmovedora…
6. una novelista entretenida…

**5-27  Y todos necesitamos…** ¿Qué debemos hacer para tener un futuro mejor? Compartan sus ideas y comuniquen sus resultados a la clase usando **tres** oraciones completas. ∎

MODELO  E1:  Hay que…

 E2:  *Hay que respetar* (respect) *y ayudar a las personas mayores.*

## 9 GRAMÁTICA

05-41 to 05-43  ¡Hola! Spanish/English Tutorials

# Los pronombres de complemento directo y la "a" personal
Expressing *what* or *whom*

**Direct objects** receive the action of the verb and answer the questions **What?** or **Whom?** Note the following examples.

A: I need to do *what?*
B: You need to buy *the concert tickets* by Monday.
A: Yes, I do need to buy *them.*

A: I have to call *whom?*
B: You have to call *your agent.*
A: Yes, I do have to call *him.*

*(continued)*

**Instructor Resources**
• PPT, Extra Activities

**EXPANSION for 5-26**
Ask students to create sentences with *hay que* for these additional people:
un/a estudiante muy bueno/a…
un/a profesor/a memorable…
unos padres perfectos…
un/a compañero/a de cuarto excelente…
un/a novio/a increíble…

**METHODOLOGY • Higher-Order Thinking**
Activities **5-26** and **5-27** require students to use critical thinking as well as to tap their previously learned vocabulary from other chapters. The aim is for your students to generate sentences such as:
Un político: *Hay que leer y escribir mucho. También hay que estudiar y escuchar a la gente.*

**HERITAGE LANGUAGE LEARNERS**
Activity **5-27** is particularly good for heritage language learners, since they may be able to take more risks with the language. You may want them to share their sentences with the entire class so that all students can benefit from their linguistic creativity.

**METHODOLOGY • *Personal a***
You may choose to present exceptions to the rule given to students regarding the personal *a*, e.g., *Tengo un hermano*, or talk about variations in the Spanish-speaking world. Your own personal philosophy, and your knowledge of your students and their abilities, will be your guide when making these types of decisions.

**NOTE for *os***
You may wish to remind your students about *vosotros*. Also, remember that the *vosotros* forms are presented as a point of information in the charts, but they are not practiced in the activities.

**NOTE for *Placement of direct object pronouns***
*¡Anda! Curso elemental* will present more information regarding accent marks in relation to direct and indirect objects in *Capítulo 10*, when commands are introduced.

Note the following examples of *direct objects* in Spanish.

| | |
|---|---|
| María toca **dos instrumentos** muy bien. | *María plays two instruments very well.* |
| Sacamos **un CD** el primero de septiembre. | *We are releasing a CD the first of September.* |
| ¿Tienes **las entradas**? | *Do you have the tickets?* |
| No conozco a **Benicio del Toro**. | *I do not know Benicio del Toro.* |
| Siempre veo a **Selena Gómez** en la televisión. | *I always see Selena Gómez on television.* |

**NOTE:** In **Capítulo 4,** you learned that to express knowing a person, you put **"a"** after the verb (*conocer + a* + person). Now that you have learned about direct objects, a more global way of stating the rule is: When direct objects refer to *people*, you must use the personal **"a."** Review the following examples.

| People | Things |
|---|---|
| ¡Veo **a** *Cameron Díaz*! | ¡Veo *el coche* de Cameron Díaz! |
| Hay que ver **a** *mis padres*. | Hay que ver *la película*. |
| ¿**A** qué *actores* conoces? | ¿Qué *ciudades* conoces? |

As in English, we can replace direct objects nouns with ***direct object pronouns.*** Note the following examples.

| | |
|---|---|
| María **los** toca muy bien. | *María plays them very well.* |
| **Lo** sacamos el primero de septiembre. | *We are releasing it the first of September.* |
| ¿**Las** tienes? | *Do you have them?* |
| No **lo** conozco. | *I do not know him.* |
| Siempre **la** veo en la televisión. | *I always see her on television.* |

In Spanish, direct object pronouns ***agree in gender and number with the nouns they replace.*** The following chart lists the direct object pronouns.

| Singular | | Plural | |
|---|---|---|---|
| **me** | *me* | **nos** | *us* |
| **te** | *you* | **os** | *you all* |
| **lo, la** | *you* | **los, las** | *you all* |
| **lo, la** | *him, her, it* | **los, las** | *them* |

## Placement of direct object pronouns

Direct object pronouns are:

1. Placed before the verb.
2. Attached to *infinitives* or to the *present participle* (**-ando, -iendo**).

| | | |
|---|---|---|
| ¿Tienes los discos compactos? | → | Sí, **los** tengo. |
| Tengo que traer los instrumentos. | → | **Los** tengo que traer. / Tengo que traer**los**. |
| Tiene que llevar su guitarra. | → | **La** tiene que llevar. / Tiene que llevar**la**. |

—¿Por qué estás escribiendo una canción para tu madre?

—**La** estoy escribiendo porque es su cumpleaños. / Estoy escribiéndo**la** porque es su cumpleaños.

*Capítulo 2, Presente indicativo de verbos regulares, pág. 67.*

**5-28** **¿Estás listo?** ¿Estás preparado/a para el concierto de Perrozompopo? Túrnate con un/a compañero/a para revisar la lista, esta vez usando **lo, la, los** o **las.** ■

**MODELO**    E1:   confirmar *la hora* del concierto

              E2:   *La confirmo hoy.*

1. comprar *las entradas*  Las compro.
2. invitar *a mis amigos*  Los invito.
3. leer *el artículo* de *The New York Times* sobre Perrozompopo  Lo leo.
4. compartir (*share*) *el artículo y los CD de Perrozompopo* con mis amigos  Los comparto.
5. preparar *comida* para un pícnic  La preparo.
6. traer *la cámara*  La traigo.

*Capítulo 3, Los quehaceres de la casa, pág. 109.*

**5-29** **¿Hay deberes?** El concierto de Perrozompopo fue increíble, pero hay que volver al mundo real. Siempre hay trabajo, sobre todo en la casa. Túrnate con un/a compañero/a para hacer y contestar las siguientes preguntas. ■

**MODELO**    E1:   ¿Lavas los pisos?

              E2:   *Sí, los lavo. / No, no/nunca los lavo.*

1. ¿Limpias la cocina?
2. ¿Arreglas tu cuarto?
3. ¿Lavas los platos?
4. ¿Guardas tus cosas?
5. ¿Sacudes los muebles?
6. ¿Haces las camas?
7. ¿Preparas la comida?
8. ¿Pones la mesa?
9. ¿Nos ayudas a arreglar el jardín?
10. ¿Me invitas a un concierto?

**5-30** **Una hora antes** Carlos Santana, como muchos músicos, es una persona muy organizada. Antes de cada concierto repasa con su ayudante (*assistant*) personal todos los preparativos (*preparations*). Aquí tienes las preguntas del ayudante. Contesta como si fueras (*as if you were*) Santana, usando **lo, la, los** o **las.** ■

**MODELO**    E1:   ¿Tienes tu anillo (*ring*) de la buena suerte?

              E2:   *Sí, lo tengo.*

1. Juan está enfermo. ¿Conoces al trompetista que toca esta noche con el conjunto?
2. ¿Traes tu guitarra nueva?
3. ¿Los cantantes saben la letra de la canción nueva?
4. ¿Traemos todos los trajes (*suits*, *outfits*)?
5. ¿Quieres unas botellas de agua (*water*)?
6. ¿Oyes al público aplaudir?
7. ¿Me van a necesitar después del concierto?
8. ¿El empresario te va a anunciar?

Carlos Santana

**METHODOLOGY •**
**Differentiated Instruction**
Differentiated instruction is when you tailor your lessons for your different types of learners. The number of types of learners and their preferences depend on which research you are consulting. Some sources maintain that there are 4 different types of learning styles, some say 7 or 8, and still others claim that there are more than 20! As instructors, what we need to remember is that students learn in different ways and progress at different rates. When assessing the progress of your students, it is important to know that for some of your students, their best performance will be to give multiple answers, while for others, their best will be one complete sentence. Differentiating instruction, in part, means to tailor our lessons so that all of our students, no matter what their style or talents, will be successful.

**ANSWERS to 5-29**
*All answers can be either sí or no.*
1. …la limpio
2. …lo arreglo
3. …los lavo
4. …las guardo
5. …los sacudo
6. …las hago
7. …la preparo
8. …la pongo
9. …los ayudo
10. …te invito

**ANSWERS to 5-30**
1. Sí, lo conozco.
2. Sí, la traigo.
3. Sí, la saben.
4. Sí, los traemos.
5. Sí, las quiero.
6. Sí, lo oigo.
7. Sí, te vamos a necesitar. / Sí, vamos a necesitarte.
8. Sí, me va a anunciar. / Sí, va a anunciarme.

**ESCUCHA**

  **5-31** ## Mis preferencias Túrnense para hacerse y contestar las siguientes preguntas usando **el pronombre de complemento directo** correcto. ■

MODELO   E1:  ¿Lees los poemas de Rubén Darío? ¿Por qué?

   E2:  *No, no los leo. No los leo porque no los conozco.*

1. ¿Escuchas música clásica? ¿Por qué?
2. ¿Tu amigo y tú tienen ganas de ver una película de acción de Matt Damon? ¿Por qué?
3. ¿Tus amigos ven todas las películas de Penélope Cruz? ¿Por qué?
4. ¿Escuchas música jazz en tu iPod? ¿Por qué?
5. ¿Tocas un instrumento? ¿Por qué?

## Planes para un concierto

05-44 to 05-46

| Estrategia | | |
|---|---|---|
| **Anticipating content** | Use all clues available to you to anticipate what you are about to hear. That includes photos, captions, and body language if you are looking at the individual(s) speaking. If there are written synopses, | it is important to read them in advance. Finally, if you are doing listening activities such as these, look ahead at the comprehension questions to give you an idea of the topic and important points. |

**5-32** ### Antes de escuchar Mira la foto y contesta las siguientes preguntas. ■

1. ¿Quiénes están en la foto?
2. ¿De qué hablan Eduardo y Cisco?

 **5-33** ### A escuchar Escucha la conversación entre Eduardo y Cisco y averigua cuál es el tema (*topic; gist*). Después, escucha una vez más para contestar las siguientes preguntas. ■

1. ¿Quién va al concierto de los Black Eyed Peas?
2. ¿Qué música prefiere Cisco?
3. Deciden no estudiar. ¿Adónde van a ir?

Eduardo y Cisco

 **5-34** ### Después de escuchar Describe una canción que te guste en **tres** oraciones y dibuja un cuadro (*picture*) que la represente. Preséntaselo a un/a compañero/a para ver si puede adivinar la canción. ■

# ¡CONVERSEMOS!
05-47

 **5-35** **En mi opinión** Hay un programa en el canal *E!* donde las personas expresan sus gustos y opiniones sobre la música y el cine ¡y tu compañero/a y tú van a participar esta semana! Entrevista a tu compañero/a sobre sus opiniones de: los mejores grupos, las mejores películas, los mejores actores y actrices. Luego, cambien de papel. ■

 **5-36** **Comparaciones** En los **Capítulos 1–4** aprendieron información sobre Los Estados Unidos (**Capítulo 1**), México (**Capítulo 2**), España (**Capítulo 3**) y Honduras, Guatemala y El Salvador (**Capítulo 4**). Con un/a compañero/a, compara estos países incluyendo la música y el cine, cuando sea posible. Usa información de los capítulos anteriores (*previous chapters*) e información de otras fuentes (*sources*). ■

MODELO    *Los países son similares y diferentes. Por ejemplo, hablan español en todos los países. España tiene influencia árabe en ciudades como (like) Granada. México no tiene influencia árabe pero sí tiene influencia de los aztecas. La música popular es similar, pero la música folclórica…*

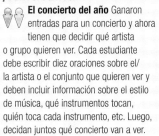

**ESCRIBE**

📖 05-48

## Una reseña (*A review*)

| **Estrategia** | Reviewing the writing of a classmate teaches you valuable editing skills that can improve your classmate's paper as well as serve to | build your confidence in your own writing by enhancing the content and syntax of your work, as well as boost your critical thinking skills. |
|---|---|---|
| **Peer review/editing** | | |

**5-37** **Antes de escribir** Piensa en una película que te gusta mucho. Anota algunas ideas sobre los aspectos que te gustan más de esa película. ■

• ¿Qué tipo de película es?
• ¿Para qué grupo(s) es apropiada?
• ¿Cuál es el tema?
• ¿Tiene una lección para el público?

**5-38** **A escribir** Organiza tus ideas y escribe una reseña (*review*), como una de las de **5-20**, de **cuatro** a **seis** oraciones. Puedes usar las siguientes preguntas para organizar tu reseña. ■

1. ¿Cómo se llama la película?
2. ¿De qué género es?
3. ¿Cómo la describes?
4. ¿A quiénes les va a gustar? ¿Por qué?
5. ¿La recomiendas? ¿Por qué?

 **5-39** **Después de escribir** En grupos de tres compartan sus reseñas. Revisen las ideas tanto de la gramática como del vocabulario. Hagan los cambios necesarios. Después, tu profesor/a va a leer las reseñas. La clase tiene que adivinar cuáles son las películas. ■

## ¿Cómo andas? II

| | Feel confident | Need to review |
|---|---|---|
| Having completed **Comunicación II**, I now can . . . | | |
| • share information about movies and television programs (p. 184) | ☐ | ☐ |
| • describe Hispanic influences in North American film (p. 186) | ☐ | ☐ |
| • rank people and things (p. 187) | ☐ | ☐ |
| • state what needs to be accomplished (p. 188) | ☐ | ☐ |
| • express *what* or *whom* (p. 189) | ☐ | ☐ |
| • anticipate content when listening (p. 192) | ☐ | ☐ |
| • communicate about music and film (p. 193) | ☐ | ☐ |
| • write a movie review and practice peer editing (p. 194) | ☐ | ☐ |

## Nicaragua

05-49

### Les presento mi país

Mauricio Morales Prado

Mi nombre es Mauricio Morales Prado y soy de Managua, Nicaragua. Mi país es conocido como la tierra de volcanes y lagos (*lakes*). Hay dos lagos principales y muchos volcanes. Siete están activos todavía y de ellos, San Cristóbal es el más alto y Masaya es el más activo. **¡Localiza estos volcanes en el mapa!** Mi familia y yo somos muy aficionados a la música. Vamos frecuentemente a los conciertos en La Concha Acústica en el Lago Managua. **¿Asistes a conciertos con tu familia o amigos?**

Teatro Nacional Rubén Darío, Managua

El volcán San Cristóbal

La Concha Acústica, Managua

### ALMANAQUE

| | |
|---|---|
| **Nombre oficial:** | República de Nicaragua |
| **Gobierno:** | República |
| **Población:** | 5.995.928 (2010) |
| **Idiomas:** | español (oficial); miskito, otros idiomas indígenas |
| **Moneda:** | Córdoba (NIO) |

### ¿Sabías que...?

- El Lago de Nicaragua es el único lago de agua dulce (*fresh water*) del mundo donde se encuentran tiburones (*sharks*) y atunes.
- El 23 de diciembre del año 1972, un terremoto (*earthquake*) desastroso de 6,5 en la escala Richter destruyó (*destroyed*) la ciudad de Managua.

### Preguntas

1. ¿Por qué se llama Nicaragua la tierra de lagos y volcanes?
2. ¿Qué tiene el Lago de Nicaragua de especial?
3. ¿Cuáles son dos lugares en Managua adonde va la gente para eventos culturales? ¿Puedes nombrar algunos posibles eventos culturales para esos dos lugares?

 Amplía tus conocimientos sobre Nicaragua en MySpanishLab.

**195**

### NOTE for *El Lago Managua*
El Lago Managua, also known as El Lago Xolotlán, covers an area of 400 square miles, measuring 16 miles from north to south and 36 miles from east to west. Managua, the capital of Nicaragua, lies on the lake's southern shore while the Momotombo volcano is on the northwestern shore. The Tipitapa River connects the lake to Lake Nicaragua.

### NOTE for *El Teatro Nacional Rubén Darío*
Named for the world-renowned Nicaraguan poet Rubén Darío, this national theater located in Managua opened in 1969. It houses theater productions, concerts, opera, ballet, art exhibitions, and many other cultural events. The theater's main hall, with its outstanding acoustics, holds 1,200 seats.

## CAPÍTULO 5

### Instructor Resources
• Text images (maps), Video resources

### SECTION GOALS for *Cultura*
By the end of the *Cultura* section, students will be able to:
- locate Nicaragua's lakes and volcanoes on a map.
- explain what *ticos* are.
- identify the national symbol of Costa Rica.
- list main exports and industries of Costa Rica.
- summarize the significance of the Panama Canal.
- identify *Los kunas* and their handicraft.
- compare and contrast Nicaragua, Costa Rica, and Panama.

### NATIONAL STANDARDS
*Cultures, Comparisons*
The cultural information about Nicaragua, Costa Rica, and Panama highlights Standards 2.1 and 2.2. Students read about each country, what makes that country unique, and some of the daily activities and products the country is known for. The cultural information presented in each chapter allows students to make comparisons among the Hispanic countries and their own countries (Standard 4.2), as well as comparisons between the Hispanic countries presented here and in earlier chapters. They learn how geography, climate, exports, and natural resources contribute to the differences among the Hispanic countries, and how those countries differ from the United States or their countries of origin.

### NOTE for *El volcán San Cristóbal*
Known as "The Land of Lakes and Volcanoes," besides its 2 large lakes (Lago Managua and Lago Nicaragua), Nicaragua has many active volcanoes including Cerro Negro, Concepción, Masaya, Momotombo, San Cristóbal, and Telica. Of these, San Cristóbal is the highest and Masaya is the most active.

### NOTE for *La Concha Acústica*
This acoustical shell that sits on the shore of Lake Managua was built in 2004 by American artist Glen Howard Small. In the form of a wave, the shell appears to surge from the lake, perfectly framing the concerts and other cultural events that take place there.

**NOTE for *Ecoturismo***
Ecotourism is big business in Costa Rica. Because the geography, flora, and fauna are so varied, there is something for everyone, such as beautiful beaches, rain and cloud forests, volcanoes, two- and three-toed sloths, howler monkeys, butterflies, tapirs, and green turtles and their nesting sites. In recent years, sailing through the trees on zip lines or walking through tree canopies over hanging bridges have been two popular diversions offered to tourists. You and your students can research additional information on the Internet by using the key words *Costa Rica* and *ecotourism*.

**NOTE for *La carreta***
The oxcart has played a big role in Costa Rica's economic history and traditions. Originally the oxcart was the only method for transporting coffee beans to coastal commerce centers. Because coffee was the economic livelihood of many farmers, the carts were extremely important. Eventually, the owners began to paint them to indicate their regions, their towns, and their own distinct personalities. These painted carts are rarely seen now, but they remain a cultural symbol and are a source of pride for many Costa Ricans, reflecting their history and industriousness. They were declared a national symbol on March 22, 1988.

**NOTE for *El café***
Costa Rican coffee ranks among the finest in the world. Costa Rican soil is perfect for coffee growing. Volcanic ashes and rich organic matter help retain humidity and facilitate oxygenation, resulting in a slight hint of acidity in the coffee's flavor.

# Cultura

## Costa Rica

CULTURA • CULTURA • CULTURA • C                    RA • C

05-50

Laura Centeno Soto

## Les presento mi país

Mi nombre es Laura Centeno Soto y soy *tica*. *Ticos* es el apodo (*nickname*) que tenemos todos los costarricenses. Soy de Guaitil, un pueblo muy pequeño entre varios parques nacionales y famoso por su cerámica. Uno de los pueblos más famosos por su artesanía, sobre todo por la carreta, un símbolo nacional de Costa Rica, es Sarchí. **¿Cuáles son algunas artesanías producidas donde tú vives?** Si piensas visitar Costa Rica, te recomiendo una visita a nuestros parques nacionales. Son bonitos y tienen flora y fauna únicas en el mundo. **¿Cuál es tu parque favorito?** ¡Costa Rica es pura vida!

El café es un producto principal de exportación.

El ecoturismo es muy importante para la economía de Costa Rica.

Una carreta pintada de Sarchí

**ALMANAQUE**

| | |
|---|---|
| **Nombre oficial:** | República de Costa Rica |
| **Gobierno:** | República democrática |
| **Población:** | 4.516.220 (2010) |
| **Idiomas:** | español (oficial); inglés |
| **Moneda:** | Colón (CRC) |

### ¿Sabías que...?

• El ejército (*army*) se abolió en Costa Rica en el año 1948. Los recursos monetarios desde aquel entonces apoyan (*support*) el sistema educativo. A causa de su dedicación a la paz (*peace*), la llaman "La Suiza de Centroamérica".

### Preguntas

1. ¿Qué artesanía es un símbolo nacional costarricense?
2. ¿Cuál es uno de los productos de exportación importantes de Costa Rica? ¿Qué otros países exportan productos similares?
3. ¿Qué otra industria es importante para la economía de Costa Rica?

 Amplía tus conocimientos sobre Costa Rica en MySpanishLab.

# Panamá

05-51

**Instructor Resources**
• Text images (maps), Video resources

## Les presento mi país

Mi nombre es Magdalena Quintero de Gracia y soy de Colón, una ciudad y puerto en la costa caribeña de Panamá. Mi país es famoso por el canal y mi ciudad está muy cerca de su entrada (*entrance*) atlántica. **¿Qué sabes tú de la historia del canal?** La economía de Panamá se basa principalmente en el sector de los servicios, la banca, el comercio y el turismo. Los turistas van al canal y también a las Islas San Blas. Allí pueden apreciar la artesanía de las mujeres indígenas. Los kunas son un grupo de indígenas que viven en este lugar y las mujeres hacen *molas* como parte de su ropa tradicional.

Magdalena Quintero de Gracia

El Canal de Panamá

Una mujer kuna vende molas, artesanía tradicional.

Las ruinas del Panamá Viejo

*Mar Caribe*

COSTA RICA
Bocas del Toro
Golfo de los Mosquitos
Barú
David
PANAMÁ
Isla de Coiba
*OCÉANO PACÍFICO*
Canal de Panamá
Colón
Balboa
Santiago
Golfo de Panamá
Panamá
La Palma
Islas San Blas
Archipiélago de las Perlas
COLOMBIA

### ALMANAQUE

| | |
|---|---|
| **Nombre oficial:** | República de Panamá |
| **Gobierno:** | Democracia constitucional |
| **Población:** | 3.410.676 (2010) |
| **Idiomas:** | español (oficial), inglés, otros idiomas indígenas |
| **Moneda:** | Balboa (PAB) |

### ¿Sabías que...?

• Richard Halliburton nadó el canal en el año 1928 y la tarifa fue (*was*) 36 centavos. La tarifa más alta fue $141.344,91 para el crucero (*cruise ship*) Crown Princess.

• Hay un palíndromo famoso en inglés asociado con el canal: *A man, a plan, a canal: ¡Panamá!*

### Preguntas

1. ¿Por qué es importante el canal?
2. Compara Panamá con Costa Rica y Nicaragua. ¿En qué son similares? ¿En qué son diferentes?
3. Compara Panamá, Costa Rica y Nicaragua con México. ¿En qué son similares? ¿En qué son diferentes?

Amplía tus conocimientos sobre Panamá en MySpanishLab.

---

**NOTE for *Palíndromo***
A palindrome is a "word, phrase, verse, or sentence which reads the same backward or forward" (*American Heritage Dictionary,* 1982). A very famous one that appears in *The American Heritage Dictionary* is "A man, a plan, a canal, Panama!" Another palindrome in Spanish is *oso.*

**SUGGESTION for *Las molas***
A brief English discussion of *molas* might include the following questions: *What is traditional clothing like in indigenous groups in the United States? (Possible answer: Some indigenous groups have animal skins or woven fabrics. The skins are natural tones, and the woven fabrics can be bright or more subdued, depending on the vegetation available for dying.) How does it compare with the molas? (Possible answer: They can be as colorful, depending on the dying materials available in nature. They reflect the culture with either geometric shapes or those of flora or fauna.)*

**NOTE for *El Canal de Panamá***
The Panama Canal reverted to Panamanian ownership and directorship on December 31, 1999. The canal greatly decreases the travel time from Atlantic Ocean destinations to Pacific Ocean ones; the trip was also much safer than going around the tip of South America. Five years after the takeover by Panama, the canal was profitable and the accident rate had been reduced.

**SUGGESTION for *El Canal de Panamá***
We believe in the need to use English at some points so that the students will have the richest experience possible. These brief questions bring forward the National Foreign Language Standards of Cultures, Comparisons, and Connections since, through culture, they have students use knowledge from political science/history and make cultural comparisons. Ask students: *Why is this canal so strategically important? Why is the Panama Canal economically important?* Ask whether anyone has ever been through the canal or through a system of locks (e.g. from lake to lake).

**NOTE for *Los kunas***
The Kuna Indians live in the Islas San Blas and in the province of Darién. The Kuna society is a matriarchal one; when a couple marries, the man moves to the woman's household. Kuna women are known for their colorful traditional dress that includes the *mola,* insets on both the front and back of a blouse with intricate patterns and/or designs. These are made by interleaving several layers of different colored cloth and cutting out shapes accordingly. This handicraft is highly prized and is a symbol of this indigenous culture.

**NOTE for *El Panamá Viejo***
Panamá Viejo, the oldest European settlement on the Pacific Coast, was founded in 1519 by the conquistador Pedrarias Dávila, or Pedro Arias de Ávila. A UNESCO World Heritage Site, Panamá Viejo is situated northeast of downtown Panama City. Once a thriving city of reportedly 10,000 inhabitants, it was a major center for merchants and landowners. The town was damaged in the 1621 earthquake, suffered additional damage by fire in 1644, and then was devastated in 1671 during Sir Henry Morgan's invasion, and was never rebuilt.

# Ambiciones siniestras
### EPISODIO 5

05-54

# Lectura

| **Estrategia** | Anticipating content |

You can often anticipate the content of a reading passage by paying attention to the title and to any available illustrations and by quickly reading through the comprehension questions that may follow a passage.

**5-40** **Antes de leer** En el **Episodio 4,** Marisol tiene sus dudas sobre Lupe. Cree que Lupe miente (*lies*) sobre su pueblo y posiblemente sobre otras cosas. En el **Episodio 4** del video, Cisco está enojado con Eduardo porque toca sus cosas. Luego, Eduardo se va misteriosamente. Teniendo esto en cuenta, contesta las siguientes preguntas. ■

- ¿Qué piensas? ¿De dónde es Lupe, de Akron, de Los Ángeles o de otro lugar?
- ¿Adónde va Eduardo?

**5-41** **A leer** Complete the following activities. ■

1. Take a look at the title of the episode, **La búsqueda de Eduardo,** and answer the following questions.

   - What verb does **búsqueda** look like?
   - Who would be looking for Eduardo?
   - What might Cisco do to look for him?

2. Now read the **Después de leer** questions. What do you glean from the questions? Employ this new reading strategy along with the others you have been learning (identifying cognates, skimming, and scanning), and enjoy the episode!

## La búsqueda de Eduardo

*no longer*
Cuando Cisco regresa a la sala, Eduardo no está. Pasa dos días haciendo llamadas y preguntándoles a otros amigos si saben algo de él. Nada. Nadie sabe nada. Cisco ya no° sabe qué hacer. ¿Debe llamar a la policía? ¿Debe avisar a los padres de Eduardo?

*clue*
Por fin va a la computadora de Eduardo para ver si hay alguna pista°. Como Cisco es muy hábil con las computadoras, puede entrar en el correo electrónico de Eduardo. ¡Allí ve unos mensajes que le dan miedo!

Lo piensa bien y finalmente decide mandarle un email a su primo Manolo. Cisco admira y respeta mucho a su primo porque tiene mucha experiencia en la vida. Piensa que Manolo

METHODOLOGY • Checking for Comprehension in English
When encouraging students to hypothesize regarding what will happen, it is acceptable to encourage them to brainstorm in English.

es muy responsable y casi siempre tiene respuestas para todo. Va a la computadora y empieza a escribir:

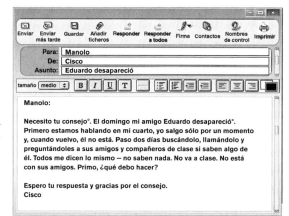

*advice / disappeared*

**Manolo:**

Necesito tu consejo°. El domingo mi amigo Eduardo desapareció°. Primero estamos hablando en mi cuarto, yo salgo sólo por un momento y, cuando vuelvo, él no está. Paso dos días buscándolo, llamándolo y preguntándoles a sus amigos y compañeros de clase si saben algo de él. Todos me dicen lo mismo — no saben nada. No va a clase. No está con sus amigos. Primo, ¿qué debo hacer?

Espero tu respuesta y gracias por el consejo.
Cisco

*distract myself*   "Bueno", piensa Cisco, "necesito algo para distraerme°. Creo que voy al concierto".

Su universidad siempre tiene buenos programas de música. Esta noche toca un grupo de fama internacional. Sus grabaciones son fenomenales y el cantante principal también tiene mucha habilidad como guitarrista. Cisco tiene todos sus CD.

"Sé quien va a estar sentada a mi lado", piensa, "aquella chica guapísima de mi clase de economía compró su entrada al mismo tiempo que yo. ¡Ay! Las cosas se ven mucho mejor ahora".

Después de regresar del concierto, Cisco está de muy buen humor. Es muy tarde pero no quiere dormir. Quiere pensar en el concierto y en la chica. Decide ir a ver si tiene un mensaje de ella o de su primo. Al abrir su correo electrónico encuentra un mensaje de Eduardo con la fecha del mismo día de la "discusión": ¡hace dos días!

¡Es increíble! Y algo igualmente increíble es que los destinatarios del mensaje sean Cisco y cuatro personas más: Alejandra Sánchez, María Soledad Valenzuela, Guadalupe Iriarte y Manolo Rodríguez. ¿Manolo? Su primo Manolo se llama *Rodríguez* también. ¿Puede ser el mismo?

**5-42** **Después de leer** Contesta las siguientes preguntas. ■

1. ¿Qué hace Cisco para buscar a Eduardo?
2. ¿A quién le escribe Cisco para pedirle consejo? ¿Por qué?
3. ¿Qué hace Cisco para distraerse? Describe el evento.
4. ¿De quién tiene Cisco un mensaje en su correo electrónico?
5. ¿Quiénes reciben el mismo mensaje?

ANSWERS to 5-42
1. Llama a sus amigos, lo busca y le escribe un email a su primo Manolo.
2. A Manolo, porque es muy inteligente y sabe qué hacer.
3. Va a un concierto. Es muy divertido y conoce a una chica bonita.
4. De Eduardo.
5. Alejandra, Marisol, Lupe y Manolo.

**Instructor Resources**
• Video script

**SECTION GOALS for *Video***
By the end of the *Video* section, students will be able to:
• discuss possible theories regarding Eduardo's whereabouts.
• report the events of the videoconference.
• predict what secrets Lupe might be hiding.

05-55 to 05-57

# Video

**5-43** **Antes del video** ¿Qué podemos hacer cuando alguien desaparece? En tu opinión, ¿por qué Cisco no llama a la policía? En la segunda parte del episodio, vas a ver una videoconferencia entre todos los estudiantes menos Eduardo. ¿Qué piensas que van a decir? También, Alejandra va a decir, "Creo que te conozco". ¿A quién crees que le dice Alejandra esa oración? ■

¿Te gusta la música latina?     Creo que te conozco.     Debemos informar a la policía.

Episodio 5

## «Se conocen»

Relájate y disfruta el video.

**5-44** **Después del video** Contesta las siguientes preguntas. ■

1. ¿Quién organiza la videoconferencia y por qué?
2. ¿De qué hablan Marisol y Lupe antes de la videoconferencia?
3. ¿Dónde están Alejandra y Manolo antes de la videoconferencia?
4. ¿Qué información comparten los estudiantes durante la videoconferencia?
5. Alejandra piensa que reconoce a alguien. ¿A quién? ¿Por qué?
6. ¿Quién desaparece al final de la videoconferencia?

**ANSWERS to 5-44**
1. Cisco, porque quiere hablar de Eduardo y del correo electrónico.
2. De la música.
3. En la biblioteca.
4. Comparten información personal como sus especialidades, etc.
5. A Lupe. Piensa que la conoce de una clase de sociología el año pasado.
6. Alejandra desaparece al final.

# Y por fin, ¿cómo andas?

|  | Feel confident | Need to review |
|---|:---:|:---:|
| Having completed this chapter, I now can . . . | | |

**Comunicación I**

| | | |
|---|:---:|:---:|
| • discuss music (p. 172) | ☐ | ☐ |
| • practice pronouncing diphthongs and linking words (MSL/SAM) | ☐ | ☐ |
| • identify people and things (Part I) (p. 175) | ☐ | ☐ |
| • identify people and things (Part II) (p. 177) | ☐ | ☐ |
| • explain how something is done (p. 179) | ☐ | ☐ |
| • describe what is happening at the moment (p. 180) | ☐ | ☐ |

**Comunicación II**

| | | |
|---|:---:|:---:|
| • share information about movies and television programs (p. 184) | ☐ | ☐ |
| • rank people and things (p. 187) | ☐ | ☐ |
| • state what needs to be accomplished (p. 188) | ☐ | ☐ |
| • express *what* or *whom* (p. 189) | ☐ | ☐ |
| • anticipate content when listening (p. 192) | ☐ | ☐ |
| • communicate about music and film (p. 193) | ☐ | ☐ |
| • write a movie review and practice peer editing (p. 194) | ☐ | ☐ |

**Cultura**

| | | |
|---|:---:|:---:|
| • discuss Hispanic music in the United States (p. 178) | ☐ | ☐ |
| • describe Hispanic influences in North American film (p. 186) | ☐ | ☐ |
| • list interesting facts about Nicaragua, Costa Rica, and Panama (pp. 195–197) | ☐ | ☐ |

**Ambiciones siniestras**

| | | |
|---|:---:|:---:|
| • anticipate content when reading and discover what Cisco does in his search for Eduardo (p. 198) | ☐ | ☐ |
| • find out who is the second student to disappear (p. 200) | ☐ | ☐ |

**Comunidades**

| | | |
|---|:---:|:---:|
| • use Spanish in real-life contexts (SAM) | ☐ | ☐ |

**Instructor Resources**
• Testing program information

# VOCABULARIO ACTIVO

| El mundo de la música | The world of music |
|---|---|
| el/la artista | artist |
| la batería | drums |
| el/la baterista | drummer |
| el/la cantante | singer |
| el concierto | concert |
| el conjunto | group; band |
| el/la empresario/a | agent; manager |
| la gira | tour |
| las grabaciones | recordings |
| la guitarra | guitar |
| el/la guitarrista | guitarist |
| el/la músico/a | musician |
| la música | music |
| la orquesta | orchestra |
| el/la pianista | pianist |
| el piano | piano |
| el tambor | drum |
| el/la tamborista | drummer |
| la trompeta | trumpet |
| el/la trompetista | trumpet player |

| Algunos verbos | Some verbs |
|---|---|
| dar un concierto | to give/perform a concert |
| ensayar | to practice/rehearse |
| grabar | to record |
| hacer una gira | to tour |
| sacar un CD | to release a CD |
| tocar | to play (a musical instrument) |

| Algunos géneros musicales | Some musical genres |
|---|---|
| el jazz | jazz |
| la música clásica | classical music |
| la música folklórica | folk music |
| la música popular | pop music |
| la música rap | rap music |
| la ópera | opera |
| el rock | rock |
| la salsa | salsa |

| Algunos adjetivos | Some adjectives |
|---|---|
| apasionado/a | passionate |
| cuidadoso/a | careful |
| fino/a | fine; delicate |
| lento/a | slow |
| suave | smooth |

| Otras palabras útiles | Other useful words |
|---|---|
| el/la aficionado/a | fan |
| la fama | fame |
| el género | genre |
| la habilidad | ability; skill |
| la letra | lyrics |
| el ritmo | rhythm |
| la voz | voice |

| El mundo del cine | The world of cinema |
|---|---|
| el actor | actor |
| la actriz | actress |
| la entrada | ticket |
| la estrella | star |
| la pantalla | screen |
| una película... | a . . . film; movie |
| de acción | action |
| de ciencia ficción | science fiction |
| documental | documentary |
| dramática | drama |
| de guerra | war |
| de humor | funny; comedy |
| de misterio | mystery |
| musical | musical |
| romántica | romantic |
| de terror | horror |

| Otras palabras útiles | Other Useful Words |
|---|---|
| el estreno | opening |
| la película | film; movie |
| una película... | a . . . movie |
| aburrida | boring |
| animada | animated |
| conmovedora | moving |
| creativa | creative |
| deprimente | depressing |
| emocionante | moving |
| entretenida | entertaining |
| épica | epic |
| de espanto | scary |
| estupenda | stupendous |
| imaginativa | imaginative |
| impresionante | impressive |
| sorprendente | surprising |
| de suspenso | suspenseful |
| trágica | tragic |

| Los números ordinales | Ordinal numbers |
|---|---|
| primer, primero/a | first |
| segundo/a | second |
| tercer, tercero/a | third |
| cuarto/a | fourth |
| quinto/a | fifth |
| sexto/a | sixth |
| séptimo/a | seventh |
| octavo/a | eighth |
| noveno/a | ninth |
| décimo/a | tenth |

| Algunos verbos | Some verbs |
|---|---|
| estrenar una película | to release a film/movie |
| presentar una película | to show a film/movie |

203

**Instructor Resources**
• IRM: Syllabi and Lesson Plans

## NATIONAL STANDARDS

### COMUNICACIÓN

• To describe your family and other families (Communication, Cultures, Comparisons)
• To relate information about your school and campus (Communication, Comparisons)
• To impart information about homes that you and your friends like and dislike (Communication, Comparisons)
• To offer opinions on what will take place in the future (Communication)
• To reveal what you and others like to do and what you need to do (Communication)
• To report on service opportunities in your community (Communication, Connections, Communities)
• To discuss music, movies, and television (Communication, Connections, Comparisons)
• To engage in additional communication practice (Communication)

### CULTURA

• To share information about Hispanic cultures in the United States, Mexico, Spain, Honduras, Guatemala, El Salvador, Nicaragua, Costa Rica, and Panama (Communication, Cultures, Comparisons)
• To compare and contrast the countries you learned about in *Capítulos 1–5* (Cultures, Comparisons)
• To explore further cultural themes (Cultures)

### AMBICIONES SINIESTRAS

• To review and create with *Ambiciones siniestras* (Communication)

### COMUNIDADES

• To use Spanish in real-life contexts (Communities)

204

# ¡Sí, lo sé!

This chapter is a recycling chapter, designed for you to see just how much Spanish you have learned thus far. The *major points* of **Capítulos 1–5** are included in this chapter, providing you with the opportunity to "put it all together." You will be pleased to realize how much you are able to communicate in Spanish.

Since this is a recycling chapter, no new vocabulary is presented. The intention is that you review the vocabulary of **Capítulos 1–5** thoroughly, focusing on the words that you personally have difficulty remembering.

Everyone learns at a different pace. You and your classmates will vary in terms of how much of the material presented thus far you have mastered and what you still need to practice.

Remember, language learning is a process. Like any skill, learning Spanish requires practice, review, and then more practice!

## METHODOLOGY • Research Guiding ¡Anda!

The programs *¡Anda! Curso elemental* and *¡Anda! Curso intermedio* are written based not only on the National Standards but also on extensive research that impacts language learning. Reading more on the topics will help to deepen understanding of the instructional delivery topics and can create excellent collegial discussions. For example, for those wishing to know more

about spiraling, please consult the work of Robert Gagné, American educational psychologist (1916–2002) whose "Nine Events of Instruction" remains a foundation of instructional delivery. Other topics of interest may be the theory of multiple intelligences proposed by Howard Gardner in 1983 or Carol Ann Tomlinson's writings on differentiated instruction.

## METHODOLOGY • Philosophy on Recycling

This chapter is unique in *¡Anda! Curso elemental* because it provides yet another opportunity for students to demonstrate the Spanish language they have acquired. In this chapter, *¡Anda! Curso elemental* has synthesized the main points of the first 5 chapters in a recycled format for students to practice the new skills they are learning. You will note that all of these

activities have the students *put it all together;* in other words, *all of the activities in Capítulo 6 are communicative.* There are no discrete point, mechanical activities. Instead, we direct the students to make use of the activities in MySpanishLab or to repeat the activities in their *Student Activities Manual,* the Extra Activities folder under Instructor's Resources, or in the textbook itself for mechanical practice.

Another way to use this chapter is to assign the activities while you are teaching each individual chapter. For example, you may have students who would benefit by additional communicative activities in addition to the *¡Conversemos!* activities. Since the Chapter 6 communicative activities have been separated by chapter, it makes it easy for you to assign them.

### OBJETIVOS

#### COMUNICACIÓN

To describe your family and other families

To relate information about your school and campus

To impart information about homes that you and your friends like and dislike

To offer opinions on what will take place in the future

To reveal what you and others like to do and what you need to do

To report on service opportunities in your community

To discuss music, movies, and television

To engage in additional communication practice (SAM)

#### CULTURA

To share information about Hispanic cultures in the United States, Mexico, Spain, Honduras, Guatemala, El Salvador, Nicaragua, Costa Rica, and Panama

To compare and contrast the countries you learned about in **Capítulos 1–5**

To explore further cultural themes (SAM)

#### AMBICIONES SINIESTRAS

To review and create with **Ambiciones siniestras**

#### COMUNIDADES

To use Spanish in real-life contexts (SAM)

205

**METHODOLOGY • Prioritizing Review Topics**

Prior to beginning the activities in this chapter, if your students choose (or you strongly encourage them) to gain more mechanical practice, repeating the activities they have already done both in the *¡Anda! Curso elemental* textbook and in their *Student Activities Manual* is an excellent start for their review. Redoing activities already done is an important review tool that is based on learning theory. This works for the following reasons: First, they are already familiar with the context of the activity, and know what they got correct and missed the first time; hence they are able to observe whether they have improved. They also are repeating the activities on a different level. Since they have already completed the activity, these repetitions go to a meta-analysis level, where they need to analyze why they continue to miss certain items. The same learning theory concept is similar in most fields/professions. For example, in the culinary arts, chefs are expected to perform the same preparations, such as cutting vegetables, in precisely the identical uniform way time and again. In music, the same scales and arpeggios are practiced over and over.

Finally, if you have advanced or heritage language learners, you may wish to skip this chapter or assign it as extra practice that the students can do by themselves.

**METHODOLOGY • Organizing a Review for Students**

Researchers and reviewers of *¡Anda! Curso elemental* agree. After giving the students strategies on how to conduct an overall review, this chapter is organized by beginning with communicative and engaging activities that focus on grammar and vocabulary beginning with *Capítulo Preliminar A.* The review continues to move through the chapters, ending with *Capítulo 5.* This is followed by *Un poco de todo,* a more comprehensive review, truly *putting it all together,* combining all of the chapters. Finally, there is a review of countries presented in *Capítulos 1–5.*

**METHODOLOGY • Recycling vs. Reviewing**

In *¡Anda! Curso elemental, recycling* up to this point has meant taking previously learned material and recombining it with new material. This concept is supported by Gagné's learning concept of spiraling information. In *Capítulo 6,* we are not presenting any new material, but rather recombining what your students have already learned and expanding the level. This also constitutes *recycling.* The concept of *review* is revisiting a topic, much like one does before an exam. *Review* is best illustrated in *Capítulo 4 (Un repaso de ser y estar),* as well as this chapter. No new information is introduced in a *review,* nor is there any true spiraling. Instead, a *review* affords students the opportunity to practice in a systematic fashion.

**METHODOLOGY • Prioritizing Review Topics**

You will note that the authors of *¡Anda! Curso elemental* have listed only 5 grammar topics that we denote as *major* and upon which we are encouraging our students to focus the majority of their review time. Students become overwhelmed when told that *everything* is major. They then tend to make poor choices regarding where to focus the majority of their time when reviewing. Truth be told, we believe there to be *one* major, overarching grammar concept, which can be broken down into subparts: *present tense of regular, irregular,* and *stem-changing verbs.* If students are able to express themselves correctly using a richness of verbs in a wide array of topics, we believe the first semester has been successful. We have listed the other 4 as "icing on the cake." Please understand that we are not diminishing the importance of concepts such as noun and adjective agreement or the differences between *saber* and *conocer.* What we are saying is that if students were to communicate with a sympathetic native speaker, they would still be understood even with mistakes in those areas. We have used as our guide descriptors such as the *ACTFL Proficiency Guidelines* as well as the *Spanish Advanced Placement* descriptors. Also guiding us is the fact that when constructing final exams, the vast majority of points fall into the *present tense* category.

**CAPÍTULO 6**

**SUGGESTION for *Prioritizing Review Topics***
If you hold review sessions or if you have students such as tutors or academic support staff that offer review sessions, suggest that students generate their questions about particular points before coming to the review. An idea to consider is that the students provide evidence of their preparation for the review session. It can serve as their "admission ticket" to the review.

**METHODOLOGY • Differentiated Instruction**
Differentiated instruction is when you tailor your lessons for your different types of learners. The number of types of learners and their preferences depend on which research you are consulting. Some sources maintain that there are four different types of learning styles, some say 7 or 8, and still others claim that there are more than 20! As instructors, what we need to remember is that students learn in different ways and progress at different rates. When assessing the progress of your students, it is important to know that for some of your students, their best performance will be to give multiple answers, while for others, their best will be one complete sentence. Differentiating instruction, in part, means to tailor our lessons so that all of our students, no matter what their style or talents, will be successful.

**PLANNING AHEAD**
You may wish to refer students to *Appendix 1. Capítulo 6,* where they can find a list of the grammar points reviewed in this chapter.

**METHODOLOGY • Organizing a Review**
*¡Anda! Curso elemental* is combining three chapters in this initial section for one important reason: Although there are a number of concepts and vocabulary words that appear in *Capítulo Preliminar A* and *Capítulo 1,* only 3 main verbs are introduced: *ser, tener,* and an abbreviated introduction of *gustar.* After completing *Capítulo 5,* your students already have a wide array of verbs and vocabulary at their fingertips. To require them to use only three in order to practice the family does not allow them to be as creative as possible. Also notice that we are suggesting that they can use verbs and vocabulary beyond *Capítulo 2.* You can differentiate instruction by directing specific students to focus on chapters beyond *Capítulo 2* if you wish.

# Organizing Your Review

There are processes used by successful language learners for reviewing a world language. The following tips can help you organize your review. There is no one correct way, but these are some suggestions that will best utilize your time and energy.

## 1 Reviewing Strategies

1. Make a list of the *major* topics you have studied and need to review, dividing them into three categories: *vocabulary, grammar,* and *culture.* These are the topics on which you need to focus the majority of your time and energy.
*Note:* The two-page chapter openers can help you determine the *major* topics.
2. Allocate a minimum of an hour each day over a period of time to review. Budget the majority of your time for the major topics. After beginning with the most important grammar and vocabulary topics, review the secondary/supporting grammar topics and the culture. Cramming the night before a test is *not* an effective way to review and retain information.
3. Many educational researchers suggest that you start your review with the most recent chapter, or in this case, **Capítulo 5.** The most recent chapter is the freshest in your mind, so you tend to remember the concepts better, and you will experience quick success in your review.
4. Spend the most amount of time on concepts in which you determine *you* need to improve. Revisit the self-assessment tools **Y por fin, ¿cómo andas?** in each chapter to see how you rated yourself. Those tools are designed to help you become good at self-assessing what you need to work on the most.

## 2 Reviewing Grammar

1. When reviewing grammar, begin with the *major* points, that is, begin with the *present tense* of regular, irregular, and stem-changing verbs. After feeling confident with using the major grammar points correctly, proceed to the additional grammar points and review them.
2. Good ways to review include redoing activities in your textbook, redoing activities in your Student Activities Manual, and (re)doing activities on MySpanishLab.

## 3 Reviewing Vocabulary

1. When studying vocabulary, it is usually most helpful to look at the English word and then say or write the word in Spanish. Make a special list of words that are difficult for you to remember, writing them in a small notebook or in an electronic file. Pull out your list every time you have a few minutes (in between classes, waiting in line at the grocery store, etc.) to review the words. The **Vocabulario activo** pages at the end of each chapter will help you organize the most important words of each chapter.
2. Saying vocabulary (which includes verbs) out loud helps you retain the words better.

## 4 Overall Review Technique

1. Get together with someone with whom you can practice speaking Spanish. If you need something to spark the conversation, take the drawings from each vocabulary presentation in *¡Anda! Curso elemental* and say as many things as you can about each picture. Have a friendly challenge to see who can make more complete sentences or create the longest story about the pictures. This will help you build your confidence and practice stringing sentences together to speak in paragraphs.
2. Yes, it is important for you to know "mechanical" pieces of information such as verb endings, or how to take a sentence and replace the direct object with a pronoun, *but* it is *much more important* that you are able to take those mechanical pieces of information and put them all together, creating meaningful and creative samples of your speaking and writing on the themes of the first 5 chapters.
3. You are well on the road to success if you can demonstrate that you can speak and write in paragraphs, using a wide variety of verbs and vocabulary words correctly. Keep up the good work!

# Comunicación

06-01 to 06-05

## Capítulo Preliminar A, Capítulo 1 y Capítulo 2

Capítulo Preliminar A, 1 y 2

**Estrategia**

Before beginning each activity, make sure that you have reviewed the identified recycled concepts carefully so that you are able to move through the activities seamlessly as you put it all together! *¡Sí, lo sabes!*

**6-1** **Nuestras familias** Completen los siguientes pasos en grupos de cuatro. ◼

**Paso 1** Con un/a compañero/a, túrnense para describir a varios miembros de sus familias usando por lo menos **diez** oraciones con un mínimo de **cinco** verbos diferentes. Incluyan (*Include*): aspectos de sus personalidades, descripciones físicas, qué hacen en su tiempo libre, cuántos años tienen, etc.

**MODELO** E1: *Mi familia no es muy grande. Mi madre es simpática, inteligente y trabajadora. Tiene cuarenta y cinco años...*

**Paso 2** Ahora describe a la familia de tu compañero/a a otro miembro del grupo usando por lo menos **cinco** oraciones. Si no recuerdas bien los detalles o si necesitas clarificación, pregúntale (*ask him/her*).

**MODELO** E2: *La familia de Adriana es pequeña. Su madre es simpática y trabajadora... Adriana, perdón, pero ¿cuántos años tiene tu madre?...*

**Estrategia**

Being a good listener is an important life skill. Repeating what your classmate said gives you practice in demonstrating how well you listen.

**Instructor Resources**
• Textbook images, Extra Activities

**METHODOLOGY • Using This Chapter**
Although most of the activities in this chapter utilize the pair icon, you will note that most can be done at home. You can choose whether you want these activities to be oral, written, or a combination of oral and written. You can also choose whether you want the activities to be prepared outside of class using MySpanishLab or done in class. The decisions are yours to personalize the chapter in a manner that best suits your and your students' needs.

Some activities may seem to be repeat activities from the original chapters. The themes are identical and need to be in order for this to qualify as a review/recycling. For example, if the students have studied the family, then the additional practice/rehearsal of this chapter needs to be about the family. Additionally, the activities in this chapter are not repeats from the original, but rather communicative practice.

The intention of this chapter is to be a culminating experience for the students. They are expected to come to class having reviewed the chapters and their concepts. You may wish to suggest that they formulate their review by going back to textbook chapter activities, the *Student Activities Manual,* and/or other available activities on MySpanishLab.

**PLANNING AHEAD**
Activity **6-1** is enhanced if students bring in photos of their families to act as advance organizers. You will note, though, that we have included a variety of family photos as visual organizers that you can suggest they use. You can also suggest that students bring in photos from magazines as their "imaginary" families. We are very sensitive to the fact that the term "family" is highly diverse in the 21st century.

**SUGGESTION for *Planning Ahead***
Students who live on campus do not always have access to personal family photos or to magazines without going home for the weekend. You might want to have pictures of families available for those students who are not able to bring in photos.

**METHODOLOGY • Reviewing Vocabulary**
Based on learning style/multiple intelligences differences, there are a variety of ways to practice vocabulary. MySpanishLab has flash cards for vocabulary practice. Another way is for the student to draw a picture of the vocabulary word on an index card with the Spanish word on the opposite side. This review method supports the learners who are strong in the Multiple Intelligence of Visual / Spatial / "Picture Smart."

**METHODOLOGY • Learning Techniques**
You may wish to remind your students that knowing mechanical information such as verb endings is not real communication. Hence, a review such

as this chapter creates important scenarios for them that are indeed real communication and real-life uses of Spanish.

**METHODOLOGY • Making Learning Meaningful for Students**
The three photos that accompany **6-1** are intended to act as advance organizer photos. Advance organizers are meant in this case to help students envision their own families. If you teach in a community that is in some way not represented by one of these three images, you may want to bring in a photo that depicts your community, or you may wish to have students bring in their own photos.

# CAPÍTULO 6

**METHODOLOGY • Quantifying Minimum Expectations**

You will note that we frequently include the minimum number of sentences expected of the students in both speaking and writing activities. If students do not know what these minimum expectations are, many will be happy with mediocre production. And they are not always the weaker students! Most of us have had bright students who are lazy and only willing to do "the minimum." Hence it is necessary for instructors to let students know what their expectations are and to encourage students to exceed the minimum.

Having provided this rationale, the decision is ultimately yours. You may choose (a) to use what we have recommended; (b) to require a different minimum level of production; or (c) not to state the level of language production. You will notice that some of the directions in this chapter are intentionally following (c). These are instructional delivery decisions that all of us must make based on a wide variety of differentiated objectives.

**EXPANSION for 6-2**

You may wish to have students consult the *Les presento mi país* sections in each chapter to search for specific information, and therefore formulate content questions.

**NOTE for 6-3**

The *modelo* includes some concepts that the students have not yet formally reviewed from *Capítulo Preliminar A*, *Capítulo 1*, and *Capítulo 2*, such as numbers beyond the hundreds and demonstrative adjectives. This should not cause a problem, as students did learn the concepts in later chapters.

## Estrategia

Although these activities are focusing on *Capítulos Preliminar A, 1*, and *2*, feel free to use additional vocabulary from later chapters to create your questions. For example, in **6-2,** you may want to use vocabulary from *Capítulo 5*.

### 6-2 ¿Cómo eres?
Conoces un poco a los estudiantes que estudiamos en **Les presento mi país** en los **Capítulos 1–5.** ¿Qué más quieres saber de ellos? Escribe por lo menos **diez** preguntas que quieres hacerles. Sé (*Be*) creativo/a. ■

**MODELO**
1. *¿Dónde estudias?*
2. *¿Te gusta leer libros de deportes?*
3. *¿Qué comes?*
4. *¿Qué idiomas hablan en tu país?*
5. ...

## Estrategia

Pay attention to the particular grammar point you are practicing. If you are supposed to write sentences using *tener*, underline each form of *tener* that you use, and then check to make sure it agrees with the subject. Using strategies such as underlining can help you focus on important points.

Rafael Sánchez Martínez

Gabriela García Cordera

Mariela Castañeda Ropero

César Alfonso Avalos

Luis Pedro Aguirre Maldonado

Claudia Figueroa Barrios

Mauricio Morales Prado

Laura Centeno Soto

Magdalena Quintero de Gracia

### 6-3 Una gira
Trabajas en tu universidad como guía para los estudiantes nuevos. Crea una gira para ellos. Incluye por lo menos **cinco** lugares y **dos** deportes. ■

**MODELO**
*Esta universidad tiene diez mil estudiantes. Esta es la biblioteca. Los estudiantes estudian aquí y usan las computadoras. Allí está el gimnasio donde juegan al básquetbol. Tenemos las especialidades de matemáticas, español...*

| Vocabulario útil | |
| --- | --- |
| **aquí** | *here* |
| **allí** | *there / over there* |
| **allá** | *over there (and potentially not visible)* |

## Rúbrica

All aspects of our lives benefit from self-reflection and self-assessment. Learning Spanish is an aspect of our academic and future professional lives that benefits greatly from just such a self-assessment. Also coming into play is the fact that, as college students, you personally are being held accountable for your learning and are expected to take ownership for your performance. Having said that, we instructors can assist you greatly by letting you know what we expect of you. It will help you determine how well you are doing with the recycling of **Capítulo Preliminar A, Capítulo 1,** and **Capítulo 2.** This rubric is meant first and foremost for you to use as a self-assessment tool, but you also can use it to peer-assess. Your instructor may use the rubric to assess your progress as well.

**Estrategia**

You and your instructor can use this rubric to assess your progress for 6-1 through 6-3.

| | 3 EXCEEDS EXPECTATIONS | 2 MEETS EXPECTATIONS | 1 APPROACHES EXPECTATIONS | 0 DOES NOT MEET EXPECTATIONS |
|---|---|---|---|---|
| **Duración y precisión** | • Has at least 8 sentences and includes all the required information. <br>• May have errors, but they do not interfere with communication. | • Has 5–7 sentences and includes all the required information. <br>• May have errors, but they rarely interfere with communication. | • Has 4 sentences and includes some of the required information. <br>• Has errors that interfere with communication. | • Supplies fewer sentences than in *Approaches Expectations* and little of the required information. <br>• If communicating at all, has frequent errors that make communication limited or impossible. |
| **Gramática nueva de los *Capítulos Preliminar A, 1 y 2*** | • Makes excellent use of the chapters' new grammar. <br>• Uses a wide variety of verbs. | • Makes good use of the chapters' new grammar. <br>• Uses a variety of verbs. | • Makes use of some of the chapters' new grammar. <br>• Uses a limited variety of verbs. | • Uses little, if any, of the chapters' new grammar. <br>• Uses few, if any, of the chapters' verbs. |
| **Vocabulario nuevo de los *Capítulos Preliminar A, 1 y 2*** | • Uses many of the vocabulary words new to Chapters Preliminary A, 1 and 2. | • Uses a variety of the new vocabulary words. | • Uses some of the new vocabulary words. | • Uses few, if any, new vocabulary words. |
| **Esfuerzo (*Effort*)** | • Clearly the student made his/her best effort. | • The student made a good effort. | • The student made an effort. | • Little or no effort went into the activity. |

**METHODOLOGY • Self-Assessment and Instructor's Use of Rubrics**

Assessing student performance is an important task that we instructors perform. Students need to know in advance what is acceptable versus unacceptable work. It is important that students are provided in advance with the rubrics so that they are clear regarding our expectations.

The rubrics provided are meant to be used either as is or to act as a guide for you. The suggestion is that **3 = A; 2 = B; 1 = C; 0 = D/F.** Also notice that there is a place for you to assess effort. As instructors, we know that there will be some students who look for and take the easy way out, even though they may have the ability. These can be gifted students or heritage language learners who choose not to work to their potential. The effort rating is a way of encouraging those students as well as giving credit to students who struggle but are working above and beyond their level of ability. These students deserve to be rewarded for their efforts.

You may wish to add other categories such as pronunciation to the rubric.

**METHODOLOGY • Assessing Effort**

Yes, commenting on and assessing a student's effort is a subjective evaluation. Nevertheless, it is something that both students and instructors need to address. The ability to realistically assess the efforts they place on tasks is a life skill students will need when they exit college. Assessing effort is also an important reality check for all students. Are they working to their highest potential? Some students truly are; others are not.

There are a variety of types of students: those who put in a great deal of effort and are successful; those who put in a great deal of effort and are not as successful as they or we would like; those who *say* they are putting in effort when in fact they are not or it is not focused; those who put in little effort and do not succeed; and those who put in little effort and still achieve at least our minimum expectation but could do extremely well with more effort. The final group is comprised of gifted students as well as heritage language learners.

**METHODOLOGY • Learning Theory**
Learning research has taught us that when reviewing/studying lists of vocabulary, it is most efficient for the brain to begin with the native language and then move to the target language word. When a beginning Spanish-language student is searching for a word in the target language, that individual defaults to the most common language—their native language. If your students are not strong speakers of English, adjust this *Estrategia* study tip to meet their needs.

**EXPANSION for 6-4**
After completing the activity, take a student poll to determine which house is the most popular. If there is a clear favorite, encourage discussion regarding their reasons for choosing it.

**METHODOLOGY • Images for 6-4**
The objective of this activity is to have students utilize the home and furnishings vocabulary of *Capítulo 3*. The images with this activity help to remind students of the vocabulary along with a variety of colors to review those as well.

**EXPANSION for 6-5**
Compare student schedules to determine who begins the day earliest, who ends the day latest, who has the most entries, which days seems to be the busiest for the majority, etc.

---

 **Capítulo 3**
06-06 to 06-10

 Capítulo 3

**6-4 Mi casa favorita**   Mira los dibujos y descríbele tu casa favorita a un/a compañero/a. Dile (*Tell him/her*) por qué te gusta la casa y explícale por qué no te gustan las otras (*the other*) casas. ◼

### Estrategia

As you study vocabulary or grammar, it might be helpful to organize the information into a word web. Start with the concept you want to practice, such as *la casa*, write the word in the center of the page, and draw a circle around it. Then, as you brainstorm how your other vocabulary fits into *la casa*, you can create circles that branch off from your main idea, for example, *la cocina, la sala, el dormitorio*, etc. and then list the furniture that belongs in each room.

---

**6-5 Mi horario personal**
Escribe tu horario (*schedule*) para una semana académica. Incluye por lo menos **siete** actividades usando **siete** verbos diferentes. Después comparte tu horario con un/a compañero/a. ◼

### Estrategia

When you are reviewing vocabulary, one strategy is to fold your paper lengthwise and have one column dedicated to the words in English and another column in Spanish. That way, you can fold the page over and look at only one set of words, testing yourself to see whether you really know the vocabulary.

**6-6** ## Quiero saber... Completa los siguientes pasos para entrevistar a un/a compañero/a.

**Paso 1**  Escribe tus preguntas usando los siguientes verbos.

| hacer | oír | querer | salir | venir |
|-------|------|--------|-------|--------|
| poder | poner | saber | traer | conocer |

**MODELO**  E1: *¿Qué traes a tus clases todos los días?*

**Paso 2**  Entrevista a tu compañero/a.

**MODELO**  E1: *¿Qué traes a tus clases todos los días?*

E2: *Traigo mi mochila a mis clases todos los días...*

**Paso 3**  Comparte la información con tus compañeros de clase.

**MODELO**  *Mi compañero Jake trae su mochila a sus clases. También,...*

**Estrategia**

With situations like those in **6-6**, it is not essential that *all* details be remembered. Nor is it essential in this type of scenario to repeat *verbatim* what someone has said; it is totally acceptable to express the same idea in different words. When necessary, ask him/her to repeat or clarify information.

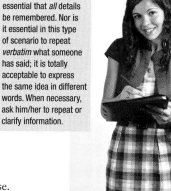

**6-7** ## ¿Qué tienen? Túrnense para describir a las personas de los dibujos usando expresiones con **tener**.

**MODELO**  *Jorge recibe una buena nota en su examen. Tiene éxito en su clase de periodismo.*

Julia

Susana   Mirta

Beatriz   Jorge

Guadalupe

Guillermo   Miguel   Beto

Adriana   David

---

**NOTE on *Actividades***

Depending on the length and frequency of your class sessions, and whether they are face to face, online, or a hybrid, you may not have time to use all the textbook activities. We encourage you to use the textbook as a tool to facilitate your students' learning, and only *you* can decide which activities will be most beneficial to your students. In some cases we have provided suggestions for adapting the directions of particular activities to suit your students' needs and to encourage you to achieve different objectives.

**NOTE for 6-6**

You may want to provide students with a specific number of questions they must write.

**EXPANSION for 6-7**

Encourage students to be creative. They can produce mini-stories about each drawing.

**METHODOLOGY • More on Assessing Effort**

Assessing a student's effort, albeit a subjective exercise, helps two major groups of students: those who find Spanish easy and are doing well but not working to their potential, and those who are giving their all and are still struggling. With regard to the latter group, many of us have our beginning Spanish classes filled with non-majors who either need the credits or want to use Spanish in some way in their future lives. Many of these individuals are giving a maximum effort and still struggling. The research on motivation would support us giving these students a grade for effort and including it into our final grading. Why? Because our goal for beginning Spanish should be to create lifelong learners, consumers, and devotees of the Spanish language. Although it is wonderful to have students decide to dedicate their lives to Spanish literature, our reality is that most of the students passing through our courses have hopes of using Spanish orally in their professional lives. Acknowledging their *esfuerzo* will motivate them to exceed even their own expectations.

## Rúbrica

**Estrategia**

You and your instructor can use this rubric to assess your progress for **6-4** through **6-7.**

| | 3 EXCEEDS EXPECTATIONS | 2 MEETS EXPECTATIONS | 1 APPROACHES EXPECTATIONS | 0 DOES NOT MEET EXPECTATIONS |
|---|---|---|---|---|
| **Duración y precisión** | • Has at least 8 sentences and includes all the required information. <br> • May have errors, but they do not interfere with communication. | • Has 5–7 sentences and includes all the required information. <br> • May have errors, but they rarely interfere with communication. | • Has 4 sentences and includes some of the required information. <br> • Has errors that interfere with communication. | • Supplies fewer sentences than in *Approaches Expectations* and little of the required information. <br> • If communicating at all, has frequent errors that make communication limited or impossible. |
| **Gramática nueva del *Capítulo 3*** | • Makes excellent use of the chapter's new grammar (e.g., **irregular present tense verbs, *tener* expressions,** and **hay**). <br> • Uses a wide variety of new verbs. | • Makes good use of the chapter's new grammar (e.g., **irregular present tense verbs, *tener* expressions,** and **hay**). <br> • Uses a variety of new verbs. | • Makes use of some of the chapter's new grammar (e.g., **irregular present tense verbs, *tener* expressions,** and **hay**). <br> • Uses a limited variety of new verbs. | • Uses little if any of the chapter's grammar (e.g., **irregular present tense verbs, *tener* expressions,** and **hay**). |
| **Vocabulario nuevo del *Capítulo 3*** | • Uses many of the new vocabulary words (e.g., **house, furniture,** and **household chores**). | • Uses a variety of the new vocabulary words (e.g., **house, furniture,** and **household chores**). | • Uses some of the new vocabulary words (e.g., **house, furniture,** and **household chores**). | • Uses little, if any, new vocabulary (e.g., **house, furniture, and household chores**). |
| ✺ **Gramática y vocabulario reciclado de los capítulos anteriores** | • Does an excellent job using recycled grammar and vocabulary to support what is being said. <br> • Uses a wide array of recycled verbs. <br> • Uses some recycled vocabulary but focuses predominantly on new vocabulary. | • Does a good job using recycled grammar and vocabulary to support what is being said. <br> • Uses an array of recycled verbs. <br> • Uses some recycled vocabulary but focuses predominantly on new vocabulary. | • Does an average job using recycled grammar and vocabulary to support what is being said. <br> • Uses a limited array of recycled verbs. <br> • Uses mostly recycled vocabulary and some new vocabulary. | • If speaking at all, relies almost completely on a few isolated words. <br> • Grammar usage is inconsistent. |
| **Esfuerzo** | • Clearly the student made his/her best effort. | • The student made a good effort. | • The student made an effort. | • Little or no effort went into the activity. |

**Capítulo 4**

06-11 to 06-15

Capítulo 4

Instructor Resources
• Textbook images, Extra Activities

 **6-8** **Lo conocemos y lo sabemos** Juntos hagan un diagrama de Venn sobre lo que conocen y saben, y sobre lo que no conocen o no saben. Escriban por lo menos **diez** oraciones. ■

MODELO

**Janet**
1. Mi familia y yo sabemos hablar español.
2. Mi amiga Julia y sus hermanos saben tocar el piano.

**Nosotras**
1. Sabemos patinar.
2. No sabemos hablar chino.
3. Conocemos a la profesora.

**Audrey**
1. Mi amiga Sally y su familia conocen al presidente de la universidad.

 **6-9** **Un cuento divertido** Escriban en grupos un cuento creativo usando los siguientes verbos. Empiecen con la oración en el modelo. ¡Incluyan muchos detalles! ■

| | | | |
|---|---|---|---|
| almorzar (nosotros) | devolver (él) | mostrar (ella) | servir (ellos) |
| cerrar (ellas) | dormir (ellos) | pedir (tú) | volver (yo) |
| costar (los libros) | encontrar (nosotros) | seguir (yo) | comenzar (él) |

MODELO

*¡Qué día tan horrible! Primero pierdo la tarea para la clase de _____.*

Vocabulario útil

| | |
|---|---|
| **entonces** | *then* |
| **después** | *afterward* |
| **finalmente** | *finally* |
| **luego** | *then* |
| **sin embargo** | *nevertheless* |

NOTE for 6-9
This activity forces practice with stem-changing verbs and with a variety of subject nouns and pronouns. With advanced students, you can make it less structured and either have them use the word bank in the textbook in the order it is given, or not. Again, the objective for this writing activity is to practice stem-changing verbs and to create a fun context. If not guided, most beginning students will look for an easier way to complete the assignment, for example, having all of their sentences begin with *yo*. Hence the structure we suggest. Encourage students to include other verbs and/or details in their sentences. For example, Student 1 might write: *Pienso, "¿Qué hago? Mi profesor pide la tarea todos los días." Finalmente, vuelvo a mi casa para buscarla.*

**6-10  Mi comunidad ideal**  Eres un/a arquitecto/a urbano/a y planeas tu ciudad ideal. ▪

**Paso 1**  Dibuja el plano de tu ciudad con los lugares más necesarios (mercados, bancos, parques, etc.).

**Paso 2**  Descríbele tu ciudad a un/a compañero/a. Usa por lo menos **diez** oraciones con una variedad de verbos y vocabulario.

**MODELO**  *Mi ciudad ideal se llama Ciudad Feliz. Hay una plaza en el centro. Tiene…*

**6-11  Querida familia:…**  Trabajas como consejero/a en un campamento de niños. Un día ayudas a los niños a escribirles cartas a sus padres y piensas que es una buena idea escribirle a un amigo también. En tu carta o email, incluye oraciones que incorporen todos los usos que puedas (*all of the uses that you can*) de **ser** y **estar**. ▪

**MODELO**

> Querido José:
>
> Estoy muy, muy cansada hoy. Tengo ganas de dormir pero ¡solamente son las 9!

**NOTE for 6-11**

For additional practice with *ser* versus *estar*, direct your students to redo activities in their *Student Activities Manual* and MySpanishLab, as well as to repeat the activities in the Extra Activities folder under Instructor's Resources and in the *¡Anda! Curso elemental* textbook.

**6-12** **Mi tiempo libre** ¡Tus compañeros y tú van a tener diez maravillosos días de vacaciones después de los exámenes! ¿Qué van a hacer? Túrnense **cinco** veces para decir oraciones usando **el futuro** (*ir + a + infinitivo*). Después de decir tu oración, repite todo lo que dijeron (*you both said*) antes (*before*). Usen también diferentes pronombres (**yo, tú, ellos, nosotros**, etc.). ■

**MODELO**  E1: *Voy a dormir diez horas cada día.*

E2: *Mis amigos van a ir a Cancún y tú vas a dormir diez horas cada día.*

E1: *Mi familia y yo vamos a nadar, tus amigos van a ir a Cancún, y voy a dormir diez horas cada día.*

E2: …

**Estrategia**

You and your instructor can use this rubric to assess your progress for **6-8** through **6-12**.

## Rúbrica

| | 3 EXCEEDS EXPECTATIONS | 2 MEETS EXPECTATIONS | 1 APPROACHES EXPECTATIONS | 0 DOES NOT MEET EXPECTATIONS |
|---|---|---|---|---|
| **Duración y precisión** | • Has at least 8 sentences and includes all the required information.<br>• May have errors, but they do not interfere with communication. | • Has 5–7 sentences and includes all the required information.<br>• May have errors, but they rarely interfere with communication. | • Has 4 sentences and includes some of the required information.<br>• Has errors that interfere with communication. | • Supplies fewer sentences than in *Approaches Expectations* and little of the required information.<br>• If communicating at all, has frequent errors that make communication limited or impossible. |
| **Gramática nueva del *Capítulo 4*** | • Makes excellent use of the chapter's new grammar (e.g., **stem-changing verbs, *ir*, *ir + a + infinitivo*,** and **affirmative and negative expressions**).<br>• Uses a wide variety of new verbs. | • Makes good use of the chapter's new grammar (e.g., **stem-changing verbs, *ir*, *ir + a + infinitivo*,** and **affirmative and negative expressions**).<br>• Uses a variety of new verbs. | • Makes use of some of the chapter's new grammar (e.g., **stem-changing verbs, *ir*, *ir + a + infinitivo*,** and **affirmative and negative expressions**).<br>• Uses a limited variety of new verbs. | • Uses little if any of the chapter's grammar (e.g., **stem-changing verbs, *ir*, *ir + a + infinitivo*,** and **affirmative and negative expressions**).<br>• Uses no new verbs. |
| **Vocabulario nuevo del *Capítulo 4*** | • Uses many of the new vocabulary words (e.g., **places** and **things to do**). | • Uses a variety of the new vocabulary words (e.g., **places** and **things to do**). | • Uses some of the new vocabulary words (e.g., **places** and **things to do**). | • Uses little, if any, new vocabulary (e.g., **places** and **things to do**). |

*(continued)*

**NOTE for 6-12**
Many of us may have played a game as youngsters where we began by saying, *"I'm going on a trip and I'm taking X."* Then the person sitting next to us says *"I'm going on a trip and I'm taking Y and X."* That is the design and goal of **6-12**. Based on educational research, repetition is an excellent way to learn. This is the same technique that is used in children's books like *The Cat in the Hat*, where the narrative has predictable repetition. This technique works with adult learners too. Although this activity can be done in larger groups, we recommend doing it in pairs, so that each student will have more opportunities to speak and hence be less likely to become distracted and go off task.

**FOLLOW-UP for 6-12**
You can modify the activity by telling your students that you need to take a vacation after grading all of their exams. You can create a scenario explaining where you are going and with whom. They can take notes and then either say or write sentences using the future and the present, e.g., *Mi profesor/a va a viajar a España, pero yo tengo que trabajar. Mi profesor/a y su familia van a nadar en la playa, pero yo necesito limpiar mi casa.*

**EXPANSION for 6-12**
Another approach would be to have students make their own list of ten things they and their family and friends are going to do. Then students can switch papers and each can say what his/her classmate and his/her friends are going to do. This would force them to change the forms of the verb *ir*. For example, if one student writes, *"Yo voy a nadar en la piscina,"* the classmate would have to say, *"Él/Ella va a nadar en la piscina."*

**Instructor Resources**
• Textbook images, Extra Activities

| | 3 EXCEEDS EXPECTATIONS | 2 MEETS EXPECTATIONS | 1 APPROACHES EXPECTATIONS | 0 DOES NOT MEET EXPECTATIONS |
|---|---|---|---|---|
| ♻ Gramática y vocabulario reciclado de los capítulos anteriores | • Does an excellent job using recycled grammar and vocabulary to support what is being said.<br>• Uses a wide array of recycled verbs.<br>• Uses some recycled vocabulary but focuses predominantly on new vocabulary. | • Does a good job using recycled grammar and vocabulary to support what is being said.<br>• Uses an array of recycled verbs.<br>• Uses some recycled vocabulary but focuses predominantly on new vocabulary. | • Does an average job using recycled grammar and vocabulary to support what is being said.<br>• Uses a limited array of recycled verbs.<br>• Uses mostly recycled vocabulary and some new vocabulary. | • If speaking at all, relies almost completely on a few isolated words.<br>• Grammar usage is inconsistent. |
| Esfuerzo | • Clearly the student made his/her best effort. | • The student made a good effort. | • The student made an effort. | • Little or no effort went into the activity. |

 **Capítulo 5**

06-16 to 06-20

 **¡El concierto del siglo!** Quieres ir al concierto de tu conjunto o cantante favorito, pero tu compañero/a no quiere ir. Creen un diálogo sobre su situación y preséntenlo a la clase. Su diálogo debe incluir por lo menos **doce** oraciones. Usen: formas de **este, ese, aquel**; unos adverbios (**-mente**); **hay que...**; y pronombres de complemento directo (**me, te, lo, la, nos, los, las**). ∎

MODELO
E1: *David, quiero ir al concierto de Marc Anthony. Es este sábado a las ocho. Las entradas no cuestan mucho. Te invito.*

E2: *No gracias, Mariela. No quiero ir. Realmente, no puedo ir. Tengo mucha tarea.*

E1: *Pero David,...*

**SUGGESTION for 6-14**
You can set this up like a talk show, such as *David Letterman* or the *Cristina* show, where you have students come to the front of the room and pretend they are on a talk show.

 **¡Bienvenido, estrella!** ¡Tienes el trabajo ideal! Puedes entrevistar a tu actor o actriz favorito/a del cine. Escribe **diez** preguntas que vas a hacerle. Después, con un/a compañero/a de clase, hagan los papeles de estrella y entrevistador/a para la clase. ∎

# Rúbrica

**Estrategia**

You and your instructor can use this rubric to assess your progress for **6-13** through **6-14**.

|  | **3 EXCEEDS EXPECTATIONS** | **2 MEETS EXPECTATIONS** | **1 APPROACHES EXPECTATIONS** | **0 DOES NOT MEET EXPECTATIONS** |
|---|---|---|---|---|
| **Duración y precisión** | • Has at least 8 sentences and includes all the required information.<br>• May have errors, but they do not interfere with communication. | • Has 5–7 sentences and includes all the required information.<br>• May have errors, but they rarely interfere with communication. | • Has 4 sentences and includes some of the required information.<br>• Has errors that interfere with communication. | • Supplies fewer sentences than in *Approaches Expectations* and little of the required information.<br>• If communicating at all, has frequent errors that make communication limited or impossible. |
| **Gramática nueva del *Capítulo 5*** | • Makes excellent use of the chapter's new grammar (e.g., **demonstrative adjectives and pronouns, adverbs,** *Hay que...,* and **direct object pronouns**).<br>• Uses a wide variety of new verbs. | • Makes good use of the chapter's new grammar (e.g., **demonstrative adjectives and pronouns, adverbs,** *Hay que...,* and **direct object pronouns**).<br>• Uses a variety of new verbs. | • Makes use of some of the chapter's new grammar (e.g., **demonstrative adjectives and pronouns, adverbs,** *Hay que...,* and **direct object pronouns**).<br>• Uses a limited variety of new verbs. | • Uses little, if any, of the chapter's new grammar (e.g., **demonstrative adjectives and pronouns, adverbs,** *Hay que...,* and **direct object pronouns**).<br>• Uses no new verbs. |
| **Vocabulario nuevo del *Capítulo 5*** | • Uses many of the new vocabulary words (e.g., **music, the movies,** and **television**). | • Uses a variety of the new vocabulary words (e.g., **music, the movies,** and **television**). | • Uses some of the new vocabulary words (e.g., **music, the movies,** and **television**). | • Uses little, if any, new vocabulary (e.g., **music, the movies,** and **television**). |
| ✪ **Gramática y vocabulario reciclado de los capítulos anteriores** | • Does an excellent job using recycled grammar and vocabulary to support what is being said.<br>• Uses a wide array of recycled verbs.<br>• Uses some recycled vocabulary but focuses predominantly on new vocabulary. | • Does a good job using recycled grammar and vocabulary to support what is being said.<br>• Uses an array of recycled verbs.<br>• Uses some recycled vocabulary but focuses predominantly on new vocabulary. | • Does an average job using recycled grammar and vocabulary to support what is being said.<br>• Uses a limited array of recycled verbs.<br>• Uses mostly recycled vocabulary and some new vocabulary. | • If speaking at all, relies almost completely on a few isolated words.<br>• Grammar usage is inconsistent. |
| **Esfuerzo** | • Clearly the student made his/her best effort. | • The student made a good effort. | • The student made an effort. | • Little or no effort went into the activity. |

**NOTE for Un poco de todo**
In the *Un poco de todo* section, each activity combines concepts from **all** of the previous chapters, resulting in comprehensive, highly communicative review activities.

**NOTE for 6-15**
You may choose to have students create a dialogue between the lottery winner and the interviewer to perform in class.

**NOTE for 6-16**
Before starting this activity, encourage students to make a list of the household chores and work-related tasks for which they might need help. This is also a great opportunity to encourage creativity and humor.

**NOTE for 6-17**
Activity **6-17** can also be done as a group activity. The class can then judge which group has created the most interesting schedule.

 **Un poco de todo**

06-21 to 06-34

 **6-15 ¡Ganaste la lotería!** Ganaste (*You won*) un millón de dólares en la lotería y te invitan a un programa de televisión para explicar qué vas a hacer con el dinero. Dile al/a la entrevistador/a (tu compañero/a) qué vas a hacer con el dinero en por lo menos **diez** oraciones. Después cambien de papel (*Take turns playing each role*). ■

 **6-16 Busco ayuda…** Con el dinero que ganaste en la lotería, decides buscar un ayudante personal (*personal assistant*) para ayudarte con los quehaceres de la casa y con algunos asuntos (*matters*) de tu trabajo. Entrevista a un/a compañero/a que hace el papel de ayudante. Después cambien de papel. ■

MODELO    E1:   *Debe mandar mis cartas y escribir unos emails.*
           E2:   *Bueno, pero no limpio las ventanas.*
           E1:   *¿Cómo? ¿No las limpia? ¿Pasa la aspiradora?*
           E2:   …

 **6-17 Mi horario para la semana** Crea un horario para una semana ideal durante el verano. Usa por lo menos **diez** verbos diferentes para explicar lo que tienes que hacer. Comparte tu horario con un/a compañero/a. ■

| junio | | | | | | |
|---|---|---|---|---|---|---|
| L | M | M | J | V | S | D |
|  | 1 | 2 | 3 | 4 | 5 | 6 |
| 7 | 8 | 9 | 10 | 11 | 12 | 13 |
| 14 | 15 | 16 | 17 | 18 | 19 | 20 |
| 21 | 22 | 23 | 24 | 25 | 26 | 27 |
| 28 | 29 | 30 |  |  |  |  |

| julio | | | | | | |
|---|---|---|---|---|---|---|
| L | M | M | J | V | S | D |
|  |  |  | 1 | 2 | 3 | 4 |
| 5 | 6 | 7 | 8 | 9 | 10 | 11 |
| 12 | 13 | 14 | 15 | 16 | 17 | 18 |
| 19 | 20 | 21 | 22 | 23 | 24 | 25 |
| 26 | 27 | 28 | 29 | 30 | 31 |  |

| agosto | | | | | | |
|---|---|---|---|---|---|---|
| L | M | M | J | V | S | D |
|  |  |  |  |  |  | 1 |
| 2 | 3 | 4 | 5 | 6 | 7 | 8 |
| 9 | 10 | 11 | 12 | 13 | 14 | 15 |
| 16 | 17 | 18 | 19 | 20 | 21 | 22 |
| 23 | 24 | 25 | 26 | 27 | 28 | 29 |
| 30 | 31 |  |  |  |  |  |

**6-18** **Mis planes para el verano** Escribe un email a un/a compañero/a de **ocho** a **diez** oraciones sobre lo que vas a hacer este verano: **cuándo, dónde** y **con quién.** ▪

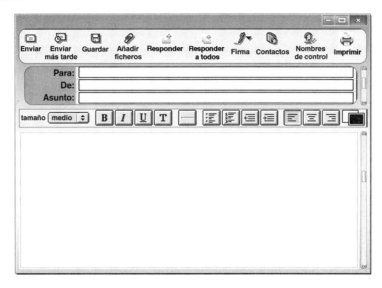

**6-19** **Para la comunidad** Escribe un poema en verso libre o una canción sobre el voluntariado y sus beneficios para los que dan y para los que reciben ayuda. ▪

**6-20** **Mi comunidad** Túrnense para describir detalladamente su comunidad o la de la foto. Incluyan en su descripción oral detalles de su pueblo o ciudad (edificios, lugares de diversión, etc.), su casa y también las oportunidades que existen para hacer trabajo voluntario. Finalmente, hagan sus presentaciones para un grupo cívico como los Rotarios (*Rotary Club*). ▪

México D.F.

**METHODOLOGY • Peer Editing**
Activities **6-18, 6-19, 6-20,** and **6-21** provide starting points for simple narrations about familiar topics. You might assign these activities for homework so that each student has something written for class. Instead of correcting the writing assignments yourself, have your students peer edit. Peer editing affords students the opportunity to read carefully in order to help their classmates. For your students who need to be reminded about peer editing, suggest that they consult the *Estrategia* for the *Escribe* section of *Capítulo 5*, p. 194.

**SUGGESTION for 6-19**
For **6-19,** you may want to provide students with a free-verse poem in English to activate schemata.

**NOTE for 6-21**

Students can begin the activity by brainstorming, jotting down the basic plot so far. They can then refer to this list to keep them on track as they add details in their oral narrations.

**METHODOLOGY • Activities related to *Ambiciones siniestras***

A technique frequently used in literature classes (both beginning and advanced) is for students to retell stories / literature in their own words and in their own order. Research reports that students learn best from other students, and activities such as **6-21** afford students the opportunity to learn from their peers. Peers also stimulate each other and they are subtly encouraged to achieve higher levels.

## 6-21 El juego de la narración
Túrnense para crear una narración oral sobre **Ambiciones siniestras**. ¡Incluyan muchos detalles! ■

**MODELO**
E1: Ambiciones siniestras *es un misterio muy imaginativo.*
E2: *Hay seis estudiantes que se llaman…*
E1: …

Cisco

Eduardo

Manolo

Alejandra

Lupe

Marisol

### Estrategia

The ability to retell information is an important language-learning strategy. Practice summarizing or retelling in your own words in Spanish the events from *Ambiciones siniestras*, chapter by chapter. Set a goal for yourself of saying or writing at least 5 important events in each episode that move the story along. Another technique is to recap as if you were retelling the story to another student who was absent.

## 6-22 ¿Me quiere?
Cisco, de **Ambiciones siniestras,** le escribe un correo electrónico a la chica que conoció (*he met*) en el concierto. En el email habla de sus planes para el fin de semana y la invita a acompañarlo (*accompany him*). Escribe ese mensaje en **diez** oraciones como si fueras (*as if you were*) Cisco. ■

**MODELO**

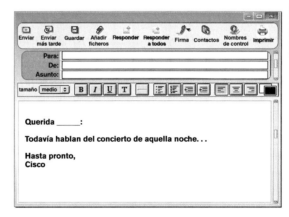

Querida _____:

**Todavía hablan del concierto de aquella noche. . .**

**Hasta pronto,**
**Cisco**

**6-23** **Su versión** En **6-21**, narraron (*you narrated*) una versión del cuento **Ambiciones siniestras**. Ahora es su turno como escritores. Sean muy creativos y creen su propia (*own*) versión creativa. Su instructor les va a explicar cómo hacerlo. Empiecen con la oración del modelo. ¡Diviértanse! ■

**MODELO** *Hay seis estudiantes de tres universidades.*

**6-24** **Tu propia película** Eres cinematógrafo y puedes crear tu propia versión de **Ambiciones siniestras**. Primero, pon las fotos en el orden correcto y luego escribe el diálogo para la película. Luego, puedes filmar tu versión. ■

**NOTE for 6-23**

This activity makes use of what we call *accordion stories*. They are a wonderful way to stimulate writing and creativity with language. You need a group of at least three students, but we recommend no more than four for this assignment. Any more than four and you will have students off task while waiting for their classmates to finish. You proceed as follows:

1. Student 1 takes the *modelo* sentence and writes it at the top of the paper. Then he/she writes a sentence that moves the story along. Student 1 then folds the paper over the original sentence and all that shows is Student 1's sentence. Student 1 passes the paper to Student 2. Student 2 reads what Student 1 has written and then adds the next sentence to the story. Student 2 then folds the paper over Student 1's sentence and passes the paper to Student 3. All Student 3 can see/read is the sentence written by Student 2. And so the process continues. You can control the number of times that the students pass the paper to each other. We suggest for this activity that each student write at least 7 sentences. For a group of 3, you will have a "story" of 21 sentences. The more sentences they write, the more involved, and usually more enjoyable, the story becomes. The students should write their sentences for up to 10 minutes. Once the 10 minutes are up, you or a member of each group can read their story aloud to the class. When the paper is unfolded, it looks like an accordion or fan.
2. Encourage students to include a wide variety of verbs and/or details in their sentences.

**EXPANSION for 6-26**
You may choose to use **6-26** as the first step, or as an organizer to be used for completing **6-27** and **6-28**.

**PLANNING AHEAD for 6-27**
You may want to encourage students to bring in travel brochures or copies of web pages from the countries mentioned in *Capítulos 1–5* to help them plan their writing.

**NOTE for 6-28**
Although this activity is similar in nature to **6-27**, you can take one of several approaches: (1) encourage your students to select a different country from the one they did in **6-27**; (2) differentiate instruction—that is, for students who are weaker, have them use **6-27** as a basis to expand for **6-28**; (3) for students who are stronger, suggest for **6-27** that they choose a country that is not necessarily their favorite but which is most suited for their clients.

**6-25** ## Los hispanos en los Estados Unidos    Escribe **cinco** influencias hispanas en los Estados Unidos. ▪

MODELO    1. *St. Augustine fue fundada por los españoles en el año 1565.*

**6-26** ## Aspectos interesantes    Escribe por lo menos **tres** cosas interesantes sobre cada uno de los siguientes países. ▪

**Estrategia**

You have read numerous cultural notes throughout the first 5 chapters. To help you organize the material, make a chart of the most important information, or dedicate a separate page in your notebook for each country, recording the unique cultural items of that particular country.

| MÉXICO | ESPAÑA | HONDURAS | GUATEMALA |
|---|---|---|---|
|  |  |  |  |
|  |  |  |  |

| EL SALVADOR | NICARAGUA | COSTA RICA | PANAMÁ |
|---|---|---|---|
|  |  |  |  |
|  |  |  |  |

**6-27** ## Un agente de viajes    Durante el verano tienes la oportunidad de trabajar en una agencia de viajes (*travel agency*). Tienes unos clientes que quieren visitar un país hispanohablante. Escoge uno de los países que estudiamos y recomienda el país en por lo menos **seis** oraciones. ▪

**6-28** ## Mi país favorito    Describe tu país favorito entre los que hemos estudiado (*we have studied*). En por lo menos **ocho** oraciones explica por qué te gusta y lo que encuentras interesante e impresionante de ese país. ▪

**6-29** ## Compáralos    Escoge dos países que estudiamos y escribe las diferencias y semejanzas (*similarities*) entre los dos. ▪

MODELO    *México es un país grande en Norteamérica y Nicaragua es más pequeño que México y está en Centroamérica.*

**6-30** **¡A jugar!** En grupos de tres o cuatro, preparen las respuestas para las siguientes categorías de *¿Lo sabes?,* un juego como *Jeopardy!,* y después las preguntas correspondientes. Pueden usar valores de dólares, pesos, euros, etc. ¡Buena suerte! ∎

## CATEGORÍAS

| VOCABULARIO | VERBOS | CULTURA |
|---|---|---|
| la vida estudiantil | verbos regulares | Estados Unidos |
| las materias y las especialidades | verbos irregulares | México |
| los deportes y los pasatiempos | **saber** y **conocer** | España |
| la casa y los muebles | **ser** y **estar** | Honduras |
| los quehaceres de la casa | **ir** | Guatemala |
| el cine | **ir** + **a** + infinitivo | El Salvador |
| la música | **estar** + **-ando, -iendo** | Nicaragua |
| el voluntariado | | Costa Rica |
| | | Panamá |

**MODELOS**

**CATEGORÍA:** LA VIDA ESTUDIANTIL

**Respuesta:** en la residencia estudiantil
**Pregunta:** *¿Dónde viven los estudiantes?*

**CATEGORÍA:** LOS DEPORTES Y LOS PASATIEMPOS

**Respuesta:** Albert Pujols
**Pregunta:** *¿Quién juega al béisbol muy bien?*

**CAPÍTULO 6**

**NOTE for 6-30**

*¡A jugar!* is based on *Jeopardy!* a highly popular, long-running television quiz show in the United States. The premise of the game is that the contestant sees the answer and must formulate the appropriate question. The "answers" are grouped by categories and each "answer" has a dollar value. Easier answers have lower dollar values. In almost every community across the United States, it is on every night of the week for 30 minutes. This game show phenomenon has been wildly successful in Spanish classrooms for decades as a review tool. It provides students with a motivating way to review categories, helps them to organize material thematically, and forces them to create questions—a skill that the research says students seldom perform since they are usually answering our questions! Use the *¡Anda! Curso elemental* transparencies/images in MSL that accompany this activity to make this activity even more enjoyable and realistic.

**NOTE for 6-30**

The images in this activity are as follows:

**¿Lo sabes?**

*México:* (top) Artesanía de Oaxaca (bottom) La biblioteca de la Universidad Nacional Autónoma de México

*España:* (top) Una tortilla española (bottom) La Pedrera (la Casa Milá) en Barcelona

*Honduras:* (top) Un charancaco *(basilisk)* de la Isla Roatán (bottom) Las ruinas de Copán

*Guatemala:* (top) Tikal (bottom) Antigua

**¿Lo sabes? Doble**

*El Salvador:* (top) Pupusas (bottom) La playa El Sunzal

*Nicaragua:* (top) Volcán San Cristóbal (bottom) La Concha Acústica

*Costa Rica:* (top) El ecoturismo (bottom) Una carreta

*Panamá:* (top) El Canal de Panamá (bottom) Una mujer kuna

# Y por fin, ¿cómo andas?

|  | Feel confident | Need to review |
|---|---|---|
| Having completed this chapter, I now can . . . | | |

**Comunicación**

| | Feel confident | Need to review |
|---|---|---|
| • describe my family and other families | ☐ | ☐ |
| • relate information about my school and campus | ☐ | ☐ |
| • impart information about homes that my friends and I like and dislike | ☐ | ☐ |
| • offer opinions on what will take place in the future | ☐ | ☐ |
| • reveal what I and others like to do and what we need to do | ☐ | ☐ |
| • report on service opportunities in my community | ☐ | ☐ |
| • discuss music, movies, and television | ☐ | ☐ |
| • engage in additional communication practice (SAM) | ☐ | ☐ |

**Cultura**

| | Feel confident | Need to review |
|---|---|---|
| • share information about the Spanish-speaking world in the United States, Mexico, Spain, Honduras, Guatemala, El Salvador, Nicaragua, Costa Rica, and Panama | ☐ | ☐ |
| • compare and contrast the countries I learned about in **Capítulos 1–5** | ☐ | ☐ |
| • explore further cultural themes (SAM) | ☐ | ☐ |

**Ambiciones siniestras**

| | Feel confident | Need to review |
|---|---|---|
| • review and create with **Ambiciones siniestras** | ☐ | ☐ |

**Comunidades**

| | Feel confident | Need to review |
|---|---|---|
| • use Spanish in real-life contexts (SAM) | ☐ | ☐ |

**Instructor Resources**
• IRM: Syllabi and Lesson Plans

## NATIONAL STANDARDS

### COMUNICACIÓN

- To greet, say good-bye, and introduce others (Communication)
- To describe yourself and others (Communication)
- To share information about school and life as a student (Communication)
- To offer opinions about sports and pastimes that you and others like and dislike (Communication)
- To describe homes and household chores (Communication)
- To identify places in and around town (Communication)
- To relate things that happen and things that have to be done (Communication)
- To convey what will take place in the future (Communication)
- To impart information about service opportunities (Communication, Connections, Communities)
- To share information about different types of music, movies, and television programs, including your personal preferences (Communication, Cultures, Comparisons)

### AMBICIONES SINIESTRAS

- To depict what has happened thus far to the protagonists: Alejandra, Manolo, Cisco, Eduardo, Marisol, and Lupe (Communication)
- To hypothesize about what you think will happen in future episodes (Communication)

### COMUNIDADES

- To use Spanish in real-life contexts (Communities)

**SECTION GOALS for** *Chapter opener*
By the end of the Chapter opener section, students will be able to:
- familiarize themselves with the text
- summarize the main points of *Capítulo Preliminar A* to *Capítulo 6*
- locate vocabulary and grammar presentations from the first half of the text
- review the *Ambiciones siniestras* storyline

**PRELIMINAR**

# B

# Introducciones y repasos

This chapter is a review of vocabulary and grammatical concepts that you are already familiar with in Spanish. Some of you are continuing with *¡Anda! Curso elemental,* while others may be coming from a different program. As you begin the second half of *¡Anda!,* it is important for all students to feel confident about what they already know about the Spanish language as they continue to acquire knowledge and proficiency. This chapter will help you determine what you already know, and also help you focus on what you personally need to improve upon.

If you are new to *¡Anda!,* you will not only want to review the grammar concepts already introduced, but also familiarize yourself with the active vocabulary used in the textbook. *¡Anda!* recycles vocabulary and grammar concepts frequently to help you learn better, and this chapter will help you with what we consider to be the basics of the preceding chapters.

226

**METHODOLOGY • Creating a Cohesive Group**
This preliminary chapter is meant to assist you with the beginning of the semester. Many of you teaching this course will have a wide array of students with different backgrounds in Spanish. It is necessary to start with a review, based on the *¡Anda! Curso elemental* chapters, which will familiarize students with the vocabulary and grammar concepts in the first half of the text to help them be successful as they continue on with their study of Spanish chapters.

**METHODOLOGY • Reviewing at the Beginning of the Term**
Learning theory informs our practice of beginning with a review before presenting new material. We recommend that this review be conducted as follows:

1. First day of class: take care of administrative details (e.g., course enrollments, going over the syllabus, which includes your expectations, etc.), followed by organizing basic speaking activities, such as having students turn to greet each other, etc.
2. Have students review *Capítulo Preliminar A* and *Capítulo 1* of *¡Anda! Curso elemental* for homework. This makes students accountable for their review. Then, the students will be able to do the pair activities in this chapter the next day in class.
3. We suggest spending from 5 to 7 days on review at the beginning of the semester. The grammar concepts and vocabulary will be recycled throughout *Capítulos 7–11.*

For all students, this chapter also reviews what has occurred to date in the thrilling episodic adventure, **Ambiciones siniestras.** Students who haven't read or viewed the first episodes will have an opportunity to do so. The episodes in the text and the video build upon each other, just like a **telenovela,** and starting in **Capítulo 7,** will continue from where the episode in **Capítulo 5** left off. **Capítulo 6** is a recycling chapter and no new episodes for **Ambiciones siniestras** were introduced.

Before you begin this chapter, you may wish to review the study and learning strategies on page 206 in **Capítulo 6.** These strategies are applicable to your other subjects as well. So on your mark, get set, let's review!

## OBJETIVOS

### COMUNICACIÓN

To greet, say good-bye, and introduce others

To describe yourself and others

To share information about school and life as a student

To offer opinions about sports and pastimes that you and others like and dislike

To describe homes and household chores

To identify places in and around town

To relate things that happen and things that have to be done

To convey what will take place in the future

To impart information about service opportunities

To share information about different types of music, movies, and television programs, including your personal preferences

### AMBICIONES SINIESTRAS

To depict what has happened thus far to the protagonists: Alejandra, Manolo, Cisco, Eduardo, Marisol, and Lupe

To hypothesize about what you think will happen in future episodes

### COMUNIDADES

To use Spanish in real-life contexts (SAM)

## THE NATIONAL STANDARDS

*¡Anda! Curso elemental* is committed to and based on the National Foreign Language Standards. These National Standards, known as *the 5 Cs,* are: Communication, Cultures, Connections, Comparisons, and Communities. The beginning of each chapter will highlight how each of the 5 Cs will be addressed.

Each of the five goal areas has corresponding standards. When possible, the goal areas have been expanded to include each standard that the activities address. In *¡Anda! Curso elemental,* you will find ways to incorporate the standards into your teaching, and sometimes we will present alternative directions or assignments in order to meet more than one standard. If you are new to *¡Anda! Curso elemental,* or you are unfamiliar with the 5 Cs, please consult the explanations provided in *Capítulo Preliminar A* or in the Preface.

## 21ST CENTURY SKILLS • DEFINITION

The Partnership for 21st Century Skills (P21) is a multidisciplinary project. The group, housed in Washington, D.C., has brought together the key national organizations representing the core academic subjects. The American Council on the Teaching of Foreign Languages (ACTFL) collaborated for a year developing the 21st Century Skills Map. The map, created by hundreds of world language educators, reflects the integration of languages and the necessary skills for a successful 21st century citizen.

## PRELIMINAR B

**METHODOLOGY • Reviewing (Capítulo Preliminar B) vs. Recycling (Capítulo 6)**

There were different goals and objectives used for creating *Capítulo 6* and this current chapter, *Capítulo Preliminar B.* The goal of *Capítulo 6* was to *recycle* material and to "put it all together," acting as culminating activities after a semester of study. Your students have been together for an extended period of time working with you and each other. They are familiar with you, your expectations, and those of *¡Anda! Curso elemental.* With *Capítulo Preliminar B,* there is the *potential* for a very different scenario. Some of you will not have taught the first semester, some of your students may have had a different instructor in the first semester, some of your students may be coming directly from high school or from another institution of higher education, and still other students may have taken time off from studying Spanish and are re-entering the course of study. Hence the intention of *Capítulo Preliminar B* is to methodically *review* and guide all students to begin at a similar point. You will notice that *Capítulo Preliminar B* moves more by small chunks of material than *Capítulo 6* does. *Capítulo Preliminar B* assumes that students need more step-by-step guidance and remediation so they can all arrive at a common starting point.

Having provided this rationale, it is up to you how (and whether!) you will use this chapter. *¡Anda! Curso elemental* was created to afford you, the instructor, the maximum flexibility in your planning. What follows are several options:

1. You may choose to use *Capítulo 6* at the end of first semester to recycle and *Capítulo Preliminar B* at the beginning of second semester as a review.
2. You may choose to use Option #1, modifying it by picking and choosing the activities in *Capítulo Preliminar B* that best suit your needs.
3. You may choose not to use *Capítulo 6* at the end of the first semester, but to begin this semester with it, and skip *Capítulo Preliminar B.*
4. You may choose to move directly to *Capítulo 7.*

The bottom line is that you know your students and your curriculum better than anyone else. Choose the option that works best for you and your circumstances.

**METHODOLOGY • Review Techniques**

As stated, this chapter is meant to jump start students while bringing together a wide array of student backgrounds and abilities. Since the suggested intention is to move students through this chapter quickly, there are no formal reading passages. Writing practice is found in the Student Activities Manual.

**SECTION GOALS for Comunicación**

By the end of the *Comunicación* section, students will be able to:
• introduce themselves and others and have polite conversations
• describe themselves, relatives, people, and classmates using *ser* and adjectives
• talk about things they and others possess using *tener*
• report about all aspects of student life
• use present tense verbs
• form questions
• count from 1 to 100,000,000
• express favorite sports and pastimes
• express likes and dislikes using *gustar*
• share what responsibilities they have
• describe things using colors
• use *ser* and *estar* in different contexts
• share information about cities and towns
• distinguish between *saber* and *conocer*
• report about future plans and events using *ir* + *a* + infinitive
• discuss service opportunities
• use affirmative and negative expressions
• share information about movies, music, and television
• talk about what they are currently doing, using the present progressive
• rank items
• identify direct objects and substitute direct objects with object pronouns

**METHODOLOGY • Review**

It is suggested that a minimal amount of time be spent on reviewing *Capítulo Preliminar A*, since all of the expressions and concepts presented there are utilized throughout the rest of the text. We recommend conducting this review in 5 to 7 days. Having said that, everyone's schedule is unique, so ultimately, you need to make choices that best fit your circumstances.

**EXPANSION for Para empezar**

You may want to have students turn to each other and practice greeting and introducing themselves to each other. You could also ask them to circulate around the class, greeting and introducing themselves to at least 5 classmates whom they do not know.

# Comunicación

### • Capítulo Preliminar A •

Greeting, saying good-bye, and introducing others

B-01

**1. Para empezar.** This chapter provided an introduction to Spanish via the following topics: greetings and farewells; classroom expressions; the alphabet; cognates; subject pronouns and the verb **ser**; adjectives of nationality; numbers 1–30; telling time; days and months; the weather; and the verb **gustar**. If you need to review any of these topics before proceeding, consult pages 2–29.

### • Capítulo 1 •

Describing yourself and others

B-02 to B-03

**2. La familia.** Review the **La familia** vocabulary on page 32 and then do the following activities.

**Estrategia**

In **B-1**, you are directed to write at least 5 sentences. See how many more than 5 you can write in the time allotted.

 **B-1** **Mi familia** Túrnense para describir a sus familias o a una de las familias de las fotos. Digan por lo menos **cinco** oraciones. ■

MODELO    *George es mi tío. Mis primos son Stacy y Scott…*

**SUGGESTION for Classroom Expressions**

You will want to review the classroom expressions presented in *Capítulo Preliminar A*. These expressions, such as commands, are useful for classroom management.

**SUGGESTION for B-1**

For **B-1**, encourage students to bring photos of their own families, to draw stick figures of their families, or to bring in pictures from magazines so that they can create "imaginary families." The latter suggestion is very successful since students tend to be very creative with the pictures they bring to class. The images make excellent visual organizers and help to break the ice for students who may not know each other well.

**SUGGESTION for La familia**

As students review this family vocabulary, encourage them to go beyond just speaking about themselves and their partners. Have them talk about the people in the photos and their families. Have them pretend that they are siblings and that one of the photos is of their family. They should try to use all of the possessive adjectives in their conversation.

**3. El verbo _tener._** Review the verb **tener** on page 34. What are all of the present tense forms of **tener**?

B-04

**B-2 Y mis amigos...**

Túrnense para hablar de las familias de unos amigos o de una familia famosa usando el verbo **tener.** Digan por lo menos **ocho** oraciones. ■

**MODELO**    *Mi amigo, Joe, tiene dos hermanos. Mis amigas Jennifer y Marty no tienen abuelos...*

**4. El singular y el plural.** Review how to make singular nouns plural on page 36 and explain the rules to your partner. Then complete the following activity.

B-05

**B-3 Te toca a ti** Digan el plural de cada palabra. ■

**MODELO**   E1:   primo
        E2:   *primos*

1. madre madres
2. francés franceses
3. taxi taxis
4. nieto nietos
5. abuela abuelas
6. joven jóvenes

**Fíjate**

The rules for accents are listed in the *Pronunciación* section for *Capítulo 2* on MySpanishLab and in the Student Activities Manual. As a reminder, some words keep their accent marks in the plural while other words lose or gain accent marks in the plural.

**5. El masculino y el femenino.** Review the differences between masculine and feminine nouns on page 37. State the rules to a partner, and then do the following activity.

B-06

**B-4 ¿Recuerdas?** Digan si las siguientes palabras son masculinas o femeninas. **¡OJO!** Hay unas excepciones. ■

**MODELO**   E1:   tía
        E2:   *femenina*

1. padrastros m
2. televisión f
3. foto f
4. universidad f
5. hermano m
6. mapa m
7. tía f
8. hijo m

**Fíjate**

Some words that end in consonants, like *profesor,* also have feminine forms: *profesora.* Pay attention to the form when making the noun plural, as in the case of *profesores* or *profesoras.*

**NOTE for *Actividades***
*¡Anda! Curso elemental* provides many activities for diverse groups of learners and learning styles. As the instructor, you should decide which activities to use based on how well they meet the needs of your students. Depending on how often your class meets, you might decide to use class time exclusively for speaking and to assign the writing activities for homework. Select and use the activities that are relevant to your learning goals. We have color-coded the activity direction lines for easy usage. The fuchsia ones are vocabulary-focused, while the blue ones are grammar-focused.

**METHODOLOGY • Helping Your Students with Their Study Habits**
References will be made to the page numbers in the first half of the book that your students can consult if they need more guidance. Students who need mechanical practice in addition to what is in this chapter will find MySpanishLab to be an excellent resource.

**EXPANSION for METHODOLOGY • Helping Your Students with Their Study Habits**
You can flag certain pages from *Capítulo Preliminar A* through *Capítulo 5* in your book and model the study skill of using sticky notes to flag important pages. If you used *¡Anda! Curso elemental* for the first half, you have a good idea of what vocabulary or grammar your students will need to review. This technique works well because it is a non-permanent way to efficiently organize the text.

**FOLLOW-UP for *El singular y el plural***
Your students should be able to form the plurals, but they will need a review of the rules for accents. In number 2, *francés,* and in number 6, *joven,* they will need a reminder about why *francés* drops the accent in the plural and why *joven* adds the accent in the plural.

**METHODOLOGY • Pair Work**
*¡Anda! Curso elemental* is based on the research that states that students learn best from other students. Stephen Krashen would explain it as *lowering the affective filter.* Still other researchers would call this a *constructivist approach* to teaching and learning. Hence, most of the activities are suggested to be pair activities. This is predicated on students changing partners daily (or nearly daily). Once again, we encourage you to determine what works best for you. You may decide that you would like to assign some of the activities as homework to be turned in for grades. Still other activities you may decide to skip altogether. The goals of *¡Anda!* are to maximize student talk time in class and to make your job as instructor as streamlined as possible, providing you with all the tools to make the best instructional delivery decisions.

**6. Los artículos definidos e indefinidos.** How do you say *the, a(n),* and *some* in Spanish? For a reminder, see page 38. Then do the following activity.

 **B-5  Vamos a practicar** Túrnense para añadir el equivalente de los artículos *the, a* o *some* a estas palabras. ■

MODELO    E1:  tías
          E2:  *las tías/unas tías*

1. abuelo el/un
2. hermanas las/unas
3. madre la/una
4. tío el/un
5. hijos los/unos
6. primas las/unas
7. nieto el/un
8. padres los/unos

**7. Los adjetivos posesivos y descriptivos.** How do you say *my, your, his, her, our,* and *their*? If you need help, see page 41. Also consult pages 43–44 to review words you may use to describe yourself and others. Then do the following activity.

 **B-6  Nuestras familias** Túrnense para describir a su familia y compararla con las familias de sus amigos. Digan por lo menos **ocho** oraciones. ■

MODELO    *Mis padres son trabajadores. La mamá de mi amigo John es trabajadora también. Nuestros primos son simpáticos…*

## • Capítulo 2 •

Sharing information about school and life as a student
Offering opinions about sports and pastimes that you and others like and dislike

**8. Las materias y las especialidades.** Review the **Las materias y las especialidades** vocabulary on page 62 of **Capítulo 2**. Then practice the vocabulary words with the following activity.

Workbooklet

 **B-7  ¿Cuál es más fácil?** Expresa tus opiniones sobre las materias y las especialidades. Comparte tus respuestas con un/a compañero/a. Puedes consultar **También se dice…** en el Apéndice 3. ■

MODELO    *Las especialidades más difíciles son las matemáticas y los negocios. Las especialidades más fáciles son…*

LAS ESPECIALIDADES…

| MÁS DIFÍCILES | MÁS FÁCILES | MÁS CREATIVAS | MÁS INTERESANTES | MÁS ABURRIDAS |
|---|---|---|---|---|
| 1. | 1. | 1. | 1. | 1. |
| 2. | 2. | 2. | 2. | 2. |

**NOTE for B-8**
Activity **B-8** is a good way for students to learn the names of their classmates and to build trust within a classroom community. When students know the names of their classmates and can talk to them on a familiar basis, they are more likely to take risks with their language learning and enjoy practicing Spanish with new people. As students report back to the class and repeat information, you can learn the names of your new students.

**9. La sala de clase.** Review the **La sala de clase** vocabulary on page 65 and then do the following activity.

B-13

Workbooklet

### B-8 ¿Qué tienen tus compañeros/as? Escoge (*Choose*) a unos/as de tus compañeros/as y completa el siguiente cuadro. ■

**MODELO**   E1:   Hablamos de Melissa. ¿Qué tiene Melissa?

E2:   Melissa tiene dos cuadernos, un libro, un bolígrafo y dos lápices.

E3:   Pero Melissa no tiene la tarea.

E2:   Ahora hablamos de _____ y _____. ¿Qué tienen. _____ y. _____?

E1:   Tienen….

**Estrategia**

For **B-8**, you and your partner may wish to ask other classmates questions such as: *¿Qué tienes en tu mochila? ¿Qué tienes en tu escritorio?*

| ESTUDIANTE _Melissa_ | ESTUDIANTES ____ Y ____ | TÚ Y YO ____ |
|---|---|---|
| (no) tiene | (no) tienen | (no) tenemos |
| 1. tiene dos cuadernos | 1. | 1. |
| 2. tiene un libro | 2. | 2. |
| 3. tiene un bolígrafo | 3. | 3. |
| 4. tiene dos lápices | 4. | 4. |
| 5. no tiene la tarea | 5. | 5. |

**METHODOLOGY • Working in Pairs**
If you are using *¡Anda! Curso elemental* for the first time, you will note that we recommend that virtually all our activities be done with students working with partners. The research is conclusive that students learn best from other students, and that working with partners in a student-centered class gives them more opportunities to become proficient in Spanish than if they were in a teacher-centered class.

**10. Presente indicativo de verbos regulares.** How do you form the *present tense* of *regular* **-ar**, **-er**, and **-ir** *verbs*? If you need help, consult pages 67–68. Finally, before you complete the following activities, review the common verbs that are presented on the those pages.

B-14 to B-15

**EXPANSION for B-9**
After completing this activity, have your students create their own examples.

**EXPANSION for B-9**
Additional questions that you may have students ask each other include: *¿Tú hablas mucho? ¿Tú corres mucho? ¿Tú vives lejos?* The students will jot down their answers and then you can ask the class: *¿Quién en la clase habla mucho? ¿Quién corre mucho? ¿Quién vive lejos?*

### B-9 ¿A quién o quiénes conoces que…? Túrnense para preguntarse y contestar para qué personas que ustedes conocen son ciertas (*true*) las siguientes afirmaciones. ■

**MODELO**   hablar poco

E1:   *¿Quién habla poco?*

E2:   *Mi hermano Evan habla poco.*

E2:   *¿Quiénes hablan poco?*

E1:   *Mis padres hablan poco. / Mis hermanos y yo hablamos poco.*

**Estrategia**

You will note that nearly all activities in *¡Anda! Curso elemental* are pair activities. You will be encouraged or required to change partners frequently, perhaps even daily. The purpose is for you to be able to practice Spanish with a wide array of speakers. Working with different classmates will help you improve your spoken Spanish more quickly.

1. hablar demasiado
2. correr mucho
3. vivir lejos
4. escribir muchos mensajes de texto
5. usar los apuntes de sus amigos
6. estudiar mucho
7. necesitar estudiar más
8. tomar un examen hoy
9. enseñar español

**ADDITIONAL ACTIVITY for *Presente indicativo de verbos regulares***

**Hay que practicar** On ten small pieces of paper, write the nouns and pronouns that follow. Then on six different slips of paper, write the six infinitives listed below. Take turns selecting a noun and a verb, and give the correct forms. After practicing the verbs listed below, select your own group of regular **-ar**, **-er**, and **-ir** verbs to practice. While doing this activity, focus not only on the forms of the verbs, but also on their meanings.

**LOS NOMBRES Y PRONOMBRES:**

| | | |
|---|---|---|
| tú | usted | yo |
| nosotros | ustedes | ellas |
| Marco | Juan y Eva | Mariela |

**LOS VERBOS:**

| | | |
|---|---|---|
| estudiar | correr | escribir |
| hablar | comer | vivir |

**MODELO**
E1:   *yo / estudiar*
E2:   *estudio*

**B-10** ⏰ 7:00 **Dime quién, dónde y cuándo** Miren el dibujo y creen juntos una historia sobre lo que ocurre en el edificio. ▪

| MODELO | E1: | *Josefina escribe una carta.* |
|---|---|---|
| | E2: | *Ella escribe cartas todos los días.* |
| | E1: | *En otro apartamento Raúl y Mariela…* |

**Estrategia**

*¡Anda! Curso elemental* encourages you to be creative when practicing and using Spanish. One way is to create mini-stories about photos or drawings that you see. Being creative includes giving individuals in drawings names and characteristics.

 **11. La formación de preguntas y las palabras interrogativas.** How do you form questions in Spanish? What are the question words in Spanish? To review this topic, consult pages 70–71 and then do the following activity.

B-16 to B-17

**B-11** ⏰ 2:00 **Preguntas y más preguntas** Túrnense para formar una pregunta con cada oración. ▪

**Fíjate**

Remember that all question words have accents. Also remember that when writing a question, there are two question marks, one at the beginning and one at the end of the question.

| MODELO | E1: | Estudio **matemáticas**. |
|---|---|---|
| | E2: | *¿Qué estudias?* |

1. Pilar estudia **en la biblioteca**. ¿Dónde estudia Pilar?
2. **Guillermo y yo** estudiamos. ¿Quiénes estudian?
3. Comen **entre las 7:00 y las 8:00 de la noche**. ¿Cuándo comen?
4. Aprendemos español **fácilmente**. ¿Cómo aprenden español?
5. Leo **tres libros**. ¿Cuántos libros lees?
6. Estudiamos español **porque nos gusta el profesor**. ¿Por qué estudian español?

**12. Los números 1–1.000.** Review the numbers 1–1,000, consulting pages 16, 47, and 72 if you need help. Then do the following activity.

B-18 to B-19

2:00 **B-12** **¡Dilo!** Túrnense para decir los precios de los artículos en el catálogo. ■

MODELO   E1:  (325 €) *El precio del armario es trescientos veinticinco euros.*
         E2:  (999 €) *El precio del sofá es…*

A  325 EUR
B  999 EUR
C  559 USD

D  444 MXN
E  815 USD
F  175 EUR
G  298 MXN

**13. El verbo *estar*.** What are the present tense forms of **estar**? When do you use **estar**? Check pages 76–77 if you need help before doing the following activity.

  **B-13** **¿Cómo se dice?** Túrnense para hacerse preguntas y contestar usando **estar**. ■

**Fíjate**
Remember that four forms of *estar* have accents in the present tense: *estás, está, estáis,* and *están.*

MODELO    el mapa / libro
    E1:  ¿Dónde está el mapa?
    E2:  El mapa está en el libro.

1. mis amigos y yo / la clase de ciencias
2. tú / el apartamento
3. los escritorios / la sala de clase
4. el papel / la silla
5. los apuntes / el cuaderno
6. Jorge y tú / la puerta
7. los libros / la mochila
8. José / bien
9. Lupe y Mariela / contento

**14. Emociones y estados.** Review the **Emociones y estados** vocabulary on page 79 and then do the following activity.

  **B-14** **¿Qué pasa?** Digan qué adjetivo describe cada una de las siguientes situaciones. ■

MODELO    E1:  Jorge y María reciben mil dólares.
    E2:  Están contentos.

1. Esperas y esperas pero tu amigo no llega. (¡Y no te llama por teléfono!)
2. Corres quince millas (*miles*).
3. Tus padres están en el hospital.
4. Tu novio/a está en Panamá y ¡no regresa!
5. El profesor de literatura lee sin parar durante una hora y quince minutos.
6. Ustedes sacan "A" en sus exámenes de español e informática.
7. Ustedes tienen un examen muy difícil hoy.

**Fíjate**
In **B-14** you see *sus exámenes de español e informática.* The word *y* changes to *e* when the *i* sound appears immediately after the *y*, as in the case of the word *informática.*

**15. En la universidad.** Review the **En la universidad** vocabulary on page 74 and do the following activity.

   **B-15** **¡Lo sé!** Digan qué lugar asocian con las siguientes palabras y acciones. Después formen una oración completa. ■

MODELO    estudiar
    E1:  Voy a la biblioteca para estudiar.
    E2:  Estudio en mi apartamento.

1. jugar al fútbol
2. comprar libros
3. comer hamburguesas, pizza, café, etc.
4. jugar al básquetbol
5. hacer experimentos científicos
6. leer libros, estudiar, escribir composiciones, etc.

B-23 to B-24

**16. El verbo *gustar*.** How do you say *to like* in Spanish? Review page 80 and then do the following activity.

 **B-16  Opiniones** Compara tu opinión sobre los siguientes temas (*topics*) con las de otros/as dos compañeros/as e informa después a la clase. ■

**Estrategia**

With **B-16,** ask each other:
*¿Qué materias te gustan?*
*¿Qué escritores te gustan?*
*¿Qué películas te gustan?*

**MODELO**  E1:  *Las materias que más me gustan son las ciencias y las matemáticas.*
             *La escritora que más me gusta es J.K. Rowling…*

           E2:  *Las materias que más le gustan a David son las ciencias y las matemáticas.*
             *La escritora que más le gusta es J.K. Rowling…*

|  | LAS MATERIAS… | LOS/AS ESCRITORES/AS… | LAS PELÍCULAS (*MOVIES*)… |
|---|---|---|---|
|  | que más me gustan son: | que más me gustan son: | que más me gustan son: |
| YO | 1. | 1. | 1. |
| ESTUDIANTE 1 | 2. | 2 | 2 |
| ESTUDIANTE 2 | 3. | 3. | 3. |
|  | que menos me gustan son: | que menos me gustan son: | que menos me gustan son: |
| YO | 1. | 1. | 1. |
| ESTUDIANTE 1 | 2 | 2 | 2 |
| ESTUDIANTE 2 | 3. | 3. | 3. |

B-25 to B-27

**17. Los deportes y los pasatiempos.** Review the **Los deportes y los pasatiempos** vocabulary on pages 81–82 and then do the following activity.

Workbooklet

 **B-17  Tus preferencias** Selecciona los **tres** deportes o pasatiempos **que más te gustan** y luego los **tres que menos te gustan**. Después de completar el cuadro, comparte la información con un/a compañero/a, según el modelo. ■

**MODELO**  *Los deportes o pasatiempos que más me gustan son patinar, bailar y leer. Los deportes o pasatiempos que menos me gustan son el fútbol, el fútbol americano y nadar.*

| LOS DEPORTES Y PASATIEMPOS QUE MÁS ME GUSTAN | LOS DEPORTES Y PASATIEMPOS QUE MENOS ME GUSTAN |
|---|---|
| 1. | 1. |
| 2. | 2. |
| 3. | 3. |

**METHODOLOGY •**
**Differentiating Instruction**
We are well aware that different students have different abilities and needs. For your heritage language learners and students who are more advanced or creative with the language, you may wish to direct them to the *También se dice…* section in *Appendix 3*. There, they will find additional vocabulary that they can incorporate into their repertoire.

**EXPANSION for B-16**
You may want to have your students try to guess what other students like and dislike and create their own categories to ask classmates about.

**METHODOLOGY • Use of English**

The majority of the reviewers/instructors involved in developing *¡Anda! Curso elemental* preferred the use of both English and Spanish in this chapter to help ease all of your students into the course. You will note that all references to grammar review are in English. This is because all grammar is presented throughout *¡Anda! Curso elemental* in English. The philosophy is that students will be more successful by quickly understanding concise explanations in English rather than laboring to decode Spanish explanations. Also, you will note that in this chapter, students are asked to review the grammar themselves and, in most cases, to state the rule(s). This is based on the learning theory concept that learners demonstrate comprehension when they can state or explain the rules. Directions to the activities are in Spanish when they are at what Krashen calls *the comprehensible input level of i + 1*.

**EXPANSION for B-18**

Have students determine at least two things that they do in each of these rooms that aren't included in this list.

**21ST CENTURY SKILLS • "THEN" AND "NOW"**

The Partnership for 21st Century Skills identified world languages as a core subject. Along with working with other disciplines, the Partnership identified how classrooms were "then" and how they need to be "now." "Then" the students learned about the language (grammar), and now, students need to be learning how to use the language. Activities like A-25 help students to interact with each other on an interpersonal level which is critical to fostering real communication.

## • Capítulo 3 •

Describing homes and household chores

**18. La casa.** Review the vocabulary about **La casa** on page 98 and do the following activities.

B-28 to B-30

 **B-18** **Las actividades** Túrnense para decir en qué parte o partes de la casa hacen las siguientes actividades. ∎

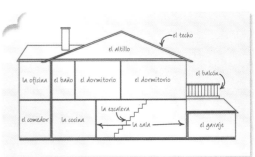

MODELO    E1:  estudiar
          E2:  *Estudio en la oficina, en el dormitorio y en la cocina.*

1. escuchar música y ver la televisión
2. organizar papeles
3. tomar una siesta
4. preparar tacos
5. tocar el piano
6. hablar por teléfono
7. tomar el sol
8. trabajar en la computadora

 **B-19** **¿Y tu casa...?** Descríbele tu casa o apartamento, o una de las viviendas de las fotos, a un/a compañero/a. O si quieres, puedes describir tu casa ideal. Usa por lo menos **ocho** oraciones. ∎

MODELO    *Mi casa tiene dos pisos. Mi dormitorio está en la planta baja. No tenemos un altillo. Mi dormitorio está al lado del baño. La cocina es pequeña....*

**19. Algunos verbos irregulares.** Review the irregular verbs on pages 101–102 and then practice them with the following activities.

B-31 to B-32

[5:00]  **B-20** **Otras combinaciones** Túrnense para formar oraciones completas combinando elementos de las tres columnas. Formen una oración distinta con cada verbo de la columna B. ■

**MODELO**    *Nosotros hacemos la tarea todos los días.*

| COLUMNA A | COLUMNA B | COLUMNA C |
|---|---|---|
| Uds. | (no) hacer | estudiar ciencias |
| el profesor | (no) oír | muchas películas |
| él, ella, Ud. | (no) querer | la tarea todos los días |
| nosotros/as | (no) salir | los libros a clase |
| ellos/ellas | (no) traer | temprano a la universidad |
| yo | (no) venir | los viernes |
| tú | (no) ver | tocar la guitarra |
| mamá y papá | (no) poder | ruidos (*noises*) por la noche |

[7:00]  **B-21** **Entrevista** Túrnense para hacerse la siguiente entrevista. ■

**MODELO**    E1:    ¿Qué te dice tu mamá siempre?
              E1:    *Mi mamá me dice…*

1. ¿Qué deporte practicas?
2. ¿Cuándo haces ejercicio?
3. ¿Qué te dice tu mamá siempre?
4. ¿Qué traes a tus clases?
5. ¿Sales los fines de semana? ¿Con quién o quiénes sales?
6. ¿Qué quieres ser (o hacer) en el futuro?
7. ¿Conoces a una persona famosa?
8. ¿Qué pones en tu mochila los lunes? ¿Los martes?
9. ¿Qué días vienes a la clase de español?
10. ¿A qué hora sales para la clase?

**Estrategia**

Getting to know your classmates helps you build confidence. It is much easier to interact with someone you know.

---

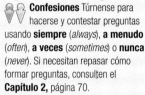

**METHODOLOGY • Lesson Planning**
Due to time constraints that all instructors have, we suggest that you decide whether you wish to formally review the cultural topics of this and previous chapters. In *Capítulo 3,* for example, one of the topics dealt with housing in the Spanish-speaking world. If you have the time in your schedule, you may wish to go to page 105 in *Capítulo 3* and select some of the questions on those topics to ask your students.

**EXPANSION for B-22**
Suggest students hypothesize about what the homes of famous people are like, and what they have in their homes. Another idea would be to have students describe a famous home they have seen, or imagine what it is like, such as the White House, the Biltmore House, etc.

**EXPANSION for B-23**
Have students hypothesize about what their partners have and do not have in their homes.

MODELO
E1: *Creo que tienes dos televisiones en tu casa.*
E2: *No tienes razón. Tengo tres televisiones.*

                    o

E2: *Sí, tienes razón. Creo que tienes una cama, dos lámparas y un estante para libros en tu dormitorio.*
E1: *…*

**20. Hay.** What does **hay** mean? Review page 119 if you need help. Then do the following activity.

 B-33 to B-34

**Fíjate**
Remember that you can form questions by adding question marks to the statement or inverting the order of the subject and the verb.

**B-22** **¿Qué hay en tu casa?** Descríbele tu casa a un/a compañero/a y averigua (*find out*) cómo es la suya (*his/hers*) usando **hay.** ■

MODELO    E1:  *En mi casa hay un garaje. ¿Hay un garaje en tu casa?*
              E2:  *Sí, en mi casa hay un garaje. / No, en mi casa no hay un garaje.*
              E1:  *Mi casa tiene dos pisos. ¿Cuántos pisos hay en tu casa?*

**21. Los muebles y otros objetos de la casa.** Review the **Los muebles y otros objetos de la casa** vocabulary on page 106. Then do the following activity.

 B-35 to B-36

**B-23** **En mi casa** ¿Qué muebles y objetos tienes o no tienes en casa? Descríbeselos a un/a compañero/a. ■

MODELO    E1:  *Yo tengo una cama y dos sillas en mi dormitorio. No tengo una televisión. ¿Qué tienes tú?*
              E2:  *Yo tengo un cuadro, una lámpara y una televisión.*

B-37 to B-38

**22. Los quehaceres de la casa y los colores.** Review the vocabulary dealing with **Los quehaceres de la casa** and **Los colores** on pages 109 and 111. Then, do the following activities.

3:00

Workbooklet

 **B-24** **Responsabilidades** ¿Cuáles son tus responsabilidades? Túrnense para contestar las siguientes preguntas y explicar cuándo hacen estos quehaceres y cuánto tiempo dedican a hacerlos. ■

**NOTE for B-24**
This activity can also be used as an interview. Each student completes the chart, answers his/her partner's questions, and then switches roles with his/her partner.

**EXPANSION for B-24**
As a follow-up to this activity, choose a student to report on his/her partner's responses. Tell everyone to listen carefully, and when he/she is finished, ask questions to verify comprehension. This encourages students to be active listeners and holds them accountable for what others say.

**Estrategia**
Group the rooms of the house with the verbs associated with each room. For example, match *comer* and *el comedor, bañarse* and *el baño, dormir* and *el dormitorio, cocinar* and *la cocina.*

MODELO     E1:  mi dormitorio

           E2:  *Tengo que limpiar mi dormitorio los lunes. Necesito dos horas porque está muy sucio.*

1. mi dormitorio
2. el baño
3. la cocina
4. la sala
5. el garaje
6. el comedor

¿Cuándo? ¿Cuánto tiempo?

dormitorio
baño
cocina
sala
garaje
comedor

| ¿QUÉ TIENES QUE HACER? | ¿CUÁNDO? | ¿CUÁNTO TIEMPO? |
| --- | --- | --- |
| limpiar mi dormitorio | los lunes | dos horas |

**B-25** **La casa ideal** ¿Cómo es tu casa ideal? ¿Y los colores? Descríbele tu casa ideal a un/a compañero/a en por lo menos **ocho** oraciones. ■

**MODELO** *Quiero una casa con una cocina amarilla…*

 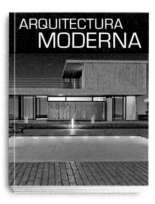 

**23. Algunas expresiones con *tener*.** Review the **tener** expressions on page 113 and then do the following activities.

B-39

 **B-26** **¿Qué tengo yo?** Túrnense para expresar cómo se sienten (*you feel*) en las siguientes situaciones. Usen las expresiones con **tener.** ■

**MODELO** E1: antes de comer

E2: *Antes de comer tengo hambre.*

1. los lunes
2. los sábados
3. tarde en la noche
4. temprano en la mañana
5. antes de tener un examen
6. cuando ves una película de terror
7. en el verano
8. en el invierno
9. durante (*during*) la semana de los exámenes finales
10. cuando sacas "A" en un examen

**B-27** **Datos personales** Túrnense para hacerse esta entrevista. ■

1. ¿Cuántos años tienes?
2. ¿Cuándo tienes hambre?
3. ¿Qué tienes que hacer hoy?
4. ¿Qué tienes ganas de hacer?
5. ¿En qué clase tienes sueño?
6. ¿En qué clase tienes mucha suerte?
7. ¿Siempre tienes razón?
8. ¿Cuándo tienes sueño?
9. Cuando tienes sed, ¿qué tomas?

**24. Los números 1.000–100.000.000.** Review the numbers on page 116 and then do the following activity.

B-40 to B-41

  **B-28 ¿Cuál es su población?** Túrnense para leer las poblaciones de las siguientes capitales del mundo hispano en voz alta. ■

1. Buenos Aires, Argentina — 12.988.000
2. La Paz, Bolivia — 1.642.000
3. Bogotá, Colombia — 8.268.000
4. La Habana, Cuba — 2.141.000
5. San José, Costa Rica — 1.416.000
6. México, D.F., México — 19.319.000

CIA World Fact Book

• **Capítulo 4** •
Identifying places in and around town
Relating things that happen and things that have to be done
Conveying what will take place in the future
Imparting information about service opportunities

**25. Los lugares.** Review the **Los lugares** vocabulary on page 134 and then do the following activity.

B-42

  **B-29 ¿Dónde está?** Tus amigos y tú están muy ocupados. Túrnate con un/a compañero/a para decir dónde están. ■

MODELO 
E1: Mi amigo quiere mandar una carta.
E2: *Está en la oficina de correos.*

1. Marta quiere leer y necesita comprar un libro.
2. Dos de mis amigos necesitan dinero.
3. Julio tiene hambre y quiere comer algo (*something*).
4. Queremos ver una exposición de arte.
5. Ustedes quieren ver una película.
6. Jorge tiene sed y quiere tomar algo.
7. Vamos a jugar al golf.
8. Tienen que ir a una boda (*wedding*).

1. Está en la librería. 2. Están en el banco. 3. Está en el restaurante / el café / el bar. 4. Estamos en el museo. 5. Están en el cine. 6. Está en el bar / el café / el restaurante. 7. Estamos en el campo de golf. 8. Están en la iglesia / el templo.

B-43 to B-44

**26.** *Saber* **y** *conocer* **and the personal** *a*. Make a list of when you use **saber** and when you use **conocer**. You can review the uses on page 137. Then do the following activity.

2:00    **B-30** **¿Lo sabes o lo conoces?** Completa cada una de las siguientes preguntas usando **sabes** o **conoces**. Después, túrnate con un/a compañero/a para hacerse y contestar las siguientes preguntas. ◼

MODELO  E1:  *¿Conoces Buenos Aires?*
       E2:  *Sí, conozco Buenos Aires. / No, no conozco Buenos Aires.*

1. ¿_Conoces / Conozco_ un buen lugar para comprar un teléfono celular?
2. ¿_Sabes / Sé_ preparar tortillas?
3. ¿_Sabes / Sé_ cuál es el mejor café de esta ciudad?
4. ¿_Conoces / Conozco_ San José, Costa Rica?
5. ¿_Sabes / Sé_ jugar al golf?
6. ¿_Sabes / Sé_ dónde están tus amigos ahora?
7. ¿_Conoces / Conozco_ al presidente de los Estados Unidos?
8. ¿_Conoces / Conozco_ el mejor restaurante chino de nuestra ciudad?
9. ¿_Sabes / Sé_ usar una computadora?
10. ¿_Conoces / Conozco_ las películas de Will Smith?

> **Fíjate**
> For more information about the personal **a**, consult *Capítulo 5*, page 190.

B-45

**27. ¿Qué tienen que hacer?** What does **tener que + infinitivo** mean? Review page 140 if you have any questions before doing this activity.

5:00    **B-31** **Entrevistas** ¿Hacen tus compañeros/as cosas similares? ◼

**Paso 1**  Usando las siguientes preguntas, entrevista a tres compañeros/as.

1. ¿Cuáles son las cosas que haces para prepararte (*prepare yourself*) bien para tus clases?
2. Generalmente, ¿qué tienes que hacer después de terminar con tus clases?

**Paso 2**  Comparte la información con otros compañeros/as de la clase. ¿Qué tienen ustedes en común?

**MODELO**  *Para prepararse bien para las clases, Jack y Sally tienen que estudiar cinco horas cada día. Sally tiene que ir a la biblioteca. Jack tiene que organizar sus apuntes. Después de terminar nuestras clases, nosotros tenemos que limpiar nuestros apartamentos…*

**28. Los verbos con cambio de raíz.** Review the stem-changing verbs on page 142 and then practice with the following activities.

B-46 to B-47

`2:00`  **B-32 ¿Quién es?** Digan a qué personas conocen que hacen las siguientes actividades. ■

**MODELO**    siempre perder la tarea

E1:  *Mi novia Carmen siempre pierde la tarea.*

E2:  *Mis primos siempre pierden la tarea.*

1. almorzar en Burger King a menudo
2. siempre entender al / a la profesor a de español
3. jugar al fútbol muy bien
4. preferir dormir hasta el mediodía
5. volver a casa tarde a menudo
6. nunca tener dinero y siempre tener que pedirlo
7. nunca encontrar sus cosas
8. querer visitar Centroamérica
9. pensar que Santa Claus existe
10. nunca mentir

`7:00`  **B-33 Un poco de mi vida** Escucha mientras tu compañero/a contesta las siguientes preguntas. Luego, repite la información a tu compañero/a. ¿Escuchaste bien? ¿Cuánta información puedes recordar? ■

1. ¿Qué clases tienes este semestre?
2. ¿A qué hora empieza tu clase preferida?
3. ¿Qué prefieres hacer si tienes tiempo entre (*between*) las clases?
4. ¿A qué hora vuelves a tu residencia / apartamento / casa?
5. ¿Qué coche tienes (o quieres tener)?
6. ¿Cuánto cuesta un coche nuevo?
7. ¿Cómo vienes a la universidad? (Por ejemplo, ¿vienes en coche?)
8. ¿Dónde prefieres vivir, en una residencia estudiantil, en un apartamento o en una casa?
9. ¿Dónde quieres vivir después de graduarte?
10. ¿Qué deporte prefieres?

**Estrategia**

Being an "active listener" is an important skill in any language. *Active listening* means that you have heard and understood what someone is saying. Being able to repeat what someone says helps you practice and perfect the skill of active listening.

**SUGGESTION for B-33**
Tell students that for **B-33,** they should have their partners answer questions 1–5. Then repeat back to their partners what they heard. Then it's their turn to do questions 1–5, and their partners will repeat what is said. Have them continue with the rest of the activity in this manner.

**ADDITIONAL ACTIVITY for *Los verbos con cambio de raíz***

**¿Conoces bien a tu compañero/a de clase?**
Túrnense para hacerse esta entrevista.
1. ¿Con quién(es) almuerzas generalmente?
2. ¿Prefieres estudiar por la noche o por la mañana?
3. ¿Cuántas horas duermes cada noche?
4. ¿A qué hora comienzas la tarea los lunes?
5. ¿Pierdes tus lápices o bolígrafos frecuentemente?
6. ¿Entiendes a tu profesor/a cuando habla español?

**EXPANSION for Additional activity for *Los verbos con cambio de raíz: ¿Conoces bien a tu compañero/a de clase?***
Have the students add original questions when they have completed the activity.

**EXPANSION for B-34**
Have students write what they are going to do, and when, on a piece of paper. Then collect the slips of paper, and read them to the class to have students guess who will do which activity at that particular time.

 **29. El verbo** *ir* e *ir + a + infinitivo.* What are the present tense forms of **ir?** How do you express the future with **ir?** Consult pages 146 and 147 if you need to do so and then do the following activities.

B-48 to B-50

**B-34** **¡Vámonos!** Completa las oraciones según el modelo. Después túrnate con un/a compañero/a para decir adónde van sus parientes (*relatives*) y sus amigos en las siguientes situaciones. ■

### Estrategia

When you write sentences that require more than one verb, as in **B-34,** make sure that your verbs match your subject throughout the sentence.

**MODELO**  E1:  Cuando tengo que estudiar…

E2:  *Cuando tengo que estudiar voy a la biblioteca.*

1. Cuando quiere comer, mi compañero de cuarto…
2. Cuando queremos hacer ejercicio, nosotros…
3. Cuando tienes ganas de bailar, tú…
4. Para almorzar muy bien, mis amigos…
5. En la primavera me gusta…
6. Cuando mi hermana quiere comprar música, ella…
7. Para ver una película, tú…
8. Cuando llueve, yo…
9. Cuando hace frío, mis padres…
10. En el verano prefiero…

**EXPANSION for B-35**
Turn this activity into an add-on game in which students sit in a circle, state their names, and each tell one thing they are going to do this week. Each student repeats what everyone has said up to that point before adding his/her information.

**MODELO**
E1:  *Soy Sally y voy a estudiar mucho.*
E2:  *Ella es Sally y va a estudiar mucho. Soy Rick y voy a jugar al fútbol.*
E3:  *Ella es Sally y va a estudiar mucho. Él es Rick y va a jugar al fútbol. Soy Tina y voy al cine…*

**B-35** **Nuestra agenda**  ¿Qué van a hacer la semana que viene? Termina las siguientes oraciones con planes diferentes. Compara tus respuestas con las de un/a compañero/a. ■

| | |
|---|---|
| **lunes** | _____ |
| **martes** | _____ |
| **miércoles** | _____ |
| **jueves** | _____ |
| **viernes** | _____ |
| **sábado** | _____ |
| **domingo** | _____ |

**MODELO**  E1:  El lunes, yo…

E2:  *El lunes voy a devolver unos libros a la biblioteca.*

1. El lunes, yo…
2. El martes, la profesora…
3. El miércoles, mis amigos…
4. El jueves, tú y yo…
5. El viernes, mis primos…
6. El sábado, tú…
7. El domingo, mi madre…

**B-36** **Qué será, será...** ¿Qué tiene el futuro para ti, tus amigos y tu familia? Hagan **cinco** predicciones de lo que va a ocurrir en el futuro y compartan sus respuestas. ■

**MODELO** *Mi primo va a ir a la Universidad Autónoma el año que viene. Nosotros vamos a estudiar mucho para sacar buenas notas. Mis padres van a trabajar en Baltimore...*

**30. Servicios a la comunidad** Review the vocabulary **Servicios a la comunidad** on page 149 and then do the following activity.

B-51

  **B-37** **Definiciones** Túrnense para leer las siguientes definiciones y decir a qué palabra o expresión corresponde cada una. ■

**MODELO** E1: personas que tienen muchos años
E2: *Las personas que tienen muchos años son los mayores.*

1. servir a las personas sin (*without*) recibir dinero a cambio (*in exchange*)
2. un lugar donde viven las personas mayores
3. acompañar a una persona a una cita (*appointment*) con el médico
4. dar un documento a las personas para obtener firmas
5. trabajar para un candidato político sin recibir dinero a cambio (*in exchange*)
6. una persona que trabaja con los niños en un campamento
7. salir en un barco (*boat*) para una o dos personas
8. disfrutar de (*enjoy*) un tipo de arte
9. "construir" una estructura portátil (no permanente) que se usa para dormir fuera de casa
10. un lugar adonde van los niños, generalmente en el verano, para hacer muchas actividades diferentes

**NOTE for B-37**
In an effort to become better acquainted with your students, and them with each other, ask them who has participated in volunteer activities, what they did, where, and when.

**EXPANSION for B-37**
Have students give examples of people who do the activities in **B-37** or describe where they might find the items in the definitions.

**ANSWERS to B-37**
1. el voluntariado
2. la residencia de ancianos
3. llevar a alguien al médico
4. circular una petición
5. apoyar a un/a candidato/a, trabajar en política, participar en una campaña política
6. el/la consejero/a
7. viajar en canoa
8. hacer artesanía
9. montar una tienda de campaña
10. el campamento de niños

**31. Las expresiones afirmativas y negativas.** Review the affirmative and negative expressions on page 151 and then do the following activity.

 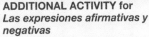 **El/La profesor/a ideal** Túrnense para decir si las siguientes características son ciertas o falsas en un profesor ideal. Usen las expresiones afirmativas y negativas en la página 151 para apoyar (*support*) sus opiniones. ■

**MODELO**    Un/a profesor/a ideal… siempre da buenas notas.
    E1: *A veces un profesor ideal da buenas notas.*
    E2: *No, el profesor ideal no siempre da buenas notas. A veces tiene que dar malas notas.*

### Un/a profesor/a ideal…

1. nunca falta (*misses*) a clase.
2. prepara algo interesante para cada clase.
3. siempre prefiere leer sus apuntes.
4. piensa que sabe más que nadie.
5. a veces organiza a sus estudiantes en grupos para discutir (*discuss*) ideas.
6. a veces llega a clase cinco minutos tarde.
7. jamás manda (da) tarea para la clase.
8. no pierde nada —por ejemplo la tarea, los exámenes, las composiciones, etc.
9. no habla con nadie después de la clase.
10. siempre está contento/a con su trabajo.

**32. Un repaso de *ser* y *estar*.** When do you use **ser** and **estar**? Write the reasons on a sheet of paper, and then check your list against the one on pages 154–155. Next, do the following activities.

 **¿Qué tal?** Adriana le escribe un email a su familia. Llenen los espacios en blanco con las formas correctas de **ser** y **estar** para conocerla mejor. ■

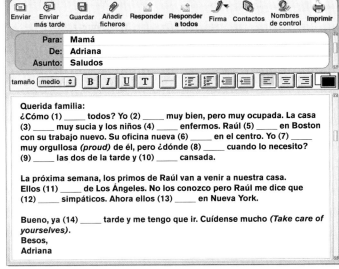

Querida familia:
¿Cómo (1) _____ todos? Yo (2) _____ muy bien, pero muy ocupada. La casa (3) _____ muy sucia y los niños (4) _____ enfermos. Raúl (5) _____ en Boston con su trabajo nuevo. Su oficina nueva (6) _____ en el centro. Yo (7) _____ muy orgullosa (*proud*) de él, pero ¿dónde (8) _____ cuando lo necesito? (9) _____ las dos de la tarde y (10) _____ cansada.

La próxima semana, los primos de Raúl van a venir a nuestra casa. Ellos (11) _____ de Los Ángeles. No los conozco pero Raúl me dice que (12) _____ simpáticos. Ahora ellos (13) _____ en Nueva York.

Bueno, ya (14) _____ tarde y me tengo que ir. Cuídense mucho (*Take care of yourselves*).
Besos,
Adriana

**ANSWERS to B-40**
1. están: *physical condition*
2. estoy: *physical condition*
3. está: *physical condition*
4. están: *physical condition*
5. está: *location*
6. está: *location*
7. estoy: *mental condition*
8. está: *location*
9. son: *tell time*
10. estoy: *physical condition*
11. son: *tell where someone is from*
12. son: *personality characteristics*
13. están: *location*
14. es: *telling time*

  **B-40  Así es**  Ahora expliquen por qué usaron (*you used*) **ser o estar** en cada parte de **B-39**. ∎

MODELO     están: *physical condition*

**B-41  A conocernos mejor**  Túrnense para hacerse y contestar las siguientes preguntas. ∎

1. ¿De dónde eres?
2. ¿A qué hora son tus clases?
3. ¿Cómo es tu casa?
4. ¿Dónde está tu casa?
5. ¿Cómo es tu dormitorio?
6. ¿Dónde está tu dormitorio?
7. ¿De qué color es tu casa?
8. ¿Cuál es tu color favorito?
9. ¿Cómo es tu novio/a (esposo/a, amigo/a)?
10. ¿Dónde está él/ella ahora (*now*)?
11. ¿Cómo eres?
12. ¿Cómo estás hoy?

## • Capítulo 5 •
Sharing information about different types of music, movies, and television programs, including your personal preferences

B-54 to B-55

**33. El mundo de la música.**  Review the **El mundo de la música** vocabulary on page 172 and then do the following activities.

 **B-42  ¿Qué quiere decir?**  Lee las siguientes descripciones. Después, túrnate con un/a compañero/a para decir a qué palabra o expresión se refieren. ∎

MODELO     E1:  dar conciertos en varias ciudades
             E2:  *Dar conciertos en varias ciudades es "hacer una gira".*

1. ser muy popular y conocido entre muchas personas  la fama
2. las palabras que cantas en una canción  la letra
3. la música de Mozart y Beethoven, por ejemplo  la música clásica
4. una persona que canta  un/a cantante
5. lo que usas para cantar y hablar  la voz
6. un instrumento de percusión  el tambor / la batería
7. sinónimo de grupo  el conjunto
8. hacer sonido bonito con un instrumento  tocar
9. cuando haces algo muy bien, dicen que tienes mucha ___habilidad___
10. la música de Jay-Z y Eminem, por ejemplo  la música rap

**SUGGESTION for B-42**
Ask students to use the Internet to research popular Hispanic groups, singers, and/or musicians. They should each choose one to report on in class, providing a photo and basic information.

**EXPANSION for B-42**
Have students play Charades to practice the vocabulary in **B-42.**

**B-43** **La música** Túrnense para hacerse esta entrevista. ■

1. ¿Cuál es tu grupo favorito?
2. ¿Cuál es tu cantante favorito/a?
3. ¿Cuál es tu instrumento favorito?
4. ¿Cuál es tu tipo de música favorito?
5. ¿Cuál es tu canción favorita?
6. ¿Sabes tocar un instrumento? ¿Cuál?
7. ¿Te gusta cantar? ¿Cuándo y dónde cantas?
8. ¿En qué tienes mucha habilidad o talento?

B-56

**34. Los adjetivos y pronombres demostrativos.** How do you say *this, that, these,* and *those* in Spanish? Review the demonstrative adjectives and pronouns on pages 175 and 177 and then do the following activities.

  **B-44** **Comparando cosas** Tu mejor amigo/a te propone una cosa pero tú siempre prefieres otra. Túrnense para responder a sus comentarios usando una forma de **este, ese** o **aquel.** ■

**MODELO**    TU MEJOR AMIGO/A:    ¿Quieres ir a este cine?

              TÚ:   *No, no quiero ir a este. Quiero ir a aquel.*

1. ¿Vamos a ir a ese teatro?
2. ¿Tus hermanos tocan en aquel grupo?
3. ¿Quieres escuchar este CD?
3. ¿Piensan ustedes arreglar este cuarto para (*for*) la fiesta?
5. ¿Vas a comprar aquellas entradas?
6. ¿Entiendes la letra de esta canción?

  **B-45** **En la universidad** Túrnense para hablar de lo que les gusta o no les gusta usando formas de **este, ese** y **aquel.** Hagan por lo menos **cinco** oraciones positivas y **cinco** oraciones negativas. ■

**MODELO**    *Me gusta esta clase. Nuestro profesor de español es interesante, pero aquel profesor de sociología es un poco aburrido. Este libro es bueno, pero ese libro de matemáticas es difícil…*

**35. Los adverbios.** In Spanish, how do most adverbs end? How are they formed? Check page 179 to verify your answers. Then do the following activity.

 **B-46** **¿Qué ocurre en el concierto?** Vas a un concierto de varios conjuntos en el estadio de tu universidad. Para saber qué pasa, completa estas oraciones con los adverbios apropiados. Comparte tus respuestas con un/a compañero/a. ■

MODELO    E1:  Vamos al concierto (rápido, cuidadoso).

          E2:  *Vamos al concierto rápidamente.*

1. La gente espera a los conjuntos (paciente, lento).
2. El primer conjunto toca (triste, feliz).
3. Un grupo llega tarde y entra al estadio (seguro, nervioso).
4. Los otros músicos escuchan (cansado, atento).
5. El conjunto toca una canción romántica y la gente empieza a bailar (lento, rápido).
6. Terminan el concierto (inmediato, final).

**36. El presente progresivo.** How do you form the present progressive in Spanish (*I am* _____ *ing, We are* _____ *ing*, etc.)? Check your answer on page 180 and then do the following activity.

 **B-47** **¿Qué están haciendo?** Túrnense para decir qué están haciendo las siguientes personas. ■

MODELO    E1:  Son las siete y media de la mañana y mi papá está en su terraza.

          E2:  *Está tomando café.*

1. A mi hermano le gusta hacer ejercicio para comenzar su día.
2. A mi prima le gusta la música folklórica y está en una tienda.
3. Mis abuelos van a tener una fiesta esta noche y no tienen comida en casa.
4. Nuestro/a profesor/a está en la computadora y resulta que tiene muchos mensajes de sus estudiantes.
5. Nuestros amigos quieren comer algo ligero (*light*) antes de ir a la fiesta.
6. Estamos con nuestros amigos en la fiesta y un grupo está tocando.

**37. El mundo del cine.** Review the **El mundo del cine** vocabulary on page 184 and practice it with the following activity.

B-59

**B-48  En mi opinión** Termina las siguientes oraciones sobre las películas que tú has visto (*have seen*). Pueden ser películas viejas o nuevas, buenas o malas. Comparte tus respuestas con un/a compañero/a. ■

**MODELO**   E1:  La mejor película de terror…

E2:  *La mejor película de terror es* Psycho.

1. La mejor película cómica…
2. Una película épica pésima…
3. La película de misterio que menos me gusta…
4. Mi actor/actriz favorito/a de las películas de acción…
5. La película animada más creativa…
6. La película más conmovedora…

 **38. Los números ordinales.** How do you say *first, second, third,* etc. in Spanish? Check your answers on page 187 and then do the following activity.

B-60

**B-49  Orden de preferencia** Asigna un orden de preferencia a las actividades de la lista: de la más importante (primero) a la menos importante (octavo). Luego compara tu lista con la de un/a compañero/a usando oraciones completas. ■

**MODELO**   *Primero, me gusta ver una película de mi actor favorito Johnny Depp. Segundo, me gusta visitar a mis parientes…*

1. ir a un concierto de un grupo fabuloso          _____
2. visitar a tus parientes                                     _____
3. ver una película de tu actor/actriz favorito/a    _____
4. leer una novela buena                                   _____
5. ir a un partido de fútbol americano               _____
6. estudiar para un examen                               _____
7. viajar a Guatemala                                        _____
8. conocer a los presidentes de los Estados Unidos  _____

**39. *Hay que + infinitivo.*** What does **hay que + infinitivo** mean? Check your answer on page 188 and then do the following activity.

B-61

  **B-50** **¿Obligaciones?** Digan qué hay que hacer o cómo hay que ser para tener las siguientes profesiones. ■

**MODELO** un pintor

E1: *Hay que pintar mucho.*

E2: *Hay que ser muy creativo.*

1. novelista
2. cantante
3. músico/a
4. actriz
5. director/a de cine
6. político/a

**40. Los pronombres de complemento directo.** What is a *direct object*? What is a *direct object pronoun*? What are the direct object pronouns in Spanish? Where do you place direct object pronouns? Review pages 189–190 and then practice with the following activities.

B-62

 **B-51** **¿Estás listo/a?** ¡Qué suerte! Vas al concierto del año en un anfiteatro. Revisa la lista de preparativos con un/a compañero/a usando **lo, la, los** o **las.** ■

**MODELO** E1: ¿Tienes que comprar *las entradas* del concierto?

E2: *Sí, las tengo que comprar hoy. / Tengo que comprarlas hoy.*

1. ¿Vamos a preparar *una comida* (meal)? Sí, vamos a prepararla. / Sí, la vamos a preparar.
2. ¿Llevamos *las bebidas* (beverages)? Sí, vamos a llevarlas. / Sí, las vamos a llevar.
3. ¿Vamos a invitar *a nuestros amigos*? Sí, los vamos a invitar. / Sí, vamos a invitarlos.
4. ¿Escuchan ellos *los CD del grupo*? Sí, los escuchan.
5. ¿Tengo que leer *la reseña* (review)? Sí, tienes que leerla. / Sí, la tienes que leer.
6. ¿Vas a llevar *la cámara*? Sí, voy a llevarla. / Sí, la voy a llevar.

**NOTE for B-51**
Prior to beginning this activity, ask students to create sentence pairs using the present progressive tense with direct objects and direct object pronouns. The first sentence should contain a direct object noun while the second sentence replaces that noun with a direct object pronoun. For example:

Mi padre está lavando el carro.
Mi padre está lavándolo. / Mi padre lo está lavando.

**B-52** **¿Hay deberes?** Siempre hay cosas que hacer. Usen **lo, la, los** y **las** para hablar de sus deberes. ■

MODELO    ¿lavar los pisos todos los días?
     E1:   *Sí, tengo que lavarlos todos los días.* /
           *Sí, los tengo que lavar todos los días.*
     E2:   *No, nunca los lavo.* / *No, los lavo los fines de semana.*

1. ¿sacudir los muebles?
2. ¿poner la mesa por la tarde?
3. ¿limpiar la cocina los sábados?
4. ¿preparar la comida todos los días?
5. ¿lavar los platos cada (*each*) día?
6. ¿hacer las camas por la mañana?
7. ¿guardar tus cosas?
8. ¿arreglar tu cuarto?

## • Ambiciones siniestras •

Depicting what has happened thus far to the protagonists:
Alejandra, Manolo, Cisco, Eduardo, Marisol, and Lupe
Hypothesizing about what you think will happen in future episodes

B-63

**41. Ambiciones siniestras.** Read and then view the synopsis of the first five text and video episodes of **Ambiciones siniestras.** Then do the following activities.

 **B-53** **¿Qué pasó?** Escribe un resumen de lo que ha pasado (*has happened*) en **Ambiciones siniestras.** Puedes describir a cada personaje o puedes escribir una síntesis de cada capítulo. ■

---

**NOTE for *AMBICIONES SINIESTRAS***

This chapter features a video synopsis of the first 5 textbook and video episodes of *Ambiciones siniestras*. Please note that this is the only time when there is only a video episode, rather than both a reading and video episode. Viewing the video will provide your students who used *¡Anda! Curso elemental* with a refresher of what happened in the first semester and it will provide your new students with an introduction to the characters and the storyline. This will help all students step into the new text and video episodes quickly beginning in *Capítulo 7*. As a reminder, starting in *Capítulo 7*, as in *Capítulos 1–5*, each chapter will have a written, textbook episode that ends in a cliffhanger. In each of those chapters, students watch an episode of the video that picks up where the textbook left off. The video episode also ends in a cliff-hanger, motivating students to read the next episode in the following chapter to discover what happens next.

7:00 **B-54** **¿Qué va a ocurrir?** Escribe un párrafo sobre lo que tú piensas que va a ocurrir en los próximos episodios de **Ambiciones siniestras.** ■

### Estrategia

The *¿Cómo andas?* and *Y por fin, ¿cómo andas?* sections are designed to help you assess your understanding of specific concepts. In *Capítulo Preliminar B*, there is one opportunity for you to reflect on how well you understand the concepts. Beginning with *Capítulo 7* there will be three opportunities in each chapter for you to stop and reflect on what you have learned. These checks help you become accountable for your own learning, and help you determine what you need to review. Also use the checklist as a way to communicate with your instructor about any concepts you still need to review. Additionally, you might also use your checklist as a way to study with a peer group or peer tutor. If you need to review a particular concept, more practice is available on MySpanishLab.

## Y por fin, ¿cómo andas?

| Having completed this chapter, I now can . . . | Feel confident | Need to review |
|---|:---:|:---:|
| **Comunicación** | | |
| • greet, say good-bye, and introduce others | ☐ | ☐ |
| • describe myself and others | ☐ | ☐ |
| • share information about school and life as a student | ☐ | ☐ |
| • offer opinions about sports and pastimes that I and others like and dislike | ☐ | ☐ |
| • describe homes and household chores | ☐ | ☐ |
| • identify places in and around town | ☐ | ☐ |
| • relate things that happen and things that have to be done | ☐ | ☐ |
| • convey what will take place in the future | ☐ | ☐ |
| • impart information about service opportunities | ☐ | ☐ |
| • share information about different types of movies, music, and television programs, including my own personal preferences | ☐ | ☐ |
| **Ambiciones siniestras** | | |
| • depict what has happened thus far to the protagonists: Alejandra, Manolo, Cisco, Eduardo, Marisol, and Lupe | ☐ | ☐ |
| • hypothesize about what I think will happen in future episodes | ☐ | ☐ |
| **Comunidades** | | |
| • use Spanish in real-life contexts (SAM) | ☐ | ☐ |

**NOTE for** *Y por fin, ¿cómo andas?*
Each chapter will normally have three *self-checks: ¿Cómo andas? I, ¿Cómo andas? II,* and the third, entitled, *Y por fin, ¿cómo andas?* Each time the students complete a self-check, they are responsible for more information and they are able to more accurately assess their progress. Since *Capítulo Preliminar B* is meant to be a quick introduction to Spanish, there is only one self-check for the students. Encourage them to use these self-checks, since they help your students become accountable for their own learning and promote self-actualization.

**SUGGESTION for** *Y por fin, ¿cómo andas?*
If you have time constraints, we recommend that these self-assessments be completed by the students outside of class. You may want to spot-check some students and ask how they are doing (e.g., "How many of you feel confident with greeting, saying goodbye, and introducing someone?"). For those students who do not raise their hands, remind them that they need to consult the pages listed to review the material. If you have time to do them in class, one approach is to have students write short answers to the topics, then check in their textbooks to verify their answers. Based on this verification, they can rate themselves on the concepts and hand in their ratings to you at the end of class.

**Instructor Resources**
• IRM: Syllabi and Lesson Plans

# 7 ¡A comer!

Comer bien es un gran placer (*pleasure*). Dentro del mundo hispanohablante hay una tremenda variedad de comidas (*foods*) y la comida tiene una función social muy importante.

**PREGUNTAS**

**1** ¿Cuáles son tus platos (*dishes*) favoritos?

**2** ¿Hay alguna comida típica de la región donde vives tú? ¿Cuáles son algunas comidas típicas de los Estados Unidos?

**3** ¿Qué platos de otras culturas te gustan? ¿Qué platos hispanos te gustan?

254

**SECTION GOALS for *Chapter opener***
By the end of the Chapter opener section, students will be able to:
• discuss their favorite dishes.
• identify regional and national cuisines of the United States.
• report about their favorite ethnic foods.

**NATIONAL STANDARDS**
*Communities*
If you have a large Hispanic population in your area, this chapter lends itself well to several service learning ideas. If you have a farmer's market or Hispanic district where local goods are sold, students can volunteer their time assisting the merchants and customers as they shop. If you have many Hispanic-owned restaurants or local businesses where the employees speak Spanish, your students could shadow someone who interacts with the Spanish-speaking public. Social services agencies that provide meals or grocery shopping services to those members of the Spanish-speaking community who are confined to homes would also be appropriate. Other suggestions include collecting food for a food bank on behalf of your Spanish class, bringing in recipes in Spanish that students can make and deliver to nursing homes, churches, after-school programs or housing projects, or inviting community members to dine at the campus. If you do not have a Hispanic population in your area, you could plan a "Taste of Hispanic Foods" night and have students prepare the Spanish language recipes you provide for a battered women's shelter, a soup kitchen, or some other social service organization in your community.

255

**METHODOLOGY • ¡Anda! Curso elemental**
If you are new to using the ¡Anda! Curso elemental program, please refer to the preface where we describe our philosophy of language education. These teacher annotations will assist you as you progress through the rest of the program to help your students acquire Spanish and become effective communicators in the language. Also, please remember that the questions that follow the brief reading on this page are meant to start with what the students already know (activating their prior knowledge), and help to entice them to learn more about the topic. We suggest you spend no more than 5–7 minutes on the chapter openers.

**WARM-UP for Chapter opener**
Students are already familiar with the word comer, introduced in Capítulo 2. This is a good opportunity to ask them to think about the types of foods and Hispanic dishes they have already learned about in previous chapters.

**METHODOLOGY • Making Topics Relevant for Students**
The text and questions for this chapter opener are completely in Spanish, just as in Capítulos 4 and 5. Note that the questions begin with your learners and their preferences, a technique we have learned from educational philosopher John Dewey. Try having your students turn to their partners and answer the questions in pairs. Then have them share the answers their partners gave. This has them practice listening and also paraphrasing.

**21ST CENTURY SKILLS • JOHN DEWEY**
Educational philosopher John Dewey (1859–1952) had a profound effect on the U.S. educational system in the most positive of ways. A man well before his time, he had insight into many of the issues that would later develop in the world of education. For example, he maintained that all learners would need to take an interdisciplinary approach to learning. ¡Anda! is based heavily on the philosophies of this visionary man.

**EXPANSION for Preguntas**
Ask students whether they are aware of dishes with the same names that are prepared differently. You may want to tell them about the difference between la tortilla mexicana (of corn or flour) and la tortilla española (potato omelet).

You may also want to ask your students the following questions:

1. En tu experiencia, ¿a qué tipo de comida se refiere la expresión "Spanish food"?
2. ¿Hay restaurantes hispanos en nuestra ciudad? ¿Qué platos tienen?

**NOTE for Chapter opener**
If your campus has a diverse student population and the students are familiar with different types of ethnic foods, you will want to anticipate the kinds of cuisine they might mention so you can tell them how to say those foods in Spanish.

**NOTE for Contenidos**
The Heritage Language activities, available in the Student Activities Manual (SAM), are not only for heritage learners, but for all of your students. The activities either require students to reflect on the usage of Spanish, or to use

Spanish in ways that encompass all of the 5 Cs. The end product will vary from student to student, which is an expected outcome of performance-based activities.

**HERITAGE LANGUAGE LEARNERS**
Ask your heritage language learners whether there is a specific comida casera they enjoy and what ingredients they use to make the dish. If the vocabulary differs from that of the Vocabulario activo, ask them to explain how the dish is made and whether the products are available in American grocery stores.

**SECTION GOALS for**
*Comunicación I*
By the end of the *Comunicación I* section, students will be able to:

• compare main dishes and cuisine from the United States and Hispanic countries.
• express preferences about food.
• categorize food into appropriate breakfast, lunch, or dinner menus.
• pronounce the letters *r* and *rr* properly.
• describe how the schedule for mealtimes differs between the United States and some Hispanic countries.
• narrate events and actions that occurred in the preterit tense.
• identify verbs with spelling changes in the preterit.
• select key words that trigger the use of the preterit.
• review the forms, uses, and placement of direct object pronouns.

**NOTE for *La comida***
The Spanish language is rich with vocabulary for food and there are many variations among countries and regions. Refer students to the *También se dice…* section in Appendix 3 for additional words.

**METHODOLOGY •**
**Assessment**
In *Capítulo 1*, we talked about the fact that assessment comes in a variety of forms. The two basic categories are *formal* and *informal*. *Formal* assessment includes the end-of-chapter written and oral tests. It also includes periodic quizzes that you may give. *Informal* assessment is the daily process that we use as instructors to evaluate the progress of our students. Some of us give class participation grades. The authors suggest a class participation grade that includes students using the target language throughout the class and the effort the students put into their assignments.

**METHODOLOGY •**
**Assessment Domains**
As previously noted, there are two main types of assessment: *formal* and *informal*. Within those two types, there are three domains/modes by which we can assess our students: *interpretive, interpersonal,* and *presentational.* When students read a passage, as with the Chapter opener, and then respond to comprehension and critical thinking questions, you are employing the *interpretive* mode. When students work in pairs / groups, you are able to assess them in the *interpersonal* mode. Finally, when students present an assignment to a partner / group, or the class, it constitutes the *presentational* mode.

# Comunicación I

**1 VOCABULARIO**    [5:00]    07-01 to 07-07

## La comida    Discussing food

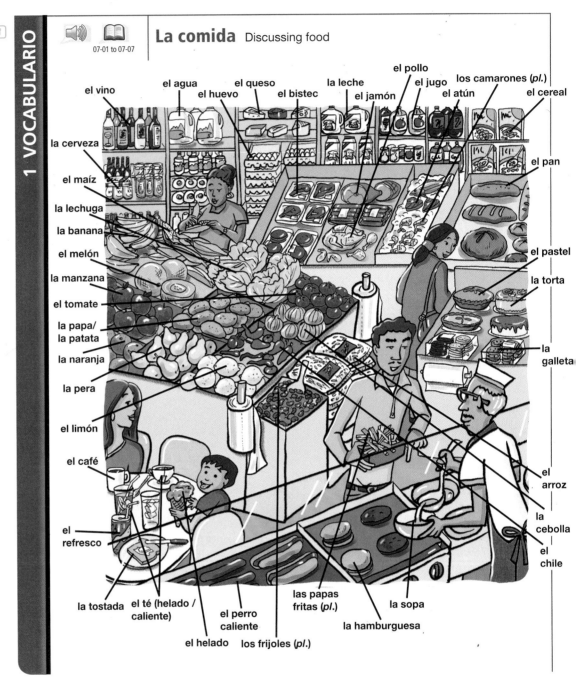

el vino · la cerveza · el maíz · la lechuga · la banana · el melón · la manzana · el tomate · la papa/ la patata · la naranja · la pera · el limón · el café · el refresco · la tostada · el té (helado / caliente) · el helado · los frijoles (*pl.*) · el perro caliente · el agua · el huevo · el queso · el bistec · la leche · el jamón · el pollo · el jugo · el atún · los camarones (*pl.*) · el cereal · el pan · el pastel · la torta · la galleta · el arroz · la cebolla · el chile · las papas fritas (*pl.*) · la sopa · la hamburguesa

**METHODOLOGY • Teaching Vocabulary**
Research concludes that learning vocabulary is best achieved when images are associated with the target words rather than learning from lists of words that are not illustrated. The "Where's Waldo?" style images created for presenting the thematic chapter vocabulary in *¡Anda! Curso elemental* are intentionally rich. They are best appreciated either online or in transparency format where the images are enlarged from the print format. What may initially be difficult to discern will be clarified when the learner makes the connection to the artwork.

**NOTE for *La comida***
*Almorzar,* introduced in *Capítulo 4,* is included in this list of new verbs to emphasize the connection between the noun for each meal and its corresponding verb.

**NOTE for *La comida***
You may want to remind students that in *Capítulo 2* they learned "tomar" as "to drink" as well as "to take."

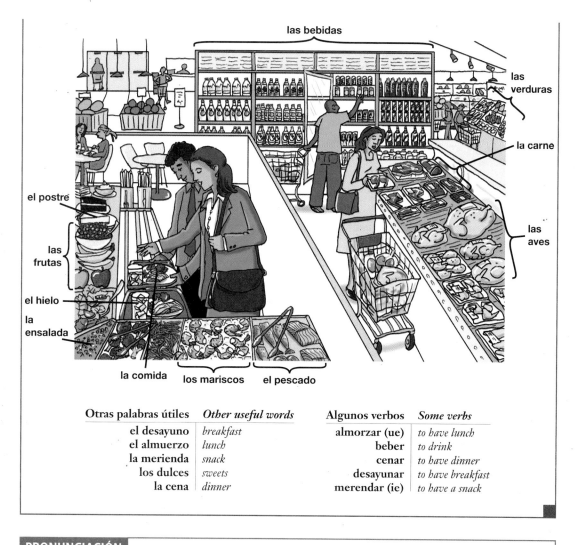

las bebidas

las verduras

la carne

las aves

el postre

las frutas

el hielo

la ensalada

la comida     los mariscos     el pescado

| Otras palabras útiles | Other useful words | Algunos verbos | Some verbs |
|---|---|---|---|
| el desayuno | breakfast | almorzar (ue) | to have lunch |
| el almuerzo | lunch | beber | to drink |
| la merienda | snack | cenar | to have dinner |
| los dulces | sweets | desayunar | to have breakfast |
| la cena | dinner | merendar (ie) | to have a snack |

## PRONUNCIACIÓN

### The different pronunciations of r and rr

07-08 to 07-11

Go to MySpanishLab / Student Activities Manual to learn about the letters r and rr.

5. Making class participation a significant component of the final grade for the class helps to keep students on task. When students understand that you expect them to speak in Spanish, to take turns, and to work well with others, AND that you will be grading them on their classroom behavior, it helps them understand the importance of their work in the classroom.

6. Not all groups will finish all items of all activities during a class period. That is fine, since students have been moving at the pace necessary for them to learn. During a subsequent class period when students are working with new partners, you can have a list of review pair activities that students can work on if they finish early. These would be the communicative activities at the end of each *chunk*. Even though your students are repeating an activity that they may have already done, the fact that they are working with a new partner and a new context will help to retain their interest.

**Fíjate**

Although *agua* and *ave* are feminine nouns, the masculine singular article *el* is used with them (*el agua, el ave*), as a way to separate and differentiate the similar stressed vowel sounds in each word (*la* and *a*). *Las* is used with the plurals of these words (*las aguas, las aves*). All adjectives describing these words are feminine (*el agua fría / las aguas frías*).

 **7-1 Concurso** Escoge **cinco** letras diferentes. Bajo cada letra escribe todas las palabras del vocabulario de **La comida** que recuerdes. Después, compara tu lista con la de un/a compañero/a. ■

| MODELO | a | d | p |
|---|---|---|---|
| | arroz | desayuno | papas fritas |
| | agua | dulce | |

 **7-2 ¡Ay, las calorías!** Túrnense para decir a qué comida corresponden las siguientes descripciones. Usen el cuadro de los valores nutritivos. ■

### CUADRO DE LOS VALORES NUTRITIVOS

| Comida | Calorías | Proteínas (gramos) | Grasas (gramos) | Carbohidratos (gramos) | Vitaminas |
|---|---|---|---|---|---|
| bistec | 455 | 27 | 36 | 0 | A, B |
| hamburguesa con queso | 950 | 50 | 60 | 54 | B |
| jugo de naranja | 100 | 1 | 0 | 16 | A, B, C |
| naranja | 50 | 1 | 0 | 16 | A, B, C |
| pan | 150 | 6 | 2 | 38 | B |
| papa | 100 | 3 | 0 | 23 | B, C |
| perro caliente | 200 | 5 | 14 | 1 | B, C |
| salmón | 200 | 24 | 10 | 0 | A, B |
| torta | 455 | 4 | 13 | 76 | A, B, C |
| lechuga | 10 | 1 | 0 | 2 | A, B, C |

Capítulo Preliminar A. Los números 0–30, pág. 16; Capítulo 1. Los números 31–100, pág. 47; Capítulo 2. Los números 100–1.000, pág. 72.

**Estrategia**

*¡Anda! Curso elemental* has provided you with recycling references to help guide your continuous review of previously learned material. Make sure to consult the indicated pages if you need to refresh your memory about numbers.

MODELO  E1: *Esta comida tiene mucha agua, es verde y tiene diez calorías.*

E2: *Es la lechuga.*

**Esta comida tiene…**

1. 60 gramos (*grams*) de grasas, 50 gramos de proteínas y 950 calorías. la hamburguesa con queso
2. muchas proteínas, es un pescado y tiene 200 calorías. el salmón
3. vitamina C, es una verdura y tiene 100 calorías. la papa
4. muchos carbohidratos y 150 calorías. el pan
5. 27 gramos de proteínas, es una carne y tiene 455 calorías. el bistec
6. 50 calorías y es una fruta. la naranja
7. 16 gramos de carbohidratos y es una bebida. el jugo de naranja
8. las vitaminas B y C, sólo un gramo de carbohidratos y 14 gramos de grasa. el perro caliente

Capítulo 2. El verbo
*gustar*, pág. 80.

Workbooklet

**7-3** **¿Cuáles son tus preferencias?** ¿Qué comidas te gustan? ▪

**Paso 1**    Completa el cuadro según tus preferencias.

**Estrategia**
You may want to talk about foods that are not included here. Refer to the *También se dice...* section in Appendix 3 for additional vocabulary.

| 1. Las carnes, las aves, el pescado y los mariscos que... | |
|---|---|
| a. más me gustan son... | b. menos me gustan son... |
| 1. | 1. |
| 2. | 2. |
| **2. Las frutas y verduras que...** | |
| a. más me gustan son... | b. menos me gustan son... |
| 1. | 1. |
| 2. | 2. |

**Paso 2**    Ahora, compara tus preferencias con las de los compañeros de la clase: ¿Cuáles son sus comidas favoritas? ¿Qué comidas les gustan menos?

**MODELO**    E1:  *¿Cuál es tu carne favorita?*

E2:  *No me gusta la carne, pero me gusta mucho el pollo. ¿Y a ti?*

Capítulo Preliminar A. La hora, pág. 18; Capítulo Preliminar A. Los días, los meses y las estaciones, pág. 20.

Workbooklet

**7-4** **La dieta de Nico** Nico es un estudiante universitario de Santiago de Chile. Mira lo que (*what*) come normalmente y cuándo lo come. Después completa los siguientes pasos. ▪

**Fíjate**
The word *galleta* means both *cookie* and *cracker*.

**LA DIETA DE NICO**

| | DESAYUNO | ALMUERZO | MERIENDA | CENA |
|---|---|---|---|---|
| | 8:30 | 12:00 | 5:30 | 8:00 |
| DÍA 1: | té con galletas | ensalada, arroz con pollo y uvas | manzana | atún con una ensalada de lechuga con tomate y fruta |
| DÍA 2: | té y pan con mantequilla | sopa, tortilla de papas y flan | galletas | pan con mermelada |

**Fíjate**
While *patata* is used in Spain, *papa* is widely used in Latin America.

**Paso 1**    Ahora completa el cuadro con tu información.

**TU DIETA**

| | DESAYUNO | ALMUERZO | MERIENDA | CENA |
|---|---|---|---|---|
| DÍA 1: | | | | |
| DÍA 2: | | | | |

**Paso 2**    Con un/a compañero/a, comparen su información con la de Nico.

**MODELO**    E1:  *Yo nunca tomo té en el desayuno. Generalmente desayuno más temprano que Nico. ¿Y tú?*

E2:  *Yo desayuno a las siete y media y generalmente como huevos y tostadas.*

**Vocabulario útil**

| | |
|---|---|
| **más temprano que** | *earlier than* |
| **más tarde que** | *later than* |

**NATIONAL STANDARDS**
*Communication*
Activity **7-4** is an excellent opportunity for students to communicate meaningful preferences. Also, if you are beginning a new semester and have new students, the next activity is a good way to help them get acquainted and build classroom community.

The interpersonal communicative activities like **7-4,** in which students are working together to piece together information, promote Standard 1.1. They are engaging in conversations, providing and obtaining information, and exchanging their opinions about their eating habits and foods they like or dislike. If you ask students to write down their daily eating schedules and menus and to present them to the class, you can satisfy Standard 1.3 as well.

**EXPANSION for 7-4**
You may wish to have each student interview another student so that when reporting, he/she will say, *Él/Ella...*

**Paso 3**   Miren la pirámide de alimentación para determinar si todos los grupos están representados en sus dietas.

**MODELO**   E1:   *Comemos pan en el desayuno y a veces en la cena.*

E2:   *Comemos papas y ensaladas de lechuga y tomate, pero no comemos muchas otras verduras.*

E1:   *Tienes razón, pero comemos mucha fruta…*

# Mi pirámide
PASOS HACIA UNA SALUD MEJOR

AGUA DIARIAMENTE

Haga ejercicio casi todos los días 30 minutos

Recomendación diaria para cada grupo de alimentos.

ACEITE GRASAS AZÚCAR OCASIONALMENTE

| GRANOS | VERDURAS | FRUTAS | PRODUCTOS LÁCTEOS | CARNES Y FRIJOLES |
|---|---|---|---|---|
| 7 onzas | 3 tazas | 2 tazas | 3 tazas | 6 onzas |
| **Consuma la mitad en granos integrales** Trate de consumir por lo menos **3 onzas y media** de granos integrales cada día | **Varíe las verduras** Intente alcanzar estas cantidades cada semana: **Verduras verdes** - 3 tazas **Verduras con almidón** - 6 tazas **Otras verduras** - 7 tazas | **Enfóquese en las frutas** Coma frutas variadas No tome mucha cantidad de jugo de frutas | **Coma alimentos ricos en calcio** Al escoger leche, yogur o queso, opte por productos bajos en contenido graso | **Escoja proteínas bajas en grasas** Escoja carnes y aves de bajo contenido graso o magras Varíe su rutina de proteínas; coma más pescado, frijoles, guisantes, nueces y semillas |

| Encuentre un equilibro entre la alimentación y la actividad física | Conozca los límites de las grasas, los azúcares y el sodio |
|---|---|
| Manténgase físicamente activo por lo menos durante 30 minutos la mayoría de los días de la semana | Su dosis de aceites es **6 cucharaditas por día** Limite las grasas sólidas y azúcares - **a 290 calorías por día** |

---

`4:00`       **7-5**   **¿Qué comes tú?**   Entrevista a un/a compañero/a usando las siguientes preguntas. ■

1. ¿Comes bien o mal? Explica.
2. ¿Qué tipo de comida prefieres?
3. ¿Qué te gusta merendar?
4. ¿Qué comidas tienen vitamina C y calcio?
5. ¿Qué comidas tienen mucha proteína?
6. ¿Qué comidas no te gustan?

## NOTA CULTURAL

## Las comidas en el mundo hispano

  07-12

La palabra "comida" significa varias cosas en español: *food, meal* y *lunch* (the main meal of the day). Las comidas en los países hispanoamericanos son similares a las comidas norteamericanas pero también existen algunas diferencias. Por ejemplo, el desayuno en el mundo hispano normalmente consiste en café y pan o panes dulces. Generalmente es una comida ligera (*light*).

El almuerzo es normalmente la comida más grande y más fuerte del día. En lugares con una cultura más tradicional, el almuerzo puede empezar a eso de (*around*) las dos de la tarde. Los niños regresan de la escuela y el papá (y la mamá si trabaja fuera [*outside*] de la casa) comen juntos en casa. Entonces, hay tiempo para descansar (*to rest*) antes de volver al trabajo y a la escuela. En los países y las zonas con más industria y comercio puede haber un horario de almuerzo similar al horario de los Estados Unidos.

La cena generalmente es una comida más ligera. La gente en los países hispanohablantes cena más tarde que la mayoría de los norteamericanos. En España, por ejemplo, ¡muchas personas no cenan hasta las diez o las once de la noche!

### Preguntas

1. ¿Cómo es un desayuno típico en el mundo hispano? ¿un almuerzo? ¿una cena?
2. Generalmente, ¿cuál es el horario de las comidas en los países hispanos?

## 2 GRAMÁTICA

 ¡Hola!
07-13 to 07-17 Spanish/English Tutorials

## Repaso del complemento directo
Communicating with less repetition

In **Capítulo 5** you learned to use **direct object pronouns** in Spanish. Return to pages 189–190 for a quick review, then answer the following questions:

¿Postre? Tenemos...

¡Los quiero todos!

### ¡Explícalo tú!

1. What are **direct objects**? What are **direct object pronouns**?
2. What are the pronouns (forms)? With what must they agree?
3. Where are direct object pronouns placed in a sentence?

 Check your answers to the preceding questions in Appendix 1.

---

**Instructor Resources**
• PPT, Extra Activities

**NATIONAL STANDARDS**
*Cultures, Comparisons*
The reading, *Las comidas en el mundo hispano*, engages your students not only in reading about meals in the Spanish-speaking world, but also in comparing the information to their own lives.

The reading explains the various meanings of the word *comida*, and how *comidas* in Hispanic countries are different from the typical meals in the United States. The reading addresses Standard 2.1 by highlighting the cultural differences in the times for meals and the types of food eaten at particular meals. Students can make comparisons between the Hispanic meal schedule and the types of foods served, and how they differ from those in the United States (Standard 4.2).

**METHODOLOGY • Planning Ahead**
Remember that all grammar explanations and culture presentations should be assigned to be read before class. Class time should be spent answering clarification questions for the grammar presentations, or answering the comprehension/critical thinking questions that follow the culture presentations.

**EXPANSION for *Las comidas en el mundo hispano***
An additional question to ask your students is: *Por lo general, ¿a qué hora tomas tú el desayuno, la comida y la cena?*

**NOTE for *Nota cultural***
The authors realize there are many variations in meals and schedules throughout the Spanish-speaking world. You may choose to highlight the practices in the countries with which you are most familiar. You may also choose to have students research the eating customs of specific countries and compare them.

**ANSWERS to *Nota cultural***
1. Un desayuno típico es ligero, como café con pan o pan dulce. Un almuerzo típico es una comida grande. Una cena típica es una comida ligera.
2. Generalmente, el desayuno es por la mañana, el almuerzo empieza a las dos y la cena es tarde.

**NOTE for *Repaso del complemento directo***
Direct object pronouns are reviewed here and recycled throughout the chapter in anticipation of the presentation of indirect object pronouns in *Capítulo 8*.

**7-6  Las dietas** ¿Piensas mucho en lo que comes? ∎

**Paso 1**   Subraya (*Underline*) los complementos directos en las siguientes preguntas. Compara tus respuestas con las de un/a compañero/a.

**MODELO**   *¿Conoces la dieta Weight Watchers?*

1. ¿Sigues la dieta Nutrisystem?
2. ¿Prefieres los postres de chocolate?
3. ¿Sabes preparar bien el arroz?
4. ¿Comes muchas frutas diferentes?
5. ¿Preparas los huevos con queso?
6. ¿Lavas la lechuga bien antes de comerla?

**Paso 2**   Ahora contesten juntos las preguntas de Paso 1, usando los pronombres de complemento directo en sus respuestas.

**MODELO**   E1:  ¿Conoces la dieta Weight Watchers?

E2:  *Sí, la conozco. / No, no la conozco.*

 **7-7  Las buenas decisiones** Túrnense para expresar cómo les gusta tomar las siguientes comidas y bebidas y con qué frecuencia las toman. ∎

nunca        algunas veces        generalmente        constantemente        siempre

**MODELO**   E1:  *la torta*

E2:  *La como con helado. La como algunas veces. / No la como nunca.*

1.

2.

3.

4.

5.

6.

**EXPANSION for 7-7**
Have students create their own lists of food and drink items, then circulate among their classmates asking how often they eat / drink them.

**3 GRAMÁTICA**

 ¡Hola!

07-18 to 07-22 Spanish/English Tutorials

# El pretérito (Parte I)
Describing things that happened in the past

Up to this point, you have been expressing ideas or actions that take place in the present and future. To talk about something you did or something that occurred in the past, you can use the **pretérito** (*preterit*). Below are the endings for regular verbs in the **pretérito.**

¿Dónde compraste el helado?

Lo compré en Big Scoop.

## Los verbos regulares

Note the endings for regular verbs in the **pretérito** below and answer the questions that follow.

|  | **-ar: comprar** | **-er: comer** | **-ir: vivir** |
|---|---|---|---|
| yo | compré | comí | viví |
| tú | compraste | comiste | viviste |
| Ud. | compró | comió | vivió |
| él/ella | compró | comió | vivió |
| nosotros/as | compramos | comimos | vivimos |
| vosotros/as | comprasteis | comisteis | vivisteis |
| Uds. | compraron | comieron | vivieron |
| ellos/as | compraron | comieron | vivieron |

### ¡Explícalo tú!

1. What do you notice about the endings for **-er** and **-ir** verbs?
2. Where are accent marks needed?

✓ Check your answers to the preceding questions in Appendix 1.

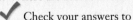

**Estrategia**

Remember that there are two types of grammar presentations in *¡Anda!*:

1. You are given the grammar rule.
2. You are given guiding questions to help *you* construct the grammar rule, and state the rule in your own words.

—¿Dónde está el vino que **compré** ayer?
—Mis primos **bebieron** la botella entera anoche.
—¿Ah, sí? ¿**Comieron** ustedes en casa?
—No, **comimos** en un restaurante chino. ¡Ellos **terminaron** el vino antes de salir a cenar!

*Where is the wine that I bought yesterday?*
*My cousins drank the whole bottle last night.*
*Really? Did you all eat at home?*
*No, we ate at a Chinese restaurant. They finished the wine before we went out to dinner!*

**7-8** **De la teoría a la práctica** Write six different infinitives on six small pieces of paper. Next, on six different small pieces of paper, write six different subject pronouns. Take turns selecting a paper from each pile and give the correct **pretérito** form of the verb. After several rounds, write another six verbs. ■

**7-9** *Tic-tac-toe* Make a grid, like one for tic-tac-toe. With a partner, select one **-ar** verb. Write a different preterit form of the verb in each blank space on your grid. Each of you should write each preterit form with a different pronoun. Do not show your partner what you have written. Take turns randomly selecting pronouns and say the corresponding verb forms. When you say a form of the verb that your partner has, your partner marks an X over the word. The first person to get three X's either vertically, horizontally, or diagonally wins the round. After doing a round with **-ar** verbs, repeat with **-er** and **-ir** verbs. ■

**MODELO**    E1: *tú comiste*
             E2: (marks X over *tu comiste*)

| tú comiste | ellos comieron | ellas comieron |
|---|---|---|
| yo comí | Uds. comieron | nosotros comimos |
| él comió | Ud. comió | ella comió |

  **7-10** **Cocinero/a** Tu compañero/a y tú van a preparar una cena especial para sus amigos. Para saber si todo está listo, túrnense para contestar las siguientes preguntas usando el pretérito y un pronombre de complemento directo (**lo, la, los, las**). ■

**MODELO**    E1: ¿Compraste la carne?
             E2: *Sí, la compré.*

1. ¿Compraste los refrescos?
2. ¿Cocinaste tus platos (*dishes*) favoritos?
3. ¿Preparaste una mesa bonita?
4. ¿Limpiaste el comedor?
5. ¿Mandaste las invitaciones?

  **7-11** **Una comida** Escribe un párrafo sobre una comida que preparaste para un amigo. Usa por lo menos **cinco** verbos en el pretérito. Lee tu párrafo a un/a compañero/a de clase y comparen sus experiencias. ■

07-23 to 07-26   Spanish/ English Tutorials

# El pretérito (Parte II)
Describing things that happened in the past

**Instructor Resources**
• PPT, Extra Activities

**METHODOLOGY • The Preterit**
The authors have chosen to present both regular and irregular preterits in the same chapter to allow for greater focus on form and practice. You will note that this is the primary grammatical focus for *Capítulo 7*. In *Capítulos 8–11*, the preterit will be continually recycled (along with the present tense) for additional practice and reinforcement.

## Los verbos que terminan en *-car*, *-zar* y *-gar* y el verbo *leer*

Several verbs have small spelling changes in the preterit. Look at the following charts.

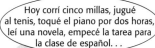

> Hoy corrí cinco millas, jugué al tenis, toqué el piano por dos horas, leí una novela, empecé la tarea para la clase de español. . .

**Fíjate**

The *-ar* and *-er* stem-changing verbs in the present tense do not have stem changes in the preterit. There may be spelling changes, however, as with *empezar* and *jugar*.

**tocar (c → qu)**

| | |
|---|---|
| yo | toqué |
| tú | tocaste |
| Ud. | tocó |
| él/ella | tocó |
| nosotros/as | tocamos |
| vosotros/as | tocasteis |
| Uds. | tocaron |
| ellos/ellas | tocaron |

* (**sacar** and **buscar** have the same spelling change)

**empezar (z → c)**

| | |
|---|---|
| yo | empecé |
| tú | empezaste |
| Ud. | empezó |
| él/ella | empezó |
| nosotros/as | empezamos |
| vosotros/as | empezasteis |
| Uds. | empezaron |
| ellos/ellas | empezaron |

* (**comenzar** and **organizar** have the same spelling change)

**jugar (g → gu)**

| | |
|---|---|
| yo | jugué |
| tú | jugaste |
| Ud. | jugó |
| él/ella | jugó |
| nosotros/as | jugamos |
| vosotros/as | jugasteis |
| Uds. | jugaron |
| ellos/as | jugaron |

* (**llegar** has the same spelling change)

**leer (i → y)**

| | |
|---|---|
| yo | leí |
| tú | leíste |
| Ud. | leyó |
| él/ella | leyó |
| nosotros/as | leímos |
| vosotros/as | leísteis |
| Uds. | leyeron |
| ellos/as | leyeron |

* (**creer** and **oír** have the same spelling change)

—**Toqué** la guitarra con el conjunto de mariachi en un restaurante mexicano anoche.
—¿A qué hora **empezaste**?
—**Empecé** a las nueve.

—¿**Jugaron** tus hermanos al béisbol hoy?
—No, **leyeron** un libro de recetas porque van a preparar una cena especial para nuestros padres.

*I played the guitar with a mariachi band at a Mexican restaurant last night.*
*At what time did you begin?*
*I began at nine.*

*Did your brothers play baseball today?*
*No, they read a recipe book because they are going to prepare a special dinner for our parents.*

*(continued)*

**Some things to remember:**

1. With verbs that end in **-car,** the **c** changes to **qu** in the **yo** form to preserve the sound of the hard **c** of the infinitive.
2. With verbs that end in **-zar,** the **z** changes to **c** before **e**.
3. With verbs that end in **-gar,** the **g** changes to **gu** to preserve the sound of the hard **g** (**g** before **e** or **i** sounds like the **j** sound in Spanish).
4. For **leer, creer,** and **oír,** change the **i** to **y** in the third-person singular and plural.

  **7-12** **¡Apúrate!** One person makes a ball out of a piece of paper, says a subject pronoun and a verb in its infinitive form, and tosses the ball to someone in the group. That person catches it, gives the corresponding form of the verb in the preterit, then says another pronoun and tosses the ball to someone else. ■

MODELO
   E1: *yo; comprar*
   E2: *compré; ellas escribir*
   E3: *escribieron; usted comer*
   E4: *comió;…*

## 7-13 Creaciones

**Paso 1**   Combinen elementos de las tres columnas para escribir **ocho** oraciones que describan lo que hicieron las siguientes personas.

MODELO   Yolanda      comprar      mucho helado
*Yolanda compró mucho helado.*

| | | |
|---|---|---|
| Yolanda | beber | la televisión durante la cena |
| usted | limpiar | cuatro botellas de agua |
| los estudiantes | preparar | mucho helado |
| yo | buscar | dos hamburguesas con queso |
| mi mejor amigo y yo | leer | la cocina después del almuerzo |
| tú | ver | una cena deliciosa |
| mis primos | comprar | el restaurante La Frontera |
| el/la profesor/a | comer | sobre el gran cocinero Emeril Lagasse |

**Paso 2**   Túrnense para preguntarse cuándo ocurrió cada actividad mencionada en **Paso 1**.

   E1: *¿Cuándo compró Yolanda mucho helado?*
   E2: *Compró mucho helado ayer. / Lo compró ayer.*

### Vocabulario útil

| | |
|---|---|
| **anoche** | *last night* |
| **anteayer** | *the day before yesterday* |
| **ayer** | *yesterday* |
| **el año pasado** | *last year* |
| **el fin de semana pasado** | *last weekend* |
| **el martes / viernes / domingo, etc., pasado** | *last Tuesday / Friday / Sunday, etc.* |
| **la semana pasada** | *last week* |

**Fíjate**

In the list of *Vocabulario útil*, note that for the words "last weekend" (*el fin de semana pasado*), the adjective *pasado* agrees with the masculine noun *el fin* and not *semana*. In contrast, for "last week" (*la semana pasada*), the word "last" agrees with the feminine noun *semana*.

Capítulo 3. La casa, pág. 98; Capítulo 3. Los quehaceres de la casa, pág. 109.

 **7-14**  **Los quehaceres de Inés**

**Paso 1**  Escribe una oración sobre cada quehacer que terminó Inés.

**MODELO**  *Inés barrió el suelo.*

1. la ropa
2. la aspiradora
3. el baño
4. los muebles
5. la basura
6. el armario

**Paso 2**  Comparte tus oraciones con un/a compañero/a.

**MODELO**  E1:  el suelo

E2:  *Inés barrió el suelo.*

E1:  *Inés…*

**Paso 3**  Túrnense para decir qué hizo Inés en el centro después de terminar sus quehaceres. Sigan el modelo.

**MODELO**  E1:  el correo

E2:  *Compró sellos.*

1. la librería
2. el cine
3. el banco
4. el cibercafé
5. la biblioteca
6. el café
7. el supermercado
8. la tienda

 **7-15**  **¿Y cuándo…?**  Entrevista a un/a compañero/a para saber cuándo ocurrieron las siguientes cosas. ■

**MODELO**  ¿Cuándo… (tú) comprar la lechuga?

E1:  *¿Cuándo compraste la lechuga?*

E2:  *La compré el sábado pasado.*

**¿Cuándo…?**

1. (tú) tocar el piano  tocaste / toqué
2. (tus amigos) visitar a sus padres  visitaron / visitaron
3. (tú) comprar un CD nuevo  compraste / compré
4. (tus amigos y tú) comer un plato increíble en un restaurante  comieron / comimos
5. (tú) empezar tus estudios universitarios  empezaste / empecé
6. (tu profesor/a) leer una novela de John Grisham  leyó / leyó
7. (tus amigos y tú) bailar el tango  bailaron / bailamos
8. (ustedes) invitar a un amigo a una fiesta  invitaron / invitamos

Capítulo 2. La formación de preguntas, pág. 70; Capítulo 5.
Los pronombres de complemento directo, pág. 189.

`5:00`
Workbooklet

**7-16** **¿Te puedo hacer una pregunta?** Entrevista a cinco estudiantes diferentes y anota sus respuestas (**sí** o **no**). Después, compara tus respuestas con las de los otros estudiantes de la clase. ¿Cuáles son las tendencias? ■

**MODELO**    arreglar el cuarto hoy

TÚ:  *¿Arreglaste tu cuarto hoy?*

E1:  *Sí, lo arreglé.*

E2:  *No, no lo arreglé.*

E3:  *Sí, arreglé mi cuarto.*

E4:  *No, no arreglé mi cuarto.*

E5:  *No, yo no lo arreglé, pero mi compañero lo arregló.*

|  | E1 | E2 | E3 | E4 | E5 |
|---|---|---|---|---|---|
| 1. arreglar el cuarto hoy |  |  |  |  |  |
| 2. comer en un restaurante el sábado pasado |  |  |  |  |  |
| 3. estudiar anoche |  |  |  |  |  |
| 4. lavar los platos ayer |  |  |  |  |  |
| 5. hablar por teléfono con los padres anteayer |  |  |  |  |  |
| 6. jugar al golf el verano pasado |  |  |  |  |  |
| 7. escribir un ensayo para la clase de inglés la semana pasada |  |  |  |  |  |
| 8. terminar la tarea para la clase de español anoche |  |  |  |  |  |

## ¿Cómo andas? I

Having completed **Comunicación I**, I now can . . .

|  | Feel confident | Need to review |
|---|---|---|
| • discuss food (p. 256) | ☐ | ☐ |
| • pronounce the different sounds of **r** and **rr** (MSL/SAM) | ☐ | ☐ |
| • discuss eating habits (p. 261) | ☐ | ☐ |
| • communicate with less repetition using direct object pronouns (p. 261) | ☐ | ☐ |
| • describe things that happened in the past (Part I) (p. 263) | ☐ | ☐ |
| • describe things that happened in the past (Part II) (p. 265) | ☐ | ☐ |

# Comunicación II

**Instructor Resources**
• Textbook images, Extra Activities

**5 VOCABULARIO**

🔊 📖 07-27 to 07-30

## La preparación de las comidas
Explaining food preparation

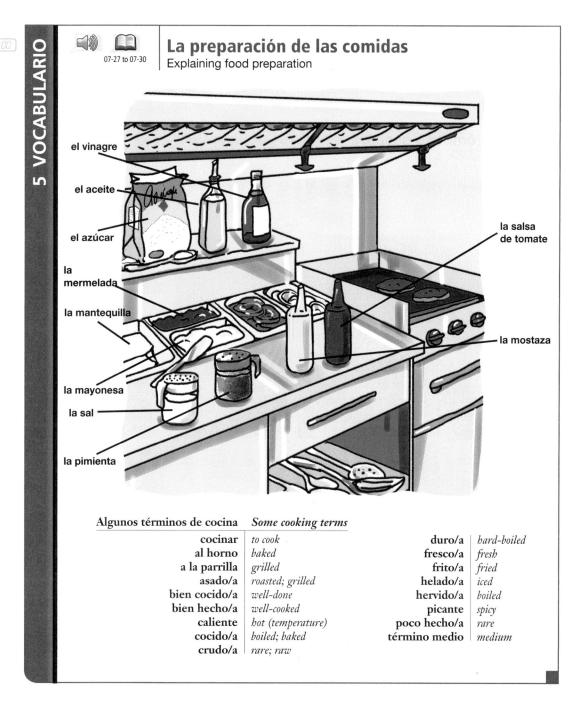

el vinagre
el aceite
el azúcar
la mermelada
la mantequilla
la mayonesa
la sal
la pimienta
la salsa de tomate
la mostaza

| Algunos términos de cocina | Some cooking terms | | |
|---|---|---|---|
| cocinar | to cook | duro/a | hard-boiled |
| al horno | baked | fresco/a | fresh |
| a la parrilla | grilled | frito/a | fried |
| asado/a | roasted; grilled | helado/a | iced |
| bien cocido/a | well-done | hervido/a | boiled |
| bien hecho/a | well-cooked | picante | spicy |
| caliente | hot (temperature) | poco hecho/a | rare |
| cocido/a | boiled; baked | término medio | medium |
| crudo/a | rare; raw | | |

**SECTION GOALS for Comunicación II**
By the end of the *Comunicación II* section, students will be able to:
• describe the various ways in which food is prepared.
• order food the way they would like it cooked.
• tell how the food tastes.
• identify regional cuisine from different parts of Spain, Mexico, the Caribbean, and South America.
• make comparisons between Hispanic foods.
• use irregular verbs correctly in the preterit.
• talk about their daily or weekly activities using the preterit.
• order a meal in a restaurant.
• describe the people and items commonly found in a restaurant.
• tell where things are located in relation to other things by using prepositions.

**21ST CENTURY SKILLS • MODES OF COMMUNICATION**
The Partnership for 21st Century Skills mirrors beautifully the National Foreign Language Standards' 5 Cs. A part of the 5 Cs are the three modes of communication: interpretive, interpersonal, and presentational. A founding principle of *¡Anda!* is to incorporate thoroughly all three modes of communication.

The interpretive mode of communication includes reading and listening. It is deciphering linguistic code. The interpersonal mode of communication is oral communication between two or more individuals. It can also be communicating via writing. Finally, the presentational mode of communication is when an individual makes a presentation to an individual or group, usually orally.

**SUGGESTION for La preparación de las comidas**
Have students brainstorm the different foods they like and dislike prepared in these different manners.

MODELO: al horno
las papas, el pavo, el pollo, etc.
Me gustan las papas al horno...

**7-17  La asociación**  Digan una palabra o expresión que asocian con cada condimento, especia o término de la siguiente lista. ■

**MODELO**      E1:  picante

                E2:  *salsa*

1. frito/a
2. la salsa de tomate
3. crudo/a

4. la mayonesa
5. el azúcar
6. a la parrilla

7. fresco/a
8. al horno

9. la mostaza
10. la mantequilla

 **7-18  ¡Cómo me gustan!**  Digan cómo les gusta preparar las siguientes comidas. ■

**MODELO**  *Me gustan los perros calientes a la parrilla con mostaza y salsa de tomate.*

1.              2.              3.              4.

5.              6.              7.              8.

> ♻ Capítulo 4. Los verbos con cambio de raíz, pág. 142. Capítulo 5. Los pronombres de complemento directo, pág. 189.

  **7-19  ¿Cómo lo prefieres?**  Entrevista a un/a compañero/a para conocer sus preferencias. Después cambien de papel. ■

**MODELO**      E1:  ¿Cómo prefieres tu hamburguesa?

                E2:  *La quiero término medio.*

1. ¿Cómo prefieres tu bistec?
2. ¿Qué condimentos usaste la última vez que comiste el bistec?
3. ¿Cómo pides tu refresco, con o sin hielo?
4. ¿Cómo preparaste los huevos la última vez que los comiste?

5. ¿Cómo prefieres la pizza?
6. ¿Cómo tomaste el té la última vez que lo bebiste, helado o caliente? ¿Lo tomaste con o sin azúcar?
7. ¿Cómo prefieres la sopa, con mucha o poca sal?
8. ¿Cómo tomaste el café esta mañana?

**SUGGESTION for 7-19**
Encourage your students to answer the questions with direct object pronouns.

## La comida hispana
07-31

La comida hispana es muy variada. En España se come mucho pescado y mariscos, pero cada región tiene sus platos típicos. Por ejemplo, en Asturias tienen la fabada (*bean stew*), en Valencia la paella y en Andalucía el gazpacho. La parte central de España es conocida por su carne asada.

La parrillada

La comida mexicana se define por sus técnicas y por los ingredientes propios del país. En México, el maíz y los chiles son ingredientes importantes en la cocina mexicana; también se destacan (*they distinguish themselves*) en la manera de cocinar verduras, carnes, mariscos, huevos, salsas, sopas y aves. Desde Baja California hasta la península de Yucatán, se encuentran platos típicos mexicanos de cada región.

Las islas del Caribe tienen en común la herencia de las culturas española, indígena y africana. Las comidas de estos países llevan una gran variedad de condimentos (*seasonings*) como la bija (*annatto*) o el achiote, el orégano, la cebolla, el ajo, el cilantro y muchos más. El arroz es indispensable en la dieta caribeña: también los plátanos, los mariscos y los frijoles (o habichuelas). El arroz es muy importante también en la dieta centroamericana, igual que el maíz, los frijoles, las tortillas, las enchiladas, las verduras, el pollo, los tamales y las frutas.

En los países de Sudamérica comen mucho arroz, frijoles, pollo, carne, frutas y mariscos. En Chile, Argentina, Paraguay y Uruguay las parrilladas o los asados (*mixed grills*) son muy populares. Las empanadas o empanadillas (un *turnover* de carne de res, legumbres, queso, mariscos o pollo) son famosas en toda la América Latina, desde Cuba hasta Argentina.

### Preguntas

1. ¿Cuáles de los platos típicos (o ingredientes) mencionados te gustan?
2. ¿Cómo se compara la comida del Caribe con la comida de otras partes del mundo hispanohablante?

**ANSWERS to *Nota cultural***

1. *Answers may vary.*
2. *Possible answer:* La comida del Caribe tiene / lleva muchos condimentos y el arroz, el plátano, los mariscos y los frijoles son importantes. El arroz y los frijoles también son importantes en los países centroamericanos y en México. La comida de Sudamérica tiene mucha carne.

## CAPÍTULO 7

**NATIONAL STANDARDS**
*Cultures, Comparisons*
The reading, *La comida hispana*, provides cultural information about various Spanish-speaking regions throughout the world. Students learn about the main dishes, the ingredients, and the seasonings commonly used in Hispanic cooking. This information explains how the geographic location affects the diet and food choices, determining which ingredients and products are readily available. Students see how geography and climate affect the practices, the products, and the perspectives of Hispanic cultures (Standards 2.1, 2.2). There is great variety in the Hispanic diet, and the reading offers a brief outline of how food differs across the regions of Spain, Mexico, the Caribbean, and South America. Students can compare how *la comida hispana* differs from their own diet, and they can also compare how it varies across Spanish-speaking countries (Standard 4.2).

**NOTE for *La comida hispana***
The authors understand that this chapter deals with the preterit tense and ideally the *Nota cultural* reading would incorporate that form. The nature of cultural notes, however, generally dictate that they be written in the present tense. For readings that contextualize both the grammar and the vocabulary of the chapter, be sure to assign and discuss the *Ambiciones siniestras* episodes.

**NOTE for *Nota cultural***
You may choose to supplement your discussion with information about Hispanic foods in the U.S., perhaps contrasting "tex-mex" food with authentic Mexican food, and African influences on Hispanic food (*Afromestizo* cooking).

**EXPANSION for *La comida hispana***
Additional questions to ask your students are:

1. ¿*Dónde preparan muchos platos con arroz?*
2. ¿*Cuál es una de las especialidades de España? ¿Cuáles son algunos de los ingredientes de los platos típicos de México?*
3. ¿*Por qué crees que comen tanta* (so much) *carne de res en Uruguay y Argentina?*
4. ¿*Cuáles son algunos platos típicos de la región donde vives? ¿Y en la región dónde vive tu familia?*

**METHODOLOGY • The Preterit**
The authors have chosen to present these irregular verbs together with regular verbs for more varied and richer practice. You may choose to divide the verbs into two or three groups and have students practice the forms with mechanical activities like **7-8.** For students who need additional practice, refer them to MySpanishLab, the Electronic Activities Cache, or the Student Activities Manual.

**SUGGESTION for *Algunos verbos irregulares en el pretérito***
If you think now is an appropriate time, point out to your students that the verbs *querer* and *saber* change meaning in the preterit. For example, in the preterit, *querer* usually means "tried to," *no querer* means "refused," and *saber* means "found out."

**6 GRAMÁTICA**

 ¡Hola! Spanish/English Tutorials
07-32 to 07-37

## Algunos verbos irregulares en el pretérito
Describing things that happened in the past

Ayer anduvimos diez millas.

In **Comunicación I** you learned about verbs that are regular in the **pretérito** and others that have spelling changes. The following verbs are *irregular* in the **pretérito**; they follow patterns of their own. Study the verb charts to determine the similarities and differences among the forms.

|  | andar (*to walk*) | estar | tener |
|---|---|---|---|
| yo | anduve | estuve | tuve |
| tú | anduviste | estuviste | tuviste |
| Ud. | anduvo | estuvo | tuvo |
| él/ella | anduvo | estuvo | tuvo |
| nosotros/as | anduvimos | estuvimos | tuvimos |
| vosotros/as | anduvisteis | estuvisteis | tuvisteis |
| Uds. | anduvieron | estuvieron | tuvieron |
| ellos/ellas | anduvieron | estuvieron | tuvieron |

—El lunes pasado llegamos a Santiago y **anduvimos** mucho por la ciudad.

—¿**Estuvieron** en un restaurante o bar interesante?

—Sí, **tuvimos** mucha suerte y comimos en el mejor restaurante de la ciudad.

*Last Monday we arrived in Santiago and walked a lot throughout the city.*

*Were you all in an interesting restaurant or bar?*

*Yes, we were very lucky and we ate at the best restaurant in the city.*

|  | conducir (*to drive*) | traer | decir |
|---|---|---|---|
| yo | conduje | traje | dije |
| tú | condujiste | trajiste | dijiste |
| Ud. | condujo | trajo | dijo |
| él/ella | condujo | trajo | dijo |
| nosotros/as | condujimos | trajimos | dijimos |
| vosotros/as | condujisteis | trajisteis | dijisteis |
| Uds. | condujeron | trajeron | dijeron |
| ellos/as | condujeron | trajeron | dijeron |

**Fíjate**
Note that the third-person plural ending of *conducir, decir,* and *traer* is *-eron.*

—¿**Condujiste** de Santiago a Valparaíso?

—No pude conducir porque no **traje** mi licencia.

—¿Qué te **dijeron** en la agencia Avis?

*Did you drive from Santiago to Valparaíso?*

*I couldn't drive because I didn't bring my driver's license.*

*What did they tell you at the Avis (car rental) agency?*

**SUGGESTION for** *Algunos verbos irregulares*
You may want to relate the following "experience" or create one of your own, using the irregular verbs presented. You can then have students make lists of the verb forms they hear, answer comprehension questions, or create an "experience" of their own with the verbs.

*Ayer fue un día muy interesante. Por la mañana conduje al campo donde anduve cinco millas. Vi muchos animales y pude tomar muchas fotos. Mis amigos vinieron conmigo y trajeron un picnic fabuloso. Prepararon unos sándwiches de jamón y queso, ensalada de fruta y limonada. El almuerzo fue delicioso. Después de almorzar dormimos la siesta. ¡Luego anduvimos otras cinco millas!*

|        | ir      | ser      |
|--------|---------|----------|
| yo     | fui     | fui      |
| tú     | fuiste  | fuiste   |
| Ud.    | fue     | fue      |
| él/ella| fue     | fue      |
| nosotros/as | fuimos | fuimos |
| vosotros/as | fuisteis | fuisteis |
| Uds.   | fueron  | fueron   |
| ellos/as | fueron | fueron  |

**Fíjate**
Note that *ser* and *ir* have the same forms in the preterit. You must rely on the context of the sentence or conversation to determine the meaning.

—¿Cómo **fue** el viaje a Chile?
—¡**Fue** increíble! Después de Valparaiso **fuimos** a Patagonia.

*How was the trip to Chile?*
*It was incredible! After Valparaiso, we went to Patagonia.*

|        | dar     | ver     | venir     |
|--------|---------|---------|-----------|
| yo     | di      | vi      | vine      |
| tú     | diste   | viste   | viniste   |
| Ud.    | dio     | vio     | vino      |
| él/ella| dio     | vio     | vino      |
| nosotros/as | dimos | vimos | vinimos |
| vosotros/as | disteis | visteis | vinisteis |
| Uds.   | dieron  | vieron  | vinieron  |
| ellos/as | dieron | vieron | vinieron |

|        | hacer     | querer     |
|--------|-----------|------------|
| yo     | hice      | quise      |
| tú     | hiciste   | quisiste   |
| Ud.    | hizo      | quiso      |
| él/ella| hizo      | quiso      |
| nosotros/as | hicimos | quisimos |
| vosotros/as | hicisteis | quisisteis |
| Uds.   | hicieron  | quisieron  |
| ellos/as | hicieron | quisieron |

**Fíjate**
The third-person singular form of *hacer* has a spelling change (*c* to *z*): *hizo.*

|        | poder     | poner     | saber     |
|--------|-----------|-----------|-----------|
| yo     | pude      | puse      | supe      |
| tú     | pudiste   | pusiste   | supiste   |
| Ud.    | pudo      | puso      | supo      |
| él/ella| pudo      | puso      | supo      |
| nosotros/as | pudimos | pusimos | supimos |
| vosotros/as | pudisteis | pusisteis | supisteis |
| Uds.   | pudieron  | pusieron  | supieron  |
| ellos/as | pudieron | pusieron | supieron |

— En Santiago **vimos** a mucha gente de la familia de Carlos.
— Sí, ¿y les **diste** los regalos que tu familia mandó?
— Mi madre **vino** con nosotros y ella misma **pudo** darles los regalos.
—¿Qué **hiciste** después de visitar a la familia de Carlos?

*In Santiago we saw a lot of people in Carlos's family.*
*Yes, and did you give them the gifts your family sent?*
*My mother came with us and she was able to give them the gifts herself.*
*What did you do after visiting Carlos's family?*

(continued)

## Verbos con cambio de raíz

The next group of verbs also follows its own pattern. In these stem-changing verbs, the first letters next to the infinitives, listed in parentheses, represent the present-tense spelling changes; the last letter indicates the spelling change in the **él/ella** and **ellos/ellas** forms of the **pretérito**.

| | dormir<br>(o → ue → u) | pedir<br>(e → i → i) | preferir<br>(e → ie → i) |
|---|---|---|---|
| yo | dormí | pedí | preferí |
| tú | dormiste | pediste | preferiste |
| Ud. | durmió | pidió | prefirió |
| él/ella | durmió | pidió | prefirió |
| nosotros/as | dormimos | pedimos | preferimos |
| vosotros/as | dormisteis | pedisteis | preferisteis |
| Uds. | durmieron | pidieron | prefirieron |
| ellos/as | durmieron | pidieron | prefirieron |

> **Fíjate**
> The *-ir* stem-changing verbs are irregular in the third-person singular and plural forms only.

—Cuando fuiste al restaurante en Valparaíso, ¿qué **pediste**?

— **Pedí** carne de res, pero mi madre **prefirió** pescado. Y después de comer mi madre **durmió** la siesta.

*What did you order when you went to the restaurant in Valparaíso?*

*I ordered beef, but my mother preferred fish. And after eating, my mother took a nap.*

---

**7-20** **Más práctica** Repite el juego de verbos de la actividad **7-8**, esta vez usando los verbos irregulares. ■

**7-21** **¿Qué dijo?** Form groups of at least six students and sit in a circle. **Estudiante 1** starts by saying his/her name and something that he/she did yesterday, last week, or last year. **Estudiante 2** gives his/her name, says something he/she did, and then tells what the preceding person (**Estudiante 1**) did. **Estudiante 3** tells his/her name, says what he/she did, and then tells what **Estudiante 2** and **Estudiante 1** did (in that order). Follow the model. ■

MODELO    E1: *Soy Fran y ayer fui a un restaurante mexicano.*

         E2: *Soy Tom y ayer jugué al tenis. Fran fue a un restaurante mexicano.*

         E3: *Soy Chris y ayer tuve que preparar la cena. Tom jugó al tenis y Fran fue a un restaurante mexicano.*

**NOTE for 7-21**
You may wish to offer students some options for stating that they do not remember. For example, they can turn to the appropriate student and ask ¿Qué dijiste? or Repite, por favor. Another possibility is to tell students that it is okay to prompt each other when a member of the circle forgets. You can also move to the next student, thus eliminating group members until one or two students are left.

**NOTE for 7-21**
You may wish to make this a writing activity: The first person writes a sentence, passes it to the next, who adds a sentence, and so on. This could be a competition to see which group has the most correct sentences after a 4- or 5-minute period.

**NOTE for 7-21**
Activity **7-21** encourages active listening. Discourage students from taking notes but rather have them prompt each other when help is needed.

**NOTE for 7-21**
As you monitor this activity, pay special attention to student pronunciation, making note of the most serious, or most common, errors. At the end of the activity, go over the mistakes with your students, modeling the correct pronunciation. In this way, this activity may also serve as focused pronunciation practice.

8-00  **7-22 El mercado** El año pasado, Amanda fue estudiante de intercambio y vivió con una familia en Asunción. Completa el siguiente párrafo sobre su primera visita al mercado y después compártelo con un/a compañero/a. ■

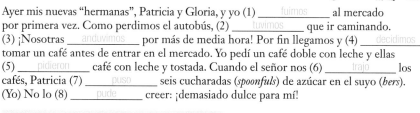

| andar | traer | decidir | ir |
|-------|-------|---------|-----|
| pedir | poder | poner | tener |

Ayer mis nuevas "hermanas", Patricia y Gloria, y yo (1) ____fuimos____ al mercado por primera vez. Como perdimos el autobús, (2) ____tuvimos____ que ir caminando. (3) ¡Nosotras ____anduvimos____ por más de media hora! Por fin llegamos y (4) ____decidimos____ tomar un café antes de entrar en el mercado. Yo pedí un café doble con leche y ellas (5) ____pidieron____ café con leche y tostada. Cuando el señor nos (6) ____trajo____ los cafés, Patricia (7) ____puso____ seis cucharadas (*spoonfuls*) de azúcar en el suyo (*hers*). (Yo) No lo (8) ____pude____ creer: ¡demasiado dulce para mí!

| comprar | decir | estar | poner |
|---------|-------|-------|--------|
| ser | tomar | ver | volver |

Al entrar en el mercado, yo (9) ____vi____ un montón (*a pile*) de verduras y frutas de muchos colores brillantes. (10) ____Fue____ impresionante. Después yo les (11) ____tomé____ varias fotos a las chicas. Primero compramos una lechuga, dos cebollas, ajo, medio kilo de zanahorias y un pimiento verde. Hablamos unos cinco minutos con la vendedora sobre su sobrina. Ella (12) ____estuvo____ seis meses en los Estados Unidos como estudiante de intercambio. Después miramos las frutas y por fin escogimos dos melones y medio kilo de peras. Las chicas (13) ____pusieron____ las verduras en el bolso grande y la fruta en el bolso más pequeño. Entonces pasamos a la parte del pescado donde nosotras (14) ____compramos____ atún. La señora lo envolvió (*wrapped*) en papel antes de ponerlo en una bolsa de plástico. Hicimos las compras en menos de media hora. A las nueve y cuarto les (15) ____dijimos____ adiós a todos y (16) ____volvimos____ a casa… esta vez en autobús.

8-00  **7-23 ¿Hay rutina en tu semana?** ¿Cuántas veces hiciste cada una de estas cosas la semana pasada? ■

**Paso 1** Di las respuestas a las siguientes preguntas, según el modelo.

**MODELO** ver una película en la televisión

E1: La semana pasada, ¿cuántas veces viste una película en la televisión?

E2: *Vi una película en la televisión una vez* (*dos veces, tres veces, etc.*).

**La semana pasada, ¿cuántas veces… ?**

1. hacer la tarea
2. dar la respuesta correcta en clase
3. venir a la clase de español
4. conducir a la universidad
5. dormir ocho horas
6. andar por el centro
7. ir al cine
8. jugar un deporte
9. ver un partido en la televisión
10. comer comida rápida

**Fíjate**

Amanda refers to a *medio kilo de zanahorias*. Remember that in most parts of the world the metric system is the preferred system of measurement.

**Estrategia**

Remember that *una vez* means *once* and *veces* means *times*: *Yo fui al restaurante una vez pero tú fuiste tres veces.* = I went to the restaurant once but you went three times.

**NOTE for 7-22**
You may prefer to have students complete this activity for homework. Then in class, you can review the answers and even use the activity as a reading comprehension activity, asking the following questions:
¿Cómo fueron las chicas al mercado?
¿Qué hicieron antes de entrar al mercado?
¿Cómo prefiere el café Patricia?
¿Qué compraron?
¿Cuánto tiempo tardaron en hacer las compras?
¿Cómo volvieron a casa?

**EXPANSION for 7-22**
Have students prepare a dialogue to perform based on the market scene in **7-22**.

**ANSWERS to 7-23 (PASO 1)**
1. hiciste / Hice
2. diste / Di
3. viniste / Vine
4. condujiste / Conduje
5. dormiste / Dormí
6. anduviste / Anduve
7. fuiste / Fui
8. jugaste / Jugué
9. viste / Vi
10. comiste / Comí

**Paso 2**   Pídele a tu compañero/a que adivine (*guess*) cuántas veces hiciste las actividades del **Paso 1.** Sigue el modelo.

**MODELO**   E1:   *La semana pasada, ¿cuántas veces piensas que (yo) hice la tarea?*

E2:   *Pienso que la hiciste tres veces.*

E1:   *Sí, tienes razón. ¡La hice tres veces!*

E1:   *¿Cuántas veces piensas que fui al cine?*

E2:   *Pienso que no fuiste.*

E1:   *No, no tienes razón. Fui una vez.*

Capítulo 2. Los deportes y los pasatiempos, pág. 81.

[5:00]  **7-24** **¿Adónde fui?** Hazle a tu compañero/a las siguientes preguntas para averiguar adónde fue de vacaciones. Después, cambien de papel. (**¡OJO!** *Before asking the last question, try to guess where he or she went.*) ■

**MODELO**   E1:   *¿Fuiste en verano?*

E2:   *No, fui en otoño. / Sí, fui en verano.*

1.  ¿Fuiste a la playa? Fui
2.  ¿Visitaste un museo? Visité
3.  ¿Viste un partido de béisbol? Vi
4.  ¿Montaste en bicicleta? Monté
5.  ¿Qué compraste? Compré
6.  ¿Comiste mariscos? Comí
7.  ¿Tomaste el sol? Tomé
8.  ¿Jugaste al golf? Jugué
9.  ¿Nadaste? Nadé
10.  ¿Dormiste en un hotel? Dormí
11.  ¿Jugaste al tenis? Jugué
12.  ¿Fuiste a un parque? Fui
13.  ¿Qué más hiciste? *Answers may vary.*
14.  ¿Adónde fuiste? Fui

[8:00]  Workbooklet  **7-25** **Chismes (*Gossip*)** Imagina que eres el/la editor/a de la columna de chismes de un periódico. Escribe en el cuadro tus respuestas a las siguientes preguntas. Después, entrevista a tres compañeros/as y anota sus respuestas. ¿Están de acuerdo? ■

1.  ¿Qué película tuvo mucho éxito el año pasado?
2.  ¿Qué actor salió en una película que **no** tuvo éxito?
3.  ¿Qué miembro del gobierno (*member of the government*) dijo algo tonto?
4.  ¿Quién hizo un CD recientemente?
5.  ¿Cuál de tus amigos estuvo en la playa recientemente?
6.  ¿Quién vino tarde a la clase una vez?
7.  ¿Quién no trajo sus libros a clase?
8.  ¿Quién les dio un examen muy difícil la semana pasada?

**NOTE for 7-24**

Activity **7-24** is based on the game "Twenty Questions." The goal of the game is to arrive at the answer by asking only *yes* or *no* questions and getting the answer before your 20 questions run out. Remind students that they need to phrase questions that can be answered just by *sí* or *no,* and they will want to keep track of their questions so they do not repeat. It might be a good idea to have them write out their questions as homework, in case they need all of the questions to find out what their classmates did last summer.

Instructor Resources
• Textbook images, Extra Activities

| YO | ESTUDIANTE 1 | ESTUDIANTE 2 | ESTUDIANTE 3 |
|----|--------------|--------------|--------------|
| 1. | | | |
| 2. | | | |
| 3. | | | |
| 4. | | | |
| 5. | | | |
| 6. | | | |
| 7. | | | |
| 8. | | | |

## 7 VOCABULARIO

07-38 to 07-42

# En el restaurante Explaining restaurant activity

el vaso

la cocinera
(el cocinero)

el camarero
(la camarera)

EL COCO LOCO

el menú

la taza

el mantel

el cuchillo

el plato      el tenedor      la servilleta   la cucharita   la cuchara

*(continued)*

**SUGGESTION for *En el restaurante***
You might want to add the word *cash* to your payment options. You can say *dinero en efectivo* for those students who pay for their meals in cash. You might also add the word *un descuento* for the university establishments that offer a discount to students with photo identification.

**SUGGESTION for *En el restaurante***
You may want to ask your students the following questions:
*¿Cuáles restaurantes en esta ciudad son caros?*
*¿Cuáles restaurantes tienen comida barata?*
*¿Cuánto dinero das de propina cuando comes en un restaurante?*
*¿Cuáles restaurantes tienen un menú grande?*
*¿Tienen especialidades de la casa en tus restaurantes favoritos?*
*¿Qué te dice el camarero cuando te sirve la comida?*
*¿Qué le dices al camarero cuando terminas la comida y quieres salir?*

| Otras palabras y expresiones útiles | Other words and useful expressions | Algunos verbos | Some verbs |
|---|---|---|---|
| barato/a | *cheap* | pagar | *to pay* |
| ¡Buen provecho! | *Enjoy your meal!* | pedir | *to order* |
| caro/a | *expensive* | reservar una mesa | *to reserve a table* |
| el/la cliente/a | *customer; client* | | |
| la especialidad de la casa | *specialty of the house* | | |
| La cuenta, por favor. | *The check, please.* | | |
| la propina | *tip* | | |
| la tarjeta de crédito | *credit card* | | |
| la tarjeta de débito | *debit card* | | |

NOTE for 7-26
This activity can also be done as a class. Have one student be the scribe for each list, with classmates supplying the items.

**[4:00]**  Workbooklet  **7-26** **La organización es clave** Juntos escriban las siguientes categorías: **cosas en la mesa, pedir y pagar** y **personas en el restaurante**. Después, organicen el vocabulario de **En el restaurante** bajo esas categorías. ■

| MODELO | COSAS EN LA MESA | PEDIR Y PAGAR | PERSONAS EN EL RESTAURANTE |
|---|---|---|---|
| | el cuchillo | la propina | el camarero |

**[2:00]**  **7-27** **¿Cómo se dice?** Túrnense para decir qué palabra o frase corresponde a las siguientes descripciones. ■

MODELO   E1:  el "Gran Especial"
         E2:  *la especialidad de la casa*

1. persona que sirve la comida  el/la camarero/a
2. dinero que das por buen servicio  la propina
3. lista de comidas y bebidas  el menú
4. es necesario para limpiar las manos  la servilleta
5. persona que prepara la comida en un restaurante  el/la cocinero/a
6. es necesario para comer *Frosted Flakes*  una cuchara/cucharita, la leche
7. es necesario para beber café  una taza
8. persona que come en el restaurante  el/la cliente/a

**Estrategia**

As you acquire more Spanish in each chapter, try to write definitions in Spanish of your new vocabulary words as in the model. Learning new vocabulary will become easier the more you practice. Also, it will help you use your new vocabulary in sentences.

Capítulo 2. El verbo *estar*, pág. 76;
Capítulo 3. *Hay*, pág. 119.

**7-28** **Una mesa bien puesta** Dibuja la mesa de tu familia o de la familia de un/a buen/a amigo/a para una cena especial con todo bien puesto (*well set*). Ahora, sin mostrar tu dibujo, descríbeselo a un/a compañero/a mientras él/ella lo dibuja. ¿Lo dibujó bien? Luego cambien de papeles. ∎

| Vocabulario útil | |
|---|---|
| **al lado (de)** | *beside; next to* |
| **a la izquierda (de)** | *to the left (of)* |
| **a la derecha (de)** | *to the right (of)* |
| **cerca (de)** | *near* |
| **debajo (de)** | *under; underneath* |
| **encima (de)** | *on top of; above* |

**7-29** **¿Qué pasó?** Miren el dibujo en la página 277 y digan por lo menos **cinco** oraciones acerca de lo que pasó anoche en el restaurante El Coco Loco. ∎

**NOTE for 7-28**
Activity **7-28** also encourages active listening, as students must pay careful attention to replicate their partners' drawings.

**EXPANSION for 7-28**
Have students bring in photos of well-set tables to describe in pairs or small groups. Also, in pairs, one student can describe his/her photo while the other student sketches what he/she hears, then switch roles. This works well as a listening comprehension activity.

## NOTE and INSTRUCTIONS
### for 7-31

This activity takes a bit of planning, but is well worth the effort. Half the class will be vendors, while the other half will be shoppers. There should be 2 meat and poultry vendors, 2 fruit and vegetable vendors, 2 bakery vendors, and 2 vendors of housewares. You may add other vendors, depending on the size of your class. The pairs of vendors sell the same types of goods but with some different varieties and/or slightly different prices. The shoppers should be given a context; for example, they may be shopping for a party or a holiday meal.

Ideally, the shops can be positioned in front of chalkboards so that the vendors can draw signs and advertisements. You can also provide them with pictures of products that are typical for their shops. The shopping lists should have drawings to represent what can be purchased, with the amounts written to the side. Shoppers may add to the lists, or simply create their own based on the type of meals or parties they choose to prepare. Encourage bargaining.

With regard to recycling prior concepts that the students have already learned, they should review and practice greetings, numbers, and interrogatives, as well as food vocabulary.

- Sample of partial list for shopper:

| | |
|---|---|
| 14 huevos | 1 mantel |
| 3 pollos | 12 tenedores |
| 2 jamones | 6 cucharas |
| 1 kilo de papas | 6 tenedores |
| 1 lechuga | servilletas de papel |
| 3 tomates | pan para 12 personas |
| 1 kilo de uvas | pasteles para 12 personas |

- Sample of partial list for vendors (in kilos except where indicated):

| | |
|---|---|
| huevos | $ ,50 each |
| pollo | $2,00 |
| jamón | $12,00 |
| bistec | $6,50 |
| lechuga | $ ,40 |
| tomates | $ ,30 |
| uvas | $ ,40 |
| pan | $ ,20 per loaf |

Attempt to make the prices as realistic as possible. Also, to keep with the country / regional theme of this chapter, you may want the prices to reflect the Chilean peso or the Paraguayan guaraní. Consult the Internet for current conversion rates.

[7:00] **7-30** ¿Me puede servir...? Vas con dos amigos/as al restaurante más popular de Asunción para cenar. ■

**Paso 1** Miren el menú y determinen qué van a pedir sabiendo que tienen 60.000 guaraníes para pagar.

**EL RESTAURANTE BUEN PROVECHO**

| SÁNDWICHES CALIENTES | |
|---|---|
| Sándwich de queso | 36.000 |
| Sándwich de pollo, jamón y queso | 48.000 |
| Sándwich de jamón | 38.000 |

| SÁNDWICHES FRÍOS | |
|---|---|
| Sándwich de pollo, tomate y lechuga | 43.000 |
| Sándwich de ensalada de pollo | 45.000 |
| Sándwich de jamón y queso | 46.000 |

| HELADOS Y POSTRES | |
|---|---|
| Tres Marías | 14.500 |
| Helado de chocolate | 12.000 |
| Helado especial | 12.000 |
| Flan de la casa | 14.500 |

| BEBIDAS Y REFRESCOS | |
|---|---|
| Café | 5.500 |
| Vaso de leche | 6.600 |
| Chocolate en taza | 7.200 |
| Té caliente | 5.500 |
| Té frío | 5.500 |
| Refrescos fríos | 7.000 |
| Cervezas | 12.500 |
| Copa de vino | 14.000 |

| SOPAS Y CREMAS | |
|---|---|
| Sopa de cebolla gratinada | 15.500 PYG |
| | 32.000 |
| Sopa de pescado | 27.000 |
| Sopa de pollo y verduras | 17.000 |
| Consomé de pollo | |

| ENSALADAS | |
|---|---|
| Mixta de verduras | 19.500 |
| Ensalada de jamón, pollo o atún | 45.000 |
| Ensalada de frutas | 35.000 |

**Paso 2** Ahora, utilizando esa información, realicen (*act out*) una escena en un restaurante para la clase. Una persona debe ser el/la camarero/a y las otras personas deben ser los clientes.

Capítulo 2. Presente indicativo de verbos regulares, pág. 67.

[10:00] **7-31** **De compras en el mercado** Algunos estudiantes van a hacer el papel de vendedores y otros de clientes. Tu profesor/a te va a dar una lista de los productos que tienes para vender o de los que necesitas comprar. Los vendedores deben ganar cincuenta mil guaraníes y los clientes sólo pueden gastar cincuenta mil guaraníes. Va a haber competencia entre los vendedores y sí, ¡puedes regatear (*bargain; negotiate the price*)! ■

## NATIONAL STANDARDS
*Communication, Cultures, Communities*

Ordering from the menu in **7-30** gives your learners the opportunity to use language in a real context and to experience the Spanish language from a part of the Spanish-speaking world that is apart from the usual. If your community has restaurants with cuisine from the Spanish-speaking world, encourage your students to use their Spanish when ordering from the menu.

## EXPANSION for 7-31

This activity can also center on a restaurant experience with some students acting as patrons and others as owners or servers. The patrons could have a certain amount to spend and the owners or servers must try to convince the patrons to order specific items (or to mount the largest bill possible). Students could create sample menus for homework or work together in groups in class.

## ESCUCHA

### 📖 Las compras en el mercado
07-43

| Estrategia | |
|---|---|
| **Combining strategies** | To begin the new term it is useful to review and combine all the listening strategies you have practiced thus far. Remember to use all clues available to you to anticipate what you are about to hear, including photos, captions, and pre-listening synopses or questions. If you are |

performing a listening activity like the one to follow, also look ahead at the comprehension questions. Once you have an idea of the context, consider what you already know about it. Taking time to think about and practice these specific strategies will enhance your ability to listen effectively.

### 7-32 Antes de escuchar Contesta las siguientes preguntas. ■

1. Mira la foto. ¿Dónde está la mujer? ¿Qué hace?
2. ¿Haces las compras (*Do you shop*) en un mercado como este, donde hay muchos vendedores en un solo lugar, o en un supermercado?
3. ¿Qué tipo de vocabulario necesitas saber para poder hacer las compras en un mercado?

### 🔊 7-33 A escuchar Escucha la conversación entre la madre de Alejandra y un vendedor para averiguar el propósito (*purpose*) de la conversación. Después, escucha una vez más para contestar las siguientes preguntas. ■

1. ¿Qué compra? Marca (✓) delante de los ingredientes o condimentos que ella compra.

| | | | |
|---|---|---|---|
| ✓ | mantequilla | | vinagre |
| | azúcar | ✓ | huevos |
| ✓ | queso | | pan |
| | mayonesa | ✓ | leche |

2. Determina si las siguientes oraciones son ciertas (**C**) o falsas (**F**).
   a. La madre necesita ingredientes para preparar un plato nuevo. C
   b. El Sr. Gómez tiene huevos blancos y marrones. F
   c. La madre compra seis huevos. C
   d. El Sr. Gómez también vende verduras. F
   e. El Sr. Gómez tiene todo lo que la madre necesita comprar. F

### 👥 7-34 Después de escuchar Realiza (*Act out*) con un/a compañero/a la escena entre la madre y el Sr. Gómez. ■

---

**NATIONAL STANDARDS**
*Communication*

The conversation in the *Escucha* section requires that students combine previously learned listening strategies such as using clues, anticipating content, previewing comprehension questions, using prior knowledge about the content, and practicing focused listening. The dialogue provides spoken Spanish, and students then understand and interpret the conversation between Alejandra's mother and the vendor (Standard 1.2). The pre-listening and post-listening activities also encourage interpersonal communication if students work in pairs or small groups (Standard 1.1). When students reenact the scene between the mother and Sr. Gómez and present the scene to the class, they use Standard 1.3, the presentational mode of communication.

**SUGGESTION for 7-34**
You may want to extend this activity by bringing in props and setting the classroom up like a market. You can assign students different roles as vendors and customers, provide shopping lists and fake money, etc.

**SECTION GOALS for *Escucha***
By the end of the *Escucha* section, students will be able to:
- combine the listening strategies they have been using in *Capítulos 1–5*.
- answer pre-listening questions in Spanish.
- predict what they are going to hear.
- determine the purpose of the conversation.
- decide whether certain statements about the conversation are true or false.
- recreate the conversation by acting out the roles.

**ANSWERS to 7-32**
1. Está en el mercado. Hace las compras.
2. *Answers may vary.*
3. *Answer may include:* necesito vocabulario para la comida, los números, saludos y despedidas, etc.

**AUDIOSCRIPT for 7-33**

| | |
|---|---|
| VENDEDOR: | Muy buenos días, señora. ¿Cómo le puedo servir hoy? |
| MADRE: | Hola, Sr. Gómez. Tengo una lista bastante larga, pero de usted sólo necesito unas cuantas cosas. |
| VENDEDOR: | Dígame. Vamos a ver. |
| MADRE: | Pues, necesito leche, mantequilla, una docena de huevos grandes —me gustan los blancos— y queso fresco. |
| VENDEDOR: | Muy bien. ¿Necesita un galón de leche? |
| MADRE: | Sí, por favor. |
| VENDEDOR: | Perdone, pero no tengo huevos blancos hoy. Sólo tengo los marrones. ¿Está bien? |
| MADRE: | Bueno, entonces sólo quiero seis. ¿Mañana va a tener los blancos? |
| VENDEDOR: | Sí, por supuesto. Aquí tiene los huevos. Y el queso, ¿cuánto necesita? (*pause as if reaching for the cheese and indicating an amount*) ¿Así está bien? |
| MADRE: | Sí. Sólo quiero un poco. Lo necesito para un plato nuevo que quiero preparar de verduras al horno con una salsa de queso. |
| VENDEDOR: | Excelente. |
| MADRE: | ¿Cuánto es? |
| VENDEDOR: | A ver —la leche, dos setenta y cinco; la mantequilla, uno cincuenta; seis huevos, 70 centavos; y el queso, uno noventa y cinco… (*pause*) son seis dólares noventa centavos. |
| MADRE: | Aquí lo tiene. Ahora necesito comprar las verduras. |
| VENDEDOR: | Muy bien. Gracias, señora. ¡Qué le vaya bien! |
| MADRE: | Adiós. Hasta mañana. |

# ¡CONVERSEMOS!

07-44

 **7-35** **De compras** Descríbele a un compañero/a lo que compraste la última vez que fuiste al supermercado. Di por lo menos **diez** oraciones e incluye detalles como los siguientes: ▪

- Lo que (no) tuviste que comprar (*tener que + infinitivo*)
- Los precios de la comida y de las bebidas
- Quien preparó la comida y cómo la preparó

Tu compañero/a va a comparar lo que él/ella compró con tus compras.

 **7-36** **¡Qué fiesta!** Colin Cowie, un famoso organizador de fiestas para las grandes estrellas de Hollywood, te contrató para ayudarle a planear una fiesta para tu músico o actor favorito. Descríbele a un/a compañero/a (Colin Cowie) en por lo menos **diez** oraciones todo lo que tuviste que hacer. Incluye la comida que compraste, lo que preparaste para comer, cómo pusiste la mesa, quiénes vinieron a la fiesta, etc. Tu compañero/a (Colin Cowie) va a decirte si le gustó lo que hiciste. ▪

**ESCRIBE**

07-45 to 07-46

## Una descripción

| Estrategia | In writing for any audience, it is important to both capture the interest of the reader with a strong topic sentence, preparing him/her | for what he/she is about to read, and end with a strong conclusion, restating or summarizing the main points for the reader. |
|---|---|---|
| **Topic sentence and conclusion** | | |

**7-37** **Antes de escribir** Piensa en el mejor día festivo que pasaste. Haz una lista de los siguientes detalles: ■

- las personas con quienes celebraste o las que fueron a la fiesta
- lo que comieron y bebieron
- las cosas que hicieron
- los regalos que dieron y recibieron

**7-38** **A escribir** Ahora, usando los detalles de la lista, escribe un párrafo bien desarrollado (*well developed*) sobre ese día, con introducción y conclusión. ■

**7-39** **Después de escribir** En grupos de cuatro o cinco estudiantes, lean los párrafos de la actividad **7-38**. Ofrezcan (*Offer*) ideas a sus compañeros para mejorar su trabajo. Después, escriban la versión final para entregársela (*turn it in*) a su profesor/a. ■

## ¿Cómo andas? II

| Having completed **Comunicación II**, I now can . . . | Feel confident | Need to review |
|---|---|---|
| • explain food preparation (p. 269) | ☐ | ☐ |
| • survey foods from different parts of the Hispanic world (p. 271) | ☐ | ☐ |
| • express things that happened in the past using irregular forms (p. 272) | ☐ | ☐ |
| • explain restaurant activity (p. 277) | ☐ | ☐ |
| • combine listening strategies (p. 281) | ☐ | ☐ |
| • communicate about food shopping and party planning (p. 282) | ☐ | ☐ |
| • relate a memory (p. 283) | ☐ | ☐ |

**SECTION GOALS for *Escribe***
By the end of the *Escribe* section, students will be able to:
- create an appropriate topic sentence and conclusion in Spanish.
- brainstorm ideas about a major childhood holiday they celebrated.
- organize and write a well-developed paragraph.
- practice reading aloud what they have written.
- revise the paragraph based on the feedback of others.
- edit the writing of others.
- finish a final draft of the paragraph.

**NATIONAL STANDARDS**
*Communication*
The *Escribe* section focuses on all three Communication Standards. First, students plan a list of details pertaining to their best childhood holiday. They write a detailed paragraph about that special day for peer review. Then, in groups of 4–5 students, they receive feedback about their writing. This requires that all students read at least 4 paragraphs that their classmates have written. Students follow Standard 1.1 when they engage in conversations and provide feedback about the writing process to their classmates. They use Standard 1.2 when they read the paragraphs written by other students, and students might also read the paragraphs aloud to their small groups. Reading aloud requires that the other group members listen to spoken Spanish. Lastly, students prepare to present their paragraphs in written form to the teacher. The teacher might display the paragraphs for an audience of readers (Standard 1.3).

**TPR activity for 7-37**
Give students simple sentences in the preterit tense that they can act out. Pretend you are remembering a birthday party from your childhood and retell the story about your presents, the cake, the decorations, etc. Here are some sample sentences:
1. *Saludé a mis amigos cuando entraron.*
2. *Recibí y abrí muchos regalos.*
3. *Comí hamburguesas con queso y perros calientes.*
4. *Mi madre me hizo una torta y la sirvió con helado.*
5. *Mis amigos y yo escuchamos música y bailamos.*
6. *Mis padres me regalaron una computadora portátil.*

**EXPANSION for 7-38**
You may wish to have students research the history of a food such as corn or potatoes. They could then write a summary, using the preterit tense and vocabulary from the chapter.

**Instructor Resources**
• Text images (maps), Video resources

**SECTION GOALS for Cultura**
By the end of the *Cultura* section, students will be able to:
• report about some geographical features of Chile.
• discuss some Chilean cultural practices such as *las onces*.
• identify Chile's national dance.
• explain the role of Paraguay's indigenous people and their language.
• compare Chile and Paraguay.
• highlight the foods and crops important to Paraguay.

**NATIONAL STANDARDS**
*Cultures, Comparisons*
The *Les presento mi país* reading about Chile and Paraguay enhances students' prior knowledge about South American countries. The Cultures Goal states that students "gain knowledge and understanding of the cultures of the world." The cultural information highlights both Standards 2.1 and 2.2 because it provides insight into the practices, products, and perspectives of the Chilean people, the Paraguayan people, and the Guaraní. For example, from the reading students learn about *las onces, la cueca*, the crops such as *la mandioca* and *la batata*, and refreshments like *el tereré*. Students can compare how Chile and Paraguay differ from their own culture, how Chile and Paraguay differ from each other, and how these South American countries differ from other Spanish-speaking countries (Standard 4.2).

**NOTE for *El pastel de choclo***
*El pastel de choclo* mixes meat and vegetables in a corn casserole.

**NOTE for *Las onces***
*Las onces, las once*, or *la once*, as it is also referred to, probably originated from a mid-morning snack, much along the lines of "*elevenses*" in England. Due to changes in the workday schedule, it gradually worked its way to the afternoon as a snack. Typical fare for *las onces* is coffee or tea, and some sort of bread or bun with butter, jam, or marmalade, but it could be as elaborate as a ham sandwich and cookies, for example.

**NOTE for *La cueca***
*La cueca* is the national dance of Chile. It represents the courtship of a rooster and a hen. The man is the rooster and dresses like a *huaso*, a Chilean cowboy. The woman is obviously the hen, and dresses in a folkloric costume as well.

# Cultura

## Chile

07-47 to 07-48

## Les presento mi país

Gino Breschi Arteaga

Mi nombre es Gino Breschi Arteaga y soy de Viña del Mar, Chile. Viña del Mar es una ciudad turística en la costa y tiene una playa hermosa. El país es muy largo y estrecho, con un promedio (*average*) de 180 kilómetros de ancho (*wide*) y aproximadamente 4.300 kilómetros de largo. Al oeste, tenemos el océano Pacífico y al este, la cordillera majestuosa de los Andes, donde hay unas minas impresionantes de carbón, oro, cobre y otros minerales importantes. **¿Prefieres vivir cerca del océano o de las montañas?** Al norte, está el desierto de Atacama, el más árido del mundo. Al sur, hay una serie de glaciares en parques nacionales. Estudié geografía y ahora trabajo para el Ministerio del Medio Ambiente, específicamente con la división que supervisa el manejo (*management*) de las áreas protegidas, como el glaciar San Rafael. **¿Cuáles áreas están protegidas en tu país?**

La playa en Viña del Mar

El pastel de choclo es un plato favorito de los chilenos

El glaciar San Rafael, Patagonia

**ALMANAQUE**

| | |
|---|---|
| **Nombre oficial:** | República de Chile |
| **Gobierno:** | República |
| **Población:** | 16.746.491 (2010) |
| **Idioma:** | español |
| **Moneda:** | Peso chileno ($) |

### ¿Sabías que...?

• Además del (*In addition to*) desayuno, el almuerzo y la cena, los chilenos toman una merienda llamada "las onces", que comen entre las 4:00 y las 7:00 de la tarde.

• El baile nacional de Chile es la cueca. Este baile se inspira en el rito de cortejo (*courting*) del gallo (*rooster*) y la gallina (*hen*).

### Preguntas

1. ¿Qué extremos geográficos y climatológicos se mencionan? ¿Hay algo parecido en los Estados Unidos?

2. ¿Qué tipos de minas hay en Chile? ¿Hay minas parecidas en los Estados Unidos?

3. Un plato popular en Chile es el pastel de choclo. ¿Cuáles son unos platos populares donde tú vives?

Amplía tus conocimientos sobre Chile en MySpanishLab.

**284**

**SUGGESTION for *La cueca***
Ask students about folkloric dances in the United States and their origins (or folkloric dances from their own countries, if they are not from the United States: e.g., square dancing, Irish contra-dancing, etc.).

**NOTE for *Chile***
The 2010 Chilean mining accident, also known as "Los 33," began as a large cave-in at the San José gold and copper mine in northern Chile on August 5, 2010. The 33 miners, who were trapped 2,300 feet underground, endured 69 days before being rescued on October 13, 2010. Once they were found to be alive, a borehole was established through which food and other provisions were passed to sustain the miners.

**EXPANSION for *Chile***
You may choose to have your students further investigate the Chilean mining accident.

**ADDITIONAL ACTIVITY for *Cultura***
Have your students do the following web activity to learn more about *la cueca*.
*¿Sabes bailar algún baile folclórico? Busca en el Internet cómo se baila la cueca y da una demostración en la clase. (Palabras clave: la cueca, cómo se baila, instrucciones para bailar la cueca)*

# Cultura

## Paraguay

07-49 to 07-50

Sandra Manrique
Esquivel

### Les presento mi país

Mi nombre es Sandra Manrique Esquivel y vivo en Villa Rica, Paraguay. Como un gran porcentaje de los paraguayos, soy bilingüe: hablo español y guaraní. **¿En qué otros países hay una población bilingüe?** El guaraní es el idioma hablado por los indígenas originales del país: los guaraníes. Hoy día, el noventa por ciento de los paraguayos somos **mestizos,** una mezcla (*mixture*) de los indígenas y los conquistadores españoles. Los indígenas cultivaron la mandioca (*yucca*), la batata (*yam*), el maíz y la yerba mate entre otras cosechas (*crops*). Villa Rica es importante por la producción de tabaco y yerba mate. Durante el día, se ve a los paraguayos tomando su **tereré,** una infusión fría de yerba mate. **¿Qué refresco te gusta tomar?**

La Represa Hidroeléctrica de Itaipú, en la frontera entre Paraguay y Brasil

El tereré, una infusión fría de yerba mate, es la bebida preferida en Paraguay

El ñandú es una especie de ave nativa y amenazada (*endangered*) de El Chaco

BOLIVIA
GRAN CHACO
Fuerte Olimpo
BRASIL
PARAGUAY
Río Paraguay
Concepción
San Pedro
Río Paraná
Asunción
Ciudad del Este
ARGENTINA

### ALMANAQUE

| | |
|---|---|
| **Nombre oficial:** | República del Paraguay |
| **Gobierno:** | República constitucional |
| **Población:** | 6.375.830 (2010) |
| **Idiomas:** | español (oficial); guaraní (oficial) |
| **Moneda:** | Guaraní (G) |

### ¿Sabías que...?

- Muchos paraguayos son aficionados a los remedios caseros (*home-made remedies*), por ejemplo los usos de la planta guaraná, un arbusto (*bush; shrub*) indígena, para calmar los nervios y ayudar con la digestión.
- El Chaco cubre el 60% de la superficie de Paraguay pero contiene solamente un 2% de la población del país.

### Preguntas

1. ¿Qué comidas se comen en Paraguay?
2. ¿Por qué son bilingües muchos paraguayos?
3. ¿En qué aspectos son Chile y Paraguay diferentes y similares? ¿Cómo se comparan con los otros países que hemos estudiado?

 Amplía tus conocimientos sobre Paraguay en MySpanishLab.

---

**ADDITIONAL ACTIVITY for *Cultura***
Have your students do the following research on the Internet.

1. *¿Qué piensas de los remedios caseros? ¿Prefieres las curas alternativas o ir al médico? ¿Por qué?*
   *Busca en el Internet más información sobre los remedios caseros y la clasificación de alimentos en la medicina herbal. (Palabras clave: la medicina herbal o alternativa, los remedios caseros)*

2. *La represa de Itaipú es un proyecto de construcción enorme. ¿Hay algún proyecto de este tipo en los Estados Unidos? ¿Por qué se llevaron a cabo estos proyectos? ¿Cuáles son los beneficios y las desventajas para los países? (Palabras clave: represas estadounidenses, proyectos hidroeléctricos, energía eléctrica)*

---

 **Instructor Resources**
- Text images (maps), Video resources

**NOTE for *El Chaco***
El Chaco, or El Gran Chaco, is a vast area of empty plains and forests. (The name *Chaco* supposedly comes from the Quechuan word for *great hunting ground*). It contains several of Paraguay's national parks and biological reserves. It is a prime area for ecotourism due to the variety of flora and fauna located there: e.g., the jaguar, the tapir, the elusive guanaco, the maned wolf, and the giant armadillo. It is also home to many aviary species, including the flamingo and the ostrich-like rhea or *ñandú*, which is endangered.

**NOTE for *La Represa Hidroeléctrica de Itaipú***
The Itaipú Hydroelectric Dam is a joint venture of enormous proportions between Brazil and Paraguay. Construction began in 1975 and was completed in 1991. Harnessing the hydroelectric potential of the Paraná River, this dam and power plant provide more than 80% of the electrical power consumption of Paraguay and more than 25% of that of Brazil. It has become a huge tourist attraction.

**NOTE for *Tereré***
*Tereré* is the cold infusion form of yerba mate, the grass-like tea that is the preferred drink in Paraguay, Uruguay, and Argentina. When it is hot, it is called *mate*; as a cold drink, it is called *tereré*.

**NOTE for *Remedios caseros***
Beliefs in herbal and folk remedies abound in Paraguay. Sometimes they are combined with modern medical practices, depending on the person with an ailment, his/her background, and his/her geographic location—rural populations being more prone to these practices. Nevertheless, in the marketplaces in Asunción, a modern capital city, medicine women set up their stalls and do brisk business.

**EXPANSION for *Preguntas***
Additional questions to ask your students are:

1. *¿Qué significa ser bilingüe?*
2. *¿Qué idiomas hablan los paraguayos? ¿Qué idiomas hablan los canadienses? ¿Los puertorriqueños?*
3. *¿Dónde vive la mayoría de los paraguayos? ¿Por qué piensas que es así?*
4. *¿Cómo se compara la comida paraguaya con la comida de otros países hispanos?*

# Ambiciones siniestras
## EPISODIO 7

07-53 to 07-54

# Lectura

| **Estrategia** | Predicting |
| --- | --- |

To predict what a reading passage is about, first anticipate the content by considering the title, visual cues (illustrations, photos), and comprehension questions. Once you have a general idea of what the passage is about, connect any personal knowledge or experience you have with it. Then, quickly skim the reading for the main idea(s). At that point you can predict what will happen in the reading.

**7-40** **Antes de leer** En el **Episodio 5**, Eduardo desaparece. Cisco no sabe qué hacer y le pide consejo a su primo, Manolo. Después, todos los estudiantes menos Eduardo y Alejandra tienen una videoconferencia. Antes de continuar con el siguiente episodio contesta las siguientes preguntas. ■

1. Mira el título. ¿Cuál es un ejemplo de un rompecabezas? ¿Qué experiencia tienes con los rompecabezas?
2. ¿Quién está en la foto? ¿Qué hace?

**7-41** **A leer** Completa los siguientes pasos. ■

1. Lee superficialmente (*skim*) el episodio para averiguar cuáles son los personajes y dónde están.
2. Escribe **dos** predicciones de lo que crees que va a ocurrir en el episodio.
3. Lee el episodio y determina si las predicciones que hiciste son correctas.

## El rompecabezas°

*riddle*

Cisco está muy preocupado por Alejandra. Por eso después de la videoconferencia llamó a Manolo y le preguntó por ella. Manolo le dijo que Alejandra no respondió al último correo electrónico. Tampoco° estuvo en la clase de literatura. Manolo le dijo a Cisco que la esperó por media hora después de la clase y no vino. No sabe nada de ella.

*Nor*

Ellos dos están muy preocupados acerca de lo que está pasando. ¿Por qué fueron escogidos°? ¿Qué pasó con Eduardo? ¿Dónde está Eduardo? ¿Y dónde está Alejandra?

*selected*

Con los nervios y la preocupación, Cisco tenía mucha hambre así que decidió ir a su restaurante favorito, Mamá Mía. Ahí siempre puede comer algo y pensar en todo lo que está pasando. Pidió lo que su madre llama *comfort food:* pollo frito, papas, maíz y frijoles. Durante la comida, conversó con sus amigos que trabajan allí. Cuando pagó, le sonó el

286

clues

teléfono celular. Cisco contestó y oyó una voz de hombre: *Cisco Quiroga. Tiene cuatro pistas° para resolver este rompecabezas o Eduardo va a morir. Aquí están:*

*Conocido por su longitud*

*Por la razón o la fuerza*

*Qué rico está el pisco*

*Para quien baile la cueca*

*Recuerde, tiene dos días para resolver el rompecabezas o Eduardo va a morir. No vaya a la policía.*

CLIC…

(colgar) hang up

Cisco se quedó sin palabras; le temblaron las manos. Tomó el teléfono y llamó a Manolo. La línea estaba ocupada. —Vamos, Manolo, cuelga° el teléfono, pensó Cisco, necesito hablar contigo. Por fin, después de llamar varias veces, Manolo contestó con voz de pánico.

—¿Quién es? —contestó Manolo.

—Soy yo, Cisco —respondió Cisco—. Mira…

*(Manolo interrumpe)*

yours

—Cisco, recibí una llamada antes de la tuya°…

—¿De un hombre con una voz muy rara? —le preguntó Cisco.

—Así que te llamó a ti también —respondió Manolo—. Cisco, tenemos que llamar a los demás. Yo llamo a Lupe y a Alejandra y tú llamas a Marisol, ¿está bien?

—De acuerdo. Muy bien —dijo Cisco.

Manolo llamó a Alejandra pero no pudo hablar con ella. La voz del contestador automático era la de un hombre… *"Lo sentimos, no estamos en casa en estos momentos. Pueden dejar un mensaje"*. Intentó llamar de nuevo. Otra vez el contestador. ¿Dónde está Alejandra? Cree que conoce la voz del hombre del contestador.

Suddenly

De repente°, Manolo, pensando en voz alta y horrorizado, gritó: ¡Por favor no… No puede ser…!

---

**7-42** **Después de leer** Contesta las siguientes preguntas. ▪

1. ¿Qué dijo Manolo de Alejandra?
2. ¿Dónde estaba (*was*) Cisco cuando recibió la llamada misteriosa?
3. ¿Qué acababa de hacer (*had just done*) cuando recibió la llamada?
4. ¿De qué se trató la llamada?
5. ¿Por qué estaba Cisco asustado (*frightened*)?
6. ¿Qué hizo Cisco después de colgar el teléfono?
7. ¿Qué ocurrió cuando Manolo llamó a Alejandra?

**NOTE for 7-42**

In an attempt to contextualize the use of the preterit, in *Episodio 7* it was necessary to also use the imperfect in a few of the comprehension questions in **7-42** and **7-44.** You may want to point out to students that this is a preview of the other past tense they will learn in *Capítulo 8* and that they will practice when to use each past tense in *Capítulo 9*.

**ANSWERS to 7-42**

1. Dijo que Alejandra no respondió al último correo electrónico y que no fue a clase.
2. Estaba en el restaurante Mamá Mía.
3. Acababa de comer *comfort food* (pollo frito, papas, maíz y frijoles).
4. Un hombre preparó un rompecabezas.
5. El hombre dijo que si no puede resolver el rompecabezas, Eduardo va a morir.
6. Llamó a Manolo.
7. No contestó y la voz del contestador automático fue la de un hombre.

287

**SECTION GOALS for *Video***

By the end of the *Video* section, students will be able to:

• summarize the main events in the video using the preterit tense.
• predict what might happen in the next video episode.
• describe the cultural items they noticed in the video.

**NOTE for 7-44**

Although this chapter presented the preterit and it would be advantageous to practice the tense with this section, there are some answers that necessitate the use of the imperfect. Rather than requiring additional grammatical explanations before the formal presentation of the imperfect, the choice was made to use the historical present.

**ANSWERS to 7-44**

1. Lupe estaba en un café y trató de resolver el rompecabezas del Sr. Verdugo. Usó la computadora para buscar información sobre el rompecabezas.
2. Cisco estaba en un café y también trató de resolver el rompecabezas.
3. Dice que está buscando información sobre comida típica de los países latinoamericanos porque piensa ir de vacaciones allí.
4. Cisco *no* les va a mencionar el correo electrónico que Eduardo escribió al Sr. Verdugo.
5. Manolo piensa que Lupe conoció a Alejandra el año pasado en la universidad.
6. Cisco cree que Manolo está diciendo que él debe saber lo que ocurrió con Eduardo.
7. Descubrió que el pisco y la cueca tienen que ver con Chile.

  # Video

07-55 to 07-57

**7-43** **Antes del video** ¿Dónde puede estar Alejandra? ¿De quién es la voz en su contestador automático? ¿Quién más recibió el rompecabezas? En la segunda parte del episodio, vas a ver a Lupe trabajando en su computadora. ¿Qué piensas que está haciendo? También Manolo, Cisco, Marisol y Lupe van a tener otra videoconferencia. ¿De qué necesitan hablar ahora? ■

¿Qué lees?

Esto es muy peligroso.

¡No tengo nada que ver con la desaparición de Eduardo!

Episodio 7

## *«¡Qué rico está el pisco!»*

Relájate y disfruta el video.

**7-44** **Después del video** Contesta las siguientes preguntas. ■

1. ¿Dónde estaba Lupe? ¿Qué hizo?
2. ¿Dónde estaba Cisco? ¿Qué hizo?
3. ¿Cuál es la mentira (*lie*) de Lupe?
4. ¿Qué **no** les va a mencionar Cisco a los otros?
5. ¿De qué le "acusó" Manolo a Lupe?
6. ¿Por qué le respondió Cisco a Manolo de una manera defensiva?
7. ¿Qué descubrió Cisco al final del episodio?

288

**HERITAGE LANGUAGE LEARNERS**

If you have heritage language learners in your class who have a grasp of the preterit and the imperfect, you may wish to ask them to answer the questions in **7-44** in those tenses.

## Y por fin, ¿cómo andas?

|                                                                                                              | Feel confident | Need to review |
|--------------------------------------------------------------------------------------------------------------|:--------------:|:--------------:|
| Having completed this chapter, I now can . . .                                                                |                |                |
| **Comunicación I**                                                                                           |                |                |
| • discuss food (p. 256)                                                                                       | ☐              | ☐              |
| • pronounce **r** and **rr** correctly (MSL/SAM)                                                             | ☐              | ☐              |
| • communicate with less repetition using direct object pronouns (p. 261)                                     | ☐              | ☐              |
| • express things that happened in the past (Part I) (p. 263)                                                 | ☐              | ☐              |
| • describe things that happened in the past (Part II) (p. 265)                                               | ☐              | ☐              |
| **Comunicación II**                                                                                          |                |                |
| • explain food preparation (p. 269)                                                                          | ☐              | ☐              |
| • express things that happened in the past using irregular forms (p. 272)                                    | ☐              | ☐              |
| • explain restaurant activity (p. 277)                                                                        | ☐              | ☐              |
| • combine listening strategies (p. 281)                                                                       | ☐              | ☐              |
| • communicate about food shopping and party planning (p. 282)                                                | ☐              | ☐              |
| • relate a memory (p. 283)                                                                                    | ☐              | ☐              |
| **Cultura**                                                                                                  |                |                |
| • compare and contrast eating habits (p. 261)                                                                 | ☐              | ☐              |
| • survey foods from different parts of the Hispanic world (p. 271)                                            | ☐              | ☐              |
| • list interesting facts about this chapter's featured countries: Chile and Paraguay (pp. 284–285)           | ☐              | ☐              |
| **Ambiciones siniestras**                                                                                    |                |                |
| • predict what will happen in a reading and discover the voice-mail message that frightens Cisco (p. 286)    | ☐              | ☐              |
| • determine who has received the riddle, and what they have figured out so far (p. 288)                       | ☐              | ☐              |
| **Comunidades**                                                                                              |                |                |
| • use Spanish in real-life contexts (SAM)                                                                     | ☐              | ☐              |

# VOCABULARIO ACTIVO

| Las carnes y las aves | Meat and poultry |
|---|---|
| las aves | poultry |
| el bistec | steak |
| la carne | meat |
| la hamburguesa | hamburger |
| el jamón | ham |
| el perro caliente | hot dog |
| el pollo | chicken |

| El pescado y los mariscos | Fish and seafood |
|---|---|
| el atún | tuna |
| los camarones (*pl.*) | shrimp |
| el pescado | fish |

| Las frutas | Fruit |
|---|---|
| la banana | banana |
| el limón | lemon |
| la manzana | apple |
| el melón | melon |
| la naranja | orange |
| la pera | pear |
| el tomate | tomato |

| Las verduras | Vegetables |
|---|---|
| la cebolla | onion |
| el chile | chili pepper |
| la ensalada | salad |
| los frijoles (*pl.*) | beans |
| la lechuga | lettuce |
| el maíz | corn |
| la papa/la patata | potato |
| las papas fritas (*pl.*) | french fries; potato chips |
| la verdura | vegetable |

| Los postres | Desserts |
|---|---|
| los dulces | candy; sweets |
| las galletas | cookies; crackers |
| el helado | ice cream |
| el pastel | pastry; pie |
| el postre | dessert |
| la torta | cake |

| Las bebidas | Beverages |
|---|---|
| el agua (con hielo) | water (with ice) |
| el café | coffee |
| la cerveza | beer |
| el jugo | juice |
| la leche | milk |
| el refresco | soft drink |
| el té (helado / caliente) | tea (iced / hot) |
| el vino | wine |

| Más comidas | More foods |
|---|---|
| el arroz | rice |
| el cereal | cereal |
| el huevo | egg |
| el pan | bread |
| el queso | cheese |
| la sopa | soup |
| la tostada | toast |

| Las comidas | Meals |
|---|---|
| el almuerzo | lunch |
| la cena | dinner |
| la comida | food; meal |
| el desayuno | breakfast |
| la merienda | snack |

| Verbos | Verbs |
|---|---|
| almorzar (ue) | to have lunch |
| andar | to walk |
| beber | to drink |
| cocinar | to cook |
| conducir | to drive |
| cenar | to have dinner |
| desayunar | to have breakfast |
| merendar | to have a snack |

| Los condimentos y las especias | Condiments and spices |
|---|---|
| el aceite | oil |
| el azúcar | sugar |
| la mantequilla | butter |
| la mayonesa | mayonnaise |
| la mermelada | jam; marmalade |
| la mostaza | mustard |
| la pimienta | pepper |
| la sal | salt |
| la salsa de tomate | ketchup |
| el vinagre | vinegar |

| Algunos términos de cocina | Cooking terms |
|---|---|
| a la parrilla | grilled |
| al horno | baked |
| asado/a | roasted; grilled |
| bien cocido/a | well done |
| bien hecho/a | well cooked |
| caliente | hot (temperature) |
| cocido/a | boiled; baked |
| crudo/a | rare; raw |
| duro/a | hard-boiled |
| fresco/a | fresh |
| frito/a | fried |
| helado/a | iced |
| hervido/a | boiled |
| picante | spicy |
| poco hecho/a | rare |
| término medio | medium |

| En el restaurante | In the restaurant |
|---|---|
| el/la camarero/a | waiter/waitress |
| el/la cliente/a | customer; client |
| el/la cocinero/a | cook |
| la cuchara | soup spoon; tablespoon |
| la cucharita | teaspoon |
| el cuchillo | knife |
| la especialidad de la casa | specialty of the house |
| el mantel | tablecloth |
| el menú | menu |
| el plato | plate; dish |
| la propina | tip |
| la servilleta | napkin |
| la tarjeta de crédito | credit card |
| la tarjeta de débito | debit card |
| la taza | cup |
| el tenedor | fork |
| el vaso | glass |

| Verbos | Verbs |
|---|---|
| pagar | to pay |
| pedir | to order |
| reservar una mesa | to reserve a table |

| Otras palabras útiles | Other useful words |
|---|---|
| anoche | last night |
| anteayer | the day before yesterday |
| el año pasado | last year |
| ayer | yesterday |
| barato/a | cheap |
| ¡Buen provecho! | Enjoy your meal! |
| caro/a | expensive |
| cerca (de) | near |
| debajo (de) | under; underneath |
| encima (de) | on top (of); above |
| el fin de semana pasado | last weekend |
| el… (jueves) pasado | last … (Thursday) |
| La cuenta, por favor. | The check, please. |
| la semana pasada | last week |
| más tarde que | later than |
| más temprano que | earlier than |

**Instructor Resources**
• IRM: Syllabi and Lesson Plans

## NATIONAL STANDARDS

### COMUNICACIÓN I
- To describe clothing (Communication, Cultures, Comparisons)
- To pronounce *ll* and *ñ* correctly (Communication)
- To state to whom and for whom things are done (Communication)
- To express likes, dislikes, needs, etc. (Communication)
- To convey information about people and things (Communication, Comparisons)
- To engage in additional communication practice (Communication)

### COMUNICACIÓN II
- To provide details about clothing (Communication)
- To relate daily routines (Communication)
- To share about situations in the past and how things used to be (Communication)
- To guess the meanings of unfamiliar words, when listening, from the context (Communication, Connections)
- To communicate about clothing and fashion (Communication)
- To write an e-mail, practicing circumlocution (Communication, Cultures, Comparisons, Connections, Communities)
- To engage in additional communication practice (Communication)

### CULTURA
- To recount information about a Spanish clothing company (Communication, Cultures, Connections, Comparisons)
- To consider shopping practices in the Spanish-speaking countries (Communication, Cultures, Connections, Comparisons)
- To share important facts about Argentina and Uruguay (Cultures, Comparisons)
- To explore the chapter's cultural themes further (Cultures)

### AMBICIONES SINIESTRAS
- To deduce the meanings of unfamiliar words, and explain the significance of the latest e-mail (Connections, Communication)
- To reveal secrets regarding Lupe (Communication)

### COMUNIDADES
- To use Spanish in real-life contexts (Communities)

## 8  ¿Qué te pones?

En los países hispanohablantes la gente lleva (*wear*) ropa (*clothing*) muy similar a la que llevan por todo el mundo pero también se usa ropa más tradicional. Por ejemplo, en México se encuentran sarapes, ponchos y huaraches y en Colombia usan ruanas (ponchos) y alpargatas (*espadrilles*).

### PREGUNTAS

**1** ¿Qué tipo de ropa te gusta? ¿Prefieres la ropa formal o la ropa informal? ¿Qué ropa llevas normalmente?

**2** ¿Te interesa la moda (*fashion*)? ¿Te gusta experimentar con diferentes estilos de ropa? Explica.

**3** ¿Cómo influye el lugar donde vive una persona en la ropa que lleva?

292

### SECTION GOALS for *Chapter opener*
By the end of the Chapter opener section, students will be able to:
- describe clothing preferences
- discuss how where one lives may affect how he/she dresses

### NATIONAL STANDARDS
*Communities*
If you have a large Hispanic community in your area, you might ask students to volunteer their time at a local church, women's shelter, or other social service agency that collects clothing. There are several organizations throughout the United States, such as Dress for Success, Goodwill, and the Salvation Army, that accept clothing donations for resale. Some churches and welfare agencies collect new and gently used items of clothing for redistribution. If you have a children's hospital, cancer treatment facility, or hospice in the area, you might consider asking students to collect clothing that can be turned into quilt squares. Then students can cut the squares for hand or machine piecing. Donate the quilts to children, the homeless, senior citizens, relatives of hospice patients, or animal shelters.

| OBJETIVOS | CONTENIDOS | |
|---|---|---|
| **COMUNICACIÓN I** | | |
| To describe clothing | **1** Clothing | 294 |
| To pronounce the letters *ll* and *ñ* | **Pronunciación:** The letters **ll** and **ñ** | MSL / SAM |
| To state to whom and for whom things are done | **2** Indirect object pronouns | 299 |
| To express likes, dislikes, needs, etc. | **3** **Gustar** and similar verbs | 302 |
| To convey information about people and things | **4** Direct and indirect object pronouns used together | 305 |
| To engage in additional communication practice | **Heritage Language** | SAM |
| **COMUNICACIÓN II** | | |
| To provide details about clothing | **5** Fabrics and materials | 309 |
| To relate daily routines | **6** Reflexive verbs | 312 |
| To share about situations in the past and how things used to be | **7** The imperfect tense | 317 |
| To guess the meanings of unfamiliar words, when listening, from the context | **ESCUCHA:** Clothes shopping **Estrategia:** Guessing meaning from context | 321 |
| To communicate about clothing and fashion | **¡Conversemos!** | 322 |
| To write an e-mail, practicing circumlocution | **ESCRIBE:** An e-mail **Estrategia:** Circumlocution | 323 |
| To engage in additional communication practice | **Heritage Language** | SAM |
| **CULTURA** | | |
| To recount information about a Spanish clothing company | **NOTA CULTURAL** Zara: la moda internacional | 298 |
| To consider shopping practices in the Spanish-speaking countries | **NOTA CULTURAL** Los centros comerciales en Latinoamérica | 316 |
| To share important facts about this chapter's featured countries: Argentina and Uruguay | **CULTURA** *Argentina y Uruguay* | 324–325 |
| To explore further the chapter's cultural themes | **MÁS CULTURA** | SAM |
| **AMBICIONES SINIESTRAS** | | |
| To deduce the meanings of unfamiliar words and explain the significance of the latest e-mail from Sr. Verdugo | **EPISODIO 8** **Lectura:** *¿Quién fue?* **Estrategia:** Guessing meaning from context | 326 |
| To reveal secrets regarding Lupe | **Video:** *El misterio crece* | 328 |
| **COMUNIDADES** | | |
| To use Spanish in real-life contexts | **Experiential Leaning:** ¿Qué me pongo? | SAM |
| | **Service Learning**: Ayuda para los que ayudan | SAM |

**293**

**NOTE for *Chapter opener***
Although *Capítulo 8* presents one primary vocabulary focus, clothing, it is rich in grammatical content. The chapter activities recycle the new vocabulary throughout, allowing students greater focus on the grammatical constructions (see *Contenidos*) while solidifying the ample list of new vocabulary words.

**NOTE for *Chapter opener***
The authors have incorporated a great deal of recycling from previous chapters in *Capítulo 8*: *La hora, Los días y las estaciones, Ir + a+ infinitive, El pretérito, Los verbos irregulares del pretérito, Los quehaceres de la casa, El mundo de la música,* and *La casa.*

**NOTE for *Chapter opener***
Ask students what they and their friends typically wear when they go to different places, e.g., a club to dance, a movie, a sporting event, an elegant restaurant, etc.

**NOTE for *Chapter opener***
Bring in photos of famous designers from the Spanish-speaking world for discussion. Assign students to research designers such as Carolina Herrera, Toledo, Narciso Rodríguez, Custodio y David DImau, Adolfo Domínguez, Silvia Tcherassi, and Óscar de la Renta.

**NATIONAL STANDARDS**
*Cultures*
It is important to reinforce the idea that students around the Spanish-speaking world share the same clothing "uniform" of jeans/slacks and T-shirts/shirts. Too often American students have the stereotypical notion that indigenous clothing is the only way of dressing. Nevertheless, it is important to share photos of indigenous peoples from the Spanish-speaking world so that your students will have a clearer picture of the diversity of *los hispanohablantes.* Activity **8-3** involves students describing the dress of indigenous people from different parts of Latin America, as depicted in the photos on p. 296.

**NOTE for *Chapter opener***
You may wish to ask your students to give their impressions regarding the photo for this chapter opener. Also, have the students read the objectives for the chapter silently. We suggest you spend no more than 5 to 7 minutes on Chapter openers.

**PLANNING AHEAD**
Inform students that they will need to bring in photos of fashion models from magazines, catalogs, or the Internet for **8-22.** You will want to have extras on hand for the students who have trouble gathering the materials or forget to bring them to class.

**METHODOLOGY • Contrasting and Comparing**
Whenever possible, every effort will be made to have students make comparisons between the culture of their homes / university communities and what they are currently learning. Additionally, as appropriate, students will be asked to compare what they are currently learning with what they learned in previous chapters.

**METHODOLOGY • Making Topics Relevant for Students**
The opening questions for each chapter begin with your learners and their preferences, something that we have learned from educational philosopher John Dewey. Try having your students turn to a partner and answer the questions in pairs. Then have them share the answers their partners gave. This has them practice listening and paraphrasing.

**METHODOLOGY • Meaningful Learning**
One purpose of the discussion questions is to begin with a topic with which your students are familiar so they can see how the major theme of the chapter relates to their lives. This facilitates learning by encouraging active mental participation in relating new material to existing knowledge, the basic tenet of Ausubel's "meaningful learning" (Ausubel, D. *Educational Psychology: A cognitive view.* New York: Holt, Rinehart & Winston 1968).

**Instructor Resources**
• Textbook images, Extra Activities

**SECTION GOALS for**
*Comunicación I*
By the end of the *Comunicación* section, students will be able to:

• talk about what people are wearing.
• pronounce the letters *ll* and *ñ* correctly.
• describe a Spanish clothing company.
• identify the indirect object in a sentence and substitute it with an indirect object pronoun.
• use the verb *gustar* and similar verbs with indirect object pronouns to express likes and dislikes.
• combine direct object pronouns and indirect object pronouns with infinitives or with present participles in a sentence.

**NATIONAL STANDARDS**
*Communication, Cultures, Comparisons*
Talking about clothing always lends itself to lively classroom discussions, since virtually everyone enjoys talking about and sharing opinions about clothes. As the chapter continues and students learn the imperfect tense, talking about what they used to wear recycles the clothing vocabulary.

*La ropa* is a topic to which students can relate. The pair activities focus on communication in the interpersonal mode (Standard 1.1), and the topic of clothing lends itself well to more creative outlets, such as a fashion show. If students become the models and announcers and narrate what each person wears as he or she walks the catwalk, you are engaging in Standard 1.3, the presentational mode. The cultural readings provide a basis for understanding the practices and perspectives (Standard 2.1) and the products and perspectives (Standard 2.2) of Hispanic people. As students discuss what types of clothing exist in the Hispanic world, what purpose a particular clothing item serves, who makes the item, and who wears the item and once they understand the cultural differences, they can compare how the concepts of clothing and fashion differ in the United States and the Hispanic world (Standard 4.2).

**METHODOLOGY •**
**Constructing Knowledge**
Since the 1940s and 1950s, educational researchers have explored how we learn and what assists in learning. When learners *construct knowledge,* the knowledge becomes internalized and transfers into long-term memory. On the other hand, memorizing lists, for example, goes into short-term memory but usually does not transfer into long-term memory. There are learning tools that help students retain information, such as mnemonic devices and connecting vocabulary with

# Comunicación I

**1 VOCABULARIO**

**La ropa**  Describing clothing

08-01 to 08-07

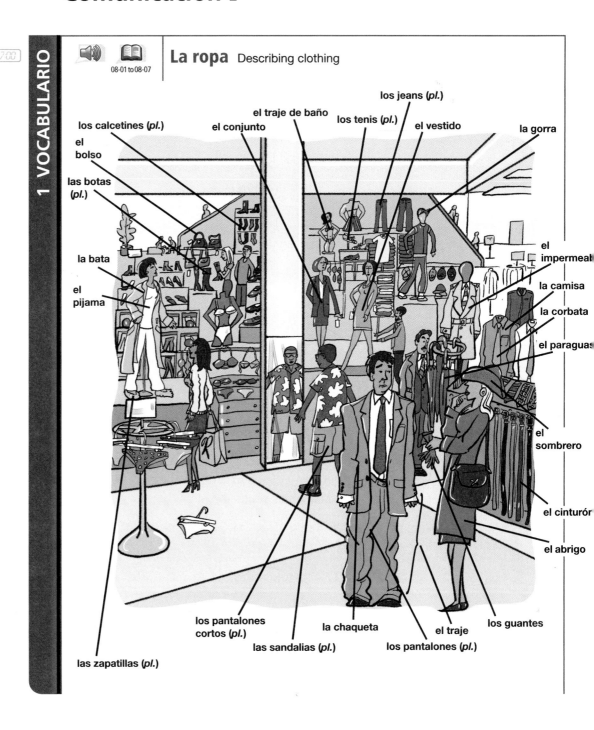

visual images. The "Where's Waldo?"–style composite visuals that *¡Anda! Curso elemental* employs to introduce vocabulary help students learn the new words. The students may need to consult with the *Vocabulario activo* pages at the end of the chapter to clarify / negotiate meaning, but that task helps them associate a visual image with a vocabulary word and acquire the meaning. These visuals will be excellent to use when you are introducing or practicing new tenses, since the students will have already associated these verbs with the images.

la camiseta

el suéter

las medias (pl.)

los zapatos (pl.)

la sudadera

la ropa interior

la falda

la blusa

| Un verbo | *A verb* | Otras palabras útiles | *Other useful words* |
|---|---|---|---|
| llevar | *to wear; to take; to carry* | la moda | *fashion; style* |
| | | las prendas | *articles of clothing* |

### Fíjate

In your vocabulary list you see the letters (*pl.*) beside words such as *las medias* or *los jeans* to indicate that they are plural in Spanish. You will also notice (*pl.*) beside *los calcetines*. Each sock is a *calcetín*.

**CAPÍTULO 8**

**METHODOLOGY • Introducing Lexical Variants**
Every effort has been made to introduce highly common vocabulary and to limit the number of words per chapter so as not to overwhelm your students. In this chapter and others, it is highly appropriate to direct your heritage language learners and advanced beginners to explore the *También se dice...* section in Appendix 3 for additional vocabulary.

**SECTION GOALS for *Pronunciación***
By the end of the *Pronunciación* section, students will be able to:
• pronounce the letters *ll* and *ñ* correctly.
• practice pronunciation skills using *dichos* and *refranes*.

## PRONUNCIACIÓN

### The letters *ll* and *ñ*

Go to MySpanishLab / Student Activities Manual to learn about the letters *ll* and *ñ*.

¡Hola! 08-08 to 08-10

---

**8-1** **Categorías** Escribe todas las palabras nuevas del vocabulario que corresponden a las siguientes categorías. Luego, compara tu lista con la de un/a compañero/a. ■

**¿Qué ropa usas para... ?** *Answers will vary but may include:*
1. hacer ejercicio y jugar a los deportes  el traje de baño, los pantalones cortos, la sudadera, los tenis
2. ir a la cama  la bata, el pijama, las zapatillas
3. cubrir (*to cover*) los pies (*feet*)  las zapatillas, los zapatos, los tenis, las botas, las sandalias, los calcetines, las medias
4. ir a clase  los jeans, los tenis, la camiseta, la sudadera
5. trabajar en una oficina  el traje, los pantalones largos, la camisa, la corbata, la falda, la blusa, la chaqueta, el conjunto, el vestido

**Fijate**

You have noticed that *¡Anda! Curso elemental* makes extensive use of pair and group work in the classroom to provide you with many opportunities during the class period to practice Spanish. When working in pairs or groups, it's imperative that you make every effort to speak only Spanish.

 **8-2  ¡Señoras y señores!**  Dibujen un diagrama de Venn según el modelo. En el círculo izquierdo, hagan una lista de la ropa que generalmente llevan las mujeres. En el círculo derecho, hagan una lista de la ropa que generalmente llevan los hombres. En el centro donde se juntan los círculos (*where the circles overlap*), hagan una lista de la ropa que los hombres y las mujeres llevan. ¿Que lista es más larga? ∎

**MODELO**

la ropa de mujeres — la ropa que sirve para hombres y mujeres — la ropa de hombres

Capítulo 3. Los colores, pág. 111.

 **8-3  ¿Cómo se visten?**  Túrnense para describir qué ropa llevan las personas en las fotos. ∎

**MODELO**  *El hombre y los chicos llevan sombreros…*

**Estrategia**

Remember that adjectives describe nouns and agree in number (singular / plural) and gender (masculine / feminine) with the nouns they are describing.

**8-4** **El juego del viaje** (*travel*)

¿Te gusta viajar? Formen un círculo de cinco estudiantes o más. Primero, decidan dónde quieren ir de viaje. Después, túrnense para decir sus nombres y un artículo de ropa que quieren llevar. Cada estudiante tiene que repetir lo que dijeron los estudiantes anteriores. **¡OJO!** Si no recuerdan (*If you don't remember*), tienen que preguntar: **¿Qué dijiste, por favor?** o **¿Puedes repetir, por favor?** ■

MODELO　　Vamos a Cancún.

E1:　*Soy Beverly y voy a llevar un traje de baño.*

E2:　*Soy Tim y voy a llevar una camiseta blanca. Beverly va a llevar un traje de baño.*

E3:　*Soy Kelly y voy a llevar una chaqueta. Tim va a llevar una camiseta blanca. Beverly va a llevar un traje de baño.*

E4:　…

### Estrategia

It is important to be supportive of your fellow classmates during these activities, which includes making suggestions and helpful comments and corrections. Because you will be learning from each other, it is good to know the following expressions to help you interact with each other:

| | |
|---|---|
| (No) Estoy de acuerdo. | *I agree. / I don't agree.* |
| Yo pienso que es… | *I think it's …* |
| ¿No debería ser…? | *Shouldn't it be … ?* |

 Capítulo Preliminar A, Los días, los meses y las estaciones, pág. 20.

 **8-5** **Señora, ¿qué debo llevar?**

Trabajas para una agencia de viajes y, para ayudar a tus clientes, tienes que preparar una lista de la ropa que deben llevar a cada destino (*destination*). Compara tu lista con la de un/a compañero/a. ■

MODELO　　La República Dominicana en agosto
*los trajes de baño, los pantalones cortos, las camisetas, los jeans, los tenis y el paraguas*

1. Argentina en julio
2. Costa Rica en junio
3. México en septiembre
4. Cuba en diciembre
5. Uruguay en marzo
6. España en febrero

### Fíjate

Remember that the seasons south of the equator are the opposite of those in the northern hemisphere, so that when it is summer in the northern hemisphere it is winter in the southern hemisphere.

**TPR activity for 8-4**
Have students act out packing their suitcases for each place. As they unpack their suitcases have them pretend they are putting on the clothing items they have mentioned for each type of weather.

**SUGGESTION for 8-4**
Some of the activity directions, such as those for **8-4,** are somewhat long—not difficult, just long. Have students read the directions for homework so that they understand what is expected of them. It will help move the class forward more efficiently.

**EXPANSION for 8-4**
You or your students can bring in clothing ads from the Sunday newspaper, clothing catalogs (many of them are free if you call the 1-800 number and request them), or the Internet. Put students into groups of four. Give each group a certain number of dollars (or the currency of the country where they will travel) and tell the students to pack suitcases with appropriate clothing for a certain number of days. See who can get the most clothing at the best prices for their trip.

**ANSWERS to 8-5**
*Sample answers include:*
1. un abrigo, unos guantes, un suéter, pantalones, jeans, camisas / blusas, zapatos
2. un traje de baño, pantalones cortos, tenis, sandalias, pantalones, camisetas, camisas / blusas
3. pantalones largos y cortos, unas camisas / blusas, una chaqueta, camisetas
4. un traje de baño, pantalones cortos, tenis, sandalias, pantalones, camisetas, camisas / blusas
5. pantalones largos y cortos, unas camisas / blusas, una chaqueta, camisetas
6. un abrigo, unos guantes, un suéter, pantalones, jeans, camisas / blusas, zapatos

Capítulo 3. Los colores, pág. 111; Capítulo 4. *Ir + a + Infinitivo*, pág. 147; Capítulo 5. Los pronombres de complemento directo, pág. 189, Capítulo 7. El pretérito, pág. 263.

**Fíjate**
The expression *acabar de + infinitive* means to have just done something. Use this expression in the present tense when you want to refer to the very recent past. As in the *modelo*, this expression is useful for establishing a context for the use of the preterit.

### 8-6 ¿Tienes un presupuesto (*budget*)?
Completa el siguiente cuadro con las prendas que acabas de comprar (*have just bought*) y con las que necesitas comprar. Luego, comparte tus respuestas con un/a compañero/a. ■

MODELO   *Acabo de comprar una blusa blanca muy elegante. La compré en Macy's la semana pasada. Pagué cuarenta y cinco dólares. Necesito comprar una falda negra.*

| ACABO DE COMPRAR... | LO(S)/LA(S) COMPRÉ... | PAGUÉ... | VOY A / NECESITO COMPRAR... |
|---|---|---|---|
| 1.  una blusa blanca | en Macy's | $45 | una falda negra |
| 2. | | | |
| 3. | | | |

**NOTA CULTURAL**

## Zara: la moda internacional

08-11 to 08-12

En España, uno de los negocios más florecientes (*flourishing*) es la empresa de ropa Zara. El fundador, Amancio Ortega Gaona, empezó el negocio (*business*) en La Coruña, en el norte de España, con unas 5.000 pesetas ($83,00 US). Ahora el Sr. Ortega es uno de los hombres más ricos de este país.

Una de las razones del gran éxito del negocio es que continuamente ofrece lo que la gente quiere. Su filosofía es vender ropa "barata y de buena calidad". Tiene unos doscientos diseñadores (*designers*) que son los responsables de crear la moda Zara. Las diferentes líneas creadas por los diseñadores proporcionan un *look* completo para hombres y mujeres.

**Fíjate**
In 2002, Spain converted to the *euro*. Previously, its currency was the *peseta*.

La mayoría de la ropa se hace en una fábrica (*factory*) muy moderna en La Coruña. Desde el momento que surge la idea hasta que la prenda llega a la tienda, sólo pasan unas tres semanas. Dos o tres veces por semana llegan productos nuevos a las tiendas y así se renueva más del cuarenta por ciento del inventario.

Ahora se puede comprar la moda Zara en más de 1.600 tiendas en 74 países, por catálogo y por el Internet. Para conocer la moda internacional del momento, hay que conocer Zara.

### Preguntas
1. ¿Quién empezó la empresa Zara y dónde? ¿Cuánto le costó?
2. ¿Por qué tiene tanto éxito el negocio?

## 2 GRAMÁTICA

08-13 to 08-17 Spanish/ English Tutorials

# Los pronombres de complemento indirecto
Stating to whom and for whom things are done

The indirect object indicates *to whom* or *for whom* an action is done. Note these examples:

A: My mom bought this dress *for whom*?

B: She bought this dress *for you*.

A: Yes, she bought *me* this dress.

Review the chart of the indirect object pronouns and their English equivalents:

¿Éste es el vestido que mi madre me compró?

### Los pronombres de complemento indirecto

| | |
|---|---|
| **me** | *to / for me* |
| **te** | *to / for you* |
| **le** | *to / for you* (Ud.) |
| **le** | *to / for him, her* |
| **nos** | *to / for us* |
| **os** | *to / for you all* (vosotros) |
| **les** | *to / for you all* (Uds.) |
| **les** | *to / for them* |

### ¡Explícalo tú!

Now study the sentences and answer the questions that follow.

| Mi madre | **me** | compra mucha ropa. |
|---|---|---|
| Mi madre | **te** | compra mucha ropa. |
| Mi madre | **le** | compra mucha ropa a usted. |
| Mi madre | **le** | compra mucha ropa a mi hermano. |
| Mi madre | **nos** | compra mucha ropa. |
| Mi madre | **os** | compra mucha ropa. |
| Mi madre | **les** | compra mucha ropa a ustedes. |
| Mi madre | **les** | compra mucha ropa a mis hermanos. |

In each of the above sentences:

1. Who is *buying* the clothing?
2. Who is *receiving* the clothing?

 Check your answers to the preceding questions in Appendix 1.

Now, look at the following examples. Identify the **direct objects** and the **indirect object pronouns**.

| | |
|---|---|
| ¿Me traes la falda gris? | *Will you bring me the gray skirt?* |
| Su novio le regaló la chaqueta más formal. | *Her boyfriend gave her the more formal jacket.* |
| Mi hermana me compró la blusa elegante. | *My sister bought me the elegant blouse.* |
| Nuestra compañera de cuarto nos lavó la ropa. | *Our roommate washed our clothes for us.* |

*(continued)*

---

---

**SUGGESTION for *Los pronombres de complemento indirecto***

The authors suggest beginning this presentation with what the students already know—a brief review of the direct object pronouns. You may want to give students a sentence like the following:

Mi madre compró un vestido azul para la fiesta.

Ask students: *¿Qué compró mi madre?* un vestido azul—remind them that direct objects answer the question "what" with regard to the action (verb).

Write two additional sentences on the board and have students tell you what the direct objects are and then rewrite the sentences replacing the direct objects with direct object pronouns.

Juan limpió las botas negras. →
Juan las limpió.

Tina necesita un conjunto nuevo. →
Tina lo necesita.

**SUGGESTION for *Los pronombres de complemento indirecto***

To facilitate learning to use indirect object pronouns you can bring food or candy to class and have students practice serving each other, or loan students objects and have them share them. (*Tom le da el dulce / la manzana / el caramelo a Gina.*) You may try this with articles of clothing as well.

**ANSWERS to 8-7**
1. Yo preparo una fiesta sorpresa para él. / Yo le preparo una fiesta sorpresa.
2. Yo mando invitaciones a todos nuestros amigos. / Yo les mando invitaciones.
3. Mis amigos y yo compramos unos regalos cómicos para ella. / Mis amigos y yo le compramos unos regalos cómicos.
4. Yo hago una torta para nosotros. / Yo nos hago una torta.
5. Mis amigos dan unas flores bonitas a mi madre. / Mis amigos le dan unas flores bonitas.
6. Nosotros cantamos a nuestro amigo una canción especial. / Nosotros le cantamos una canción especial.

**Some things to remember:**

1. Like direct object pronouns, indirect object pronouns *precede* verb forms and can also be *attached to infinitives and present participles* (**-ando, -iendo**).

¿**Me** quieres dar la chaqueta?
¿Quieres dar**me** la chaqueta?
} *Do you want to give me the jacket?*

¿**Me** vas a dar la chaqueta?
¿Vas a dar**me** la chaqueta?
} *Are you going to give me the jacket?*

¿**Me** estás dando la chaqueta?
¿Estás dándo**me** la chaqueta?
} *Are you giving me the jacket?*

Manolo **te** puede comprar la gorra en la tienda.
Manolo puede comprar**te** la gorra en la tienda.
} *Manolo can buy you the cap at the store.*

Su hermano **le** va a regalar una camiseta.
Su hermano va a regalar**le** una camiseta.
} *Her brother is going to give her a T-shirt.*

2. To clarify or emphasize the indirect object, a prepositional phrase (**a** + *prepositional pronoun*) can be added, as in the following sentences. Clarification of **le** and **les** is especially important since they can refer to different people (*him, her, you, them, you all*).

**Le** presto el abrigo **a él** pero no **le** presto nada **a ella**.
*I'm loaning him my coat, but I'm not loaning her anything.* (clarification)

¿**Me** preguntas **a mí**?
*Are you asking me?* (emphasis)

3. It is common for Spanish speakers to include both an indirect object noun and pronoun in the same sentence, especially when the third person form is used. This is most often done to clarify or emphasize something.

> **Fíjate**
> Remember that indirect object pronouns indicate to whom (*a quién*) and for whom (*para quién*) something is done.

---

  **8-7** **Amigos perfectos** Cuando sus mejores amigos celebran sus cumpleaños, tu compañero/a y tú siempre organizan las fiestas. Juntos escriban oraciones sobre las cosas que hacen, usando **me, te, nos, le** y **les**. ■

MODELO    E1: yo / preparar / las fiestas de cumpleaños / para mis amigos

        E2: *Yo preparo las fiestas de cumpleaños para mis amigos. / Les preparo las fiestas.*

1. yo / preparar / una fiesta sorpresa (*surprise*) / para él
2. yo / mandar / invitaciones / a todos nuestros amigos
3. mis amigos y yo / comprar / unos regalos cómicos / para ella
4. yo / hacer / una torta / para nosotros
5. mis amigos / dar / unas flores bonitas / a mi madre
6. nosotros / cantar / a nuestro amigo / una canción especial

**EXPANSION for 8-8**
Play the role of the counselor and have students respond with the appropriate verb and indirect object pronoun changes.

**8-8  ¿Qué me recomienda?** Una persona hace el papel de consejero/a y la otra de estudiante de primer año (*freshman*). Deben hacer y contestar las siguientes preguntas según el modelo. Luego, cambien de papel. ∎

**MODELO**   E1:   ¿Me recomienda usted la clase de Conversación 101?
             E2:   *No, no le recomiendo esa clase. Le recomiendo la clase de civilización española.*

1. ¿Me está pidiendo usted información sobre mi familia?
2. ¿Me recomienda usted algunas clases fáciles?
3. ¿Me ayuda usted con mis estudios?
4. ¿Me recomienda usted jugar algún deporte?
5. ¿Me recomienda usted hablar con mis profesores fuera de clase?
6. ¿Me recomienda usted la cafetería?

Capítulo 3. Los quehaceres de la casa, pág. 109;
Capítulo 7. El pretérito, pág. 263.

**8-9  ¡Qué suerte!** Haz una lista de por lo menos **cuatro** cosas que tú hiciste por tu compañero/a de cuarto o tu familia la semana pasada. Después, haz otra lista de tres o cuatro cosas que esa persona hizo por ti. Compara tu lista con la de un/a compañero/a. ∎

**MODELO**   E1:   *A mi compañero de cuarto le arreglé la sala, le contesté el teléfono…*
             E2:   *Mi compañera de cuarto me buscó unos libros en la biblioteca. También me preparó la comida…*

Capítulo 7. El
pretérito, pág. 263.

**ADDITIONAL ACTIVITY for *Los pronombres de complemento indirecto***

**¡Qué consejos!** Los consejeros normalmente les dan mucha información a los estudiantes nuevos durante la orientación. De los siguientes comentarios posibles, ¿cuáles son probables y cuáles son improbables?

**MODELO**
Les digo que tenemos una universidad muy buena.
E1:  *Nos dice que tenemos una universidad muy buena. Es probable.*
1. Les pido información sobre sus familias.
2. Les pregunto cuáles son sus especialidades.
3. Les doy las reglas (*rules*) de la universidad.
4. Les prometo mi ayuda.
5. Les recomiendo la cafetería.
6. También les recomiendo el restaurante El Pollo Loco.
7. Les explico que no deben (*should not, must not*) estudiar mucho.
8. Les recomiendo clases fáciles.
9. Les digo que pueden salir hasta muy tarde todas las noches.
10. Les digo que no tienen que regresar a la residencia hasta las dos de la mañana.
11. Finalmente, les recomiendo que tomen una clase de español.

**Fíjate**

As in English, there are word "families." *El regalo* (noun) means "gift" and *regalar* (verb) means "to give a gift."

**8-10  Los regalos** ¿Te regalaron muchas cosas este año? ¿Regalaste muchas cosas tú? Escribe una lista de **cuatro** regalos que te dieron y de **cuatro** cosas que tú les regalaste. Luego, comparte tu lista con un/a compañero/a según el modelo. ¡Hay que ser creativos! ∎

**MODELO**   E1:   *Le di una corbata a mi padre.*
             E2:   *¿Ah sí? ¿De qué color? ¿Le gustó a tu padre?*
             E1:   *Sí, le gustó mucho la corbata azul. Y mis padres me regalaron una bicicleta.*
             E2:   *¡Qué suerte! ¿Te gusta montar en bicicleta?*

**NOTE for 8-10**
You may wish to prepare a list of possible "presents" for the students to choose from if time is a factor.

**3 GRAMÁTICA**

08-18 to 08-21 Spanish Tutorial

## *Gustar* y verbos como *gustar*
Expressing likes, dislikes, needs, etc.

¡Me encanta el vestido!

As you already know, the verb **gustar** is used to express likes and dislikes. **Gustar** functions differently from other verbs you have studied so far.

• The person, thing, or idea that is liked is the *subject* (S) of the sentence.
• The person who likes the other person, thing, or idea is the *indirect object* (IO).

Consider the chart below:

| | | | |
|---|---|---|---|
| (A mí) | **me** | gusta el traje. | *I like the suit.* |
| (A ti) | **te** | gusta el traje. | *You like the suit.* |
| (A Ud.) | **le** | gusta el traje. | *You like the suit.* |
| (A él) | **le** | gusta el traje. | *He likes the suit.* |
| (A ella) | **le** | gusta el traje. | *She likes the suit.* |
| (A nosotros/as) | **nos** | gusta el traje. | *We like the suit.* |
| (A vosotros/as) | **os** | gusta el traje. | *You (all) like the suit.* |
| (A Uds.) | **les** | gusta el traje. | *You (all) like the suit.* |
| (A ellos/as) | **les** | gusta el traje. | *They like the suit.* |

**Note the following:**

1. The construction **a** + *pronoun* (**a mí, a ti, a él,** etc.) or **a** + *noun* is optional most of the time. It is used for clarification or emphasis. Clarification of **le gusta** and **les gusta** is especially important since the indirect object pronouns **le** and **les** can refer to different people (*him, her, you, them, you all*).

**A él le gusta** llevar ropa cómoda. (clarification) — *He likes to wear comfortable clothes.*
**A Ana le gusta** llevar pantalones cortos. (clarification) — *Ana likes to wear shorts.*
**Me gustan** esos pantalones largos. — *I like those long pants.*
**A mí me gustan** más esos cortos. (emphasis) — *I like those short ones even more.*

2. Use the plural form **gustan** when what is liked (the subject of the sentence) is plural.

Me gusta **el traje.** → Me gusta**n los trajes.**
*I like the suit.* — *I like the suits.*

3. To express the idea that one likes *to do* something, **gustar** is followed by an infinitive. In that case you always use the singular **gusta,** even when you use more than one infinitive in the sentence:

**Me gusta ir** de compras por la mañana. — *I like to go shopping in the morning.*
A Pepe **le gusta leer** revistas de moda y **llevar** ropa atrevida. — *Pepe likes to read fashion magazines and wear daring clothing.*
**Nos gusta llevar** zapatos cómodos cuando hacemos ejercicio. — *We like to wear comfortable shoes when we exercise.*

**ADDITIONAL ACTIVITY for**
*Gustar y verbos como gustar*

**Ideas incompletas** Completa las siguientes oraciones. Después, compártelas con un/a compañero/a.

1. En invierno me encanta(n)…
2. A mis profesores les molesta(n)…
3. A mi mejor amigo/a no le importa(n)…
4. A los estudiantes de español les fascina(n)…
5. A mis compañeros de clase y a mí nos hace(n) falta…

**NOTE for Gustar *y verbos como* gustar**

The authors have chosen to introduce a manageable number of verbs at this point. You may prefer to add some additional verbs such as *aburrir, faltar, interesar,* and *parecer.* Students will practice *quedar bien* and *quedar mal* in *Comunicación II.*

**EXPANSION for 8-11**

Challenge students to create as many sentences as they can in a set amount of time with *gustar* and *gustar*-type verbs using music as the context. Then give students another context and repeat.

The verbs listed below function like **gustar**:

| | |
|---|---|
| **encantar** | *to love; to like very much* |
| **fascinar** | *to fascinate* |
| **hacer falta** | *to need; to be lacking* |
| **importar** | *to matter; to be important* |
| **molestar** | *to bother* |

**Me encanta** ir de compras.

*I love to go shopping. (I like shopping very much.)*

A Doug y a David **les fascina** la tienda de ropa Rugby.

*The Rugby clothing store fascinates (is fascinating to) Doug and David.*

¿**Te hace falta** dinero para comprar el vestido?

*Do you need (are you lacking) money to buy the dress?*

A Juan **le importa** el precio de la ropa, no la moda.

*The price of the clothing, not the style, matters (is important) to Juan.*

**Nos molestan** las personas que llevan sandalias en invierno.

*People who wear sandals in the winter bother us.*

 Capítulo 5. El mundo de la música, pág. 172.

 **8-11 Hablando de la música…** A Jaime y a Celia les gusta mucho la música. Completa las siguientes oraciones para descubrir sus preferencias. Después, comparte tu párrafo con un/a compañero/a. ■

**MODELO**     A nosotros *nos fascina* (fascinar) la música rap.

A nosotros (1) __nos encanta__ (encantar) la música rock. A mí (2) __me gustan__ (gustar) los grupos como AC/DC y Metallica. Mi cantante favorito es Dave Matthews y (3) __me gusta__ (gustar) su grupo también. A Celia (4) __le fascina__ (fascinar) el grupo Nickleback. Celia tiene casi todos los CD pero, (5) __le hace falta__ (hacer falta) uno que se llama *Running with Dark Horse*. A nuestros compañeros (6) __les molesta__ (molestar) tener que escuchar nuestra música favorita. Ellos prefieren la música jazz. A Celia y a mí no (7) __nos importa__ (importar) su opinión, ¡somos amigos pero no nos tienen que gustar las mismas cosas siempre!

3:00  Workbooklet

**8-12 ¿Qué opinas?** Da tu opinión sobre esta ropa poniendo una equis (**X**) en la columna apropiada de cada hilera (*row*). Luego, comparte tu opinión con un/a compañero/a. ■

MODELO
E1: *¿Te fascinan los vestidos de Carolina Herrera?*
E2: *Sí, me fascinan. / No, no me importan mucho. / No sé, no los conozco.*

| | (NO) ME FASCINA(N) | (NO) ME ENCANTA(N) | NO ME IMPORTA(N) MUCHO | NO LO(S)/LA(S) CONOZCO |
|---|---|---|---|---|
| 1. los vestidos de Carolina Herrera | | | | |
| 2. un traje de Armani | | | | |
| 3. una camisa y corbata de Zara | | | | |
| 4. una sudadera | | | | |
| 5. un conjunto | | | | |

**Instructor Resources**
• PPT, Extra Activities

Capítulo 2. Las materias y las especialidades, pág. 62; En la universidad, pág. 74; Los deportes y los pasatiempos, pág. 81.

Workbooklet

**8-13 En mi opinión...** ¿Qué te gusta y no te gusta de tu universidad? ■

**Paso 1** Completa el siguiente cuadro según tu opinión.

| ME MOLESTA(N)... | ME ENCANTA(N)... | NOS HACE(N) FALTA... |
|---|---|---|
| 1. | 1. | 1. |
| 2. | 2. | 2. |
| 3. | 3. | 3. |

**Paso 2** Ahora, circula por la clase para pedirles a tres compañeros sus opiniones.

**MODELO** E1 (Tú): ¿Qué te molesta?

E2: Me molesta la comida de la cafetería.

| A _____ LE MOLESTA(N)... | A _____ LE ENCANTA(N)... | NOS HACE(N) FALTA... |
|---|---|---|
| 1. | 1. | 1. |
| 2. | 2. | 2. |
| 3. | 3. | 3. |

**ADDITIONAL ACTIVITY for Gustar y verbos como gustar**

**Preferencias** ¿Qué opinas? Responde a estas situaciones usando **encantar, fascinar, importar** y **molestar**. Comparte tus respuestas con un/a compañero/a.

MODELO
E1: *comprar ropa en Target*
E2: *Me encanta comprar ropa en Target. / No me gusta comprar ropa en Target.*
1. llevar sandalias en el invierno
2. tener que ponerme (*put on*) ropa formal
3. correr con zapatos elegantes
4. ponerme un traje de baño
5. llevar pantalones sin cinturón

**METHODOLOGY • Grammar Presentations**
In addition to having students read the grammar presentations outside of class, you can assign two to three mechanical activities from the Student Activities Manual or MySpanishLab for students to practice the new grammar point. This allows students to come to class better prepared and more confident. You also have available the Extra Activities where you can find additional practice to offer your students. *¡Anda! Curso elemental* offers a great deal of student support and additional practice on MySpanishLab.

**ADDITIONAL ACTIVITY for Los pronombres de complemento indirecto**
If your students need additional practice with direct object pronouns prior to studying indirect object pronouns, try this activity:

**¿Quién habla?** Estás en una tienda de ropa y escuchas una conversación entre una madre y su hija. Aquí tienes partes de esa conversación. ¿Quién dijo cada oración: la madre o la hija?

MODELO Debes comprar ropa más formal.
*Lo dijo la madre.*
1. Te recomiendo comprar ropa menos atrevida.
2. Te prometo estudiar mucho.
3. Te compro estos pantalones azules si sacas buenas notas en el examen de español.
4. Kiko me invitó a un baile formal. ¿Me compras un vestido elegante?
5. Considera la ropa más barata.

 ¡Hola! Spanish Tutorial

08-22 to 08-26

**4 GRAMÁTICA**

# Los pronombres de complemento directo e indirecto usados juntos
Conveying information about people and things

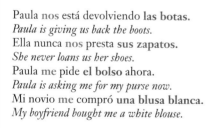

¡Me encanta la elegante blusa verde!

¿Sí, amor? Pues, entramos. Te la compro ahora mismo.

You have worked with two types of object pronouns, direct and indirect. Now, note how they are used together in the same sentence.

Paula **nos** está devolviendo **las botas**.
*Paula is giving us back the boots.*
→ Paula **nos las** está devolviendo.
*Paula is giving them back to us.*

Ella nunca **nos** presta **sus zapatos**.
*She never loans us her shoes.*
→ Ella nunca **nos los** presta.
*She never loans them to us.*

Paula **me** pide **el bolso** ahora.
*Paula is asking me for my purse now.*
→ Paula **me lo** pide ahora.
*Paula is asking me for it now.*

Mi novio **me** compró **una blusa blanca**.
*My boyfriend bought me a white blouse.*
→ Mi novio **me la** compró.
*My boyfriend bought it for me.*

*(continued)*

## ¡Explícalo tú!

1. You know that direct and indirect objects come after verbs. Where do you find the direct and indirect object pronouns?
2. Reading from left to right, which pronoun comes first (direct or indirect)? Which pronoun comes second?

 Check your answers for the preceding questions in Appendix 1.

**¡OJO!** A change occurs when you use **le** or **les** along with a direct object pronoun that begins with **l:** (**lo, la, los, las**): **le** or **les** changes to **se.**

**le → se**

| | |
|---|---|
| Paula le pide **el bolso** a mi hermana. | → Paula se **lo** pide. |
| Su novio no le compró **una chaqueta.** | → Su novio no se **la** compró. |
| Su novio le va a comprar **un traje.** | → Su novio se **lo** va a comprar. |

**les → se**

| | |
|---|---|
| Paula les devuelve **las botas.** | → Paula se **las** devuelve. |
| Yo le presto **mis zapatos.** | → Yo se **los** presto. |
| Paula nunca les presta **sus cosas.** | → Paula nunca se **las** presta. |

Direct and indirect object pronouns may also be attached to infinitives and present participles. Note that when attached, an accent is placed over the final vowel of the infinitive and the next-to-last vowel of the participle.

¿Aquel abrigo? Mi madre **me lo** va a comprar.
¿Aquel abrigo? Mi madre va a comprár**melo.** } *That coat over there? My mother is going to buy it for me.*

**Me lo** está comprando ahora.
Está comprándo**melo** ahora. } *She is buying it for me now.*

[3:00]

Capítulo 7: El pretérito, pág. 263; Algunos verbos irregulares en el pretérito, pág. 272.

## 8-14 Combinaciones

Escribe oraciones completas sobre lo que dijo Pablo sobre su hermano Antonio. Sigue el modelo, primero usando el complemento indirecto y después los pronombres de complemento indirecto y directos juntos. Comparte tus oraciones con un/a compañero/a. ■

**MODELO**    Mi hermano Antonio / prestar / (a mí) / sus zapatos favoritos / ayer
*Mi hermano Antonio* **me prestó** *sus zapatos favoritos ayer.*
*Mi hermano Antonio* **me los** *prestó ayer.*

1. Yo / dar / (a Antonio) / unos jeans / la semana pasada
2. Mis padres / regalar / (a Antonio) / un traje formal / el año pasado
3. Yo / lavar / la ropa / (a Antonio) / anteayer
4. Antonio / pedir / dinero para comprar una gorra / (a mí) / anoche
5. Antonio y yo / decir / la verdad sobre el accidente / (a nuestros padres) / ayer

**8-15** **Antonio, ¿me prestas…?** Ahora Pablo va a una fiesta y quiere usar la ropa de su hermano Antonio. Túrnense para hacer los papeles de Pablo y Antonio usando los pronombres de complemento directo e indirecto. ■

**MODELO**   prestar / un abrigo

    E1 (Pablo):    *¿Me prestas el abrigo?*

    E2 (Antonio):    *Sí, te lo presto. / No, no te lo presto.*

1. prestar / los zapatos negros
2. prestar / la corbata azul
3. prestar / una camiseta blanca y una camisa azul de manga larga (*long sleeved*)
4. prestar / el cinturón negro
5. prestar / tu abrigo nuevo

---

Workbooklet

**8-16** **Mis recomendaciones** ¿Qué recomiendas? Lee la lista y pon una equis (**X**) en la columna apropiada. Después, comparte tus opiniones con un/a compañero/a según el modelo. ■

**MODELO**   los libros de Tom Clancy (a tus primas)

    E1:    *¿Les recomiendas los libros de Tom Clancy a tus primas?*

    E2:    *No, no se los recomiendo.*

| | SÍ | NO |
|---|---|---|
| 1. las novelas de Stephen King (a tus tíos) | | |
| 2. la música de Eminem (a tu compañero/a de cuarto) | | |
| 3. el restaurante Taco Bell (a nosotros) | | |
| 4. la tienda Macy's (a tu amiga que no tiene mucho dinero) | | |
| 5. la película *Drácula* (a tus primos de cinco años) | | |
| 6. Disney World (a tu hermano) | | |
| 7. el Museo de Arte Moderno (a tu profesor/a) | | |
| 8. la clase de español (a tu mejor amigo/a) | | |

**ANSWERS to 8-15**

1. ¿Me prestas los zapatos negros? Sí, te los presto. / No, no te los presto.
2. ¿Me prestas la corbata azul? Sí, te la presto. / No, no te la presto.
3. ¿Me prestas una camiseta blanca y una camisa azul de manga larga? Sí, te las presto. / No, no te las presto.
4. ¿Me prestas el cinturón negro? Sí, te lo presto. / No, no te lo presto.
5. ¿Me prestas tu abrigo nuevo? Sí, te lo presto. / No, no te lo presto.

**EXPANSION for 8-16**
Have students personalize this activity by substituting the proper nouns with their own choices and/or changing the persons to whom the recommendations are given.

**EXPANSION for 8-16**
Take a survey and compile results of what students would recommend and what they would not recommend to the persons indicated.

**EXPANSION for 8-16**
Have students work in small groups to create a new list of things to recommend (or not) to specific people. You may choose to encourage them to be as creative and/or humorous as possible.

**EXPANSION for 8-17**

Have students create a new set of questions between employer and employee beginning with a different phrase (or a variety of phrases), e.g., *¿Me puede decir por qué usted no me contestó los emails que le mandé ayer? (No se los contesté porque no tuve tiempo.) ¿Me puede decir por qué no me trajo el periódico esta mañana? (No se lo traje porque no lo pude encontrar.) ¿Me puede decir por qué no me dio la información sobre el nuevo cliente? (No se la di porque el nuevo cliente decidió no trabajar con nosotros.) ¿Me puede decir por qué no me buscó unas recepcionistas nuevas? (No se las busqué porque tuve que hacer muchas otras cosas esta semana.)* You may also want to change the scenario to designer / model, restaurant cook / waiter, professor / student, parent / child, etc.

**EXPANSION for 8-17**

After completing this activity, have students role-play the situations between the assistant and his/her boss.

**ANSWERS to 8-17**

1. Sí, se lo puedo traer. / Sí, puedo traérselo.
2. Sí, se los puedo comprar. / Sí, puedo comprárselos.
3. Sí, se los puedo arreglar. / Sí, puedo arreglárselos.
4. Sí, se lo puedo buscar. / Sí, puedo buscárselo.
5. Sí, se la puedo reservar. / Sí, puedo reservársela.
6. Sí, se las puedo comprar. / Sí, puedo comprárselas.

[4:00]  **8-17** **¿En qué puedo servirle?**

Acabas de empezar una pasantía (*internship*). En vez de (*Instead of*) tareas asociadas con la profesión que te interesa seguir, te dan el trabajo de ayudante de una de las vicepresidentas. Túrnense para contestar sus preguntas. ∎

**MODELO**    E1:   ¿Me puede comprar un periódico?

           E2:   *Sí, se lo puedo comprar. / Sí, puedo comprárselo.*

**Estrategia**

Remember that when addressing an employer, you would use *usted*, not *tú*. Also, be sure to practice both ways of structuring the sentence with two object pronouns, as in the *modelo*.

1. ¿Me puede traer un café?
2. ¿Me puede comprar los boletos (*tickets*) para un viaje a Nueva York?
3. ¿Me puede arreglar los apuntes y los papeles para la reunión de esta tarde?
4. ¿Me puede buscar un artículo en el periódico?
5. ¿Me puede reservar una mesa en un restaurante elegante para esta noche?
6. ¿Me puede comprar unas rosas para la recepcionista? Es su cumpleaños hoy.

## ¿Cómo andas? I

|  | Feel confident | Need to review |
|---|:---:|:---:|
| Having completed **Comunicación I**, I now can . . . | | |
| • describe clothing (p. 294) | ☐ | ☐ |
| • pronounce the letters *ll* and *ñ* (MSL / SAM) | ☐ | ☐ |
| • recount information about a Spanish clothing company (p. 298) | ☐ | ☐ |
| • state to whom and for whom things are done (p. 299) | ☐ | ☐ |
| • express likes, dislikes, needs, etc., (p. 302) | ☐ | ☐ |
| • convey information about people and things (p. 305) | ☐ | ☐ |

# Comunicación II

**Instructor Resources**
- Textbook images, Extra Activities

**SECTION GOALS for**
*Comunicación II*
By the end of the *Comunicación* section, students will be able to:
- describe textures and patterns of articles of clothing and suggest appropriate clothing for different seasons and occasions.
- discuss their daily routines using reflexive and non-reflexive verbs.
- describe shopping centers in Latin America.
- use the imperfect forms for regular and irregular verbs correctly.
- explain when to use the imperfect.
- recognize key words that signal the imperfect.
- narrate what they used to do as children using the imperfect.

**METHODOLOGY • Teaching Vocabulary**
Help students organize the new vocabulary by using drawings, examples, and semantic maps. For teaching *la tela,* for example, you could bring in clothing made of each fabric and allow them to feel the texture as you explain what each word is. You could point out the patterns of students' clothing or draw examples on the board of *cuadros, lunares,* and *rayas.* Find photos that illustrate the adjectives or draw stick figures on the board and describe each item. You could also organize the vocabulary by theme, such as fabric, and draw a thematic map on the board to help them organize their learning.

## 5 VOCABULARIO

**Las telas y los materiales** Providing details about clothing

08-27 to 08-29

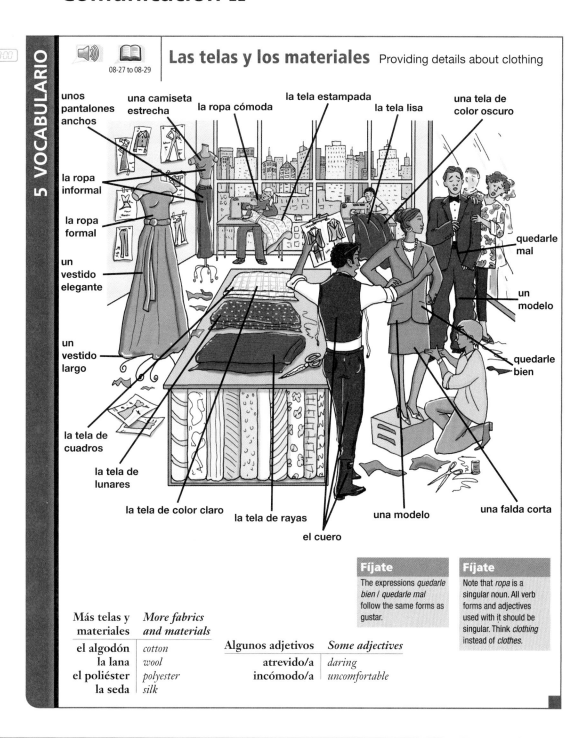

unos pantalones anchos
una camiseta estrecha
la ropa cómoda
la tela estampada
la tela lisa
una tela de color oscuro
la ropa informal
la ropa formal
un vestido elegante
quedarle mal
un modelo
un vestido largo
quedarle bien
la tela de cuadros
la tela de lunares
la tela de color claro
la tela de rayas
el cuero
una modelo
una falda corta

| **Fíjate** |
| --- |
| The expressions *quedarle bien / quedarle mal* follow the same forms as *gustar.* |

| **Fíjate** |
| --- |
| Note that *ropa* is a singular noun. All verb forms and adjectives used with it should be singular. Think *clothing* instead of *clothes.* |

| Más telas y materiales | *More fabrics and materials* |
| --- | --- |
| el algodón | *cotton* |
| la lana | *wool* |
| el poliéster | *polyester* |
| la seda | *silk* |

| Algunos adjetivos | *Some adjectives* |
| --- | --- |
| atrevido/a | *daring* |
| incómodo/a | *uncomfortable* |

**ADDITIONAL ACTIVITY for *Las telas y los materiales***
**¿Tienes una memoria fotográfica?** Mira alrededor de la clase por quince segundos. Cierra los ojos y en un minuto, describe con detalles quién lleva puesto qué. Di por lo menos cinco oraciones. Túrnense.

**MODELO**
*Mark lleva una camiseta estampada y unos pantalones negros. Brenda lleva unas botas negras, una falda y un suéter. Julie lleva unos tenis, unos jeans y una chaqueta azul. Los tenis son amarillos. La chaqueta es estrecha e informal.*

**8-18 Los opuestos** Túrnense para decir el opuesto de cada una de las siguientes palabras. ■

1. ancho   estrecho
2. formal   informal
3. quedarle bien   quedarle mal
4. claro   oscuro
5. corto   largo
6. liso   estampado

**8-19 Definiciones** Túrnense para elegir una palabra o expresión para completar cada oración. ■

1. Cuando hace mucho frío, prefiero llevar un abrigo de…
   a. rayas   b. poliéster   c. lana

2. El padre de Ana está furioso porque ella salió de casa con un vestido muy…
   a. elegante   b. atrevido   c. ancho

3. La tela de ___algodón___ viene de una planta.
   a. algodón   b. cuero   c. poliéster

4. A mi madre no le importa mucho ___la moda___. Siempre prefiere llevar ropa cómoda y barata.
   a. el modelo   b. la moda   c. la seda

5. Mi padre dice que quiere proteger (*protect*) los animales. Por eso nunca lleva ropa…
   a. lisa   b. estampada   c. de cuero

6. A mi amigo le encanta la ropa ___oscura___ porque dice que "su color" es el negro.
   a. lisa   b. clara   c. oscura

**8-20 ¡A dibujar!** Completa los siguientes pasos. ■

**Paso 1** Dibuja a un hombre o una mujer con cualquier (*whatever*) ropa que quieras. Incluye diferentes telas y materiales en el dibujo.

**Paso 2** Descríbele tu dibujo a un/a compañero/a, quien tiene que dibujar lo que tú le dices. Luego cambien de papel.

**MODELO** *El hombre lleva un sombrero negro muy elegante. Lleva un traje azul oscuro muy elegante, una camisa blanca y una corbata azul con rayas rojas…*

METHODOLOGY • Visual
Organizers
It is helpful to have a file of pictures of
clothing from magazines, preferably
mounted on stiff paper. These can be
used in a variety of ways, from activities
like **8-22** to warm-ups for class. If you do
not have pictures already collected and
in your files, have students gather them
for you.

**8-21** **¿Cuál es tu conjunto favorito?** Usa las siguientes
preguntas para entrevistar a un/a compañero/a sobre su conjunto favorito. ■

1. ¿Cuál es tu conjunto favorito?
2. ¿De qué color es?
3. ¿De qué tela es?
4. ¿De qué estilo es?
5. ¿Lo compraste tú? Si no, ¿quién te lo compró?
6. ¿Cuándo lo compraste o cuándo te lo compraron?
7. ¿Dónde lo compraste o dónde te lo compraron?
8. ¿Cuándo lo llevas?
9. ¿Por qué te gusta tanto?

**8-22** **¿Qué está de moda?** Trae a la clase tres o cuatro fotos de
modelos (pueden ser de una revista [*magazine*], un catálogo o del Internet).
Túrnate con un/a compañero/a para describir en por lo menos **tres** oraciones la
ropa que llevan los modelos. Digan qué ropa les gusta más y qué ropa no les gusta.
¿Están de acuerdo? ■

MODELO   *La primera modelo de Carolina Herrera lleva un vestido corto. Es negro y muy*
         *elegante. Su bolso es beige y es pequeño…*

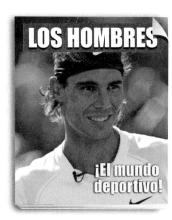

**8-23** **¿Quién puede ser?** Escoge a una persona de tu clase y piensa en
la ropa que lleva incluyendo el estilo (*style*), el color y la tela. Describe **cuatro** de sus
prendas a tu compañero/a, quien tiene que adivinar a quién describes. Túrnense para
describir a **tres** compañeros de clase. ■

Capítulo 3, Los colores,
pág. 111.

MODELO   E1:  *Esta persona lleva unos pantalones largos de rayas blancas, una camiseta*
              *oscura, una chaqueta informal y unos tenis blancos.*
         E2:  *Es Mayra.*

**6 GRAMÁTICA**

08-30 to 08-35   ¡Hola! Spanish/English Tutorials

## Las construcciones reflexivas   Relating daily routines

Study the captions for the
following drawings.

In each drawing:

• Who is performing / doing the
  action?
• Who or what is receiving the
  action?

**When the subject both performs
and receives the action of
the verb, a reflexive verb and
pronoun are used.**

• Which of the drawings and
  captions demonstrate reflexive
  verbs?

Look at the following chart: the
reflexive pronouns are highlighted.

La fiesta **los** despierta.

Alberto **la** acuesta.

Beatriz **lo** lava.

Raúl y Gloria **se**
despiertan.

Alberto **se** acuesta.

Beatriz **se** lava.

**Reflexive pronouns**

| Yo | me | divierto | en las fiestas. |
|----|----|----------|-----------------|
| Tú | te | diviertes | en las fiestas. |
| Usted | se | divierte | en las fiestas. |
| Él / Ella | se | divierte | en las fiestas. |
| Nosotros | nos | divertimos | en las fiestas. |
| Vosotros | os | divertís | en las fiestas. |
| Ustedes | se | divierten | en las fiestas. |
| Ellos / Ellas | se | divierten | en las fiestas. |

Reflexive pronouns follow the same rules for position as other object pronouns. Reflexive pronouns:

1. precede conjugated verbs.
2. can be attached to *infinitives* and *present participles* (**-ando, -iendo**).

**Te** vas a dormir.
Vas a dormir**te**.  } *You are falling asleep.*

¿**Se** van a dormir esta noche?
¿Van a dormir**se** esta noche?  } *Are they going to fall asleep tonight?*

¿**Se** están durmiendo?
¿Están durmiéndo**se**?  } *Are you all falling asleep?*

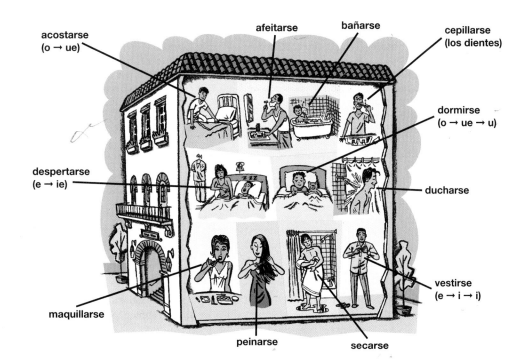

acostarse (o → ue)
afeitarse
bañarse
cepillarse (los dientes)
despertarse (e → ie)
dormirse (o → ue → u)
ducharse
maquillarse
peinarse
secarse
vestirse (e → i → i)

### Algunos verbos reflexivos

| | | | |
|---|---|---|---|
| acordarse de (o → ue) | to remember | ponerse (nervioso/a) | to get (nervous) |
| arreglarse | to get ready | probarse (o → ue) la ropa | to try on clothing |
| callarse | to get / keep quiet | quedarse | to stay; to remain |
| divertirse (e → ie → i) | to enjoy oneself; to have fun | quitarse (la ropa) | to take off (one's clothes) |
| irse | to go away; to leave | reunirse | to get together; |
| lavarse | to wash oneself | | to meet |
| levantarse | to get up; to stand up | sentarse (e → ie) | to sit down |
| llamarse | to be called | sentirse (e → ie → i) | to feel |
| ponerse (la ropa) | to put on (one's clothes) | | |

**Note:** To identify all of the previous verbs as *reflexive*, the infinitives end in **-se.**

### Estrategia

When a new infinitive is presented, if it is a stem-changing verb, the irregularities will be given in parentheses. For example, if you see *divertirse (e → ie → i)* you know that this infinitive is an *-ir* stem-changing verb, that the first "e" in the infinitive changes to "ie" in the present indicative, and that the "e" changes to "i" in the third-person singular and plural of the preterit.

### Fíjate

Some verbs change their meanings slightly between non-reflexive and reflexive verbs, for example: *dormir* (to sleep) and *dormirse* (to fall asleep); *ir* (to go) and *irse* (to leave).

**METHODOLOGY • Recycling**
This is a good opportunity to recycle and remind students what the **e → ie → i** notation means.

**METHODOLOGY • Reviewing and Recycling Grammatical Concepts**
You may wish to have a warm-up each day at the beginning of class in which you select different verbs and vocabulary words from this and previous chapters. For example, you can do a quick mechanical drill with the forms of different tenses, such as the *pretérito* from *Capítulo 7*. You can also end a class with a quick mechanical drill. These quick reviews should last no more than 2 minutes.

**ADDITIONAL ACTIVITY for *Las construcciones reflexivas***

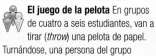 **El juego de la pelota** En grupos de cuatro a seis estudiantes, van a tirar (*throw*) una pelota de papel. Turnándose, una persona del grupo nombra uno de los verbos reflexivos y un sujeto, y tira la pelota a un/a compañero/a. Si el/la compañero/a dice la forma correcta, gana un punto y tiene que continuar el juego. Cuando terminen, jueguen otra vez con los verbos en el pretérito.

MODELO
E1: ducharse… yo (tira la pelota)
E2: *me ducho*
E2: vestirse… mi madre (tira la pelota)
E3: *mi madre se viste*
E3: acordarse… tú (tira la pelota)
E4: *te acuerdas*

**NOTE for 8-25**

**INSTRUCTIONS:** Draw a 9-square tic-tac-toe board and write a different reflexive verb in each of the 9 squares. With a partner, and without showing your squares, play tic-tac-toe. For example, your partner says one of the verbs. If the verb is in your square, mark an X on the verb; if not, you don't have to do anything. Now you have to say one of your verbs, and you take turns until one of you has 3 Xs in a row going horizontally, vertically, or diagonally.

**NOTE for 8-25**

You may wish to tell your students that Tic-tac-toe is "Tres en raya" or "Taeti"

**METHODOLOGY • Pair Work**

You will want to identify daily who is Student "A" and who is Student "B," and then ask Student "A" to do the even-numbered items while Student "B" does the odd items. It is important for you to tell students explicitly to take turns when working in pairs. If not, one student may tend to monopolize the pair work.

**NOTE for 8-26**

You may wish to begin this activity by having students change the preterit forms of the reflexive verbs into the present tense.

**TPR ACTIVITY for 8-26**

Use **8-26** as a model to narrate a typical day using reflexive verbs. You can talk about your day or what we do, as in *primero nos despertamos y nos levantamos,* and have students act out the actions along with you. If you add extra information that is not in the book, make sure you write down those verbs so they can see them as they act out the day.

**HERITAGE LANGUAGE LEARNERS**

Have each student create his/her own complete "Un día en la vida" for a particular day and time of the year, school-related or not. Then collect their "lists" and read them aloud as they guess who wrote each one. Finally, discuss the similarities and differences in their days.

**ANSWERS for 8-26**

**El día de María**

1. Se levantó.
2. Se duchó.
3. Se secó.
4. Se maquilló. / Se vistió.
5. Se maquilló. / Se vistió.
6. Antes de irse a la universidad, se acordó de la tarea que no hizo para su clase de historia.
7. Llegó a la clase de historia y se quitó el abrigo.

**El día de Tomás**

1. Se despertó tarde.
2. Se levantó rápidamente a las ocho.
3. Se fue para la clase de química.
4. Después de las clases se fue con los amigos para pasar el fin de semana en la playa.
5. Se divirtió con sus amigos.
6. Se acostó tarde.
7. No se durmió inmediatamente.

  **8-24** ## El juego de la asociación   Juntos decidan qué verbos reflexivos asocian con las siguientes palabras y expresiones. ■

1. no decir nada   callarse
2. una silla   sentarse
3. recordar algo   acordarse
4. tener sueño   dormirse
5. no recordar algo   olvidarse de

6. triste o alegre, por ejemplo   ponerse / sentirse
7. un sombrero   ponerse
8. estar sucio   lavarse / ducharse / bañarse
9. no ir a ningún lugar   quedarse

**8-25** ## ¡Batalla!   Va a jugar con un/a compañero/a a *tic-tac-toe.* Escuchen mientras el/la profesor/a les explica el juego. ■

 Capítulo 7. El pretérito, pág. 263. Algunos verbos irregulares en el pretérito, pág. 272.

**8-26** ## Un día en la vida   Ordena las actividades diarias de María y Tomás, estudiantes universitarios en Argentina, de forma cronológica. Luego, compara tu lista con la de un/a compañero/a. ■

**El día de María**

1. Antes de irse a la universidad, se acordó de la tarea que no hizo para su clase de historia.
2. Se duchó.
3. Se maquilló.
4. Llegó a la clase de historia y se quitó el abrigo.
5. Se vistió.
6. Se secó.
7. Se levantó.

**El día de Tomás**

1. Se acostó tarde.
2. Se levantó rápidamente a las ocho.
3. Se despertó tarde.
4. No se durmió inmediatamente.
5. Se divirtió con sus amigos.
6. Después de las clases se fue con los amigos para pasar el fin de semana en la playa.
7. Se fue para la clase de química.

Capítulo Preliminar
A. La hora, pág. 18.

**8-27** **Un día normal** Escribe por lo menos **cinco** actividades que haces normalmente y a qué hora las haces. Usa verbos reflexivos. Después, comparte tu lista con un/a compañero/a. ■

**8-28** **Para conocerte mejor** Túrnense para hacerse esta entrevista y conocer mejor sus hábitos. ■

MODELO     E1:  ¿Qué te pones para ir al cine?

E2:  *Me pongo los jeans con una camiseta. ¿Y tú? ¿Qué te pones?*

E1:  *Generalmente me pongo pantalones con una blusa o un suéter.*

E2:  *¿Qué…?*

1. ¿Qué te pones cuando sales con esa "persona especial"?
2. Cuando estás durmiéndote, ¿te acuerdas de las cosas que no hiciste durante el día?
3. ¿Cómo te diviertes?
4. Si tienes tiempo, ¿con quién(es) te reúnes?
5. ¿Cuándo te pones nervioso/a?
6. ¿Cuándo te sientes feliz?

**8-29** **Mímica** Hagan mímica (*charades*) en grupos de cuatro. Túrnense para escoger un verbo reflexivo para representar al grupo. El grupo tiene que adivinar qué verbo es. Sigan jugando hasta que cada estudiante represente **cuatro** verbos diferentes. ■

**8-30** **¿Conoces bien a tus compañeros?** Trabaja en grupos de cuatro para hacer esta actividad. ■

Paso 1     Un/a compañero/a debe salir de la sala de clase por un momento. Los otros estudiantes escriben **cinco** preguntas sobre la vida diaria del/de la compañero/a, usando los verbos reflexivos.

MODELO     *¿A qué hora te despiertas?*

*¿Te duchas todos los días?*

Paso 2     Antes de entrar el/la compañero/a, el grupo de estudiantes debe adivinar cuáles van a ser las respuestas a esas preguntas.

MODELO     *Se despierta a las siete.*

*Sí, se ducha todos los días.*

Paso 3     Entra el/la compañero/a y los otros le hacen las preguntas.

Paso 4     Comparen las respuestas del grupo con las del/de la compañero/a. ¿Tenían razón? Pueden repetir la actividad con los otros miembros del grupo.

**NOTE for 8-27**
You may choose to make **8-27** a writing activity:

MODELO     *Me despierto a las ocho y me levanto inmediatamente. Después…*

**EXPANSION for 8-27**
You may wish to ask your students about their daily routines this morning and last night: e.g., *¿Qué hiciste esta mañana? ¿Qué hiciste anoche?*

**FOLLOW-UP for 8-28**
You can ask questions so that your students use the third person: e.g., *¿Qué se pone _____ cuando sale con esa "persona especial"? ¿Cómo se divierten _____ y _____ cuando salen? ¿Cuándo se sienten _____ y _____ felices?* etc.

## NOTA CULTURAL

`4:00`

# Los centros comerciales en Latinoamérica

08-36

Ir de compras en Latinoamérica se asocia muchas veces con los mercados al aire libre donde se vende la artesanía y la comida típica de la región. Es cierto que estos lugares existen y son muy populares, sobre todo con los turistas. Pero en las últimas décadas ha surgido (*has emerged*) la cultura del centro comercial y los grandes almacenes en las sociedades latinoamericanas.

Los grandes centros comerciales, como los Unicentros en El Salvador y los centros Sambil en Venezuela, las tiendas de Falabella en Chile, Argentina y Perú, y los almacenes Liverpool en México, son buenos ejemplos de mercados modernos que atraen a la población latina de varias clases económicas. Estas tiendas son modernas y ofrecen de todo a los clientes que buscan una gran variedad de productos como, por ejemplo, ropa, artículos y aparatos domésticos y muebles.

La gente va a los centros comerciales para pasear, mirar y entretenerse (*to entertain oneself*). En muchos hay hipermercados donde se puede comprar comida y artículos diversos para el hogar. Los centros comerciales son lugares para citas, para pasar el tiempo, para ir al cine, para reunirse con amigos, para observar a la gente, para ojear las vitrinas (*window shop*) y para enterarse de las últimas tendencias de la moda. Verdaderamente, estos centros han cambiado (*have changed*) mucho el estilo de vida de la gente hoy en día.

### Preguntas

1. Antes de leer "Los centros comerciales en Latinoamérica", ¿qué entendías tú (*did you understand*) por "mercado latinoamericano"? ¿Qué imagen tenías (*did you used to have*)?
2. ¿Qué hace la gente en los centros comerciales latinoamericanos? ¿Cómo se comparan estas actividades con las de los centros comerciales estadounidenses?

**7 GRAMÁTICA**

 ¡Hola! Spanish/English Tutorials
08-37 to 08-41

## El imperfecto
Sharing about situations in the past and how things used to be

Cuando Pepe vivía en la playa, nadaba en el mar todas las mañanas.

In **Capítulo 7** you learned how to express certain ideas and notions that happened in the past with the preterit. Spanish has another past tense, **el imperfecto,** that *expresses habitual or ongoing past actions, provides descriptions,* or *describes conditions.*

|            | -ar: hablar | -er: comer | -ir: vivir |
|------------|-------------|------------|------------|
| yo         | hablaba     | comía      | vivía      |
| tú         | hablabas    | comías     | vivías     |
| Ud.        | hablaba     | comía      | vivían     |
| él, ella   | hablaba     | comía      | vivía      |
| nosotros/as| hablábamos  | comíamos   | vivíamos   |
| vosotros/as| hablabais   | comíais    | vivíais    |
| Uds.       | hablablan   | comían     | vivían     |
| ellos/as   | hablaban    | comían     | vivían     |

There are only *three irregular verbs* in the imperfect: **ir, ser,** and **ver.**

|            | ir      | ser     | ver      |
|------------|---------|---------|----------|
| yo         | iba     | era     | veía     |
| tú         | ibas    | eras    | veías    |
| Ud.        | iba     | era     | veía     |
| él, ella   | iba     | era     | veía     |
| nosotros/as| íbamos  | éramos  | veíamos  |
| vosotros/as| ibais   | erais   | veíais   |
| Uds.       | iban    | eran    | veían    |
| ellos/as   | iban    | eran    | veían    |

**The imperfect is used to:**

**1. provide background information, set the stage, or express a condition that existed**

| | |
|---|---|
| **Llovía** mucho. | *It was raining a lot.* |
| **Era** una noche oscura y nublada. | *It was a dark and cloudy night.* |
| **Estábamos** en el segundo año de la universidad. | *We were in our second year of college.* |
| Adriana **estaba** enferma y no **quería** levantarse. | *Adriana was ill and didn't want to get up / get out of bed.* |

**2. describe habitual or often repeated actions**

| | |
|---|---|
| **Íbamos** al centro comercial todos los viernes. Nos **divertíamos** mucho. | *We went (used to go) to the mall / shopping district every Friday. We had a lot of fun.* |
| Cuando **era** pequeño, Lebron **jugaba** al básquetbol por lo menos dos horas al día. | *When he was little, Lebron played (used to play) basketball for at least two hours a day.* |
| Mis padres siempre **se vestían muy bien** los domingos para ir a la iglesia. | *My parents always dressed very well on Sundays to go to church.* |

*(continued)*

**CAPÍTULO 8**

**Instructor Resources**
• PPT, Extra Activities

**NOTE for** *El imperfecto*
Preferences for presenting the preterit and imperfect tenses can be highly personal. We break down the use of the imperfect into 4 categories; you may prefer to combine them in a different way. The goal is to reach the learning styles of as many students as possible.

**SUGGESTION for** *El imperfecto*
Drill *el imperfecto* by giving infinitives and subject pronouns and having the class respond chorally with the correct forms.

**SUGGESTION for** *El imperfecto*
Drill with directed questions such as: *¿Dónde vivías? ¿Quién era tu mejor amigo/a? ¿Cómo era? ¿Cómo se llamaba tu mejor amigo/a de la escuela primaria? ¿Qué te ponías cuando tenías 5 años? Cuando tenías 5 años, ¿con quién jugabas? ¿Qué no te gustaba comer que ahora te gusta?*

**SUGGESTION for** *El imperfecto*
Remember that you can assign grammar tutorials in English and Spanish and PowerPoint presentations to supplement your lessons.

Some words or expressions for describing habitual and repeated actions are:

| | | | |
|---|---|---|---|
| **a menudo** | *often* | **muchas veces** | *many times* |
| **casi siempre** | *almost always* | **mucho** | *a lot* |
| **frecuentemente** | *frequently* | **normalmente** | *normally* |
| **generalmente** | *generally* | **siempre** | *always* |
| **mientras** | *while* | **todos los días** | *every day* |

3. express *was* or *were* + *-ing*

¿**Dormías**?                                      *Were you sleeping?*
**Me duchaba** cuando Juan llamó.        *I was showering when Juan called.*
Alberto **leía** mientras Alicia **escuchaba** música.    *Alberto was reading while Alicia was listening to music.*

4. tell time in the past

**Era** la una y yo todavía **estudiaba**.            *It was 1:00 and I was still studying.*
**Eran** las diez y los niños **dormían**.          *It was 10:00 and the children were sleeping.*

---

*3:00* **8-31** **La práctica** Repitan el juego de la actividad **7-8** en la página 264, esta vez para practicar el imperfecto. ■

---

*5:00* **8-32** **Cuando era joven** Completa el párrafo sobre Eva Perón para saber cómo pudo ser su vida cuando era joven. Después, compara tus respuestas con las de un/a compañero/a. ■

| | | | | |
|---|---|---|---|---|
| ayudar | encantar | gustar | poder | querer |
| preferir | sentirse | ser | tener | trabajar |

María Eva Duarte, como primero se llamaba, nació en una provincia de
Buenos Aires en el año 1919. Cuando (1) ____tenía____ seis o siete años su
padre murió. Eva y sus cuatro hermanos (2) __se sentían__ muy tristes y la vida
(3) ____era____ muy difícil para ellos porque les faltaban dinero y comida. La
madre (4) __trabajaba__ como costurera (*seamstress*) y los niños la (5) __ayudaban__
en la casa. Nos imaginamos que a Eva le (6) __encantaba__ el verano cuando
(7) ____podía____ estar en casa con sus hermanos. No le (8) __gustaban__ las muñecas y (9) __prefería__ inventar juegos
o imaginar situaciones diferentes. Parece que desde el principio (*from the start*) Eva (10) __quería__ ser actriz.

Workbooklet

**8-33 En el colegio...** ¿Qué hacías cuando estabas en el colegio? ¿Con qué frecuencia? Escribe una equis (**X**) en la columna apropiada de cada hilera (*row*). Luego, compara tus respuestas con las de un/a compañero/a. ■

**MODELO**
E1: *¿Escuchabas música de Cristina Aguilera?*
E2: *No, nunca escuchaba música de Cristina Aguilera. / Sí, a veces escuchaba música de Cristina Aguilera.*

| | TODOS LOS DÍAS | MUCHAS VECES | A VECES | NUNCA |
|---|---|---|---|---|
| 1. escuchar música de Cristina Aguilera | | | | |
| 2. nadar en la playa | | | | |
| 3. leer obras de Shakespeare | | | | |
| 4. bañarse por la noche | | | | |
| 5. acostarse temprano | | | | |
| 6. dormirse en las clases | | | | |
| 7. ponerse nervioso/a antes de un examen | | | | |
| 8. reunirse con los amigos | | | | |
| 9. vestirse como querías | | | | |
| 10. querer ir a la escuela | | | | |
| 11. levantarse muy tarde | | | | |
| 12. no hacer nada por la noche | | | | |

Capítulo 3. La casa, pág. 98; Los colores, pág. 111.

**8-34 Mi primera casa** ¿Cómo era tu primera casa o la casa de tu amigo/a? Descríbesela a un/a compañero/a dándole por lo menos **cinco** detalles. Luego, cambien de papel. ■

**MODELO**
*Mi primera casa estaba en una ciudad pequeña. Tenía dos dormitorios. La cocina era amarilla. El comedor blanco y la sala azul eran pequeños. Tenía solamente (only) un baño.*

**¿Cierto o falso?** Lee las frases siguientes y decide si son ciertas o falsas en tu caso. Después, túrnate con un/a compañero/a para hacer preguntas y contestar según el modelo.

**MODELO**

E1: *Antes de venir a la universidad, ¿vivías en un apartamento?*

E2: *No, no vivía en un apartamento. Vivía con mis padres en una casa.*

Antes de venir a la universidad…
1. vivir en un apartamento
2. tener una mascota (*pet*)
3. ver mucho la televisión
4. gustarte comer verduras
5. ser un/a buen/a estudiante
6. tener muchos amigos
7. estudiar todo el tiempo
8. tener mucho dinero para gastar
9. llevar pantalones cortos
10. tocar un instrumento
11. sacar la basura
12. manejar mucho

---

`4:00`  **8-35** **¡Cómo cambia la vida!**

Miren el dibujo y escriban **siete** oraciones que contesten la pregunta "¿cómo era la vida en los años setenta?". Usen verbos como **tener, estar, ser, haber, ayudar, limpiar** y **jugar**. ¡Sean creativos! ∎

---

`8:00`
Workbooklet

**8-36** **Preguntas personales** Cuando tenían dieciséis años, ¿qué hacían tus compañeros/as de clase? Circula por la clase para preguntárselo. ∎

**MODELO**

E1: *¿Jugabas al fútbol con los amigos?*

E2: *Sí, jugaba todos los días después de salir del colegio.*

E3: *Sí, jugaba con el equipo del colegio.*

E4: *No, nunca jugaba al fútbol. No me gustaba.*

| | ESTUDIANTE 1: | ESTUDIANTE 2: | ESTUDIANTE 3: |
|---|---|---|---|
| 1. ¿Te quedabas en casa los fines de semana? | | | |
| 2. ¿Qué hacías los fines de semana? | | | |
| 3. ¿Manejabas (*Did you drive*)? | | | |
| 4. ¿Tenías coche (*car*)? | | | |
| 5. ¿Trabajabas? | | | |
| 6. ¿Qué hacías cuando hacía mal tiempo? | | | |
| 7. ¿Qué hacías cuando hacía buen tiempo? | | | |
| 8. ¿Qué hacías cuando tenías dinero? | | | |
| 9. ¿Qué hacías cuando no tenías dinero? | | | |
| 10. ¿Qué hacías para divertirte? | | | |

## ESCUCHA

08-42 to 08-43

# En el centro comercial

**Estrategia**

**Guessing meaning from context**

You do not need to know every word to understand a listening passage or to get the gist of a conversation. Think about the overall message, then use the surrounding words or sentences to guess at meaning.

### 8-37 Antes de escuchar

Beatriz, la prima de Marisol, es estudiante de intercambio en Buenos Aires. Va de compras con su "hermana" argentina, Luz. Están en la tienda Zara, comprando ropa. ▪

1. ¿Cómo es la tienda Zara?
2. ¿Piensas que ir de compras a Zara en Buenos Aires es igual que ir de compras a Zara en Nueva York (o en cualquier otra ciudad)?

Beatriz y Luz van de compras.

### 8-38 A escuchar

Completa las siguientes actividades. ▪

1. Escucha la conversación entre Beatriz y Luz y después selecciona la opción que mejor conteste la pregunta.

   ¿De qué se trata (*What is the gist of*) la conversación?

   _____ a. A Beatriz no le gustan las blusas de la tienda y tampoco la tienda. Jamás va de compras allí.

   _____ b. A Beatriz le encanta el dependiente. Vive cerca de Luz.

   _____ c. A Luz le gustan los perros negros. Alguien tiene un perro que se llama Toro o posiblemente Goro.

2. Escucha una vez más y termina las siguientes oraciones.

   a. Marisol y Beatriz visitaron una de las tiendas Zara... (dónde y cuándo)
   b. Marisol y Beatriz no compraron nada porque...
   c. Luz no quiere comprar la blusa de seda o la falda de lana porque...
   d. Beatriz reconoce (*recognizes*) al dependiente porque...

3. ¿Qué significa "dependiente"?

### 8-39 Después de escuchar

En grupos de tres, realicen (*act out*) la escena entre Beatriz, Luz y el dependiente. ▪

---

**NATIONAL STANDARDS**

*Communication*

The new strategy in *Capítulo 8* is guessing meaning from context. The two Communication Standards incorporated in the *Escucha* section are Standard 1.2 and Standard 1.3. Standard 1.2 focuses on understanding and interpreting spoken Spanish, whereas Standard 1.3 focuses on presenting information, concepts, and ideas to an audience of listeners. Depending on how the instructor chooses to implement the *Después de escuchar* section, students can present the scene to the class (Standard 1.3) or they could also communicate interpersonally in small groups (Standard 1.1)

**ANSWERS to 8-37**

1. Zara es una tienda española. Vende ropa de buena calidad, pero no es muy cara.
2. *Answers may vary.*

**ANSWERS to 8-38**

1. b
2. a. ...en Nueva York el verano pasado.
   b. ...no tenían mucho dinero.
   c. ...los colores no le quedan bien.
   d. ...vive cerca de Luz / es el vecino de Luz.
3. Significa "salesperson".

---

**SECTION GOALS for *Escucha***

By the end of the *Escucha* section, students will be able to:

- employ a new listening strategy of guessing meaning from context.
- incorporate previously learned listening strategies.
- get the main idea of the conversation.
- recreate the conversation by acting it out.

**AUDIOSCRIPT for 8-38**

Luz: Esta es mi tienda favorita. ¿Conoces la ropa de Zara? Es una empresa española.

Beatriz: Sí. Mi prima Marisol y yo fuimos a una de las tiendas en Nueva York el verano pasado. ¡Fue increíble!

Luz: ¿Compraron algo?

Beatriz: No. Estábamos de vacaciones y era el último día en la ciudad. No teníamos mucho dinero.

Luz: Yo no puedo hacer muchas compras pero me encanta tener prendas especiales para complementar mi ropa.

Beatriz: Vamos a ver... ¿Te gusta esta blusa de seda? ¿Y esta falda de lana?

Luz: Son muy bonitas pero estos colores no me quedan muy bien. Mmmmm... pero me encanta el dependiente que está allí en la sección de hombres.

Beatriz: ¡Luz! ¿No es ese el hombre guapísimo que vive en el edificio al lado del tuyo? Tú sabes... ¿el hombre con el perro negro grande?

Luz: Es curioso... me acuerdo del perro pero no de él.

Beatriz: Sí, ¡es él! Se levanta todos los días muy temprano para correr en el parque con su perro. No recuerdo el nombre del perro... es algo como... Toro o Goro o Gorro...

Luz: Shhhh... aquí viene.

Dependiente: Buenos días. ¿En qué puedo servirles? Tenemos unas blusas de seda con un 25 por ciento de descuento. Los colores son perfectos para ustedes —muy vibrantes.

Luz: ¡Me fascinan! Voy a comprar la blusa amarilla. ¿Y tú, Beatriz?

Beatriz: ¿Cómo? ¿Qué dices? [*distracted*] Oh... la blusa. No, prefiero el hombre azul —quiero decir... [*stumbling over her words*] el perro blanco... Ay... ¡qué vergüenza! Escucha... ¿oyes mi teléfono celular? [*voice is rising...*] ¡Me llaman! Gracias. ¡Adiós! [*she rushes off*]

Dependiente: Tu amiga es un poco rara, ¿no? ¿Qué le pasa?

Luz: Ah, no es nada. Es su primera vez en Zara y está un poco emocionada. [*They laugh.*]

**SECTION GOALS for *¡Conversemos!***

By the end of the *¡Conversemos!* section, students will be able to:

- describe clothing in the presentational and interpersonal modes.
- discuss past clothing styles and compare them to present styles in the presentational and interpersonal modes.
- utilize previously learned/recycled vocabulary and grammatical concepts such as *gustar* and *gustar*-type verbs and the imperfect form.

**NOTE for *¡Conversemos!***

Creating a fashion show in class is excellent for communication practice. Among the many options, one is to have students write up their own descriptions and then wear what they describe to class. Another option is to have students give their written descriptions to classmates to be read as they model their outfits.

# ¡CONVERSEMOS!
08-44

 **8-40** **Los modelos** Crea un desfile de moda (*fashion show*) con un/a compañero/a. Describe la ropa que lleva tu compañero/a. Si quieres, trae fotos de ropa de unas revistas y descríbela como si fueras un comentarista de moda para *Style.com*. Incluye **por lo menos diez** oraciones. ■

 **8-41** **¿Qué llevaban?** Piensa en la ropa que tus amigos, tu familia y tú llevaban cuando eran más jóvenes. ¿Cómo se compara el estilo de antes con el estilo de ahora? Describe con detalles la ropa que se llevaba en **por lo menos diez** oraciones. ■

## ESCRIBE

 **Un email**
08-45

| Estrategia | It is common when learning a language not to know or remember the exact word(s) you need to communicate an idea. Thinking of another way to express something is called *circumlocution*—essentially using several words to describe something simple. | For example, if you don't know or remember the word for "tía," you could say "la hermana de mi padre." If you can't remember the word for "cine," you could get your point across by writing "todos los sábados íbamos al centro para ver una película." |
|---|---|---|
| **Circumlocution** | | |

**8-42 Antes de escribir** ¿Qué te gustaba hacer de niño/a? ¿Te levantabas temprano para jugar con tus amigos? ¿Tus padres te dejaban comer caramelos y otros dulces a menudo? Haz una lista de las **ocho** cosas que más te gustaba hacer cuando eras niño/a, usando "circumlocution" cuando sea necesario. ■

**8-43 A escribir** Organiza tus ideas y escribe un email a tu hermano/a (o a tu mejor amigo/a), recordando las cosas que hacías en tu niñez. ■

 **8-44 Después de escribir** Tu profesor/a va a leer los emails a la clase para ver si ustedes pueden adivinar quiénes los escribieron. ■

## ¿Cómo andas? II

Having completed **Comunicación II,** I now can . . .

| | Feel confident | Need to review |
|---|---|---|
| • provide details about clothing (p. 309) | ☐ | ☐ |
| • relate daily routines (p. 312) | ☐ | ☐ |
| • consider shopping practices in the Spanish-speaking countries (p. 316) | ☐ | ☐ |
| • share about situations in the past and how things used to be (p. 317) | ☐ | ☐ |
| • guess the meanings of unfamiliar words, when listening, from the context (p. 321) | ☐ | ☐ |
| • communicate about clothing and fashion (p. 322) | ☐ | ☐ |
| • write an e-mail, practicing circumlocution (p. 323) | ☐ | ☐ |

**SECTION GOALS for Cultura**
By the end of the Cultura section, students will be able to:
• explain the ethnic roots represented in Argentina.
• describe the geographical diversity of Argentina.
• discuss the climate and culture of Uruguay.
• compare Argentina and Uruguay, and also these two countries with previously featured countries.

**NATIONAL STANDARDS**
*Cultures, Comparisons*
In *Les presento mi país*, the readings highlight the unique features of Argentina and Uruguay. Students learn about the culture of these two countries (Standard 2.1), and with the information presented they can make comparisons about how these countries differ from the United States (Standard 4.2). One comparison they learn is that many Italians immigrated to Argentina and therefore many Argentines have Italian surnames; also, Italian cuisine has been incorporated into the Argentine and Uruguayan diet. In Uruguay there is a temperate climate, which differs from the extreme temperature variations in regions across the United States.

**NOTE for *Les presento mi país***
One of the goals of *¡Anda! Curso elemental* is to expose students to new countries, ways of living, and ways of thinking. For many, this may be their first exposure to foreign cultures so a sampling of each country of focus is important as an introduction to the Spanish-speaking world. You may choose to highlight different points for these countries, given your background and interests. For example, you may choose to emphasize the history of Argentina touching on Evita Perón, los gauchos, Borges, etc., or spend more time on the national issues that Argentina and Uruguay face today.

**NOTE for *Les presento mi país***
People from the city of Buenos Aires are called *porteños*. They are said to have their own mannerisms and idiomatic expressions as well as accent. The pronunciation of *y* and *ll* are closer to the *sh* sound in English than in Spanish elsewhere.

# Cultura
## Argentina

CULTURA • CULTURA • CULTURA • C ... A • C

08-46 to 08-48

## Les presento mi país

María Graciela
Martelli Paz

Mi nombre es María Graciela Martelli Paz y vivo en Rosario, una ciudad cerca de Buenos Aires. Realmente soy porteña (*una persona de Buenos Aires*) porque nací allí. Mi primer apellido es italiano porque mis abuelos paternos eran de Nápoles. Muchos argentinos tienen apellidos italianos a causa de la gran inmigración europea a fines del siglo diecinueve. **¿De qué herencia sos vos, che?** Mi país es grande y la geografía es muy variada: desde la montaña más alta del hemisferio occidental, el Cerro Aconcagua, hasta la ciudad más sureña (*del sur*) del mundo, Ushuaia. También tenemos lugares naturales como los glaciares, las pampas, la región de la Patagonia, las cataratas del Iguazú y unas playas hermosas, como la de Mar del Plata. **¿Qué regiones y riquezas naturales hay en tu país?**

las cataratas del Iguazú en la frontera con Brasil y Argentina

el tango en San Telmo, un antiguo barrio en la capital

galerías Pacífico en la calle Florida

### ALMANAQUE 🇦🇷

| | |
|---|---|
| **Nombre oficial:** | República de Argentina |
| **Gobierno:** | República |
| **Población:** | 41.343.201 (2010) |
| **Idioma:** | español |
| **Moneda:** | Peso argentino ($) |

### ¿Sabías que...?

• El **lunfardo** es un dialecto o jerga que tuvo su origen en los barrios de Buenos Aires a finales del siglo XIX. Es la lengua del tango y también la jerga de las prisiones a principios del siglo XX. Se forman palabras diciendo las sílabas al revés (*reversing the syllables*): "tango" en lunfardo es *gotán*.

### Preguntas

1. ¿Cuáles son tres de las distintas regiones geográficas del país? Cuando es verano en Argentina, ¿en qué estación estamos aquí? ¿Por qué?
2. ¿Dónde puedes ir de compras en Buenos Aires?
3. ¿Qué tiene Argentina en común con otros países de Sudamérica?

 Amplía tus conocimientos sobre Argentina en MySpanishLab.

324

**NOTE for *Les presento mi país***
Argentines use *che* to call attention to people, to begin sentences, as a nickname, and as a sentence interjection. It is an all-purpose word. In some indigenous languages, it means "man" or "people." It was, of course, the nickname of Ernesto Guevara, the revolutionary from Rosario, Argentina.

**NOTE for *Les presento mi país***
While *voseo*, the use of the pronoun *vos* for second person singular, is widespread throughout many parts of Latin America, it is very widespread in

Argentina. Though it is not taught in Spanish textbooks in the United States, millions of people in the Southern Cone and elsewhere use this linguistic form on a daily basis.

**EXPANSION for *Preguntas***
Additional questions include: *¿Cómo se usa la palabra "che" en Argentina? ¿Por qué se dice que Buenos Aires es una ciudad cosmopolita? ¿Qué es el lunfardo?*

# Uruguay

08-46 to 08-47, 08-49

## Les presento mi país

Mi nombre es Francisco Tomás Bacigalupe Bustamante, aunque de pequeño me llamaban Paquito. Soy de Montevideo, la capital de Uruguay. Mi país es pequeño, pero también es tranquilo y bonito. La mayoría de la población, el ochenta por ciento, vive en los centros urbanos. El clima es templado (no hace mucho calor ni mucho frío) y es perfecto para nuestras playas increíbles. Cuando era niño las playas eran nuestro destino favorito para ir de vacaciones. **¿Dónde ibas tú de vacaciones?** Tenemos mucho en común con nuestros vecinos los argentinos: el tango, la yerba mate, los gauchos y una dieta que contiene mucha carne. También comemos mucha pizza y pasta, debido a nuestra herencia italiana. **¿Qué comida de otros países te gusta comer?**

Francisco Tomás Bacigalupe Bustamante

...a del Este es un ...eario (*resort*) ...turístico.

El chivito es un plato típico uruguayo.

el puerto de Montevideo

### ALMANAQUE

**Nombre oficial:** República Oriental del Uruguay

**Gobierno:** República democrática

**Población:** 3.510.386 (2010)

**Idiomas:** español (oficial); portuñol/brasilero

**Moneda:** Peso uruguayo ($U)

### ¿Sabías que...?

- Debido al índice de alfabetización (*literacy*), el clima agradable y templado, la belleza del paisaje y la hospitalidad de la gente, a Uruguay se le conoce como "la Suiza de América".

### Preguntas

1. ¿Dónde vive la mayoría de los uruguayos?
2. Muchos uruguayos son de herencia italiana. ¿En qué se ve esta herencia?
3. ¿Qué tiene en común Uruguay con su país vecino Argentina?

Amplía tus conocimientos sobre Uruguay en MySpanishLab.

**325**

**CAPÍTULO 8**

**NOTE for *Montevideo***
Montevideo, Uruguay, is the southernmost capital in South America. This vibrant city lies on the northeastern bank of the Río de la Plata, the river that separates the southern coast of Uruguay from the northern coast of Argentina. With a rich culture influenced by many European immigrants, it is also an important center of commerce and higher education in Uruguay.

**SUGGESTION for *Montevideo***
Ask students what influences might occur by having Montevideo just across the river from Argentina. Ask them whether they know of other cities that are located at the mouths of rivers, or are even split by them, and how they might be different from cities that are land locked.

**NOTE for *Punta del Este***
Punta del Este is one of the most popular resorts in all of South America. It is a mecca for glamorous tourists who enjoy golfing, casinos, beautiful beaches, and other resort pastimes.

**SUGGESTION for *Punta del Este***
Ask students: What are some famous resorts in the United States? Are some more exclusive than others? Why do they think that happens?

**NOTE for *El chivito***
*El chivito* is a steak sandwich that contains cheese, ham, bacon, tomatoes, eggs, lettuce, and mayonnaise. It is the Uruguayan version of "fast food," and is quite popular. Another typical dish is *asado*, also common in Argentina. Italian food is also popular, due to the large number of people of Italian descent in the country.

**SUGGESTION for *El chivito***
Ask students: What is our most common fast food? (hamburgers); Do we have food in common with other cultures, or is it exclusively "United Statesian"?

**EXPANSION for *Preguntas***
Additional questions to ask your students are:
1. ¿Cómo es Uruguay? ¿Por qué crees que la mayoría de la gente vive en los centros urbanos?
2. ¿Qué plato de "comida rápida" es típico en Uruguay? ¿Cómo se compara este plato con la "comida rápida" estadounidense? ¿Y con la comida de los otros países que hemos estudiado?

## SECTION GOALS for *Lectura*

By the end of the *Lectura* section, students will be able to:

- utilize the new reading strategy of guessing from the context.
- apply the new strategy in combination with the previous strategies.
- narrate the main events of the reading.

## RECAP of *AMBICIONES SINIESTRAS* Episodio 7

**Lectura:** In *Capítulo 7, El rompecabezas*, Cisco called Manolo to check on Alejandra and learned that no one had heard from her. Cisco went to his favorite restaurant to do some thinking and received a phone call from a man who said he would have two days to solve a riddle or Eduardo would die. Upon further investigation, Cisco learned from Manolo that he too had received the mysterious phone call. When Manolo called Alejandra, he heard a man's voice on her answering machine.

**Video:** In *Episodio 7, ¡Qué rico está el pisco!*, Cisco organized a videoconference about Eduardo's and Alejandra's disappearances. Both Cisco and Lupe acted very mysteriously when asked about the disappearances. It appeared that Lupe was hiding her true identity, and that Cisco knew more about the disappearances than he was letting on. At the end of the episode, Cisco suspected that the answer to the riddle was Chile, and he wondered if Sr. Verdugo could be holding Eduardo in Chile.

## NATIONAL STANDARDS
### Communication

The *Lectura* provides authentic text in Spanish that students have to read and interpret for understanding (Standard 1.2). The video provides listening practice as students interpret what is happening and why, and how these actions might affect future actions (Standard 1.2). The new strategy, guessing meaning from the context, prepares students to become more efficient readers as they scan for the main ideas and supporting ideas for enhanced understanding. If students work together to discuss the comprehension questions, they engage in conversations and provide and obtain information (Standard 1.1).

## ANSWERS to 8-45

1. Marisol y Manolo estaban preocupados porque Eduardo desapareció y no sabían dónde estaba Alejandra.
2. Tenían que resolver el rompecabezas para salvar la vida de Eduardo.
3. Manolo pensaba que Cisco sabía algo de Eduardo, y Marisol no sabía si Lupe le estaba diciendo la verdad.

---

# Ambiciones siniestras — EPISODIO 8

📖 08-52 to 08-53

# Lectura

**Estrategia** — Guessing meaning from context

Before consulting a dictionary, always try to guess the meaning of an unfamiliar word from the context. Look closely at the surrounding words and sentences to help you determine the meaning. Even without an exact translation, you can get the general idea of what the word means.

---

**8-45 Antes de leer** En el **Episodio 7**, los protagonistas seguían preocupados por Eduardo y tampoco sabían dónde estaba Alejandra. Para prepararte bien para el **Episodio 8**, contesta las siguientes preguntas basadas en el **Episodio 7**. ■

1. ¿Cómo se sentía Marisol? ¿Manolo? Explica.
2. ¿Por qué era importante resolver el rompecabezas?
3. ¿Cuáles eran las dudas que tenían?

**8-46 A leer** Completa las siguientes actividades. ■

1. Al empezar el episodio, sabemos que Marisol estaba "preocupada". Cuando ella fue a su computadora *"Tenía varios mensajes, pero inmediatamente vio uno del hombre del concurso. Empezó a <u>temblar</u> sin saber por qué"*.

   ¿Qué significa la palabra "temblar"? ¿Cómo podía sentirse Marisol? ¿feliz?, ¿asustada? Creemos que Marisol se puso nerviosa, entonces "temblar" es más una reacción de miedo, ¿no? En realidad, "temblar" significa "*to tremble*".

2. Lee el episodio y subraya (*underline*) las palabras que no conoces. Intenta adivinar el significado, según el contexto. (Sigue el proceso indicado en el apartado 1.) Después, compara tus palabras con las de tu compañero/a.

 **¿Quién fue?**

Eran las ocho y Marisol estaba en la cama, preocupada y confusa. No quería levantarse. No tenía ganas de arreglarse… no podía comer porque no tenía hambre ni para sus dulces favoritos.

Sonó el teléfono pero Marisol decidió no contestarlo. Prefería escuchar un mensaje que hablar con alguien en estos momentos. Nada: nadie dejó un mensaje. Decidió levantarse e ir a la computadora para leer su correo electrónico. Tenía varios mensajes, pero inmediatamente vio uno del hombre del concurso. Empezó a temblar sin saber por qué. Por fin lo abrió y leyó:

326

---

**EXPANSION for 8-45**

Additional questions to ask your students are:

*¿Quién puede ser el hombre que deja el mensaje en el contestador automático?*

*¿Dónde piensas que están Eduardo y Alejandra? ¿Qué pasó con ellos?*

**METHODOLOGY • Reading**
*¡Anda! Curso elemental* supports both top-down and bottom-up approaches to reading. In the top-down, or reader-driven, approach, the pre-existing knowledge the reader brings to the text is critical to comprehension. The *Antes de leer* section supports this approach. The text-driven, or bottom-up, approach relies on the decoding of words, phrases, and sentences.

**NATIONAL STANDARDS**
*Communication, Comparisons*
Note that the readings are kept at a level of comprehensible input that entices the students to read. Also, follow-up questions encourage students to think beyond the content of the story and make informed guesses about what they would do in the same circumstance.

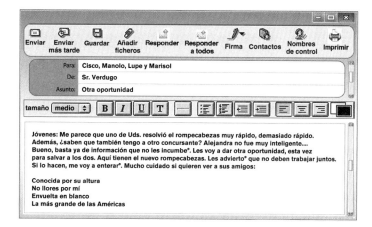

*you do not need to know*
*warn*
*find out*

**Jóvenes:** Me parece que uno de Uds. resolvió el rompecabezas muy rápido, demasiado rápido. Además, ¿saben que también tengo a otro concursante? Alejandra no fue muy inteligente.... Bueno, basta ya de información que no les incumbe°. Les voy a dar otra oportunidad, esta vez para salvar a los dos. Aquí tienen el nuevo rompecabezas. Les advierto° que no deben trabajar juntos. Si lo hacen, me voy a enterar°. Mucho cuidado si quieren ver a sus amigos:

Conocida por su altura
No llores por mí
Envuelta en blanco
La más grande de las Américas

*nightmare*
*She had nothing to do with that / behaving / was hiding / was*

Marisol no podía creerlo. ¡Qué pesadilla°! ¿Quién resolvió el primer rompecabezas? Ella no tuvo nada que ver con eso°. ¿Y qué pasó con Lupe en estos últimos días? Estaba portándose° muy rara y misteriosamente. Dijo que las cosas no eran importantes, pero sí, lo son. Parecía que escondía° algo. ¡Podía ser que este último mensaje fuera° de ella! En ese momento sonó el teléfono.

—Marisol, soy Manolo. Encontré tu número en el Internet.

—Manolo, gracias por llamar —respondió Marisol —Tengo que hablar contigo. Tengo mucho miedo. ¿Recibiste el nuevo rompecabezas? ¿Fuiste tú quien solucionó el primer rompecabezas? —le preguntó.

—Sí, —explicó Manolo, —recibí el nuevo pero no, no fui yo quien solucionó el primero —explicó Manolo.

—¿Sabes qué? —empezó a decir Marisol—. Creo que es Lupe quien nos manda los emails. Creo que ella es el «Sr. Verdugo» —le dijo muy convencida.

—¿Sí? —respondió Manolo—, y yo creía que era Cisco. Él tiene mucho talento con las computadoras. Me da mucho miedo. Creo que Cisco sí sabe lo que pasa con Eduardo y no nos dice nada. Temo que él sea el culpable°.

*I'm afraid he may be the guilty one*
*approach*

—No sé —le refutó Marisol—. No lo sé. Hay cosas muy misteriosas con Lupe también. Siempre está en Internet y cuando me acerco° a ella, cierra su computadora y me dice que no está haciendo nada. ¿Qué hacemos? —le preguntó.

—Tal vez debemos llamar a la policía —contestó Manolo—, pero ¿qué decimos? No sabemos nada en concreto ni de Eduardo ni de Alejandra. Vamos a pensarlo bien. ¿Y si es una broma° de mal gusto? Te llamo pronto.

*joke*

—Bueno —respondió Marisol angustiada—. Adiós.

*screamed*

Marisol, temblando de nuevo, volvió a sus mensajes. Miró la lista y vio una dirección que no reconoció: muchasuerte@comando.com. Abrió el mensaje y gritó°.

327

**Instructor Resources**
• Video script

**ANSWERS to 8-47**

1. Eran las ocho. Marisol estaba en la cama.
2. «*Conocida por su altura*
   *No llores por mí*
   *Envuelta en blanco*
   *La más grande de las Américas*»
3. Cisco, Manolo y Marisol no deben trabajar juntos para resolver el rompecabezas si quieren ver a sus amigos.
4. Manolo llamó a Marisol.
5. Manolo cree que Cisco es el Sr. Verdugo y que sabe lo que pasó con Eduardo. Marisol cree que Lupe es el Sr. Verdugo.

**EXPANSION for 8-47**

Additional questions to ask your students are:

*Según Manolo, todo eso puede ser "una broma de mal gusto". ¿Qué opinas?*

*¿Por qué gritó Marisol?*

**SECTION GOALS for *Video***

By the end of the *Video* section, students will be able to:

• review the events of the previous episode.
• retell the main points of the story.
• predict future events.

**METHODOLOGY • Video**

The video episode in each chapter, as well as the episode in the text, contextualizes the new vocabulary words and grammatical structures. This feature is a critical part of the ¡Anda! Curso elemental program, as each episode (reading and video) ends in a mini-cliffhanger that is furthered or resolved in the subsequent episode. If either the reading or the video is omitted, students will not be able to follow the story and will miss a wonderful learning opportunity. Note that the video script is available on MySpanishLab.

**METHODOLOGY • Checking for Comprehension in English**

When you are encouraging students to hypothesize regarding what will happen, it is acceptable to ask them to brainstorm in English.

---

**8-47 Después de leer** Contesta las siguientes preguntas. ■

1. ¿Qué hora era? ¿Qué hacía Marisol al empezar el episodio?
2. ¿Cuál era el nuevo rompecabezas?
3. ¿Qué amenaza (*threat*) había al final de su mensaje?
4. ¿Quién llamó por teléfono?
5. ¿Cuáles eran las dudas de Manolo?, ¿y de Marisol?

  # Video

08-54 to 08-55

**8-48 Antes del video** En la segunda parte del episodio vas a saber quién resolvió el rompecabezas, pero vas a tener más dudas sobre algunos de los protagonistas. Manolo va a hablar de algo peligroso (*dangerous*). Y finalmente, ¿quién tiene una pistola? ■

Eso es todo lo que necesito.

Cisco, te lo digo en serio, esto puede ser muy peligroso.

Oye, Manolo. Perdón pero tengo que irme.

*«El misterio crece»*

Episodio 8

Relájate y disfruta el video.

**8-49 Después del video** Contesta las siguientes preguntas. ■

1. ¿Qué hacía Lupe mientras hablaba con Manolo?
2. ¿Quién resolvió el primer rompecabezas? ¿Cuál era la respuesta?
3. Según Lupe, ¿quién debía saber algo sobre Eduardo?
4. ¿Qué ocurrió justo antes de colgar (*just prior to hanging up*) los teléfonos?
5. ¿Por qué se puso nervioso Manolo al final del episodio?
6. ¿A quién vimos al final del episodio?

328

---

**ANSWERS to 8-49**

1. Miraba su computadora donde vio a Eduardo y a Alejandra en diferentes lugares.
2. Lupe resolvió el primer rompecabezas. "Chile" era la respuesta.
3. Dice que Cisco debía saber algo sobre Eduardo.
4. Manolo y Lupe oyeron un ruido extraño en el teléfono.
5. Recordó que no deben trabajar juntos para resolver el rompecabezas y ellos escucharon un ruido cuando Cisco empezó a resolverlo.
6. Vimos a Cisco buscando un papel.

**EXPANSION for 8-49**

Additional questions to ask your students are:

*¿Adónde va Cisco y qué piensas que va a hacer allí?*

*¿Por qué tiene una pistola Lupe? ¿Crees que es una estudiante como ella dice?*

# Y por fin, ¿cómo andas?

|  | Feel confident | Need to review |
|---|---|---|
| Having completed this chapter, I now can . . . | | |

### Comunicación I

- describe clothing (p. 294) — ☐ ☐
- pronounce *ll* and *ñ* correctly (MSL / SAM) — ☐ ☐
- state to whom and for whom things are done (p. 299) — ☐ ☐
- express likes, dislikes, needs, etc. (p. 302) — ☐ ☐
- convey information about people and things (p. 305) — ☐ ☐

### Comunicación II

- provide details about clothing (p. 309) — ☐ ☐
- relate daily routines (p. 312) — ☐ ☐
- share about situations in the past, and how things used to be (p. 317) — ☐ ☐
- guess the meanings of unfamiliar words, when listening, from the context (p. 321) — ☐ ☐
- communicate about clothing and fashion (p. 322) — ☐ ☐
- write an e-mail, practicing circumlocution (p. 323) — ☐ ☐

### Cultura

- recount information about a Spanish clothing company (p. 298) — ☐ ☐
- consider shopping practices in Spanish-speaking countries (p. 316) — ☐ ☐
- share important facts about this chapter's featured countries: Argentina and Uruguay (pp. 324–325) — ☐ ☐

### Ambiciones siniestras

- deduce the meanings of unfamiliar words in a reading passage and explain the significance of the latest e-mail from Sr. Verdugo (p. 326) — ☐ ☐
- reveal secrets regarding Lupe (p. 328) — ☐ ☐

### Comunidades

- use Spanish in real-life contexts (SAM) — ☐ ☐

**Instructor Resources**
• Testing program information

# VOCABULARIO ACTIVO

| La ropa | Clothing |
|---|---|
| el abrigo | overcoat |
| la bata | robe |
| la blusa | blouse |
| el bolso | purse |
| las botas (pl.) | boots |
| los calcetines (pl.) | socks |
| la camisa | shirt |
| la camiseta | T-shirt |
| la chaqueta | jacket |
| el cinturón | belt |
| el conjunto | outfit |
| la corbata | tie |
| la falda | skirt |
| la gorra | cap |
| los guantes | gloves |
| el impermeable | raincoat |
| los jeans (pl.) | jeans |
| las medias (pl.) | stockings; hose |
| la moda | fashion |
| los pantalones (pl.) | pants |
| los pantalones cortos (pl.) | shorts |
| el paraguas | umbrella |
| el pijama | pajamas |
| las prendas | articles of clothing |
| la ropa interior | underwear |
| las sandalias (pl.) | sandals |
| el sombrero | hat |
| la sudadera | sweatshirt |
| el suéter | sweater |
| los tenis (pl.) | tennis shoes |
| el traje | suit |
| el traje de baño | swimsuit; bathing suit |
| el vestido | dress |
| las zapatillas (pl.) | slippers |
| los zapatos (pl.) | shoes |

| Algunos verbos | Some verbs |
|---|---|
| llevar | to wear; to take; to carry |
| prestar | to loan; to lend |

| Algunos verbos como *gustar* | Verbs similar to gustar |
|---|---|
| encantar | to love; to like very much |
| fascinar | to fascinate |
| hacer falta | to need; to be lacking |
| importar | to matter; to be important |
| molestar | to bother |

| Las telas y los materiales | Fabrics and materials |
|---|---|
| el algodón | cotton |
| el cuero | leather |
| la lana | wool |
| el poliéster | polyester |
| la seda | silk |
| la tela | fabric |

## Algunos adjetivos — *Some adjectives*

| | |
|---|---|
| ancho/a | *wide* |
| atrevido/a | *daring* |
| claro/a | *light (colored)* |
| cómodo/a | *comfortable* |
| corto/a | *short* |
| de cuadros | *checked* |
| de lunares | *polka-dotted* |
| de rayas | *striped* |
| elegante | *elegant* |
| estampado/a | *print; with a design or pattern* |
| estrecho/a | *narrow; tight* |
| formal | *formal* |
| incómodo/a | *uncomfortable* |
| informal | *casual* |
| largo/a | *long* |
| liso/a | *solid-colored* |
| oscuro/a | *dark* |

## Otra palabra útiles — *Another useful word*

| | |
|---|---|
| el/la modelo | *model* |

## Un verbo — *A verb*

| | |
|---|---|
| quedarle bien / mal | *to fit well / poorly* |

## Algunos verbos reflexivos — *Some reflexive verbs*

| | |
|---|---|
| acordarse de (o → ue) | *to remember* |
| acostarse (o → ue) | *to go to bed* |
| afeitarse | *to shave* |
| arreglarse | *to get ready* |
| bañarse | *to bathe* |
| callarse | *to get / keep quiet* |
| cepillarse (el pelo, los dientes) | *to brush (one's hair, teeth)* |
| despertarse (e → ie) | *to wake up; to awaken* |
| divertirse (e → ie → i) | *to enjoy oneself; to have fun* |
| dormirse (o → ue → u) | *to fall asleep* |
| ducharse | *to shower* |
| irse | *to go away; to leave* |
| lavarse | *to wash oneself* |
| levantarse | *to get up; to stand up* |
| llamarse | *to be called* |
| maquillarse | *to put on make up* |
| peinarse | *to comb one's hair* |
| ponerse (la ropa) | *to put on (one's clothes)* |
| ponerse (nervioso/a) | *to get (nervous)* |
| probarse (o → ue) la ropa | *to try on clothing* |
| quedarse | *to stay; to remain* |
| quitarse (la ropa) | *to take off (one's clothes)* |
| reunirse | *to get together; to meet* |
| secarse | *to dry off* |
| sentarse (e → ie) | *to sit down* |
| sentirse (e → ie → i) | *to feel* |
| vestirse (e → i → i) | *to get dressed* |

## NATIONAL STANDARDS

### COMUNICACIÓN I
• To describe the human body (Communication)
• To pronounce the letters *d* and *t* (Communication)
• To share about people, actions, and things (Communication)
• To explain ailments and treatments (Communication)
• To make emphatic and exclamatory statements (Communication)
• To engage in additional communication practice (Communication, Communities)

### COMUNICACIÓN II
• To narrate in the past (Communication)
• To explain how long something has been going on and how long ago something occurred (Communication, Communities)
• To ask yourself questions when listening to organize and summarize what you hear (Communication, Connections)
• To communicate about ailments and healthy living (Communication)
• To write a summary, sequencing past events (Communication, Comparisons)
• To engage in additional communication practice (Communication, Communities)

### CULTURA
• To relate the importance of water in maintaining good health (Communication, Connections)
• To consider pharmacies in Spanish-speaking countries and how they differ from those in the United States (Communication, Comparisons, Connections)
• To list important information about this chapter's featured countries: Peru, Bolivia, and Ecuador (Communication, Cultures, Connections, Comparisons)
• To explore further the chapter's cultural themes (Communication, Cultures)

### AMBICIONES SINIESTRAS
• To create check questions to facilitate comprehension when reading, and give details about the new e-mail message (Communication, Connections)
• To discover the progress the characters are making in deciphering the new riddle (Communication)

# 9
# Estamos en forma

Todos queremos tener una buena calidad de vida y prolongarla lo más posible. No podemos cambiar nuestra herencia genética transmitida de padres a hijos, pero sí tenemos control sobre decisiones que pueden afectar nuestro estilo de vida: el ejercicio, la dieta, la prevención de accidentes y el uso de sustancias adictivas como el tabaco.

## PREGUNTAS

**1** ¿Vives una vida sana (*healthy*)? ¿Qué haces (o no haces) para tener una vida más sana?

**2** ¿Qué tipo de ejercicio te gusta hacer?

**3** ¿Cuáles son algunas de las decisiones específicas que tomamos que pueden afectar nuestra salud (*health*)?

332

**COMUNIDADES**
• To use Spanish in real-life contexts (Communities)

**SECTION GOALS for *Chapter opener***
By the end of the Chapter opener section, students will be able to:
• list environmental and personal factors that contribute to longevity.
• compare healthy lifestyle choices with unhealthy choices.
• narrate how their choices contribute to or detract from living healthily.

**NATIONAL STANDARDS**
*Communities*
This chapter is about health and wellness. If you have a health/wellness major at your school (especially nutrition/dietetics or exercise science) you could ask a faculty member to provide materials that your students could translate and use to make presentations to the Hispanic community about topics such as MyPlate, the food pyramid, diet, exercise, and preventive medical care. They could get healthy recipes and translate those into Spanish for the Spanish-speaking community as well. You could also ask local health clinics or doctors' offices if they have simple materials or signs they would like to post in Spanish, such as to whom to make checks, the rules of the office regarding the use of cell phones, or fees for certain services like flu shots or copies of forms. If you have a sizable Hispanic community, you could ask the hospital for upcoming wellness programs and have students make flyers in Spanish, posting the details of the events. As always, use good judgment when thinking of service projects, remember the skill level of your students, and consider how they could serve the community.

**METHODOLOGY • Teacher Talk**
In the classroom, although we simplify our language when we speak, attempting to stay within the range of *i + 1*, we should strive to deliver our speech at a speed that is as close to natural as possible. As the semester progresses, that speed gradually increases.

333

**Instructor Resources**
• Textbook images, Extra Activities

**SECTION GOALS for**
*Comunicación I*
By the end of the first *Comunicación* section, students will be able to:
• identify body parts and things associated with the human body.
• pronounce the letters *d* and *t* correctly.
• match body parts with clothing items worn on the body.
• review formation and placement of direct and indirect object pronouns and reflexive pronouns.
• describe ailments and medical treatments for ailments.
• tell where to go to treat certain symptoms and explain what symptoms they have.
• read about the importance of water to health.
• use *qué* and *cuánto* for exclamations.

**NATIONAL STANDARDS**
*Communication*
Talking about how one feels appeals to the basic sense that we all have; we love to talk about ourselves! Your students will enjoy the associated activities that help them acquire the vocabulary. The vocabulary associated with *El cuerpo humano* and *Algunas enfermedades y tratamientos médicos* is rich with communicative possibilities because the topic is universal. Most of the activities are for pairs and small groups: thus, students are engaging in interpersonal communication (Standard 1.1). If you have students play doctor and patient, pretending to have ailments, or act out ailments you suggest, you satisfy Standard 1.3, the presentational mode. You could bring in the Spanish dosage instructions from packages of over-the-counter medications for students to read and discuss, and that would meet Standard 1.2, the interpretive mode. You could also read the instructions to them and use that as a listening activity.

# Comunicación I

**1 VOCABULARIO**

09-01 to 09-07

## El cuerpo humano  Describing the human body

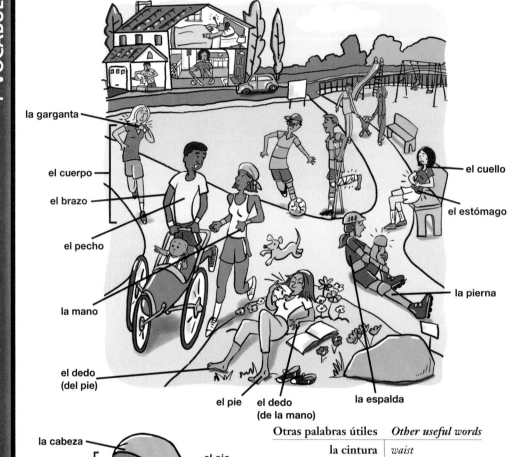

la garganta
el cuerpo
el brazo
el pecho
la mano
el dedo (del pie)
el pie
el dedo (de la mano)
el cuello
el estómago
la pierna
la espalda

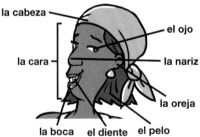

la cabeza
la cara
la boca
el diente
el pelo
el ojo
la nariz
la oreja

| Otras palabras útiles | *Other useful words* |
|---|---|
| la cintura | *waist* |
| el corazón | *heart* |
| el oído | *inner ear* |
| la salud | *health* |
| la sangre | *blood* |

| Algunos verbos | *Some verbs* |
|---|---|
| doler (ue) | *to hurt* |
| estar enfermo/a | *to be sick* |
| estar sano/a; saludable | *to be healthy* |
| ser alérgico/a (a) | *to be allergic (to)* |

## PRONUNCIACIÓN

09-08 to 09-11

### The letters *d* and *t*

Go to MySpanishLab / Student Activities Manual to learn about the letters *d* and *t*.

---

[4:00]  **9-1 Simón dice** Escuchen mientras su instructor/a les da las instrucciones de esta actividad. ■

 Capítulo 8. La ropa, pág. 294.

---

[2:00] **9-2 ¿Cómo nos vestimos?** Túrnense para decir qué partes del cuerpo asocian con la ropa indicada. ■

MODELO  E1:  los zapatos
        E2:  *los pies*

1. las botas  los pies
2. los guantes  las manos
3. los pantalones  las piernas
4. la gorra  la cabeza
5. la corbata  el cuello
6. la camiseta  el pecho/la espalda
7. los tenis  los pies
8. la chaqueta  el pecho/la espalda/los brazos

---

[2:00] **9-3 Categorías** Juntos escriban todas las palabras del vocabulario nuevo que corresponden a las siguientes partes del cuerpo. ■

MODELO  E1:  la cabeza
        E2:  *la cara, el pelo,* etc.

1. la cabeza
2. de la cintura para arriba (*from the waist up*)
3. de la cintura para abajo (*from the waist down*)
4. la cara

---

[2:00] **9-4 ¿Cómo se escribe?** Escribe la primera y la última letra de una de las palabras del vocabulario. Un/a compañero/a tiene que terminarla. Túrnense para practicar la ortografía de por lo menos **ocho** palabras. ■

MODELO  E1:  e _ _ _ _ _ a
        E2:  e s p a l d a

**SECTION GOALS for** *Pronunciación*

By the end of the *Pronunciación* section, students will be able to:
- pronounce the letters *d* and *t* correctly.
- practice pronunciation skills using *dichos* and *refranes*.

**INSTRUCTIONS for 9-1**

Play *Simón dice* with your students to practice the body parts. Here are the instructions for how to play the game:

Tell students that they should all obey you if you first say the words "Simón dice" and that they are out of the game if they follow an order that doesn't begin with "Simón dice," or if they fail to do what Simón says to do.

Begin by saying something like, "Simón dice, tócate la cabeza." Look to make sure all have touched their heads. Give another order such as, "Simón dice, tócate el brazo." Check again. Continue giving orders. Mix it up and say something like, "levanta la mano derecha," without the preface "Simón dice." Call out the players who raise their right hands. Play until one person is left. That is the winner.

**METHODOLOGY • Pairing Students**

What follows are some suggestions for pairing students using the body parts:

1. You will need one small piece of paper for each student. Write different body parts on half of the slips. On the other half of the slips, write related body parts or other words. For example, you might write *las manos* on one slip, and *los dedos* on another; *el ojo* on one, and *ver* on yet another. Put your slips of paper in a hat, box, or bag, and let each student draw a paper. Then tell them to get up and find the person who has the body part / word most closely "related" to their own. This is a critical thinking activity.

2. Again, you will need one slip of paper for each student in your class. Write the first part of a word on one slip, and finish word on a second slip. For example, one slip might have *ca* ... and its mate would have ... *ra*. Another pair could be *estó* ... and its partner would be ... *mago*.

3. A third way is to write a body part on one slip and draw it on another (or cut the pictures out of a magazine). For example, on one slip of paper you write *la nariz* and on its match you draw (or cut out) a nose.

You will want to collect these slips of paper at the end of the activity so that you can reuse them in the future. A good way to organize them is to put them in sandwich bags and mark on the bags what vocabulary topic they are and to which chapter they correspond in *Curso elemental.*

## INSTRUCTIONS for 9-7

This activity has two parts. Draw a monster on the board, a transparency, etc., and have students work in pairs with one student facing the drawing and the other with his/her back to the drawing. The student facing the drawing describes what he/she sees (the instructor's drawing) and the other student draws it. When finished, the student compares the drawing he/she created with the original and then the students switch places and repeat the activity.

## SUGGESTION for 9-7

Make your "monster" as unusual as you like, since the more you deviate from a real person, the more closely the student who is drawing must listen to his/her partner. Perhaps the monster you draw has 1 eye, 3 noses, 2 mouths, 1 tooth, 1 big ear, 1 small ear, 3 legs, and 5 hearts. If you have an odd number of students, 1 pair has to draw while the third student gives directions. Also, you may ask the extra student to draw the second monster after you have modeled the procedure. You may wish to teach additional words like *cuadrado*, *círculo*, *línea*, *triángulo*, etc. Finally, encourage the student giving the directions *not* to use his/her hands since this is a listening activity and he/she needs to work toward making himself/herself understood. By the way, this is a very popular activity with students and instructors alike. The students feel a real sense of accomplishment when they are able to carry on extended descriptions.

## NOTE for 9-7

The objective of this activity is for students to listen to each other and to instantly demonstrate comprehension via the drawing. If the student who has his/her back to the *monstruo* does not understand, he/she must ask questions for clarification. Although couched in an enjoyable context where students are practicing their new vocabulary, the objective is much more important. Your students are communicating on an interpersonal level in an attempt to be mutually understood.

---

**9-5** **¿Qué te duele?** Con una/a compañero/a, creen preguntas y respuestas para ver lo que les duele a las siguientes personas. ■

MODELO  a Ricardo / los brazos

E1: *¿Qué le duele a Ricardo?*

E2: *Le duelen los brazos.*

1. A Julia / la cabeza  ¿Qué le duele? Le duele la cabeza.
2. A Marco y a Miguel / las piernas  ¿Qué les duele? Les duelen las piernas.
3. A ti / el estómago  ¿Qué te duele? Me duele el estómago.
4. A tu primo / la garganta  ¿Qué le duele a tu primo? Le duele la garganta.
5. A ustedes / los ojos  ¿Qué les duele? Nos duelen los ojos.

> **Fíjate**
>
> The verb *doler* functions like *gustar*.
>
> Me duelen los brazos.
> *My arms hurt (me).*

---

**9-6** **Una obra de arte** Miren el cuadro y descríbanlo usando las siguientes preguntas como guía. ■

1. ¿Cuántas personas hay en el cuadro?  dos
2. ¿Cuántas caras hay?  cuatro
3. ¿Cuántas manos pueden ver?  seis
4. ¿Cuántos ojos pueden ver?  cinco
5. ¿Cuántas narices hay?  cuatro
6. ¿Qué otras cosas ven en el cuadro?  pelo, cabezas, etc.
7. Estas personas son…  madre e hijo
8. El cuadro representa…  *Answers may vary.*

> **Fíjate**
>
> Note that *la mano* is irregular; it ends in *o* but the word is feminine.

Capítulo 3. *Hay,* pág. 119.

---

**9-7** **¿Es un monstruo o una obra de arte?** Su instructor/a va a dibujar un monstruo. Descríbele a un/a compañero/a cómo es el monstruo y él/ella tiene que dibujarlo. Al terminar, cambien de papel para describir un monstruo nuevo. ■

**El monstruo tiene…**

| a la derecha | a la izquierda | encima de | debajo de |
|---|---|---|---|

> **Estrategia**
>
> Being an "active listener" is an important skill in any language; it means that you have heard and understood what someone is saying. Being able to demonstrate that you have understood correctly, as in reproducing this drawing of the monster, helps you practice and perfect the skill of active listening.

---

**ADDITIONAL ACTIVITY for** *El cuerpo humano*

The following activity requires markers (or crayons) and end roll or butcher-type paper. If your institution does not have any paper readily available, you can acquire end rolls from your local newspaper. Newspapers usually donate end rolls to educators.

**Vamos a dibujar** Su profesor/a les va a dar un papel largo y unos marcadores (*markers*). Una persona del grupo va a acostarse (*lie down*) encima del papel. Otra persona va a trazar una línea (*trace*) alrededor del/de la compañero/a. Después, cada persona en el grupo tiene que marcar (*label*) por lo menos tres partes del cuerpo.

**2 GRAMÁTICA**

 09-12 to 09-17   Spanish/English Tutorials

## Un resumen de los pronombres de complemento directo e indirecto y reflexivos
Sharing about people, actions, and things

You have already learned the forms, functions, and positioning of the *direct* and *indirect object pronouns*, as well as the *reflexive pronouns*. The following is a review:

| LOS PRONOMBRES DE COMPLEMENTO **DIRECTO** | LOS PRONOMBRES DE COMPLEMENTO **INDIRECTO** | LOS PRONOMBRES **REFLEXIVOS** |
|---|---|---|
| Direct object pronouns tell *what* or *who* receives the action of the verb. They replace direct object nouns and are used to avoid repetition. | Indirect object pronouns tell *to whom* or *for whom* something is done or given. | Reflexive pronouns indicate that the *subject* of a sentence or clause *receives the action of the verb.* |

| | | | | | | | |
|---|---|---|---|---|---|---|---|
| **me** | *me* | **me** | *to/for me* | **me** | *myself* |
| **te** | *you* | **te** | *to/for you* | **te** | *yourself* |
| **lo, la** | *you* | **le (se)** | *to/for you* | **se** | *yourself* |
| **lo, la** | *him/her/it* | **le (se)** | *to/for him/her* | **se** | *himself/herself* |
| **nos** | *us* | **nos** | *to/for us* | **nos** | *ourselves* |
| **os** | *you (all)* | **os** | *to/for you (all)* | **os** | *yourselves* |
| **los, las** | *you (all)* | **les (se)** | *to/for you (all)* | **se** | *yourselves* |
| **los, las** | *them/you* | **les (se)** | *to/for them/you* | **se** | *themselves/yourselves* |

Compré la medicina ayer. **La** compré en la Farmacia Fénix. Tengo que dárse**la** a mi hijo.

*I bought the medicine yesterday. I bought it it at Fénix Pharmacy. I have to give it to my son.*

**Le** compré la medicina ayer. **Le** voy a dar la medicina esta noche.

*I bought him the medicine yesterday. I am going to give him the medicine tonight.*

**Me** cepillo los dientes tres veces al día.

*I brush my teeth three times a day.*

Remember the following guidelines on position and sequence:

## Position

• Object pronouns and reflexive pronouns come **before** the verb.

El doctor Sánchez **le** dio una inyección a David.     *Dr. Sánchez gave David a shot.*

Después **se** sintió aliviado.     *Then he felt relieved.*

*(continued)*

- Object pronouns and reflexive pronouns can also be placed before or be attached to the end of:

  a. **infinitives**

La enfermera **me** va a llamar.
La enfermera va a llamar**me.** } *The nurse is going to call me.*

Después **se** va a ir a su casa.
Después va a ir**se** a su casa. } *Then she is going to go home.*

  b. **present participles (*-ando*, *-endo*, and *-iendo*)**

**La** está tomando ahora.
Está tomándo**la** ahora. } *He is taking it now.*

**Se** está poniendo nervioso.
Está poniéndo**se** nervioso. } *He is getting nervous.*

## Sequence

- When a direct (DO) and indirect object (IO) pronoun are used together, ***the indirect object precedes the direct object.***
- If both the direct and the indirect object pronouns begin with the letter "*l*" the indirect object pronoun changes from **le** or **les** to **se,** as in the following example.

Quiero mandar la carta al director ahora.

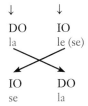

DO     IO
la     le (se)

IO     DO
se     la

*I want to send the letter to the director now.*

DO     IO

**Se la** quiero mandar ahora mismo.
Quiero mandár**se la** ahora mismo. } *I want to send it to him right now.*

*Capítulo 1. Los adjetivos descriptivos, pág. 43.*

---

**EXPANSION for 9-8**
Have your students each draw their own *animal muy extraño*, and repeat **9-8,** using their own drawings.

**EXPANSION for 9-8**
Challenge students to bring in photos of the strangest animals they can find for the class to describe. Then take a class vote to determine which is the strangest.

**EXPANSION for 9-8**
Have students describe their favorite animals, and have their classmates guess which animals they are describing.

[3:00]  **9-8 Un animal muy extraño**

Juntos respondan a las siguientes oraciones exclamativas con el pronombre de complemento directo apropiado y un adjetivo. ■

**MODELO**    E1: ¡Mira la nariz!

        E2: *Sí, la tiene muy grande (pequeña/fea/ bonita…).*

**Fíjate**
In Spanish, an animal's legs are referred to as *patas. Pierna(s)* is only used for people.

1. ¡Mira la boca!
2. ¡Mira las orejas!
3. ¡Mira los dientes!
4. ¡Mira las patas!
5. ¡Mira la cabeza!
6. ¡Mira el estómago!
7. ¡Mira la cara!
8. ¡Mira el cuello!

Capítulo 8. *Gustar* y verbos como *gustar*, pág. 302.

## 9-9 Las preferencias

Escribe oraciones completas usando los pronombres de complemento indirecto. Después compara tus oraciones con las de un/a compañero/a. ▪

**MODELO** A Betty / gustar despertarse temprano
*A Betty le gusta despertarse temprano.*

1. A mis padres / importar el dinero  A mis padres les importa el dinero.
2. A mí / molestar las personas irresponsables  (A mí) Me molestan las personas irresponsables.
3. A Manolo / encantar las novelas de Mario Vargas Llosa  A Manolo le encantan las novelas de Mario Vargas Llosa.
4. A nosotros / hacer falta estudiar mucho más  (A nosotros) Nos hace falta estudiar mucho más.
5. A nuestro/a profesor/a / fascinar el cine japonés  (A nuestro/a profesor/a) Le fascina el cine japonés.

## 9-10 En el restaurante

¿Qué les pasó ayer a Paco y a Pati en el Restaurante Boca Grande? ▪

**Paso 1** Completa las siguientes oraciones con los pronombres de complemento directo, indirecto o reflexivo apropiados. Después, compara tus respuestas con las de un/a compañero/a.

Paco y Pati se conocieron en el gimnasio hace varias semanas. Anoche decidieron salir juntos. Llegaron al restaurante con mucha hambre. (1) ____Se, R____ sentaron en una mesa grande al lado de las ventanas. Primero pidieron el menú. El camarero (2) ____se, IO____ (3) ____lo, DO____ trajo en seguida (inmediatamente). Después, (4) ____les, IO____ recomendó unos platos muy ricos. Paco pidió un bistec para él y a Pati (5) ____le, IO____ pidió pollo asado con ajo. ¡Pati no (6) ____lo, DO____ podía creer! ¡Paco ni (7) ____le, IO____ preguntó qué quería! Ella (8) ____se, R____ sentía muy incómoda —ningún hombre, excepto su padre, (9) ____la, DO____ había tratado (*had treated*) así antes. Pati (10) ____se, R____ calló mientras Paco hablaba de su día, su trabajo y su familia. Cuando por fin el camarero (11) ____les, IO____ sirvió la comida, Pati miró su plato y (12) ____se, R____ levantó gritando. ¡Su plato era del "Menú para niños"!

**Paso 2** Digan qué tipo de pronombre usaron en cada oración.

**EXPANSION for 9-9**
Have students replace the subjects of each of these sentences with as many options as possible, and then complete new sentences.

**MODELO**
A mis padres/importar el dinero.
A mis padres/importar la salud.
*A mis padres les importa la salud.*

**NOTE for 9-9**
You may want to share with students that Mario Vargas Llosa is a Peruvian author and Nobel Prize winner.

**METHODOLOGY • Oral Practice**
Research strongly supports our belief that classroom time should be spent engaging the students almost exclusively in meaningful *oral* activities. You have noted that virtually all of the activities in *¡Anda! Curso elemental* are meant to be done orally, in pairs or groups. This is to maximize students' opportunities to speak and use Spanish in *i + 1* settings that help build their confidence in the language. Research confirms that strong oral skills translate into better writing skills. Therefore, we need to provide our students with a controlled environment in class to practice speaking so that outside of class they will be more successful and confident writers.

**EXPANSION for 9-10**
You may want to also use the passage as a reading comprehension activity, and ask the following questions:
  1. ¿Dónde se conocieron Pati y Paco?
  2. ¿Adónde fueron después?
  3. ¿Quién pidió la comida? ¿Qué pidió?
  4. ¿Por qué se enojó Pati?

**EXPANSION for 9-10**
You may want to convert **9-10** into a TPR activity. Choose three students to play the roles of Paco, Pati, and the waiter. Either call on students to read each sentence, or do the reading yourself, sentence by sentence. As each sentence is being read, the students perform the actions, providing a visual representation of how direct object, indirect object, and reflexive pronouns work.

Capítulo 4. *Ir + a + infinitivo*, pág. 147;
Capítulo 5. El presente progresivo, pág. 180.

**9-11** **¿Quién...?** Jacobo está enfermo y no puede levantarse de la cama. Es un poco exigente (*demanding*) y quiere saber quiénes lo van a atender (*wait on him*). Contesta sus preguntas y después comparte tus respuestas con un/a compañero/a. ■

MODELO      ¿Quién va a traerme la tarea? (hermano)
*Tu hermano te la va a traer. / Tu hermano va a traértela.*

1. ¿Quién va a traerme los libros que pedí? (Patricia)   Patricia te los va a traer. / Patricia va a traértelos.
2. ¿Quién está comprándome la medicina que necesito? (Marcelo)   Marcelo te la está comprando. / Marcelo está comprándotela.
3. ¿Quién me va a limpiar el cuarto? (Guadalupe y Lina)   Guadalupe y Lina te lo van a limpiar. / Guadalupe y Lina van a limpiártelo.
4. ¿Quién me está lavando la ropa? (tu madre)   Tu madre te la está lavando. / Tu madre está lavándotela.
5. ¿Quién está preparándome la comida? (Tina y Luisa)   Tina y Luisa te la están preparando. / Tina y Luisa están preparándotela.
6. ¿Quién me va a hacer la tarea? (nadie)   Nadie te la va a hacer. / Nadie va a hacértela.

**9-12** **Hay que ayudar a Pepito** Pepito tiene tres años y necesita ayuda para hacerlo todo. Túrnense para formar los pedidos (*requests*) del niño y las respuestas. ■

MODELO      los dedos / limpiar
       E1:   *¿Me los limpias?*
       E2:   *Sí, te los limpio.*

1. el pelo / secar   ¿Me lo secas? / Sí, te lo seco.
2. las manos / lavar   ¿Me las lavas? / Sí, te las lavo.
3. las orejas / limpiar   ¿Me las limpias? / Sí, te las limpio.
4. los dientes / cepillar   ¿Me los cepillas? / Sí, te los cepillo.
5. los ojos / mirar   ¿Me los miras? / Sí, te los miro.

## 3 VOCABULARIO

09-18 to 09-23

**Algunas enfermedades y tratamientos médicos**
Explaining ailments

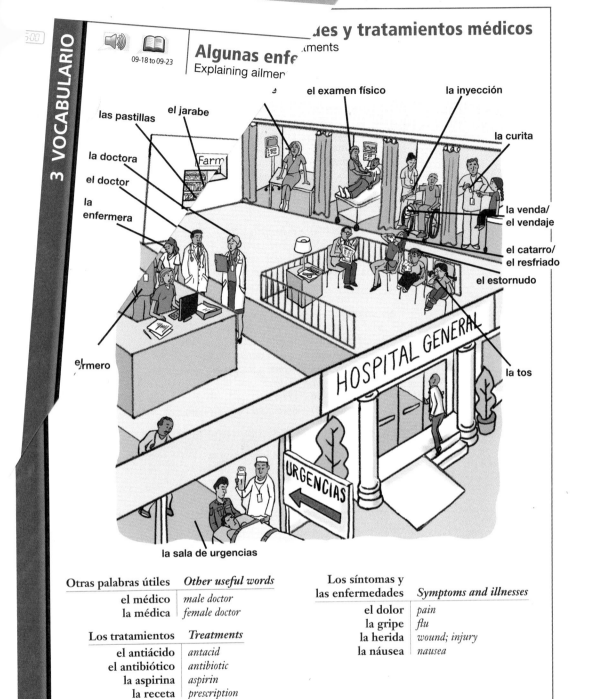

- el examen físico
- la inyección
- las pastillas
- el jarabe
- la doctora
- el doctor
- la enfermera
- la curita
- la venda/ el vendaje
- el catarro/ el resfriado
- el estornudo
- el enfermero
- la tos
- HOSPITAL GENERAL
- URGENCIAS
- la sala de urgencias

| Otras palabras útiles | Other useful words |
|---|---|
| el médico | male doctor |
| la médica | female doctor |

| Los tratamientos | Treatments |
|---|---|
| el antiácido | antacid |
| el antibiótico | antibiotic |
| la aspirina | aspirin |
| la receta | prescription |

| Los síntomas y las enfermedades | Symptoms and illnesses |
|---|---|
| el dolor | pain |
| la gripe | flu |
| la herida | wound; injury |
| la náusea | nausea |

*(continued)*

**Instructor Resources**
- Textbook images, Extra Activities

**NATIONAL STANDARDS**
*Communication, Comparisons, Connections*

The vocabulary about illness, injury, and explaining symptoms to medical personnel encompasses many of the National Standards. Any of the pair or small group activities that require students to engage in conversations, provide and obtain information, express their feelings and emotions, and exchange opinions address Standard 1.1. The idea of using verbs reflexively and non-reflexively or the concept of using articles with body parts instead of using possessive adjectives helps students see the differences between Spanish and English. They make comparisons (Standard 4.1) between how they express pain or discomfort in Spanish and in English. They are able to connect their prior knowledge of science/health with the new vocabulary in Spanish.

**SUGGESTION for *Algunas enfermedades y tratamientos médicos***

Ask students to describe the emergency room scene.

**SUGGESTION for *Algunas enfermedades y tratamientos médicos***

As a listening exercise, you may want to ask students true/false questions about the drawing:

1. La mujer en la bata rosada tiene un brazo roto.
2. La niña de la camiseta anaranjada se cortó el dedo.
3. Los doctores llevan batas blancas.
4. La mujer de la camiseta rosada se rompió la pierna.
5. El señor en la silla de ruedas (*wheelchair*) recibe una inyección.
6. Los niños están muy enfermos y necesitan tratamiento urgentemente.

| Algunos verbos | |
| --- | --- |
| acabar de + infinitivo | *to h...* |
| caer(se) | *to fall...* |
| cortar(se) | *to cut (bed + (something)* |
| curar(se) | *to cure; to...* |
| enfermar(se) | *to get sick* |
| estornudar | *to sneeze* |
| evitar | *to avoid* |
| guardar cama | *to stay in bed* |
| lastimar(se) | *to get hurt* |
| mejorar(se) | *to improve; to get bette...* |
| ocurrir | *to occur* |
| quemar(se) | *to burn; to get burned* |
| romper(se) | *to break* |
| tener... | |
| alergia (a) | *to be allergic (to)* |
| (un) catarro, resfriado | *to have a cold* |
| (la/una) gripe | *to have the flu* |
| una infección | *to have an infection* |
| tos | *to have a cough* |
| un virus | *to have a virus* |
| tener dolor de... | |
| cabeza | *to have a headache* |
| espalda | *to have a backache* |
| estómago | *to have a stomachache* |
| garganta | *to have a sore throat* |
| toser | *to cough* |
| tratar de | *to try to* |
| vendar(se) | *to bandage (oneself); to dress (a wound)* |

---

**Fíjate**

A verb with **se** in parentheses indicates that it can be also used as a reflexive verb.

| | |
| --- | --- |
| *quemar(se):* Ayer me quemé. (reflexive) | *Yesterday I burned myself.* |
| Ayer quemé los papeles viejos. | *Yesterday I burned the old papers.* |

---

2:00    **9-13** **No corresponde** ¿Qué palabra o expresión no pertenece (*doesn't belong*) a cada uno de los siguientes grupos de palabras? Túrnense para leer la lista y contestar. ∎

**MODELO**    E1:  el estómago, la cara, el ojo, la nariz

E2:  *el estómago*

1. el hospital, el doctor, el enfermero, el oído  el oído
2. toser, estornudar, la receta, tener catarro  la receta
3. el jarabe, la farmacia, las pastillas, quemarse  quemarse
4. lastimarse, la sala de urgencias, la tos, romperse la pierna  la tos
5. la venda, la herida, cortarse, el resfriado  el resfriado

booklet

## 9-14 Algunos tratamientos

¿Adónde tienes que ir para poder curarte o buscar tratamiento para las siguientes condiciones? Pon una equis (**X**) en la columna apropiada. Después, túrnate con un/a compañero/a para decir adónde van. ∎

**MODELO**  un brazo roto (*broken*)

E1:  *Si tengo un brazo roto, voy a la sala de urgencias.*

| CONDICIÓN | A LA CAMA | A LA FARMACIA | AL CONSULTORIO DEL MÉDICO | AL HOSPITAL | A LA SALA DE URGENCIAS |
|---|---|---|---|---|---|
| 1. tos | | | | | |
| 2. náusea | | | | | |
| 3. (la) gripe | | | | | |
| 4. (un) dolor de garganta | | | | | |
| 5. una infección de la sangre | | | | | |
| 6. una herida en la pierna | | | | | |
| 7. (un) catarro | | | | | |
| 8. fiebre | | | | | |

**Fíjate**

Body parts are usually referred to with an article, not a possessive adjective.

*Me duele la mano.*
*My hand hurts.*

## 9-15 ¿Por qué?

Túrnense para describir lo que les pasa a estas personas y ofrecer una causa posible de su(s) problema(s). ∎

**MODELO**

Selena

*Selena tiene una herida porque se cortó con un cuchillo.*

1.

Antonio

2.

Umberto y Ricardo

3.

Juliana y Memo

4.

María Jesús

5.

Rafael

**NOTE for 9-16**

*Soroche,* or altitude sickness, can strike anyone, regardless of whether he/she is in good or poor health. People in really good physical shape can fall victim to *soroche,* and feeble folks can be immune. The best remedy is to move slowly, avoid alcohol, meat, and tobacco the first few days, and acclimatize. Symptoms can also be lessened by drinking a tea made from the coca leaves, a local herbal remedy.

 **9-16  El soroche** El verano pasado Nina fue a Bolivia como voluntaria para ayudar a construir una escuela en el altiplano (*high plateau*). ■

El altiplano en los Andes de Bolivia

**Paso 1**    Juntos terminen la conversación entre Nina y su padre con las palabras de la lista.

| corazón | enfermedad | evitar | me duele |
|---------|------------|--------|----------|
| mejorar | náusea | pastillas | estómago |

NINA:    Hola, papá.

PAPÁ:    ¡Ay, Nina! ¿Cómo estás, hija? ¿Llegaste bien?

NINA:    Sí. Ayer llegamos bien pero hoy me siento enferma. (1) __Me duele__ la cabeza. No me duele mucho el (2) __estómago__ pero tengo (3) __náusea__ cuando pienso en la comida —me entran ganas (*I get the urge*) de vomitar.

PAPÁ:    Pobrecita. ¿Qué te pasa? ¿Comiste ayer?

NINA:    Sí, un poco. Pero desde que (*since*) llegamos no tengo mucha hambre.

PAPÁ:    ¿Tienes otros síntomas?

NINA:    Sí. El (4) __corazón__ me late (*is beating*) rápidamente y no puedo respirar (*breathe*) muy bien. ¿Crees que tengo alguna (5) __enfermedad__?

PAPÁ:    Nina, me parece que tienes soroche.

NINA:    ¿Soroche? ¿Qué es eso?

PAPÁ:    Es el mal de altura (*altitude sickness*). Debes empezar a sentirte mejor (*better*) en un par de días. Mientras tanto, necesitas intentar relajarte, tomar mucha agua y (6) __evitar__ el alcohol y el tabaco. También puedes tomar unas (7) __pastillas__ de ibuprofeno y beber un té medicinal hecho de (*made from*) hojas de coca (*coca leaves*).

NINA:    Gracias, papá. Ya que entiendo qué me ocurre, creo que me voy a (8) __mejorar__ pronto.

**Paso 2**    Ahora, contesten las siguientes preguntas.

1. ¿Qué es el soroche?
2. ¿Cuáles son los síntomas?
3. ¿Qué tratamiento le recomienda su papá?

**ANSWERS to 9-16**

Paso 2
1. Es la enfermedad de la altura.
2. Con el soroche puedes tener dolor de cabeza, náusea, no tener hambre, el corazón late rápidamente y no puedes respirar bien.
3. Le recomienda tomar ibuprofeno, descansar/relajarse, beber mucha agua, evitar el alcohol y el tabaco y tomar un té de hojas de coca.

**21ST CENTURY SKILLS •
SOCIAL AND CROSS-
CULTURAL SKILLS**

All activities in *¡Anda!*, including the information gap activities in which students need to circulate throughout the class build social and cross-cultural skills. The activities require students to listen and speak at appropriate times as well as be respectful of their classmates. By changing partners frequently (if not daily) students learn to work with a wide range of people.

## 9-17 ¿Qué debemos hacer?

En grupos de cuatro o cinco, cada estudiante escribe dos enfermedades u otros problemas médicos que tuvo, acaba de tener o que podría (*could*) tener. Después túrnense para compartir la información mientras los compañeros dicen lo que debe hacer. ■

**MODELO**    E1:   *Tengo una pierna rota.*
              E2:   *Debes ir a la sala de urgencias.*
              E3:   *Debes guardar cama.*
              E4:   *Debes tomar medicina para el dolor.*

Workbooklet

## 9-18 Para evitar lo inevitable

¿Cómo tratan de evitar tus compañeros las siguientes enfermedades y condiciones? Circula por la clase para hacerles las siguientes preguntas. Necesitas **tres** respuestas para cada pregunta. ■

**MODELO**    TÚ:   ¿Cómo tratas de evitar el dolor de garganta?
              E1:   *Bebo mucho jugo de naranja.*
              E2:   *Llevo una bufanda (scarf) en el cuello.*
              E3:   *Tomo mucha vitamina C.*

| | |
|---|---|
| 1. ¿Cómo tratas de evitar el dolor de cabeza?<br>E1: _____<br>E2: _____<br>E3: _____ | 4. ¿Cómo evitas enfermarte?<br>E1: _____<br>E2: _____<br>E3: _____ |
| 2. ¿Cómo tratas de evitar el dolor de estómago?<br>E1: _____<br>E2: _____<br>E3: _____ | 5. ¿Cómo evitas cortarte?<br>E1: _____<br>E2: _____<br>E3: _____ |
| 3. ¿Cómo tratas de evitar el dolor de espalda?<br>E1: _____<br>E2: _____<br>E3: _____ | 6. ¿Cómo evitas caerte?<br>E1: _____<br>E2: _____<br>E3: _____ |

## NOTA CULTURAL

### El agua y la buena salud

09-24 to 09-25

¿Sabías que tres cuartas partes de tu peso corporal (*body weight*) son de agua? Tu vida empezó en un mar de líquido amniótico y ahora, como adulto, alrededor del 85 por ciento de la sangre, el 70 por ciento de los músculos y el 22 por ciento de tu cerebro consisten en agua.

Para mantener la buena salud se debe beber por lo menos 2 litros (6 a 8 vasos) de agua al día. El cuerpo elimina de unos 500 a 700 centímetros cúbicos diarios de agua al sudar (*sweat*) y es muy importante reponer esa cantidad y más.

Los alimentos son una fuente (*source*) importante de agua para el cuerpo, sobre todo las frutas y las verduras. También cuentan otras bebidas además del agua, pero hay que considerar que algunas tienen el efecto contrario. El café y las bebidas alcohólicas deshidratan. Para compensar esta deshidratación hay que beber agua. Por ejemplo, por cada vaso de cerveza se debe tomar otro vaso de agua.

### Preguntas

1. ¿Por qué es importante beber tanta (*so much*) agua? ¿Cuántos vasos de agua bebes al día?
2. ¿Qué otros beneficios tiene beber suficiente agua al día?

## 4 GRAMÁTICA

 09-26 to 09-29

### ¡Qué! y ¡cuánto! Making emphatic and exclamatory statements

So far you have used **qué** and **cuánto** as interrogative words, but these words can also be used in exclamatory sentences.

—Felipe, ¡**qué** fiebre tienes!
—María, ¡**cuánto** estornudas!

—Mi cabeza, ¡**qué** dolor!
—**Cuánto** lo siento.

*Felipe, what a fever you have!*
*María, you are sneezing so much!*

*My head—what pain!*
*I'm so sorry. (How sorry I am.)*

NATIONAL STANDARDS
*Communication*

Making exclamations enriches the ability of the language learner to communicate in an expressive manner. The exclamatory phrases beginning with *¡qué!* or *¡cuánto!* provide a basis for communicating in natural contexts, as native speakers do. These expressions allow students to express their feelings and emotions and exchange opinions with others about their likes and dislikes (Standard 1.1). The exclamatory phrases are an easy way to communicate with native speakers and to be understood in multiple contexts.

—¡**Qué** susto! ¡Se cortó el dedo!     *What a scare! He cut his finger!*
—Se ve muy mal. ¡**Qué** feo!     *It looks really bad. How awful! (It looks awful/ugly.)*

—¡**Qué** doctor! Le salvó la vida.     *What a doctor! He saved his life.*
—**Cuánto** se lo agradezco.     *I'm so thankful. (How grateful I am.)*

Note that in the examples above, **cuánto** accompanies *verbs* and is masculine and singular. When **cuánto** accompanies *nouns* it must agree with them in gender and number:

—¡**Cuántas** recetas y todavía estoy tosiendo!     *So many prescriptions and I am still coughing!*
—Sí, y ¡**cuántos** estudiantes con la misma infección!     *Yes, and so many students with the same infection!*

---

 **9-19** **¿Cómo respondes?** Elige la respuesta apropiada para cada comentario. Después, comparte tus respuestas con un/a compañero/a. ■

1. __d__ ¡Ay, el estómago!
2. __c__ Su novia se graduó con honores.
3. __h__ Pepe me compró veinticuatro rosas rojas.
4. __e__ Esta comida es deliciosa.
5. __f__ Este doctor es el novio de aquella enfermera.
6. __g/b__ Mi madre preparó tapas para cincuenta personas.
7. __a__ Tiene la cara de un monstruo.
8. __b__ Tengo que leer dos libros para mi clase de historia y preparar un informe.

a. ¡Qué feo!
b. ¡Cuánto trabajo!
c. ¡Qué inteligente!
d. ¡Cuánto me duele!
e. ¡Cuánto me gusta!
f. ¡Qué interesante!
g. ¡Cuánta comida!
h. ¡Qué romántico!

---

 **9-20** **¡El amor es increíble!** Juntos respondan a estas situaciones. Pueden utilizar las siguientes expresiones o pueden responder con sus propias expresiones. ■

*Possible answers include:*

*1. ¡Cuánto tiempo!, ¡Qué romántico!, ¡Qué interesante!*

*2. ¡Qué triste!, ¡Qué cruel!, etc.*

*3. ¡Qué romántico!, ¡Qué interesante!*

*4. ¡Qué mala suerte!, ¡Qué horrible!, ¡Qué triste!, etc.*

*5. ¡Qué cruel!, ¡Qué dolor!*

*6. ¡Qué suerte!, ¡Qué interesante!*

| | | |
|---|---|---|
| ¡Qué (mala) suerte! | ¡Qué cruel! | ¡Qué dolor! |
| ¡Qué horrible! | ¡Qué romántico! | ¡Cuánto tiempo! |
| ¡Qué triste! | ¡Qué interesante! | |

1. Mis padres celebran este mes su aniversario de boda —¡25 años ya!
2. Félix, no te quiero desilusionar (*disappoint*) después de tantos meses juntos, pero quiero salir con otros hombres.
3. Silvia es la mujer más increíble del mundo. Quiero ser más que su novio. Quiero pasar mi vida con ella.
4. Nadie quiere salir conmigo (*with me*). Nadie me mira. Me gusta ir al cine, comer en buenos restaurantes, ir a partidos de básquetbol, bailar —pero no me gusta hacer estas cosas solo (*alone*).
5. Soy muy joven para tener novia. Me divertí contigo (*with you*) anoche en la fiesta pero me divierto con muchas mujeres…
6. Adriano es el hombre perfecto para mí. Es muy respetuoso y me trata bien siempre.

[3:00]  **9-21** **¿Qué tiene?** ¿Cómo responden ustedes a las siguientes situaciones? ■

MODELO   E1:  Tito está muy mal porque tiene un dolor terrible de estómago.

         E2:  *¡Cuánto le duele!*

         E1:  Yo no puedo hablar porque estoy tosiendo mucho.

         E2:  *¡Qué tos tienes!*

1. No puedo respirar, me duele la garganta, estornudo todo el tiempo y no tengo hambre.  ¡Qué catarro/resfriado tienes!
2. A mi hermano siempre le ocurre algo malo: se cae, se rompe algo…  ¡Qué mala suerte tiene!
3. ¡Ay! Necesito un antiácido ahora mismo, por favor.  ¡Cuánto te duele el estómago!
4. Mi abuelo acaba de salir del hospital después de pasar mucho tiempo allí. No tiene seguro médico (*health insurance*).  ¡Qué caro! ¡Cuánto dinero le va a costar!
5. Tú tienes mucha fiebre y te duele el cuerpo.  ¡Qué enfermo/a estoy!

## ¿Cómo andas? I

|  | Feel confident | Need to review |
|---|---|---|
| Having completed **Comunicación I,** I now can . . . | | |
| • describe the human body (p. 334) | ☐ | ☐ |
| • pronounce the letters **d** and **t** (MSL / SAM) | ☐ | ☐ |
| • share about people, actions, and things (p. 337) | ☐ | ☐ |
| • explain ailments and treatments (p. 341) | ☐ | ☐ |
| • relate the importance of water in maintaining good health (p. 346) | ☐ | ☐ |
| • make emphatic and exclamatory statements (p. 349) | ☐ | ☐ |

# Comunicación II

09-30 to 09-35  ¡Hola! Spanish/English Tutorials

## El pretérito y el imperfecto  Narrating in the past

Fuimos a Cuzco y subimos a
Machu Picchu. Hacía buen tiempo.

In **Capítulos 7** and **8** you learned about two aspects of the past tense in Spanish, **el pretérito** and **el imperfecto,** which are not interchangeable. Their uses are contrasted below.

**THE PRETERIT IS USED:**

1. To relate an event or occurrence that refers to *one specific time in the past*
   - **Fuimos** a Cuzco el año pasado.
     *We went to Cuzco last year.*
   - **Comimos** en el restaurante El Sol y **nos gustó** mucho.
     *We ate at El Sol restaurant and liked it a lot.*

2. To relate an act *begun or completed in the past*
   - **Empezó** a llover.
     *It started to rain.*
   - **Comenzaron** los juegos.
     *The games began.*
   - La gira **terminó.**
     *The tour ended.*

3. To relate a *sequence of events or actions*, each completed and moving the narrative along toward its conclusion
   - **Llegamos** en avión, **recogimos** las maletas y **fuimos** al hotel.
     *We arrived by plane, picked up our luggage, and went to the hotel.*
   - Al día siguiente **decidimos** ir a Machu Picchu.
     *The next day we decided to go to Machu Picchu.*
   - **Vimos** muchos ejemplos de la magnífica arquitectura incaica. Después **anduvimos** un poco por el camino de los incas. **Nos divertimos** mucho.
     *We saw many examples of the magnificent Incan architecture. Afterward we walked a bit on the Incan road. We had a great time.*

**THE IMPERFECT IS USED:**

1. To express *habitual* or often *repeated actions*
   - **Íbamos** a Cuzco todos los veranos.
     *We used to go to Cuzco every summer.*
   - **Comíamos** en el restaurante El Sol todos los lunes.
     *We used to eat at El Sol Restaurant every Monday.*

2. To express *was/were + -ing*
   - **Llovía** sin parar.
     *It rained without stopping.*
   - **Comenzaban** los juegos cuando llegamos.
     *The games were beginning when we arrived.*
   - La gira **transcurría** sin ningún problema.
     *The tour continued without any problems.*

3. To provide *background* information, set the stage, or express a pre-existing condition
   - **Era** un día oscuro. **Llovía** de vez en cuando.
     *It was a dark day and it rained once in a while.*
   - Los turistas **llevaban** pantalones cortos y lentes de sol.
     *The tourists were wearing shorts and sunglasses.*
   - El camino **era** estrecho y **había** muchos turistas.
     *The path was narrow and there were many tourists.*

*(continued)*

---

## Instructor Resources
- PPT, Extra Activities

**SECTION GOALS for**
*Comunicación II*
By the end of the second *Comunicación* section, students will be able to:
- explain the uses of the preterit and imperfect.
- identify key words that trigger the preterit or imperfect.
- contrast the use of the preterit or imperfect in a sentence.
- narrate a story in the past tense.
- discuss the role of pharmacies in the Spanish-speaking world.
- use expressions with *hacer.*

**NATIONAL STANDARDS**
*Communication*
Learning the differences between the preterit and the imperfect may be one of the greater challenges for your students in the first year of Spanish. *¡Anda! Curso elemental* makes strong use of enjoyable activities to help students acquire the concept.

The narration of events in the past tense, using either the preterit or imperfect, allows for greater flexibility in communication. When students engage in conversations about activities that they used to do as children, or what they did last week, they are communicating in the interpersonal mode (Standard 1.1). If they read a story in Spanish, written in the past tense, they are using Standard 1.2, and if they listen to the story, as well as read it, they have met the Standard. If they narrate a past tense event and present it to the class either orally or as a written story, that addresses Standard 1.3—the presentational mode.

**METHODOLOGY • Chunking**
*¡Anda! Curso elemental* believes in the pedagogical concept of "chunking." *Chunking* means taking large, broad concepts and breaking them into manageable chunks. This is what we have done with the important grammar concept of the past tense. In *Capítulo 7*, the preterit was introduced; in *Capítulo 8*, the imperfect. Now in this chapter we review the formation of these two tenses, and then proceed to contrast their uses, breaking them into manageable rules.

---

**SUGGESTION for *El pretérito y el imperfecto***
Begin each class with directed questions using both the *pretérito* and the *imperfecto*. Some sample questions include: ¿A qué hora te acostaste anoche? ¿A qué hora te acostabas el verano pasado? ¿Qué te pusiste ayer? ¿Qué te ponías cuando tenías cinco años?, etc.

**SUGGESTION for *El pretérito y el imperfecto***
To assist in remembering the *pretérito* and *imperfecto* and the rules for each, have students recall humorous stories from their childhoods. Have students write their stories in English and decide which verbs in their stories would be *preterit* and which would be *imperfect*. They can use the examples from their humorous stories to help them remember which to use and why.

**Una mañana muy extraña** Lee el siguiente texto sobre una experiencia muy extraña. Señala si cada verbo debe estar en pretérito (P) o imperfecto (I) y explica por qué.

**MODELO**

1. was (P/I) #4 *(To relate an action that took place within a specified or specific amount [segment] of time— "yesterday morning.")*

Yesterday morning (1) was (P/I) strange. When I (2) woke up (P/I), I (3) was feeling (P/I) a little sick. My head (4) was hurting (P/I) and my back (5) ached (P/I) as well. The weather (6) was (P/I) damp and cold so I (7) was (P/I) not anxious to get out of bed. Suddenly I (8) heard (P/I) a crash. I (9) glanced (P/I) at the clock and (10) saw (P/I) that it (11) was (P/I) already 8:45. My roommate always leaves by 8:00, so I (12) believed (P/I) that I (13) was (P/I) alone. I (14) jumped (P/I) out of bed and (15) ran (P/I) to the window. I (16) didn't see (P/I) anything unusual. I (17) was thinking (P/I) I (18) should look (P/I) around outside when I (19) heard (P/I) an eerie sound, like a cross between a whimper and a howl.

By that time my head (20) was throbbing (P/I) along with my back, but I (21) could not pay attention (P/I) to the pain. I (22) struggled (P/I) to overcome it so I (23) could focus (P/I) on the situation at hand. Without grabbing a coat, I (24) ran out the door. I (25) did not realize (P/I) that the wooden steps (26) were (P/I) icy and I immediately (27) slipped (P/I) and (28) fell (P/I). I (29) banged (P/I) both my back and my head on the hard, wooden steps. I (30) screamed (P/I) loudly but (31) did not feel (P/I) the fall because to my right there (32) was (P/I) a big black bear digging in our garbage can. He (33) was staring (P/I) at me, apparently (34) feeling (P/I) just as startled as I (35) was (P/I). At exactly the same moment we (36) began (P/I) to back away from each other—me up the steps and the bear away from the garbage can. As I (37) was reaching (P/I) up to open the screen door, the bear (38) turned (P/I) and (39) ran (P/I).

Once I (40) calmed (P/I) down I (41) realized (P/I) that I (42) was no longer feeling (P/I) pain. The fear and the hard fall had cured me!

---

| THE **PRETERIT** IS USED: | THE **IMPERFECT** IS USED: |
|---|---|
| **4.** To relate an action that took place within a specified or *specific amount* (segment) *of time*<br>**Caminé** (por) dos horas.<br>*I walked for two hours.*<br>**Hablamos** (por) cinco minutos.<br>*We talked for five minutes.*<br>**Contemplaron** el templo un rato.<br>*They contemplated the temple for a while.*<br>**Viví** en Ecuador (por) seis años.<br>*I lived in Ecuador for six years.* | **4.** To *tell time* in the past<br>**Era** la una.<br>*It was 1:00.*<br>**Eran** las tres y media.<br>*It was 3:30.*<br>**Era** muy tarde.<br>*It was very late.*<br>**Era** la medianoche.<br>*It was midnight.* |
| | **5.** To describe physical and emotional states or characteristics<br>Después del viaje **queríamos** descansar. Yo **tenía** dolor de cabeza y no **me sentía** muy bien.<br>*After the trip we wanted to rest. I had a headache and did not feel well.* |

**Fíjate** The use of *por* is optional in these cases.

### WORDS AND EXPRESSIONS THAT COMMONLY SIGNAL:

| PRETERIT | IMPERFECT |
|---|---|
| anoche | a menudo |
| anteayer | cada semana/mes/año |
| ayer | con frecuencia |
| de repente *(suddenly)* | de vez en cuando *(once in a while)* |
| el fin de semana pasado | frecuentemente |
| el mes pasado | mientras |
| el lunes pasado/el martes pasado, etc. | muchas veces |
| esta mañana | siempre |
| una vez, dos veces, etc. | todos los lunes/martes, etc. |
| | todas las semanas |
| | todos los días/meses/años |

**NOTE:** The **pretérito** and the **imperfecto** can be used in the same sentence.

**Veían** la televisión cuando **sonó** el teléfono.

*They were watching television when the phone rang.*

In the preceding sentence, an action was going on (**veían**) when it was interrupted by another action (**sonó el teléfono**).

## 9-22 Una (muy) breve historia de los incas
¿Qué sabes sobre los incas? Completa los siguientes pasos. ■

Machu Picchu, la ciudad perdida de los incas

El imperio de los incas

**Paso 1**  Lee el siguiente fragmento.

El imperio de los incas fue uno de los imperios más importantes de las civilizaciones precolombinas. Se encontraba (*It was located*) en lo que es hoy Perú, Bolivia, el norte de Chile y parte de Ecuador. El imperio se dividía en tres partes iguales: una tercera parte pertenecía (*pertained/belonged to*) a los indígenas y pasaba de padre a hijo; otra tercera parte era del Inca, o sea, del Gobierno; la otra tercera parte pertenecía a la Iglesia.

Los incas adoraban al hijo del Sol. Según la leyenda (*legend*), el hijo cayó en algún lugar cerca del lago Titicaca. Con él llegó su hermana y según la leyenda, ellos eran los padres de todos los incas. Esta civilización practicaba sacrificios de animales y algunas veces sacrificios humanos. También le ofrecían objetos preciosos y joyas (*jewels*) al Sol. El último cacique (o jefe político) famoso de los incas fue Atahualpa.

**Paso 2**  Subrayen los verbos.

**Paso 3**  Digan cuáles son **pretéritos** y cuáles son **imperfectos** y expliquen por qué se usaron cada uno de estos tiempos verbales.

**CAPÍTULO 9**

**NOTE for 9-22**
The lost city of Machu Picchu (8,000 feet, 2,438 meters) was rediscovered in 1911 by Hiram Bingham, an archaeologist from Yale University. It had been hidden for centuries in the mountains of the Andes northwest of Cuzco. Its amazing construction and architecture demonstrate the achievements of the Incan civilization. The stones of the buildings there are cut precisely to fit together tightly; not even a knife blade can be inserted between them. There is no mortar holding the stones in place. As the Incas did not use the wheel, it is a mystery how they could construct such massive buildings so high up in the mountains. The Urubamba River snakes along 2,000 feet (610 meters) below. Cuzco is at 11,000 feet (3,353 meters), much higher than Machu Picchu.

**NOTE for 9-22**
In some texts you will see definite articles before the names of countries, as in *el Perú* or *el Ecuador.* We have not included the articles here in *Una (muy) breve historia de los incas,* but you have the option to use them.

**EXPANSION for 9-22**
You may want to ask students the following comprehension questions:
1. ¿Dónde se encontraba el imperio de los incas?
2. ¿Cómo se dividía el imperio?
3. ¿En qué consiste la leyenda del hijo del Sol?
4. ¿Qué practicaban los incas?

⏱ 4:00  **9-23** **Un cuento de hadas** En grupos de tres o cuatro personas, pongan las siguientes oraciones en orden cronológico para terminar el cuento de Ricitos de Oro (*Goldilocks*). Después, analicen los usos **del pretérito** y **el imperfecto** dentro del cuento y expliquen por qué usaron cada uno de estos tiempos verbales. ■

Había una vez una niña muy curiosa. Un día, mientras caminaba por el bosque, encontró una casa muy bonita. En la casa vivían tres osos. Mientras los osos no estaban…

| | |
|---|---|
| 9 | Los osos la asustaron (*scared her*). |
| 3 | Entró en el dormitorio de los osos. |
| 7 | Mientras ella dormía entraron los osos. |
| 10 | La niña se levantó y salió corriendo de la casa. |
| 2 | Tenía sueño. |
| 4 | Buscó una cama. |
| 1 | La niña entró en la casa. |
| 5 | Vio que una cama era muy grande, otra era muy pequeña y la otra tenía el tamaño perfecto. |
| 8 | Encontraron a la niña dormida en la cama. |
| 6 | Se acostó. |

 Capítulo 8. Las construcciones reflexivas, pág. 312.

⏱ 6:00  **9-24** **En el consultorio** Completa el siguiente pasaje con la forma correcta **del pretérito** o **el imperfecto** de cada verbo entre paréntesis. Después, comparte las respuestas con un/a compañero/a y explícale por qué usaste el pretérito o el imperfecto. ■

Ayer en el consultorio del Dr. Fuentes (1. haber) ___había___ mucha actividad. Muchos pacientes (2. esperar) ___esperaban___ al médico y yo no (3. encontrar) ___encontraba___ dónde sentarme. Dos horas (4. pasar) ___pasaron___ lentamente. (5. Ser) ___Eran___ las once cuando por fin la recepcionista me (6. llamar) ___llamó___ y la enfermera (7. salir) ___salió___ para buscarme. Juntas (8. entrar) ___entramos___ al cuarto donde (9. estar) ___estaba___ el médico. El Dr. Fuentes (10. levantarse) ___se levantó___ y me (11. mirar) ___miró___ con mucha curiosidad. (12. Empezar) ___Empezó___ a examinarme y a hacerme preguntas.

Yo (13. ponerse) ___me puse___ nerviosa y (14. callarse) ___me callé___. Sólo (15. esperar) ___esperaba___ un examen anual típico pero las preguntas (16. ser) ___eran___ demasiado específicas. Por ejemplo, me (17. preguntar) ___preguntó___ si (18. sentirse) ___me sentía___ mareada (*faint*) por la mañana y si (19. comer) ___comía___ bien cuando (20. tener) ___tenía___ hambre.

Por fin (21. darse cuenta [*to realize*]: yo) ___me di cuenta___ de lo que (22. ocurrir) ___ocurría___. ¡El Dr. Fuentes (23. pensar) ___pensaba___ que yo (24. estar) ___estaba___ embarazada (*pregnant*)! Por lo visto la enfermera (25. equivocarse [*to be mistaken*]) ___se equivocó___ y ¡le (26. dar) ___dio___ al médico la información de otra paciente!

**9-25** **En el pasado** Termina las siguientes oraciones. Después, compártelas con un/a compañero/a. ■

MODELO     Cuando era niño/a…

E1:  *Cuando era niño, hacía ejercicio todos los días. Y tú, ¿qué hacías?*

E2:  *Cuando era niña, siempre jugaba en el parque con mi hermana.*

1. Cuando era niño/a…
2. Cuando tenía dieciséis años, frecuentemente…
3. Una vez el verano pasado…

4. Ayer tenía ganas de _____ pero…
5. Anoche…
6. Cuando vivía con mis padres, todas las semanas…

**9-26** **Nuestro cuento** En grupos de tres, van a contar una historia (en el pasado) basada en los dibujos. Al terminar van a compartir sus historias con los otros miembros de la clase. ■

**Estrategia**

In this variation of "Cinderella," remember to use the *imperfect* for *description* and *background* information. Use the *preterit* for *sequences of actions*.

**La Cenicienta**

**NOTE for 9-27**

This medical form is similar to what a student might encounter in a real-life emergency room visit. While at first glance the activity may appear labor intensive, in reality the form can be completed quickly, allowing plenty of time for *Pasos 2* and *3*.

Workbooklet

**9-27 Y en el hospital** Imagina que trabajas como enfermero/a en la sala de urgencias de un hospital. Un día entra un joven de unos veinte años con unos síntomas raros. ■

**Paso 1**  Llena el siguiente formulario médico para el joven enfermo como si fueras un/a enfermero/a.

---

### FORMULARIO MÉDICO

Por favor complete este formulario con la mayor precisión posible.  Toda la infomación en este formulario es confidencial y será utilizada en caso de emergencia.  Por favor escriba legiblemente.

**HISTORIA MÉDICA**

Nombre _____
Dirección _____
Ciudad y estado _____
Código postal _____
Número de teléfono _____
Edad _____
Fecha de nacimiento _____
Sexo _____ Peso _____ Altura _____
Grupo sanguíneo _____

1. ¿Está bajo tratamiento por alguna enfermedad? Explique._____
   _____

2. ¿Toma algún tipo de medicamento? _____
   _____

3. ¿Tiene algún tipo de alergia?_____
   _____

4. ¿Ha tenido cirugía alguna vez?_____
   _____

**CONDICIONES MÉDICAS**

Por favor marque cualquier enfermedad que haya tenido en el pasado y la fecha en que comenzó.

| | | |
|---|---|---|
| _____artritis | _____asma | _____dolor de espalda |
| _____mareos | _____tos crónica | _____dolor de pecho |
| _____diabetes | _____epilepsia | _____fracturas |
| _____dolor de cabeza | _____hernia | _____presión alta |

¿Ha tenido otra condición que no hemos mencionado?_____
_____

---

**Paso 2**  Crea **seis** preguntas para determinar cuál es su problema, según el modelo.

**MODELO**  E1:  ¿Dar / todos sus datos / en recepción?

E2:  *¿Dio todos sus datos en recepción?*

1. ¿Cuándo / llegar / la sala de urgencias?  ¿Cuándo llegó Ud. a la sala de urgencias?
2. ¿Cuándo / empezar / a dolerle?  ¿Cuándo le empezó a doler?
3. ¿Qué / hacer / cuando / empezar / a dolerle?  ¿Qué hacía cuando le empezó a doler?
4. ¿Quién / estar / con Ud.?  ¿Quién estaba con Ud.?
5. ¿Cómo / sentirse / cuando / acostarse / anoche?  ¿Cómo se sentía Ud. cuando se acostó anoche?
6. ¿Qué / causar / el dolor?  ¿Qué le causó el dolor?

**Paso 3**  Crea un diálogo con un/a compañero/a entre el joven y el/la enfermero/a usando las preguntas que escribiste.

**9-28** ## La última vez que nos enfermamos  Túrnense para describir la última vez que ustedes, un amigo, o un pariente se enfermaron. ■

- ¿Cuándo fue?
- ¿Cómo se sentían?
- ¿Cuáles fueron los síntomas?
- Si fueron al médico, ¿qué les hizo? ¿Qué les dijo?
- ¿Les recetó (recetar = *to prescribe*) algo? ¿Cuánto pagaron por la visita? Si no fueron al médico, ¿qué hicieron para curarse?
- ¿Cuánto tiempo duró (durar = *to last*) la enfermedad?

**Fíjate**

Use the term *médico* when referring to the profession of a doctor. Use *doctor* for the title of the person.

*El doctor Ramírez es un médico excelente.*

---

 **9-29** ### ¿Y ayer?  Descríbele a un/a compañero/a tu día de ayer en por lo menos **cinco** oraciones. ■

MODELO    *Ayer hacía mal tiempo cuando me desperté. No quería levantarme, pero por fin salí de la cama y fui a mi clase de español. El profesor nos dio mucha tarea. Luego fui a la biblioteca. Estudiaba cuando llegó mi mejor amigo Jeff.*

**Fíjate**

When the preterit and imperfect are used together in narratives in which events are retold, you will notice that the *imperfect* provides the background information such as the time, weather, and location. The *preterit* relates the specific events that occurred.

---

Capítulo 5. El mundo del cine, pág. 184.

**9-30** ### Luces, cámara, acción  ¿Te gustan las películas? ¿Vas al cine a menudo? Cuéntale (*Narrate*) a un/a compañero/a una película que hayas visto (*you have seen*) últimamente. Usa por lo menos **siete** oraciones. ¡Recuerda! Generalmente **el imperfecto** se usa para la descripción y **el pretérito** para la acción. ■

**ADDITIONAL ACTIVITY for** *El pretérito y el imperfecto*

**Los días del verano** ¿Qué hiciste el verano pasado? Usando por lo menos cinco oraciones, descríbele a un/a compañero/a un día normal, y después, en otras cinco oraciones, un día que fue diferente.

**ADDITIONAL ACTIVITY for** *El pretérito y el imperfecto*

**Un accidente** Entrevista a un/a compañero/a sobre un accidente que sufrió. Debes incluir la siguiente. información:
- que hacía cuando ocurrió
- cuándo ocurrió
- dónde ocurrió
- cómo ocurrió el accidente
- quién le ayudó
- qué pasó después

**ADDITIONAL ACTIVITY for** *El pretérito y el imperfecto*

This grammar topic is the perfect opportunity for a round robin story. Divide students into 5 or 6 groups. Write the first sentence or two of a possible story on the board (e.g., *Era una noche oscura. Roberto estaba solo en su casa…*; *Había una vez una niña muy, muy mala…*). Tell the groups to continue the story. Give them five or six minutes to write collectively. Then, have each group pass their story to the group to their left (or right). The groups now read what the previous group has written and continue that story for another 5 or 6 minutes. This continues until all groups have contributed to each story. At that time, the stories go back to their original groups to be finished. You may want to devote an entire class to this activity or divide it over two class periods.

## NOTA CULTURAL

`3:00`

### Las farmacias en el mundo hispanohablante

En Latinoamérica, las farmacias son, por la mayor parte, dispensarios de medicina únicamente. El farmacéutico (*pharmacist*) muchas veces ofrece consejos sobre los medicamentos (medicinas). Es fácil conseguir muchos tipos de medicina sin receta en las farmacias. Por ejemplo, puedes ir a la farmacia, describir los síntomas que tienes (como tos y fiebre) y pedir que te den unos antibióticos. Todo ello sin consultar al médico. Muchos países tienen *farmacias de turno* o *de guardia* que atienden al público las veinticuatro horas del día.

En algunos países (como Argentina, Chile y Perú) hay un nuevo tipo de farmacia al estilo estadounidense, que vende de todo. Estas farmacias pertenecen a grandes cadenas (Farmacity en Argentina, FASA en Chile, Inka Farma en Perú) que atraen a los consumidores con una gran variedad de productos, aparte de los medicamentos.

#### Preguntas
1. ¿Qué es una "farmacia de turno" o "farmacia de guardia"? ¿Existe este sistema en los Estados Unidos?
2. ¿Qué diferencias hay entre las farmacias hispanas tradicionales y las de los Estados Unidos?

## 6 GRAMÁTICA

`4:00`

 ¡*Hola!* Spanish Tutorial
09-37 to 09-40

### Expresiones con *hacer* Explaining how long something has been going on and how long ago something occurred

The verb **hacer** means *to do* or *to make*. You have also used **hacer** in idiomatic expressions dealing with weather. There are some additional special constructions with **hacer** that deal with time. **Hace** is used:

1. **to discuss an action that began in the past but is still going on in the present.**

> **hace** + *period of time* + **que** + *verb in the present tense*

**Hace** cuatro días **que** tengo la gripe.              *I've had the flu for four days (and still have it).*
**Hace** dos años **que** soy enfermera.                  *I've been a nurse for two years.*

2. **to ask how long something has been going on.**

> **cuánto (tiempo)** + **hace** + **que** + *verb in present tense*

¿Cuántos años **hace que** estudias medicina?         *How many years have you been studying medicine?*
¿Cuánto tiempo **hace que** estudias medicina?        *How long have you been studying medicine?*
¿Cuántos meses **hace que** tu abuela guarda          *How many months has your grandmother been staying*
  cama?                                                 *in bed?*
¿Cuánto tiempo **hace que** tu abuela guarda cama?   *How long has your grandmother been staying in bed?*

3. **in the preterit to tell how long ago something happened.**

> **hace** + *period of time* + **que** + *verb in the preterit*

**Hace** cuatro años **que** empecé a estudiar medicina.  *I began to study medicine four years ago.*
**Hace** seis años **que** me mudé aquí para estudiar.    *I moved here six years ago to study.*

or

> *verb in the preterit* + **hace** + *period of time*

Empecé a estudiar medicina **hace** cuatro años.      *I began to study medicine four years ago.*
Me mudé aquí **hace** seis años.                       *I moved here six years ago.*

Note that in this construction **hace** can either precede or follow the rest of the sentence. When it follows, **que** is not used.

4. **to ask how long ago something happened.**

> **cuánto (tiempo)** + **hace** + **que** + *verb in preterit*

¿Cuánto tiempo **hace que** empezaste a estudiar      *How long ago did you begin to study medicine?*
  medicina?
¿Cuánto tiempo **hace que** te enfermaste?            *How long ago did you get sick?*

**NOTE for** *Expresiones con hacer*
Discuss the difference in meaning in the sentences between having the verbs in the present tense vs. the preterit with students.

**ADDITIONAL ACTIVITY for** *Expresiones con* **hacer**
**Creando oraciones**

**Paso 1** Escribe seis oraciones diferentes utilizando palabras de cada columna, más otras palabras necesarias. Comparte las oraciones con un/a compañero/a.

MODELO
*Hace una hora que estudio francés.*

| Hace | una hora | que estudiar… |
|      | un día   | escuchar la música de… |
|      | una semana | ir a un museo de… |
|      | un mes   | comprar… |
|      | un año   | visitar a… |
|      | mucho tiempo | viajar a… |

**Paso 2** Juntos pongan los verbos en las oraciones en el pretérito. ¿Cómo cambia el significado de las oraciones?

MODELO
Hace una hora que estudio francés.
*Hace una hora que estudié francés.*

**9-31** **¿Qué pasa?** Juntos completen el diálogo entre Julián, Mari Carmen y su mamá con las palabras apropiadas. ■

_Julián, ¡ese sofá es horrible!_

MAMÁ: Julián (1) ¿ __Cuánto__ tiempo hace (2) __que__ vives en esta casa?

JULIÁN: Bueno, creo que (3) __hace__ unos dos años que vivo aquí.

MAMÁ: Y (4) ¿ __cuánto__ __tiempo__ __hace__ que tienes ese sofá? Está muy sucio.

JULIÁN: No sé, mamá. Fue un regalo de un amigo. Lo tenía en su apartamento.

MAMÁ: Creo que (5) __hace__ por lo menos diez años (6) __que__ tiene esas manchas (_stains_) negras. ¡Es horrible!

JULIÁN: Mamá, (7) __hace__ media hora (8) __que__ criticas mi casa y…

MARI CARMEN: ¡Mamá! (9) ¡ __Hace__ cinco minutos (10) __que__ te estoy llamando! ¡Tráeme agua!

Workbooklet

**9-32** **Firma aquí** Circula por la clase hasta encontrar a un estudiante que pueda contestar afirmativamente tus preguntas. ■

**Fíjate**

Note that _cuánto_ agrees with the amount of time: _cuánto tiempo; cuántas semanas/horas; cuántos años/días._

MODELO empezar a estudiar español hace menos de (_less than_) un año

E1: _¿Empezaste a estudiar español hace menos de un año?_

E2: _No, empecé a estudiar español hace dos años._

E1: (a otro estudiante) _¿Empezaste a estudiar español hace menos de un año?_

E3: _Sí, empecé a estudiar español hace seis meses._

E1: _Muy bien. Firma (Sign) aquí por favor._

_Janet_

| | |
|---|---|
| 1. empezar a estudiar español hace menos de un año | _____ |
| 2. graduarse de la escuela secundaria (_high school_) hace dos años | _____ |
| 3. conocer a su mejor amigo/a hace muchos años | _____ |
| 4. ver una película de terror hace dos o tres semanas | _____ |
| 5. ir a un concierto hace uno o dos meses | _____ |
| 6. tomar café hace una hora | _____ |
| 7. comer en un restaurante elegante hace unos días | _____ |
| 8. hacer ejercicio hace unas horas | _____ |
| 9. hablar con alguien de su familia hace una semana | _____ |
| 10. enfermarse hace una semana | _____ |

**NOTE for 9-32**

Encourage students to move around the room, asking questions to as many different classmates as possible. You may want to make this a competition—the student who gets the most signatures in the amount of time you set wins.

**9-33** **Conversando** Habla con varios compañeros de clase utilizando las siguientes preguntas para guiar la conversación. ■

1. ¿Cuánto tiempo hace que vives en este estado (*state*)? ¿Dónde vivías antes?
2. ¿Cuánto tiempo hace que estudias en esta universidad? ¿En qué año te gradúas?
3. ¿Cuánto tiempo hace que conoces a tu mejor amigo/a? ¿Dónde lo/la conociste?
4. ¿Cuánto tiempo hace que viste a tus padres? ¿Volviste a casa o te visitaron?
5. ¿Cuánto tiempo hace que fuiste al médico? ¿Qué te recomendó?

fui

se sentía

quería

Eran,

hacía

llegué

decidimos

ESCUCHA

## Síntomas y tratamientos
09-41 to 09-43

**Estrategia**

**Asking yourself questions**

A useful tool for boosting comprehension is asking yourself check questions to help you organize information and summarize what you have heard. You will practice this strategy in the **A escuchar** section.

**9-34 Antes de escuchar** Marisol no se siente bien y llama a su madre para pedirle consejo. Cuando tú no te sientes bien, ¿qué haces generalmente: llamas al médico, hablas con un/a amigo/a, llamas a tu madre u otro pariente o te cuidas solo/a (*take care of yourself*)? ■

Marisol llama a su madre.

**9-35 A escuchar** Completen las siguientes actividades. ■

1. La conversación entre Marisol y su madre se divide en tres partes. Escucha la primera parte y después escoge la pregunta que mejor resuma (*summarizes*) lo que escuchaste. Repite el proceso con cada parte.

**PRIMERA PARTE** b
a. ¿Por qué llama Marisol a su madre?
b. ¿Cuáles son los síntomas de Marisol?
c. ¿Qué hizo Marisol cuando se levantó?

**SEGUNDA PARTE** c
a. ¿Con quiénes salió Marisol anoche?
b. ¿A Marisol le gustan las galletas?
c. ¿Qué comió Marisol anoche?

**TERCERA PARTE** c
a. ¿Debe ir a clase?
b. ¿Debe comer mucho hoy?
c. ¿Qué puede hacer Marisol para sentirse mejor?

 2. Escucha una vez más para averiguar si escogiste las preguntas apropiadas. Compáralas con las de un/a compañero/a. Expliquen por qué son las mejores preguntas.

3. Ahora escucha la conversación por última vez para contestar las siguientes preguntas.
   a. ¿Por qué llama Marisol a su madre? Llama a su madre porque no se siente bien y no sabe qué hacer.
   b. ¿Cuáles son sus síntomas? Le duele mucho la cabeza y el estómago. No tiene ganas de comer.
   c. ¿Qué comió Marisol anoche? Comió dos hamburguesas con queso y papas fritas, helado y galletas.
   d. ¿Cuál es el consejo de su mamá? Le dice que no debe comer mucho pero debe beber mucha agua y té. Si come, debe comer cosas ligeras como sopa, arroz y fruta.

 **9-36 Después de escuchar** Realicen la escena entre Marisol y su madre. ■

# ¡CONVERSEMOS!
09-44

 **9-37** **Los pacientes** Tienes un trabajo como voluntario/a en un hospital. Describe a tres pacientes (ficticios) con quienes estuviste ayer. Tu compañero/a te hace las siguientes preguntas para guiar tu descripción: ◾

1. ¿Cómo son?
2. ¿Cuáles son las enfermedades o condiciones de los pacientes?
3. ¿Qué tratamientos recibieron?

Incluye por lo menos **diez** oraciones en tu descripción.

**9-38** **¿Qué hicieron?** Piensa en alguien que conoces que antes no vivía una vida sana, pero que recientemente cambió su vida. Descríbele a tu compañero/a de clase qué hacía antes y qué hizo para cambiar. Piensa bien si debes usar **el pretérito** o **el imperfecto** para explicar su situación. Tu compañero/a te va a hacer preguntas para clarificar y recibir más información. ◾

CAPÍTULO 9

SECTION GOALS for
*¡Conversemos!*
By the end of the *¡Conversemos!* section, students will be able to:

- describe possible conditions, ailments, and treatments of hospital patients using presentational and interpersonal modes.
- share information about someone's previously unhealthy lifestyle and the changes he/she has made using presentational and interpersonal modes.
- utilize previously learned/recycled vocabulary and grammatical concepts such as the preterit and imperfect tenses.

**ESCRIBE**

09-45

## Un resumen

| Estrategia | When writing a summary in Spanish about things that occurred in the past, you must choose appropriately between the preterit and the imperfect. For example, if you are relating a chain or sequence of events—actions that occurred one after the other—you will most likely need to use the preterit. If you | are describing situations, what used to happen, or what was going on when something else happened, you will most likely use the imperfect. At this stage of your learning, it is a good idea to bookmark the list of words and expressions that commonly signal the preterit and the imperfect on page 350 to also help guide you. |
|---|---|---|
| **Sequencing events** | | |

**9-39** **Antes de escribir** Piensa en el Episodio 8 de **Ambiciones siniestras.**
Haz una lista de los **ocho** acontecimientos (*events*) más importantes de *¿Quién fue?* y *El misterio crece.* ■

**9-40** **A escribir** Escribe un resumen del Episodio 8 de **Ambiciones siniestras,** utilizando tu lista e incorporando un poco de descripción sobre los personajes y la escena: dónde estaban, qué hacían, cómo se sentían, etc. ■

 **9-41** **Después de escribir** Comparte tu resumen con un/a compañero/a.
¿Tienen el mismo contenido? Enfóquense en los verbos. ¿Usaron de manera correcta el pretérito y el imperfecto? ■

## ¿Cómo andas? II

| | Feel confident | Need to review |
|---|:---:|:---:|
| Having completed **Comunicación II,** I now can . . . | | |
| • narrate in the past (p. 349) | ☐ | ☐ |
| • consider pharmacies in Spanish-speaking countries and how they differ from those in the United States (p. 356) | ☐ | ☐ |
| • explain how long something has been going on and how long ago something occurred (p. 356) | ☐ | ☐ |
| • ask myself questions when listening to organize and summarize what I hear (p. 360) | ☐ | ☐ |
| • communicate about ailments and healthy living (p. 361) | ☐ | ☐ |
| • write a summary, sequencing past events (p. 362) | ☐ | ☐ |

# Perú

09-46 to 09-47

## Les presento mi país

Diana Ávila Peralta

Mi nombre es Diana Ávila Peralta y soy de Ayacucho, Perú. Estudio historia en la Universidad Nacional Mayor de San Marcos en Lima y mientras estudio, vivo con unos parientes en Miraflores, un barrio de la capital. **¿Dónde viven los estudiantes de tu universidad generalmente?** Quiero ser profesora porque me fascina la historia de mi país y quiero compartir mi pasión con otras personas. Hay muchas ruinas de la civilización incaica en Perú. **¿Qué sabes de la historia de tu país y sus pueblos antiguos?** Perú es un país de extremos geográficos: tenemos la costa, al nivel del mar, los Andes, montañas impresionantes, cañones profundos, la selva y los principios del río Amazonas con flora y fauna magníficas. ¡Puedes mantenerte en forma caminando por estas regiones!

Las líneas de Nazca

Loros en la selva amazónica

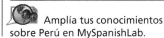

Miraflores, en las afueras de Lima, Perú

OCÉANO PACÍFICO

---

### ALMANAQUE

| | |
|---|---|
| **Nombre oficial:** | República del Perú |
| **Gobierno:** | República constitucional |
| **Población:** | 29.907.003 (2010) |
| **Idiomas:** | español (oficial); quechua (oficial); idiomas indígenas |
| **Moneda:** | Nuevo sol (S/) |

### ¿Sabías que...?

- Las líneas de Nazca, que se encuentran en un desierto del sur del país, son un enigma. Consisten en una serie de dibujos de diferentes animales, plantas y flores, y figuras geométricas que se reconocen solamente desde el aire.
- Hay casi 3,5 millones de llamas en los Andes.

### Preguntas

1. ¿Por qué Diana quiere ser profesora?
2. ¿Por qué se dice que Perú es un país de geografía muy variada?
3. ¿Qué otros países comparten algunas de las características geográficas de Perú?

Amplía tus conocimientos sobre Perú en MySpanishLab.

**363**

---

**NOTE for Las líneas de Nazca**
Las líneas de Nazca are still a mystery today. There are hundreds of different figures, plus additional cross-hatching lines, spread out over an area of 400 square miles. Some of the figures are distinctive (e.g., a monkey, a humming-bird, a spider, flowers), and others are difficult to decipher even now. Several theories exist as to the origin and meaning of the lines.

**NOTE for La selva amazónica**
It has been reported that the Andes Mountain range and the Amazon rainforest are home to more than half of the world's species of flora and fauna. The Scarlet Macaw is a member of the parrot family. Known for their vibrant colors and loud call, these birds can be seen gathering by the hundreds on the clay cliffs of the Amazon River where they feed on the rich minerals found there. Macaws build their nests high up in the canopy trees of the Amazon rainforest and mate for life. They can reach 32 inches long, more than half of which consists of a pointed tail, and an average weight of about 2.2 lbs.

---

**Instructor Resources**
• Text images (maps), Video resources

**SECTION GOALS for Cultura**
By the end of the *Cultura* section, students will be able to:
- discuss the geography of Peru.
- highlight geographical and historical sites in Peru.
- contrast Peru with Bolivia.
- identify the indigenous people of Bolivia.
- describe the indigenous ruins in Bolivia.
- explain how Bolivia differs from other South American countries.
- describe the geographical variation in Ecuador.
- explain the role of the shaman.
- make comparisons between Peru, Bolivia, and Ecuador.

**NATIONAL STANDARDS**
*Communication, Cultures, Connections, Comparisons*
The readings from *Les presento mi país* relate to Communication, Cultures, Connections, and Comparisons. The readings encompass interpretive communication because students are reading written Spanish and they have to interpret and understand the information (Standard 1.2). If you also read the cultural notes aloud, they would be interpreting and understanding spoken Spanish (Standard 1.2). Your students are engaging in interpersonal communication when discussing the readings in small groups and answering the questions that follow (Standard 1.1). The readings about Peru, Bolivia, and Ecuador explain how the cultures differ between the three countries, and students can relate to how the cultural differences shape the practices, perspectives, and products of the countries (Standards 2.1, 2.2). These cultural differences provide the basis for making comparisons between these cultures and the cultures of the United States (Standard 4.2). Students can also make connections between their studies in history, geography, and science to the new information about Peru, Bolivia, and Ecuador.

**NOTE for Les presento mi país**
The University of San Marcos was founded May on 12, 1551, by an order of Dominican friars; it is the oldest university in Latin America.

**NOTE for Miraflores**
An upscale neighborhood of Lima, this area is known for its excellent shopping, restaurants, parks, and beaches. It is also a cultural center with many art galleries and theaters.

### Instructor Resources
• Text images (maps), Video resources

**NOTE for *Los aymaras***
The Aymara indigenous people have a distinctive style of dress. The women wear layers of bright skirts (called *polleras*) and bowler hats. The hat is worn to the side of her head if the woman is unmarried, and in the center if she is married. The men wear striped ponchos and woven hats with earflaps, called *chullos*. The earflaps are a necessity for protection against the cold in the regions where they live.

**SUGGESTION for *Aymaras***
Ask students: Do we have regional or indigenous costumes in the United States? Do we have a way of telling someone's civil status from apparel or some outward appearance (e.g., wedding rings)?

**NOTE for *El lago Titicaca***
Lake Titicaca is the highest navigable lake in the world at 12,500 feet (3,810 meters). The Floating Islands of the Uros are here. These islands are constructed from layers of totora reeds, which are replaced from the top while those underneath decompose. The Uros people live on the islands and visitors are welcome, but you have to keep moving in order not to sink!

**SUGGESTION for *El lago Titicaca***
Ask students whether they can imagine living on a floating island. What would that be like? Would the sensation be like sleeping on a waterbed?

**NOTE for *Las chullpas***
*Chullpas*, ancient Aymara burial towers, can be found across the *Altiplano* in Bolivia and Peru. Corpses, placed in fetal position, were entombed along with some personal belongings. In the northern part of the *Altiplano* the *chullpas* are circular and made of stone while those in the southern part are rectangular and made of adobe.

**NOTE for *La papa***
The potato is originally from South America, and scores of varieties are cultivated in Andean countries. It is a staple in the diet of Bolivians. Another staple is an Incan grain, *quinoa*. This grain has been called "the most complete protein" food and is extremely nutritious. Bolivians have their own version of "hot sauce" called *la llagua*. This is a condiment found on tables everywhere in Bolivia and consists of tomatoes, onions, and very hot peppers called *locotos*.

# Cultura

## Bolivia

CULTURA • CULTURA • CULTURA • CU

09-46, 09-48

## Les presento mi país

Mi nombre es Jorge Gustavo Salazar y soy de Sucre, una de las dos capitales de mi país y la sede (*headquarters*) constitucional donde se mantiene el Tribunal Supremo de Bolivia. La Paz, la capital administrativa, es la capital más alta del mundo, a unos 3.650 m.s.n.m. en los Andes. **¿A qué altura está tu ciudad?** La gente indígena constituye más del cincuenta por ciento de la población del país, y muchos viven en el altiplano, un área cerca del lago Titicaca, que es el lago navegable más alto del mundo. En el altiplano se encuentran las ruinas de una civilización antigua preincaica, anterior a los aymara, que pueblan la región hoy en día. **¿Hay ruinas de antiguas civilizaciones cerca de donde tú vives?**

Jorge Gustavo Salazar

**Fíjate**
The abbreviation *m.s.n.m.* means *metros sobre nivel del mar*, or meters above sea level.

En las islas flotantes del lago Titicaca viven algunos indígenas.

Una mujer aymara con ropa tradicional

Unas chullpas en el altiplano

### ALMANAQUE

| | |
|---|---|
| **Nombre oficial:** | República de Bolivia |
| **Gobierno:** | República |
| **Población:** | 9.947.418 (2010) |
| **Idiomas:** | español (oficial); quechua (oficial); aymara (oficial) |
| **Moneda:** | Boliviano (Bs) |

### ¿Sabías que...?

• La papa, nativa de Sudamérica, es un alimento básico en Bolivia. Se cultivan más de doscientos tipos de papa en el país.

• Aunque no tiene salida al mar, Bolivia tiene una fuerza marina: la Armada Boliviana.

### Preguntas

1. ¿Por qué crees que Bolivia tiene tres idiomas oficiales?
2. ¿Qué distinción tiene La Paz como capital?
3. ¿Qué riesgo para la salud (*health risk*) comparten Bolivia y Perú?

Amplía tus conocimientos sobre Bolivia en MySpanishLab.

364

# Ecuador

CULTURA • CULTURA • CULTURA • CULTURA •

09-46, 09-49

## Les presento mi país

Yolanda Pico Briones

Mi nombre es Yolanda Pico Briones y soy de Quito, la capital de Ecuador. Mi país tiene tres diferentes tipos de geografía: la costa, la sierra y el oriente o la selva. La población, principalmente mestiza e indígena, se concentra en la sierra y la costa. **¿Dónde vive la mayoría de la población en tu país?** Uno de los grupos indígenas de Ecuador son los tsáchilas, también llamados "los colorados", debido a la costumbre de los hombres de pintarse (*dye*) el pelo de color rojo. Los chamanes (*shamans*) de esta tribu tienen gran conocimiento de las plantas medicinales y, por lo tanto, tienen mucho poder en la comunidad. **¿Es popular la medicina alternativa donde tú vives?**

Las islas Galápagos

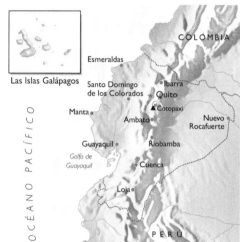

Un sombrero panamá

Las plantas medicinales son importantes en la medicina alternativa.

### ALMANAQUE

**Nombre oficial:** República del Ecuador
**Gobierno:** República
**Población:** 14.790.608 (2010)
**Idiomas:** español (oficial), quechua y otros idiomas indígenas
**Moneda:** El dólar estadounidense ($)

### ¿Sabías que...?

• El famoso sombrero panamá es en realidad de Ecuador.
• El volcán Cotopaxi se considera el volcán activo más alto del mundo.

### Preguntas

1. ¿Cuál es una costumbre de los tsáchilas?
2. ¿Qué tiene Ecuador en común geográficamente con Perú y Bolivia?
3. ¿En qué otros países se encuentra un gran porcentaje de mestizos e indígenas?

 Amplía tus conocimientos sobre Ecuador en MySpanishLab.

365

---

**NOTE for Los tsáchilas**
The Tsáchilas or *Colorados* are a distinctive indigenous group in the province of Pichincha, some 40 miles west of Quito. Although many of their traditions are being lost due to the encroachment of modernization and the lure of the big cities for the younger members of the community, this group maintains some easily recognizable traits. The men wear a rectangular piece of cloth, navy blue and white striped, which resembles a skirt. They shave their heads up to the crown, maintaining the hair on top rather long. This is then coated with a mixture of a vaseline-like substance tinted with the *achiote* seed, which makes it bright orange-red. The women weave a cloth of many colors for their skirts and wear necklaces of glass beads. Both sexes paint their bodies with black lines. The shamans of the Tsáchilas are well known for their knowledge and use of medicinal plants.

**SUGGESTION for Los tsáchilas**
Ask students: Why is it hard to maintain tribal or community customs in the present day? What do you think of shamans? Can they cure people? Why do you think they can or can't?

**SUGGESTION for El sombrero panamá**
Ask students: Can you think of other products or practices that have geographic misnomers, e.g., have names that do not truly reflect their origins (e.g., the Russian flu, which didn't begin in Russia, but was first documented there)?

**NOTE for El sombrero panamá**
Despite the name, Panama hats (*el sombrero panamá*) are made only in Ecuador. They are woven by hand from the toquilla plant. Monticristi and Jipijapa are two places where the hats are made. The true Panama hat is woven so tightly that it passes the water test: Turn the hat upside down and pour water into it. The best hats yield not a drop of water leaking out!

**NOTE for Las islas Galápagos**
The Galapagos Islands are an archipelago of volcanic islands that lie approximately 500 miles off the coast of Ecuador. Some 23,000 inhabitants live in this Ecuadorian province that encompasses a biological marine reserve and a national park. The islands are well known for their wildlife and the vast number of endemic species.

---

**NOTE for Las islas Galápagos**
Charles Darwin spent a good deal of time studying the vast array of animal species found there during the voyage of the *Beagle*. His collections and observations contributed to Darwin's theory of natural selection.

# Ambiciones siniestras

# Lectura

**Estrategia** · · · · Asking yourself questions

Just as with listening, it is helpful to learn to ask yourself check questions as you read, which help you summarize and organize information.

---

**9-42** **Antes de leer** En el **Episodio 8** Marisol y Manolo hablan de las dudas que tienen sobre Lupe y Cisco. Teniendo esto en cuenta, contesta las siguientes preguntas. ■

- ¿Es posible que Lupe sea (*is*) el Sr. Verdugo?
- ¿Por qué actúa Cisco de manera tan misteriosa?
- Si resuelven el nuevo rompecabezas, ¿van a poder salvar (*save*) a Alejandra y a Eduardo?

---

**9-43** **A leer** Completa los siguientes pasos. ■

**Paso 1** Lee el primer párrafo y elige la pregunta que mejor lo resuma (*summarizes it*).
    a. ¿Dónde están los protagonistas?
    b. ¿Cómo están Eduardo y Alejandra?
    c. ¿Qué saben Manolo, Cisco, Marisol y Lupe de Eduardo y Alejandra?

**Paso 2** Ahora lee el segundo párrafo y elige la pregunta que mejor lo resuma.
    a. ¿Por qué tienen miedo Manolo, Cisco, Marisol y Lupe?
    b. ¿Por qué Manolo, Cisco, Marisol y Lupe participaron en el concurso?
    c. ¿Por qué desaparecieron Eduardo y Alejandra?

**Paso 3** Continúa leyendo el episodio pero ahora, en vez de elegir la mejor pregunta, tú vas a escribir una pregunta para cada sección indicada (secciones de 3 a 9). Al terminar, compara tus preguntas con las de tus compañeros.

## ¡Qué mentira!

[1] En distintas partes del país hay cuatro estudiantes universitarios muy preocupados. Todavía no saben ni dónde ni cómo están Eduardo y Alejandra. Sólo saben que desaparecieron y que un tal Verdugo tiene algo que ver con todo eso°.

*has something to do with it*
*lie*

[2] El concurso —¡Qué mentira°!— ¿Cómo pudieron creerlo? Este tipo de cosas tan increíbles generalmente terminan siendo falsas. Para Manolo, Cisco, Marisol y Lupe es mucho más serio. Hay dos desaparecidos° ya y los otros con el miedo de no saber si les va a pasar lo mismo a ellos. El Sr. Verdugo les dijo que no hablaran° con nadie —especialmente

*missing*
*not to talk*

366

---

*would hurt all of them* con la policía— o les haría daño a todos°. Así que todos los días se levantan y se acuestan con miedo.

*scared* [3] Hoy Manolo se despertó asustado° y se levantó inmediatamente. Durmió mal anoche y ahora le duele todo el cuerpo. Decidió tomar tres aspirinas y volvió a acostarse. Pocos minutos después, sonó el teléfono celular. Era Cisco.

[4] —¿Manolo? ¿Estás levantado?

—Sí —respondió Manolo— hace media hora. ¿Qué pasa?

—Acabamos de recibir otro mensaje. Este hombre está loco —explicó Cisco.

—Voy a leer el mensaje y te llamo más tarde —le dijo Manolo.

*They hung up* [5] Colgaron°. Otra llamada. Esta vez fue Marisol.

—¿Manolo? Tienes que leer el último mensaje. No sé qué hacer…

—Mira Marisol, voy a leerlo ahora mismo. Ya me llamó Cisco hace unos minutos. Llama tú a Lupe y dentro de diez minutos te llamo. ¿Está bien? ¿Estás en tu teléfono celular?

—Sí. Bueno, te espero.

*turned on* [6] Manolo encendió° la computadora y leyó:

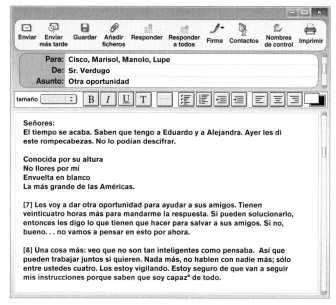

Enviar | Enviar más tarde | Guardar | Añadir ficheros | Responder | Responder a todos | Firma | Contactos | Nombres de control | Imprimir

**Para:** Cisco, Marisol, Manolo, Lupe
**De:** Sr. Verdugo
**Asunto:** Otra oportunidad

tamaño | B *I* U T

Señores:
El tiempo se acaba. Saben que tengo a Eduardo y a Alejandra. Ayer les di este rompecabezas. No lo podían descifrar.

Conocida por su altura
No llores por mí
Envuelta en blanco
La más grande de las Américas.

[7] Les voy a dar otra oportunidad para ayudar a sus amigos. Tienen veinticuatro horas más para mandarme la respuesta. Si pueden solucionarlo, entonces les digo lo que tienen que hacer para salvar a sus amigos. Si no, bueno. . . no vamos a pensar en esto por ahora.

[8] Una cosa más: veo que no son tan inteligentes como pensaba. Así que pueden trabajar juntos si quieren. Nada más, no hablen con nadie más; sólo entre ustedes cuatro. Los estoy vigilando. Estoy seguro de que van a seguir *capable* mis instrucciones porque saben que soy capaz° de todo.

*dial* [9] Con un gran suspiro, Manolo buscó su teléfono y empezó a marcar°... De pronto dejó de *threw it* marcar, se quedó mirando el teléfono un momento y lo tiró° con fuerza contra la pared...

---

CAPÍTULO 9 · NATIONAL STANDARDS

**Communication, Comparisons**
Note that the readings are kept at a level of comprehensible input that entices the students to read. Also, the follow-up questions encourage your students to think beyond the content of the story and make informed guesses about what they would do in the same circumstances. The *Ambiciones siniestras* reading for *Capítulo 9* focuses on asking questions while reading. If students work together and discuss the questions as they read, they are communicating interpersonally (Standard 1.1). The students can also make comparisons between the past tense in English and the preterit and imperfect in Spanish (Standard 4.1) as they read the story and decide why parts of the story required the preterit or the imperfect.

**NATIONAL STANDARDS**
**Communication, Connections**
The reading and writing activities from *Ambiciones siniestras* are designed to practice the new strategy of asking oneself questions. Students read the passage or engage in pre-writing activities that facilitate their communication in Spanish (Standard 1.2), and if they communicate with others in the interpersonal mode, they also apply Standard 1.1. They can use this new strategy and apply it to other subjects as they read for comprehension (Standard 3.1) while they strengthen their reading skills and increase their comprehension in other disciplines.

**SUGGESTION for Lectura**
You may want to explain that *Verdugo* means "tormenter."

🎙 **Instructor Resources**
• Video script

**ANSWERS to 9-44**
1. No saben si ellos también van a desaparecer.
2. Durmió mal y le duele el cuerpo. También está asustado.
3. Cisco y Marisol llaman a Manolo para saber si él recibió y leyó el mensaje nuevo.
4. Dice que pueden trabajar juntos y que él los está vigilando.
5. El Sr. Verdugo dice que los está vigilando y que es "capaz de todo".

**SECTION GOALS for *Video***
By the end of the *Video* section, students will be able to:
• answer pre-viewing questions.
• make predictions about what will happen based on the previous episode.

**ANSWERS to 9-46**
1. Estaban en la biblioteca.
2. Trataban de descifrar el rompecabezas.
3. Tenía un libro de Perú que hablaba de la cordillera de los Andes, una zona de gran altura.
4. Lupe dijo que todos los países de los Andes, Chile, Argentina, Perú, Bolivia, Ecuador, Colombia y Venezuela tienen grandes alturas.
5. Decidieron llamarlos para compartir sus ideas sobre el rompecabezas.
6. Dijo que es una frase famosa que dijo Eva Perón, la esposa del Presidente argentino Juan Perón.
7. Manolo propuso dividir el trabajo — la tercera pista para las chicas y la cuarta para Cisco y él.
8. Tenían doce horas.
9. Marisol no se encontraba bien y Lupe le dijo que pensaba que Cisco no les estaba diciendo la verdad. Cisco la oyó decirlo.

---

**9-44** **Después de leer** Contesta las siguientes preguntas. ▪

1. ¿Por qué se levantan y se acuestan con miedo nuestros protagonistas?
2. ¿Cómo se sentía Manolo cuando se levantó?
3. ¿Quiénes llamaron a Manolo? ¿Por qué?
4. Además de un rompecabezas, ¿qué información nueva contiene el mensaje?
5. En tu opinión, ¿qué fue lo más aterrador (*frightening*) de todo lo que dijo el mensaje?

  # Video

09-53 to 09-54

**9-45** **Antes del video** ¿Por qué crees que Manolo tiró el teléfono contra la pared? ¿Los protagonistas van a poder descifrar ese nuevo rompecabezas? ¿Van a trabajar juntos esta vez? ¿Van a poder salvar a Eduardo y a Alejandra? ▪

Sin embargo, creo que ya tenemos una pista (*clue*).

Todo este lío (*mess*) con los rompecabezas me tiene bastante nerviosa.

Tengo que confesar algo.

Episodio 9

## «No llores por mí»

Relájate y disfruta el video.

---

**9-46** **Después del video** Contesta las siguientes preguntas. ▪

1. ¿Dónde estaban Marisol y Lupe?
2. ¿Qué hacían ellas?
3. ¿Qué información tenía Marisol que creía que podía ayudar con la primera pista?
4. ¿Cómo respondió Lupe a su idea?
5. ¿Por qué decidieron ellas llamar a Cisco y a Manolo?
6. ¿Qué dijo Cisco sobre la segunda pista, "No llores por mí"?
7. ¿Qué propuso Manolo sobre las dos últimas pistas?
8. ¿Cuántas horas tenían para terminar de descifrar el rompecabezas?
9. ¿Cómo terminó el episodio?

368

# Y por fin, ¿cómo andas?

|  | Feel confident | Need to review |
|---|---|---|

Having completed this chapter, I now can . . .

**Comunicación I**

- describe the human body (p. 334) ☐ ☐
- pronounce the letters **d** and **t** (MSL / SAM) ☐ ☐
- share about people, actions, and things (p. 337) ☐ ☐
- explain ailments and treatments (p. 341) ☐ ☐
- make emphatic and exclamatory statements (p. 346) ☐ ☐

**Comunicación II**

- narrate in the past (p. 349) ☐ ☐
- explain how long something has been going on and how long ago something occurred (p. 356) ☐ ☐
- ask myself questions when listening to organize and summarize what I hear (p. 360) ☐ ☐
- communicate about ailments and healthy living (p. 361) ☐ ☐
- write a summary, sequencing past events (p. 362) ☐ ☐

**Cultura**

- relate the importance of water in maintaining good health (p. 346) ☐ ☐
- consider pharmacies in Spanish-speaking countries and how they differ from those in the United States (p. 356) ☐ ☐
- list important information about this chapter's featured countries: Peru, Bolivia, and Ecuador (pp. 363–365) ☐ ☐

**Ambiciones siniestras**

- create check questions to facilitate comprehension when reading, and give details about the new e-mail message (p. 366) ☐ ☐
- discover the progress the characters are making in deciphering the new riddle (p. 368) ☐ ☐

**Comunidades**

- use Spanish in real-life contexts (SAM) ☐ ☐

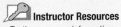

**Instructor Resources**
• Testing program information

# VOCABULARIO ACTIVO

| El cuerpo humano | *The human body* |
|---|---|
| la boca | *mouth* |
| el brazo | *arm* |
| la cabeza | *head* |
| la cara | *face* |
| la cintura | *waist* |
| el corazón | *heart* |
| el cuello | *neck* |
| el cuerpo | *body* |
| el dedo (de la mano) | *finger* |
| el dedo (del pie) | *toe* |
| el diente | *tooth* |
| la espalda | *back* |
| el estómago | *stomach* |
| la garganta | *throat* |
| la mano | *hand* |
| la nariz | *nose* |
| el oído | *inner ear* |
| el ojo | *eye* |
| la oreja | *ear* |
| el pecho | *chest* |
| el pelo | *hair* |
| el pie | *foot* |
| la pierna | *leg* |

| Algunos verbos | *Some verbs* |
|---|---|
| doler (ue) | *to hurt* |
| estar enfermo/a | *to be sick* |
| estar sano/a; saludable | *to be healthy* |
| ser alérgico/a (a) | *to be allergic (to)* |

| Otras palabras útiles | *Other useful words* |
|---|---|
| la salud | *health* |
| la sangre | *blood* |

| Algunas enfermedades y tratamientos médicos | *Illnesses and medical treatments* |
|---|---|
| el antiácido | *antacid* |
| el antibiótico | *antibiotic* |
| la aspirina | *aspirin* |
| el catarro / el resfriado | *cold* |
| la curita | *adhesive bandage* |
| el/la doctor/a | *doctor* |
| el dolor | *pain* |
| el/la enfermero/a | *nurse* |
| el estornudo | *sneeze* |
| el examen físico | *physical exam* |
| la farmacia | *pharmacy* |
| la fiebre | *fever* |
| la gripe | *flu* |
| la herida | *wound; injury* |
| el hospital | *hospital* |
| la inyección | *shot* |
| el jarabe | *cough syrup* |
| el/la médico/a | *doctor* |
| la náusea | *nausea* |
| las pastillas | *pills* |
| la receta | *prescription* |
| la sala de urgencias | *emergency room* |
| la tos | *cough* |
| la venda / el vendaje | *bandage* |

| Algunos verbos | Some verbs |
|---|---|
| **acabar de + *infinitivo*** | *to have just finished + (something)* |
| **caer(se)** | *to fall down* |
| **cortar(se)** | *to cut (oneself)* |
| **curar(se)** | *to cure; to be cured* |
| **enfermar(se)** | *to get sick* |
| **estornudar** | *to sneeze* |
| **evitar** | *to avoid* |
| **guardar cama** | *to stay in bed* |
| **lastimar(se)** | *to get hurt* |
| **mejorar(se)** | *to improve; to get better* |
| **ocurrir** | *to occur* |
| **quemar(se)** | *to burn; to get burned* |
| **romper(se)** | *to break* |
| **tener…** | |
| **alergia (a)** | *to be allergic (to)* |
| **(un) catarro, resfriado** | *to have a cold* |
| **(la/una) gripe** | *to have the flu* |
| **una infección** | *to have an infection* |
| **tos** | *to have a cough* |
| **un virus** | *to have a virus* |
| **tener dolor de…** | *to have a…* |
| **cabeza** | *headache* |
| **espalda** | *backache* |
| **estómago** | *stomachache* |
| **garganta** | *sore throat* |
| **toser** | *to cough* |
| **tratar de** | *to try to* |
| **vendar(se)** | *to bandage (oneself); to dress (a wound)* |

**Instructor Resources**
• IRM: Syllabi and Lesson Plans

## NATIONAL STANDARDS

### COMUNICACIÓN I
• To discuss modes of transportation (Communication, Comparisons)
• To pronounce the letters *b* and *v* (Communication)
• To influence others and give advice (Communication)
• To give orders and instructions (Communication)
• To engage in additional communication practice (Communication, Communities)

### COMUNICACIÓN II
• To share about travel (Communication)
• To state what belongs to you and others (Communication)
• To compare people, places, and things (Communication, Comparisons)
• To focus on linguistic cues (Communication, Connections)
• To communicate about travel plans (Communication)
• To write and present a report using linking words (Communication, Cultures, Connections)
• To engage in additional communication practice (Communication, Communities)

### CULTURA
• To list some public transportation options and discuss procedures for getting a driver's license (Communication, Cultures, Connections, Comparisons)
• To investigate travel and tourism opportunities in Venezuela (Communication, Cultures)
• To impart important facts about this chapter's featured countries: Colombia and Venezuela (Communication, Cultures, Comparisons)
• To explore further the chapter's cultural themes (Communication, Cultures)

### AMBICIONES SINIESTRAS
• To determine when it is appropriate to skip unfamiliar words and to discover the truth about what Cisco knows (Communication, Comparisons)
• To confirm that Lupe is not who she appears to be (Communication)

### COMUNIDADES
• To use Spanish in real-life contexts (Communities)

# 10 ¡Viajemos!

¿Te gusta viajar (*travel*)? ¿Adónde? ¿Cómo? ¿Cuándo? Exploremos muchas opciones. ¡Viajemos!

## PREGUNTAS

1 Cuando viajas, ¿adónde vas generalmente?

2 ¿Cuándo viajas? ¿Por qué?

3 En el futuro, ¿adónde quieres ir?

372

**SECTION GOALS for *Chapter opener***
By the end of the Chapter opener section, students will be able to:
• list preparations of smart travelers.
• make suggestions for planning a trip.

**NATIONAL STANDARDS**
*Communities*
There are several service learning options available for integrating travel, transportation, and the use of Spanish. If you have a large Hispanic population, you could plan a travel fair, where students have a table or booth for each Spanish-speaking country. You could invite community members from those countries to represent their countries of origin with realia, photos, souvenirs, artifacts, or food. This could be done during the day, during your class time, at night, or on a weekend. Students could research the countries of their Hispanic partners and act as the travel agents for the public, offering advice for what to see, excursions to take, and general travel tips. If you do not have a large Hispanic population, you could ask the students to do research as if they were travel agents and offer a "get to know my country" event where community members could find out what each Spanish-speaking country has to offer tourists. Students could research the current cost of travel, immunizations, and documentation required, and the best places to see; they could also plan a virtual trip using the Internet.

**EXPANSION for _Preguntas_**
Ask your students the following questions: _¿Tuviste problemas alguna vez en un viaje? Explica. ¿Qué puedes hacer para evitar ese problema en futuros viajes?_

**PLANNING AHEAD**
Assign **10-31** several days in advance, so that students can plan well their sentences.

**METHODOLOGY • Student Motivation**
Motivation plays a large role in learning another language. All of the activities in _¡Anda! Curso elemental_ focus on having students interact with each other in a non-threatening and highly engaging way. You should notice your students becoming more and more comfortable and confident as they learn Spanish. This chapter continues our goal of providing students with fun, enjoyable opportunities to practice Spanish with their classmates.

373

**SECTION GOALS for**
*Comunicación I*

By the end of the *Comunicación* section, students will be able to:
• discuss different modes of transportation.
• identify the parts of a car and their functions.
• pronounce the letters *b* and *v* correctly.
• give affirmative and negative *tú* commands.
• give affirmative and negative *Ud.* and *Uds.* commands.
• contrast public transportation options in the United States and abroad, and report about learning how to drive in Colombia.

**NATIONAL STANDARDS**
*Communication*

The vocabulary and activities in this section are highly motivational since a number of the transportation words are cognates. Also, it is very easy for students to access and use this vocabulary in real-life situations using the Internet, since there is an abundance of travel web sites for each country.

Depending on where one lives, there are multiple modes of transportation available. In the large cities, people walk or use public transportation such as trains or buses, whereas in small cities and suburbs many people drive cars. In *Capítulo 10,* students learn about different modes of transportation and how in many Hispanic countries there is a greater reliance on public transportation than on cars. They are able to make comparisons (Standard 4.2) about how transportation options differ among countries.

The vocabulary in *Capítulo 10* is focused on transportation, the parts of a car, and verbs associated with driving and maintaining vehicles. Students communicate in the interpersonal mode when they identify the parts of a car and discuss proper car maintenance (Standard 1.1). They can use this information, coupled with commands, to express themselves to others (rental car agents, mechanics, police, cab drivers, chauffeurs, bus drivers, etc.) about their transportation needs when traveling abroad (Standard 2.2). Students are able to connect what they already know about transportation and car parts with the new information they have learned in Spanish (Standard 3.1).

# Comunicación I

**1 VOCABULARIO**

7:00   10-01 to 10-08

## Los medios de transporte   Discussing modes of transportation

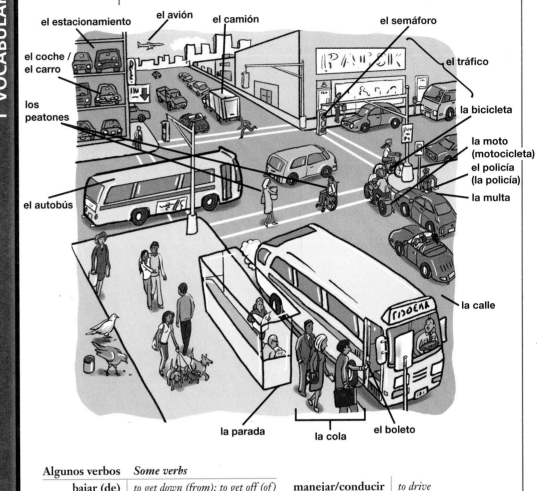

el estacionamiento · el avión · el camión · el semáforo · el coche / el carro · el tráfico · los peatones · la bicicleta · la moto (motocicleta) · el policía (la policía) · la multa · el autobús · la calle · la parada · la cola · el boleto

| Algunos verbos | *Some verbs* | | |
|---|---|---|---|
| **bajar (de)** | *to get down (from); to get off (of)* | **manejar/conducir** | *to drive* |
| **cambiar** | *to change* | **revisar** | *to check; to overhaul* |
| **doblar** | *to turn* | **sacar la licencia** | *to get a driver's license* |
| **entrar** | *to enter* | **subir (a)** | *to go up; to get on* |
| **estacionar** | *to park* | **viajar** | *to travel* |
| **funcionar** | *to work; to function* | **visitar** | *to visit* |
| **llenar** | *to fill* | | |

**NOTE for *Los medios de transporte***

If you wish, point out other ways of saying some of the following vocabulary. For example: *el autobús/camión (Mex.)/guagua (Caribe); el coche/el carro/el auto; el boleto/el billete*. If you choose to expand their knowledge by explaining that different countries have different ways of saying things, we recommend that you explain to beginning students that they will still be understood using the basic vocabulary we are presenting in *¡Anda! Curso elemental*. Otherwise, they will become frustrated, thinking that native speakers in country X will not understand them. As always, remind them of the *También se dice...* section in Appendix 3.

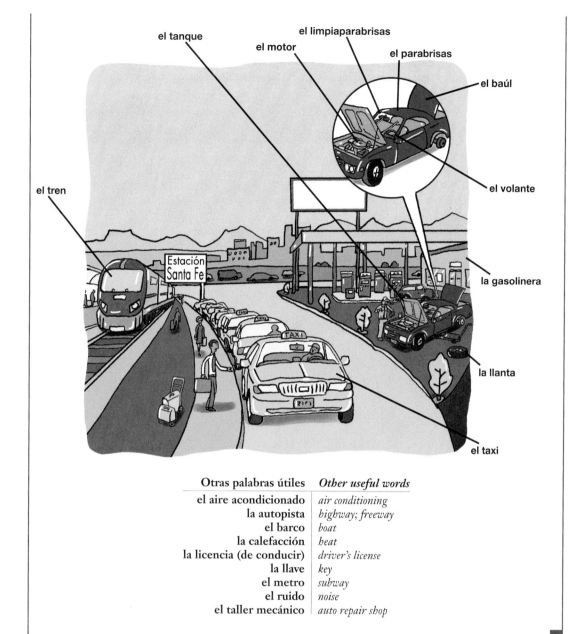

el tanque
el motor
el limpiaparabrisas
el parabrisas
el baúl
el tren
el volante
Estación Santa Fe
la gasolinera
la llanta
el taxi

| Otras palabras útiles | Other useful words |
|---|---|
| el aire acondicionado | *air conditioning* |
| la autopista | *highway; freeway* |
| el barco | *boat* |
| la calefacción | *heat* |
| la licencia (de conducir) | *driver's license* |
| la llave | *key* |
| el metro | *subway* |
| el ruido | *noise* |
| el taller mecánico | *auto repair shop* |

## PRONUNCIACIÓN

10-09 to 10-12

### The letters *b* and *v*

Go to MySpanishLab / Student Activities Manual to learn about the letters *b* and *v*.

**SECTION GOALS for *Pronunciación***

By the end of the *Pronunciación* section, students will be able to:
- pronounce the letters *b* and *v* correctly.
- state the rules that state when the *v* is pronounced like *b*.
- pronounce some popular *dichos y refranes* with *v* and *b* sounds in them.

**CAPÍTULO 10**

**METHODOLOGY • Timing Activities**

You will see that in some cases suggested times for activities may be slightly longer than in past chapters. As students are able to manipulate and create more with the language, more time may be allotted for activities in which students are encouraged to elaborate on responses or engage in more extended conversation. Whenever possible, extend your follow-up to engage students further by posing related questions and holding them accountable for what classmates are saying. For example, after a student responds to a question affirmatively, e.g., that she changed the oil in her car, you might ask another student: *¿Cambió Carla el aceite de su coche?*

**METHODOLOGY • Following Up Activities Efficiently**

When following up pair and group activities it is important to be efficient. In most cases, you should not have every group report, but rather call on two or three. In more mechanical activities, answers can be checked quickly, by calling on different students, and only checking items you know are not completely straightforward. Follow-up may take from 20 seconds to 2 minutes, depending on the length of the activity. For activities that require more manipulation or creation of language, follow-up will take longer but should not last longer than 2 or 3 minutes. The key is to be efficient and maintain a lively pace.

**ADDITIONAL ACTIVITY for *Los medios de transporte***

 **No pertenece** ¿Qué palabra no pertenece a cada uno de los siguientes grupos? Túrnense para leer la lista y contestar.

1. el parabrisas, el tráfico, el limpiaparabrisas, el baúl
2. el carro, el semáforo, la moto, el metro
3. revisar, estacionar, manejar, caminar
4. el tanque, el motor, la rueda, la multa
5. el taxi, el coche, el avión, el camión

**ANSWERS:**
1. el tráfico
2. el semáforo
3. caminar
4. la multa
5. el avión

---

  5:00 Workbooklet **10-1 ¿Qué tienen en común?** Escriban características específicas de cada medio de transporte en cada uno de los círculos pequeños. En el círculo grande del centro, escriban lo que todos estos medios de transporte tienen en común. Después comparen su diagrama con los de otros compañeros. ∎

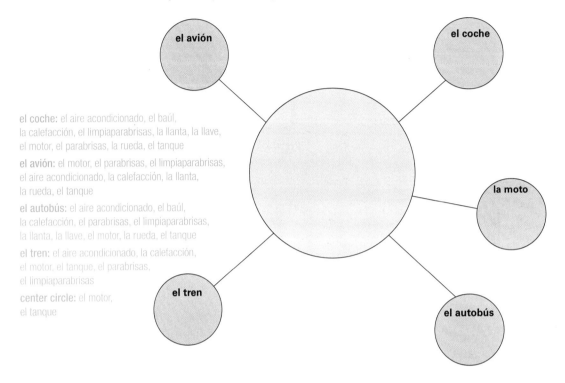

el coche: el aire acondicionado, el baúl, la calefacción, el limpiaparabrisas, la llanta, la llave, el motor, el parabrisas, la rueda, el tanque

el avión: el motor, el parabrisas, el limpiaparabrisas, el aire acondicionado, la calefacción, la llanta, la rueda, el tanque

el autobús: el aire acondicionado, el baúl, la calefacción, el parabrisas, el limpiaparabrisas, la llanta, la llave, el motor, la rueda, el tanque

el tren: el aire acondicionado, la calefacción, el motor, el tanque, el parabrisas, el limpiaparabrisas

center circle: el motor, el tanque

---

4:00 **10-2 ¿Es verdad?** Decide si las siguientes oraciones son ciertas (**C**) o falsas (**F**). Si son falsas, corrígelas (*correct them*). Compara tus respuestas con las de un/a compañero/a. ∎

**Estrategia**

When correcting true/false statements, instead of simply adding a negative word, correct the word that is false to make the statement true.

MODELO    Un carro tiene seis llantas.

    E1:  *Un carro tiene seis llantas.*

    E2:  *Falso. Un carro tiene cuatro llantas.*

1. Hay semáforos en las autopistas. F  en las calles
2. Para llegar a la universidad yo puedo tomar el autobús o ir a pie. C/F
3. Ir en avión es más rápido que ir en tren. C
4. Un coche no puede funcionar sin limpiaparabrisas. F  un motor, gasolina, etc.
5. Hay que cambiar el aceite de un coche cada 100.000 millas. F  de cada 3.000 a 5.000
6. Puedes llenar el tanque con gasolina en la gasolinera. C
7. Usamos la calefacción en el verano. F  Usamos la calefacción en el invierno.
8. Si manejamos muy rápido el policía nos puede dar una llave. F  una multa

**10-3** ¿Cómo vas? Completa los siguientes pasos. ■

Paso 1     Pon una equis (X) en la columna apropiada. Después, pregúntale a un/a compañero/a qué medios de transporte usa él/ella.

| ¿QUÉ USAS...? | A MENUDO | A VECES | NUNCA |
|---|---|---|---|
| bicicleta | | | |
| autobús | | | |
| avión | | | |
| carro | | | |
| tren | | | |

MODELO    E1:   *¿Qué medio de transporte usas a menudo?*

             E2:   *Uso el autobús a menudo. ¿Y tú?*

             E1:   *Uso el carro.*

             E2:   *¿Qué medio de transporte usas a veces?*

             E1:   *Uso la bicicleta a veces. ¿Y tú?*

Paso 2     Túrnense para hacerse y contestar las siguientes preguntas.

          ¿Qué medio de transporte usas…

1. más?
2. menos?
3. para ir a la universidad?
4. para ir al centro comercial?
5. para ir a visitar a tus amigos?
6. para ir a la casa de tus padres o de unos parientes?
7. para ir a Los Ángeles?
8. para ir a Caracas, Venezuela?
9. para ir a Europa?

**10-4** Cinco preguntas En grupos de tres o cuatro estudiantes, escriban **cinco** preguntas interesantes relacionadas con **Los medios de transporte**. Después, para cada pregunta, deben escoger a una persona de otro grupo para contestarla. ■

MODELO     GRUPO 1:   *¿Cambiaste el aceite del coche la semana pasada?*

   GRUPO 2 (PHILIP):   *No, no cambié el aceite la semana pasada, pero tengo que cambiarlo pronto.*

         GRUPO 1:   *¿Viajaste a México el verano pasado?*

   GRUPO 2 (GENA):   *Sí, fui a Cancún con mi familia.*

**378** CAPÍTULO 10

**NOTE for 10-5**

As with all activities like **10-5,** insist that students answer truthfully, the purpose being that students will need to interact with a variety of others in the class.

**ADDITIONAL ACTIVITY for**
*Los medios de transporte*

You may choose to use this activity as a teacher-led listening activity or as a paired activity.

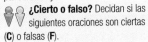 **¿Cierto o falso?** Decidan si las siguientes oraciones son ciertas (**C**) o falsas (**F**).

1. Se compra la gasolina en galones en los Estados Unidos.
2. Se puede manejar sin llantas.
3. Cuesta más viajar en avión que viajar por autobús.
4. Hay que tener una licencia especial para conducir una moto.
5. Cuesta menos comprar un coche con aire acondicionado.
6. Las llaves sirven para abrir el baúl.
7. Se puede estacionar en la autopista.
8. Un coche puede funcionar sin aceite.

**ANSWERS:**
1. C
2. F
3. C
4. C
5. F
6. C/F
7. F
8. F

---

 Workbooklet

**Estrategia**

When performing a signature search (or *Firma aquí*) activity, remember to circulate around the classroom, speaking to many different classmates. You should try to have a different student's signature for each item.

 **10-5** **Firma aquí** Circula por la clase hasta encontrar a un estudiante que pueda contestar afirmativamente a tu pregunta. **¡OJO!** Debes usar **el pretérito** en la mayoría de las preguntas. ■

MODELO   manejar un camión el verano pasado

E1: *¿Manejaste un camión el verano pasado?*

E2: *Sí, manejé un camión el verano pasado.*

E1: *Pues, firma aquí.*

_____Rosario_____

| manejar un camión el verano pasado | ir a una gasolinera esta mañana | saber manejar un barco |
|---|---|---|
| tener más de tres llaves contigo | ir a la universidad por la autopista. | tener un coche sin (*without*) calefacción |
| perder las llaves alguna vez | viajar a algún lugar exótico durante las últimas vacaciones | recibir una multa el año pasado |
| tener un accidente de coche en los últimos dos años | llevar el coche al taller mecánico el mes pasado | viajar en tren el año pasado |

---

 **10-6** **¡No funciona!** Necesitan llevar su coche a un mecánico. Hagan los papeles del conductor y el mecánico. Tienen que descubrir qué problema tiene el coche, hablar de posibles soluciones y decidir cuánto tiempo se necesita para repararlo. ■

## 2 GRAMÁTICA

10-13 to 10-18 · ¡Hola! Spanish/English Tutorials

# Los mandatos informales
## Influencing others and giving advice

*¡A la derecha, Pepe! Dobla a la derecha, no a la izquierda...*

When you need to give orders, advise, or ask people to do something, you use commands. If you are addressing a friend or someone you normally address as **tú**, you use informal commands. You have been responding to **tú** commands since the beginning of *¡Anda! Curso elemental*: **escucha, escribe, abre tu libro en la página,** etc.

**1.** The affirmative *tú* command form is the same as the **él, ella, Ud.** form of the present tense of the verb:

| Infinitive | | Present tense | Affirmative *tú* command |
|---|---|---|---|
| llen**ar** | él, ella, Ud. | llen**a** | llen**a** |
| le**er** | él, ella, Ud. | le**e** | le**e** |
| ped**ir** | él, ella, Ud. | pid**e** | pid**e** |

Llen**a** el tanque.      *Fill the tank.*
Dobl**a** a la derecha.      *Turn to the right.*
Conduc**e** con cuidado.      *Drive carefully.*
Pid**e** permiso.      *Ask permission.*

**There are eight common verbs that have irregular affirmative *tú* commands:**

| decir → **di** | ir → **ve** | salir → **sal** | tener → **ten** |
|---|---|---|---|
| hacer → **haz** | poner → **pon** | ser → **sé** | venir → **ven** |

**Sé** respetuoso con los peatones.      *Be respectful of pedestrians.*
**Ten** cuidado al conducir.      *Be careful when driving.*
**Ven** al aeropuerto con tu pasaporte.      *Come to the airport with your passport.*
**Pon** las llaves en la mesa.      *Put the keys on the table.*

*(continued)*

---

---

**Instructor Resources**
• PPT, Extra Activities

**NATIONAL STANDARDS**
*Communication*
Students enjoy learning the command forms since it provides them the linguistic opportunity to give directions to others. The communicative activities related to the parts of a car and the vocabulary about driving offer a starting point for conversation. Most students are aware of the responsibilities of driving and maintaining a car, and they are able to state their likes and dislikes about driving and practice posing questions to their classmates (Standard 1.1).

**NOTE for *Los mandatos informales***
You may wish to point out that accent marks are not needed when one pronoun is attached to a command of one syllable; for example, *ponlo, dime,* etc.

**NOTE for *Los mandatos informales***
As stated at the beginning of *¡Anda! Curso elemental,* the forms of *vosotros* are not practiced. If you wish to include them here, please do so.

**SUGGESTION for *Los mandatos informales***
Drill *tú* commands by saying an infinitive and having the students tell you the command.

**ADDITIONAL ACTIVITY for *Los mandatos informales***
**¿Qué hago?** Di las formas afirmativas y negativas de los mandatos informales de los siguientes verbos.

**MODELO**
E1: *beber*
E2: *¡Bebe! ¡No bebas!*

1. hablarme
2. comer
3. tomarla
4. llevarlo
5. usarlas
6. estudiar menos
7. ser bueno
8. ponerlo aquí
9. salir temprano
10. venir ahora
11. tenerlo
12. hacerlo
13. decírmelo
14. dormirse
15. vestirse

**2. To form the negative *tú* (informal) commands:**

1. Take the **yo** form of the present tense of the verb.
2. Drop the **-o** ending.
3. Add *-es* for **-ar** verbs, and add *-as* for **-er** and **-ir** verbs.

| Infinitive | Present tense | | Negative *tú* command |
|---|---|---|---|
| llen**ar** | yo llen**ø** | + es | no llen**es** |
| le**er** | yo le**ø** | + as | no le**as** |
| ped**ir** | yo pid**ø** | + as | no pid**as** |

| | |
|---|---|
| No llen**es** el tanque. | *Don't fill the tank.* |
| No dobl**es** a la derecha. | *Don't turn to the right.* |
| No conduz**cas** muy rápido. | *Don't drive very fast.* |
| No pid**as** permiso. | *Don't ask permission.* |

Verbs ending in **-car, -gar,** and **-zar** have a spelling change in the negative **tú** command. These spelling changes are needed to preserve the sounds of the infinitive endings.

| Infinitive | Present tense | | Negative *tú* command |
|---|---|---|---|
| sa**car** | yo sa**co** | c → qu | no sa**ques** |
| lle**gar** | yo lle**go** | g → gu | no lle**gues** |
| empe**zar** | yo empie**zo** | z → c | no empie**ces** |

**Fíjate**

The verb *conducir* has an irregular *yo* form, similar to *conocer* (conocer → cono**zco**; conducir → condu**zco**).

**Fíjate**

These are the same spelling changes with which you were presented when you learned the irregular preterit tense of these verbs.

**3. Object and reflexive pronouns are used with *tú* commands in the following ways:**

**a.** They are *attached* to the ends of *affirmative* commands. When the command is made up of more than two syllables after the pronoun(s) is/are attached, a written accent mark is placed over the stressed vowel.

| | |
|---|---|
| Se me pinchó una llanta. **¡Cámbiamela!** | *I got a flat tire. Change it for me!* |
| Tu bicicleta no funciona. **Revísala.** | *Your bike does not work. Check it.* |
| Me gusta tu coche. **Préstamelo.** | *I like your car. Lend it to me.* |
| Es tarde. **Duérmete** mientras conduzco. | *It's late. Sleep while I drive.* |

**b.** They are placed *before negative* **tú** commands.

| | |
|---|---|
| No se nos pinchó una llanta. ¡No **me la** cambies! | *We don't have a flat tire. Don't change it for me!* |
| Tu bicicleta funciona. No **la** revises. | *Your bicycle works. Don't check it.* |
| No me gusta tu coche. No **me lo** prestes. | *I don't like your car. Don't lend it to me.* |
| Es tarde. No **te duermas** mientras conduces. | *It's late. Don't fall asleep while you drive.* |

**10-7 ¿Qué diría el profesor?** Túrnense para decir cuál de los dos mandatos diría (*would say*) un/a profesor/a de una escuela de conducir. ◾

**MODELO**    a. Toma apuntes mientras hablo.
         b. No tomes apuntes mientras hablo.
         E1: *Toma apuntes mientras hablo.*

1. (a.) Estudia las reglas (*rules*) en el manual de conducir.    b. No estudies las reglas.
2. a. Ven tarde a la clase.    (b.) No vengas tarde a la clase.
3. (a.) Lee el manual con cuidado.    b. No leas el manual con cuidado.
4. (a.) Practica fuera de la clase.    b. No practiques fuera de la clase.
5. a. Ponte nervioso/a.    (b.) No te pongas nervioso/a.
6. (a.) Conduce con cuidado.    b. No conduzcas con cuidado.
7. (a.) Sal de la clase antes de tiempo.    (b.) No salgas de la clase antes de tiempo.
8. (a.) Trae tu manual a clase.    b. No traigas tu manual a clase.

 **10-8 Hazlo, por favor** Túrnense para expresar mandatos afirmativos y negativos usando los pronombres de complemento directo. ◾

Capítulo 5. Los pronombres de complemento directo, pág. 189.

**MODELO**    esperar el autobús
      E1: *¡Espéralo!*
      E2: *¡No lo esperes!*

**Estrategia**

For activities like **10-8** you can take turns by having one student do the even-numbered items while the other does the odd-numbered ones. Or, one can give the affirmative commands while the other gives the negatives; then switch roles.

1. tomar el autobús
2. prestarme las llaves
3. conducir el carro
4. usar la calefacción
5. hacer ruido
6. limpiar el parabrisas
7. subir la ventana
8. estacionar el coche en el garaje
9. buscar un estacionamiento

 **10-9 El sobrinito** Tu hermana está enferma y necesita ir al médico. Tú tienes que quedarte en su casa con Abel, su hijo de cuatro años. Dile lo que puede y no puede hacer en las siguientes situaciones. ◾

**MODELO**    Abel quiere comer un plato de donas (*donuts*).
      *¡No comas todas las donas!*

**Abel quiere...**

1. mirar un programa de *Sesame Street* ¡Mira Sesame Street!
2. llamar por teléfono a Big Bird ¡No llames a Big Bird!
3. dibujar en la pared ¡No dibujes en la pared!
4. limpiar su cuarto ¡Limpia tu cuarto!
5. mirar una película de terror ¡No mires la película de terror!
6. poner el gato (*cat*) en la lavadora ¡No pongas el gato en la lavadora!
7. beber una Coca-Cola ¡No bebas Coca-Cola!
8. dormir la siesta ¡Duerme la siesta!

**NOTE for 10-8**
You may prefer to offer additional practice with the command forms prior to adding all the pronouns by taking advantage of the suggestions and additional activities offered in the instructor annotations for this section, the Extra Activities folder under Instructor Resources, and on MySpanishLab.

**ANSWERS to 10-8**
1. ¡Tómalo! ¡No lo tomes!
2. ¡Préstamelas! ¡No me las prestes!
3. ¡Condúcelo! ¡No lo conduzcas!
4. ¡Úsala! ¡No la uses!
5. ¡Hazlo! ¡No lo hagas!
6. ¡Límpialo! ¡No lo limpies!
7. ¡Súbela! ¡No la subas!
8. ¡Estaciónalo en el garaje! ¡No lo estaciones en el garaje!
9. ¡Búscalo! ¡No lo busques!

**21ST CENTURY SKILLS • LIFE AND CAREER SKILLS**
The Partnership for 21st Century Skills requires that education include preparing students for the world of work. That includes the skills of managing goals and time, working independently, and being self-directed learners. *¡Anda!* provides Estrategias at the point of need to help learners become successful, independent, life-long learners. Perhaps more important are the curricular suggestions for *¡Anda!* users, one of which is assigning topics like grammar presentations and cultural readings to be done before class. This approach ensures the creation of independent, self-directed learners.

**382** CAPÍTULO 10

## ADDITIONAL ACTIVITY for *Los mandatos informales*

 **Por favor...** ¿Qué les pides a tus amigos? Con un/a compañero/a, da los mandatos siguientes.

**MODELO**
E1: llamarme mañana
E2: *Llámame mañana, por favor.*

1. venir a verme
2. tener paciencia conmigo
3. decirme la verdad siempre
4. divertirse
5. no salir con personas antipáticas
6. acordarse de la fiesta
7. no ser tonto/a
8. no vestirse de manera atrevida

**ANSWERS:**
1. Ven a verme, por favor.
2. Ten paciencia conmigo, por favor.
3. Dime la verdad siempre, por favor.
4. Diviértete, por favor.
5. No salgas con personas antipáticas, por favor.
6. Acuérdate de la fiesta, por favor.
7. No seas tonto/a, por favor.
8. No te vistas de manera atrevida, por favor.

## METHODOLOGY • Teaching Commands

There are several approaches to teaching the commands. We have made the conscious decision to chunk the material to present the familiar commands first for several reasons. First, they are the commands that students will tend to use the most among themselves. Next, the affirmative commands are very easy to form, something they already know. Finally, the negative familiar commands prepare the students for the formal commands to follow, and ultimately, the subjunctive. You may want to point out to students that they have seen formal commands in the activity direction lines throughout the text.

---

`4:00`  **10-10** **¡Ayúdame!** ¡Tu compañero/a de apartamento te vuelve loco/a! ∎

**Paso 1** Usa los siguientes verbos para decirle lo que debe y no debe hacer y compara tus respuestas con las de un/a compañero/a.

**MODELO** no poner tus libros en mi cama
*No pongas tus libros en mi cama.*

1. no dormirse en el sofá No te duermas en el sofá.
2. sacar la basura Saca la basura.
3. no comer en la sala No comas en la sala.
4. no beber de mi vaso No bebas de mi vaso.
5. decirme la verdad siempre Dime la verdad siempre.
6. no vestirse en la cocina No te vistas en la cocina.
7. tener más paciencia con mi gato Ten más paciencia con mi gato.
8. no invitar siempre a los amigos después de las once de la noche No invites siempre a tus amigos después de las once de la noche.

**Paso 2** Para cada mandato negativo que dieron juntos, den otra alternativa.

**MODELO** E1: *No pongas tus libros en mi cama.*
E2: *Ponlos en la mesa.* Answers will vary.

---

`5:00`  **10-11** **¡Una fiesta!** Tu compañero/a y tú organizan una fiesta para sus amigos. Tienen mucho que hacer: limpiar el apartamento, organizar la música, comprar y preparar la comida, vestirse, etc. Un amigo se ofrece a ayudarles. Hagan una lista de las cosas que él puede hacer. ∎

**MODELO**

> 1. Organiza los CD.

---

`5:00`  **10-12** **El transporte** Revisa el vocabulario de **Los medios de transporte.** Escoge seis de los verbos y haz una lista de mandatos afirmativos y negativos, usando los verbos. ¡Sé creativo! Después, comparte tu lista con un/a compañero/a. ∎

**MODELO** revisar → *Revisa el motor de tu coche.*

**3 GRAMÁTICA**

**10-19 to 10-22** Spanish/English Tutorials

## Los mandatos formales — Giving orders and instructions

When you need to influence others by making a request, giving advice, giving instructions, or giving orders to people you normally treat as **Ud.** or **Uds.**, you are going to use a different set of commands: **formal** commands. The forms of these commands are similar to the negative **tú** command forms.

¡Volaba!

Muéstreme su licencia, por favor.

¿Iba muy rápido, señor policía?

1. **To form the *Ud.* and *Uds.* commands:**
   1. Take the **yo** form of the present tense of the verb.
   2. Drop the **-o** ending.
   3. Add **-e(n)** for **-ar** verbs, and add **-a(n)** for **-er** and **-ir** verbs.

| Infinitive | Present tense | | Ud. commands | Uds. commands |
|---|---|---|---|---|
| limpi**ar** | yo limpi**ø** | + e(n) | (no) limpi**e** | (no) limpi**en** |
| le**er** | yo le**ø** | + a(n) | (no) le**a** | (no) le**an** |
| ped**ir** | yo pid**ø** | + a(n) | (no) pid**a** | (no) pid**an** |

| | |
|---|---|
| **Llene** el tanque. **Llénelo.** | *Fill up the tank. Fill it.* |
| **No limpie** el parabrisas. **No lo limpie.** | *Don't clean the windshield. Don't clean it.* |
| **Conduzca** el camión. **Condúzcalo.** | *Drive the truck. Drive it.* |
| **No ponga** esa gasolina cara en el coche. | *Don't put that expensive gasoline in the car.* |
| **No la ponga** en el coche. | *Don't put it in the car.* |
| **Traiga** su licencia. **Tráigala.** | *Bring your license. Bring it.* |
| **No busquen** sus llaves. **No las busquen.** | *Don't look for your keys. Don't look for them.* |

### ¡Explícalo tú!

1. Where do the object pronouns appear in affirmative commands? Where do they appear in negative commands? In what order?
2. Why are there written accents added to some of the commands and not to others?

 Check your answers to the preceding questions in Appendix 1.

2. Verbs ending in *-car*, *-gar*, and *-zar* have a spelling change in the *Ud.* and *Uds.* commands. These spelling changes are needed to preserve the sounds of the infinitive endings.

| Infinitive | Present tense | | Ud/Uds. commands |
|---|---|---|---|
| sac**ar** | yo sa**c**o | c → qu | sa**qu**e(n) |
| lleg**ar** | yo lle**g**o | g → gu | lle**gu**e(n) |
| empez**ar** | yo empie**z**o | z → c | empie**c**e(n) |

*(continued)*

**Instructor Resources**
• PPT, Extra Activities

**NOTE for *Los mandatos formales***
The formal commands are introduced at this point since the students have already begun the imperative with the familiar commands. Note that students have already seen some formal commands in *Capítulo Preliminar A*. The formal commands provide pre-practice for the subjunctive. Students are now able to perform the imperative with both singular and plural subjects.

**NOTE for *Los mandatos formales***
Remind students that the verbs that are stem-changing in the present tense also have stem changes in the command forms, e.g., *pedir → pida, dormir → duerma, volver → vuelva*, etc.

**NOTE for *Los mandatos formales***
Remind students that *conducir* has an irregular *yo* form and it maintains this change in the negative *tú* command. This is also true for the rest of the verbs with irregular *yo* forms that you have learned thus far (*hacer, conocer, decir, poner*, etc.).

**NOTE for *Gramática***
This is an inductive grammar presentation in which the students are given examples of a grammar concept and, through the use of guiding questions, they formulate the rule in their own words. Research indicates that students remember and internalize grammar rules better when they construct their own knowledge.

**NOTE for *Los mandatos formales***

*¡Anda! Curso elemental* will use the *Uds.* commands throughout this program. If you use the *vosotros* forms, please point out the linguistic difference.

**SUGGESTION for *Los mandatos formales***

As a warm-up activity, drill command forms by saying an infinitive and asking for a choral class response for the command. Start with just the command form, then add more information.
For example: *hablar (más despacio), regresar (temprano), levantarse (por favor), comprar (estos zapatos), comer (verduras), beber (leche), traer (su traje de baño), ponerse (guantes), divertirse (esta noche).*

**3. These verbs also have irregular forms for the *Ud./Uds.* commands:**

| | | | | | | | | |
|---|---|---|---|---|---|---|---|---|
| dar | → | **dé(n)** | | ir | → | **vaya(n)** | ser → | **sea(n)** |
| estar | → | **esté(n)** | | saber | → | **sepa(n)** | | |

**Finally, compare the forms of the *tú* and *Ud./Uds.* commands:**

| | *Tú* commands | | *Ud./Uds.* commands | |
|---|---|---|---|---|
| | affirmative | negative | affirmative | negative |
| hablar | habla | no hables | hable(n) | no hable(n) |
| comer | come | no comas | coma(n) | no coma(n) |
| pedir | pide | no pidas | pida(n) | no pida(n) |

Capítulo 8. Las construcciones reflexivas, pág. 312.

**10-13 Consejos** Dos estudiantes de intercambio (*exchange students*) van a llegar a tu universidad y necesitan tu ayuda con lo que deben y no deben hacer antes de venir a los Estados Unidos. Hazles una lista con tus consejos y comparte la lista con un/a compañero/a. ■

**MODELO**    E1: acostarse temprano la noche antes de viajar

          E2: *Acuéstense temprano la noche antes de viajar.*

1. levantarse temprano el día del viaje   Levántense temprano el día del viaje.
2. preparar el equipaje (*luggage*) el día anterior   Preparen el equipaje el día anterior.
3. llevar ropa cómoda   Lleven ropa cómoda.
4. no ponerse nervioso/a   No se pongan nerviosos.
5. evitar el alcohol   Eviten el alcohol.
6. tener su pasaporte a mano (*on hand*)   Tengan su pasaporte a mano.
7. sentarse en el asiento correcto   Siéntense en el asiento correcto.
8. dormirse en el avión   Duérmanse en el avión.

**10-14 La multa** Termina el diálogo entre Mayra y el policía. Después presenta la escena con un/a compañero/a. ■

MAYRA: Buenas noches. ¿Iba muy rápido, señor policía?

POLICÍA: Sí, señorita. (1) _Muéstreme_ (mostrarme) su licencia, por favor.

MAYRA: Aquí la tiene (*here you go*), señor. Sé que la foto es muy mala.

POLICÍA: No (2) _se preocupe_ (preocuparse). Ahora, (3) _cuénteme_ (contarme), señorita: ¿A qué velocidad (*speed*) iba?

MAYRA: Pues… la verdad es que no estoy segura. (4) _Dígamelo_ (decírmelo) usted.

POLICÍA: Iba a ochenta kilómetros por hora y el límite aquí es sesenta y cinco.

MAYRA: ¡Ay! ¡Mi padre me va a matar! Por favor, no (5) _me dé_ (darme) una multa. Lo siento. Le aseguro que voy a manejar mucho más lento ahora.

POLICÍA: No es mi decisión. Es la ley (*law*).

MAYRA: Entonces, por lo menos no (6) _escriba_ (escribir) ochenta kilómetros por hora en la multa. (7) _Ponga_ (poner) setenta, por favor.

POLICÍA: No puedo hacer eso. Bueno, (8) _tómela_ (tomarla).

MAYRA: (*silencio*)

POLICÍA: Y no (9) _maneje_ (manejar) tan rápido en el futuro. (10) _Tenga_ (tener) más cuidado.

**10-15 El transporte rápido** El Transmilenio es un sistema de transporte masivo de pasajeros (*passengers*) en autobús que permite llegar rápidamente a cualquier (*any*) lugar de la ciudad de Bogotá. Lee las siguientes reglas del Transmilenio y completa la lista con mandatos formales. Luego, compártela con un/a compañero/a. ■

| | | | |
|---|---|---|---|
| entrar | llevar | pagar | pararse (*to stand*) |
| permitir | respetar | evitar | transitar (*to enter/exit*) |

**MODELO** Siempre *evite* correr.

- Instrucciones para el uso adecuado (*suitable*) del sistema:

1. Cuando espere al autobús, _párese_ detrás de la línea amarilla de seguridad.
2. Antes de entrar, _permita_ que salgan los pasajeros.
3. _Pague_ con su tarjeta al entrar.
4. Al usar las rampas, túneles o plataformas, _transite_ por la derecha.
5. No _lleve_ paquetes (*packages*) grandes ni mascotas (*pets*).
6. No _entre_ en el autobús bebiendo o fumando ni en estado de embriaguez (*intoxication*).
7. _Respete_ las sillas azules que son para personas con discapacidad, mujeres embarazadas, niños pequeños y ancianos.

**NOTE for 10-15**
In addition to the *Transmilenio* bus system, Bogotá has more than 20,000 buses and microbuses that transport around 7 million passengers daily. For more information on the *Transmilenio* bus system, research it using the Internet.

**EXPANSION for 10-15**
Ask students whether these regulations are any different from the ones that apply to public transportation where they live.

**NOTA CULTURAL**

## ¿Cómo nos movemos?

El saber manejar un auto no suele ser tan importante en los países hispanohablantes como en los Estados Unidos. Por lo general, la gente camina más y usa el transporte público, ya sea el autobús, el metro o el taxi. Las personas que sí quieren conducir generalmente tienen que tomar un curso en una escuela privada de conducir.

En Colombia, por ejemplo, para obtener (*get*) una licencia de conducir es necesario:

- tener 16 años.
- saber leer y escribir.
- aprobar un examen teórico o presentar un certificado de aptitud en conducción (*driving*) emitido por una escuela aprobada (*approved*) por el Ministerio de Educación Nacional en coordinación con el Ministerio de Transporte.
- presentar un certificado de aptitud física y mental expedido por (*completed by*) un médico.

Una de las escuelas de conducir más conocidas en Colombia es Conducir Colombia. Los cursos y los precios varían según la experiencia previa del estudiante. Hay cursos básicos de diez clases por unos ciento cincuenta y nueve dólares hasta cursos avanzados de catorce clases por unos doscientos dólares.

### Preguntas

1. ¿Sabes conducir? ¿Cuándo aprendiste? ¿Quién te enseñó? ¿Cuándo sacaste la licencia de conducir? *Answers may vary.*
2. Según la lectura, ¿crees que es generalmente más fácil o más difícil obtener una licencia en Colombia que en los Estados Unidos? Explica. *Puede ser más difícil obtener una licencia de conducir en Colombia porque es necesario presentar un certificado de aptitud física y mental.*

 Capítulo 8: Los pronombres de complemento indirecto, pág. 299; Los pronombres de complemento directo e indirecto usados juntos, pág. 305.

 **10-16** **La gasolinera** Ustedes acaban de llegar a una gasolinera con taller mecánico. Túrnense para decirle al mecánico lo que necesitan. ■

**MODELO**  No pueden abrir el baúl.
*Ábranos el baúl, por favor. / Ábranoslo, por favor.*

1. Necesitan gasolina.
2. El parabrisas está sucio.
3. El limpiaparabrisas no funciona.
4. El motor tiene un ruido extraño.
5. Las llantas necesitan aire.
6. El aceite está sucio.

Capítulo 2. La sala de clase, pág. 65.

**3:00**  **10-17** **¿Cómo contestaría tu profe de español?** Túrnense para hacer los papeles de profesor/a (**P**) y estudiante (**E**). ■

MODELO    E: ¿Debemos hacer la tarea para mañana?

             P: *Sí, hagan la tarea para mañana. / Sí, háganla para mañana.*

1. ¿Debemos traer el cuaderno a la clase?
2. ¿Podemos llegar cinco minutos tarde?
3. ¿Hay que hablar en español todo el tiempo?
4. ¿Tenemos que tomar un examen pasado mañana?
5. ¿Podemos usar nuestros apuntes durante el examen?
6. ¿Está bien si no venimos a clase mañana?
7. ¿Podemos desayunar en la sala de clase?
8. ¿Buscamos la lectura en el Internet?
9. ¿Empezamos la tarea en clase?
10. ¿Podemos salir temprano?

Capítulo 3. La casa, pág. 100; Los muebles y otros objetos de la casa, pág. 108; Los quehaceres de la casa, pág. 111.

**5:00**  **10-18** **¡A su servicio!** Ustedes son compañeros/as de apartamento y acaban de ganar el concurso ¡A su servicio! Reciben como premio la ayuda de Jaime, un mayordomo (*butler*), por una semana. Díganle **ocho** cosas que quieren que haga (*you want him to do*) para ayudarlos hoy con los quehaceres. Después, díganle **tres** cosas que no debe hacer. ■

MODELO    *Jaime, saque la basura, por favor.*

## ¿Cómo andas? I

| Having completed **Comunicación I**, I now can . . . | Feel confident | Need to review |
|---|:---:|:---:|
| • discuss modes of transportation (p. 374) | ☐ | ☐ |
| • pronounce the letters **b** and **v** (MSL / SAM) | ☐ | ☐ |
| • influence others and give advice (p. 379) | ☐ | ☐ |
| • give orders and instructions (p. 383) | ☐ | ☐ |
| • list some public transportation options and discuss procedures for getting a driver's license (p. 386) | ☐ | ☐ |

**ADDITIONAL ACTIVITY for**
*Los mandatos formales*

 **Los compañeros de cuarto del infierno** Este año tus compañeros de cuarto/apartamento (¡o unos miembros de tu familia!) son horribles. Haz una lista de cinco cosas que deben (o no deben) hacer. Después, comparte tu lista con un/a compañero/a. (Verbos posibles: *cerrar, dejar, limpiar, sacar, sacudir, pasar la aspiradora, lavar*)

MODELO
*Cierren la puerta del refrigerador.*
*No dejen la ropa sucia en el suelo.*

🔑 **Instructor Resources**
• Textbook images, Extra Activities

**SECTION GOALS for**
*Comunicación II*

By the end of the *Comunicación II* section, students will be able to:

• talk about traveling and planning trips.
• read about vacation opportunities in Venezuela.
• state what belongs to someone using possessive pronouns.
• make equal and unequal comparisons and use comparatives and superlatives.

**NATIONAL STANDARDS**
*Communication*

We have broken the vocabulary dealing with travel into manageable chunks. Students will be able to recycle the vocabulary they learned in the first *Comunicación* section.

The communicative activities allow students to converse about their travel plans and all things associated with going on a trip. Most of the activities require students to engage in conversations, provide and obtain information, express feelings and emotions, and exchange opinions (Standard 1.1).

**METHODOLOGY •**
**Pronunciation**

As always, pronounce the words and have students repeat them after you. Remember that it is important to say the words several times and have the students repeat after you each time. It is excellent for modeling, along with their laboratory exercises.

**SUGGESTION for** *El viaje*

Practice the vocabulary with directed questions, such as *¿Tienes un pasaporte? ¿Tuviste que comprar boletos para un viaje?, ¿para tomar el autobús para venir a la universidad? ¿Prefieres ir a un lago o a las montañas para pasar un fin de semana tranquilo?*, etc.

# Comunicación II

**4 VOCABULARIO**

🔊 📖 **El viaje**  Sharing about travel
10-24 to 10-29

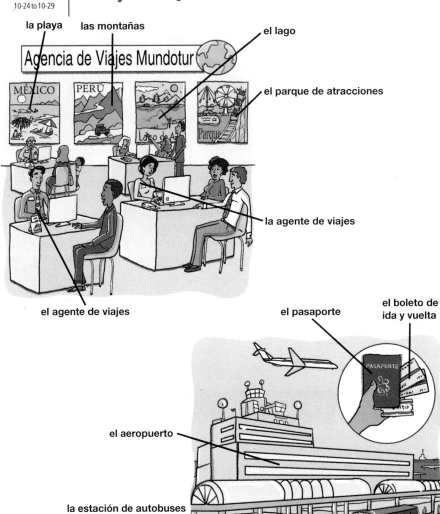

la playa  las montañas  el lago

Agencia de Viajes Mundotur

el parque de atracciones

la agente de viajes

el agente de viajes  el pasaporte  el boleto de ida y vuelta

el aeropuerto

la estación de autobuses

el cuarto individual

arreglar / hacer la maleta

la maleta

la propina

el barco

el cuarto doble

el botones

| Otras palabras útiles | Other useful words | Algunos verbos útiles | Some useful verbs |
|---|---|---|---|
| la agencia de viajes | travel agency | caminar, ir a pie | to walk; to go on foot |
| la estación de tren | train station | dejar | to leave |
| el extranjero | abroad | ir de vacaciones | to go on vacation |
| la recepción | front desk | ir de viaje | to go on a trip |
| la reserva | reservation | irse del hotel | to leave the hotel; to check out |
| el sello | postage stamp | registrarse (en el hotel) | to check in |
| la tarjeta postal | postcard | volar (o → ue) | to fly; to fly away |
| las vacaciones | vacation | | |
| los viajeros | travelers | | |
| el vuelo | flight | | |

**SUGGESTION for El viaje**
Have students brainstorm names of hotels, airports, and travel agencies with which they are familiar to personalize this vocabulary section.

**HERITAGE LANGUAGE LEARNERS**
Have heritage language learners role-play the following situations:
1. in a travel agency
2. in an airport
3. a train or bus station
4. a hotel

Challenge them to create a problem that they must resolve.

**EXPANSION for 10-19**
Have students create their own grid relating to their university, city, or area.

**METHODOLOGY • Pace of Instruction**
Maintaining a lively pace in the classroom keeps students engaged and on their toes. Group work should be stopped when two or three groups have completed the activity, not when all groups are done. In addition, follow-up should be quick and, unless you are checking a skill-acquiring activity, there is no need to go over every item.

 Workbooklet

**10-19 Categorías** Tienes tres minutos para escribir todas las palabras que pertenecen (*pertain*) a las siguientes categorías. No debes repetir palabras. Después, compara tus listas con las de un/a compañero/a. Date un punto por cada palabra que tienes que tu compañero/a no tiene. ■

| EL AEROPUERTO | EL HOTEL | LAS VACACIONES |
|---|---|---|
| | | |

**10-20 La competencia** En grupos de cuatro o cinco estudiantes, escriban la oración más larga (y lógica) posible usando las palabras nuevas de **El viaje**. ■

**ADDITIONAL ACTIVITY for**
*El viaje*

**¿Adónde van?** Ustedes trabajan en una agencia de viajes y un/a cliente quiere ir de viaje a la isla de Margarita en Venezuela. Tiene un presupuesto de 2.000 dólares.

**Paso 1** Escriban una conversación entre el/la agente de viajes y el/la cliente. Incluyan:
1. como mínimo dos preguntas sobre las preferencias del cliente.
2. los planes —el destino, cómo va a viajar, cuánto cuesta el boleto, qué puede hacer y ver allí y qué ropa necesita para hacer la maleta.

**Paso 2** Realicen la escena para la clase.

While the students are writing, circulate often among them to offer suggestions and make corrections. That way, when they present their skits there won't be as many errors. You may also have them turn the skits in, correct them, and give them back the following class for students to act out. How you handle *Paso 2* will determine the amount of time you need to set aside for the activity.

**NOTE for 10-22**
The authors have used Venezuela as the destination in this activity because it is one of the countries highlighted in this chapter. You may prefer to assign a different country or allow students to decide where the friend must go on the business trip.

**NOTE for 10-23**
Prior to preparing the interview, you may want to show your students on a world map where the Seven Summits are located. You may also want to investigate Jordan Romero's latest adventures to include in the information you provide. You may even choose to have students research Jordan Romero on the Internet and bring their own facts to share with the class.

**NOTE for 10-23**
Share the following information with your students as either a listening or a reading passage:
Jordan Romero (n. el 12 de julio del año 1996), en Bear Lake, California, es un joven extraordinario. El 22 de mayo del año 2010, junto con su padre y un equipo, se convirtió en la persona más joven en escalar el monte Everest. Así, con sólo trece años cumplió la meta de escalar las "Siete cumbres" (*Seven Summits*). Cuando tenía sólo 10 años, subió al Kilimanjaro (África, 5.981 metros) en julio del año 2006. En abril del año 2007, alcanzó el Kosciuszko (Australia continental, 2.228 metros), y

**10-21 ¿Quiénes lo hacen?** Circula por la clase hasta encontrar a un/a estudiante que pueda contestar afirmativamente a tu pregunta. ¡OJO! Debes usar el pretérito (P) en algunas de las preguntas. ■

*Capítulo 7. El pretérito, pág. 263.*

**MODELO**    ¿Quién...?

siempre dejar una buena propina para el/la camarero/a (*housekeeper*) cuando va a un hotel

TIFFANY:    *¿Siempre dejas una buena propina para el camarero cuando vas a un hotel?*

ROB:    *Sí, siempre dejo una buena propina.*

TIFFANY:    *Pues, firma aquí.*

_____ *Rob* _____

| ¿QUIÉN...? | | |
|---|---|---|
| siempre dejar una buena propina para el/la camarero/a cuando va a un hotel | ir a un parque de atracciones el año pasado | viajar al extranjero |
| ir a la playa el verano pasado | volar en avión | recibir tarjetas postales |
| quedarse en un hotel elegante una vez | esquiar en las montañas | tener más de dos maletas |

**10-22 Antes de ir** Tu amigo tiene que ir a Venezuela para una reunión (*meeting*) de negocios. Dale **cinco** consejos sobre lo que debe o no debe hacer para prepararse para el viaje y compara tu lista con la de tu compañero/a. ■

**MODELO**    1.   *Busca tu pasaporte.*

**10-23 Un joven increíble** Su profesor/a les va a dar información sobre Jordan Romero, un alpinista mexicoamericano muy interesante. Luego, van a preparar una entrevista entre Jordan y un/a reportero/a. Completen los siguientes pasos. ■

**Paso 1**    Preparen una lista de preguntas para Jordan.

**MODELO**    1.   *¿Cuándo y dónde naciste?*

           2.   *¿Cuándo empezaste a hacer alpinismo?*

**Paso 2**    Inventen respuestas lógicas a las preguntas.

**MODELO**    E1:   *¿Cuándo y dónde naciste?*

           E2:   *Nací en Bear Lake, California, el doce de julio del año 1996.*

**Paso 3**    Hagan los papeles de Jordan y el/la reportero/a.

el mismo año subió también al Elbrus (Europa, 5.642 metros) y al Aconcagua (Sudamérica, 6.962 metros). En el año 2008 completó la ascensión al monte McKinley (Norteamérica, 6.236 metros) y en septiembre del año 2009, al Carstensz Pyramid (Oceanía, 4.884 metros).

**10-24 Las mejores vacaciones** Piensa en tus mejores vacaciones al contestar las siguientes preguntas. Después, circula por la clase para entrevistar a tus compañeros/as. ∎

1. ¿Adónde fuiste?
2. ¿Cómo viajaste?
3. ¿Dónde te quedaste?
4. ¿Cuánto tiempo estuviste allí?

5. ¿Qué hiciste durante aquellas vacaciones especiales?
6. ¿A quién le mandaste una tarjeta postal?, ¿una tarjeta electrónica?

## NOTA CULTURAL

## Venezuela, país de aventuras

10-30

**Venezuela,** ¿Es Ud. aventurero/a? En Venezuela tenemos muchas oportunidades para conocer nuestro país a base de la aventura. Le proponemos (*propose*) una excursión de dos días en el Canaima. El primer día le ofrecemos un paseo en barco por la laguna Ucaima y una visita al Salto Ucaima. La excursión del segundo día le permite conocer el Salto Ángel, donde podemos nadar al pie de la cascada (*waterfall*).

Si le gusta hacer trekking, puede disfrutar de una excursión a los tepuyes (una palabra

**país de aventuras** indígena que significa "montaña"). Se puede subir el Pico Humboldt; a unos 4.942 m.s.n.m. es el segundo pico del país. Una excursión de este tipo está dentro de los considerados "deportes extremos" que se pueden practicar.

Si quiere combinar la aventura con una estancia en un hotel de lujo (*luxury*), debe considerar La isla de Margarita. Está situada al norte de Caracas a sólo treinta y cinco minutos en avión o a un par de horas en ferry. Allí puede disfrutar de todos los deportes de agua, pescar, jugar al golf y explorar las numerosas y variadas playas. Por la noche hay restaurantes, clubes de baile, bares y casinos. Para informarse mejor, póngase en contacto hoy con su agencia de viajes preferida.

**Preguntas**

1. ¿Qué puedes hacer durante la excursión en el Canaima?, ¿en la excursión a los tepuyes?, ¿en la isla de Margarita?
2. De las aventuras que ofrece Venezuela, ¿cuál prefieres? ¿Por qué?
3. ¿Eres aventurero/a? ¿Cuál es la aventura más atrevida que has tenido (*you have had*)?

# CAPÍTULO 10

🔑 **Instructor Resources**
• PPT, Extra Activities

**METHODOLOGY •**
**Differentiated Instruction**
Differentiating instruction can take the form of utilizing different methods or having different assignments that are leveled for different abilities or interests. In the interest of differentiation, if you have students who are at risk of not achieving a high level of success, the long form of possessive adjectives and possessive pronouns is not an essential grammatical concept and one that can be skipped for them. They already have one way of expressing possession from *Capítulo 1,* and at this point in the chapter, you could ask them to review *Capítulo 1,* and then hold them accountable for just that way of forming the possessive.

**SUGGESTION for *Otras formas del posesivo***
Have students engage in a round of verbal "one-upmanship." One student begins by describing a common possession, in very general terms. The next student describes to a partner his/hers and goes one better. This continues until nothing can be added, and then another round begins. Students are encouraged to embellish the truth!

E1:   *Tengo una bicicleta roja.*
E2:   *La mía es roja y tiene ruedas especiales.*
E3:   *La mía es una bicicleta de carrera y puede ir muy rápido.*
E4:   *La mía me costó mil dólares y…*

**NOTE for *Gramática***
This is an inductive grammar presentation in which the students are given examples of a grammar concept and, through the use of guiding questions, they formulate the rule in their own words. Research indicates that students remember and internalize grammar rules better when they construct their own knowledge.

---

**5 GRAMÁTICA**

10-31 to 10-33   Spanish/English Tutorials   ¡Hola!

## Otras formas del posesivo
Stating what belongs to you and others

¿Dónde están tus llaves? Tengo las mías aquí.

Pues, las llaves mías deben estar en el carro.

In **Capítulo 1,** you learned how to say *my, your, his, ours,* etc. (**mi/s, tu/s, su/s, nuestro/a/os/as, vuestro/a/os/as, su/s**). In Spanish you can also show possession with the long (or stressed) forms, the equivalents of the English *of mine, of yours, of his, of hers, of ours,* and *of theirs.*

| Singular | | Plural | | |
|----------|----------|----------|----------|----------|
| **Masculine** | **Feminine** | **Masculine** | **Feminine** | |
| **mío** | **mía** | **míos** | **mías** | *mine* |
| **tuyo** | **tuya** | **tuyos** | **tuyas** | *yours* (fam.) |
| **suyo** | **suya** | **suyos** | **suyas** | *his, hers, yours* (for.), *theirs* (form.) |
| **nuestro** | **nuestra** | **nuestros** | **nuestras** | *ours* |
| **vuestro** | **vuestra** | **vuestros** | **vuestras** | *yours* (fam.) |

Study the following examples.

| | | |
|---|---|---|
| **Mi** coche funciona bien. | **El coche mío** funciona bien. | **El mío** funciona bien. |
| **Nuestros** boletos cuestan mucho. | **Los boletos nuestros** cuestan mucho. | **Los nuestros** cuestan mucho. |
| ¿Dónde están **tus** llaves? | ¿Dónde están **las llaves tuyas**? | ¿Dónde están **las tuyas**? |
| **Su** multa es de $100. | **La multa suya** es de $100. | **La suya** es de $100. |

**¡Explícalo tú!**

Compare the possessives in the sentences above.
1. What is the position of each possessive in the left-hand column? the middle column?
2. How do the possessive adjectives and pronouns agree?
3. What do the sentences in the column on the right mean? What has been removed from each previous sentence?

✔   Check your answers to the preceding questions in Appendix 1.

\*Note that the third-person forms (**suyo/a/os/as**) can have more than one meaning. To avoid confusion, you can use:

el coche suyo $\left\{ \begin{array}{l} \textit{article} + \textit{noun} + \text{de} + \textit{subject pronoun:} \\ \text{el coche de él/ella} \\ \text{el coche de Ud.} \\ \text{el coche de ellos/ellas} \\ \text{el coche de Uds.} \end{array} \right.$

3:00  **10-25** **Entre hermanos**

Cambia todos los posesivos a la forma nueva (larga) en la conversación entre Marco y Mari. Después compara los cambios con los de un/a compañero/a. ∎

**MODELO**  El problema que tienes con tu coche es serio.
*El problema que tienes con el coche tuyo es serio.*

MARCO: Mari, parece que tu llanta pierde aire.

MARI: Ah, ¿sí? Tampoco funciona bien mi coche.

MARCO: Pues, mi mecánico es muy bueno.

MARI: Gracias, pero pienso llevar el coche a nuestro mecánico. Hace muchos años que Tom y yo lo conocemos.

MARCO: ¿Él tiene su negocio en la calle Bolívar?

MARI: Sí, y trabaja con uno de sus hermanos.

MARCO: ¿Puedes usar uno de sus coches mientras arregla el tuyo?

MARI: Sí, pero prefiero sacar tu BMW del garaje. Nunca lo manejas.

MARCO: Escucha, hermana. Ese BMW es un tesoro (*treasure*) y nadie lo maneja.

Capítulo 8. La ropa, pág. 294; Las telas y los materiales, pág. 309.

4:00  **10-26** **¡Problemas!** Están de viaje con algunos de sus mejores amigos. El hotel les lavó la ropa pero ahora ustedes no saben de quiénes son las prendas. Túrnense para hacer y contestar las preguntas de Ana, quien está intentando organizar la ropa. ∎

**MODELO**  E1 (ANA): Los calcetines rojos, ¿son tuyos? (de Felipe)

E2: *No, son de Felipe.*
*Los calcetines son suyos.*

1. Los pantalones cortos azules, ¿son tuyos? (de Tina) No, son de Tina. Los pantalones (cortos azules) son suyos.
2. La camisa de rayas, ¿es mía? (de Susana) No, es de Susana. La camisa (de rayas) es suya.
3. Los calcetines estampados, ¿son tuyos? (mío) Sí, son míos. Los calcetines (estampados) son míos.
4. La chaqueta negra, ¿es tuya? (de Felipe) No, es de Felipe. La chaqueta (negra) es suya.
5. El suéter de algodón, ¿es tuyo? (mío) Sí, es mío. El suéter (de algodón) es mío.
6. Las camisetas blancas, ¿son tuyas? (de Tina) No, son de Tina. Las camisetas (blancas) son suyas.

**NATIONAL STANDARDS**
*Communication*
The activities that accompany the presentation of possessive pronouns help students master speech typical of native speakers. They have already learned the possessive adjectives and how to use *de* for possession, and now they have learned another way to express possession. The activities recycle the possessive adjectives in combination with the new material, and students are able to communicate in the interpersonal mode (Standard 1.1) about what they and others possess.

**SUGGESTION for 10-25**
You may want to begin the activity by having students identify the possessive adjectives in the conversation by underlining them.

**EXPANSION for 10-25**
Ask students to create a list of their 5 favorite possessions. Then have them circulate around the room and offer those possessions to other students.
E.g., Mi iPod negro.→ ¿Quieres el iPod negro mío?
No, no quiero el iPod tuyo. / Sí, quiero el iPod tuyo.

**EXPANSION for 10-26**
Ask students to point out and discuss the clothing they and their classmates are wearing using possessive forms.

**NATIONAL STANDARDS**
*Communication, Comparisons*
In *Capítulo 10*, students learn how to compare things that are similar and dissimilar. They also learn how to form comparatives and superlatives. This new information allows for greater depth of conversation with others when they express their feelings and emotions and exchange opinions. They can discuss familiar topics in Spanish with classmates (Standard 1.1), and, if they travel abroad, they can form useful questions, such as where the cheapest place to stay is, or what restaurant has the best food. If they are deciding between two things featured in their guidebooks, they can ask which one is better. The new grammar allows them to compare how to phrase comparisons in English and Spanish (Standard 4.1).

**SUGGESTION for *El comparativo y el superlativo***
Use your students and objects in the classroom to demonstrate forming comparisons and superlatives. Have two students stand up. Offer a couple of comparisons as a model (e.g., *Mary es más baja que Gena. El pelo de Gena es tan rubio como el pelo de Mary.*). Then have students create as many comparisons of equality and inequality as possible on their own. Together, create superlative statements about the students and the classroom. Another great topic for comparison is your institution with a rival institution.

**NOTE for *El comparativo y el superlativo***
You may want to point out to students that *tan* is an adverb and therefore its form does not change, while *tanto* is an adjective, and as such, must agree with the noun that follows it.

---

[5:00]  **10-27 Personalmente...** Termina las siguientes oraciones sobre tu mejor amigo/a y tú y después compártelas con un/a compañero/a. ∎

1. El mejor amigo mío...
2. La casa suya...
3. La especialidad mía...
4. La materia favorita suya...
5. El restaurante favorito nuestro...
6. A los otros amigos nuestros les encanta(n)...

## 6 GRAMÁTICA

[6:00]

📖 ¡Hola!
10-34 to 10-39 Spanish/English Tutorials

## El comparativo y el superlativo
Comparing people, places, and things

### El comparativo

Just as English does, Spanish uses comparisons to specify which of two people, places, or things has a lesser, equal, or greater degree of a particular quality.

1. **The formula for comparing unequal things follows the same pattern as in English:**

| | |
|---|---|
| **más** + *adjective/adverb/noun* + **que** | *more . . . than* |
| **menos** + *adjective/adverb/noun* + **que** | *less . . . than* |

El Hotel Hilton es **más** caro **que** el Motel 6. — *The Hilton is **more** expensive **than** Motel 6.*
El Motel 6 hace reservas **más** rápidamente **que** el Hotel Hilton. — *Motel 6 makes reservations **faster than** the Hilton.*
En esta ciudad hay **menos** hoteles **que** moteles. — *In this city there are **fewer** hotels **than** motels.*

• When comparing numbers, **de** is used instead of **que**:

El Hilton de Bogotá tiene **más de** doscientos cuartos. — *The Bogotá Hilton has **more than** two hundred rooms.*

2. **The formula for comparing two or more *equal* things also follows the same pattern as in English:**

| | |
|---|---|
| **tan** + *adjective/adverb* + **como** | *as . . . as* |
| **tanto(a/os/as)** + *noun* + **como** | *as much/many . . . as* |

La agencia de viajes Mundotur es **tan** conocida **como** Meliá. — *The Mundotur travel agency is **as** well known **as** Meliá.*
Estos vuelos son **tan** caros **como** esos. — *These flights are **as** expensive **as** those.*
Mi coche va **tan** rápido **como** un Ferrari. — *My car is **as** fast as a Ferrari.*
No tengo **tantas** maletas **como** tú. — *I don't have **as many** suitcases **as** you (do).*
No hay **tanto** tráfico **como** ayer. — *There isn't **as much** traffic **as** yesterday.*

## El superlativo

¡Éstas son las mejores vacaciones de mi vida!

¡Éstas son las peores vacaciones de mi vida!

1. **To compare three or more people or things, use the superlative. The formula for expressing the superlative is:**

> **el, la, los, las** (*noun*) + **más/menos** + *adjective* (+ **de**)

La agencia de viajes Viking es **la** agencia **más** popular **de** nuestro pueblo.

*The Viking Travel Agency is the most popular (travel) agency in our town.*

—¿Es el aeropuerto Hartsfield de Atlanta **el** aeropuerto **más** concurrido **de** los Estados Unidos?

*Is Atlanta's Hartsfield Airport the busiest airport in the United States?*

—Sí, ¡y el aeropuerto de mi ciudad es **el menos** concurrido!

*Yes, and my city's airport is the least busy!*

2. **The following adjectives have irregular comparative and superlative forms.**

| Adjective | | Comparative | | Superlative | |
|-----------|------|-------------|--------|--------------|-------------|
| bueno/a | *good* | mejor | *better* | el/la mejor | *the best* |
| malo/a | *bad* | peor | *worse* | el/la peor | *the worst* |
| joven | *young* | menor | *younger* | el/la menor | *the youngest* |
| viejo/a | *old* | mayor | *older* | el/la mayor | *the eldest* |

## Comparative:

Mi clase de español es **mejor que** mis otras clases.     *My Spanish class is better than my other classes.*

## Superlative:

Mi clase de español es **la mejor de** mis clases.     *My Spanish class is the best (one) of my classes.*

**SUGGESTION for *El superlativo***
As a class, create as many superlatives as possible in 2 to 3 minutes about your Spanish class and/or your institution.

[4:00]

**10-28 ¿Cierto o falso?** ¿Qué sabes de la geografía? Indica si las siguientes oraciones son ciertas (**C**) o falsas (**F**); si son falsas, corrígelas. Después, comparte tus oraciones con las de un/a compañero/a siguiendo el modelo. ■

**MODELO** México es más grande que Uruguay.

E1: *¿Es México más grande que Uruguay?*

E2: *Sí. México es mucho más grande que Uruguay. ¿Es Chile tan grande como Argentina?*

E1: *No. Chile es más pequeño que Argentina, pero creo que es tan grande como Venezuela.*

1. México es más pequeño que Colombia.  F   México es más grande que Colombia.
2. Venezuela es casi tan grande como Colombia.  C
3. Panamá es más grande que Venezuela.  F   Panamá es más pequeño que Venezuela.
4. De estos países, Panamá es el más pequeño.  C
5. Colombia es más grande que los Estados Unidos.   F  Colombia es más pequeño que los Estados Unidos.
6. Caracas es tan grande como México, D.F.
      F   Caracas no es tan grande como México, D.F.

 Capítulo 1, Los adjetivos descriptivos, pág. 43.

[4:00]

**10-29 ¡Así son!** Cada persona tiene su opinión. Vamos a descubrir sus opiniones. ■

**Paso 1** Con un/a compañero/a, hagan una lista de tres o cuatro adjetivos para describir a la persona de cada categoría.

**MODELO** persona de la clase

E1: *alto/a, interesante*

E2: *cómico/a, simpático/a*

1. actriz de la televisión
2. actor del cine
3. jugador de fútbol/béisbol/tenis/etc.
4. cantante de rock/jazz/ópera
5. profesor/a de la universidad
6. persona de la política

**Paso 2** Ahora creen preguntas y luego respuestas para cada categoría.

E1: *¿Quién es la persona más alta de la clase?*

E2: *Catalina es la persona más alta de la clase.*

Workbooklet

**Estrategia**

You can also use the following expressions to express your opinions: *Pienso que…, Creo que…, Estoy de acuerdo, No estoy de acuerdo,* and *En mi opinión…*

## 10-30 ¿El mejor o el peor?

Circula por la clase para averiguar qué opinan los estudiantes sobre "los mejores" y "los peores". Necesitas al menos **dos** opiniones para cada categoría. ■

MODELO  E1: *¿Cuál es el mejor supermercado?*

E2: *En mi opinión, Whole Foods es el mejor supermercado. Y tú, ¿qué piensas?*

E1: *Creo que el mejor supermercado es Kroger.*

| | ESTUDIANTE 1 | ESTUDIANTE 2 |
|---|---|---|
| 1. el mejor supermercado | | |
| el peor supermercado | | |
| 2. el mejor almacén | | |
| el peor almacén | | |
| 3. el mejor restaurante | | |
| el peor restaurante | | |
| 4. el mejor aeropuerto | | |
| el peor aeropuerto | | |
| 5. el mejor hotel | | |
| el peor hotel | | |
| 6. el mejor parque de atracciones | | |
| el peor parque de atracciones | | |
| 7. la mejor playa | | |
| la peor playa | | |
| 8. el mejor lugar para la luna de miel (*honeymoon*) | | |
| el peor lugar para la luna de miel | | |
| 9. la mejor aerolínea (*airline*) | | |
| la peor aerolínea | | |
| 10. el mejor coche | | |
| el peor coche | | |

**Estrategia**

One way to approach **10-31** is to arrange your clues from most general to most specific.

## 10-31 Adivina, adivinanza

Trae un objeto personal a la clase y escribe **cuatro** oraciones sobre él, usando las formas comparativas. No digas el nombre de tu objeto. Lee las oraciones en grupos de cuatro o cinco estudiantes para ver si los compañeros pueden adivinar (*guess*) lo que es. ■

MODELO  un bolígrafo

E1: 1. Es más grande que un anillo.
2. Es tan importante como un libro.
3. Es menos largo que mi zapato.
4. Seguramente ustedes lo usan tanto como yo.
5. Es tan útil como un lápiz.

E2: *¡Es un bolígrafo!*

**NOTE for 10-30**
Have students report their findings, asking them to give reasons for their choices. Then compile classroom opinions as a group, or tally responses for them and present the results during the next class as part of the warm-up.

**EXPANSION for 10-30**
Have students revise the categories, e.g., *el supermercado más grande/ más popular, el almacén más grande/ pequeño/popular/caro/barato…,* and repeat the activity.

**SUGGESTION for 10-31**
Assign **10-31** for homework so that students come to class prepared to play this guessing game. Have each group choose their best riddle to present to the class.

**SUGGESTION for 10-31**
Model this activity by giving clues about an object you have brought to class.

**10-32 El transporte** Habla con un/a compañero/a sobre todos los medios de transporte que usan o han usado (*have used*) y compárenlos, pensando en los aspectos positivos y negativos de cada uno. ■

MODELO   E1: *Uso el coche más que el metro pero el metro es más rápido que el coche.*

E2: *Nunca voy en metro porque no hay metro en mi ciudad. Voy mucho en autobús porque es más barato que un taxi y es más rápido que mi bicicleta.*

Capítulo 7. El pretérito, pág. 263; Algunos verbos irregulares en el pretérito, pág. 272; Capítulo 8. El imperfecto, pág. 317; Capítulo 9. El pretérito y el imperfecto, pág. 349.

 **10-33 Los mejores recuerdos (*memories*)** Escoge uno de los siguientes temas y descríbele la situación a un/a compañero/a. Debes mencionar cuándo y dónde ocurrió, quiénes estaban contigo y qué pasó. Túrnense. ■

1. el mejor regalo que recibí
2. el mejor regalo que regalé (*gave*)
3. el mejor día de mi vida
4. el peor día de mi vida
5. las mejores vacaciones que tomé
6. las peores vacaciones que tomé

# ESCUCHA

## Las vacaciones

**10-40 to 10-41**

### Estrategia

**Listening for linguistic cues**

You can enhance comprehension by listening for linguistic cues. For example, verb endings can tell you who is participating and whether the incident is taking place now, already took place in the past, or will take place in the future. ■

**10-34** **Antes de escuchar** Los amigos de Manolo están en una fiesta. Oyen por casualidad una conversación entre varias personas sobre algunos viajes que ya tomaron y otros viajes que quieren tomar en el futuro. ■

1. ¿Cuáles fueron tus viajes más memorables?
2. ¿Hay un viaje en particular que le puedes recomendar a un/a amigo/a?
3. ¿A dónde quieres ir en tu próximo viaje?

Memo, Cristina y Rosa hablan de unos viajes interesantes.

**10-35** **A escuchar**

**Paso 1** Escucha la conversación entre Memo, Cristina y Rosa para tener una idea general de lo que dicen.

**Paso 2** Cristina habla de Venezuela. Escucha otra vez y apunta todos los verbos que puedas que ella usa. ¿Cuál es el tiempo verbal que usa más? Entonces, es un viaje que...
a. hizo ya.
b. va a hacer.
c. quiere hacer.

**Paso 3** Escucha una vez más para poder completar la siguiente actividad.
1. ¿Quién sale mañana para Colombia? Escribe los verbos que usa esta persona para hablar de su viaje.
2. ¿Habla Rosa de un viaje que hizo ya, va a hacer o quiere hacer? ¿Cómo lo sabes?

**10-36** **Después de escuchar** En grupos de tres o cuatro estudiantes, hablen de dos o tres lugares turísticos diferentes que conozcan (*you know*). ¿Qué tienen en común? ■

---

**NATIONAL STANDARDS**
*Communication, Connections*
The new listening strategy, listening for linguistic cues, facilitates communication. The strategy is effective for interpersonal communication (Standard 1.1), as well as for Standard 1.2, being able to understand and interpret spoken Spanish. Students can also apply this strategy when listening to others present information in Spanish (Standard 1.3). The example of listening for verb endings to guide their understanding of the time frame of the story is a skill they are not used to using in English. They have to connect this new strategy to their other listening strategies from learning English because it is extremely beneficial when learning a foreign language (Standard 3.2).

**ANSWERS to 10-35**
**Paso 3**
1. Memo: salgo, tengo, estoy pensando, conocer
2. Habla de un viaje que hizo ya y también habla de un viaje que quiere hacer. Fue a Uruguay el año pasado, pero quiere ir a Bogotá para ver el museo de Botero.

---

**SECTION GOALS for *Escucha***
By the end of the *Escucha* section, students will be able to:
- practice listening for linguistic cues.
- identify key cues that aid comprehension.
- use the pre-listening questions to guide their listening.
- discuss what they heard in the passage.

**AUDIOSCRIPT for 10-35**

MEMO: Cristina, ¿adónde fuiste de vacaciones el verano pasado?

CRISTINA: Fui a Venezuela con mi prima. Pasamos una semana en Caracas y cuatro días en la playa.

ROSA: Ah, ¿sí? ¿En qué playa?

CRISTINA: Nos quedamos en La Costa Azul de la Isla de Margarita. Está como a media hora de Caracas en avión, pero nosotras cruzamos en ferry y tardamos dos horas, más o menos.

MEMO: ¿Qué tal el hotel?

CRISTINA: El hotel se llamaba Playa Princesa. Era pequeño, de unos cien cuartos, pero bastante lujoso. Dicen que es famoso porque tiene el mejor restaurante de la isla y la piscina es la más grande de Venezuela. ¿Por qué, Memo? ¿Estás planeando un viaje a Venezuela?

MEMO: ¿No te lo dije? Salgo mañana para Colombia. Tengo una conferencia de trabajo, pero estoy pensando escaparme un par de días para conocer un poco de Venezuela.

ROSA: ¡Qué suerte! Me encantaría ir contigo, Memo. Hace mucho tiempo que quiero ir a Colombia, sobre todo a Bogotá. Como ya saben, mi artista favorito es Fernando Botero y él es colombiano. Me dicen que hay un museo fabuloso…

CRISTINA: Pero, Rosa, ¿no viajaste a Sudamérica el año pasado?

ROSA: Sí, pero estuve en Uruguay para visitar a la familia de mi madre. No tuve tiempo de ir a Colombia y, además, Montevideo está muy lejos de Bogotá.

MEMO: Pues, vente conmigo mañana.

ROSA: ¡Ojalá!

*[They laugh]*

# ¡CONVERSEMOS!

10-42

**10-37** **Ayudante indispensable**

Tu jefe/a viaja mucho para el negocio y necesita que
tú le hagas los arreglos (*make the arrangements*)
para su próximo viaje a Colombia. Crea un itinerario
para tu jefe/a y dile lo que necesita hacer y
cuándo, usando por lo menos **siete** mandatos. Tu
compañero/a de clase va a ser el/la jefe/a y tiene que
responder a tus arreglos, usando mandatos cuando
sea necesario. ¿Van a usar mandatos formales o
informales? ■

**10-38** **¡Buen viaje!** Tienes fondos (*funds*) sin límite para tus próximas
vacaciones. Planea un viaje para tu compañero/a de clase y tú. Después, descríbele el viaje
a tu compañero/a y dile qué necesita hacer y cuándo, usando por lo menos **siete** mandatos.
Tu compañero/a tiene que responder, también usando mandatos cuando sea necesario.
¿Van a usar mandatos formales o informales? ■

**ESCRIBE**

10-43

## Un reportaje

| Estrategia | Linking words help you connect ideas and sentences so you can communicate more effectively. As you write your travel review, practice linking your ideas and sentences. Linking words | you know include *y, o, pero, porque, que, cuando, antes de, después de, durante, para empezar, entonces, antes, después, de repente, finalmente, al final, por fin,* and *mientras.* |
|---|---|---|
| **Using linking words** | | |

**10-39　Antes de escribir** Escoge un lugar turístico de Colombia o Venezuela e investígalo en el Internet. Toma apuntes sobre los aspectos que encuentres más interesantes del lugar. ■

**10-40　A escribir** Organiza tus ideas y escribe un reportaje para una revista turística que incluya como mínimo la siguiente información: ■

1. dónde está
2. cómo llegar allí
3. qué actividades se pueden hacer
4. dónde uno puede quedarse (hotel de lujo, etc.)

5. el precio del viaje
6. este lugar es más interesante que...
7. este lugar es más/menos barato que...
8. este lugar es el más _____ porque...

**10-41　Después de escribir** Presenta tu reportaje a los compañeros de clase. Después de todas las presentaciones deben votar para elegir los **tres** lugares que desean visitar. ■

## ¿Cómo andas? II

|  | Feel confident | Need to review |
|---|---|---|
| Having completed **Comunicación II,** I now can . . . | | |
| • share about travel (p. 388) | ☐ | ☐ |
| • investigate travel and tourism opportunities in Venezuela (p. 391) | ☐ | ☐ |
| • state what belongs to me and others (p. 392) | ☐ | ☐ |
| • compare people, places, and things (p. 394) | ☐ | ☐ |
| • focus on linguistic cues (p. 399) | ☐ | ☐ |
| • communicate about travel plans (p. 400) | ☐ | ☐ |
| • write and present a report using linking words (p. 401) | ☐ | ☐ |

**SECTION GOALS for** *Escribe*
By the end of the *Escribe* section, students will be able to:

- research information about Colombia and Venezuela using the Internet.
- organize their research and select key points to highlight.
- write an article for a travel magazine about what they learned using linking words.
- present their report to their classmates.
- listen to others present and decide which places they would most like to visit.

**NATIONAL STANDARDS**
*Communication, Cultures, Connections*
The *Escribe* section focuses on the two countries highlighted in the chapter—Colombia and Venezuela. The research on the Internet requires them to focus on the most important things Colombia and Venezuela have to offer tourists, and if you require evidence of reading Internet articles in Spanish, they practice Standard 1.2. The report that they write focuses on Standard 1.3, the presentational mode, because they are writing a report to be read by others and presented to the class. The countries highlighted provide contact with the culture (Standard 2.1), and students can then connect what they learned about the countries with what they already knew about them (Standard 3.2).

**Instructor Resources**
• Text images (maps), Video resources

**SECTION GOALS for *Cultura***
By the end of the *Cultura* section, students will be able to:
• discuss public transportation in Colombia.
• analyze the importance of oil in Venezuela.
• highlight cultural places of interest such as Colombia's Museo del Oro and La Catedral de Sal de Zipaquirá.
• identify Simón Bolívar.
• contrast Colombia and Venezuela.

**NATIONAL STANDARDS**
*Communication, Cultures, Comparisons*
The readings from *Les presento mi país* require students to understand and interpret written Spanish (Standard 1.2). If they discuss the questions that follow in pairs or small groups, they are engaging in conversations in the interpersonal mode (Standard 1.1). The cultural information presented in the readings provides an in-depth understanding of what makes these countries unique (Standard 2.1). Students read the information presented and make comparisons about how these countries differ from the United States (Standard 4.2) and how these differences affect the Spanish-speaking people.

**NOTE for *La Catedral de Sal de Zipaquirá***
The cathedral is constructed approximately 600 feet inside a salt mountain. The salt deposits were formed 200 million years ago. Zipaquirá is a town of approximately 120,000 people. The cathedral was first opened in 1954, and then closed in 1990 due to safety concerns. It was then reopened in 1995.

**NOTE for *El Museo del Oro***
The Museo del Oro de Bogotá is considered one of, if not the premier, gold museum in the world. Located in the Banco de la República, it offers an impressive collection of gold not only from the indigenous empires of western South America, but from around the world.

**NOTE for *¿Sabías que...?***
Simón Bolívar (1782–1830) was born in Caracas, Venezuela. He was a political and military figure credited with leading several independence movements against the Spanish Empire (known as Bolívar's War).

# Cultura

# Colombia

CULTURA • CULTURA • CULTURA • CU

10-44 to 10-46

## Les presento mi país

Rosa María Gutiérrez Murcia

Mi nombre es Rosa María Gutiérrez Murcia y soy de Medellín, la segunda ciudad de Colombia. El setenta y cinco por ciento de la población colombiana se concentra en los centros urbanos y las regiones montañosas del país. En Medellín disfrutamos del único sistema de metro del país que proporciona transporte a la gente que vive en las afueras de la ciudad. **¿Qué tipos de transporte público hay en tu pueblo o ciudad?** Bogotá tiene el sistema más extenso de ciclorrutas (caminos para bicicletas) del país; gracias a él, la gente puede circular y disfrutar de los espacios públicos y verdes de la capital. Mi país es muy bello y tiene muchas atracciones para los turistas. Además, es el único país de Sudamérica que tiene costa en el Océano Pacífico y en el Mar Caribe.

Bogotá, Colombia

La Catedral de Sal de Zipaquirá

El Museo del Oro en Bogotá

**ALMANAQUE**

| | |
|---|---|
| Nombre oficial: | República de Colombia |
| Gobierno: | República |
| Población: | 44.205.293 (2010) |
| Idioma: | español |
| Moneda: | Peso colombiano (COP/$) |

### ¿Sabías que...?
• En Zipaquirá, Colombia, hay una catedral única. ¡La catedral está situada a 600 pies adentro de una montaña de sal!
• Simón Bolívar es conocido por ser *El Libertador*. Se considera un héroe en Colombia, Venezuela, Ecuador, Perú, Panamá y Bolivia, entre otros países hispanoamericanos.

### Preguntas
1. ¿Qué tiene Colombia que no tiene ningún otro país del continente?
2. ¿Cómo se comparan los medios de transporte de Medellín y Bogotá con los de tu área?
3. ¿Qué tienen en común Colombia, Perú y Chile?

 Amplía tus conocimientos sobre Colombia en MySpanishLab.

402

**SUGGESTION for *ciclorrutas***
Ask students the following questions: Are there bike paths where you live? Why? Do you think a system of bike paths is ecologically sound? Explain.

# Venezuela

10-44 to 10-45, 10-47

Joaquín Navas Posada

## Les presento mi país

Mi nombre es Joaquín Navas Posada y soy de Maracaibo, Venezuela. Hace dos años que vivo con mi hermano mayor y su esposa en la capital, Caracas, porque estudio arte en la Universidad Central de Venezuela. Mi hermano es ingeniero y trabaja en la industria petrolera. Venezuela es miembro de la Organización de Países Exportadores de Petróleo, conocida como la OPEP. **¿Qué papel tiene Venezuela en la OPEP?** Me encanta vivir con mi hermano porque es el mejor cocinero de Venezuela y sabe preparar todas las comidas tradicionales venezolanas como las arepas, las hallacas y el pabellón criollo. ¡Qué ricos! Vivir en la capital, es decir, en la costa, es muy agradable, porque hay mucho que hacer, tanto para nosotros como para los turistas.

Caracas tiene cuatro millones de habitantes.

Las arepas, un plato típico venezolano

La industria petrolera es muy importante para la economía venezolana.

Mar Caribe

OCÉANO ATLÁNTICO

Esmeralda — Isla de Margarita

Caracas

Maracaibo — Barcelona

Barquisimeto

Tucupita

Barinas

Mérida — Río Orinoco

Río Apure — San Fernando de Apure — Ciudad Bolívar

VENEZUELA — GUYANA

COLOMBIA

Río Orinoco

BRASIL

### ALMANAQUE

**Nombre oficial:** República Bolivariana de Venezuela

**Gobierno:** República federal

**Población:** 27.223.228 (2010)

**Idiomas:** español (oficial); lenguas indígenas

**Moneda:** Bolívar (BOB)

### ¿Sabías que...?

- El Salto Ángel, a unos 978 metros de altura, es la catarata más alta del mundo. El agua cae desde la cima del Auyan-tepuy, que está en el Parque Nacional Canaima, en el sureste del país.
- En Mérida hay una heladería que ha figurado en el libro Mundial de Récords Guinness por el mayor número de helados: tienen más de 600 sabores. Por costumbre hay 110 sabores disponibles diariamente.

### Preguntas

1. ¿Dónde vive Joaquín? ¿Le gusta? Explica.
2. ¿Cuál es la base principal de la economía venezolana actualmente?
3. La bandera de Venezuela es muy parecida a la de Colombia y a la de Ecuador. ¿Por qué piensas que es así? ¿En qué se diferencian las banderas y a qué se deben estas diferencias?

Amplía tus conocimientos sobre Venezuela en MySpanishLab.

**403**

**Instructor Resources**
- Text images (maps), Video resources

**NOTE for *Les presento mi país***
The discovery of oil reserves in Venezuela in the early 20th century has had a major impact on the Venezuelan economy. Venezuela relies heavily on its oil reserves to keep its economy booming. Projected oil income is looking to new methods of extracting valuable minerals from the earth. The Oil Belt of the Orinoco, *La Faja del Orinoco*, is an example of an oil reserve that is coming into increasing importance for its deposits of extra heavy crude oil and bitumen, both products that will be commercially producible and will contribute to the world oil reserves.

**NOTE for *La Universidad Central de Venezuela***
Founded in 1721, the Universidad Central de Venezuela is the oldest university in Venezuela and one of the oldest in Latin America. It is a public institution with more than 60,000 students and 8,000 professors. UNESCO has designated it a World heritage Site, or *Patrimonio de la Humanidad* in Spanish.

**SUGGESTION for *La Universidad Central de Venezuela***
Additional questions to ask your students are: How many students attend your university? How many professors do you think are employed there? Do students live in dorms or in apartments or with family members, as in many Latin American countries?

**NOTE for *La arepa, el pabellón criollo y la hallaca***
The *arepa* is the "bread" of Venezuela. Made with corn meal, it is served plain, stuffed, or filled with cheese, beans, meat, or just about anything. It is eaten as an accompaniment, as a main course, or as "fast food" on the run. The *pabellón criollo* is a dish of shredded beef, black beans (*caraotas negras*), rice, and fried plantains. The *hallaca* is a traditional Christmas confection, a mixture of chopped beef, chicken, pork, onions, green peppers, tomatoes, raisins, olives, and spices mixed into corn dough. It is then wrapped in banana leaves and steamed.

**METHODOLOGY • Cultural Expansion**
Many countries in the Spanish-speaking world have constantly changing political and economic conditions. We recommend that you have your students consult the Internet to research the latest news taking place in Venezuela and Colombia.

# Ambiciones siniestras
## EPISODIO 10

📖 10-50 to 10-51

# Lectura

**Estrategia**  Skipping words

If you have attempted to guess the meanings of unfamiliar words from context and are still having problems understanding, you may want to skip unfamiliar words and follow these steps:

1. Identify the subject and main verb of each sentence.
2. Find descriptions of the subject in the sentence(s).
3. Identify words and phrases that indicate time and place, cause and effect.
4. Ignore words set off by commas.
5. Summarize the content of each paragraph and look for information to fill in gaps.

**10-42  Antes de leer** En preparación para el **Episodio 10**, contesta las siguientes preguntas basadas en el **Episodio 9**. ■

1. ¿Crees que Manolo, Cisco, Lupe y Marisol pueden solucionar el nuevo rompecabezas?
2. ¿Crees que van a poder salvar a Eduardo y Alejandra si lo solucionan?
3. ¿Qué le pasa a Marisol? ¿Está enferma?
4. En tu opinión, ¿qué tiene que confesar Cisco?

**10-43  A leer** Completa las siguientes actividades. ■

1. Lee superficialmente el episodio y subraya las palabras que no conoces.
2. A continuación hay unas oraciones de la lectura con posibles palabras problemáticas subrayadas. Léelas y responde.
   a. *Cisco estaba <u>destrozado</u>. —Me siento responsable por todo —les dijo.*
      - El sujeto de la primera oración es _____ y el verbo es _____. La palabra <u>destrozado</u> describe a _____.
      - Por las tres oraciones que siguen sabemos que Cisco se siente:
        1. muy bien         2. muy mal         3. regular
   b. *En medio de su <u>remordimiento</u> Manolo lo interrumpió.*
   Si dividimos esa oración en dos partes, *"En medio de su remordimiento"* y *"Manolo lo interrumpió"*:
      - ¿Cuál es la parte más importante para la comprensión de la lectura?
   c. *"Cisco, ¿no te dijo nada?" <u>imploró</u> Manolo.*
      - ¿Por qué *no* es crítico saber lo que significa "imploró" en esta oración?
   d. *Aquí les mando como documento <u>adjunto</u> el resto de lo que encontré en la computadora de Eduardo el día que desapareció.*
      - La palabra "adjunto" es:
        1. un sustantivo (*noun*).     2. un verbo.     3. un adjetivo.
      - Si ignoras la palabra, ¿puedes entender la oración?
3. Lee el episodio otra vez, empleando esa estrategia con cualquier otra palabra que no comprendas (*you do not understand*).

404

### ¿Qué sabía?

*had told them*

Cisco les confesó todo a Manolo, Marisol y Lupe en la videoconferencia. Les dijo que sabía más del caso de lo que les había dicho°. Les mandó el email de Eduardo el cual descubrió el día que éste desapareció.

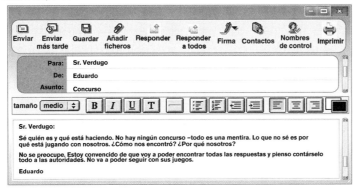

Cisco estaba destrozado.

—Me siento responsable por todo —les dijo—. Me pregunto por qué no fui a la policía en seguida. ¡Soy el hombre más tonto del mundo!

En medio de su remordimiento Manolo lo interrumpió.

*how he found out*

—¿Qué sabía Eduardo? Era obvio por su mensaje que sabía que el concurso era fraudulento, pero me pregunto cómo se enteró°. ¿Cómo y dónde descubrió esa información? ¿Cuándo empezó a tener dudas? Cisco, ¿no te dijo nada? —imploró Manolo.

Cisco se quedó mirando la pantalla por varios minutos antes de responder:

*to defraud*
*evil*

*proof*

—Aquí les mando como documento adjunto el resto de lo que encontré en la computadora de Eduardo el día que desapareció. Les tengo que confesar que yo también tuve dudas e investigué varias ideas que tenía sobre el concurso. Descubrí que era una conspiración Ponzi para estafar° a la gente. El Sr. Verdugo buscaba jóvenes inteligentes que le ayudaran con su malvado° plan. Eduardo encontró los papeles con mis apuntes que tenía al lado de mi computadora y desapareció con ellos. Yo iba a contactar a las autoridades pero cuando Eduardo se fue con toda mi información, yo tenía que reproducirlo todo. Sin las pruebas°, ¿quién me iba a creer? Lo siento mucho, perdónenme…

Manolo, Marisol y Lupe escucharon atentamente y recibieron el documento adjunto de Cisco casi al mismo tiempo en sus computadoras y lo leyeron. Marisol fue la primera en responder:

—Me pregunto si Eduardo pudo hablar con las autoridades antes de desaparecer. ¿Se fue en su coche en busca del Sr. Verdugo? ¿Sabía adónde tenía que ir? ¿Qué piensan?

—Eso es precisamente lo que yo estaba pensando —Manolo les respondió—. —Y algo más: ¿qué tenía que ver Alejandra con todo esto? No podemos olvidarnos de ella.

*dial*

La única persona que no respondió fue Lupe. Ella también recibió los mensajes y seguía la teleconferencia entre ellos sin participar. De repente abrió otra ventana en su pantalla y empezó a escribir algo muy detallado. Al mismo tiempo, tomó su teléfono celular y empezó a marcar°…

**CAPÍTULO 10**

**NOTE for** *Episodio 10*
In a Ponzi scheme, named for Italian Charles Ponzi, a fraudulent operator offers an unusually high return to investors on an initial investment. The extremely high returns advertised (and paid) necessitate an ever-increasing flow of money from investors to keep the scam going, and greed fuels investing more money. The scheme collapses either by the police being notified or by the Ponzi operator disappearing with the money. In 2009, Bernard Madoff was convicted of the largest Ponzi scheme ever, with losses estimated at $65 billion dollars.

**METHODOLOGY • Checking for Comprehension in English**
When encouraging students to hypothesize regarding what will happen, it is acceptable to encourage them to brainstorm in English.

**Instructor Resources**
- Video script

**ANSWERS to 10-44**
1. Les confesó que sabía más de lo que dijo y que Eduardo encontró los papeles de Cisco y le mandó un email al Sr. Verdugo antes de desaparecer.
2. Era una conspiración Ponzi.
3. Querían saber si Eduardo pudo hablar con las autoridades antes de desaparecer, si salió en busca del Sr. Verdugo y qué tiene que ver Alejandra con todo esto.
4. Lupe
5. Miró la pantalla de la computadora, escribió algo y empezó a marcar.

**SECTION GOALS for *Video***
By the end of the *Video* section, students will be able to:
- implement the new strategy, listening for linguistic cues, when the characters are talking.
- contrast their previous predictions with what really happened in the episode.
- predict what will happen in the next video.
- summarize the main events.

**ANSWERS to 10-46**
1. Marisol
2. Le dice que no, que es peligroso.
3. Parece que un hombre la está persiguiendo/vigilando.
4. Le mandan un email con la respuesta al Sr. Verdugo. Luego tienen una videoconferencia con Manolo y Cisco y les dan la solución.
5. Quiere llamar a la policía.
6. Marisol dice que hay cosas que no tienen sentido, que sabe que Lupe miente sobre quién es y también sobre su vida.
7. Lupe dice que va a ser sincera y saca una pistola.

---

**10-44**  **Después de leer** Contesta las siguientes preguntas. ■

1. Por fin, ¿qué les confesó Cisco a Marisol, Manolo y Lupe?
2. Si no había (*If there wasn't*) ningún concurso, ¿en qué consistía "el juego" del Sr. Verdugo?
3. ¿Cuáles eran las preguntas que tenían Manolo y Marisol ahora?
4. ¿Quién no dijo nada?
5. ¿Qué hizo Lupe al final del episodio?

10-52 to 10-54

# Video

**10-45** **Antes del video** ¿Qué habrá hecho Eduardo (*What must Eduardo have done*) con la información sobre la conspiración Ponzi? ¿Qué escribe Lupe en la computadora y a quién llama? En la segunda parte del episodio vas a saber quién resuelve el rompecabezas y vas a ver una confrontación entre Marisol y Lupe. ■

¡Marisol, no salgas de tu casa! ¡Estás en peligro!

Chicos, tenemos buenas noticias.

Hace mucho tiempo que descubrí que tú no eres la persona que dices ser.

Episodio 10

# «*Falsas apariencias*»

Relájate y disfruta el video.

**10-46** **Después del video** Contesta las siguientes preguntas. ■

1. ¿Quién resuelve el rompecabezas?
2. ¿Cómo responde Lupe cuando Marisol le dice que va a ir a su casa?
3. ¿Por qué tiene miedo Marisol?
4. ¿Qué hacen Lupe y Marisol con la respuesta del rompecabezas?
5. ¿Qué quiere hacer Cisco?
6. ¿Qué prueba (*proof*) tiene Marisol de que Lupe no es quien dice ser?
7. ¿Cómo termina el episodio?

## Y por fin, ¿cómo andas?

|  | Feel confident | Need to review |
|---|---|---|
| Having completed this chapter, I now can . . . | | |

**Comunicación I**

| | | |
|---|---|---|
| • discuss modes of transportation (p. 374) | ☐ | ☐ |
| • pronounce the letters **b** and **v** (MSL / SAM) | ☐ | ☐ |
| • influence others and give advice (p. 379) | ☐ | ☐ |
| • give orders and instructions (p. 383) | ☐ | ☐ |

**Comunicación II**

| | | |
|---|---|---|
| • share about travel (p. 388) | ☐ | ☐ |
| • state what belongs to me and others (p. 392) | ☐ | ☐ |
| • compare people, places, and things (p. 394) | ☐ | ☐ |
| • focus on linguistic cues (p. 399) | ☐ | ☐ |
| • communicate about travel plans (p. 400) | ☐ | ☐ |
| • write and present a report using linking words (p. 401) | ☐ | ☐ |

**Cultura**

| | | |
|---|---|---|
| • list some public transportation options and discuss procedures for getting a driver's license (p. 386) | ☐ | ☐ |
| • investigate travel and tourism opportunities in Venezuela (p. 391) | ☐ | ☐ |
| • impart important facts about this chapter's featured countries: Colombia and Venezuela (pp. 402–403) | ☐ | ☐ |

**Ambiciones siniestras**

| | | |
|---|---|---|
| • determine when it is appropriate to skip unfamiliar words and to discover the truth about what Cisco knows (p. 404) | ☐ | ☐ |
| • confirm that Lupe is not who she appears to be (p. 406) | ☐ | ☐ |

**Comunidades**

| | | |
|---|---|---|
| • use Spanish in real-life contexts (SAM) | ☐ | ☐ |

# VOCABULARIO ACTIVO

| El transporte | Transportation |
|---|---|
| el autobús | bus |
| el avión | airplane |
| la bicicleta | bicycle |
| el camión | truck |
| el carro / el coche | car |
| el metro | subway |
| la moto(cicleta) | motorcycle |
| el taxi | taxi |
| el tren | train |

| Algunas partes de un vehículo | Parts of a vehicle |
|---|---|
| el aire acondicionado | air conditioning |
| el baúl | trunk |
| la calefacción | heat |
| el limpiaparabrisas | windshield wiper |
| la llanta | tire |
| la llave | key |
| el motor | motor; engine |
| el parabrisas | windshield |
| el tanque | gas tank |
| el volante | steering wheel |

| Otras palabras útiles | Other useful words |
|---|---|
| la autopista | highway; freeway |
| el boleto | ticket |
| la calle | street |
| la cola | line (of people) |
| el estacionamiento | parking |
| la gasolinera | gas station |
| la licencia (de conducir) | driver's license |
| la multa | traffic ticket; fine |
| la parada | bus stop |
| el peatón | pedestrian |
| el/la policía | policeman/policewoman |
| el ruido | noise |
| el semáforo | traffic light |
| el taller mecánico | auto repair shop |
| el tráfico | traffic |

| Algunos verbos útiles | Some useful verbs |
|---|---|
| arreglar / hacer la maleta | to pack a suitcase |
| bajar (de) | to get down (from); to get off (of) |
| cambiar | to change |
| caminar, ir a pie | to walk; to go on foot |
| dejar | to leave |
| doblar | to turn |
| entrar | to enter |
| estacionar | to park |
| funcionar | to work; to function |
| ir de vacaciones | to go on vacation |
| ir de viaje | to go on a trip |
| irse del hotel | to leave the hotel; to check out |
| llenar | to fill |
| manejar / conducir | to drive |
| registrarse (en el hotel) | to check in |
| revisar | to check; to overhaul |
| sacar la licencia | to get a driver's license |
| subir (a) | to go up; to get on |
| viajar | to travel |
| visitar | to visit |
| volar (o → ue) | to fly, to fly away |

| El viaje | The trip |
|---|---|
| el aeropuerto | airport |
| la agencia de viajes | travel agency |
| el/la agente de viajes | travel agent |
| el barco | boat |
| el boleto de ida y vuelta | round-trip ticket |
| la estación (de tren, de autobús) | (train, bus) station |
| el extranjero | abroad |
| la maleta | suitcase |
| el pasaporte | passport |
| la reserva | reservation |
| el sello | postage stamp |
| la tarjeta postal | postcard |
| las vacaciones | vacation |
| los viajeros | travelers |
| el vuelo | flight |

| El hotel | The hotel |
|---|---|
| el botones | bellman |
| el cuarto doble | double room |
| el cuarto individual | single room |
| la recepción | front desk |

| Algunos lugares | Some places |
|---|---|
| el lago | lake |
| las montañas | mountains |
| el parque de atracciones | theme park |
| la playa | beach |

**Instructor Resources**
• IRM: Syllabi and Lesson Plans

# 11 El mundo actual

¿Qué peligros existen hoy en día para el medio ambiente (*environment*)? Hay más de 5.000 especies de animales en peligro (*danger*) de extinción, el 70% del aire en las ciudades está contaminado, y las selvas (*jungles*), las cuales contienen más del 50% de todas las especies de plantas y animales existentes, se reducen drásticamente cada año.

## PREGUNTAS

**1** ¿Dónde hay selvas tropicales?

**2** ¿Puedes nombrar algunos animales que están en peligro de extinción?

**3** ¿Dónde está contaminado el aire en los Estados Unidos?

410

**411**

**21ST CENTURY SKILLS • WORLD LANGUAGES SKILLS MAP**
A world language skills map was created that incorporates all of the 21st century skills identified by the Partnership for 21st Century Skills. The map illustrates sample outcomes for the skills in ACTFL terms. Examples of the skills are provided in the Novice, Intermediate, and Advanced ranges. This tool is available at www.P21.org.

**EXPANSION for Preguntas**
Additional questions to ask your students are: *¿Por qué es tan importante proteger las selvas? ¿Por qué es la destrucción de la selva tropical tan peligrosa para el mundo?*

**WARM-UP for Chapter opener**
This chapter is about the environment and all aspects related to being responsible citizens in a global village. Start out by asking your students how they contribute to or detract from the well-being of the environment. What changes do they think each person can make to help make the environment cleaner and safer for future generations? Ask your students what endangered animals they can name and where those animals are found.

**NOTE for Chapter opener**
Draw a semantic map or word web on the board and discuss the categories of animals (mammals, reptiles, birds, amphibians) and list the endangered animals from each group. You could also brainstorm things like ethanol fuels, wind power, cisterns, hybrid cars, bamboo, etc., that students can list as responsible choices that individuals and government could make in the future.

**NATIONAL STANDARDS**
*Communities*
Depending on the area in which you live, you might want to consider the following service learning options. If you have a large Hispanic population, you could team up with a local school, zoo, or animal sanctuary and start an environmental campaign about the dangers facing humans and animals and how the Hispanic community can band together to make small changes for big gains (recycling, using less electricity, carpooling, using environmentally friendly products, etc.). Students could partner with the science faculty and other students at your school to make presentations (in Spanish) to the Hispanic community about endangered natural resources and how each community member can do his or her part to preserve nature and the environment. If you do not have a large Hispanic population in your community, students could campaign to have local businesses sell green merchandise and set up recycling projects in your community. You could report the results in Spanish on your school web site. At your university, you could invite the community to a showing of a documentary on environmental issues as a solo project or as part of Earth Week, or whatever science-themed activities your school does, and discuss the film and its implications in Spanish after the viewing. You might also hold a fundraiser and have your students donate the money to "sponsor" an animal at a local zoo or aquarium (many animals in danger of extinction can be sponsored for as little as $20—check with your local animal welfare agency for details). The animal can be one that is indigenous to a Spanish-speaking country.

**SECTION GOALS for**
*Comunicación I*

By the end of the *Comunicación* section, students will be able to:

- name different types of animals and organize them into categories.
- state the rules for accents.
- discuss the environment and natural disasters.
- plan ways to conserve and protect the environment.
- locate El Yunque and describe highlights of the rain forest.
- differentiate between the indicative and the subjunctive moods.
- form the present subjunctive of regular and irregular verbs.
- use the subjunctive to express opinions, doubt, and probability, as well as wishes and hopes.
- give advice to others using the subjunctive.

**NATIONAL STANDARDS**
*Communication, Cultures, Connections, Comparisons, Communities*

In this final chapter of new material in *¡Anda! Curso elemental,* students are now able to combine a great deal of basic language and express thoughtful ideas, both in speaking and in writing. This chapter lends itself well to comparisons of the United States and Hispanic cultures, while connecting to other disciplines such as environmental science, government, biology, and the like.

This chapter encompasses all 5 Goal Areas of the National Standards. Students communicate in the interpersonal mode (Standard 1.1) when they share their opinions with others about environmental issues in the United States and abroad and possible solutions for a changing population and environment. If students present their ideas for preserving habitats and improving air quality to an audience, they are communicating in the presentational mode (Standard 1.3). They have to consider how the practices and perspectives of Hispanic people and their cultures affect the environment (for example, in the El Yunque rainforest or in South America) (Standard 2.1). The environment is something that students study in political science, geography, business, religion, science, sociology, and numerous other disciplines. They take the knowledge they have learned from these courses and make connections (Standards 3.1 and 3.2), using Spanish to express their opinions regarding possible solutions, while also considering

how the cultures of Spanish-speaking people affect the environment. They might consider, for example, how in the United States there is a greater dependence on oil than in Hispanic countries, and how transportation choices affect the environment; this allows them to compare how people in the United States and Hispanic countries differ (Standard 4.2). Finally, if your students participate in environmental campaigns by reading, attending meetings, or traveling abroad, they can use their Spanish to participate in the communities in which they live or in the communities to which they travel (Standard 5.1).

# Comunicación I

7:00   11-01 to 11-05

## Los animales   Describing animals and their habitats

### Los animales de la granja

| Otras palabras útiles | *Other useful words* | Algunos verbos | *Some verbs* |
|---|---|---|---|
| los animales de la granja | *farm animals* | cuidar | *to take care of* |
| los animales domésticos / | *domesticated animals;* | preocuparse (por) | *to worry about;* |
| las mascotas | *pets* | | *to concern oneself with* |
| la granja / la finca | *farm* | | |

## Los animales salvajes

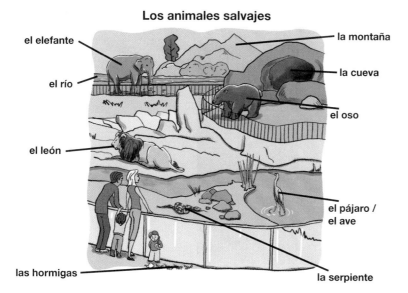

el elefante

el río

el león

las hormigas

la montaña

la cueva

el oso

el pájaro / el ave

la serpiente

| Otras palabras útiles | Other useful words |
|---|---|
| los animales salvajes | *wild animals* |
| los animales en peligro de extinción | *endangered species* |
| el bosque | *forest* |
| el océano | *ocean* |
| peligroso/a | *dangerous* |
| la selva | *jungle* |

### PRONUNCIACIÓN

¡Hola!

11-06 to 11-10

#### Review of Word Stress and Accent Marks

Go to MySpanishLab / Student Activities Manual to review word stress and accent marks.

Workbooklet

**11-1** **La fauna** Organiza los animales del vocabulario con un/a compañero/a según las siguientes categorías: **insecto, reptil, mamífero, ave** y **anfibio.** ■

| INSECTO | REPTIL | MAMÍFERO | AVE | ANFIBIO |
|---|---|---|---|---|
|  |  |  |  |  |
|  |  |  |  |  |
|  |  |  |  |  |
|  |  |  |  |  |
|  |  |  |  |  |

[2:00] 🍦🍦 **11-2** **¿Dónde viven?** Digan en qué lugar vive los siguientes animales. ■

1. ___e___    a. la selva

2. ___a___    b. un lago

3. ___f___    c. una granja

4. ___d___    d. el bosque

5. ___b___    e. un hoyo

6. ___c___    f. un árbol

[3:00] 🍦🍦 **11-3** **¿Qué sabemos?** Termina las siguientes oraciones con lo que sabes de los animales y dónde viven. Después compara tus oraciones con las de un/a compañero/a. ■

♻ Capítulo 10; El comparativo y el superlativo, pág. 394.

**MODELO**    Los insectos más molestos son…
              *Los insectos más molestos son las moscas y los mosquitos.*

1. Los animales de la granja más grandes son…
2. Los animales de la granja más pequeños son…
3. Los animales domésticos más comunes en mi familia y entre mis amigos son…
4. El animal salvaje más peligroso es…
5. El animal salvaje más grande es…
6. Los animales del bosque más interesantes son…

**EXPANSION for 11-3**
Encourage students to create more superlatives and also some comparisions for the animals.

**ANSWERS for 11-3**
1. Los animales de la granja más grandes son los toros, los caballos y las vacas.
2. Los animales de la granja más pequeños son el ratón, la rata, la rana y el pez.
3. Los animales domésticos más comunes en mi familia y entre mis amigos son los gatos y los perros. (*Answers may vary.*)
4. El animal salvaje más peligroso es el león / el elefante / la serpiente. (*Answers may vary.*)
5. El animal salvaje más grande es el elefante.
6. Los animales más interesantes del bosque son los osos, las serpientes, los pájaros y los insectos. (*Answers may vary.*)

Capítulo 8. *Gustar* y verbos como *gustar*, pág. 302.

  **11-4** **Las preferencias**  Completa los siguientes pasos. ■

**Paso 1**  Escribe los nombres de los **tres** animales que más te gustan y de los **tres** que menos te gustan y explica por qué. Usa verbos como **gustar, fascinar, encantar, hacer falta** y **molestar.** Después, comparte tus respuestas con un/a compañero/a.

**MODELO**  *El animal que más me gusta es el caballo porque es muy fuerte y me encanta montar a caballo* (go horseback riding). *También me gustan los gatos y los perros porque puedo tenerlos en casa. Los tres animales que menos me gustan son… porque…*

**Paso 2**  Presenten sus respuestas a los compañeros de la clase. ¿Cuál es el animal que más les gusta? ¿Y el que menos les gusta?

 Workbooklet

**11-5** **¿Qué opinas?**  Circula por la clase para averiguar (*find out*) con quiénes asocian tus compañeros las siguientes actividades. ■

**MODELO**  tener miedo de las serpientes

E1:  *Hola Sarah. ¿Quién tiene miedo de las serpientes?*

E2:  *Hola Tomás. Mi madre tiene mucho miedo de las serpientes.*

| ¿QUIÉN…? | | |
|---|---|---|
| tener miedo de las serpientes | ver un oso el año pasado | gustarle los perros |
| E1: <u>La madre de Sarah</u> | E1: _____ | E1: _____ |
| E2: _____ | E2: _____ | E2: _____ |
| E3: _____ | E3: _____ | E3: _____ |
| tener un animal doméstico | odiar los insectos | saber ordeñar (*to milk*) una vaca |
| E1: _____ | E1: _____ | E1: _____ |
| E2: _____ | E2: _____ | E2: _____ |
| E3: _____ | E3: _____ | E3: _____ |
| ver un elefante o un león | gustarle cuidar animales | tener un caballo |
| E1: _____ | E1: _____ | E1: _____ |
| E2: _____ | E2: _____ | E2: _____ |
| E3: _____ | E3: _____ | E3: _____ |

**11-6 Una encuesta** ¿Qué experiencias tienen ustedes con los animales? ■

**Paso 1** Háganse preguntas sobre los siguientes animales.

**MODELO** los perros

E1: *Sarah, ¿tienes perros?*

E2: *Sí, tengo dos perros. Se llaman Duke y Spot. ¿Y ustedes?*

E3: *Sí, en mi casa tenemos dos perros grandes. Se llaman Sissie y Pepper. Son viejos porque ya tienen ocho años.*

E4: *Nosotros no tenemos perrros. Tenemos dos gatos que se llaman Snuggles y Lucky.*

E1: *Tengo un perro pequeño. Es chihuahua y se llama Bullet…*

1. los perros
2. los gatos
3. las ranas
4. los caballos
5. los pájaros
6. las serpientes
7. los osos
8. las vacas
9. ¿?

**Paso 2** Organicen las respuestas y compártanlas con los otros grupos.

**MODELO** *En nuestro grupo todos tenemos perros menos Jack. Los perros se llaman Duke, Spot, Sissie, Pepper y Bullet. Jack tiene dos gatos…*

## EXPANSION for *El medio ambiente*
Give students 3 or 4 minutes to study the list of new words. Then have them close their books and in 3 minutes write all the words they can remember. You may wish to make this a competition by asking who has the longest list.

## EXPANSION for *El medio ambiente*
Ask students for details on specific occurrences of the natural disasters listed.

### MODELO
El derrame de petróleo:
*Un ejemplo ocurrió en los Estados Unidos en el año 2010 en el Golfo de México que afectó principalmente la costa de Luisiana, Mississippi y Florida.*

## SUGGESTION for *El medio ambiente*
Ask students what is involved in cleanup after specific disasters.

## SUGGESTION for *El medio ambiente*
Have students rank by least harmful to most harmful the things human beings do to harm the environment.

**2 VOCABULARIO**

## El medio ambiente Sharing details about the environment

11-11 to 11-18

### Los desastres

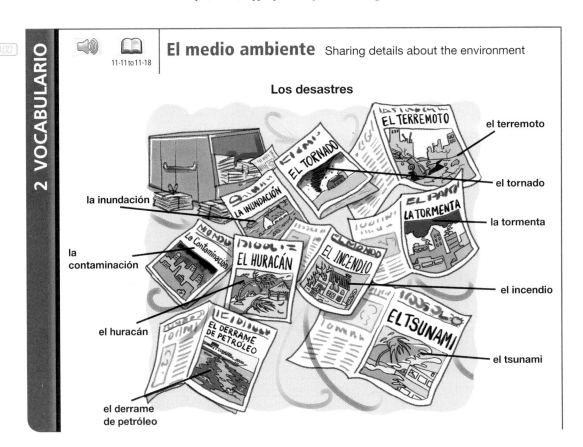

- el terremoto
- el tornado
- la tormenta
- la inundación
- la contaminación
- el incendio
- el huracán
- el tsunami
- el derrame de petróleo

## El reciclaje

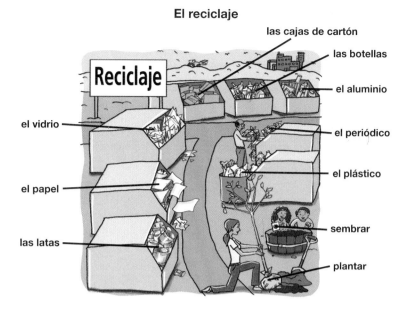

las cajas de cartón

las botellas

el aluminio

el vidrio

el periódico

el plástico

el papel

las latas

sembrar

plantar

| El planeta | *The planet* |
|---|---|
| el cielo | *sky; heaven* |
| la naturaleza | *nature* |
| el recurso natural | *natural resource* |
| la selva (tropical) | *jungle; (tropical) rain forest* |
| la tierra | *land; soil* |
| la Tierra | *Earth* |

| Otras palabras útiles | *Other useful words* |
|---|---|
| el aire | *air* |
| la basura | *garbage* |
| la calidad | *quality* |
| la ecología | *ecology* |
| puro/a | *pure* |
| el vertedero | *dump* |
| vivo/a | *alive; living* |

| Los desastres | *Disasters* |
|---|---|
| la destrucción | *destruction* |
| el efecto invernadero | *global warming* |
| la lluvia ácida | *acid rain* |
| la tragedia | *tragedy* |

| Algunos verbos | *Some verbs* |
|---|---|
| botar | *to throw away* |
| contaminar | *to pollute* |
| evitar | *to avoid* |
| hacer daño | *to (do) damage; to harm* |
| matar | *to kill* |
| proteger | *to protect* |
| reciclar | *to recycle* |
| reforestar | *to reforest* |
| reutilizar | *to reuse* |

**11-7** **Asociaciones** Túrnense para decir qué asocian con cada una de las siguientes palabras o expresiones. ■

MODELO    E1:  reutilizar
          E2:  *reciclar*

1. la basura
2. hacer daño
3. el recurso natural
4. puro
5. proteger
6. la lluvia ácida

**EXPANSION for *El medio ambiente***

This vocabulary lends itself to practicing affirmative and negative commands by creating sentences about what one should do to protect the environment and should not do to avoid harming it.

**ADDITIONAL ACTIVITY for *El medio ambiente***

**¿Cómo aprendemos?** Mira el vocabulario de *El medio ambiente* y sigue los pasos:

Paso 1. Escribe una lista de las palabras que ya conoces.

Paso 2. Escribe una lista de las palabras que son cognados.

Paso 3. Escribe una lista de las palabras que ya asocias con imágenes (piensas en la palabra y "ves" el objeto o la acción) o nombres específicos (el huracán Irene) o situaciones (la lluvia ácida destruye los árboles donde vivo).

Paso 4. Escribe las palabras que quedan que no están en tus listas.

Paso 5. Comparte tus listas con un/a compañero/a. Después, hablen de estratégias para aprender y recordar las palabras del Paso 4.

[3:00]  **11-8** **¿Qué es...?** Aquí tienen las definiciones. ¿Cuáles son las palabras? ■

> **Fijate**
> Note that *la Tierra* (Earth) is capitalized in Spanish but *la tierra* (land, soil) is not.

MODELO   E1: lo opuesto de contaminado

E2: *puro*

1. plantar árboles donde antes los había   reforestar
2. el estudio de la protección del medio ambiente   la ecología
3. un lugar designado donde botamos la basura   el vertedero
4. no botar; buscar un uso nuevo para una lata, botella, etc.   reutilizar
5. estas plantas grandes protegen la Tierra de la potencia del sol   los árboles
6. ensuciar el agua o el aire   contaminar
7. lo opuesto de muerto   vivo
8. el posible resultado de la contaminación del aire   el efecto invernadero

[3:00]  **11-9** **Hay que reciclar** ¿Qué hacen tu familia, tu comunidad y tu universidad para proteger el medio ambiente? Explícale a un/a compañero/a quién hace qué para proteger el medio ambiente. Después, cambien de papel. ■

MODELO   *Yo voy a la universidad en bicicleta para evitar la contaminación del aire. Mi familia y yo reciclamos el plástico. Mi pueblo ofrece programas de prevención contra incendios. La universidad dio un seminario sobre el efecto invernadero y la destrucción de la capa de ozono.*

[5:00]  **11-10** **Entrevista** Circula por la clase haciéndoles a tus compañeros las siguientes preguntas. ■

1. ¿Cuáles son los recursos naturales más importantes donde vivimos?
2. ¿Dónde está el vertedero más cerca de aquí?
3. ¿Qué haces con tu basura?

4. ¿Dónde podemos reciclar en nuestra universidad?
5. ¿Qué reciclamos en nuestra universidad?
6. ¿Cómo es la calidad del aire donde vivimos?

[12:00] **11-11** **El reportaje** ¿Cómo podemos proteger el medio ambiente? ■

Paso 1   Escribe un párrafo de **seis** a **ocho** oraciones sobre qué podemos hacer en el futuro para proteger el medio ambiente. Puedes usar las ideas de la siguiente lista.

- sembrar muchas plantas
- reciclar y/o reutilizar el plástico, el vidrio, el papel y el cartón
- usar carros eléctricos
- proteger los animales en peligro de extinción
- apoyar las instituciones de conservación de los recursos naturales

- proteger la selva tropical
- reforestar los bosques
- usar el carro lo menos posible
- usar energía solar
- no prender (*turn on*) a menudo el aire acondicionado

MODELO   *Para evitar la destrucción de los bosques y la selva tropical, no debemos cortar más árboles. En el futuro, debemos plantar más árboles para reforestar el bosque...*

 Paso 2   Después, en grupos pequeños, comparen sus oraciones y juntos escriban un reportaje corto con sus recomendaciones para proteger el medio ambiente.

**NOTE for 11-11**

You may choose to make **11-11** a project/presentation for groups or individuals. Topics can be chosen or assigned.

**Instructor Resources**
• PPT, Extra Activities

# NOTA CULTURAL

## El Yunque: tesoro tropical

11-19 to 11-20

El Bosque Nacional del Caribe también se conoce como El Bosque Lluvioso de El Yunque, en honor al dios bondadoso (*kind*) indígena Yuquiyú. El Yunque es el único bosque lluvioso tropical que pertenece al Sistema de Bosques Nacionales de los Estados Unidos. Más de 100 billones de galones de agua de lluvia caen anualmente en el bosque sobre el monte El Toro (a 1.076 metros).

El Yunque es el bosque nacional más viejo y pequeño de las Américas. Sin embargo, cuenta con la mayor diversidad de flora. Hay más de 240 especies de árboles en un área de poco más de 11.760 hectáreas (28,000 acres). Además, sirve de refugio a muchas especies de pájaros incluyendo la cotorra o loro (*parrot*) puertorriqueño, el cual está en peligro de extinción. Después del huracán Hugo en el año 1989 quedaron solo veinte loros. En esa época se empezó un programa para salvarlos y hoy en día existen unos ochenta y cinco. La ranita (rana pequeña) llamada *coquí* es original de Puerto Rico y hay muchas clases diferentes de coquíes en el Yunque.

El Bosque Nacional del Caribe es el lugar de Puerto Rico más frecuentado por los turistas. También lo frecuentan mucho las familias puertorriqueñas durante los fines de semana para pasar el día.

### Preguntas

1. ¿Por qué es tan importante El Yunque? *Es el único bosque lluvioso tropical del sistema de Bosques Nacionales de los Estados Unidos.*
2. ¿Cuáles son algunas de las características del Yunque que lo hacen tan especial? *Tiene una gran diversidad de flora, sirve de refugio para muchas especies de pájaros como la cotorra y para muchas clases diferentes de coquí.*

## 3 GRAMÁTICA

11-21 to 11-25 ¡Hola! Spanish/English Tutorials

### El subjuntivo  Commenting on what is necessary, possible, probable, and improbable

In Spanish, *tenses* such as the present, past, and future are grouped under two different moods, the **indicative** mood and the **subjunctive** mood.

 Up to this point you have studied tenses grouped under the *indicative* mood (with the exception of commands) to report what happened, is happening, or will happen. The *subjunctive* mood, on the other hand, is used to express doubt, insecurity, influence, opinion, feelings, hope, wishes, or desires that can be happening now, have happened in the past, or will happen in the future. In this chapter you will learn the present tense of the *subjunctive mood*.

Es una lástima que no quieran reciclar el plástico, el vidrio, el aluminio y el papel.

*(continued)*

**NOTE for *Nota cultural***
El Yunque is the only tropical rainforest in the United States—technically so because Puerto Rico is a United States territory. (Alaska has a *temperate* rainforest.) El Yunque has reported up to 250 inches of rainfall a year! El Yunque was a sacred place to the Taíno Indians, the original inhabitants of the island. The rainforest is home to many different types of flora, including some orchids the size of a fingernail, and many types of fauna such as frogs (*coquíes*), parrots, and bats. Though the rainforest looks vast from within, it is greatly diminished from its original size. It has suffered deforestation over the centuries; at this point in time, about 85% of the forest that Christopher Columbus saw at the end of the 15th century is gone. Research on the Internet for additional information.

**NATIONAL STANDARDS**
*Communication, Connections, Comparisons*
The *Nota cultural* reading on El Yunque provides an authentic text for students to interpret and understand written Spanish (Standard 1.2). They can make connections between their prior knowledge of tropical forests with the new information about *el coquí, los loros,* and the protection the park receives from the United States (Standards 3.1 and 3.2). Also, the reading provides the basis for making comparisons between the flora and fauna in El Yunque with other flora and fauna that students have learned about, and how this rainforest compares with others they have studied (Standard 4.2).

**EXPANSION for *El Yunque: tesoro tropical***
Additional questions to ask your students are: *¿Visitaste alguna vez una selva? ¿Qué esperas encontrar en una selva? ¿Qué razones puede haber para que el loro esté en peligro de extinción? ¿Cómo crees que se puede proteger a los pájaros? ¿Por qué crees que el coquí se ha convertido (*has become*) en un símbolo de Puerto Rico?*

**NATIONAL STANDARDS**
*Communication, Communities*
The introduction of the subjunctive mode provides a new way for students to express themselves (as native speakers would). Communication Standard 1.1 states that students express feelings and emotions and exchange opinions, which now they are able to do in a more authentic way. They can disagree and justify their responses, make suggestions or recommendations to others, and express desires. These skills are also beneficial in the presentational mode because now they are able to debate about certain topics with others in front of an audience (Standard 1.3). They are able to interact with native Spanish speakers now that they have been introduced to the subjunctive, which is an important resource when communicating outside of the school environment. Students are able to engage in conversation with the Spanish-speaking community (Standard 5.1).

## Present subjunctive

To form the subjunctive, take the **yo** form of the present indicative, drop the final **-o,** and add the following endings.

**Fíjate**

You are already somewhat familiar with the subjunctive forms from your practice with *usted* (*¡Estudie!*) and negative *tú* (*¡No hables!*) commands.

| Present indicative | *yo* form | | Present subjunctive |
|---|---|---|---|
| estudiar | estudiø | + e | estudie |
| comer | comø | + a | coma |
| vivir | vivø | + a | viva |

| | estudiar | comer | vivir |
|---|---|---|---|
| yo | estudie | coma | viva |
| tú | estudies | comas | vivas |
| Ud. | estudie | coma | viva |
| él, ella | estudie | coma | viva |
| nosotros/as | estudiemos | comamos | vivamos |
| vosotros/as | estudiéis | comáis | viváis |
| Uds. | estudien | coman | vivan |
| ellos/as | estudien | coman | vivan |

## Irregular forms

- Verbs with irregular **yo** forms maintain this irregularity in all forms of the present subjunctive. Note the following examples.

| | conocer | hacer | poner | venir |
|---|---|---|---|---|
| yo | conozca | haga | ponga | venga |
| tú | conozcas | hagas | pongas | vengas |
| Ud. | conozca | haga | ponga | venga |
| él, ella | conozca | haga | ponga | venga |
| nosotros/as | conozcamos | hagamos | pongamos | vengamos |
| vosotros/as | conozcáis | hagáis | pongáis | vengáis |
| Uds. | conozcan | hagan | pongan | vengan |
| ellos/as | conozcan | hagan | pongan | vengan |

- Verbs ending in **-car, -gar,** and **-zar** have a spelling change in all present subjunctive forms, in order to maintain the sound of the infinitive.

| | | Present indicative | Present subjunctive |
|---|---|---|---|
| **buscar** | c → qu | yo busco | busque |
| **pagar** | g → gu | yo pago | pague |
| **empezar** | z → c | yo empiezo | empiece |

|  | **buscar** | **pagar** | **empezar** |
|---|---|---|---|
| yo | busque | pague | empiece |
| tú | busques | pagues | empieces |
| Ud. | busque | pague | empiece |
| él, ella | busque | pague | empiece |
| nosotros/as | busquemos | paguemos | empecemos |
| vosotros/as | busquéis | paguéis | empecéis |
| Uds. | busquen | paguen | empiecen |
| ellos/as | busquen | paguen | empiecen |

## Stem-changing verbs

In the present subjunctive, stem-changing **-ar** and **-er** verbs make the same vowel changes that they do in the present indicative: **e → ie** and **o → ue**.

|  | **pensar (e → ie)** | **poder (o → ue)** |
|---|---|---|
| yo | piense | pueda |
| tú | pienses | puedas |
| Ud. | piense | pueda |
| él, ella | piense | pueda |
| nosotros/as | pensemos | podamos |
| vosotros/as | penséis | podáis |
| Uds. | piensen | puedan |
| ellos/as | piensen | puedan |

The pattern is different with the **-ir** stem-changing verbs. In addition to their usual changes of **e → ie**, **e → i**, and **o → ue**, in the **nosotros** and **vosotros** forms the stem vowels change **ie → i** and **ue → u**.

|  | **sentir (e → ie, i)** | **dormir (o → ue, u)** |
|---|---|---|
| yo | sienta | duerma |
| tú | sientas | duermas |
| Ud. | sienta | duerma |
| él, ella | sienta | duerma |
| nosotros/as | sintamos | durmamos |
| vosotros/as | sintáis | durmáis |
| Uds. | sientan | duerman |
| ellos/as | sientan | duerman |

*(continued)*

**NOTE for** *El subjuntivo*
*¡Anda! Curso elemental* is research based and coordinated with the National Standards. In addition, hundreds of reviewers were consulted, and they determined that the present subjunctive should at least be introduced in the first year. This chapter's theme lends itself well to expressing opinions, making suggestions and recommendations, and finding solutions to problems. These types of language skills are important to communication, especially in the interpersonal mode (Standard 1.1) and when making presentations (Standard 1.3). Students learned the commands in previous chapters and therefore already learned how to form subjunctive endings. A more in-depth treatment of the subjunctive continues in *¡Anda! Curso intermedio.*

**NOTE for *El subjuntivo***
You may have learned these fixed expressions as impersonal expressions with *ser*. In *¡Anda! Curso elemental,* we have chosen to simply call them, "fixed expressions," under the headings of opinions, doubts, probabilities, wishes, desires, and hopes. This eliminates any confusion between "personal" and "impersonal," because these expressions can be used regardless of the relationship to the speaker.

The **e → i** stem-changing verbs keep the change in all forms.

| | pedir (e → i, i) |
|---|---|
| yo | pida |
| tú | pidas |
| Ud. | pida |
| él, ella | pida |
| nosotros/as | pidamos |
| vosotros/as | pidáis |
| Uds. | pidan |
| ellos/as | pidan |

## Irregular verbs in the present subjunctive

- The following verbs are irregular in the subjunctive.

| | dar | estar | saber | ser | ir |
|---|---|---|---|---|---|
| yo | dé | esté | sepa | sea | vaya |
| tú | des | estés | sepas | seas | vayas |
| Ud. | dé | esté | sepa | sea | vaya |
| él, ella | dé | esté | sepa | sea | vaya |
| nosotros/as | demos | estemos | sepamos | seamos | vayamos |
| vosotros/as | deis | estéis | sepáis | seáis | vayáis |
| Uds. | den | estén | sepan | sean | vayan |
| ellos/as | den | estén | sepan | sean | vayan |

**Dar** has a written accent on the first- and third-person singular forms (**dé**) to distinguish them from the preposition **de.** All forms of **estar,** except the **nosotros** form, have a written accent in the present subjunctive.

## Using the subjunctive

One of the uses of the subjunctive is with fixed expressions that communicate opinion, doubt, probability, and wishes. They are always followed by the subjunctive.

¡Es increíble que este capítulo sea el último!

### Opinion

| | |
|---|---|
| Es bueno / malo / mejor que… | *It's good / bad / better that . . .* |
| Es importante que… | *It's important that . . .* |
| Es increíble que… | *It's incredible that . . .* |
| Es una lástima que… | *It's a pity that . . .* |
| Es necesario que… | *It's necessary that . . .* |
| Es preferible que… | *It's preferable that . . .* |
| Es raro que… | *It's rare that . . .* |

## Doubt and probability

| | |
|---|---|
| Es dudoso que… | It's doubtful that . . . |
| Es imposible que… | It's impossible that . . . |
| Es improbable que… | It's unlikely that . . . |
| Es posible que… | It's possible that . . . |
| Es probable que… | It's likely that . . . |

## Wishes and hopes

| | |
|---|---|
| Ojalá (que)… | Let's hope that . . . / Hopefully . . . |

**Es necesario que** protejamos los animales en peligro de extinción.

*It's necessary that we protect endangered species.*

**Es una lástima que** algunas personas no quieran reciclar el plástico, el vidrio, el aluminio y el papel.

*It's a shame that some people don't want to recycle plastic, glass, aluminum, and paper.*

**Ojalá (que)** haya menos destrucción del medio ambiente en el futuro.

*Let's hope that there is less destruction of the environment in the future.*

**Fíjate**

The subjunctive of *hay* is *haya*.

### ¡Explícalo tú!

1. What is the difference between the subjunctive and the indicative moods?
2. What other verb forms look like the subjunctive?
3. Where does the subjunctive verb come in relation to the word **que**?

✔ Check your answers to the preceding questions in Appendix 1.

---

 **11-12** **¡Corre!** Escuchen mientras su profesor/a les explica cómo jugar con las formas de los verbos en el subjuntivo. ■

---

 **11-13** **Opciones** Túrnense para crear oraciones completas usando los sujetos indicados en cada frase. ■

**MODELO**  Es preferible que ella / nosotros / tú (reciclar el vidrio)

  E1:  *Es preferible que ella recicle el vidrio.*

  E2:  *Es preferible que nosotros reciclemos el vidrio.*

  E3:  *Es preferible que tú recicles el vidrio.*

1. Es dudoso que tú / Marta y yo / ella (reutilizar las botellas de plástico) reutilices / reutilicemos / reutilice
2. Es necesario que el gobierno / ellos / Uds. (reforestar los bosques) reforeste / reforesten / reforesten
3. Ojalá que ellos / él / nosotros (conservar las selvas tropicales) conserven / conserve / conservemos
4. Es posible que yo / tú / Uds. (poder evitar la lluvia ácida) pueda / puedas / puedan
5. Es importante que mi país / los jóvenes / nosotros (respetar la naturaleza) respete / respeten / respetemos
6. Es una lástima que papá / tú / tus hermanos (botar basura por las calles) bote / botes / boten

**NOTE and INSTRUCTIONS for 11-12**

**11-12** is a fun way to practice verb forms.

**INSTRUCTIONS:** Have your students sit in rows. Each row is a team, so each team/row should have an equal number of people. Each person at the head of the row has a piece of paper with as many subject pronouns written on it as there are people in the row. Do not list the pronouns in their conjugation order.

Write any infinitive on the board. The first student writes the subjunctive form of that verb that corresponds to the first pronoun listed. That student then passes the sheet of paper over his/her head. The second student writes the correct form of the subjunctive of the second pronoun and passes the paper to the student sitting behind him/her. The process continues with all of the students in the row. The last student in the row brings the completed sheet to you. The first row to finish with all forms correct wins that round.

Additional rules:

1. After each round, have students each move back one seat, with the person in the last seat of the row moving to the front.
2. Allow any students to correct any forms that came before.

**NOTE for 11-14**
You may prefer to have your students complete this activity for homework and, after checking the answers in class, ask basic comprehension questions.

**EXPANSION for 11-14**
**11-14** can also be used as a reading comprehension activity that can be done outside of class. You can ask students to complete the following questions for homework or in small groups and check them as a class.

1. Generalmente, ¿dónde vive la mayoría de los cocodrilos?
2. ¿Qué tipos de cocodrilos están en peligro de extinción?
3. ¿En qué lugares se encuentra el cocodrilo americano?
4. ¿Cuál cocodrilo tiene más peligro de extinción y por qué?
5. ¿Es peligroso para los humanos el cocodrilo cubano? ¿Por qué?
6. ¿Qué "talento" tiene el cocodrilo americano que le ayuda a matar?
7. ¿Cómo podemos proteger los cocodrilos?
8. ¿Qué sugerencias tienes para vivir en armonía con los cocodrilos?

**NOTE for 11-15**
When practicing these fixed expressions, you may wish to point out to students that if they do not wish to refer to anyone in particular, they should use the infinitive:
*Es preferible comer menos.*

**11-14** **El cocodrilo** Completa el siguiente párrafo con la forma correcta del verbo apropiado en el subjuntivo. Después, compara tus respuestas con las de un/a compañero/a. ■

> **Fíjate**
> The *yo* form of the present tense (indicative mode) of *proteger* is *protejo*. Therefore, the subjunctive of *proteger* is *proteja*, *protejas*, etc.

El cocodrilo cubano

| estar | proteger | haber | matar |
|-------|----------|-------|-------|
| poder | existir | ser | vivir |

Es raro que los cocodrilos (1) __vivan / existan__ en el hemisferio occidental. ¡Siempre pienso en el continente de África como hábitat para este animal! Es una lástima que el cocodrilo americano y el cocodrilo cubano (2) __estén__ en peligro de extinción. Es bueno que el cocodrilo americano (3) __exista / viva__ en varias partes del hemisferio (Florida, algunas islas del Caribe y varias zonas costeras del Golfo de México y el océano Pacífico), porque así tiene menos peligro de extinción que el cocodrilo cubano, el cual (*which*) existe solamente en el sureste de Cuba. Es posible que el cocodrilo americano (4) __sea__ peligroso para los humanos. Son tan grandes que pueden atacar y comer animales de gran tamaño cuando se acercan a beber agua. Es improbable que el cocodrilo cubano (5) __mate__ a una persona porque es mucho más pequeño y prefiere aves, pequeños mamíferos, peces y otros animales acuáticos. Es increíble que el cocodrilo americano (6) __pueda__ caminar distancias cortas, lo que significa que puede matar fuera del agua también. Es necesario que nosotros (7) __protejamos__ estos reptiles y ojalá que (8) __haya__ muchos más en el futuro.

**11-15** **Mis mejores consejos...** Completa el cuadro con tus mejores consejos. Después, comparte tu información con un/a compañero/a. ■

Workbooklet

| PARA PROTEGER LOS RÍOS Y LOS OCÉANOS | PARA EVITAR LA CONTAMINACIÓN DEL AIRE | PARA MANTENER LAS CALLES LIMPIAS |
|---|---|---|
| 1. Es importante que no botemos la basura en los ríos. | 1. | 1. |
| 2. | 2. | 2. |
| 3. | 3. | 3. |

**11-16** **¿Para quién es necesario que...?** Túrnense para hacer y contestar las preguntas sobre las siguientes situaciones usando las expresiones de la pág. 422. ■

MODELO  estudiar esta noche
   E1: *Es probable que estudie esta noche. ¿Y tú?*
   E2: *Tengo que estudiar, pero es posible que vaya al cine.*

1. estudiar este fin de semana
2. comer menos comida rápida
3. arreglar su cuarto
4. gastar menos dinero
5. buscar un/a nuevo/a compañero/a de cuarto
6. dormir más
7. sacar mejores notas
8. comprar un coche nuevo
9. reciclar más

**11-17** **Posibles determinaciones** ¿Cuáles pueden ser tus determinaciones (*resolutions*) para el próximo año? Descríbelas y después compártelas con un/a compañero/a. ■

MODELO   *Es mejor que no coma tanto chocolate el próximo año, pero es dudoso que pueda evitarlo. ¡Me fascina el chocolate! Es importante que haga más ejercicio. Es una lástima que no me guste hacerlo.*

 **11-18** **Es importante que...** Juntos escojan una de las siguientes situaciones para desarrollar en forma de diálogo. Usando las expresiones que acaban de (*have just*) aprender, den consejos según la situación. Después, presenten el diálogo a los compañeros de clase. ■

---

**Situación A:**

La doctora Pérez es especialista en nutrición. María Cecilia es una joven universitaria de dieciocho años que va a hacerle una consulta a la doctora sobre cómo mejorar el cutis (*complexion*).

---

**Situación C:**

El sargento López está enamorado de la linda Carolina, pero es tan tímido que nunca la invita a salir con él. Su amiga Carmen trata de ayudarlo.

---

**Situación B:**

Bruno quiere comprar un carro usado y le pide a su amigo Manolo, quien trabaja en una agencia de carros, que le ayude.

---

**Situación D:**

Patricio se mata estudiando para el examen de matemáticas. Un día antes del examen se da cuenta (*he notices*) de que no tenía un examen de matemáticas, ¡sino de español! Va a su consejero para ver qué le aconseja.

---

## ¿Cómo andas? I

|  | Feel confident | Need to review |
|---|---|---|
| Having completed **Comunicación I,** I now can . . . | | |
| • describe animals and their habitats (pp. 412–413) | ☐ | ☐ |
| • pronounce words following the rules for accentuation and stress (MSL / SAM) | ☐ | ☐ |
| • share details about the environment (p. 416) | ☐ | ☐ |
| • describe El Yunque, the rain forest of Puerto Rico (p. 419) | ☐ | ☐ |
| • comment on what is necessary, possible, probable, and improbable (p. 419) | ☐ | ☐ |

**SECTION GOALS for**
*Comunicación II*
By the end of the *Comunicación* section, students will be able to:

• discuss how governments are organized and administered.
• debate with others about politics and the environment.
• contrast the political history of the United States with that of Latin America and Spain.
• suggest ways to improve politics in the future.
• identify the uses of *por* and *para*.
• use common prepositions and prepositional phrases.
• form prepositions with the correct pronouns.
• explain where items are located in relation to one another using prepositions.
• use infinitives after prepositions.

**NATIONAL STANDARDS**
*Communication, Cultures, Connections, Comparisons*
This final vocabulary presentation in *¡Anda! Curso elemental* provides students with a sophisticated vocabulary that helps them talk and write about current events both in the United States and abroad. Since politics change so rapidly, you may want your students to check the web sites of Spanish-speaking countries to note their current political climates.

The vocabulary for *la política* allows students to talk about current events and reflect on the rapidly changing political policies and leaders. With this vocabulary, students can read news articles from Spanish-language web sites (Standard 1.2) using authentic text to read and interpret written Spanish. They can also engage in conversations with others in the interpersonal mode (Standard 1.1) about what is going on in the world, and they can present to an audience of listeners or readers about their political views (especially interesting during an election year) and debate important issues (Standard 1.3). They can use this information to analyze the cultural differences between the way the United States is governed and its relationship to other countries (Standards 2.1 and 2.2), and how the government affects the practices, products, and perspectives of the people. Students can make connections between their understanding of U.S. government and diplomatic and economic relationships with Hispanic countries (Standard 3.2). They can compare the government, election process, and rights of the people to see how the culture in the United States differs from Hispanic cultures and how they are governed (Standard 4.2).

# Comunicación II

## La política   Discussing government and current affairs

**4 VOCABULARIO**

11-26 to 11-29

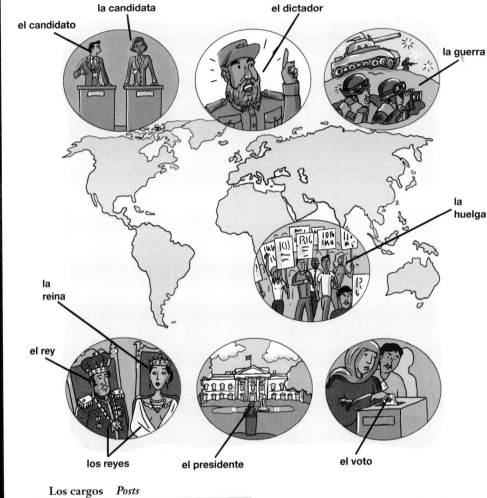

| Los cargos | Posts | | |
|---|---|---|---|
| el alcalde | *mayor (male)* | la gobernadora | *governor (female)* |
| la alcaldesa | *mayor (female)* | el juez | *judge (male)* |
| la dictadora | *dictator (female)* | la jueza | *judge (female)* |
| el diputado | *deputy; representative (male)* | la presidenta | *president (female)* |
| la diputada | *deputy; representative (female)* | el senador | *senator (male)* |
| el gobernador | *governor (male)* | la senadora | *senator (female)* |

| Las administraciones y los regímenes | *Administrations and regimes* |
|---|---|
| **el congreso** | *congress* |
| **la democracia** | *democracy* |
| **la dictadura** | *dictatorship* |
| **el estado** | *state* |
| **el gobierno** | *government* |
| **la ley** | *law* |
| **la monarquía** | *monarchy* |
| **la presidencia** | *presidency* |

| Las cuestiones políticas | *Political matters* |
|---|---|
| **el bienestar** | *well-being; welfare* |
| **la corte** | *court* |
| **la defensa** | *defense* |
| **la delincuencia** | *crime* |
| **el desempleo** | *unemployment* |
| **la deuda (externa)** | *(foreign) debt* |
| **el impuesto** | *tax* |
| **la inflación** | *inflation* |
| **el juicio** | *trial* |

| Algunos verbos | *Some verbs* |
|---|---|
| **apoyar** | *to support* |
| **combatir** | *to fight; to combat* |
| **elegir** | *to elect* |
| **estar en huelga** | *to be on strike* |
| **llevar a cabo** | *to carry out* |
| **luchar** | *to fight; to combat* |
| **meterse en política** | *to get involved in politics* |
| **resolver (o → ue)** | *to resolve* |
| **votar** | *to vote* |

---

 **11-19** **Al revés** Generalmente ustedes reciben las definiciones y tienen que advinar la palabra o expresión. Esta vez van a elegir **seis** palabras o expresiones de **La política** y escribir las definiciones. ∎

**MODELO**     el impuesto
        *El dinero que tenemos que pagar al gobierno cuando compramos algo. Es un porcentaje del costo.*

---

Workbooklet

**11-20** **Batalla** Completa cada parte del cuadro con el nombre de un lugar o una persona según la descripción. Después, compara tus respuestas con las de un/a compañero/a. Dense un punto por cada acierto (*match*). ∎

| 1. una reina | 5. un país con alta inflación | 9. el nombre del segundo presidente de los Estados Unidos |
|---|---|---|
| 2. un estado en el Noreste | 6. un país con baja inflación | 10. el nombre de un senador de tu estado |
| 3. un país con monarquía | 7. una ciudad de los Estados Unidos con mucha delincuencia (*crime*) | 11. el nombre de una guerra muy larga |
| 4. un rey | 8. un alcalde | 12. un/a juez/a de la Corte Suprema de los Estados Unidos |

CAPÍTULO 11    **427**

---

**NOTE for *La política***
Tell students that *el alcalde* has an irregular feminine counterpart, *la alcaldesa*. Another similar pair is *el rey* and *la reina*.

**SUGGESTION for *La política***
Have students note how many of the words in this list are cognates. They may want to master these words first, and then add those that are unfamiliar to them.

**NOTE for 11-19**
Students may need additional guidance and support as they work through this activity. While a bit challenging for some, this activity is designed to help students develop the skill of circumlocution.

**EXPANSION for 11-20**
Have students share the reasoning behind their choices, e.g., why they believe a particular country has such a high rate of inflation or why President X was the best.

**11-21  Reportando**  Imagínense que son periodistas y tienen que hacer un reportaje sobre unas charlas y discursos de unos políticos. Formen oraciones lógicas, añadiendo otras palabras cuando sea necesario. ■

MODELO      encuesta / mostrar / el 65% de las personas / no votar / elecciones
*La encuesta mostró que el 65% de las personas no votaron en las elecciones.*

1. alcalde / no resolver / problemas / huelgas
2. jefe / partido politico / decir / (él) meterse en política / para combatir / alta inflación
3. senadora / confirmar / senado / votar por / nuevos impuestos
4. reyes / preocuparse por / bienestar / personas / provincias
5. presidente / dedicarse a / luchar contra / delincuencia, desempleo, deuda externa

**NOTA CULTURAL**

## La política en el mundo hispano

11-30

La historia política de Latinoamérica es la historia de la lucha dramática del ser humano contra fuerzas destructivas como la colonización, el imperialismo, la esclavitud y el genocidio en siglos anteriores y, en épocas más recientes, la pobreza, la corrupción, el nepotismo, la división rígida de clases y el militarismo. Muchos países hispanohablantes han sufrido severas dictaduras o democracias débiles e ineficaces. Esta lucha ahora se traduce en la búsqueda de una relación más justa con el mundo desarrollado y en particular con los Estados Unidos.

Evo Morales, elegido por segunda vez el 6 de diciembre del año 2009, es el primer presidente indígena de Bolivia.

En décadas recientes, España ha surgido como un país moderno y avanzado, con un rey progresista y amante de la democracia. Latinoamérica, a su vez, experimentó un periodo de paz y esperanza en la segunda mitad del siglo XX. La guerra que azotó (*whipped*) a Centroamérica en la década de los ochenta acabó y, aunque sus efectos aún se sienten y la recuperación es lenta en algunos países, el estándar de vida en Centroamérica ha aumentado (*has grown*), así como el comercio y el deseo de fortalecer las instituciones democráticas.

### Preguntas

1. ¿Cuáles fueron algunos de los problemas en la historia política de los países hispanos?
2. ¿Qué cambios han experimentado (*have they experienced*) muchos de los países hispanos en los últimos quince o veinte años?

Capítulo 7, El pretérito, pág. 263; Capítulo 7, Algunos verbos irregulares en el pretérito, pág. 272.

🔑 **Instructor Resources**
• PPT, Extra Activities

  **11-22** **¿Qué sabes de...?** Juntos contesten las siguientes preguntas para mostrar sus conocimientos políticos. ■

1. ¿En qué año fue la última campaña para la presidencia de los Estados Unidos?
2. ¿Cómo se llama el/la gobernador/a de tu estado?
3. ¿Quién fue un/a dictador/a infame? ¿De qué país? ¿Cuándo fue dictador/a?
4. ¿Qué países tienen un rey o una reina? ¿Cómo se llaman?
5. ¿Cuántos senadores hay en el senado de los Estados Unidos?
6. ¿Cuántos jueces hay en la Corte Suprema de los Estados Unidos?

 **11-23** **El futuro político** Escribe algunas ideas sobre lo que debe pasar en el futuro en tu ciudad, estado, país o en el mundo. Después, en grupos de tres, escriban un párrafo colectivo para la clase. Usen las expresiones que requieren el subjuntivo cuando sea posible. ■

**MODELO**   *Es necesario que los partidos políticos no combatan tanto entre sí* (among themselves). *También es importante que el presidente resuelva problemas económicos como la inflación. Es dudoso que podamos bajar la deuda nacional porque todos quieren dinero para sus programas.*

 **11-24** **Los partidos políticos** En grupos de cinco o seis estudiantes van a crear un partido político nuevo. Tienen que determinar el nombre del partido y el programa (*platform*). Después, presenten sus partidos a los otros grupos y juntos decidan cuál(es) de los partidos mejor representa(n) las opiniones de la clase. ■

**NOTE for 11-24**
If you find that **11-24** is too challenging for your students, you could start by brainstorming a list of local governmental issues or (non-partisan) problems that the community and/or your state face, and then have students react to the statements. Some ideas include general problems across the United States:
   *El desempleo en la Compañía X es muy alto.*
   *Los empleados de la Fábrica X están en huelga.*
   *Hay más problemas con el clima y la temperatura alta que en años previos.*
   *En los Estados Unidos hay mucha basura y no hay suficiente reciclaje.*

## 5 GRAMÁTICA

📖 11-31 to 11-34

### Por y para   Expressing time, deadlines, movement, destination, means, purpose, etc.

As you have seen, Spanish has two main words to express *for*: **por** and **para.** They have distinct uses and are not interchangeable.

¿Por cuánto tiempo ocupa el presidente la presidencia?

*(continued)*

**POR is used to express:**

**1. Duration of time (*during, for*)**
El presidente ocupa la presidencia **por** cuatro años consecutivos.
*The president holds the presidency for four consecutive years.*
El alcalde habló **por** más de media hora.
*The mayor spoke for more than a half hour.*

**2. Movement or location (*through, along, past, around*)**
Los candidatos andan **por** la calle y hablan con la gente.
*The candidates are going through the streets talking with the people.*
El rey saluda **por** la ventana.
*The king is waving through the window.*

**3. Motive (*on account of, because of, for*)**
Decidimos meternos en política **por** nuestros hijos. Queremos asegurarles un futuro mejor.
*We decided to get involved in politics because of our children. We want to assure them a better future.*
En resumen, nos dijeron que hay que reciclar **por** el futuro de nuestro planeta.
*In short, they told us that we must recycle for the future of our planet.*

**4. Exchange (*in exchange for*)**
Gracias **por** su ayuda, señora Presidenta.
*Thank you for your help, Madam President.*
Limpiaron el vertedero **por** diez mil dólares.
*They cleaned the dump for ten thousand dollars.*

**5. Means (*by*)**
Los diputados discutieron los resultados de las elecciones **por** teléfono.
*The representatives argued about the election results over the phone.*
¿Los reyes van a viajar **por** barco o **por** avión?
*Are the king and queen going to travel by ship or by plane?*

**PARA is used to express:**

**1. Point in time or a deadline (*for, by*)**
Es dudoso que todos los problemas se solucionen **para** el final de su presidencia.
*It is doubtful that all problems will be solved by the end of her presidency.*
Es importante que bajemos los impuestos **para** el próximo año.
*It is important that we lower taxes by next year.*

**2. Destination (*for*)**
La reina sale hoy **para** Puerto Rico.
*The queen leaves for Puerto Rico today.*
Los diputados se fueron **para** el Capitolio.
*The representatives left for the Capitol.*

**3. Recipients or intended person or persons (*for*)**
Mi hermano escribe discursos **para** la gobernadora.
*My brother writes speeches for the governor.*
Necesitamos un avión **para** el dictador.
*We need a plane for the dictator.*

**4. Comparison (*for*)**
**Para** un hombre que sabe tanto de la política, no tiene ni idea sobre la delincuencia de nuestras calles.
*For a man who knows so much about politics, he has no idea about the crime on our streets.*
La tasa de desempleo es bastante baja **para** un país en desarrollo.
*The unemployment rate is quite low for a developing country.*

**5. Purpose or goal (*to, in order to*)**
**Para** recibir más votos, la candidata necesita proponer soluciones **para** los problemas con la deuda externa.
*(In order) to receive more votes, the candidate needs to propose solutions for the problems with foreign debt.*
Hay que luchar contra la contaminacón **para** proteger el medio ambiente.
*One needs to fight pollution to protect the environment.*

**11-25** **Los políticos** Hoy en día, los políticos son muy activos y están en todas partes. Completen las oraciones de manera lógica. ■

> MODELO    La candidata Dávila tuvo una entrevista y habló por…
> *La candidata Dávila tuvo una entrevista y habló por tres horas.*

1. El alcalde dijo que se metió en política para…
2. Las diputadas Meana y Caballero dijeron que hay que elegir a un gobernador nuevo para…
3. Nuestro presidente les dio las gracias a las organizadoras por…
4. El dictador se comunicó por…
5. Después del discurso el rey salió para…
6. La senadora, acompañada por _____, caminó por…

**11-26** **Razones** Túrnense para decir para quiénes están haciendo ustedes las siguientes cosas. ■

> MODELO    comprar / libro sobre la inflación
> E1:   *¿Para quién estás comprando el libro sobre la inflación?*
> E2:   *Estoy comprando el libro para mis padres.*

1. hacer / campaña
2. escribir / discurso
3. pedir / donación (*contribution*)
4. buscar / empleo
5. circular / peticiones
6. proteger / el medio ambiente

**11-27** **Mi hermana Leonor** Mi hermana Leonor me dio una gran sorpresa para mi cumpleaños. ■

**Paso 1**    Para saber qué pasó, completa cada espacio en blanco del siguiente párrafo con **por** o **para**.

Leonor, mi hermana, estuvo en mi casa (1) ___por___ un mes el verano pasado. Vino (2) ___para___ mi cumpleaños. Leonor llegó con tres maletas y una enorme caja misteriosa. El día de mi cumpleaños me dijo que (yo) tenía que estar lista (3) ___para___ las cinco de la tarde. Efectivamente, a las cinco en punto estaba sentada en la sala cuando vi (4) ___por___ la ventana a un grupo de amigos. Venían con un trío de guitarras. ¡Era una serenata (5) ___para___ mí! ¡Qué emoción tan grande! La serenata comenzó y Leonor bajó (6) ___por___ la escalera con una caja.
—Es (7) ___para___ ti —me dijo. La abrí y ¡qué sorpresa! Era una hamaca de yute (*jute hammock*) de la República Dominicana, donde Leonor había vivido (*had lived*) (8) ___por___ varios meses.
—¡Una hamaca (9) ___para___ el patio —exclamé— (10) ___para___ leer y dormir al sol! ¡Qué delicia! —Y en seguida pregunté:— Pero, Leonor, ¿cómo trajiste esta hamaca desde Santo Domingo? ¿La trajiste (11) ___por___ avión o la mandaste (12) ___por___ correo?
Leonor se rió y me contestó: —(13) ___Para___ una hermana como tú, todo es posible. Me la traje en avión. (14) ___Para___ ser una caja tan grande la verdad es que no me causó tantos problemas. ¡Feliz cumpleaños!

**Paso 2**    Comparte tus respuestas con un/a compañero/a y explícale por qué usaste **por o para** en cada una.

**CAPÍTULO 11**

**NOTE for 11-25 and 11-26**
These two activities require that students focus on meaning before they begin to make choices between *por* and *para* in **11-27**

**ANSWERS TO 11-26**
1. ¿Para quién estás haciendo campaña?
   Estoy haciendo campaña para
2. ¿Para quién estás escribiendo un discurso?
   Estoy escribiendo un discurso para…
3. ¿Para quién estás pidiendo una donación?
   Estoy pidiendo una donación para…
4. ¿Para quién estás buscando empleo?
   Estoy buscando emplea para…
5. ¿Para quién estás circulando peticiones?
   Estoy circulando peticiones para…
6. ¿Para quién estás protegiendo el medio ambiente?
   Estoy protegiendo el medio ambiente para…

**SUGGESTION for 11-27**
You may choose to have your students complete *Paso 1* for homework to maximize class time.

**EXPANSION for 11-27**
Activity **11-27** can also be used as a comprehension activity. You can assign the following activity for homework, or for use in small groups.
Decide si las siguientes oraciones son **ciertas** (C) o **falsas** (F). Si son falsas, corrígelas.
1. _____ Leonor pasó todo el verano pasado en la casa de su hermana.
2. _____ Ella vino a pasar sus vacaciones de verano con su hermana.
3. _____ Leonor trajo mucho equipaje a la casa de su hermana.
4. _____ Leonor hizo planes con su hermana por la tarde.
5. _____ Apareció en la casa un grupo de cantantes.
6. _____ Leonor le dio una caja de guitarras a su hermana.
7. _____ La hermana de Leonor vivió en la República Dominicana.
8. _____ Leonor trajo una hamaca a la casa de su hermana.
9. _____ La hermana reaccionó con mucho gusto al ver el paquete.
10. _____ Leonor envió la hamaca desde la República Dominicana a la casa de su hermana.

**TPR ACTIVITY for *Las preposiciones***

Prepositions lend themselves well to TPR activities. These can be simple, like using classroom objects and giving amusing instructions for the students to follow, e.g., *Pon el lápiz encima de tu cabeza.*

If you want to incorporate world geography with the prepositions, have students work in groups with a map of South America and Central America, with the countries cut out into individual shapes. Create a new map by giving directions such as *Brasil está lejos de Honduras* or *Chile está cerca de Argentina* and have them put their new maps together. See which groups' maps match yours. You can also assign countries to individual students and, based on their classmates' suggestions, they form a "human" map of Central and South America.

**NOTE for *Los pronombres preposicionales***

In addition to *conmigo* and *contigo*, you may choose to present the form *consigo*.

---

**11-28 Preguntas personales** Túrnense para contestar las siguientes preguntas. ■

1. ¿Por cuánto tiempo viste las noticias en la televisión anoche?
2. ¿Por cuánto tiempo estudiaste anoche?
3. ¿Qué veías por la ventana de tu cuarto cuando eras joven?
4. Cuando estabas en la escuela primaria, ¿ibas al colegio en autobús, carro o a pie?
5. ¿Por quién votaste la primera vez que pudiste votar?
6. ¿Qué puede hacer un estudiante universitario para ser más activo en la política?
7. ¿Sabes si hay un centro de reciclaje por aquí? ¿Por dónde voy para llegar allí?
8. ¿Qué necesitamos hacer para evitar la contaminación?

Capítulo 7, El pretérito, pág. 263; Algunos verbos irregulares en el pretérito, pág 272; Capítulo 8, El imperfecto, pág. 317.

## 6 GRAMÁTICA

11-35 to 11-37  Spanish/English Tutorials

# Las preposiciones y los pronombres preposicionales
### Specifying location and other information

Sin duda, su apoyo es esencial. Con ustedes podemos hacer grandes cambios sin dificultades.

Besides the prepositions **por** and **para,** there is a variety of useful prepositions and prepositional phrases, many of which you have already been using throughout *¡Anda! Curso elemental.* Study the following list to review the ones you already know and to acquaint yourself with those that may be new to you.

| | | | |
|---|---|---|---|
| **a** | *to; at* | **después de** | *after* |
| **a la derecha de** | *to the right of* | **detrás de** | *behind* |
| **a la izquierda de** | *to the left of* | **en** | *in* |
| **acerca de** | *about* | **encima de** | *on top of* |
| **(a)fuera de** | *outside of* | **enfrente de** | *across from; facing* |
| **al lado de** | *next to* | **entre** | *among; between* |
| **antes de** | *before (time/space)* | **hasta** | *until* |
| **cerca de** | *near* | **lejos de** | *far from* |
| **con** | *with* | **para** | *for; in order to* |
| **de** | *of; from; about* | **por** | *for; through; by; because of* |
| **debajo de** | *under; underneath* | **según** | *according to* |
| **delante de** | *in front of* | **sin** | *without* |
| **dentro de** | *inside of* | **sobre** | *over; about* |
| **desde** | *from* | | |

El centro de reciclaje está **a la derecha del** supermercado.

*The recycling center is to the right of the supermarket.*

La alcadesa va a hablar **acerca de** los problemas que tenemos con la protección del cocodrilo cubano.

*The mayor is going to speak about the problems we are having with the protection of the Cuban crocodile.*

Vimos un montón de plástico **encima del** papel.

*We saw a mountain of plastic on top of the paper.*

Quieren sembrar flores **enfrente del** vertedero.

*They want to plant flowers in front of the dump.*

El proyecto no puede tener éxito **sin** el apoyo del gobierno local.

*The project cannot be successful without the support of the local government.*

## Los pronombres preposicionales

Study the list of pronouns that are used following prepositions.

<table>
<tr><td rowspan="5">**Fíjate**<br><br>The list of pronouns that follow prepositions is the same as the list of subject pronouns, except for the first two (*mí* is used instead of *yo*, and *ti* instead of *tú*).</td><td>**mí**</td><td>*me*</td><td>**nosotros/as**</td><td>*us*</td></tr>
<tr><td>**ti**</td><td>*you*</td><td>**vosotros/as**</td><td>*you*</td></tr>
<tr><td>**usted**</td><td>*you*</td><td>**ustedes**</td><td>*you*</td></tr>
<tr><td>**él**</td><td>*him*</td><td>**ellos**</td><td>*them*</td></tr>
<tr><td>**ella**</td><td>*her*</td><td>**ellas**</td><td>*them*</td></tr>
</table>

**Para mí,** es muy importante resolver el problema de la lluvia ácida.

*For me, it's really important to solve the problem of acid rain.*

¿Qué candidato está sentado **enfrente de ti**?

*Which candidate is seated in front of you?*

Se fueron de la huelga **sin nosotros.**

*They left the strike without us.*

Trabajamos **con ellos** para proteger el medio ambiente.

*We work with them to protect the environment.*

Note that **con** has two special forms:

**1.** con + mí = **conmigo** *with me*
—¿Vienes **conmigo** al discurso?
*Are you coming with me to the speech?*

**2.** con + ti = **contigo** *with you*
—Sí, voy **contigo.**
*Yes, I'm going with you.*

---

**11-29** **Hablando del candidato** Termina la conversación entre Celia y Manolo sobre el candidato Carlos Arroyo con los pronombres preposicionales apropiados y después comparte tus respuestas con un/a compañero/a. ■

CELIA: Manolo, ¿qué opinas tú de (1) ___él___?

MANOLO: Pues, te digo que para (2) ___mí___ está muy claro. El señor Arroyo no piensa en (3) ___nosotros___ ni en nuestros problemas.

> **Fíjate**
> Remember that when *a + el* and *de + el* appear together in a sentence, you must use the contractions (*al, del*).

CELIA: Sí, siempre está con las personas ricas e influyentes (*influential*), tratando de conseguir dinero de (4) ___ellos___ para su campaña.

MANOLO: También creo que vive parte del año aquí y parte en la costa. Para (5) ___mí___ eso significa que quiere ser nuestro líder pero no quiere vivir con (6) ___nosotros___. ¿Y para (7) ___ti___, Celia?

CELIA: Creo que tienes razón. Me gusta hablar con ___tigo (contigo)___ (8) porque me haces pensar en las cosas que no son tan obvias.

**ADDITIONAL ACTIVITY for** *Las preposiciones*

**Ahora, dibújenlo ustedes**

Pensando en los verbos *ser* y *estar* y en las preposiciones, imaginen seis escenas / situaciones diferentes. Hagan un dibujo simple para ilustrar cada escena / situación y después describan la escena en dos o tres oraciones.

**MODELO**

Estos gatos están cansados. Son enormes.

*Los gatos son enormes. Están cansados y duermen encima de la mesa.*

1. Estas tres botellas son de vidrio, son muy pequeñas y están enfrente de una caja de cartón grande.
2. Estas latas son de sopa y atún. Están debajo de la silla.
3. Este hombre es veterinario. El pájaro está enfermo. El veterinario examina el pájaro al lado de una ventana.
4. Hay un peligroso incendio en el bosque, pero está lejos de la ciudad.

**11-30** **Descríbemelo** Juntos describan el dibujo usando las siguientes preposiciones. ■

**MODELO**  *El gato está al lado del árbol.*

1. al lado de
2. a la derecha de
3. a la izquierda de
4. cerca de

5. debajo de
6. delante de
7. detrás de
8. lejos de

**11-31** **Una política joven** Completa el párrafo sobre Martina Peña, una candidata nueva en el mundo político, con las preposiciones de la lista. Después compara tu párrafo con el de un/a compañero/a. ■

| a | antes de | con (2 veces) | de |
|---|----------|---------------|-----|
| después de | entre | sobre | sin |

(1) ___Antes de___ meterse en la política. Martina compartió sus ideas (2) ___con___ mucha gente. (3) ___Entre___ otras personas se reunió (4) ___con___ políticos importantes y, (5) ___de___ ellos, aprendió mucho (6) ___sobre___ el bienestar, los derechos humanos, la violencia, el desempleo y la inflación. (7) ___Después de___ escuchar todo lo que tenían que decir, ella volvió (8) ___a___ su casa y empezó a convertir sus ideas en discursos. El próximo paso fue buscar apoyo y dinero. Sabía perfectamente que (9) ___sin___ ese apoyo no iba a ser posible ganar las elecciones.

## 11-32 ¿Dónde están?

Con un/a compañero/a, expliquen dónde están los siguientes lugares en El Viejo San Juan en Puerto Rico, usando siempre las preposiciones apropiadas. ■

Viejo San Juan

**MODELO**   E1: *¿Dónde está el Campo del Morro?*

E2: *Está entre el Castillo y La Casa Blanca, al lado del Cementerio de San Juan.*

1. La Fortaleza, casa del gobernador
2. El Capitolio, edificio de las oficinas de los senadores y representantes
3. La Plaza de Armas
4. El Castillo de San Felipe del Morro
5. La Casa Blanca, casa de la familia de Juan Ponce de León
6. La Alcaldía / El Ayuntamiento, edificio donde el alcalde tiene sus oficinas
7. Correos
8. El Banco Popular
9. La puerta de San Juan
10. La catedral de San Juan

Capítulo 2. En la universidad, pág. 74.

## 11-33 La universidad

Túrnense para explicar dónde están los siguientes lugares en su universidad. ■

**MODELO**   *La biblioteca está detrás del centro estudiantil.*

1. la biblioteca
2. el gimnasio
3. el centro estudiantil
4. la librería

5. la cafetería
6. tu cuarto o residencia estudiantil
7. el centro de salud
8. el estadio de fútbol

## 11-34 ¿Con quién...?

Decide quién hace las siguientes actividades contigo y después comparte las respuestas con un/a compañero/a. ■

**MODELO**   E1: *¿Quién... habla contigo por teléfono todos los días?*

E2: *Mi madre habla conmigo por teléfono todos los días.*

### ¿Quién...?

1. viene a clase contigo
2. se sienta contigo en la sala de clase
3. hace las actividades de clase contigo
4. estudia contigo fuera de clase
5. almuerza o cena contigo
6. sale contigo por la tarde (para ir al cine / bar / club de baile, etc.)

**NOTE for 11-32**
These buildings are historical sites located in Viejo San Juan, near El Castillo de San Felipe del Morro. Many of them are open to the public and serve as museums or tourist sites, while others are used for government business and officials.

**NOTE for 11-32**
Activity **11-32** lends itself well to a cultural expansion activity. Students can research San Juan sites such as El Morro on the Internet and present their findings to the class.

**ADDITIONAL ACTIVITY for**
*Las preposiciones*
**En nuestra clase...** Creen diez oraciones con preposiciones que describan su clase de español.

**MODELO**
*Ryan se sienta al lado de George. / Los libros de mi profesor están encima de su escritorio. / Las ventanas están lejos de nosotros.*

**7 GRAMÁTICA**

 11-38 to 11-40

## El infinitivo después de preposiciones
Providing more information about location, time, and other subjects

¡No me digas que todos tienen que comer antes de salir nosotros!

In Spanish, if you need to use a verb immediately after a preposition, it must always be in the **infinitive** form. Study the following examples:

**Antes de reciclar** las latas debes limpiarlas.
*Before recycling the cans, you should clean them.*

**Después de pisar** la hormiga la niña empezó a llorar.
*After stepping on the ant, the little girl began to cry.*

Es fácil decidir **entre reciclar** y **botar.**
*It is easy to decide between recycling and throwing away.*

Necesitamos trabajar con personas de todos los países **para proteger** mejor la Tierra.
*We need to work with people from all countries in order to better protect the Earth.*

Ganaste el premio **por estar** tan interesado en el medio ambiente.
*You won the prize for being so interested in the environment.*

No podemos vivir **sin trabajar** juntos.
*We cannot live without working together.*

Capítulo 10. El viaje, pág. 388.

 **11-35** **De viaje** Forma oraciones lógicas usando **antes de** o **después de**. Después, compártelas con un/a compañero/a. ■

**MODELO**     E1:  salir / hacer la maleta

E2:  *Antes de salir, necesito hacer la maleta.  /  Antes de salir, tengo que hacer la maleta.*

1. comprar el boleto / ir al banco   Antes de comprar el boleto, tengo que ir al banco.
2. pasar por recepción / ir al cuarto   Después de ir al cuarto, tengo que pasar por recepción.
3. llegar al aeropuerto / mostrar el pasaporte   Después de llegar al aeropuerto, tengo que mostrar el pasaporte
4. hacer la maleta / lavar la ropa   Antes de hacer la maleta, necesito lavar la ropa.
5. ir de vacaciones / dejar el gato con mis padres   Antes de ir de vacaciones, necesito dejar el gato con mis pa

**EXPANSION for 11-36**
Have students create a new "story" following this model. They should replace *perro* with another noun every time it appears and make any other necessary adjustments.

[3:00]   **11-36** **Lo que pasó con el perro** Termina las siguientes oraciones de forma lógica según el modelo. Después, comparte tus respuestas con un/a compañero/a. ■

**MODELO**   E1:  Es importante que sepas que el perro se escapó para…

E2:  *Es importante que sepas que el perro se escapó para jugar con esa perra bonita del vecino.*

1. Es mejor que busquemos el perro antes de…
2. Es probable que el perro nos evite para…
3. Es posible que el perro tenga hambre después de…
4. Sí, es raro que no venga para…
5. Es dudoso que se vaya con otra persona después de…
6. Ojalá que lo encontremos sin…

[5:00]   **11-37** **Mis decisiones** Termina las siguientes oraciones y después compártelas con un/a compañero/a. ■

**MODELO**   E1:  No me voy de aquí sin…

E2:  *No me voy de aquí sin terminar la tarea.*

1. Necesito pensar en el futuro antes de…
2. Quiero hablar con mis padres / mi mejor amigo sobre…
3. Voy a buscar un trabajo después de…
4. Tengo que escoger entre…
5. Me quedo en este lugar hasta…
6. Después pienso ir a _____ para…

**ESCUCHA**

## Un anuncio político

11-41 to 11-43

| **Estrategia** | | |
|---|---|---|
| **Using visual organizers** | Once you know the topic or gist of a passage, it may be helpful to mentally organize what you are about to hear. | Determine whether a list, chart, or diagram could be useful in helping you keep track of the information. |

**11-38** **Antes de escuchar** Fania Marte Lozada tiene un anuncio político en la radio. ◼

1. ¿Qué es un anuncio político?
2. ¿Escuchaste alguna vez un anuncio político de un candidato en la radio o viste uno de estos anuncios en la televisión?
3. ¿Qué información contiene generalmente un anuncio de este tipo?

Fania Marte Lozada, candidata

**11-39** **A escuchar** Completa los siguientes pasos. ◼

1. Escucha el anuncio para sacar la idea general.
2. Decide de qué forma quieres organizar la información (*list, chart, diagram,* etc.).
3. Escucha otra vez para completar tu diagrama o lista con la información esencial.
4. Escucha una vez más para añadir algunos detalles.

**11-40** **Después de escuchar** En grupos de tres o cuatro, compartan su información y juntos decidan si la Dra. Marte Lozada sería (*would be*) una buena alcaldesa. Expliquen. ◼

# ¡CONVERSEMOS!

11-44

 **11-41** **Nuestro mundo**

Junto con un/a compañero/a, creen una conversación entre un ciudadano y un candidato sobre los problemas más críticos del medio ambiente y las posibles soluciones y fondos (*funding*). Necesitan incluir por lo menos **diez** oraciones y usar el **subjuntivo por lo menos cinco veces.** Después, presenten la entrevista para los compañeros de la clase. ■

**11-42** **La política** Tu companero/a y tú son reporteros de noticias. Juntos creen un reportaje sobre algún aspecto de la política del mundo y de lo que pasó hoy. Incluyan por lo menos **diez** oraciones. ■

**SECTION GOALS for**
*¡Conversemos!*
By the end of the *¡Conversemos!* section, students will be able to:

- discuss environmental issues, along with potential solutions and funding sources using presentational and interpersonal modes.
- share information about a politically-related current event using presentational and interpersonal modes.
- utilize previously learned/recycled vocabulary and grammatical concepts such as the subjunctive mood, *por* and *para*, and other prepositions.

**ESCRIBE**

## Un anuncio de servicio público

11-45

| Estrategia | In writing a public announcement, your goal is to influence the listeners to support your cause and become better environmentalists. To create the most effective announcement, consider the elements of persuasive writing: appeal to reason, emotions, and good character (ethical, morals, and concern for the well-being of the | audience); define any key terms that may not be clear; reference an authority and/or supporting evidence to back your claims; and anticipate counterarguments and address them. You must develop a rational argument, making sure the conclusion logically follows the claims you make. |
|---|---|---|
| **Persuasive writing** | | |

**11-43 Antes de escribir** Vas a crear un anuncio de publicidad para la radio sobre algún aspecto de la protección del medio ambiente. Debe durar (*last*) unos quince segundos. Decide de qué quieres hablar y haz una lista de los puntos más importantes que quieres incluir. ■

**11-44 A escribir** Organiza tus ideas y escribe un anuncio. Debe estar dirigido (*directed*) a los adultos jóvenes. ■

 **11-45 Después de escribir** Presenta tu anuncio a los compañeros de clase. ■

## ¿Cómo andas? II

|  | Feel confident | Need to review |
|---|---|---|
| Having completed **Comunicación II**, I now can . . . | | |
| • discuss government and current affairs (p. 426) | ☐ | ☐ |
| • relate specific facts about politics in the Spanish-speaking world (p. 428) | ☐ | ☐ |
| • express time, deadlines, movement, destination, means, purpose, etc. (p. 429) | ☐ | ☐ |
| • specify location and other information (p. 432) | ☐ | ☐ |
| • provide more information about location, time, and other subjects (p. 436) | ☐ | ☐ |
| • listen to a radio announcement and practice using visual organizers to enhance comprehension (p. 438) | ☐ | ☐ |
| • communicate about world issues (p. 439) | ☐ | ☐ |
| • employ persuasive writing to create a public announcement (p. 440) | ☐ | ☐ |

# Cultura

## Cuba

CULTURA • CULTURA • CULTURA •                                                    LTURA •

11-46 to 11-47
[10:00]

### Les presento mi país

Alicia Ortega Mujica

Mi nombre es Alicia Ortega Mujica y soy de La Habana, la capital de Cuba. La mayoría de los cubanos tenemos herencia española, africana o una mezcla (*mixture*) de las dos. La influencia africana se nota sobre todo en la música cubana, especialmente en la salsa. Celia Cruz, "la reina de la salsa", siempre alababa estas raíces africanas en sus canciones. **¿Qué influencia africana se siente en la música de tu país?** Antes, la economía cubana dependía mayormente de la producción de azúcar, pero ahora el turismo es muy importante y el gobierno invierte recursos para desarrollar esa infraestructura a fin de (*in order to*) atraer más visitantes al país.

La Plaza de la Revolución

El ajiaco, un plato típico cubano

FLORIDA
BAHAMAS
Matanzas — Santa Clara
La Habana
Morón — OCÉANO ATLÁNTICO
Pinar del Río
CUBA
Isla de la Juventud — Camagüey — Nuevitas
Cienfuegos — Holguín
Manzanillo
ISLAS CAIMANES — Santiago de Cuba
Guantánamo
Mar Caribe — JAMAICA

El Gran Teatro de La Habana y El Ballet Nacional de Cuba

### ALMANAQUE

**Nombre oficial:** República de Cuba
**Gobierno:** Estado/Régimen comunista
**Población:** 11.477.459 (2010)
**Idioma:** español
**Moneda:** Peso cubano (CUP) y Peso convertible (CUC)

### ¿Sabías que...?

- El zunzuncito, el pájaro más pequeño del mundo, es endémico (*common*) de Cuba. Mide menos de seis centímetros y pesa menos de dos gramos. Es una especie de colibrí (*hummingbird*).

### Preguntas

1. ¿Cuál es la composición étnica de la población cubana?
2. ¿Cuáles son las bases principales de la economía cubana?
3. ¿Qué tipo de música es popular en Cuba? ¿Es popular en otras partes del mundo?

 Amplía tus conocimientos sobre Cuba en MySpanishLab.

441

---

**EXPANSION for *El ajiaco***
Additional questions to ask your students are: *¿Tenemos una sopa nacional? ¿un plato nacional? ¿Cuál es tu sopa favorita? ¿cómo se prepara?*

**SUGGESTION for *El Ballet Nacional de Cuba***
Additional questions to ask your students are: *¿Hay alguna compañía de ballet famosa en los Estados Unidos? Nombra algún bailarín famoso. ¿Adónde puedes ir a ver un ballet?*

---

 **Instructor Resources**
• Text images (maps), Video resources

**SECTION GOALS for *Cultura***
By the end of the *Cultura* section, students will be able to:
• name the cultural influences in Cuba.
• list important agricultural products in Cuba.
• discuss the wildlife common to Cuba.
• identify the natural resources of Puerto Rico.
• state the relationship of Puerto Rico to the United States.
• report about the major products of the Dominican Republic.
• explain how the geography of the Dominican Republic differs from that of other Hispanic countries.
• contrast Cuba, Puerto Rico, and the Dominican Republic with other Hispanic countries.

**NATIONAL STANDARDS**
***Communication, Cultures, Comparisons***
Students read about three Hispanic countries: Cuba, Puerto Rico, and the Dominican Republic, in *Les presento mi país*. The reading provides written Spanish and students are able to interpret and understand the cultural information presented (Standard 1.2). They can discuss in pairs or small groups how the three featured countries differ and how they are different from other Hispanic countries they have learned about (Standard 1.1). The information explains how the cultures differ from country to country, and students can compare how the history and geography of these countries affect their products, practices, and perspectives (Standards 2.1 and 2.2). They can then make comparisons between the cultural practices of Cubans, Puerto Ricans, and Dominicans and how they are similar to or different from those of the United States (Standard 4.2).

**NOTE for *Cultura***
You may live in a part of the country that has a large number of people whose heritage is Puerto Rican, Cuban, or Dominican. At this point in *Capítulo 11,* and as you approach the end of *¡Anda! Curso elemental,* you can include students from these countries in a discussion of their heritage, which will enrich the learning of the entire class.

**SUGGESTION for *La Plaza de la Revolución***
Additional questions to ask your students are: *¿Qué lugares públicos en los Estados Unidos se usan para las demostraciones públicas, tanto políticas como de otro tipo?* (e.g., Times Square in NYC), *¿Cómo se honra en los Estados Unidos a los héroes políticos y militares?*

**Instructor Resources**
• Text images (maps), Video resources

**NOTE for *Vista de San Juan***
San Juan is located in the northern coastal plains in the Karstic region of Puerto Rico. (Karst contains such features as caves, sinkholes, springs, and sinking streams. These landforms are created by water dissolving the bedrock over many thousands of years.) San Juan is an excellent natural harbor. Founded in 1521, it is technically the oldest city in the United States, founded by Juan Ponce de León five years before he reached St. Augustine, FL. *La ciudad amurallada* is a nickname of San Juan.

**EXPANSION for *Vista de San Juan***
Additional questions to ask your students are: *¿Hay alguna ciudad amurallada en los Estados Unidos? ¿Por qué crees que la muralla fue importante para San Juan en su momento?*

**NOTE for *El coquí***
The *coquí* is the "national" frog, or symbol of Puerto Rico. It is a tiny amphibian of about 1 inch in length. About 16 different species live on the island, and 13 of those are found in *El Yunque*, the Caribbean National Forest. The *coquí* is so named because of the sound or call made by the male of the species at dusk: co-quí, co-quí.

**EXPANSION for *El coquí***
Additional questions to ask your students are: *¿Cuál es el símbolo oficial de los Estados Unidos? ¿Había otros posibles "candidatos" cuando fue escogido? ¿Cuál prefieres tú y por qué?*

**NOTE for *El radiotelescopio de Arecibo***
The single-dish radio telescope at the Arecibo Observatory is the largest of its kind in the world. This important scientific facility is open to scientists worldwide on the basis of competitive research proposals and projects. It is located at the National Astronomy and Ionosphere Center in Arecibo, Puerto Rico. It has even appeared in several movies: *GoldenEye* (James Bond), *Contact*, and *Species*. To learn more about this facility research it on the Internet.

**EXPANSION for *El radiotelescopio de Arecibo***
Additional questions to ask your students are: *¿Qué instalaciones para la investigación científica hay en los Estados Unidos? ¿dónde están?* (e.g., NASA in Texas and NORAD in Colorado)

# Cultura

# Puerto Rico

CULTURA • CULTURA • CULTURA • C ... A • C

11-46, 11-48

## Les presento mi país

Pablo Colón Padín

Mi nombre es Pablo Colón Padín y soy de San Germán, Puerto Rico, conocido como la Ciudad de las Lomas (*hills*). Actualmente soy estudiante del Recinto Universitario de Mayagüez, donde han asistido, entre muchos otros, algunos ingenieros de NASA. **¿Te interesan los estudios del espacio y de los planetas?** El Observatorio de Arecibo, sitio del radiotelescopio de un solo plato más grande del mundo, está a unas setenta millas de mi universidad. También se puede estudiar una naturaleza muy diversa en mi isla: desde un área de cuevas del norte hasta El Yunque, bosque lluvioso del este. Puerto Rico es territorio de los Estados Unidos pero la cuestión de la independencia y la estadidad (*statehood*) se siguen debatiendo. **¿Qué opinas tú de esta cuestión?**

El radiotelescopio del Observatorio de Arecibo

Vista de San Juan, la capital

El coquí, el famoso símbolo de Puerto Rico

**ALMANAQUE**

| | |
|---|---|
| **Nombre oficial:** | Estado Libre Asociado de Puerto Rico |
| **Gobierno:** | Territorio de los Estados Unidos; Estado Libre Asociado |
| **Población:** | 3.978.702 (2010) |
| **Idiomas:** | español e inglés |
| **Moneda:** | Dólar estadounidense ($) |

### ¿Sabías que...?

• Puerto Rico tiene tres bahías fosforescentes habitadas por millones de microorganismos (dinoflagelados) que emanan (*emanate*) luz cuando son alborotados (*stirred up*). Se puede observar este fenómeno por la noche. ¡Qué maravilla!

### Preguntas

1. ¿Qué evidencia del desarrollo avanzado de las ciencias hay en Puerto Rico?
2. Describe la variedad natural de la isla.
3. ¿Hay otros países de Centroamérica que tienen bosques lluviosos?

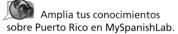 Amplía tus conocimientos sobre Puerto Rico en MySpanishLab.

442

# La República Dominicana

11-46, 11-49

## Les presento mi país

Amparo Burgos Báez

Mi nombre es Amparo Burgos Báez y soy de la República Dominicana, que comparte la isla de La Española con Haití. Mi país es muy montañoso y áspero (*rough*), con cuatro sistemas principales de cordilleras (*mountain ranges*), pero también tiene unas playas increíbles de arena fina y agua cristalina. **¿Prefieres las montañas o la playa?** Uno de nuestros platos más típicos es *la bandera dominicana,* que consiste en arroz, habichuelas rojas, carne, ensalada y tostones (*plantain chips*)… Si nos visitas, vas a escuchar el merengue y la bachata con sus ritmos contagiosos. Otras aficiones del país son los deportes acuáticos y el béisbol. **¿Sabes qué jugadores dominicanos juegan para equipos estadounidenses?**

Santa María La Menor, la primera catedral del Nuevo Mundo

Los cigarros dominicanos son de los mejores del mundo.

OCÉANO ATLÁNTICO

Puerto Plata
Santiago
Samaná
HAITÍ
Cotuí
Punta Cana
LA REPÚBLICA
DOMINICANA
San Juan
Santo Domingo
La Romana
Barahona
San Pedro de Macoris

Mar Caribe

El merengue, la música nacional

### ALMANAQUE

**Nombre oficial:** La República Dominicana
**Gobierno:** Democracia representativa
**Población:** 9.823.821 (2010)
**Idioma:** español (oficial)
**Moneda:** Peso dominicano ($RD)

### ¿Sabías que…?

- Cristóbal Colón descubrió la isla en su primer viaje y la nombró La Española. Santo Domingo fue la primera ciudad europea fundada en el Nuevo Mundo y hoy en día casi la mitad de la población vive ahí, en la capital.
- La mayoría de los beisbolistas hispanos en las Grandes Ligas son dominicanos.

### Preguntas

1. ¿Cómo es la geografía dominicana y qué tiene de especial?
2. ¿Qué es "la bandera dominicana"?
3. ¿Qué tienen en común la República Dominicana y los otros países del Caribe que has estudiado?

Amplía tus conocimientos sobre la República Dominicana en MySpanishLab.

443

**Instructor Resources**
- Text images (maps), Video resources

**NOTE for *Los cigarros***
Tabacco is the Dominican Republic's oldest crop, cultivated by the Taino Indians before Columbus landed, and is a stable agricultural export. The Association of Cigar Producers (Procigar) estimates that more than 70,000 Dominicans make their living off the crop. The United States is the number one importer of Dominican cigars.

**NOTE for *La Catedral Santa María La Menor***
Also known as the *Catedral Primada de América*, the church was begun in 1514 and completed in 1540. The architecture is a blend of Gothic, baroque, and plateresque styles and the façade is made of coral and limestone.

**NOTE for *El merengue***
*Merengue* means whipped egg whites and sugar in Spanish, similar to the English word meringue. It is unclear as to why this name became the name of a style of music from the Dominican Republic. But, perhaps, we can trace its meaning to a dance move that resembles an egg beater in action.
    This style of music was created by Ñico Lora in the 1920s and eventually became the country's national music and dance style. World-famous merengue singers include Los Hermanos Rosario, Juan Luis Guerra, Wilfredo Vargas, Sergio Vargas, Johnny Ventura, Kinito Mendez, Josie Esteban y la Patrulla 15, Pochy y su Cocoband, Fernando Villalona, Cuco Valoy, Elvis Crespo, Miriam Cruz y Las Chicas del Can, Conjunto Quisqueya, and Omega.

# Ambiciones siniestras — EPISODIO 11

11-52

# Lectura

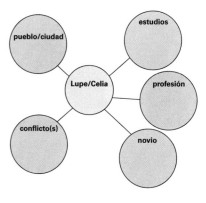

**Estrategia** — Using visual organizers

After you have read a text, it may be useful to create a visual organizer for the information
contained therein. In *¡Anda! Curso elemental*, you have already worked with timelines,
semantic maps (or web diagrams), charts, and Venn diagrams in completing activities.
Try these organizers as you read.

**11-46** **Antes de leer** En el **Episodio 10** tuvimos una confesión de Cisco y
surgieron más dudas sobre Lupe. Parece que tiene secretos. Teniendo esto en cuenta,
contesta las siguientes preguntas. ■

1. ¿Quién es Lupe?
2. ¿Cuáles pueden ser sus secretos?
3. ¿Está en peligro Marisol?

**11-47** **A leer** Complete the following steps. ■

1. Skim the episode and think about which
   visual organizer(s) would best summarize
   what you learn about Lupe.
2. Create the visual organizer(s), then read
   the passage carefully to gather all the
   information you can to complete your
   organizer. Finally, share it with your
   classmates. Did you all create the same type
   of visual organizer? Which one(s) proved to
   be most beneficial?

pueblo/ciudad · estudios · Lupe/Celia · profesión · conflicto(s) · novio

 ## Celia

*stayed there*
*sighed*

Marisol tenía una cara de terror. Lupe se quedó° mirando la pistola que tenía en la mano.
Por fin la puso en la mesa y suspiró° lentamente.

*hurt*

—Bueno —dijo Lupe—. Veo que es necesario que te lo cuente todo ahora. Pensaba hacerlo,
pero no en este momento. Creía que te protegía… No quise hacerle daño° a nadie, Marisol.
Me mandaron aquí para ayudar.

444

—¿Protegerme? ¿Ayudarme? —respondió Marisol—. No sé qué creer. No sé quién eres. No sé qué quieres de mí… de nosotros.

—Marisol, no soy estudiante. Soy agente del FBI.

—¿Cómo? ¿Cómo que eres una agente? No lo comprendo —dijo Marisol—. Te ves tan joven.

*I haven't been*
*lies*

—Yo sé que no he sido° honesta —respondió Lupe—. No estoy nada orgullosa de las falsas apariencias y de tantas mentiras°. A veces tengo la sensación de que mi vida es una mentira… pero después pienso en las personas a las que estoy ayudando.

—¿A quiénes estás ayudando? —preguntó Marisol—. Estoy desilusionada… muy desilusionada.

—Escuche —imploró Lupe.

—¿Escuche? —preguntó Marisol, incrédula—. ¿Ahora me tratas de «usted»? ¡Éramos amigas! Confiaba en ti.

—Bueno, Marisol. *Te* lo cuento todo pero tienes que dejarme hablar —dijo Lupe.

—Te escucho… ojalá que sea la verdad —respondió Marisol con voz desesperada.

Entonces se sentaron juntas y Lupe empezó a explicárselo todo:

*that I had*
*ever met*
*as soon as*
*I graduated*

*he had not been*

*involved*
*required that he leave*
*undercover*

*dead*

—Mi nombre verdadero es Celia Cortez y soy de Los Ángeles. Me gradué hace ocho años de la Universidad de Georgetown con una especialidad en ciencias políticas. Mientras estaba en el último año, conocí a un hombre increíble y me enamoré de él en seguida. Era el hombre más inteligente, más atractivo, más interesante que había conocido jamás°. Tenía un trabajo muy bueno con el gobierno federal. Era mi mejor amigo… Decidimos casarnos en cuanto me graduara°. Una noche dábamos un paseo por el centro de Washington cuando me dijo que tenía que contarme algo muy importante, que no había sido° totalmente honesto conmigo. Me dijo entonces que trabajaba para el FBI, no para el Departamento de Estado como yo pensaba. Le pregunté por qué decidió contármelo todo aquella noche y me respondió que era porque estaba involucrado° en un trabajo que requería que saliera° de Washington por varias semanas. Me explicó que no iba a poder estar en contacto conmigo mientras tanto. Sin preguntar, imaginaba que iba encubierto°. Nunca pensé en el peligro que le podía esperar. Yo era muy joven y realmente no sabía nada de su trabajo. Dos semanas después recibí la llamada que cambió mi vida por completo: mi amor estaba muerto°. Lo mataron. Yo estaba perdida…

—Ay Lupe… perdón, Celia —respondió Marisol—. Lo siento. ¿Qué hiciste entonces?

—Me gradué y fui a trabajar para la misma agencia para conocer mejor quién era él, para poder saber más de su vida y para sentirme más unida a él. Eso fue, como te dije, hace ocho años.

Sonó el teléfono celular de Celia. Contestó y se quedó escuchando sin decir nada. Cortó y le dijo a Marisol:

—Perdona. Es muy importante que hable con esta persona. Tengo que salir ahora pero después vuelvo para contestar tus preguntas. Y no te preocupes por Eduardo y Alejandra. Todo eso fue una mentira también.

445

**Instructor Resources**
• Video script

**ANSWERS to 11-48**
1. Celia Cortez
2. Los Ángeles
3. la Universidad de Georgetown; Ciencias políticas
4. Es agente del FBI.
5. Hace ocho años; en la universidad
6. Iba encubierto y lo mataron.
7. Se graduó y consiguió un trabajo en la misma agencia.
8. Celia está hablando por teléfono y después se va.

**SECTION GOALS for Video**
By the end of the *Video* section, students will be able to:
• brainstorm how they think the episode will end based on the information from the *Lectura*.
• reveal the ending of *Ambiciones siniestras*.
• discuss their opinions and feelings about the ending.
• summarize the plot from the first episode to the final episode.

**ANSWERS to 11-50**
1. Celia estaba en el aeropuerto.
2. Fueron al centro comercial.
3. No encontraron a nadie.
4. Después de que Eduardo contactó al FBI, ellos decidieron ponerlo bajo protección. Después de reconocer Alejandra a Lupe/Celia, el FBI la contactó y ella se infiltró en su organización para mandarle información a Celia.
5. Lupe/El primer rompecabezas vino del Sr. Verdugo. Celia escribió el segundo porque quería distraer a Cisco, Manolo y Marisol para protegerlos.
6. Marisol está viendo las noticias en la televisión. En la televisión hablan sobre el caso y dicen que capturaron al Sr. Verdugo. En ese momento recibe un email sobre otro concurso.

---

**11-48** **Después de leer** Contesta las siguientes preguntas. ■

1. ¿Cómo se llama Lupe en realidad?
2. ¿De dónde es?
3. ¿Dónde estudió y cuál era su especialidad?
4. ¿Cuál es su trabajo ahora?
5. ¿Cuándo y dónde conoció a su novio?
6. ¿Qué le pasó al novio?
7. ¿Qué hizo ella después?
8. ¿Cómo termina la lectura?

 11-53 to 11-54

# Video

**11-49** **Antes del video** ¿Qué crees que sabe Celia del Sr. Verdugo? ¿De Eduardo y Alejandra? ¿Quién llama a Celia? ¿Adónde va ella? En la segunda parte del episodio vas a encontrar todas las respuestas, y más. ■

Buenas tardes. Soy la agente Celia Cortez.   Llegamos demasiado tarde. Todos se fueron.   Eduardo, ¿estás bien?

 Episodio 11

## «El desenlace»

Relájate y disfruta el video.

**11-50** **Después del video** Contesta las siguientes preguntas. ■

1. ¿Dónde estaba Celia cuando empezó el episodio del video?
2. ¿Adónde fueron?
3. ¿A quién(es) encontraron allí?
4. ¿Qué les pasó a Eduardo y Alejandra cuando desaparecieron?
5. ¿Quién escribió los rompecabezas? ¿Por qué?
6. ¿Cómo termina **Ambiciones siniestras**?

# Y por fin, ¿cómo andas?

|  | Feel confident | Need to review |
|---|:---:|:---:|

Having completed this chapter, I now can . . .

### Comunicación I

- describe animals and their habitats (pp. 412–413) ☐ ☐
- pronounce words following the rules for accentuation and stress (MSL / SAM) ☐ ☐
- share details about the environment (p. 416) ☐ ☐
- comment on what is necessary, possible, probable, and improbable (p. 419) ☐ ☐

### Comunicación II

- discuss government and current affairs (p. 426) ☐ ☐
- express time, deadlines, movement, destination, means, purpose, etc. (p. 429) ☐ ☐
- specify location and other information (p. 432) ☐ ☐
- provide more information about location, time, and other subjects (p. 436) ☐ ☐
- listen to a radio announcement and practice using visual organizers to enhance comprehension (p. 438) ☐ ☐
- communicate about world issues (p. 439) ☐ ☐
- employ persuasive writing to create a public announcement (p. 440) ☐ ☐

### Cultura

- describe El Yunque, the rain forest of Puerto Rico (p. 419) ☐ ☐
- relate specific facts about politics in the Spanish-speaking world (p. 428) ☐ ☐
- share important facts about Cuba, Puerto Rico, and the Dominican Republic (pp. 441–443) ☐ ☐

### Ambiciones siniestras

- use visual organizers when reading, and explain who Lupe really is (p. 444) ☐ ☐
- relate what happened to Eduardo and Alejandra (p. 446) ☐ ☐

### Comunidades

- use Spanish in real-life contexts (SAM) ☐ ☐

# VOCABULARIO ACTIVO

| Algunos animales | *Some animals* |
|---|---|
| el caballo | *horse* |
| el cerdo | *pig* |
| el conejo | *rabbit* |
| el elefante | *elephant* |
| la gallina | *chicken; hen* |
| el gato | *cat* |
| la hormiga | *ant* |
| el insecto | *insect* |
| el león | *lion* |
| la mosca | *fly* |
| el mosquito | *mosquito* |
| el oso | *bear* |
| el pájaro / el ave | *bird* |
| el perro | *dog* |
| el pez (*pl.*, los peces) | *fish* |
| la rana | *frog* |
| la rata | *rat* |
| el ratón | *mouse* |
| la serpiente | *snake* |
| el toro | *bull* |
| la vaca | *cow* |

| Algunos verbos | *Some verbs* |
|---|---|
| cuidar | *to take care of* |
| preocuparse (por) | *to worry about; to concern oneself with* |

| Las cuestiones políticas | *Political issues* |
|---|---|
| el bienestar | *well-being; welfare* |
| la defensa | *defense* |
| la delincuencia | *crime* |
| el desempleo | *unemployment* |
| la deuda (externa) | *(foreign) debt* |
| el impuesto | *tax* |
| la inflación | *inflation* |

| Otras palabras útiles | *Other useful words* |
|---|---|
| los animal domésticos / las mascotas | *domesticated animals; pets* |
| los animales en peligro de extinción | *endangered species* |
| los animales salvajes | *wild animals* |
| el árbol | *tree* |
| el bosque | *forest* |
| la cueva | *cave* |
| la finca | *farm* |
| la granja | *farm* |
| el hoyo | *hole* |
| el lago | *lake* |
| la montaña | *mountain* |
| el océano | *ocean* |
| peligroso/a | *dangerous* |
| el río | *river* |
| la selva | *jungle* |

| El medio ambiente | *The environment* |
|---|---|
| el aluminio | *aluminum* |
| la botella | *bottle* |
| la caja (de cartón) | *(cardboard) box* |
| la contaminación | *pollution* |
| el derrame de petróleo | *oil spill* |
| el huracán | *hurricane* |
| el incendio | *fire* |
| la inundación | *flood* |
| la lata | *can* |
| el periódico | *newspaper* |
| el plástico | *plastic* |
| el terremoto | *earthquake* |
| la tormenta | *storm* |
| el tornado | *tornado* |
| el tsunami | *tsunami* |
| el vidrio | *glass* |

## Algunos verbos — *Some verbs*

| | |
|---|---|
| apoyar | *to support* |
| botar | *to throw away* |
| combatir | *to fight; to combat* |
| contaminar | *to pollute* |
| cuidar | *to take care of* |
| elegir | *to elect* |
| estar en huelga | *to be on strike* |
| evitar | *to avoid* |
| hacer daño | *to (do) damage; to harm* |
| llevar a cabo | *to carry out* |
| luchar | *to fight; to combat* |
| matar | *to kill* |
| meterse en política | *to get involved in politics* |
| plantar | *to plant* |
| proteger | *to protect* |
| reciclar | *to recycle* |
| reforestar | *to reforest* |
| reutilizar | *to reuse* |
| resolver (o → ue) | *to resolve* |
| sembrar (e → ie) | *to sow* |
| votar | *to vote* |

## La política — *Politics*

| | |
|---|---|
| el alcalde / la alcaldesa | *mayor* |
| el/la candidato/a | *candidate* |
| el/la dictador/a | *dictator* |
| el/la diputado/a | *deputy; representative* |
| el/la gobernador/a | *governor* |
| la guerra | *war* |
| la huelga | *strike* |
| el/la juez/a | *judge* |
| el juicio | *trial* |
| el/la presidente/a | *president* |
| el rey / la reina | *king / queen* |
| el/la senador/a | *senator* |

## Las preposiciones — *Prepositions*

*See page 432.*

## Las administraciones y los regímenes — *Administrations and regimes*

| | |
|---|---|
| el congreso | *congress* |
| la corte | *court* |
| la democracia | *democracy* |
| la dictadura | *dictatorship* |
| el estado | *state* |
| el gobierno | *government* |
| la ley | *law* |
| la monarquía | *monarchy* |
| la presidencia | *presidency* |
| la provincia | *province* |
| la región | *region* |
| el senado | *senate* |

## Las elecciones — *Elections*

| | |
|---|---|
| la campaña | *campaign* |
| el discurso | *speech* |
| la encuesta | *survey; poll* |
| el partido político | *political party* |
| el voto | *vote* |

## Otras palabras útiles — *Other useful words*

| | |
|---|---|
| el aire | *air* |
| la basura | *garbage* |
| la calidad | *quality* |
| la capa de ozono | *ozone layer* |
| el cielo | *sky; heaven* |
| el desastre | *disaster* |
| la destrucción | *destruction* |
| la ecología | *ecology* |
| el efecto invernadero | *global warming* |
| la lluvia ácida | *acid rain* |
| la naturaleza | *nature* |
| el planeta | *planet* |
| puro/a | *pure* |
| el recurso natural | *natural resource* |
| la selva tropical | *jungle; (tropical) rain forest* |
| la Tierra | *Earth* |
| la tierra | *land; soil* |
| la tragedia | *tragedy* |
| el vertedero | *dump* |
| vivo/a | *alive; living* |

**Instructor Resources**
• IRM: Syllabi and Lesson Plans

# Y por fin, ¡lo sé!

This final chapter is designed for you to see just how much Spanish you have acquired thus far. The *major points* of **Capítulos 7–11** are recycled in this chapter. No new vocabulary is presented.

All learners are different in terms of what they have mastered and what they still need to practice. Take the time with this chapter to determine what you feel confident with, and what you personally need to work on. And remember, language learning is a process. Like any skill, learning Spanish requires practice, review of the basics, and then more practice!

Before we begin revisiting the important grammar concepts, go to the end of each chapter, to the **Vocabulario activo** summary sections, and review the vocabulary that you have learned. Doing so now will help you successfully and creatively complete the following recycling activities. Consult the **Vocabulario activo** pages as needed as you progress through this chapter.

450

**METHODOLOGY • Philosophy on Recycling**

This chapter is unique in *¡Anda! Curso elemental* because it presents an opportunity for instructors and students to have yet another assessment regarding language acquired. In this chapter, *¡Anda!* has synthesized the main points of the final 5 chapters in a recycled format for students to practice the new skills they are learning. You will note that all of these activities have the students *put it all together;* in other words, *virtually all of the activities in Capítulo 12 are communicative.* There are no discrete-point mechanical

activities; some are structured, meaningful activities that help students build towards communicative practice. For mechanical practice, we direct students to make use of the activities in MySpanishLab, or to repeat the activities in their Student Activities Manual or in the textbook itself.

Finally, if you have advanced or heritage language learners, this is an excellent chapter for them, since most of the activities afford them the opportunity to be highly creative.

## OBJETIVOS

### COMUNICACIÓN

To communicate preferences regarding food and clothing

To relate ideas about past experiences and your daily routine

To convey information about people and things

To express ideas on topics such as health, travel, animals, the environment, and politics

To make requests and give advice using commands

To articulate desires and opinions on a variety of topics

### CULTURA

To share information about Chile, Paraguay, Argentina, Uruguay, Perú, Bolivia, Ecuador, Venezuela, Colombia, Cuba, Puerto Rico, and La República Dominicana

To compare and contrast the countries you learned about in **Capítulos 7–11**

### AMBICIONES SINIESTRAS

To go behind the scenes of **Ambiciones siniestras**

### COMUNIDADES

To use Spanish in real-life contexts (SAM)

**METHODOLOGY • Organizing a Review for Students**
Researchers and reviewers of *¡Anda! Curso elemental* agree: after giving students strategies on how to conduct an overall review, this chapter is organized by beginning with communicative and engaging activities that focus on grammar and vocabulary from *Capítulo 7*. The recycling continues to move through the chapters, ending with *Capítulo 11*. This is followed by *Un poco de todo*, a more comprehensive review, after which students are truly *putting all the chapters together*. Finally, there is a recycling of countries presented in *Capítulos 7–11* as well as *Ambiciones siniestras*.

**METHODOLOGY • Recycling vs. Reviewing**
In *¡Anda! Curso elemental, recycling* has meant taking previously learned material and recombining it with new material. This concept is supported by Gagné's learning concept of spiraling information. The concept of *review* is revisiting a topic, much like one does before an exam. *Review* is best illustrated in *Capítulo 7 (Un repaso del complemento directo)*, as well as in this chapter. No new information is presented, but rather a review affords students the opportunity to practice in a systematic fashion.

**PLANNING AHEAD**
You may wish to point out to your students Appendix 1, *Capítulo 12*, where they can find a list of the grammar points reviewed in this chapter.

451

# Organizing Your Review

There are processes used by successful language learners for reviewing a world language. The following tips can help you organize your review. There is no one correct way, but these are some suggestions that will best utilize your time and energy.

## 1 Reviewing Strategies

1. Make a list of the *major* topics you have studied and need to review, dividing them into categories: *vocabulary, grammar,* and *culture.* These are the topics where you need to focus the majority of your time and energy.
   *Note:* The two-page chapter openers can help you determine the *major* topics.
2. Allocate a minimum of an hour each day over a period of days to review. Budget the majority of your time with the major topics. After beginning with the major grammar and vocabulary topics, review the secondary/supporting grammar topics and the culture. Cramming the night before a test is *not* an effective way to review and retain information.
3. Many educational researchers suggest that you start your review with the most recent chapter, or for this review, **Capítulo 11.** The most recent chapter is the freshest in your mind, so you tend to remember the concepts better, and you will experience quick success in your review.
4. Spend the most amount of time on concepts in which you determine *you* need to improve. Revisit the self-assessment tools from **Y por fin, ¿cómo andas?** in each chapter to see how you rated yourself. Those tools are designed to help you become good at self-assessing what *you* need to work on the most.

## 2 Reviewing Grammar

1. When reviewing grammar, begin with the *major* points, that is, begin with the *preterit, imperfect, pronouns (direct, indirect, and reflexive), commands,* and the *subjunctive.* After feeling confident using the major grammar points correctly, then proceed with the additional grammar points and review them.
2. Good ways to review include redoing activities in your textbook, redoing activities in your Student Activities Manual, and (re)doing activities on MySpanishLab.

## 3 Reviewing Vocabulary

1. When studying vocabulary, it is usually most helpful to look at the English word, and then say or write the word in Spanish. Make a special list of words that are difficult for you to remember, writing them in a small notebook or in an electronic file. Pull out the notebook every time you have a few minutes (in between classes, waiting in line at the grocery store, etc.) to review the words. The **Vocabulario activo** pages at the end of each chapter will help you organize the most important words of each chapter.
2. Saying vocabulary (which includes verbs) out loud helps you retain the words better.

## 4 Overall Review Technique

1. Get together with someone with whom you can practice speaking Spanish. It is always good to structure the oral practice. If you need something to spark the conversation, take the drawings from each vocabulary presentation in *¡Anda! Curso elemental* and say as many things as you can about each picture. Have a friendly challenge to see who can make more complete sentences or create the longest story about the pictures. This will help you build your confidence and practice stringing sentences together to speak in paragraphs.
2. Yes, it is important for you to know "mechanical" pieces of information such as verb endings, or how to take a sentence and replace the direct object with a pronoun. *But,* it is *much more important* for you to be able to take those mechanical pieces of information and put them all together, creating meaningful and creative samples of your speaking and writing on the themes of **Capítulos 7–11.** Also remember that **Capítulos 7–11** are built upon previous knowledge that you acquired in the beginning chapters of *¡Anda! Curso elemental.*
3. You are on the road to success if you can demonstrate that you can speak and write in paragraphs, using a wide variety of verbs and vocabulary words correctly. Keep up the good work!

# Comunicación

 **Capítulo 7**

to 12-07

Capítulo 7

 **¡Fiesta!**  Decidieron tener una fiesta y tienen que trabajar mucho para prepararlo todo. Organícense, siguiendo el modelo y utilizando **el pretérito**, para organizar la fiesta. ■

MODELO  ¿Comprar / tú / las bebidas?

E1:  *¿Compraste las bebidas?*

E2:  *Sí, las compré ayer.*

> ### Estrategia
> Before beginning each activity, make sure that you have reviewed carefully the concepts in each given chapter so that you are able to move through the activities seamlessly as you put it all together.

1. ¿Pedir / ustedes / los mariscos?
2. ¿Preparar / tu compañero / los perros calientes?
3. ¿Comprar / tu amiga / el pastel?
4. ¿Limpiar / tú / la sala?

5. ¿Lavar / ustedes / los manteles?
6. ¿Encontrar / Manuel y Manuela / las servilletas?
7. ¿Traer/ Jorge / los CD?
8. ¿Invitar / tú / al profesor?

 **Después de la fiesta**  ¡La fiesta de la actividad **12-1** fue un éxito! Describan lo que pasó en la fiesta y qué hicieron cuando se fueron los invitados. Sean creativos y usen por lo menos **siete** oraciones. ■

MODELO  *¡Nuestra fiesta fue un éxito! Vinieron muchos invitados. La gente bailó, comió y se divirtió mucho. Escuchamos música salsa y rock. Después, tuvimos que pasar la aspiradora…*

**Instructor Resources**
• Textbook images, Extra Activities

**METHODOLOGY • Quantifying Minimum Expectations**
You will note that we frequently include the minimum number of sentences expected of the students, both in speaking and writing activities. If students do not know what these minimum expectations are, many will be happy with mediocre production. Most of us have had bright students who are lazy and unmotivated and are only willing to do the minimum. Hence it is necessary for instructors to let students know what their expectations are and to encourage them to exceed the minimum.

Having provided this rationale, the decision is ultimately yours. You may choose
1. to use what we have recommended;
2. to require a different minimum level of production;
3. not to state the level of language production.

You will notice that some of the directions in this chapter intentionally follow option 3. These are instructional delivery decisions that all of us must make based on a wide variety of differentiated objectives.

**METHODOLOGY • Recycling**
Note that this chapter helps recycle and remind students of concepts learned before *Capítulo 7*. Direct your students to the correct chapters to refresh their memories about concepts presented in the previous semester.

**EXPANSION for 12-3**
Have students compare schedules. Another option is to ask students what activities they have in common.

**METHODOLOGY • Self-Assessment and Instructor's Use of Rubrics**
Assessing student performance is an important task that we instructors perform. Students need to know in advance what is acceptable versus unacceptable work. It is important that students are provided in advance with the rubrics so that they are clear regarding our expectations.

The rubrics provided are meant to be used either as is or to act as a guide for you. The suggestion is that **3 = A; 2 = B; 1 = C; 0 = D/F.** Also notice that there is a place for you to assess effort. As instructors, we know that there will be some students who look for and take the easy way out, even though they may have the ability. These can be gifted students or heritage language learners who choose not to work to their potential. The effort rating is a way of encouraging those students as well as giving credit to students who struggle but are working above and beyond their level of ability. These students deserve to be rewarded for their efforts.

You may wish to add other categories such as pronunciation to the rubric as well.

 **12-3 La semana pasada** Túrnense para describir qué hicieron y adónde fueron **la semana** pasada, usando por lo menos **siete** oraciones en **el pretérito** con verbos diferentes. ■

MODELO
*La semana pasada hice muchas cosas. Por ejemplo, vi una película en la televisión. Estudié mucho también. Conduje a la universidad el martes en vez de tomar el autobús porque tuve que ir al médico por la tarde. El miércoles por la noche mi amigo y yo fuimos al concierto de Juanes. Dormí muy poco toda la semana…*

| l | m | m | j | v | s | d |
|---|---|---|---|---|---|---|
| estudiar, ver una película | ir al médico | ir al concierto de Juanes | | | ir al café Chulo | |
| | | | | | | |
| | | | | | | |

## Rúbrica

**Estrategia**
You and your instructor can use this rubric to assess your progress for activities **12-1** through **12-3**.

All aspects of our lives benefit from self-reflection and self-assessment. Learning Spanish is an aspect of our academic and future professional lives that benefits greatly from just such a self-assessment. Also coming into play is the fact that as college students, you personally are being held accountable for your learning and are expected to take ownership for your performance. Having said that, we instructors can assist you greatly by letting you know what we will expect of you. It will help you determine how well you are doing with the recycling of **Capítulo 7.** This rubric is meant first and foremost for you to use as a self-assessment, but you also can use it to peer-assess. Your instructor may use the rubric to assess your progress as well.

| | **3 EXCEEDS EXPECTATIONS** | **2 MEETS EXPECTATIONS** | **1 APPROACHES EXPECTATIONS** | **0 DOES NOT MEET EXPECTATIONS** |
|---|---|---|---|---|
| **Duración y precisión** | • Has at least 8 sentences and includes all the required information.<br>• May have errors, but they do not interfere with communication. | • Has 5–7 sentences and includes all the required information.<br>• May have errors, but they rarely interfere with communication. | • Has 4 sentences and includes some of the required information.<br>• Has errors that interfere with communication. | • Supplies fewer sentences and little of the required information in *Approaches Expectations.*<br>• If communicating at all, has frequent errors that make communication limited or impossible. |
| **Gramática nueva del *Capítulo 7*** | • Makes excellent use of the chapter's new grammar (e.g., direct object pronouns and the preterit).<br>• Uses a wide variety of verbs when appropriate. | • Makes good use of the chapter's new grammar (e.g., direct object pronouns and the preterit).<br>• Uses a variety of verbs when appropriate. | • Makes use of some of the chapter's new grammar (e.g., direct object pronouns and the preterit).<br>• Uses a limited variety of verbs when appropriate. | • Uses little, if any, of the chapter's new grammar (e.g., direct object pronouns and the preterit).<br>• Uses few, if any, of the chapter's verbs. |

*(continued)*

| | 3 EXCEEDS EXPECTATIONS | 2 MEETS EXPECTATIONS | 1 APPROACHES EXPECTATIONS | 0 DOES NOT MEET EXPECTATIONS |
|---|---|---|---|---|
| Vocabulario nuevo del *Capítulo 7* | • Uses many of the new vocabulary words (e.g., foods, food preparation, and the restaurant). | • Uses a variety of the new vocabulary words (e.g., foods, food preparation, and the restaurant). | • Uses some of the new vocabulary words (e.g., foods, food preparation, and the restaurant). | • Uses few, if any, new vocabulary words (e.g., foods, food preparation, and the restaurant). |
| ✪ Gramática y vocabulario reciclado de los capítulos anteriores | • Does an excellent job using recycled grammar and vocabulary to support what is being said. <br> • Uses a wide array of recycled verbs. <br> • Uses some recycled vocabulary, but focuses predominantly on new vocabulary. | • Does a good job using recycled grammar and vocabulary to support what is being said. <br> • Uses an array of recycled verbs. <br> • Uses some recycled vocabulary, but focuses predominantly on new vocabulary. | • Does an average job using recycled grammar and vocabulary to support what is being said. <br> • Uses a limited array of recycled verbs. <br> • Uses mostly recycled vocabulary and some new vocabulary. | • If speaking at all, relies almost completely on a few isolated words. <br> • Usage of previously learned grammar is inconsistent. |
| Esfuerzo | • Clearly the student made his/her best effort. | • The student made a good effort. | • The student made an effort. | • Little or no effort went into the activity. |

 ## Capítulo 8

to 12-14

Capítulo 8

 **12-4  La boda del siglo**  David y Adriana se casan. Tu compañero/a y tú están invitados y están planeando cómo vestirse. Túrnense para hablar del evento siguiendo el modelo. ▪

MODELO      tú / prestar / a mí / pantalones / amarillo

     E1:  *¿Me prestas tus pantalones amarillos?*

     E2:  *Sí, te los presto. / No, no te los presto.*

1. tú / prestar / a mí / zapatos / negro
2. tú / prestar / a Julieta / blusa / azul / seda
3. ellas / prestar / a Mariela / falda / corto / atrevido
4. Raúl y Rafa / prestar / a Leo / el cinturón / de cuero / negro
5. Ud. / prestar / a Jaime / coche / nuevo

**METHODOLOGY • Assessing Effort**

Yes, commenting on and assessing a student's effort is a subjective evaluation. Nevertheless, it is something that both students and instructors need to address. The ability to realistically assess the efforts they place on tasks is a life skill students will need when they exit college. Assessing effort is also an important reality check for all students. Are they working to their highest potential? Some students truly are; others are not.

There are a variety of types of students: those who put in a great deal of effort and are successful; those who put in a great deal of effort and are not as successful as they or we would like; those who *say* they are putting in effort when in fact they are not or it is not focused; those who put in little effort and do not succeed; and those who put in little effort and still achieve at least our minimum expectation but could do extremely well with more effort. The final group is comprised of gifted students as well as heritage language learners.

**METHODOLOGY • Reviewing Vocabulary**

You will note that students are encouraged to review each chapter's vocabulary on their own. We recommend that they begin their vocabulary review with the two-page list of *Vocabulario activo* that is found at the end of each chapter.

 **12-5  La recomendación fue...** ¿Cuáles fueron sus recomendaciones a las siguientes personas? Túrnense para formar preguntas y contestar según el modelo. ▪

**MODELO**  tú / las blusas de Kohls (a tus primas)

E1:  *¿Les recomendaste las blusas de Kohls a tus primas?*

E2:  *No, no se las recomendé. / Sí, se las recomendé.*

1. ellos / los museos de arqueología (a tu profesor/a)
2. tú / el café Starbucks (a tus padres)
3. tu hermano / el hotel Ritz (a su amiga que no tiene dinero)
4. nosotros / la música de Shakira (a unos compañeros)
5. yo / la película *Shrek* (a mis primos de cinco años)
6. ustedes / las novelas de Gabriel García Márquez (a sus tíos)
7. tú / la clase de español (a tu mejor amigo/a)

**Estrategia**

You can elaborate on your answers as to why you recommended or did not recommend something by adding **porque** and a short explanation. In the model, you could say *No, no se las recomendé porque son muy caras.*

Workbooklet   **12-6  Una encuesta** Usa las siguientes expresiones para crear una encuesta de **diez** preguntas. Hazles las preguntas a diez personas diferentes y comparte tus resultados con la clase. ▪

| PREGUNTA | ME ENCANTA(N) | ME MOLESTA(N) | ME IMPORTA(N) | ME HACE(N) FALTA | ME FASCINA(N) |
|---|---|---|---|---|---|
| ¿Te gustan los animales salvajes? ¿Cuáles? | | | | | Erika: Sí, me fascinan los tigres. |
| ¿Te gusta la ropa elegante? | | Alex: No, me molesta. Prefiero la ropa informal. | | | |
| | | | | | |
| | | | | | |

**EXPANSION for 12-7**
As a follow-up to this activity, ask
students to report on what their partners
read, thus encouraging active listening,
summarizing, and reporting back using a
different form of the reflexive verbs.

 **12-7** **¿Qué hiciste ayer?** Escribe un párrafo sobre lo que hiciste ayer.
Incluye por lo menos **diez** actividades usando un mínimo de **siete** verbos reflexivos.
Después, léeselo a un/a compañero/a. ■

MODELO      *Ayer me levanté a las seis de la mañana.*
            *Me duché en tres minutos. Me puse los*
            *pantalones rojos con rayas blancas...*

 **12-8** **Para conocerte mejor** Cuando tenías quince años, ¿qué hacías
en las siguientes situaciones? ■

Paso 1      Contesta las siguientes preguntas.

MODELO      E1:  ¿Qué hacías por las tardes, después de salir del colegio?

            E2:  *Yo jugaba al tenis. ¿Qué hacías tú?*

            E1:  *Hacía la tarea y ayudaba a mi madre con los quehaceres de la casa.*

1. ¿Qué te ponías cuando salías con esa "persona especial"?
2. Antes de dormirte, ¿pensabas en tu día?
3. ¿Tenías un perro?
4. ¿Cómo te divertías?
5. ¿Siempre te acordabas de hacer toda la tarea?
6. Si tenías tiempo, ¿con quién(es) te reunías?
7. ¿Dónde te gustaba sentarte en el cine, adelante o atrás? ¿Por qué?
8. ¿Qué querías ser de mayor?
9. ¿En qué situaciones te ponías nervioso/a?
10. ¿Cuándo te sentías feliz?

> **Estrategia**
>
> Being a good listener is
> an important life skill.
> Repeating what your
> classmate said gives you
> practice in demonstrating
> how well you listened.

Paso 2      Escucha las respuestas de tu compañero/a. ¿Cuántas preguntas contestaron
            ustedes de manera similar? ¿De manera diferente?

**EXPANSION for 12-8**
You may want to collect selected
information as students report back in
order to compile class statistics (e.g.,
how many students had dogs, what they
wanted to be when they grew up, etc.).
You may also want to add additional
questions, thus personalizing the activity
for your students, regarding other pets
they may have had, what they did on
weekends, which sports and pastimes
were their favorites, etc.

**SUGGESTION for 12-9**
Have students bring in photos of their first home or a "fictitious" first home image from the Internet.

 **12-9  Mi primera casa**  ¿Cómo era tu primera casa o la de un/a amigo/a de tu infancia? Descríbesela a un/a compañero/a en por lo menos **diez** oraciones incluyendo todos los detalles posibles (los muebles, los colores, etc.). ◼

MODELO    *Mi primera casa estaba en una ciudad pequeña. Tenía dos dormitorios. La cocina era amarilla. El comedor y la sala eran pequeños. Tenía solamente* (only) *un baño…*

### Estrategia

You and your instructor can use this rubric to assess your progress for activities **12-4** through **12-9**.

## Rúbrica

| | 3<br>EXCEEDS EXPECTATIONS | 2<br>MEETS EXPECTATIONS | 1<br>APPROACHES EXPECTATIONS | 0<br>DOES NOT MEET EXPECTATIONS |
|---|---|---|---|---|
| **Duración y precisión** | • Has at least 8 sentences and includes all the required information.<br>• May have errors, but they do not interfere with communication. | • Has 5–7 sentences and includes all the required information.<br>• May have errors, but they rarely interfere with communication. | • Has 4 sentences and includes some of the required information.<br>• Has errors that interfere with communication. | • Supplies fewer sentences and little of the required information in *Approaches Expectations*.<br>• If communicating at all, has frequent errors that make communication limited or impossible. |
| **Gramática nueva del *Capítulo 8*** | • Makes excellent use of the chapter's new grammar (e.g., the imperfect, object pronouns, reflexive verbs, and verbs like *gustar*).<br>• Uses a wide variety of verbs when appropriate. | • Makes good use of the chapter's new grammar (e.g., the imperfect, object pronouns, reflexive verbs, and verbs like *gustar*).<br>• Uses a variety of verbs when appropriate. | • Makes use of some of the chapter's new grammar (e.g., the imperfect, object pronouns, reflexive verbs, and verbs like *gustar*).<br>• Uses a limited variety of verbs when appropriate. | • Uses little, if any, of the chapter's new grammar (e.g., the imperfect, object pronouns, reflexive verbs, and verbs like *gustar*).<br>• Uses few, if any, of the chapter's verbs. |
| **Vocabulario nuevo del *Capítulo 8*** | • Uses many of the new clothing-related vocabulary words. | • Uses a variety of the new clothing-related vocabulary words. | • Uses some of the new clothing-related vocabulary words. | • Uses few, if any, new clothing-related vocabulary words. |

*(continued)*

| | 3<br>EXCEEDS<br>EXPECTATIONS | 2<br>MEETS<br>EXPECTATIONS | 1<br>APPROACHES<br>EXPECTATIONS | 0<br>DOES NOT MEET<br>EXPECTATIONS |
|---|---|---|---|---|
| ⊕ **Gramática y vocabulario reciclado de los capítulos anteriores** | • Does an excellent job using recycled grammar and vocabulary to support what is being said.<br>• Uses a wide array of recycled verbs.<br>• Uses some recycled vocabulary, but focuses predominantly on new vocabulary. | • Does a good job using recycled grammar and vocabulary to support what is being said.<br>• Uses an array of recycled verbs.<br>• Uses some recycled vocabulary, but focuses predominantly on new vocabulary. | • Does an average job using recycled grammar and vocabulary to support what is being said.<br>• Uses a limited array of recycled verbs.<br>• Uses mostly recycled vocabulary and some new vocabulary. | • If speaking at all, relies almost completely on a few isolated words.<br>• Usage of previously learned grammar is inconsistent. |
| **Esfuerzo** | • Clearly the student made his/her best effort. | • The student made a good effort. | • The student made an effort. | • Little or no effort went into the activity. |

## Capítulo 9

Capítulo 9

to 12-21

**12-10** **Un diálogo** Imaginen que trabajan como voluntarios con un médico. Creen un diálogo entre el médico y el paciente con respecto a sus síntomas y su tratamiento. Escriban por lo menos **catorce** oraciones. ■

MODELO  E1 (MÉDICO):  *¿Cómo está? ¿Qué le duele?*

E2 (PACIENTE):  *Creo que tengo catarro o un virus. Me duele todo.*

E1:  *¿Tiene fiebre? ¿Tose? ¿Estornuda?*

E2:  *No, no tengo fiebre pero sí tengo tos. Y sí, estornudo mucho. ¡También me quemé!*

E1:  *¿Se quemó? ¿Cómo?*

E2:  *…*

**12-11** **¡Me enfermé!** ¿Cuándo fue la última vez que se enfermaron? ¿Qué hicieron? ¿Qué pasó? ■

Paso 1  Descríbele a un/a compañero/a tu última enfermedad en por lo menos **diez** oraciones.

MODELO  *Hace dos semanas que me enfermé. Tuve gripe y guardé cama por una semana. Mi madre me llevó al médico porque me dolía el cuerpo y tenía fiebre…*

Paso 2  Describe en tus propias (*own*) palabras la enfermedad de tu compañero/a de clase.

### Estrategia
It is rare that people remember *everything* that they hear! It is important that you feel comfortable asking someone to repeat information or asking for clarification.

## Rúbrica

| | 3 EXCEEDS EXPECTATIONS | 2 MEETS EXPECTATIONS | 1 APPROACHES EXPECTATIONS | 0 DOES NOT MEET EXPECTATIONS |
|---|---|---|---|---|
| **Duración y precisión** | • Has at least 8 sentences and includes all the required information. <br>• May have errors, but they do not interfere with communication. | • Has 5–7 sentences and includes all the required information. <br>• May have errors, but they rarely interfere with communication. | • Has 4 sentences and includes some of the required information. <br>• Has errors that interfere with communication. | • Supplies fewer sentences and little of the required information in *Approaches Expectations*. <br>• If communicating at all, has frequent errors that make communication limited or impossible. |
| **Gramática nueva del** *Capítulo 9* | • Makes excellent use of the chapter's new grammar (e.g., preterit and imperfect). <br>• Uses a wide variety of verbs when appropriate. | • Makes good use of the chapter's new grammar (e.g., preterit and imperfect). <br>• Uses a variety of verbs when appropriate. | • Makes use of some of the chapter's new grammar (e.g., preterit and imperfect). <br>• Uses a limited variety of verbs when appropriate. | • Uses little, if any, of the chapter's new grammar (e.g., preterit and imperfect). <br>• Uses few, if any, of the chapter's verbs. |
| **Vocabulario nuevo del** *Capítulo 9* | • Uses many of the new vocabulary words (e.g., the body and medical terms). | • Uses a variety of the new vocabulary words (e.g., the body and medical terms). | • Uses some of the new vocabulary words (e.g., the body and medical terms). | • Uses few, if any, new vocabulary words (e.g., the body and medical terms). |
| ✹ **Gramática y vocabulario reciclado de los capítulos anteriores** | • Does an excellent job using recycled grammar and vocabulary to support what is being said. <br>• Uses a wide array of recycled verbs. <br>• Uses some recycled vocabulary, but focuses predominantly on new vocabulary. | • Does a good job using recycled grammar and vocabulary to support what is being said. <br>• Uses an array of recycled verbs. <br>• Uses some recycled vocabulary, but focuses predominantly on new vocabulary. | • Does an average job using recycled grammar and vocabulary to support what is being said. <br>• Uses a limited array of recycled verbs. <br>• Uses mostly recycled vocabulary and some new vocabulary. | • If speaking at all, relies almost completely on a few isolated words. <br>• Usage of previously learned grammar is inconsistent. |
| **Esfuerzo** | • Clearly the student made his/her best effort. | • The student made a good effort. | • The student made an effort. | • Little or no effort went into the activity. |

**Capítulo 10**

o 12-27

 **12-12** **Los días de vacaciones** ¿Qué hiciste durante las últimas vacaciones? Descríbele a tu compañero/a, en por lo menos **diez** oraciones y usando una variedad de verbos y vocabulario, tus últimas vacaciones. Incluye las siguientes palabras: ▪

| todos los días | todas las noches | generalmente | normalmente |
| un día | una vez | una mañana | nunca |

**MODELO**    *Durante las últimas vacaciones nosotros fuimos a Punta Cana. Fue la primera vez que visitamos la República Dominicana. Todos los días íbamos a la playa. Allí nadábamos…*

 **12-13** **Mis vacaciones favoritas** ¿Adónde fuiste y cómo fueron tus vacaciones favoritas? Descríbeselas a un/a compañero/a en por lo menos **siete** oraciones usando el pretérito y una variedad de verbos. ▪

**MODELO**    *Mis vacaciones en Argentina fueron mis mejores vacaciones. Fuimos a la playa, donde mi familia y yo anduvimos muchas horas. Bebí mate por primera vez…*

**SUGGESTION for 12-12 and 12-13**
Both of these activities could also take the form of travel diaries, in which you ask students to write commentaries for 4 or 5 days of a real or imagined trip.

**EXPANSION for 12-13**
Have students each create their own poster or web project featuring the Spanish-speaking country they would most like to visit. Students could then share them in class or post the electronic version online.

**SUGGESTION for reviewing commands**
You could encourage students to create a list of commands more closely related to their experiences. For example, they could include commands for professors, fellow students, coaches, cafeteria managers, campus police, administrators, politicians, etc.

 **12-14  Y también...** Imagina que tienes un hijo y que, por primera vez, él va a salir solo con sus amigos y se va a llevar el coche. ¿Qué le aconsejas? Túrnense para hacer **mandatos informales** con los siguientes verbos.

MODELO    E1:  leer / el manual

E2:  *Lee el manual.*

1. conducir / con cuidado
2. llevar / el permiso
3. tener cuidado / los peatones
4. llenar el tanque / gasolina
5. no mandar / mensajes de texto
6. no perder / llaves
7. no abrir / ventanas / si llueve
8. no estacionarse / en lugares prohibidos
9. no doblar a la izquierda / sin mirar
10. no comer ni beber / en el coche
11. limpiar / parabrisas
12. no ir / muy rápido

 **12-15  ¡Me molestas!** ¿En tu vida hay alguien que te está volviendo loco/a (*is driving you crazy*)? Túrnense para decirle a tu compañero/a lo que debe y no debe hacer. Pueden usar las palabras y expresiones de la lista y otras también. ¡Sean creativos! ◼

**Estrategia**
Organize your thoughts in chronological order, and use transitions in your paragraphs. Consider words like *primero, segundo, tercero, próximo, después,* and *finalmente.*

| | |
|---|---|
| guardar tu comida | tener más paciencia |
| no dejar la ropa sucia en el piso | no estornudar |
| lavar los platos | mejorarte |
| sacar la basura | cuidarte |
| no invitar siempre a tus amigos | no ponerte mi ropa |

MODELO    *Raúl, por favor, ¡me estás volviendo loca! Primero, guarda tu comida en el refrigerador, no la pongas en el sofá. Segundo, ¡no estornudes encima de la comida! Ponte el abrigo porque hace frío. Cuídate, por favor...*

**12-16  En la gasolinera** Están en una gasolinera. Túrnense para decirle al empleado (*attendant*) lo que necesitan. ◼

MODELO    *Ponga aire en las llantas, por favor. También, abra el baúl, por favor. Yo no puedo abrirlo...*

**12-17** **¡Por fin!** ¡Este es el momento que esperabas! ¡Por fin ustedes son los profesores de español! Túrnense para decirles a sus estudiantes por lo menos **ocho** cosas que deben o no deben hacer. ¡Sean creativos! ▪

MODELO *Hagan la tarea para mañana. También, hablen en español durante toda la clase…*

 **12-18** **Comparando** Estás planeando unas vacaciones. Dile a tu compañero/a cuáles son, en tu opinión, los mejores y los peores servicios y destinos. Usa comparaciones y superlativos. Crea por lo menos **diez** oraciones. ▪

MODELO *El aeropuerto de Austin es más pequeño que el aeropuerto de Dallas, pero en mi opinión es mejor porque no es muy grande. Para mí, la agencia Travel Experts es la mejor porque saben preparar unos viajes estupendos. Por ejemplo, la playa de Ixtapa en México es tan bonita como la playa de Cancún, y los hoteles no cuestan tanto como los hoteles de Cancún…*

**NOTE for 12-18**
Encourage students to be creative here and to feel free to invent when necessary. Many students may have little travel experience.

**Rúbrica**

> **Estrategia**
> You and your instructor can use this rubric to assess your progress for activities **12-12** through **12-18**.

|  | 3 EXCEEDS EXPECTATIONS | 2 MEETS EXPECTATIONS | 1 APPROACHES EXPECTATIONS | 0 DOES NOT MEET EXPECTATIONS |
|---|---|---|---|---|
| **Duración y precisión** | • Has at least 8 sentences and includes all the required information.<br>• May have errors, but they do not interfere with communication. | • Has 5–7 sentences and includes all the required information.<br>• May have errors, but they rarely interfere with communication. | • Has 4 sentences and includes some of the required information.<br>• Has errors that interfere with communication. | • Supplies fewer sentences and little of the required information in *Approaches Expectations*.<br>• If communicating at all, has frequent errors that make communication limited or impossible. |
| **Gramática nueva del *Capítulo 10*** | • Makes excellent use of the chapter's new grammar (e.g., formal and informal commands, the comparative and superlative).<br>• Uses a wide variety of verbs when appropriate. | • Makes good use of the chapter's new grammar (e.g., formal and informal commands, the comparative and superlative).<br>• Uses a variety of verbs when appropriate. | • Makes use of some of the chapter's new grammar (e.g., formal and informal commands, the comparative and superlative).<br>• Uses a limited variety of verbs when appropriate. | • Uses little, if any, of the chapter's new grammar (e.g., formal and informal commands, the comparative and superlative).<br>• Uses few, if any, of the chapter's verbs. |

*(continued)*

| | 3 EXCEEDS EXPECTATIONS | 2 MEETS EXPECTATIONS | 1 APPROACHES EXPECTATIONS | 0 DOES NOT MEET EXPECTATIONS |
|---|---|---|---|---|
| **Vocabulario nuevo del *Capítulo 10*** | • Uses many of the new travel-related vocabulary words. | • Uses a variety of the new travel-related vocabulary words. | • Uses some of the new travel-related vocabulary words. | • Uses few, if any, new travel-related vocabulary words. |
| ✤ **Gramática y vocabulario reciclado de los capítulos anteriores** | • Does an excellent job using recycled grammar and vocabulary to support what is being said.<br>• Uses a wide array of recycled verbs.<br>• Uses some recycled vocabulary, but focuses predominantly on new vocabulary. | • Does a good job using recycled grammar and vocabulary to support what is being said.<br>• Uses an array of recycled verbs.<br>• Uses some recycled vocabulary, but focuses predominantly on new vocabulary. | • Does an average job using recycled grammar and vocabulary to support what is being said.<br>• Uses a limited array of recycled verbs.<br>• Uses mostly recycled vocabulary and some new vocabulary. | • If speaking at all, relies almost completely on a few isolated words.<br>• Usage of previously learned grammar is inconsistent. |
| **Esfuerzo** | • Clearly the student made his/her best effort. | • The student made a good effort. | • The student made an effort. | • Little or no effort went into the activity. |

## Capítulo 11

12-28 to 12-32

 **12-19** **Mis deberes** Siempre hay algo que podemos hacer para mejorar. Dile a tu compañero/a por lo menos **diez** cosas que debes hacer ahora o que te propones (*you intend*) hacer en el futuro. Usa **el subjuntivo** cuando sea necesario. ■

MODELO   *Primero, es necesario que estudie más en el futuro. También es importante que no coma tanto chocolate, pero es dudoso que pueda evitarlo. Entonces, es importante que compre cosas saludables. Pero, ¡qué lástima! ¡Me fascina el chocolate! Pues, como me gusta tanto, es importante que haga más ejercicio. ¡Es una lástima que no me guste hacerlo!*

**SUGGESTION for 12-19**
You may choose to have students write these suggestions for another person rather than for themselves. They could also write the suggestions from the point of view of a parent, friend, physician, therapist, professor, employer, spouse, etc.

**12-20  Mi casa ideal** ¿Cómo esperas que sea tu casa en diez años? ▪

**Paso 1**  Descríbesela a un/a compañero/a con todo detalle (los cuartos, los muebles, los colores, etc.). Incluye por lo menos **cinco** preposiciones diferentes en la descripción.

**MODELO**  *Espero que mi casa tenga cinco dormitorios. Al lado de la puerta quiero que haya una sala y una cocina detrás de la sala. ¡Ojalá que tenga una cocina muy grande!*

**Paso 2**  Repite lo que tu compañero/a te dijo. Es importante que uses y practiques las preposiciones.

> **Estrategia**
> You may want to draw the floor plan of your house and label the rooms. That way, it will be easier to talk about where each room is located in relation to other rooms. When working with a partner, you might want to draw your partner's house as you hear it described, taking note of the prepositions he/she has mentioned.

## Rúbrica

> **Estrategia**
> You and your instructor can use this rubric to assess your progress for activities **12-19** through **12-20**.

| | 3 EXCEEDS EXPECTATIONS | 2 MEETS EXPECTATIONS | 1 APPROACHES EXPECTATIONS | 0 DOES NOT MEET EXPECTATIONS |
|---|---|---|---|---|
| **Duración y precisión** | • Has at least 8 sentences and includes all the required information. <br>• May have errors, but they do not interfere with communication. | • Has 5–7 sentences and includes all the required information. <br>• May have errors, but they rarely interfere with communication. | • Has 4 sentences and includes some of the required information. <br>• Has errors that interfere with communication. | • Supplies fewer sentences and little of the required information in *Approaches Expectations*. <br>• If communicating at all, has frequent errors that make communication limited or impossible. |
| **Gramática nueva del *Capítulo 11*** | • Makes excellent use of the chapter's new grammar (e.g., the subjunctive and prepositions). <br>• Uses a wide variety of verbs when appropriate. | • Makes good use of the chapter's new grammar (e.g., the subjunctive and prepositions). <br>• Uses a variety of verbs when appropriate. | • Makes use of some of the chapter's new grammar (e.g., the subjunctive and prepositions). <br>• Uses a limited variety of verbs when appropriate. | • Uses little, if any, of the chapter's new grammar (e.g., the subjunctive and prepositions). <br>• Uses few, if any, of the chapter's verbs. |

*(continued)*

**Instructor Resources**
• Textbook images, Extra Activities

|  | 3 EXCEEDS EXPECTATIONS | 2 MEETS EXPECTATIONS | 1 APPROACHES EXPECTATIONS | 0 DOES NOT MEET EXPECTATIONS |
|---|---|---|---|---|
| Vocabulario nuevo del *Capítulo 11* | • Uses many of the new vocabulary words (e.g., animals, the environment, and politics). | • Uses a variety of the new vocabulary words (e.g., animals, the environment, and politics). | • Uses some of the new vocabulary words (e.g., animals, the environment, and politics). | • Uses few, if any, new vocabulary words (e.g., animals, the environment, and politics). |
|  Gramática y vocabulario reciclado de los capítulos anteriores | • Does an excellent job using recycled grammar and vocabulary to support what is being said.<br>• Uses a wide array of recycled verbs.<br>• Uses some recycled vocabulary, but focuses predominantly on new vocabulary. | • Does a good job using recycled grammar and vocabulary to support what is being said.<br>• Uses an array of recycled verbs.<br>• Uses some recycled vocabulary, but focuses predominantly on new vocabulary. | • Does an average job using recycled grammar and vocabulary to support what is being said.<br>• Uses a limited array of recycled verbs.<br>• Uses mostly recycled vocabulary and some new vocabulary. | • If speaking at all, relies almost completely on a few isolated words.<br>• Usage of previously learned grammar is inconsistent. |
| Esfuerzo | • Clearly the student made his/her best effort. | • The student made a good effort. | • The student made an effort. | • Little or no effort went into the activity. |

 **Un poco de todo**

12-33 to 12-41

---

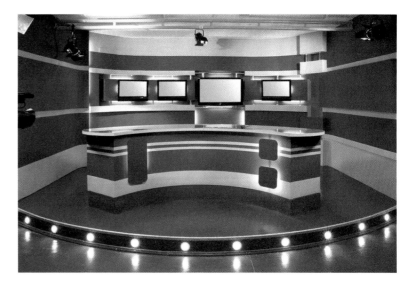

**12-21 Nuestro medio ambiente y más aún** Creen juntos un reportaje (*report*) para la televisión sobre uno de los siguientes temas. ■

**TEMAS**
1. el medio ambiente
2. la política
3. el tiempo
4. el arte, la música, los deportes y otros eventos

**NOTE for *Un poco de todo***
In the *Un poco de todo* section, each activity combines concepts from all of the previous chapters resulting in comprehensive, highly communicative review activities.

**NOTE for *Un poco de todo***
In the *Un poco de todo* section, students put together all the information they have learned thus far. These activities show students how much they have progressed in their competence with Spanish and their ability to communicate. You might decide to film the *entrevistas* and *reportajes* as examples for future students, using the MediaShare feature in MySpanishLab. Additionally, these videos will demonstrate to your current students how much they have learned throughout the course. If you have "potential" Spanish minors/majors in the course, this would be useful for their language learning portfolio.

**SUGGESTION for 12-21**
You may want to ask your students to make a PowerPoint presentation, video, or podcast based on this activity.

**12-22** **¿Cómo eres?** Conoces un poco a los estudiantes de los países que estudiamos en los capítulos anteriores. ¿Qué más quieres saber de ellos? Escribe por lo menos **diez** preguntas que quieras hacerles. Usa **el pretérito, el imperfecto** y **el subjuntivo** en tus preguntas. ▪

MODELO
1. ¿Qué estudiaste el semestre pasado?
2. ¿Adónde fuiste el verano pasado?
3. ¿Es posible que viajes este verano?
4. ...

Gino Breschi Arteaga

Sandra Manrique Esquivel

María Graciela Martelli Paz

Francisco Tomás Bacigalupe Bustamante

Diana Ávila Peralta

Jorge Gustavo Salazar

Yolanda Pico Briones

Rosa María Gutiérrez Murcia

Joaquín Navas Posada

Alicia Ortega Mujica

Pablo Colón Padín

Amparo Burgos Báez

**CAPÍTULO 12**

**NOTE for *Actividades***
The *actividades* in the *Cultura* section allow instructors great flexibility in deciding how they want to implement them. You will notice that many of the activities can be assigned as homework, as individual practice, in small groups, as oral practice, as whole class practice, or for individual and/or group projects. Many of the more in-depth topics would be excellent for your heritage language learners and students with special testing needs or alternative assessment needs, as well as anyone needing extra practice.

**METHODOLOGY • Question Formation**
Research tells us that students need more practice creating questions, since most times they answer them. **12-22** helps students practice question formation while focusing on the featured tenses.

**EXPANSION for 12-22**
Have students ask the featured students about their home countries.

**SUGGESTION for 12-23**
Have students state the capital of each country in the photos.

**EXPANSION for 12-23**
You may choose to collect and expand the information given, turning it into a *Jeopardy!*-type game.

**EXPANSION for 12-23**
Have students each read a fact from their list and have the class guess what country they are referring to.

Workbooklet

**12-23 ¿Sabías que...?** Completa los siguientes pasos. ◾

**Paso 1** Escribe dos cosas interesantes que no sabías antes pero que aprendiste sobre cada uno de los siguientes países.

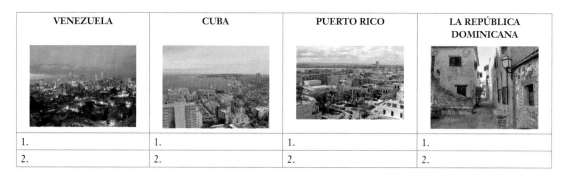

| CHILE | PARAGUAY | ARGENTINA | URUGUAY |
|---|---|---|---|
| 1. | 1. | 1. | 1. |
| 2. | 2. | 2. | 2. |

| PERÚ | BOLIVIA | ECUADOR | COLOMBIA |
|---|---|---|---|
| 1. | 1. | 1. | 1. |
| 2. | 2. | 2. | 2. |

| VENEZUELA | CUBA | PUERTO RICO | LA REPÚBLICA DOMINICANA |
|---|---|---|---|
| 1. | 1. | 1. | 1. |
| 2. | 2. | 2. | 2. |

**Paso 2** Compara la información con el lugar donde vives. ¿Qué cosas son similares? ¿Qué diferencias hay?

**12-24** **¡A cocinar!** Vas a preparar una cena latina para tus amigos con platos representativos de varios países. Selecciona por lo menos **tres** platos y **una** bebida. Indica el país de origen de cada plato y los ingredientes. Si varios países comparten el plato, menciónalos también. ▪

**SUGGESTION for 12-24**
You may wish to make this a class activity where students bring the *platos* to class, along with the recipes. You could compile the recipes to "publish" a class cookbook. Your students could also share the recipes with your school's food service and perhaps have a Hispanic or international foods day.

La parrillada

El chivito

**12-25** **Los símbolos nacionales** Escoge **tres** países distintos y un símbolo para cada uno de ellos. Describe estos símbolos nacionales y habla de cómo y por qué son representativos del país. Después, haz una comparación entre los países y sus símbolos. ▪

**EXPANSION for 12-25**
Have students compare their chosen symbols with symbols of their own country.

**12-26** **¿El ecoturismo o una expedición antropológica?**
¡Qué suerte! Recibiste la distinción de ser el/la mejor estudiante de español y puedes elegir entre un viaje de ecoturismo o una expedición antropológica. Piensa en lo que aprendiste de cada país y decide adónde quieres ir para divertirte e investigar más. Después, describe el lugar específico que vas a visitar y di por qué, cómo, cuándo, etc. Si hay dos países con lugares similares, compáralos e indica por qué seleccionaste uno en particular. ▪

**NOTE for 12-27**
*Episodio 12* is a behind-the-scenes compilation of *Ambiciones siniestras*. The video includes outtakes as well as interviews with the actors.

**SUGGESTION for 12-27**
Film your students' versions of *Ambiciones siniestras II* using the MediaShare feature in MySpanishLab and have the class vote on their favorite version.

Episodio 12

**12-27**   **Tus propias ambiciones siniestras**   ¡Ahora te toca a ti! Puedes seleccionar entre las siguientes actividades basadas en **Ambiciones siniestras.** ■

1. Imagina que eres David Letterman o Cristina y que tienes la oportunidad de entrevistar a los actores de **Ambiciones siniestras.** Prepara la entrevista con un/a compañero/a.

2. Escribe tu propia versión resumida de **Ambiciones siniestras.** ¿Termina igual que el original? Compara tu versión con la de un/a compañero/a.

3. Escribe y filma **Ambiciones siniestras II.** Al final, ¿qué pasa con el Sr. Verdugo? Preséntale tu película a la clase.

**NOTE to Instructors**
To our esteemed colleagues: our most heartfelt thank you for using the *¡Anda! Curso elemental* instructional program. We encourage you to submit any comments or questions you may have to your local sales representative, or to the World Languages Division at Pearson Arts & Sciences. If you have enjoyed teaching with *¡Anda! Curso elemental* as much as we have enjoyed creating the program, please consider using *¡Anda! Curso intermedio* for your intermediate courses.

# Y por fin, ¿cómo andas?

Having completed this chapter, I now can . . .

| | Feel confident | Need to review |
|---|---|---|

### Comunicación

- communicate preferences regarding food and clothing ☐ ☐
- relate ideas about past experiences and my daily routine ☐ ☐
- convey information about people and things ☐ ☐
- express ideas on topics such as health, travel, animals, the environment, and politics ☐ ☐
- make requests and give advice using commands ☐ ☐
- articulate desires and opinions on a variety of topics ☐ ☐

### Cultura

- share information about Chile, Paraguay, Argentina, Uruguay, Perú, Bolivia, Ecuador, Venezuela, Colombia, Cuba, Puerto Rico, and La República Dominicana ☐ ☐
- compare and contrast the countries I learned about in **Capítulos 7–11** ☐ ☐

### Ambiciones siniestras

- go behind the scenes of **Ambiciones siniestras** ☐ ☐

### Comunidades

- use Spanish in real-life contexts (SAM) ☐ ☐

# Appendix 1

## Answers to ¡Explícalo tú!
## (Inductive Grammar Answers)

### 12. Gustar

1. To say you like or dislike one thing, what form of **gustar** do you use?
   **gusta**
2. To say you like or dislike more than one thing, what form of **gustar** do you use?
   **gustan**

### 9. El verbo *gustar*

1. To say you like or dislike one thing, what form of **gustar** do you use?
   **gusta**
2. To say you like or dislike more than one thing, what form of **gustar** do you use?
   **gustan**
3. Which words in the examples mean *I?* (**Me**) *You?* (**Te**) *He/she?* (**le**)
4. If a verb is needed after **gusta/gustan,** what form of the verb do you use?
   **the infinitive form of the verb**

### 4. Los verbos con cambio de raíz

1. Which verb forms look like the infinitive **cerrar**?
   **nosotros, vosotros**
2. Which verb forms have a spelling change that differs from the infinitive **cerrar**?
   **yo, tú, él, ella, usted, ellos, ellas, ustedes**

1. Which verb forms look like the infinitive **pedir**?
   **nosotros, vosotros**
2. Which verb forms have a spelling change that differs from the infinitive **pedir**?
   **yo, tú, él, ella, usted, ellos, ellas, ustedes**

1. Which verb forms look like the infinitive **encontrar**?
   **nosotros, vosotros**
2. Which verb forms have a spelling change that differs from the infinitive **encontrar**?
   **yo, tú, usted, él, ella, ustedes, ellos, ellas**

**A1**

1. Which verb forms look like the infinitive **jugar**?
   **nosotros, vosotros**
2. Which verb forms have a spelling change that differs from the infinitive **jugar**?
   **yo, tú, usted, él, ella, ustedes, ellos, ellas**
3. Why does **jugar** not belong with the verbs like **encontrar**?
   **because the change is** $u \rightarrow ue$**, not** $o \rightarrow ue$ **like** *encontrar*

**To summarize . . .**

1. What is a rule that you can make regarding all four groups of stem-changing verbs and their forms?
   *Nosotros/vosotros* **look like the infinitive. All the other forms have the spelling change.**
2. With what group of stem-changing verbs would you put **querer**?
   **e → ie**
3. With what group of stem-changing verbs would you put the following verbs:
   demostrar        *to demonstrate* **o → ue**
   devolver         *to return (an object)* **o → ue**
   encerrar         *to enclose* **e → ie**
   perseguir        *to chase* **e → i**

## 6. *Ir + a + infinitivo*

1. When do the actions in these sentences take place: in the *past, present,* or *future?*
   **future**
2. What is the first bold type verb you see in each sentence?
   **a form of** *ir*
3. In what form is the second bolded verb?
   **infinitive**
4. What word comes between the two verbs?
   **a**
   Does this word have an equivalent in English?
   **no**
5. What is your rule, then, for expressing future actions or statements?
   **use a form of** *ir + a +* **infinitive**

## 8. Las expresiones afirmativas y negativas

1. When you use a negative word (**nadie, nunca**, etc.) in a sentence, does it come before or after the verb?
   **The negative word can go either before or after the verb.**
2. When you use the word **no** and then a negative word in the same sentence, does **no** come before or after the verb?
   *No* **comes before the verb.**

   Where does the negative word come in these sentences?
   **The negative word can go either before or after the verb.**
3. Does the meaning change depending on where you put the negative word? (E.g., **Nadie llama** *versus* **No llama nadie**.)
   **No, the meaning stays the same.**

A2

### 9. Un repaso de *ser* y *estar*

1. Why do you use a form of **ser** in the first sentence?
   **because it is a characteristic that remains relatively constant**
2. Why do you use a form of **estar** in the second sentence?
   **because it describes a physical or personality characteristic that can change, or a change in condition**

## Capítulo 5

### 2. Los adjetivos demostrativos

1. When do you use **este, ese,** and **aquel**?
   **when you want to point out *one* masculine person or object**
2. When do you use **esta, esa,** and **aquella**?
   **when you want to point out *one* feminine person or object**
3. When do you use **estos, esos,** and **aquellos**?
   **when you want to point out *two or more* masculine persons or objects, or a mix of masculine and feminine persons or objects**
4. When do you use **estas, esas,** and **aquellas**?
   **when you want to point out *two or more* feminine persons or objects**

### 5. El presente progresivo

1. What is the infinitive of the first verb in each sentence that is in *italics*?
   **estar**
2. What are the infinitives of **haciendo, estudiando, escuchando, tocando, viendo,** and **escribiendo**?
   **hacer, estudiar, escuchar, tocar, ver, escribir**
3. How do you form the verb forms in **boldface**?
   **Take the infinitive, drop the *-ar, -er,* or *-ir,* and add *-ando* or *-iendo*.**
4. In this new tense, the *present progressive*, do any words come between the two parts of the verb?
   **no**
5. Therefore, your formula for forming the present progressive is:
   **a form of the verb *estar* + a verb ending in *-ando* or *-iendo***

## Capítulo 6

### Major grammar points to be reviewed

1. Present tense of:
   Regular **-ar, -er, -ir** verbs
   Irregular verbs
   Stem-changing verbs **e → ie, e → i, o → ue, u → ue**
2. Future tense *ir + a +* **infinitive**
3. Use of direct object pronouns

**A3**

4. Correctly using **ser** and **estar**
5. Correctly using **gustar**

## Major vocabulary to be reviewed

1. The *Vocabulario activo* at the end of each chapter

## Major cultural information to be reviewed

1. At least two facts about each of the feature countries
2. At least one point about each of the two culture presentations in each chapter

## Capítulo 7

### 2. Repaso del complemento directo

1. What are direct objects?
   **Direct objects receive the action of verbs, answering the questions *what* and *whom*.**
   What are direct object pronouns?
   **Direct object pronouns replace direct objects.**
2. What are the pronouns (forms)? With what must they agree?
   **The pronoun forms are *me, te, lo, la, nos, los, las*. They must agree with direct objects.**
3. Where are direct object pronouns placed in a sentence?
   **They are placed either before verbs or attached to infinitives, *-ando*, or *-iendo*.**

### 3. El pretérito (Parte I)

1. What do you notice about the endings for **-er** and **-ir** verbs?
   **They are the same.**
2. Where are accent marks needed?
   **Accent marks are needed on the *yo* and *él/ella/usted* forms.**

## Capítulo 8

### 2. Los pronombres de complemento indirecto

1. Who is buying the clothing?
   *Mi madre.*
2. Who is receiving the clothing?
   Mi madre **me** compra mucha ropa.
   **I am receiving the clothes.**
   Mi madre **te** compra mucha ropa.

A4

**You are receiving the clothes.**
Mi madre **le** compra mucha ropa a usted.
**You are receiving the clothes.**
Mi madre **le** compra mucha ropa a mi hermano.
**My brother is receiving the clothes.**
Mi madre **nos** compra mucha ropa.
**We are receiving the clothes.**
Mi madre **os** compra mucha ropa.
**You all are receiving the clothes.**
Mi madre **les** compra mucha ropa a ustedes.
**You all are receiving the clothes.**
Mi madre **les** compra mucha ropa a mis hermanos.
**My brothers are receiving the clothes.**

| | |
|---|---|
| ¿Me (i.o.) traes la falda gris (d.o.)? | *Will you bring me the gray skirt?* |
| Su novio le (i.o.) regaló la chaqueta mas formal (d.o.). | *Her boyfriend gave her the more formal jacket.* |
| Mi hermana me (i.o.) compró la blusa elegante (d.o.). | *My sister bought me the elegant blouse.* |
| Nuestra compañera de cuarto nos (i.o.) lavó la ropa (d.o.). | *Our roommate washed our clothes for us.* |

## 4. Los pronombres de complemento directo e indirecto usados juntos

1. You know that direct and indirect objects come after verbs. Where do you find direct and indirect object pronouns?
   **before verbs or attached to infinitives or present participles**
2. Reading from left to right, which pronoun comes first (direct or indirect)? Which pronoun comes second?
   **The indirect object pronoun comes first, and the direct object pronoun comes second.**

## 6. Las construcciones reflexivas

In each drawing:

Who is performing / doing the action?
   a. La fiesta
   b. Alberto
   c. Beatriz
   d. Raúl y Gloria
   e. Alberto
   f. Beatriz

Who or what is receiving the action?
   a. neighbors
   b. daughter
   c. car
   d. Raúl and Gloria
   e. Alberto
   f. Beatriz

Which of the drawings and captions demonstrate reflexive verbs?
**the bottom row (Raúl y Gloria se despiertan. / Alberto se acuesta. / Beatriz se lava.)**

A5

### 3. Los mandatos formales

1. Where do the object pronouns appear in affirmative commands?
   **attached to the command**
   In negative commands?
   **before the command and not attached**

   In what order?
   **i.o. / d.o.**
2. Why are there written accents on some of the commands and not on others?
   **because some commands would change pronunciation without the accent marks**

### 5. Otras formas del posesivo

1. What is the position of each possessive in the left-hand column? the middle column?
   **before the noun; after the noun**
2. How do the possessive adjectives and pronouns agree?
   **They agree in number and gender with the nouns they describe or replace.**
3. What do the sentences mean in the column on the right?
   **Mine works fine; Ours cost a lot; Where are yours? His/hers/yours is $100.**

   What have you removed from the previous sentence?
   **the noun**

### 3. El subjuntivo

1. What is the difference between the subjunctive and the indicative moods?
   **The subjunctive expresses concepts such as doubts, emotions, wishes, and desires. The indicative reports events and happenings.**
2. What other verb forms look like the subjunctive?
   **The *Usted* and *Ustedes* (formal) commands.**
3. Where does the subjunctive verb come in relation to the word **que?**
   **after the word *que***

### Major grammar points to be reviewed

1. Past tenses:
   Regular and irregular preterit
   Regular and irregular imperfect
   Uses of the preterit and imperfect
2. Pronouns:
   Direct object
   Indirect object
   Reflexive
   Placement of pronouns

3. Commands:
   Informal affirmative and negative
   Formal affirmative and negative

4. Subjunctive:
   Formation
   Usage

## Major vocabulary to be reviewed

1. The *Vocabulario activo* at the end of each chapter

## Major cultural information to be reviewed

1. At least two facts about each of the feature countries
2. At least one point about each of the two culture presentations in each chapter

A7

# Appendix 2

## Verb Charts

### Regular Verbs: Simple Tenses

| Infinitive / Present Participle / Past Participle | Indicative | | | | | Subjunctive | | Imperative |
|---|---|---|---|---|---|---|---|---|
| | Present | Imperfect | Preterit | Future | Conditional | Present | Imperfect | Commands |
| hablar / hablando / hablado | hablo / hablas / habla / hablamos / habláis / hablan | hablaba / hablabas / hablaba / hablábamos / hablabais / hablaban | hablé / hablaste / habló / hablamos / hablasteis / hablaron | hablaré / hablarás / hablará / hablaremos / hablaréis / hablarán | hablaría / hablarías / hablaría / hablaríamos / hablaríais / hablarían | hable / hables / hable / hablemos / habléis / hablen | hablara / hablaras / hablara / habláramos / hablarais / hablaran | habla (tú), no hables / hable (usted) / hablemos / hablad (vosotros), no habléis / hablen (Uds.) |
| comer / comiendo / comido | como / comes / come / comemos / coméis / comen | comía / comías / comía / comíamos / comíais / comían | comí / comiste / comió / comimos / comisteis / comieron | comeré / comerás / comerá / comeremos / comeréis / comerán | comería / comerías / comería / comeríamos / comeríais / comerían | coma / comas / coma / comamos / comáis / coman | comiera / comieras / comiera / comiéramos / comierais / comieran | come (tú), no comas / coma (usted) / comamos / comed (vosotros), no comáis / coman (Uds.) |
| vivir / viviendo / vivido | vivo / vives / vive / vivimos / vivís / viven | vivía / vivías / vivía / vivíamos / vivíais / vivían | viví / viviste / vivió / vivimos / vivisteis / vivieron | viviré / vivirás / vivirá / viviremos / viviréis / vivirán | viviría / vivirías / viviría / viviríamos / viviríais / vivirían | viva / vivas / viva / vivamos / viváis / vivan | viviera / vivieras / viviera / viviéramos / vivierais / vivieran | vive (tú), no vivas / viva (usted) / vivamos / vivid (vosotros), no viváis / vivan (Uds.) |

A8

# Regular Verbs: Perfect Tenses

| | Indicative | | | | | Subjunctive | |
| --- | --- | --- | --- | --- | --- | --- | --- |
| | Present Perfect | Past Perfect | Preterit Perfect | Future Perfect | Conditional Perfect | Present Perfect | Past Perfect |
| he | hablado | había | hablado | hube | hablado | habré | hablado | habría | hablado | haya | hablado | hubiera | hablado |

| | Present Perfect | Past Perfect | Preterit Perfect | Future Perfect | Conditional Perfect | Present Perfect | Past Perfect |
| --- | --- | --- | --- | --- | --- | --- | --- |
| he | hablado | había | hablado | hube | hablado | habré | hablado |
| has | comido | habías | comido | hubiste | comido | habrás | comido |
| ha | vivido | había | vivido | hubo | vivido | habrá | vivido |
| hemos | | habíamos | | hubimos | | habremos | |
| habéis | | habíais | | hubisteis | | habréis | |
| han | | habían | | hubieron | | habrán | |

| Conditional Perfect | | Present Perfect | | Past Perfect | |
| --- | --- | --- | --- | --- | --- |
| habría | hablado | haya | hablado | hubiera | hablado |
| habrías | comido | hayas | comido | hubieras | comido |
| habría | vivido | haya | vivido | hubiera | vivido |
| habríamos | | hayamos | | hubiéramos | |
| habríais | | hayáis | | hubierais | |
| habrían | | hayan | | hubieran | |

# Irregular Verbs

| Infinitive / Present Participle / Past Participle | Indicative | | | | | Subjunctive | | Imperative |
| --- | --- | --- | --- | --- | --- | --- | --- | --- |
| | Present | Imperfect | Preterit | Future | Conditional | Present | Imperfect | Commands |
| andar andando andado | ando andas anda andamos andáis andan | andaba andabas andaba andábamos andabais andaban | anduve anduviste anduvo anduvimos anduvisteis anduvieron | andaré andarás andará andaremos andaréis andarán | andaría andarías andaría andaríamos andaríais andarían | ande andes ande andemos andéis anden | anduviera anduvieras anduviera anduviéramos anduvierais anduvieran | anda (tú), no andes ande (usted) andemos andad (vosotros), no andéis anden (Uds.) |
| caer cayendo caído | caigo caes cae caemos caéis caen | caía caías caía caíamos caíais caían | caí caíste cayó caímos caísteis cayeron | caeré caerás caerá caeremos caeréis caerán | caería caerías caería caeríamos caeríais caerían | caiga caigas caiga caigamos caigáis caigan | cayera cayeras cayera cayéramos cayerais cayeran | cae (tú), no caigas caiga (usted) caigamos caed (vosotros), no caigáis caigan (Uds.) |
| dar dando dado | doy das da damos dais dan | daba dabas daba dábamos dabais daban | di diste dio dimos disteis dieron | daré darás dará daremos daréis darán | daría darías daría daríamos daríais darían | dé des dé demos deis den | diera dieras diera diéramos dierais dieran | da (tú), no des dé (usted) demos dad (vosotros), no deis den (Uds.) |
| decir diciendo dicho | digo dices dice decimos decís dicen | decía decías decía decíamos decíais decían | dije dijiste dijo dijimos dijisteis dijeron | diré dirás dirá diremos diréis dirán | diría dirías diría diríamos diríais dirían | diga digas diga digamos digáis digan | dijera dijeras dijera dijéramos dijerais dijeran | di (tú), no digas diga (usted) digamos decid (vosotros), no digáis digan (Uds.) |

## Irregular Verbs (continued)

| Infinitive Present Participle Past Participle | Indicative | | | | | | Subjunctive | | Imperative |
|---|---|---|---|---|---|---|---|---|---|
| | Present | Imperfect | Preterit | Future | Conditional | Present | Imperfect | Commands |
| estar estando estado | estoy estás está estamos estáis están | estaba estabas estaba estábamos estabais estaban | estuve estuviste estuvo estuvimos estuvisteis estuvieron | estaré estarás estará estaremos estaréis estarán | estaría estarías estaría estaríamos estaríais estarían | esté estés esté estemos estéis estén | estuviera estuvieras estuviera estuviéramos estuvierais estuvieran | está (tú), no estés esté (usted) estemos estad (vosotros), no estéis estén (Uds.) |
| haber habiendo habido | he has ha hemos habéis han | había habías había habíamos habíais habían | hube hubiste hubo hubimos hubisteis hubieron | habré habrás habrá habremos habréis habrán | habría habrías habría habríamos habríais habrían | haya hayas haya hayamos hayáis hayan | hubiera hubieras hubiera hubiéramos hubierais hubieran | |
| hacer haciendo hecho | hago haces hace hacemos hacéis hacen | hacía hacías hacía hacíamos hacíais hacían | hice hiciste hizo hicimos hicisteis hicieron | haré harás hará haremos haréis harán | haría harías haría haríamos haríais harían | haga hagas haga hagamos hagáis hagan | hiciera hicieras hiciera hiciéramos hicierais hicieran | haz (tú), no hagas haga (usted) hagamos haced (vosotros), no hagáis hagan (Uds.) |
| ir yendo ido | voy vas va vamos vais van | iba ibas iba íbamos ibais iban | fui fuiste fue fuimos fuisteis fueron | iré irás irá iremos iréis irán | iría irías iría iríamos iríais irían | vaya vayas vaya vayamos vayáis vayan | fuera fueras fuera fuéramos fuerais fueran | ve (tú), no vayas vaya (usted) vamos, no vayamos id (vosotros), no vayáis vayan (Uds.) |
| oír oyendo oído | oigo oyes oye oímos oís oyen | oía oías oía oíamos oíais oían | oí oíste oyó oímos oísteis oyeron | oiré oirás oirá oiremos oiréis oirán | oiría oirías oiría oiríamos oiríais oirían | oiga oigas oiga oigamos oigáis oigan | oyera oyeras oyera oyéramos oyerais oyeran | oye (tú), no oigas oiga (usted) oigamos oíd (vosotros), no oigáis oigan (Uds.) |

A10

# Irregular Verbs (continued)

| Infinitive / Present Participle / Past Participle | Indicative | | | | | Subjunctive | | Imperative |
|---|---|---|---|---|---|---|---|---|
| | Present | Imperfect | Preterit | Future | Conditional | Present | Imperfect | Commands |
| poder<br>pudiendo<br>podido | puedo<br>puedes<br>puede<br>podemos<br>podéis<br>pueden | podía<br>podías<br>podía<br>podíamos<br>podíais<br>podían | pude<br>pudiste<br>pudo<br>pudimos<br>pudisteis<br>pudieron | podré<br>podrás<br>podrá<br>podremos<br>podréis<br>podrán | podría<br>podrías<br>podría<br>podríamos<br>podríais<br>podrían | pueda<br>puedas<br>pueda<br>podamos<br>podáis<br>puedan | pudiera<br>pudieras<br>pudiera<br>pudiéramos<br>pudierais<br>pudieran | |
| poner<br>poniendo<br>puesto | pongo<br>pones<br>pone<br>ponemos<br>ponéis<br>ponen | ponía<br>ponías<br>ponía<br>poníamos<br>poníais<br>ponían | puse<br>pusiste<br>puso<br>pusimos<br>pusisteis<br>pusieron | pondré<br>pondrás<br>pondrá<br>pondremos<br>pondréis<br>pondrán | pondría<br>pondrías<br>pondría<br>pondríamos<br>pondríais<br>pondrían | ponga<br>pongas<br>ponga<br>pongamos<br>pongáis<br>pongan | pusiera<br>pusieras<br>pusiera<br>pusiéramos<br>pusierais<br>pusieran | pon (tú),<br>no pongas<br>ponga (usted)<br>pongamos<br>poned (vosotros),<br>no pongáis<br>pongan (Uds.) |
| querer<br>queriendo<br>querido | quiero<br>quieres<br>quiere<br>queremos<br>queréis<br>quieren | quería<br>querías<br>quería<br>queríamos<br>queríais<br>querían | quise<br>quisiste<br>quiso<br>quisimos<br>quisisteis<br>quisieron | querré<br>querrás<br>querrá<br>querremos<br>querréis<br>querrán | querría<br>querrías<br>querría<br>querríamos<br>querríais<br>querrían | quiera<br>quieras<br>quiera<br>queramos<br>queráis<br>quieran | quisiera<br>quisieras<br>quisiera<br>quisiéramos<br>quisierais<br>quisieran | quiere (tú),<br>no quieras<br>quiera (usted)<br>queramos<br>quered (vosotros),<br>no queráis<br>quieran (Uds.) |
| saber<br>sabiendo<br>sabido | sé<br>sabes<br>sabe<br>sabemos<br>sabéis<br>saben | sabía<br>sabías<br>sabía<br>sabíamos<br>sabíais<br>sabían | supe<br>supiste<br>supo<br>supimos<br>supisteis<br>supieron | sabré<br>sabrás<br>sabrá<br>sabremos<br>sabréis<br>sabrán | sabría<br>sabrías<br>sabría<br>sabríamos<br>sabríais<br>sabrían | sepa<br>sepas<br>sepa<br>sepamos<br>sepáis<br>sepan | supiera<br>supieras<br>supiera<br>supiéramos<br>supierais<br>supieran | sabe (tú),<br>no sepas<br>sepa (usted)<br>sepamos<br>sabed (vosotros),<br>no sepáis<br>sepan (Uds.) |
| salir<br>saliendo<br>salido | salgo<br>sales<br>sale<br>salimos<br>salís<br>salen | salía<br>salías<br>salía<br>salíamos<br>salíais<br>salían | salí<br>saliste<br>salió<br>salimos<br>salisteis<br>salieron | saldré<br>saldrás<br>saldrá<br>saldremos<br>saldréis<br>saldrán | saldría<br>saldrías<br>saldría<br>saldríamos<br>saldríais<br>saldrían | salga<br>salgas<br>salga<br>salgamos<br>salgáis<br>salgan | saliera<br>salieras<br>saliera<br>saliéramos<br>salierais<br>salieran | sal (tú),<br>no salgas<br>salga (usted)<br>salgamos<br>salid (vosotros),<br>no salgáis<br>salgan (Uds.) |

A11

## Irregular Verbs (continued)

| Infinitive Present Participle Past Participle | Indicative | | | | | | Subjunctive | | Imperative |
|---|---|---|---|---|---|---|---|---|---|
| | Present | Imperfect | Preterit | Future | Conditional | Present | Imperfect | Commands |
| ser siendo sido | soy eres es somos sois son | era eras era éramos erais eran | fui fuiste fue fuimos fuisteis fueron | seré serás será seremos seréis serán | sería serías sería seríamos seríais serían | sea seas sea seamos seáis sean | fuera fueras fuera fuéramos fuerais fueran | sé (tú), no seas sea (usted) seamos sed (vosotros), no seáis sean (Uds.) |
| tener teniendo tenido | tengo tienes tiene tenemos tenéis tienen | tenía tenías tenía teníamos teníais tenían | tuve tuviste tuvo tuvimos tuvisteis tuvieron | tendré tendrás tendrá tendremos tendréis tendrán | tendría tendrías tendría tendríamos tendríais tendrían | tenga tengas tenga tengamos tengáis tengan | tuviera tuvieras tuviera tuviéramos tuvierais tuvieran | ten (tú), no tengas tenga (usted) tengamos tened (vosotros), no tengáis tengan (Uds.) |
| traer trayendo traído | traigo traes trae traemos traéis traen | traía traías traía traíamos traíais traían | traje trajiste trajo trajimos trajisteis trajeron | traeré traerás traerá traeremos traeréis traerán | traería traerías traería traeríamos traeríais traerían | traiga traigas traiga traigamos traigáis traigan | trajera trajeras trajera trajéramos trajerais trajeran | trae (tú), no traigas traiga (usted) traigamos traed (vosotros), no traigáis traigan (Uds.) |
| venir viniendo venido | vengo vienes viene venimos venís vienen | venía venías venía veníamos veníais venían | vine viniste vino vinimos vinisteis vinieron | vendré vendrás vendrá vendremos vendréis vendrán | vendría vendrías vendría vendríamos vendríais vendrían | venga vengas venga vengamos vengáis vengan | viniera vinieras viniera viniéramos vinierais vinieran | ven (tú), no vengas venga (usted) vengamos venid (vosotros), no vengáis vengan (Uds.) |
| ver viendo visto | veo ves ve vemos veis ven | veía veías veía veíamos veíais veían | vi viste vio vimos visteis vieron | veré verás verá veremos veréis verán | vería verías vería veríamos veríais verían | vea veas vea veamos veáis vean | viera vieras viera viéramos vierais vieran | ve (tú), no veas vea (usted) veamos ved (vosotros), no veáis vean (Uds.) |

# Stem-Changing and Orthographic-Changing Verbs

| Infinitive / Present Participle / Past Participle | Indicative | | | | | Subjunctive | | Imperative |
|---|---|---|---|---|---|---|---|---|
| | Present | Imperfect | Preterit | Future | Conditional | Present | Imperfect | Commands |
| almorzar (ue) (c) almorzando almorzado | almuerzo almuerzas almuerza almorzamos almorzáis almuerzan | almorzaba almorzabas almorzaba almorzábamos almorzabais almorzaban | almorcé almorzaste almorzó almorzamos almorzasteis almorzaron | almorzaré almorzarás almorzará almorzaremos almorzaréis almorzarán | almorzaría almorzarías almorzaría almorzaríamos almorzaríais almorzarían | almuerce almuerces almuerce almorcemos almorcéis almuercen | almorzara almorzaras almorzara almorzáramos almorzarais almorzaran | almuerza (tú), no almuerces almuerce (usted) almorcemos almorzad (vosotros), no almorcéis almuercen (Uds.) |
| buscar (qu) buscando buscado | busco buscas busca buscamos buscáis buscan | buscaba buscabas buscaba buscábamos buscabais buscaban | busqué buscaste buscó buscamos buscasteis buscaron | buscaré buscarás buscará buscaremos buscaréis buscarán | buscaría buscarías buscaría buscaríamos buscaríais buscarían | busque busques busque busquemos busquéis busquen | buscara buscaras buscara buscáramos buscarais buscaran | busca (tú), no busques busque (usted) busquemos buscad (vosotros), no busquéis busquen (Uds.) |
| corregir (i, i) (j) corrigiendo corregido | corrijo corriges corrige corregimos corregís corrigen | corregía corregías corregía corregíamos corregíais corregían | corregí corregiste corrigió corregimos corregisteis corrigieron | corregiré corregirás corregirá corregiremos corregiréis corregirán | corregiría corregirías corregiría corregiríamos corregiríais corregirían | corrija corrijas corrija corrijamos corrijáis corrijan | corrigiera corrigieras corrigiera corrigiéramos corrigierais corrigieran | corrige (tú), no corrijas corrija (usted) corrijamos corregid (vosotros), no corrijáis corrijan (Uds.) |
| dormir (ue, u) durmiendo dormido | duermo duermes duerme dormimos dormís duermen | dormía dormías dormía dormíamos dormíais dormían | dormí dormiste durmió dormimos dormisteis durmieron | dormiré dormirás dormirá dormiremos dormiréis dormirán | dormiría dormirías dormiría dormiríamos dormiríais dormirían | duerma duermas duerma durmamos durmáis duerman | durmiera durmieras durmiera durmiéramos durmierais durmieran | duerme (tú), no duermas duerma (usted) durmamos dormid (vosotros), no durmáis duerman (Uds.) |
| incluir (y) incluyendo incluido | incluyo incluyes incluye incluimos incluís incluyen | incluía incluías incluía incluíamos incluíais incluían | incluí incluiste incluyó incluimos incluisteis incluyeron | incluiré incluirás incluirá incluiremos incluiréis incluirán | incluiría incluirías incluiría incluiríamos incluiríais incluirían | incluya incluyas incluya incluyamos incluyáis incluyan | incluyera incluyeras incluyera incluyéramos incluyerais incluyeran | incluye (tú), no incluyas incluya (usted) incluyamos incluid (vosotros), no incluyáis incluyan (Uds.) |

## Stem-Changing and Orthographic-Changing Verbs (continued)

| Infinitive Present Participle Past Participle | Indicative | | | | | Subjunctive | | Imperative |
|---|---|---|---|---|---|---|---|---|
| | Present | Imperfect | Preterit | Future | Conditional | Present | Imperfect | Commands |
| llegar (gu) llegando llegado | llego llegas llega llegamos llegáis llegan | llegaba llegabas llegaba llegábamos llegabais llegaban | llegué llegaste llegó llegamos llegasteis llegaron | llegaré llegarás llegará llegaremos llegaréis llegarán | llegaría llegarías llegaría llegaríamos llegaríais llegarían | llegue llegues llegue lleguemos lleguéis lleguen | llegara llegaras llegara llegáramos llegarais llegaran | llega (tú), no llegues llegue (usted) lleguemos llegad (vosotros), no lleguéis lleguen (Uds.) |
| pedir (i, i) pidiendo pedido | pido pides pide pedimos pedís piden | pedía pedías pedía pedíamos pedíais pedían | pedí pediste pidió pedimos pedisteis pidieron | pediré pedirás pedirá pediremos pediréis pedirán | pediría pedirías pediría pediríamos pediríais pedirían | pida pidas pida pidamos pidáis pidan | pidiera pidieras pidiera pidiéramos pidierais pidieran | pide (tú), no pidas pida (usted) pidamos pedid (vosotros), no pidáis pidan (Uds.) |
| pensar (ie) pensando pensado | pienso piensas piensa pensamos pensáis piensan | pensaba pensabas pensaba pensábamos pensabais pensaban | pensé pensaste pensó pensamos pensasteis pensaron | pensaré pensarás pensará pensaremos pensaréis pensarán | pensaría pensarías pensaría pensaríamos pensaríais pensarían | piense pienses piense pensemos penséis piensen | pensara pensaras pensara pensáramos pensarais pensaran | piensa (tú), no pienses piense (usted) pensemos pensad (vosotros), no penséis piensen (Uds.) |
| producir (zc) (j) produciendo producido | produzco produces produce producimos producís producen | producía producías producía producíamos producíais producían | produje produjiste produjo produjimos produjisteis produjeron | produciré producirás producirá produciremos produciréis producirán | produciría producirías produciría produciríamos produciríais producirían | produzca produzcas produzca produzcamos produzcáis produzcan | produjera produjeras produjera produjéramos produjerais produjeran | produce (tú), no produzcas produzca (usted) produzcamos producid (vosotros), no produzcáis produzcan (Uds.) |
| reír (i, i) riendo reído | río ríes ríe reímos reís ríen | reía reías reía reíamos reíais reían | reí reíste rio reímos reísteis rieron | reiré reirás reirá reiremos reiréis reirán | reiría reirías reiría reiríamos reiríais reirían | ría rías ría riamos riáis rían | riera rieras riera riéramos rierais rieran | ríe (tú), no rías ría (usted) riamos reíd (vosotros), no riáis rían (Uds.) |

# Stem-Changing and Orthographic-Changing Verbs (continued)

| Infinitive / Present Participle / Past Participle | Indicative | | | | | Subjunctive | | Imperative |
|---|---|---|---|---|---|---|---|---|
| | Present | Imperfect | Preterit | Future | Conditional | Present | Imperfect | Commands |
| seguir (i, i) (ga) siguiendo seguido | sigo sigues sigue seguimos seguís siguen | seguía seguías seguía seguíamos seguíais seguían | seguí seguiste siguió seguimos seguisteis siguieron | seguiré seguirás seguirá seguiremos seguiréis seguirán | seguiría seguirías seguiría seguiríamos seguiríais seguirían | siga sigas siga sigamos sigáis sigan | siguiera siguieras siguiera siguiéramos siguierais siguieran | sigue (tú), no sigas siga (usted) sigamos seguid (vosotros), no sigáis sigan (Uds.) |
| sentir (ie, i) sintiendo sentido | siento sientes siente sentimos sentís sienten | sentía sentías sentía sentíamos sentíais sentían | sentí sentiste sintió sentimos sentisteis sintieron | sentiré sentirás sentirá sentiremos sentiréis sentirán | sentiría sentirías sentiría sentiríamos sentiríais sentirían | sienta sientas sienta sintamos sintáis sientan | sintiera sintieras sintiera sintiéramos sintierais sintieran | siente (tú), no sientas sienta (usted) sintamos sentid (vosotros), no sintáis sientan (Uds.) |
| volver (ue) volviendo vuelto | vuelvo vuelves vuelve volvemos volvéis vuelven | volvía volvías volvía volvíamos volvíais volvían | volví volviste volvió volvimos volvisteis volvieron | volveré volverás volverá volveremos volveréis volverán | volvería volverías volvería volveríamos volveríais volverían | vuelva vuelvas vuelva volvamos volváis vuelvan | volviera volvieras volviera volviéramos volvierais volvieran | vuelve (tú), no vuelvas vuelva (usted) volvamos volved (vosotros), no volváis vuelvan (Uds.) |

A15

# Appendix 3

## También se dice...

### Los saludos/Greetings

¿Cómo andas? *How are you doing?*
¿Cómo vas? *How are you doing?*
El gusto es mío. *Pleased to meet you; The pleasure is all mine.*
Hasta entonces. *Until then.*
¿Qué hubo? *How's it going? What's happening? What's new?*
¿Qué pasa? *How's it going? What's happening? What's new?*
¿Qué pasó? *How's it going? What's happening? What's new?*

### Las despedidas/Farewells

Nos vemos. *See you.*
Que te vaya bien. *Hope everything goes well.*
Que tenga(s) un buen día. *Have a nice day.*
Vaya con Dios. *Go with God.*

### Las presentaciones/Introductions

Me gustaría presentarle a... *I would like to introduce you to . . . (formal)*
Me gustaría presentarte a... *I would like to introduce you to . . . (familiar)*

### Expresiones útiles para la clase/Useful classroom expressions

#### Preguntas y respuestas/Questions and answers

(No) entiendo. *I (don't) understand.*
¿Puede repetir, por favor? *Could you repeat, please?*

#### Expresiones de cortesía/Polite expressions

Muchas gracias. *Thank you very much.*
No hay de qué. *Not at all.*

#### Mandato para la clase/Instruction for class

Saque(n) un bolígrafo/papel/lápiz. *Take out a pen/a piece of paper/a pencil.*

### Las nacionalidades/Nationalities

argentino/a *Argentinian*
boliviano/a *Bolivian*
chileno/a *Chilean*
colombiano/a *Colombian*
costarricense *Costa Rican*
dominicano/a *Dominican*
ecuatoriano/a *Ecuadorian*
guatemalteco/a *Guatemalan*
hondureño/a *Honduran*
nicaragüense *Nicaraguan*
panameño/a *Panamanian*
peruano/a *Peruvian*
uruguayo/a *Uruguayan*
venezolano/a *Venezuelan*

### Expresiones del tiempo/Weather expressions

el arco iris *rainbow*
el chirimiri *drizzle (Spain)*
Está despejado. *It's clear.*
Hace fresco. *It's cool.*
Hay neblina/niebla. *It's foggy.*
la humedad *humidity*
los copos de nieve *snowflakes*
las gotas de lluvia *raindrops*
el granizo *hail*
el hielo *ice*
el huracán *hurricane*
la llovizna *drizzle*
el pronóstico *weather forecast*
el/los rayo/s, el relámpago *lightning*
la tormenta *storm*
el tornado *tornado*
el/los trueno/s *thunder*

### La familia/Family

el/la ahijado/a *godchild*
el bisabuelo *great-grandfather*
la bisabuela *great-grandmother*
el/la cuñado/a *brother-in-law/sister-in-law*
la familia política *in-laws*
el/la hermanastro/a *stepbrother/stepsister*
el /la hijastro/a *stepson/stepdaughter*
el/la hijo/a único/a *only child*

la madrina *godmother*
el/la medio/a hermano/a *half brother/half sister*
los medios hermanos *half brothers and sisters*
la mami *Mommy; Mom (Latin America)*
el marido *husband*
la mujer *wife*
los nietos *grandchildren*
la nuera *daughter-in-law*
el padrino *godfather*

**A16**

el papi *Daddy; Dad (Latin America)*
el pariente *relative*
el/la prometido/a *fiancé(e)*
los sobrinos *nieces and nephews*
el/la suegro/a *father-in-law/mother-in-law*
los suegros *in-laws*
la tatarabuela *great-great-grandmother*
el tatarabuelo *great-great-grandfather*
la tía abuela *great-aunt*
el tío abuelo *great-uncle*
el/la viudo/a *widower/widow*
el yerno *son-in-law*

### Otra palabra útil/*Another useful word*

divorciado/a *divorced*

### La gente/*People*

el bato *friend; guy (in SE USA slang)*
el/la chaval/a *young man/young woman (Spain)*
el chamaco *young man (Cuba, Honduras, Mexico, El Salvador)*
el/la fulano/a *unknown man/woman*

## Los adjetivos/*Adjectives*

### La personalidad y otros rasgos/*Personality and other characteristics*

amable *nice; kind*
bobo/a *stupid; silly*
el/la bromista *person who likes to play jokes*
cariñoso/a *loving; affectionate*
chistoso/a *funny*
cursi *pretentious; affected*
divertido/a *funny*
educado/a *well mannered; polite*

elegante *elegant*
empollón/ona *bookworm; nerd*
encantador/a *charming; lovely*
espabilado/a *smart; vivacious; alert (Latin America)*
frustrado/a *frustrated*
gracioso/a *funny*
grosero/a *unpleasant*
histérico/a *crazed*
impaciente *impatient*
indiferente *indifferent*
irresponsable *irresponsible*
malvado/a *evil; wicked*
majo/a *pretty; nice (Spain)*
mono/a *pretty; nice (Spain, Caribbean)*
odioso/a *unpleasant*
pesado/a *annoying person*
pijo/a *posh; snooty (Spain)*
progre *liberal; progressive (Spain)*
sabelotodo *know-it-all*
viejo/a *old*

### Las características físicas/*Physical characteristics*

atlético/a *athletic*
bello/a *beautiful (Latin America)*
blando/a *soft*
esbelto/a *slender*
flaco/a *thin*
frágil *fragile*
hermoso/a *beautiful; lovely*
musculoso/a *muscular*
robusto/a *sturdy*

### Otras palabras útiles/*Other useful words*

demasiado/a *too much*
suficiente *enough*

## Capítulo 2

### Las materias y las especialidades/*Subjects and majors*

la agronomía *agriculture*
la antropología *anthropology*
el cálculo *calculus*
las ciencias políticas *political sciences*
las comunicaciones *communications*
la contabilidad *accounting*
la economía *economics*
la educación física *physical education*
la enfermería *nursing*
la filosofía *philosophy*
la física *physics*
la geografía *geography*
la geología *geology*
la historia *history*
la ingeniería *engineering*
la literatura comparada *comparative literature*
el mercadeo *marketing (Latin America)*
la mercadotecnia (el márketing) *marketing (Spain)*

la medicina del deporte *sports medicine*
la química *chemistry*
los servicios sociales *social work*
la sociología *sociology*
la terapia física *physical therapy*

### En la sala de clase/*In the classroom*

el aula *classroom*
el/la alumno/a *student*
la bombilla *light bulb*
la cámara proyectora *overhead camera*
el cielorraso *ceiling*
el enchufe *wall socket*
el interruptor *light switch*
las luces *lights*
el ordenador *computer (Spain)*
la pantalla *screen*
el proyector *projector*
la prueba *test*
el pupitre *student desk*

A17

el rotulador *marker*
el sacapuntas *pencil sharpener*
el salón de clase *classroom*
el suelo *floor*
la tarima *dais; platform*

### Los verbos/*Verbs*

apuntar *to point*
asistir a clase *to attend class*
beber *to drink*
entrar *to enter*
entregar *to hand in*
mirar *to look; to observe*
prestar atención *to pay attention*
repasar *to review*
responder *to answer*
sacar *to take out*
sacar buenas/malas notas *to get good/bad grades*
tomar apuntes *to take notes*

### Las palabras interrogativas/*Interrogative words*

¿Con cuánto/a/os/as? *With how many . . . ?*
¿Con qué? *With what . . . ?*
¿Con quién? *With whom . . . ?*
¿De dónde? *From where . . . ?*
¿De qué? *About what . . . ?*
¿De quién? *Of whom . . . ?*

### Emociones y estados/*Emotions and states of being*

agotado/a *exhausted*
agradable *nice*
alegre *happy*
asombrado/a *amazed; astonished*
asqueado/a *disgusted*
asustado/a *scared*
deprimido/a *depressed*
desanimado/a *discouraged; disheartened*
disgustado/a *upset*
dormido/a *sleepy*
emocionado/a *moved; touched*
entusiasmado/a *delighted*
fastidiado/a *annoyed; bothered*
ilusionado/a *thrilled*
optimista *optimistic*
pesimista *pessimistic*
retrasado/a *late*
sonriente *smiling*
soñoliento/a *sleepy (Spain)*

### Los lugares/*Places*

el apartamento estudiantil *student apartment*
el campo de fútbol *football field*
el campus *campus*
la cancha de tenis/baloncesto *tennis/basketball court*
la/s casa/s de hermandad/es *fraternity and sorority housing*
el centro comercial *mall*
el comedor estudiantil *student dining hall*
la habitación *room*
la matrícula *registration*

el museo *museum*
la oficina de consejeros *guidance/advising office*
el supermercado *supermarket*
el teatro *theater*

### La residencia/*The dorm*

los bafles *speakers (Spain)*
el calendario *calendar*
la cama *bed*
el iPod *iPod*
el Internet *Internet*
las literas *bunkbeds*
la llave *memory stick*
la mesita de noche *nightstand*
el móvil *cell phone (Spain)*
la redacción/la composición *essay*
la tarjeta de crédito *credit card*
la tarjeta de identidad; el carnet *ID card*
los videojuegos *video games*

### Los deportes y los pasatiempos/*Sports and pastimes*

cazar *to hunt*
conversar con amigos *to talk with friends*
escalar *to go mountain climbing*
esquiar *to ski*
estar en forma *to be in shape*
hablar por teléfono *to talk on the phone*
hacer alpinismo *to go hiking*
hacer footing *to go jogging (Spain)*
hacer gimnasia *to exercise*
hacer senderismo *to hike*
hacer pilates *to do Pilates*
hacer yoga *to do yoga*
ir al centro comercial *to go the mall; to go downtown*
ir a fiestas *to go to parties*
ir a un partido de... *to go to a . . . game*
jugar al ajedrez *to play chess*
jugar al boliche *to bowl*
jugar al ráquetbol *to play racquetball*
jugar a videojuegos *to play video games*
levantar pesas *to lift weights*
ver videos *to watch videos*
montar a caballo *to go horseback riding*
pasear *to go out for a ride; to take a walk*
pasear en barco *to sail*
ir a navegar *to sail*
pescar *to fish*
practicar boxeo *to box*
practicar ciclismo *to cycle*
practicar lucha libre *to wrestle*
practicar las artes marciales *to do martial arts*
salir a cenar/comer *to go out to dinner/eat*
tirar un platillo volador *to throw a Frisbee*

### Palabras asociadas con los deportes y los pasatiempos/*Words associated with sports and pastimes*

el/la aficionado/a *fan*
el bate *bat*

el campo *field*
los libros de…
    acción *action books*
    aventura *adventure books*
    cuentos cortos *short stories*
    ficción (ciencia-ficción) *fiction (science fiction)*
    horror *horror books*

misterio *mystery books*
romance *romance books*
espías *spy books*
el palo de golf *golf club*
la pista *track*
la pista y el campo *track and field (Spain)*
la raqueta *racket*

## Capítulo 3

### La casa/*The house*
la alcoba *bedroom*
el armario empotrado *closet (Spain)*
el ático *attic*
la bodega *cellar*
la buhardilla *attic*
el clóset *closet (Latin America)*
el corredor *hall*
el cuarto *bedroom*
el despacho *office*
el desván *attic*
el pasillo *hallway*
el patio *patio; yard*
el placar *closet (Argentina)*
el portal *porch*
el porche *porch*
la recámara *bedroom (Mexico)*
el salón *salon; lounge; living room*
el tejado *roof*
la terraza *terrace; porch*
el vestíbulo *entrance hall*

### En la sala y el comedor/*In the living room and dining room*
la banqueta/el banquillo *small seating stool*
la estantería *bookcase*
la mecedora *rocking chair*
la moqueta *carpet (Spain)*

### En la cocina/*In the kitchen*
el congelador *deep freezer*
el friegaplatos *dishwasher*
el frigorífico *refrigerator (Spain)*
el horno *oven*
el lavavajillas *dishwasher (Spain)*
el taburete *bar stool*

### Otras palabras/*Other words*
el aparato eléctrico *electric appliance*
la chimenea *chimney*
la cómoda *dresser*
las cortinas *curtains*
el espejo *mirror*
el fregadero *sink*
los gabinetes *cabinets*

la lavadora *washer*
la secadora *dryer*
el librero *bookcase (Mexico)*
la nevera *refrigerator*
las persianas *shutters; window blinds*

### En el baño/*In the bathroom*
la cisterna *toilet water tank*
el espejo *mirror*
los grifos *faucets*
la jabonera *soap dish*
el toallero *towel rack*

### En el dormitorio/*In the bedroom*
el edredón *comforter*
la frazada *blanket (Latin America)*

### Los quehaceres de la casa/*Household chores*
barrer *to sweep*
cortar el césped *to cut the grass*
fregar los platos *to wash the dishes*
fregar los suelos *to clean the floors*
guardar la ropa *to put away clothes*
lavar la ropa *to do laundry*
ordenar *to put in order*
planchar la ropa *to iron*
quitar el polvo *to dust*
recoger *to clean up in general*
recoger la mesa *to clean up after a meal*
regar las plantas *to water the plants*
sacudir las alfombras *to shake out the rugs*
sacudir el polvo *to dust*

### Expresiones con *tener*/*Expressions with* tener
tener celos *to be jealous*
tener novio/a *to have a boyfriend/girlfriend*

### Los colores/*Colors*
color café *brown*
púrpura *purple (Spain)*
azul/verde claro *light blue/green*
azul/verde oscuro *dark blue/green*
rosa *pink (Spain)*

## Capítulo 4

**Lugares en una ciudad o pueblo/*Places in a city or town***

la alberca  *swimming pool; sports complex (Mexico)*
el ambulatorio  *medical center (not a hospital) (Spain)*
el aseo  *public restroom*
la catedral  *cathedral*
el campo de golf  *golf course*
la capilla  *chapel*
la clínica  *clinic*
el consultorio  *doctor's office*
el convento  *convent*
la cuadra  *block (Latin America)*
la ferretería  *hardware store*
la fogata  *bonfire*
la frutería  *fruit store*
la fuente  *fountain*
la gasolinera  *gas station*

la heladería  *ice cream shop*
la manzana  *block (Spain)*
el mercadillo  *open-air market*
la mezquita  *mosque*
la papelería  *stationary store*
la panadería  *bread store*
la pastelería  *pastry shop*
la pescadería  *fish shop; fishmonger*
la piscina  *pool*
el polideportivo  *sports center*
el quiosco  *newsstand*
los servicios  *public restrooms*
la sinagoga  *synagogue*
la tienda de juguetes  *toy store*
la tienda de ropa  *clothing store*
el zócalo  *plaza (Mexico)*

## Capítulo 5

**El mundo de la música/*The world of music***

la musica…
    alternativa *alternative music*
    bluegrass *bluegrass music*
el coro  *choir*
el cuarteto  *quartet*
el equipo de cámara/sonido  *camera/sound crew*
el/la mánager  *manager*
el merengue  *merengue*
la música popular  *popular music*
el/la organista  *organist*
la pandilla  *gang; posse*
los/las seguidores/as  *groupies*
el teclado  *keyboard*

**El mundo del cine/*The world of film***

**Gente/*People***

el/la cinematógrafo/a  *cinematographer*
el/la director/a  *director*
el/la guionista  *scriptwriter*

**Las películas/*Movies***

el cortometraje  *short (film)*
los dibujos animados  *cartoons*
el guión  *script*
el montaje  *montage*

## Capítulo 7

**Las carnes y las aves/*Meats and poultry***

las aves de corral  *poultry*
la carne de cerdo  *pork*
la carne de cordero  *lamb*
la carne de res  *beef*
la carne molida  *ground beef*
la carne picada  *ground beef (Spain)*
el chorizo  *highly seasoned pork sausage*
la chuleta  *chop*
el chuletón  *T-bone (Spain)*
el jamón serrano  *prosciutto ham (Spain)*
el pavo  *turkey*
la salchicha  *sausage; hot dog*
el salchichón  *spiced sausage (Spain)*
la ternera  *veal*
el tocino  *bacon*

**El pescado y los mariscos/*Fish and seafood***

las almejas  *clams*
las anchoas  *anchovies*

los calamares  *squid*
el cangrejo  *crab*
el chillo  *red snapper (Puerto Rico)*
las gambas  *shrimp*
el huachinango  *red snapper (Mexico)*
la langosta  *lobster*
el lenguado  *flounder*
la ostra  *oyster*
el pulpo  *octopus*
la sardina  *sardines*

**Las frutas/*Fruits***

el aguacate  *avocado*
el albaricoque  *apricot*
el ananá  *pineapple (Latin America)*
el banano  *banana; banana tree*
la cereza  *cherry*
la china  *orange (Puerto Rico)*
la ciruela  *plum*
el durazno  *peach*

A20

la fresa *strawberry*
el melocotón *peach*
la papaya *papaya*
la piña *pineapple*
el pomelo *grapefruit*
la sandía *watermelon*
la toronja *grapefruit*

## Las verduras/*Vegetables*

las aceitunas *olives*
la alcaparra *caper*
el apio *celery*
la berza *cabbage (Spain)*
el calabacín *zucchini*
la calabaza *squash; pumpkin*
los champiñones *mushrooms*
la col *cabbage*
la coliflor *cauliflower*
los espárragos *asparagus*
las espinacas *spinach*
los guisantes *peas*
las habichuelas *kidney beans*
los hongos *mushrooms (Latin America)*
la judías verdes *green beans*
el pepinillo *pickle*
el pepino *cucumber*
el pimiento *pepper*
el plátano *plantain*
el repollo *cabbage*
la salsa *sauce*
las setas *wild mushrooms (Spain)*
la zanahoria *carrot*

## Los postres/*Desserts*

el arroz con leche *rice pudding*
la batida *milkshake*
el batido *milkshake (Spain)*
los bocaditos *bite-size sandwiches*
los bollos *sweet bread*
el bombón *sweets; candy*
el caramelo *sweets; candy*
los chocolates *chocolates*
los chuches *candies in general (Spain)*
la dona *donut*
el dónut *donut (Spain)*
el flan *caramel custard*
la natilla *custard*
los pastelitos *turnover; pastry; finger cakes*
la tarta *cake*

## Las bebidas/*Beverages*

el champán *champagne*
la sidra *cider*
el zumo *juice (Spain)*

## Más comidas/*More foods*

el ajo *garlic*
la avena *oatmeal*
el caldo *broth*
el consomé *clear soup*
los fideos *noodles (in soup)*
la harina *flour*

la jalea *jelly; marmalade (Spain, Puerto Rico)*
la margarina *margarine*
la miel *honey*
el pan dulce *sweet roll*
el panqueque *pancake*
las tortas americanas *pancakes (Spain)*

## Las comidas/*Meals*

el aperitivo *appetizer*
las tapas *hors d'oeuvres*

## Los condimentos y las especias/*Condiments and spices*

el aderezo *seasoning; dressing*
el aliño *seasoning; dressing (Spain)*

## Algunos términos de la cocina/*Some cooking terms*

agregar *to add*
asar *to roast; to broil*
aumentar libras/kilos *to gain weight*
batir *to beat*
calentar *to heat*
derretir *to melt*
espesarse *to thicken*
freír *to fry*
mezclar *to mix*
revolver *to stir*
servir *to serve*
unir *to combine*
verter *to pour*

## Otras palabras útiles/*Other useful words*

aclararse *to thin*
añadir *to add*
el batidor *beater*
la batidora *hand-held mixer*
la cacerola *saucepan*
cocer *to cook*
la copa *goblet; wine glass*
el cuenco *bowl; mixing bowl*
echar (algo) *to add*
el fuego (lento, mediano, alto) *(low, medium, high) heat*
la fuente *serving platter/dish*
el ingrediente *ingredient*
el kilogramo *kilogram (or 2.2 pounds)*
el nivel *level*
la olla *pot*
el pedazo *piece*
el platillo *saucer*
el plato hondo *bowl*
el plato sopero *soup bowl*
la receta *recipe*
recalentar *to reheat*
remover *to stir (Spain)*
la sartén *frying pan*
el/la sopero/a *soup serving bowl*

## En el restaurante/*In the restaurant*

la cucharilla *teaspoon (Spain)*
el friegaplatos *dishwasher (person)*
el/la mesero/a *waiter/waitress (Latin America)*
el/la pinche *kitchen assistant*

**A21**

## Capítulo 8

### La ropa y la joyería/Clothing and jewelry

el albornoz *bathrobe (Spain)*
las alpargatas *espadrille shoes (Spain)*
el anorak *rain-proof coat*
los aretes *earrings*
la bolsa *bag*
la bufanda *scarf*
la capa de agua *raincoat (Puerto Rico)*
la cartera *pocketbook, purse*
el chubasquero *raincoat (Spain)*
el collar *necklace*
la correa *belt*
el gorro *wool cap; hat*
los mahones *jeans (Puerto Rico)*
las pantallas *earrings (Puerto Rico)*
el peine *comb*
la peinilla *comb (Latin America)*
los pendientes *earrings*
la pulsera *bracelet*
la sombrilla *parasol; umbrella*
los vaqueros *jeans*
las zapatillas de tenis *sneakers; tennis shoes (Spain)*

### Más palabras útiles/More useful words

de buena/mala calidad *good/poor quality*
de goma *(made of) rubber*
de lino *(made of) linen*
de manga corta/larga/media *short/long/half sleeve*

de nilón *nylon*
de oro *(made) of gold*
de plata *(made) of silver*
de platino *platinum*
de puntitos *polka dotted*

### Para comprar ropa/To go clothes shopping

el escaparate *store window*
el/la dependiente/a *clerk*
la ganga *bargain*
la liquidación *clearance sale*
el maniquí *mannequin*
el mostrador *counter*
la oferta *offer; sale*
la rebaja *sale; discount*
el tacón alto/bajo *high/low heel*
la venta *clearance sale*
la vitrina *store window*
los zapatos planos/de cuña *flat/wedge shoes*

### Algunos adjetivos/Some adjectives

amplio/a *wide*
apretado/a *tight*

### Un verbo reflexivo/A reflexive verb

desvestirse (e → i → i) *to get undressed*

## Capítulo 9

### El cuerpo humano/The human body

la arteria *artery*
el cabello *hair*
la cadera *hip*
la ceja *eyebrow*
el cerebelo *cerebellum*
el cerebro *brain*
la cintura *waist*
el codo *elbow*
la costilla *rib*
la frente *forehead*
el hombro *shoulder*
el hueso *bone*
el labio *lip*
la lengua *tongue*
las mejillas *cheeks*
la muñeca *wrist*
el músculo *muscle*
el muslo *thigh*
los nervios *nerves*
la pestaña *eyelash*
la piel *skin*
el pulmón *lung*
la rodilla *knee*
el talón *heel*

el trasero *buttocks (Spain)*
el tobillo *ankle*
la uña *nail*
las venas *veins*

### Algunas enfermedades/Some illnesses

el alcoholismo *alcoholism*
la alta tensión *high blood pressure*
el ataque del corazón *heart attack*
la baja tensión *low blood pressure*
el cáncer *cancer*
la depresión *depression*
la diabetes *diabetes*
el dolor de cabeza *headache*
el/la drogadicto/a *drug addict*
la hipertensión *high blood pressure*
el infarto *heart attack*
la inflamación *inflammation*
el mareo *dizziness*
la narcomanía *drug addiction*
la presión alta/baja *high/low blood pressure*
la quemadura *burn*
el sarampión *measles*
el SIDA *AIDS*
la varicela *chicken pox*

A22

### Otros verbos útiles/Other useful verbs

contagiarse de *to catch (an illness)*
desmayarse *to faint*
desvanecerse *to faint*
doblarse *to sprain*
enyesar *to put on a cast*
fracturar(se) *to break; to fracture*
hacer gárgaras *to gargle*
hinchar *to swell*
pegársele *to catch something*
recetar *to prescribe*
respirar *to breathe*
sacar la sangre *to draw blood*
tomarle la presión *to take someone's blood pressure*
tomarle el pulso *to take someone's pulse*
tomarle la temperatura *to check someone's temperature*
torcerse *to sprain*
vomitar *to vomit*

### Otras palabras útiles/Other useful words

las alergias *allergies*
el antihistamínico *antihistamine*

la camilla *stretcher*
la cura *cure*
la dosis *dosage*
la enfermedad *illness*
las gotas para los ojos *eyedrops*
los medicamentos *medicines*
las muletas *crutches*
operar *to operate*
el/la paciente *patient*
la penicilina *penicillin*
el pulso *pulse*
las pruebas médicas *medical tests*
la radiografía *X-ray*
el resultado *result*
retorcerse *to sprain*
el termómetro *thermometer*
la tirita *bandage*
la vacuna *vaccination*

## Capítulo 10

### El transporte y otras palabras/Transportation and other words

el aparcamiento *parking lot*
el atasco *traffic jam*
el billete *ticket*
el camino *dirt road*
el camión *bus (Mexico)*
la camioneta *pickup truck; van; station wagon*
el carnet *driver's license (Spain)*
la carretera *highway*
enviar *to send; to dispatch*
la goma *tire (Latin America)*
la guagua *bus (Caribbean)*
el guía *steering wheel*
el paso de peatones *crosswalk*
el seguro del coche *car insurance*
el tiquete *ticket*
la velocidad *speed*

### Algunas partes de un vehículo/Some parts of a car

el acelerador *accelerator; gas pedal*
el cinturón de seguridad *seat belt*
el claxon *horn*
el espejo retrovisor *rearview mirror*
los frenos *brakes*
las luces *lights*

el maletero *car trunk (Spain)*
el parachoques *bumper*
la transmisión *transmission*

### Un verbo útil/A useful verb

perderse *to get lost*

### El viaje/Travel

los cheques de viajero *traveler's checks*
la dirección *address*
el equipaje *luggage*
la estampilla *(postage) stamp*
la oficina de turismo *tourist office*
el paquete *package*
el pasaje de ida y vuelta *round-trip ticket*
los pasajes *(travel) tickets*
el sobre *the envelope*

### El hotel/The hotel

el/la camarero/a *service maid*
el/la guardia de seguridad *security guard*
el/la portero/a *doorman/woman*
el/la recepcionista *receptionist*
el servicio *room service (cleaning)*
el/la telefonista *telephone operator*

## Capítulo 11

### Algunos animales/*Some animals*

la abeja *bee*
la ardilla *squirrel*
la ballena *whale*
la cabra *goat*
el cangrejo *crab*
el ciervo *deer*
el cochino *pig*
la culebra *snake*
el dinosaurio *dinosaur*
la foca *seal*
el gallo *rooster*
el gorila *gorilla*
la iguana *iguana*
la jirafa *giraffe*
el lobo *wolf*
el loro *parrot*
la mariposa *butterfly*
el marrano *pig*
el mono *monkey*
el nido *nest*
la oveja *sheep*
la paloma *pigeon; dove*
el pato *duck*
el puerco *pig*
el pulpo *octopus*
el puma *puma*
el rinoceronte *rhinoceros*
el saltamontes *grasshopper*
el tiburón *shark*
el tigre *tiger*
la tortuga *turtle*
el venado *deer*
el zorro *fox*

### El medio ambiente/*The environment*

el aerosol *aerosol*
el agua subterránea *ground water*
la Antártida *Antarctica*
el Ártico *the Arctic*
la atmósfera *atmosphere*
el aumento *increase*
el bióxido de carbono *carbon dioxide*
el carbón *coal*
el central nuclear *nuclear plant*
el clorofluorocarbono *chlorofluorocarbon*
el combustible fósil *fossil fuel*
la cosecha *crop; harvest*
la descomposición *decomposition*
el desperdicio de patio *yard waste*
el ecosistema *ecosystem*
la energía *energy*
la energía eólica (molinos de viento) *wind power (windmills)*

la industria *industry*
insoportable *unbearable; unsustainable*
el medio ambiente *environment*
el oxígeno *oxygen*
el país *country*
el pesticida *pesticide*
el petróleo *petroleum*
la piedra *rock; stone*
las placas solares *solar panels*
la planta eléctrica *power plant*
el plomo *lead*
el polvo *dust*
el rayo de sol *ray of sunlight*
el rayo ultravioleta *ultraviolet ray*
el riesgo *risk*

### Algunos verbos/*Some verbs*

atrapar *to trap*
conseguir *to achieve*
corroer *to corrode*
dañar *to damage*
desarrollar *to evolve; to develop*
descongelarse *to melt; melt down*
destruir *to destroy*
hacer huelga *to go on strike*
hundirse *to sink*
luchar en contra *to fight against*
prevenir *to prevent*
realizar *to achieve*
tirar *to throw away (Spain)*

### La política/*Politics*

la constitución *constitution*
la ciudadanía *citizenship*
el/la ciudadano/a *citizen*
el/la congresista *congressman/woman*
el gobierno *the government*
la monarquía constitucional *constitutional monarchy*
el paro general *general strike*
el/la primer/a ministro/a *prime minister*
el/la secretario/a de estado *secretary of state*

### Las cuestiones políticas/*Political issues*

el aborto *abortion*
el abuso de menores *child abuse*
el derecho de trabajadores *workers' rights*
la eutanasia *euthanasia*
el genocidio *genocide*
la inmigración ilegal *illegal immigration*
la pena capital *death penalty*
la seguridad social *social security*
la violencia doméstica *domestic violence*

# Appendix 4

## Spanish-English Glossary

**A**

**a** to; at (**11**); **~ cambio** in exchange (**4**, **PB**); **~ eso de** around (**7**); **~ fin de** in order to (**11**); **~ la derecha (de)** to the right (of ) (**3**, **11**); **~ la izquierda (de)** to the left (of ) (**3**, **11**); **~ la parrilla** grilled (**7**); **~ mano** on hand (**10**); **~ menudo** often (**2**, **3**); **¿~ qué hora...?** At what time? (**PA**); **~ veces** sometimes; from time to time (**2**, **3**, **4**); **~ ver** let's see (**2**)

**abarcar** to encompass (**5**)

**Abra(n) el libro en la página...** Open your book to page . . . (**PA**)

**abrazo, el** hug (**PA**)

**abrigo, el** coat; overcoat (**3**, **8**)

**abrir** to open (**2**)

**abuelo/a, el/la** grandfather/ grandmother (**1**)

**abuelos, los** grandparents (**1**)

**aburrido/a** boring; bored (*with* **estar**) (**1**, **2**, **5**)

**acabar con** end (**4**)

**acabar de + infinitivo** to have just finished + (*something*) (**3**, **9**)

**aceite, el** oil (**7**)

**acerca de** about (**11**)

**acercar** to approach (**8**)

**acierto, el** match (**11**)

**acompañar** to accompany (**6**)

**acordarse (o, ue) de** to remember (**8**)

**acostarse (o, ue)** to go to bed (**8**)

**actor, el** actor (**5**)

**actriz, la** actress (**5**)

**además de** furthermore; in addition to (**2**, **7**)

**Adiós.** Good-bye. (**PA**)

**adivinar** to guess (**7**)

**adjetivos, los** adjectives (**1**)

**administración de empresas, la** business (**2**)

**¿Adónde?** To where? (**2**)

**advertir** to warn (**8**)

**aerolínea, la** airline (**10**)

**aeropuerto, el** airport (**10**)

**afeitarse** to shave (**8**)

**aficionado/a, el/la** fan (**5**)

**afuera de** outside of (**11**)

**afueras, las** outskirts (**3**)

**agencia de viajes, la** travel agency (**6**, **10**)

**agente de viajes, el/la** travel agent (**10**)

**agua, el** water; **~ (con hielo)** water (with ice) (**5**, **7**); **~ dulce** fresh water (**5**)

**ahora** now (**PB**)

**aire, el** air (**11**); **~ acondicionado** air conditioning (**10**)

**al horno** baked (**7**)

**al lado (de)** beside; next to (**3**, **11**)

**alborotado/a** stirred up (**11**)

**alcalde, el** mayor (**11**)

**alcaldesa, la** mayor (**11**)

**alebrijes, los** painted wooden animals (**2**)

**alemán/alemana** German (**PA**)

**alfabetización, la** literacy (**8**)

**alfombra, la** rug; carpet (**3**)

**algo** something; anything (**4**, **PB**)

**algodón, el** cotton (**8**)

**alguien** someone (**4**)

**algún** some; any (**4**)

**alguno/a/os/as** some; any (**3**, **4**)

**allá** over there (*and potentially not visible*) (**6**)

**allí** there / over there (**4**, **6**)

**almacén, el** department store (**4**)

**almohada, la** pillow (**3**)

**almorzar (ue)** to have lunch (**4**, **7**)

**almuerzo, el** lunch (**7**)

**alpargatas, las** espadrilles (**8**)

**altillo, el** attic (**3**)

**altiplano, el** high plateau (**9**)

**alto/a** tall (**1**)

**aluminio, el** aluminum (**11**)

**amarillo** yellow (**3**)

**ambulante** roving (**4**)

**amenaza, la** threat (**8**)

**amenazada** endangered (**7**)

**amigo/a, el/la** friend (**1**)

**amor, el** love (**4**)

**amueblado/a** furnished (**3**)

**anaranjado** orange (**3**)

**ancho** wide (**7**, **8**)

**andar** to walk (**7**)

**anillo, el** ring (**5**)

**animada** animated (**5**)

**animal, el** animal (**11**); **~ doméstico** domesticated animal; pet (**11**); **~ en peligro de extinción** endangered species (**11**); **~ salvaje** wild animal (**11**)

**año pasado, el** last year (**7**)

**anoche** last night (**7**)

**ante** before (**6**)

**anteayer** the day before yesterday (**7**)

**anterior** previous (**5**)

**antes de** before (time/space) (**11**)

**antiácido, el** antacid (**9**)

**antibiótico, el** antibiotic (**9**)

**antiguo/a** old (**3**)

**antipático/a** unpleasant (**1**)

**anuncio, el** ad (**3**)

**apartamento, el** apartment (**2**)

**apasionado/a** passionate (**5**)

**apéndice, el** appendix (**4**)

**apodo, el** nickname (**5**)

**apoyar** to support (**5**, **PB**, **11**); **~ a un/a candidato/a** to support a candidate (**4**)

**aprender** to learn (**2**)

**aprobado/a** approved (**10**)

**apuntes, los** (*pl.*) notes (**2**)

**aquel/la** that, that one (*way over there/not visible*) (**5**)

**aquellos/as** that, those (*way over there/not visible*); those ones (**5**)

**aquí** here (**6**)

**árbol, el** tree (**11**)

**arbusto, el** bush; shrub (**7**)

**armario, el** armoire; closet; cabinet (**3**)

**arquitectura, la** architecture (**2**)

**arreglar** to straighten up; to fix (**3**); **~se** to get ready (**8**); **~ la maleta** to pack a suitcase (**10**)

**arroz, el** rice (**7**)

**arte, el** art (**2**)

**artículo, el** article (**1**); **~ definido** definite article (**1**); **~ indefinido** indefinite article (**1**)

**artista, el/la** artist (**5**)
**asado/a** roasted; grilled (**7**)
**áspero/a** rough (**11**)
**aspirina, la** aspirin (**9**)
**asunto, el** matter (**6**)
**asustado/a** frightened (**7**)
**asustar** to scare (**9**)
**atender** to wait on (**9**)
**aterredor/a** frightening (**9**)
**atletismo, el** track and field (**2**)
**atrevido/a** daring (**8**)
**atún, el** tuna (**7**)
**aumentar** to grow (**11**)
**autobús, el** bus (**10**)
**autopista, la** highway; freeway (**10**)
**ave, el** bird (**11**)
**averiguar** to find out (**4, PB**)
**aves, las** poultry (**7**)
**avión, el** airplane (**10**)
**ayer** yesterday (**7**)
**ayudante, el/la** assistant (**5**)
**ayudar** to help (**3**); ~ **a las personas mayores/los mayores** to help elderly people (**4**)
**azotar** to whip (**11**)
**azúcar, el** sugar (**7**)
**azul** blue (**3**)

**B**

**bailar** to dance (**2**)
**bajar (de)** to get down (from); to get off (of) (**10**)
**bajo/a** short (**1**)
**balcón, el** balcony (**3**)
**banana, la** banana (**7**)
**bañarse** to bathe (**8**)
**banco, el** bank (**4**)
**bañera, la** bathtub (**3**)
**baño, el** bathroom (**3**)
**bar, el** bar (**4**)
**barato/a** cheap (**7**)
**barco, el** boat (**4, 10, PB**)
**barro negro, el** black clay (**2**)
**Bastante bien.** Just fine. (**PA**)
**basura, la** garbage (**11**)
**bata, la** robe (**8**)
**batata, la** yam (**7**)
**batería, la** drums (**5**)
**baterista, el/la** drummer (**5**)
**baúl, el** trunk (**10**)
**beber** to drink (**7**)
**bebida, la** beverage (**7, PB**)
**beige** beige (**3**)
**bella** beautiful (**4**)
**besito, el** little kiss (**PA**)

**biblioteca, la** library (**2**)
**bicicleta, la** bicycle (**10**)
**bidet, el** bidet (**3**)
**bien: bien cocido/a** well done (**7**); ~ **hecho/a** well cooked (**7**); ~**, gracias.** Fine, thanks. (**PA**)
**bienestar, el** well-being; welfare (**11**)
**biología, la** biology (**2**)
**bistec, el** steak (**7**)
**blanco** white (**3**)
**blusa, la** blouse (**8**)
**boca, la** mouth (**9**)
**boda, la** wedding (**4, 6**)
**boleto, el** ticket (**8, 10**); ~ **de ida y vuelta** round-trip ticket (**10**)
**bolígrafo, el** ballpoint pen (**2**)
**bolso, el** purse (**8**)
**bondadoso/a** kind (**11**)
**bonito/a** pretty (**1**)
**borrador, el** eraser (**2**)
**bosque, el** forest (**11**)
**botar** to throw away (**11**)
**botas, las** (*pl.*) boots (**8**)
**botella, la** bottle (**11**)
**botones, el** bellman (**10**)
**brazo, el** arm (**9**)
**broma, la** joke (**3, 8**)
**buceo, el** scuba diving (**4**)
**¡Buen provecho!** Enjoy your meal! (**7**)
**bueno/a** good (**1, 10**)
**Buenos días.** Good morning. (**PA**)
**Buenas noches.** Good evening. (**PA**)
**Buenas tardes.** Good afternoon. (**PA**)
**bufanda, la** scarf (**9**)
**bullicio, el** hubbub (**4**)
**buscar** to look for (**4**)

**C**

**caballo, el** horse (**11**)
**cabeza, la** head (**9**)
**cada** each (**3**)
**cadena, la** chain (**3**)
**caer(se)** to fall down (**9**)
**café, el** café (**4, 7**)
**cafetería, la** cafeteria (**2**)
**caja, la (de cartón)** (cardboard) box (**11**)
**cajero automático, el** ATM (**4**)
**calcetines, los** (*pl.*) socks (**8**)
**calculadora, la** calculator (**2**)
**calefacción, la** heat (**10**)
**calidad, la** quality (**11**)

**caliente** hot (temperature) (**7**)
**callarse** to get / keep quiet (**8**)
**calle, la** street (**3, 10**)
**cama, la** bed (**3**)
**camarero/a, el/la** waiter/waitress (**7**); housekeeper (**10**)
**camarones, los** (*pl.*) shrimp (**7**)
**cambiar** to change (**10**)
**caminar** to walk (**2**); to walk; to go on foot (**10**)
**camión, el** truck (**10**)
**camisa, la** T-shirt (**5**); shirt (**8**)
**camiseta, la** T-shirt (**8**)
**campamento de niños, el** summer camp (**4**)
**campaña, la** campaign (**11**)
**campo, el** country (**3**)
**canadiense** Canadian (**PA**)
**candidato/a, el/la** candidate (**11**)
**cansado/a** tired (**2**)
**cantante, el/la** singer (**5**)
**capa de ozono, la** ozone layer (**11**)
**capítulo, el** chapter (**5**)
**cara, la** face (**9**)
**cargos, los** posts (**11**)
**carne, la** meat (**7**); ~ **de cerdo** pork (**7**)
**caro/a** expensive (**4, 7**)
**carro, el** car (**10**)
**casa, la** house (**3**)
**casado/a** married (**1**)
**cascada, la** waterfall (**10**)
**castillo, el** castle (**3**)
**catarro, el** cold (**9**)
**catorce** fourteen (**PA**)
**cebolla, la** onion (**7**)
**cena, la** dinner (**7**)
**cenar** to have dinner (**7**)
**centro, el** downtown (**4**); ~ **comercial** mall; business/ shopping district (**4**); ~ **estudiantil** student center; student union (**2**)
**cepillarse (el pelo, los dientes)** to brush (one's hair, teeth) (**8**)
**cerca (de)** near (**2, 7, 11**)
**cerdo, el** pig (**11**)
**cereal, el** cereal (**7**)
**cero** zero (**PA**)
**cerrar (ie)** to close (**4**)
**cerveza, la** beer (**7**)
**cestería, la** basket making (**2**)
**chamán, el** shaman (**9**)
**Chao.** Bye. (**PA**)
**chaqueta, la** jacket (**8**)
**chico/a, el/la** boy/girl (**1**)

**chile, el** chili pepper (**7**)
**chino/a** Chinese (**PA**)
**cibercafé, el** Internet café (**4**)
**cielo, el** sky; heaven (**11**)
**cien** one hundred (**2**); ~ **mil** one hundred thousand (**3**); ~ **millones** one hundred million (**3**); ~ **one** hundred (**1**)
**ciencias, las** ( *pl.*) science (**2**)
**Cierre(n) el/los libros/s.** Close your book/s. (**PA**)
**cierto/a** true (**4**)
**cinco** five (**PA**)
**cincuenta** fifty (**1**)
**cine, el** movie theater (**4**)
**cintura, la** waist (**9**); **de la ~ para arriba** from the waist up (**9**)
**cinturón, el** belt (**8**)
**circular una petición** to circulate a petition (**4**)
**cita, la** appointment (**4**, **PB**)
**ciudad, la** city (**3**, **4**)
**claro/a** light (colored) (**8**)
**cliente/a, el/la** customer; client (**7**)
**club, el** club (**4**); ~ **de campo** country club (**4**)
**coche, el** car (**8**, **10**)
**cocido/a** boiled; baked (**7**)
**cocina, la** kitchen (**3**)
**cocinar** to cook (**7**)
**cocinero/a, el/la** chef (**4**, **7**)
**cognado, el** cognate (**PA**)
**cola, la** line (of people) (**10**)
**colcha, la** bedspread; comforter (**3**)
**colgar** to hang up (**7**)
**colibrí, el** hummingbird (**11**)
**color, el** color (**3**)
**combatir** to fight; to combat (**11**)
**comedor, el** dining room (**3**)
**comenzar (ie)** to begin (**4**)
**comer** to eat (**2**)
**cómico/a** funny; comical (**1**)
**comida, la** food; meal (**7**, **PB**)
**¿Cómo?** What? How? (**PA**, **2**); **¿~ está usted?** How are you? (*for.*) (**PA**); **¿~ estás?** How are you? (*fam.*) (**PA**); **¿~ se dice... en español?** How do you say . . . in Spanish? (**PA**); **¿~ se llama usted?** What is your name? (*for.*) (**PA**); **¿~ te llamas?** What is your name? (*fam.*) (**PA**)
**como** like (**5**)
**cómodo/a** comfortable (**8**)
**compañero/a de clase, el/la** classmate (**2**)

**compartir** share (**3**, **5**)
**composición, la** composition (**2**)
**comprar** to buy (**2**)
**comprender** to understand (**2**)
**Comprendo.** I understand. (**PA**)
**computadora, la** computer (**2**)
**con** with (**11**)
**concierto, el** concert (**5**)
**concurso, el** contest (**3**)
**condimento, el** condiment; seasoning (**7**)
**conducción, la** driving (**10**)
**conducir** to drive (**7**, **8**, **10**)
**conejo, el** rabbit (**11**)
**congreso, el** congress (**11**)
**conjunto, el** group; band (**5**); outfit (**8**)
**conmigo** with me (**9**)
**conmovedora** moving (**5**)
**conocer** to be acquainted with (**3**)
**consejo, el** advice (**5**)
**contaminación, la** pollution (**11**)
**contaminar** to pollute (**11**)
**contar** to narrate (**9**)
**contemporáneo/a** contemporary (**3**)
**contento/a** content; happy (**2**)
**contestar** to answer (**2**)
**Conteste(n).** Answer. (**PA**)
**contigo** with you (**9**)
**corazón, el** heart (**9**)
**corbata, la** tie (**8**)
**cordillera, la** mountain range (**11**)
**corregir** to correct (**3**, **10**)
**correo basura, el** spam (**3**)
**correos, el** post office (**4**)
**correr** to run (**2**)
**cortar(se)** to cut (oneself) (**9**)
**corte, la** court (**11**)
**cortejo, el** courting (**7**)
**corto/a** short (**8**)
**cosa, la** thing (**3**)
**cosecha, la** crop (**7**)
**costar (ue)** to cost (**4**)
**costurero/a, el/la** tailor/seamstress (**8**)
**crear** create (**4**)
**creativa** creative (**5**)
**creer** to believe (**2**)
**crucero, el** cruise ship (**5**)
**crudo/a** rare; raw (**7**)
**cuaderno, el** notebook (**2**)
**cuadro, el** picture; painting (**3**, **5**)
**cual** which (**11**)
**¿Cuál?** Which (one)? (**2**); **¿~ es la fecha de hoy?** What is today's date? (**PA**)

**cualquier** whatever (**8**)
**¿Cuándo?** When? (**2**)
**¿Cuánto/a?** How much?, How many? (**2**)
**cuarenta** forty (**1**)
**cuarto, el** room (**2**, **3**); ~ **doble** double room (**10**); ~ **individual** single room (**10**)
**cuarto/a** fourth (**5**)
**cuatro** four (**PA**)
**cuatrocientos** four hundred (**2**)
**cubano/a** Cuban (**PA**)
**cubrir** to cover (**8**)
**cuchara, la** soup spoon; tablespoon (**7**)
**cucharada, la** spoonful (**7**)
**cucharita, la** teaspoon (**7**)
**cuchillo, el** knife (**7**)
**cuello, el** neck (**9**)
**cuenta, la** bill; account (**4**)
**cuero, el** leather (**8**)
**cuerpo humano, el** human body (**9**)
**cuestiones políticas, las** political issues (**11**)
**cueva, la** cave (**11**)
**cuidadoso/a** careful (**5**)
**cuidar** to take care of (**3**, **11**)
**culpable, el/la** guilty (**8**)
**curandero/a, el/la** folk healer (**4**)
**curar(se)** to cure; to be cured (**9**)
**curita, la** adhesive bandage (**9**)
**curso, el** course (**2**)

## D

**dañar** to hurt (**11**)
**dar** to give (**3**); to find (**2**); ~ **un concierto** to give/perform a concert (**5**); ~ **vida** give life (**5**)
**de** of; from; about (**11**); ~ **cuadros** checked (**8**); **¿~ dónde?** From where? (**2**); ~ **la mañana** in the morning (**PA**); ~ **la noche** in the evening (**PA**); ~ **la tarde** in the afternoon (**PA**); ~ **lunares** polka-dotted (**8**); ~ **nada.** You're welcome. (**PA**); **¿~ qué se trata... ?** What is the gist of . . . ? (**8**); ~ **rayas** striped (**8**); ~ **repente** suddenly (**PB**); ~ **suspenso** suspenseful (**5**)
**debajo (de)** under; underneath (**7**, **11**)
**deber, el** obligation; duty (**4**); ~ ought to; should (**4**)
**débil** weak (**1**)

décimo/a tenth (5)
decir to say; to tell (3)
dedo, el (de la mano) finger (9);
  ~ (del pie) toe (9)
defensa, la defense (11)
dejar to leave (10)
delante de in front of (11)
delgado/a thin (1)
delincuencia, la crime (11)
demás, los others (4)
democracia, la democracy (11)
demostrar (ue) to demonstrate (4)
dentro de inside of (11)
deporte, el sport (2)
derecho, el law (2)
derrame de petróleo, el oil spill
  (11)
desaparecer to disappear (5)
desaparecido/a missing (9)
desastre, el disaster (11)
desayunar to have breakfast (7)
desayuno, el breakfast (7)
descansar to rest (7)
desde from (11)
desempleo, el unemployment (11)
desfile de moda, el fashion show (8)
desilusionar to disappoint (9)
desordenado/a messy (3)
despedida, la farewell (PA)
despertador, el alarm clock (2)
despertarse (e, ie) to wake up; to
  awaken (8)
después afterward (6); after (11)
destacar stand out (5); to
  distinguish (7)
destino, el destination (8)
destrucción, la destruction (11)
destruir to destroy (5)
detrás (de) behind (4, 11)
deuda, la (externa) (foreign)
  debt (11)
devolver (ue) to return
  (an object) (4)
día, el day (PA); ~ festivo
  holiday (7)
dibujo, el drawing (3)
dictador/a, el/la dictator (11)
dictadura, la dictatorship (11)
diente, el tooth (9)
diez ten (PA)
difícil difficult (2)
dinero, el money (2)
diputado/a, el/la deputy;
  representative (11)
disco compacto, el (el CD) compact
  disk, CD (2)

discurso, el speech (11)
discutir to discuss (PB)
diseñador/a, el/la designer (8)
disfrutar de enjoy (4, PB)
distraer to distract (5)
divertirse (e, ie) to enjoy oneself; to
  have fun (8)
dividido por divided by (1)
doblar to turn (10)
doce twelve (PA)
doctor/a, el/la doctor (9)
doler (ue) to hurt (9)
dolor, el pain (9)
domingo, el Sunday (PA)
dona, la donut (10)
¿Dónde? Where? (2)
dormir (ue) to sleep (4); ~se (o, ue)
  to fall asleep (8)
dormitorio, el bedroom (3)
dos two (PA)
dos millones two million (3)
doscientos two hundred (2)
ducha, la shower (3)
ducharse to shower (8)
dulce, el candy; sweets (7)
durante during (PB)
durar to last (9, 11)
duro/a hard-boiled (7)
DVD, el (pl. los DVD) DVD/s (2)

**E**

echar una siesta take a nap (PB)
ecología, la ecology (11)
edificio, el building (2)
efecto invernadero, el global
  warming (11)
ejército, el army (5)
él he, him (PA, 11)
el/la/los/las the (1)
elecciones, las elections (11)
elefante, el elephant (11)
elegante elegant (8)
elegir to elect (11)
ella she (PA); her (11)
ellos/as they (PA); them (11)
emanar to emanate (11)
embarazada pregnant (9)
embriaguez, el intoxication (10)
emocionante moving (5)
emociones, las emotions (2)
empanada, la turnover (meat) (7)
empezar (ie) to begin (4)
empleado/a, el/la attendant (12)
empresario/a, el/la agent;
  manager (5)

en in (11); ~ frente de in front of
  (2); ~ vez de instead of (8)
encantar to love; to like very
  much (8)
Encantado/Encantada. Pleased to
  meet you. (PA)
encender to turn on (9)
encerrar (ie) to enclose (4)
encima (de) on top (of ); above
  (3, 7, 11)
encontrar (ue) to find (4)
encubierto/a undercover (11)
encuesta, la survey; poll (11)
endémico/a common (11)
enfermar(se) to get sick (9)
enfermedad illness (9)
enfermero/a, el/la nurse (9)
enfermo/a ill; sick (2)
enfrente (de) in front (of) (4); across
  from; facing (11)
enojado/a angry (2)
ensalada, la salad (7)
ensayar to practice/rehearse (5)
ensayo, el essay (2)
enseñar to teach; to show (2)
entender (ie) to understand (4)
enterar to find out (8, 10)
entonces then (4)
entrada, la ticket (5); ~ gratis free
  ticket (5); ~ entrance (5)
entrar to enter (10); ~ ganas get the
  urge (9)
entre among; between (4, PB, 11)
entregar to turn in (7)
entretenerse to entertain oneself (8)
entretenido/a entertaining (5)
entrevista, la interview (3)
envolver to wrap (7)
épica epic (5)
equipaje, el luggage (10)
equipo, el team (2)
equivocarse to be mistaken (9)
es: ~ la... It's . . . o'clock. (PA);
  ~ necesario que it's necessary
  that (11); ~ una lástima it's a
  shame (11)
escalera, la staircase (3, 11)
esconder to hide (8)
escribir to write (2)
Escriba(n). Write. (PA)
escritorio, el desk (2)
escuchar: escuchar música to listen
  to music (2)
Escuche(n). Listen. (PA)
escuela secundaria, la high
  school (9)

**ese/a** that, that one (**5**)

**esos/as** those over there; those ones (**3**, **5**)

**espalda, la** back (**9**)

**español/española** Spaniard (**PA**)

**espantosa** scary (**5**)

**especialidad, la: ~ de la casa** specialty of the house (**7**); **~es** majors (**2**)

**especias, las** spices (**7**)

**esperar** to wait for; to hope (**2**)

**esposo/a, el/la** husband/wife (**1**)

**Está nublado.** It's cloudy. (**PA**)

**estación, la (de tren, de autobús)** (train, bus) station (**10**); **~** season (**PA**)

**estacionamiento, el** parking (**10**)

**estacionar** to park (**10**)

**estadidad, la** statehood (**11**)

**estadio, el** stadium (**2**)

**estado, el** state (**2**, **9**, **11**)

**estadounidense (norteamericano/a)** American (**PA**)

**estafar** to defraud (**10**)

**estampado/a** print; with a design or pattern (**8**)

**estante, el** bookcase (**3**)

**estar** to be (**2**); **~ de acuerdo** to agree (**4**); **~ en huelga** to be on strike (**11**); **~ enfermo/a** to be sick (**9**); **~ sano/a; saludable** to be healthy (**9**)

**este/a** this, this one (**5**)

**estilo, el** style (**8**)

**esto** this (**3**)

**estómago, el** stomach (**9**)

**estornudar** to sneeze (**9**)

**estornudo, el** sneeze (**9**)

**estos/as** these (**5**)

**estrecho/a** narrow; tight (**8**)

**estrella, la** star (**5**)

**estrenar una película** to release a film/movie (**5**)

**estreno, el** opening (**5**)

**estudiante, el/la** student (**2**)

**estudiar** to study (**2**, **6**)

**estufa, la** stove (**3**)

**estupendo/a** stupendous (**5**)

**evitar** to avoid (**9**, **11**)

**evolucionar** evolve (**5**)

**examen, el** exam (**2**); **~ físico** physical exam (**9**)

**exigente** demanding (**9**)

**experimentar** to experience (**11**)

**expresión, la** expression (**PA**); **~ de cortesía** polite expression (**PA**)

**extranjero, el** abroad (**10**)

**extraño/a** strange (**4**)

## F

**fabada, la** bean stew (**7**)

**fábrica, la** factory (**8**)

**fácil** easy (**2**)

**falda, la** skirt (**8**)

**faltar** to miss (**4**, **PB**)

**fama, la** fame (**5**)

**familia, la** family (**1**)

**farmacéutico/a, el/la** pharmacist (**9**)

**farmacia, la** pharmacy (**9**)

**fascinar** to fascinate (**8**)

**feliz** happy (**2**)

**feo/a** ugly (**1**)

**fiebre, la** fever (**9**)

**fiesta, la** party (**3**)

**fila, la** row (**5**)

**fin de semana, el** weekend (**7**)

**finalmente** finally (**6**)

**finca, la** farm (**11**)

**fino/a** fine; delicate (**5**)

**firma, la** signature (**4**)

**físico/a** physical (**1**)

**floreciente** flourishing (**8**)

**fondos, los** funds (**10**)

**formal** formal (**8**)

**foto, la** photo (**1**)

**francés/francesa** French (**PA**)

**fresco/a** fresh (**7**)

**frijoles, los** (*pl.*) beans (**7**)

**frito/a** fried (**7**)

**fruta, la** fruit (**7**)

**fuente, la** source (**5**, **9**)

**fuera** outside (**7**)

**fuerte** strong (**1**); loud (**3**)

**funcionar** to work; to function (**10**)

## G

**galleta, la** cookie; cracker (**7**)

**gallina, la** chicken, hen (**7**, **11**)

**gallo, el** rooster (**7**)

**ganar** to win (**6**)

**garaje, el** garage (**3**)

**garganta, la** throat (**9**)

**gasolinera, la** gas station (**10**)

**gato, el** cat (**10**, **11**)

**género, el** genre (**5**)

**gente, la** people (**1**)

**gimnasio, el** gymnasium (**2**)

**gira, la** tour (**5**)

**gobernador/a, el/la** governor (**11**)

**gobierno, el** government (**11**)

**gordo/a** fat (**1**)

**gorra, la** cap (**8**)

**grabación, la** recording (**5**)

**grabar** to record (**5**)

**Gracias.** Thank you. (**PA**)

**graduar** to graduate (**11**)

**gramo, el** gram (**7**)

**grande** big; large (**1**, **10**)

**granja, la** farm (**11**)

**gripe, la** flu (**9**)

**gris** gray (**3**)

**gritar** to scream (**8**)

**guantes, los** gloves (**8**)

**guapo/a** handsome/pretty (**1**)

**guardar** to put away; to keep (**3**); **~ cama** to stay in bed (**9**)

**guerra, la** war (**11**)

**guía, la** guide (**5**)

**guitarra, la** guitar (**5**)

**guitarrista, el/la** guitarist (**5**)

**gustar** to like (**PA**)

## H

**habilidad, la** ability; skill (**5**)

**hablar** to speak (**2**)

**hace: ~ buen tiempo.** The weather is nice. (**PA**); **~ calor.** It's hot. (**PA**); **~ frío.** It's cold. (**PA**); **~ mal tiempo.** The weather is bad. (**PA**); **~ sol.** It's sunny. (**PA**); **~ viento.** It's windy. (**PA**)

**hacer** to do; to make (**3**, **9**); **~ artesanía** to make arts and crafts (**4**); **~ daño** to (do) damage; to harm (**11**); **~ ejercicio** to exercise (**2**); **~ falta** to need; to be lacking (**8**); **~ la cama** to make the bed (**3**); **~ mímica** to play charades (**8**); **~ una caminata** to take a walk (**4**); **~ una gira** to tour (**5**); **~ una hoguera** to light a campfire (**4**)

**hamaca, la** hammock (**11**)

**hamburguesa, la** hamburger (**7**)

**hasta** until (**11**); **~ luego.** See you later. (**PA**); **~ mañana.** See you tomorrow. (**PA**); **~ pronto.** See you soon. (**PA**)

**hay** there is; there are (**2**); **~ que + infinitivo** it is necessary . . . / you must . . . / one must/should . . . (**5**)

**helado, el** ice cream; iced (**7**)

**herida, la** wound; injury (**9**)

**hermano/a, el/la** brother/sister (**1**)

**hermanos, los** brothers and sisters; siblings (**1**)

**hervido/a** boiled (**7**)
**hijo/a, el/la** son/daughter (**1**)
**hijos, los** sons and daughters; children (**1**)
**hispanohablante** Spanish-speaking (**3**)
**hojalatería, la** tin work (**2**)
**¡Hola!** Hi! (**PA**)
**hombre, el** man (**1**)
**hora, la** time (**PA**)
**horario, el (de clases)** schedule (of classes) (**2, 6**)
**hormiga, la** ant (**11**)
**hospital, el** hospital (**9**)
**hotel, el** hotel (**10**)
**hoyo, el** hole (**11**)
**huelga, la** strike (**11**)
**huevo, el** egg (**7**)
**humilde** humble (**3**)
**huracán, el** hurricane (**11**)

**I**

**idiomas, los** (*pl.*) languages (**2**)
**iglesia, la** church (**4**)
**Igualmente.** Likewise. (**PA**)
**imaginativo/a** imaginative (**5**)
**impermeable, el** raincoat (**8**)
**importar** to matter; to be important (**8**)
**impresionante** impressive (**5**)
**impuesto, el** tax (**11**)
**incendio, el** fire (**11**)
**incómodo/a** uncomfortable (**8**)
**incumbir** to concern (**8**)
**inflación, la** inflation (**11**)
**influyente** influential (**11**)
**informal** casual (**8**)
**informática, la** computer science (**2**)
**inglés/inglesa** English (**PA**)
**inodoro, el** toilet (**3**)
**insecto, el** insect (**11**)
**inteligente** intelligent (**1**)
**interesante** interesting (**1**)
**interesar** to be interested in (**2**)
**inundación, la** flood (**11**)
**invierno, el** winter (**PA**)
**involucrado/a** involved (**11**)
**inyección, la** shot (**9**)
**ir** to go (**4**); **~ de camping** to go camping (**4**); **~ de compras** to go shopping (**2**); **~ de excursión** to take a short trip (**4**); **~ de vacaciones** to go on vacation (**10**); **~ de viaje** to go on a trip (**10**); **~se del hotel** to leave the hotel; to check out (**10**); **~se** to go away; to leave (**8**)

**J**

**jamás** never; not ever (*emphatic*) (**4,** 11)
**jamón, el** ham (**7**)
**japonés/japonesa** Japanese (**PA**)
**jarabe, el** cough syrup (**9**)
**jardín, el** garden (**3**)
**jazz, el** jazz (**5**)
**jeans, los** (*pl.*) jeans (**8**)
**joven** young; young man/young woman (**1, 10**)
**joya, la** jewel (**9**)
**jueves, el** Thursday (**PA**)
**juez/a, el/la** judge (**11**)
**jugar (ue)** to play (**4**); **~ al básquetbol** to play basketball; **~ al béisbol** to play baseball; **~ al fútbol** to play soccer; **~ al fútbol americano** to play football; **~ al golf** to play golf; **~ al tenis** to play tennis (**2**)
**jugo, el** juice (**7**)
**juicio, el** jury (**11**)

**L**

**La cuenta, por favor.** The check, please. (**7**)
**laboratorio, el** laboratory (**2**)
**lado, el** side (**2**)
**lago, el** lake (**5, 10, 11**)
**lámpara, la** lamp (**3**)
**lana, la** wool (**8**)
**lápiz, el** pencil (**2**)
**largo/a** long (**8**)
**lastimar(se)** to get hurt (**9**)
**lata, la** can (**11**)
**latir** to beat (heart) (**9**)
**lavabo, el** sink (**3**)
**lavaplatos, el** dishwasher (**3**)
**lavar los platos** to wash dishes (**3**); **~se** to wash oneself (**8**)
**le** to/for him, her (**8**)
**Lea(n).** Read. (**PA**)
**leche, la** milk (**7**)
**lechuga, la** lettuce (**7**)
**leer** to read (**2**)
**lejos de** far from (**2, 11**)
**lento/a** slow (**3, 5**)
**león, el** lion (**11**)
**les** to/for them (**8**)
**letra, la** lyrics (**5**)
**levantarse** to get up; to stand up (**8**)
**ley, la** law (**10, 11**)
**leyenda, la** legend (**9**)

**librería, la** bookstore (**2**)
**libro, el** book (**2**)
**licencia, la (de conducir)** driver's license (**10**)
**ligero/a** light (**PB**)
**limón** lemon (**7**)
**limpiaparabrisas, el** windshield wiper (**10**)
**limpiar** to clean (**3**)
**limpio/a** clean (**3**)
**lío, el** mess (**9**)
**liso/a** solid-colored (**8**)
**literatura, la** literature (**2**)
**llamarse** to be called (**8**)
**llanta, la** tire (**10**)
**llave, la** key (**10**)
**llegar** to arrive (**2**)
**llenar** to fill (**10**)
**llevar** to wear; to take; to carry (**8**); **~ a alguien al médico** to take someone to the doctor (**4**); **~ a cabo** to carry out (**11**)
**Llueve.** It's raining. (**PA**)
**lluvia, la** rain (**PA**); **~ ácida** acid rain (**11**)
**Lo sé.** I know. (**PA**)
**lo, la** him, her, it, you (**5**)
**loma, la** hill (**11**)
**loro, el** parrot (**11**)
**los, las** them; you all (**5**)
**lucha libre, la** wrestling (**2**)
**luchar** to fight; to combat (**11**)
**luego** then (**6**)
**lugar, el** place (**2**)
**lugareños, los** locals (*pl.*) (**4**)
**luna de miel, la** honeymoon (**10**)
**lunes, el** Monday (**PA**)

**M**

**madrastra, la** stepmother (**1**)
**madre, la** mother (**1**)
**maíz, el** corn (**7**)
**mal de altura, el** altitude sickness (**9**)
**maleta, la** suitcase (**10**)
**malo/a** bad (**1, 10**)
**malvado/a** evil (**10**)
**mamá, la** mom (**1**)
**mandar una carta** to send/mail a letter (**4**)
**mandato, el** instruction, command (**PA**)
**mandioca, la** yucca (**7**)
**manejar** to drive (**8, 10**)
**manejo, el** management (**7**)
**mano, la** hand (**1, 9**)

**manta, la** blanket (3)
**mantel, el** tablecloth (7)
**mantequilla, la** butter (7)
**manzana, la** apple (7)
**mapa, el** map (2)
**maquillarse** to put on make up (8)
**marcar** to dial (9)
**mariscos, los** seafood (7)
**marrón** brown (3)
**martes, el** Tuesday (PA)
**más** + *adjective/adverb/noun* + **que** more . . . than (10)
**más** plus (1); **~ o menos.** So-so. (PA); **~ tarde que** later than (7); **~ temprano que** earlier than (7)
**mascota, la** domesticated animal; pet (10, 11)
**matar** to kill (11)
**matemáticas, las** (*pl.*) mathematics (2)
**materia, la** subject (2)
**material, el** material (8)
**mayonesa, la** mayonnaise (7)
**mayor** old; older (1); the eldest (10); the largest (5); bigger (10)
**mayordomo, el** butler (10)
**me** me (5); to/for me (8)
**Me llamo...** My name is . . . (PA)
**medianoche, la** midnight (PA)
**medias, las** (*pl.*) stockings; hose (8)
**medicina, la** medicine (2)
**médico/a, el/la** doctor (9)
**medio ambiente, el** environment (11)
**medio** medium (7)
**mediodía, el** noon (PA)
**mejor, el/la** the best (4, 10); better (10); **~(se)** to improve; to get better (9)
**melón, el** melon (7)
**menor** smaller; younger; the smallest; the youngest (10)
**menos** + *adjective/adverb/noun* + **que** less . . . than (10)
**menos** minus (1)
**mensaje, el** message (3)
**mentir (ie)** to lie (4)
**mentira, la** lie (5, 7)
**menú, el** menu (7)
**mercado, el** market (4)
**merendar** to have a snack (7)
**merienda, la** snack (7)
**mermelada, la** jam; marmalade (7)
**mes, el** month (PA)
**mesa, la** table (2)
**meterse en política** to get involved in politics (11)
**metro, el** subway (10)

**mexicano/a** Mexican (PA)
**mezcla, la** mixture (7)
**mí** me (11)
**mi, mis** my (1)
**microondas, el** microwave (3)
**mientras** while (2)
**miércoles, el** Wednesday (PA)
**mil** one thousand (2)
**milla, la** mile (PB)
**millón** one million (3)
**mío/a/os/as** mine (10)
**mirar** to look at (1)
**mochila, la** bookbag; knapsack (2)
**moda, la** fashion (8)
**modelo, el/la** model (8)
**moderno/a** modern (3)
**molestar** to bother (8)
**monarquía, la** monarchy (11)
**montaña, la** mountain (10, 11)
**montañoso/a** mountainous (4)
**montar: ~ (a caballo)** to ride a horse (11); **~ en bicicleta** to ride a bike (2); **~ una tienda de campaña** to put up a tent (4)
**montón, el** pile (7)
**morado** purple (3)
**morir (ue)** to die (4)
**mosca, la** fly (11)
**mosquito, el** mosquito (11)
**mostaza, la** mustard (7)
**mostrar (ue)** to show (4)
**moto(cicleta), la** motorcycle (1, 10)
**motor, el** motor; engine (10)
**muchacho/a, el/la** boy/girl (1)
**Mucho gusto.** Nice to meet you. (PA)
**mueble, el** piece of furniture (3)
**muebles, los** furniture (*pl.*) (3)
**muerto/a** dead (11)
**mujer, la** woman (1)
**multa, la** traffic ticket; fine (10)
**museo, el** museum (4)
**música, la** music (2); **~ clásica** classical music (5); **~ folklórica** folk music (5); **~ popular** pop music (5); **~ rap** rap music (5)
**musical** musical (5)
**músico/a, el/la** musician (5)
**muy** very (1)
**Muy bien.** Really well. (PA)

## N

**nacionalidad, la** nationality (PA)
**nada** nothing (4)
**nadar** to swim (2)

**nadie** no one; nobody (4)
**naranja, la** orange (7)
**nariz, la** nose (9)
**narrar** to narrate (6)
**naturaleza, la** nature (11)
**náusea, la** nausea (9)
**necesitar** to need (2)
**negocio, el** business (8)
**negro** black (3)
**nervioso/a** upset; nervous (2)
**ni... ni** neither . . . nor (4)
**ni** nor (3)
**nieto/a, el/la** grandson/granddaughter (1)
**nieve, la** snow (PA)
**nigeriano/a** Nigerian (PA)
**ningún** none (4)
**ninguno/a/os/as** none (3, 4)
**niño/a, el/la** little boy/little girl (1)
**no: ~ comprendo.** I don't understand. (PA); **~ lo sé.** I don't know. (PA); **~.** No. (PA)
**noreste, el** northeast (2)
**nos** us (5); to/for us (8)
**nosotros/as** us (PA); we (11)
**novecientos** nine hundred (2)
**noveno/a** ninth (5)
**noventa** ninety (1)
**novio/a, el/la** boyfriend/girlfriend (1)
**nube, la** cloud (PA)
**nuestro/a/os/as** our/s (1, 10)
**nueve** nine (1)
**nuevo/a** new (3)
**número, el** number (PA); **~ ordinal** ordinal number (5)
**nunca** never (2, 3, 4)

## O

**o... o** either . . . or (4)
**objeto, el** object (3)
**obtener** to get (10)
**océano, el** ocean (11)
**ochenta** eighty (1)
**ocho** eight (PA)
**ochocientos** eight hundred (2)
**octavo/a** eighth (5)
**ocurrir** to occur (9)
**oeste, el** west (2)
**oferta, la** offer (3)
**oficina, la** office (3); **~ de correos** post office (4)
**ofrecer** offer (2)
**oído, el** inner ear (9)
**oír** to hear (3)
**ojalá que** let's hope (11)

**A31**

ojear las vitrinas to window shop (8)
ojo, el eye (9)
once eleven (PA)
ópera, la opera (5)
oreja ear (9)
organizar to organize (4)
orgulloso/a proud (4)
orquesta, la orchestra (5)
os to/for you all (5, 8)
oscuro/a dark (8)
oso, el bear (11)
otoño, el fall (PA)
otro/a another (PA)

**P**

paciente, el/la patient (1)
padrastro, el stepfather (1)
padre, el father (1)
padres, los parents (1)
pagar to pay (7)
paisaje, el countryside (3)
pájaro, el bird (11)
palabra, la word (PA)
pan, el bread (7)
pantalla, la screen (5)
pantalones, los (pl.) pants (8);
    ~ cortos (pl.) shorts (8)
papá, el dad (1)
papa, la potato (7)
papas fritas, las (pl.) french fries;
    potato chips (7)
papel, el paper (2)
paquete, el package (10)
para for (PB); in order to (11)
parabrisas, el windshield (10)
parada, la bus stop (10)
paraguas, el umbrella (8)
pararse to stand (10)
parecer seem (4)
pared, la wall (2)
parientes, los relatives (pl.) (2)
parque, el park (4); ~ de atracciones
    theme park (10)
parrillada, la mixed grill (7)
participar en una campaña política
    to participate in a political
    campaign (4)
partido político, el political party
    (11)
pasajero, el passenger (10)
pasaporte, el passport (10)
pasar: ~ to happen (PB); ~ la
    aspiradora to vacuum (3)
pasatiempos, los pastimes (2)
pastel, el pastry; pie (7)

pastilla, la pill (9)
pata, la leg (of an animal) (9)
patata, la potato (7)
patinar to skate (2)
paz, la peace (5)
peatón, el pedestrian (10)
pecho, el chest (9)
pedagogía, la education (2)
pedido, el request (9)
pedir (i) to ask for (4); to order (7)
peinarse to comb one's hair (8)
película, la film (4, 5); ~ de acción
    action movie (5); ~ de ciencia
    ficción science fiction movie (5);
    ~ documental documentary (5);
    ~ dramática drama (5); ~ de
    guerra war movie (5); ~ de humor
    funny movie; comedy (5); ~ de
    misterio mystery movie (5); ~
    musical musical (5); ~ romántica
    romantic movie (5); ~ de terror
    horror movie (5)
peligro, el danger (11)
peligroso/a dangerous (8, 11)
pelo, el hair (9)
pelota, la ball (2)
pensar (ie) to think (4)
peor worse, the worst (4, 10)
pequeño/a small (1, 10)
pera, la pear (7)
perder (ie) to lose; to waste (4)
perdido/a lost (4)
perezoso/a lazy (1)
periódico, el newspaper (11)
periodismo, el journalism (2)
pero but (2)
perro: ~ dog (3, 11); ~ caliente hot
    dog (7)
perseguir (i) to chase (4)
personalidad, la personality (1)
pertenecer to belong (9)
pesadilla, la nightmare (8)
pescado, el fish (7)
pésimo/a heavy; depressing (5)
peso corporal, el body weight (9)
pez, el (pl., los peces) fish (11)
pianista el/la pianist (5)
piano, el piano (5)
picante spicy (7)
pie, el foot (8, 9)
pierna, la leg (9)
pijama, el pajamas (8)
pimienta, la pepper (7)
pintar to dye (9)
piso, el floor; story (3)
pista, la clue (5, 7)

pizarra, la chalkboard (2)
placer, el pleasure (7)
planeta, el planet (11)
planta baja, la ground floor (3)
plantar to plant (11)
plástico, el plastic (11)
plato, el plate; dish (7)
playa, la beach (10)
plaza, la town square (4)
pobre poor (1)
poco (un) (a) little (1); ~ hecho/a
    rare (7)
poder to be able to (3)
policía, el policeman (10)
poliéster, el polyester (8)
política, la politics (11)
pollo, el chicken (7)
poner to put; to place (3); ~ la mesa
    to set the table (3); ~se (la ropa)
    to put on (one's clothes) (8); ~se
    (nervioso/a) to get (nervous) (8)
por times; by (1); ~ for; through; by;
    because of (11); ~ favor. Please.
    (PA); ~ lo menos at least (3);
    ~ ciento percent (1); ¿~ qué?
    Why? (2)
portarse to behave (8)
postre, el dessert (7)
preferir (ie) to prefer (4)
preguntar to ask (a question) (2)
prenda, la article of clothing (8)
preocupado/a worried (2)
preocuparse (por) to worry about;
    to concern (11)
preparar to prepare; to get ready (2);
    ~ la comida to prepare a meal (3)
preparativo preparation (5)
presentación, la introduction (PA)
presentar una película to show a
    film/movie (5)
presentarlo to introduce (3)
presidencia, la presidency (11)
presidente/a, el/la president (11)
prestar to loan; to lend (8)
presupuesto, el budget (8)
primavera, la spring (PA)
primer first (5); ~ piso second
    floor (3)
primero/a first (5)
primo/a, el/la cousin (1)
primos, los cousins (1)
principio, el start (8)
probarse (o, ue) la ropa to try on
    clothing (8)
profesor/a, el/la professor (2)
programa, el platform (11)

A32

**promedio, el** average (7)
**propina, la** tip (7)
**propio/a** own (6)
**proponer** propose (5)
**próposito, el** purpose (7)
**proteger** to protect (11)
**provincia, la** province (11)
**prueba, la** proof (10)
**psicología, la** psychology (2)
**pueblo, el** town; village (4)
**puerta, la** door (2)
**puertorriqueño/a** Puerto Rican (PA)
**puro/a** pure (11)

## Q

**que** what (3)
**¿Qué?** What? (2); **¿~ día es hoy?**
  What day is today? (PA); **¿~ es
  esto?** What is this? (PA);
  **¿~ hora es?** What time is it?
  (PA); **¿ ~ significa?** What does
  it mean? (PA); **¿~ tal?** How's it
  going? (PA); **¿~ tiempo hace?**
  What's the weather like? (PA)
**quedar** to stay (11)
**quedarle bien / mal** to fit well /
  poorly (8)
**quedarse** to stay; to remain (8)
**quehaceres, los** (*pl.*) chores (3)
**quemar(se)** to burn; to get
  burned (9)
**querer** to want; to love (2, 3)
**queso, el** cheese (7)
**¿Quién/es?** Who? (PA, 2)
**quiero: ~ presentarle a...** I would
  like to introduce you to . . . (*for.*)
  (PA); **~ presentarte a...** I would
  like to introduce you to . . . (*fam.*)
  (PA)
**quince** fifteen (PA)
**quinientos** five hundred (2)
**quinto/a** fifth (5)
**quitarse (la ropa)** to take off (one's
  clothes) (8)

## R

**radio, el/la** radio (2)
**rana, la** frog (11)
**rasgo, el** characteristic (1)
**rata, la** rat (11)
**ratón, el** mouse (11)
**realizar** to act out (7)
**rebozo, el** poncho (8)
**recepción, la** front desk (10)

**receta, la** prescription (9)
**recetar** to prescribe (9)
**recibir** to receive (2)
**reciclar** to recycle (11)
**recomendar (ie)** to recommend (4)
**reconocer** to recognize (8)
**recordar (ue)** to remember (4)
**recuerdo, el** memento (3);
  memory (7)
**recurso natural, el** natural
  resource (11)
**reforestar** to reforest (11)
**refresco, el** soft drink (7)
**refrigerador, el** refrigerator (3)
**regalo, el** gift (8)
**regatear** to bargain (7)
**regímenes, los** regimes (11)
**región, la** region (11)
**registrarse (en el hotel)** to check
  in (10)
**regresar** to return (2)
**Regular.** Okay. (PA)
**reina, la** queen (11)
**reírse** to laugh (4)
**reloj, el** clock; watch (2)
**remedio casero, el** home-made
  remedy (7)
**repartir comidas** to hand out/deliver
  food (4)
**repetir (i)** to repeat (4)
**Repita(n).** Repeat. (PA)
**reportaje, el** report (12)
**reproductor de CD/DVD, el** CD/
  DVD player (2)
**requerir** to require (11)
**reseña, la** review (PB, 5)
**reserva, la** reservation (10)
**reservar una mesa** to reserve a
  table (7)
**resfriado, el** cold (9)
**residencia, la** dorm (2); **~
  estudiantil** dormitory (2)
**resolver (o, ue)** to resolve (11)
**respetar** to respect (5)
**responsable** responsible (1)
**restaurante, el** restaurant (4, 7)
**resumir** to summarize (9)
**reunirse** to get together; to meet (8)
**reutilizar** to reuse (11)
**revisar** to check; to overhaul (10)
**revista, la** magazine (8)
**rey, el** king (11)
**rico/a** rich (1)
**riesgo, el** risk (9)
**río, el** river (11)
**ritmo, el** rhythm (5)

**rock, el** rock (5)
**rojo** red (3)
**rompecabeza, el** riddle (7)
**romper(se)** to break (9)
**ropa, la** clothes; clothing (3, 8);
  **~ interior** underwear (8)
**rosado** pink (3)
**roto** broken (9)
**ruido, el** noise (3, PB, 10)

## S

**sábado, el** Saturday (PA)
**sábana, la** sheet (3)
**saber** to know (4)
**sacar: ~ la basura** to take out the
  garbage (3); **~ la licencia** to get a
  driver's license (10); **~ un CD** to
  release a CD (5)
**sacudir los muebles** to dust (3)
**sal, la** salt (7)
**sala, la: ~ de clase** classroom (2);
  **~ de urgencias** emergency room
  (9); **~** living room (3)
**salir** to leave; to go out (3)
**salsa, la** salsa (5); **~ de tomate**
  ketchup (7)
**salud, la** health (9)
**saludo, el** greeting (PA)
**salvar** to save (9)
**sano/a** healthy (9)
**sandalia, la** sandal (8)
**sangre, la** blood (9)
**secarse** to dry off (8)
**seda, la** silk (8)
**sede, la** seat (of government) (9)
**seguir (i)** to follow; to continue
  (doing something) (4)
**según** according to (3, 11)
**segundo/a** second (5)
**segundo piso, el** third floor (3)
**seguridad, la** security (2)
**seguro médico, el** health insurance
  (9)
**seis** six (PA)
**seiscientos** six hundred (2)
**sello, el** postage stamp (10)
**selva, la** jungle (11); **~ tropical**
  jungle; (tropical) rain forest (11)
**semáforo, el** traffic light (10)
**semana, la** week (PA); **~ pasada** last
  week (7)
**sembrar (e, ie)** to sow (11)
**semejanza, la** similarity (6)
**semestre, el** semester (2)
**senado, el** senate (11)

A33

**senador/a, el/la** senator (**11**)
**señor, el (Sr.)** man; gentleman; Mr. (**1**)
**señora, la (Sra.)** woman; lady; Mrs. (**1**)
**señorita, la (Srta.)** young woman; Miss (**1**)
**sentarse (e, ie)** to sit down (**8**)
**sentido, el** meaning (**3**)
**sentir** to feel (**PB**); **~se (e, ie)** to feel (**8**)
**séptimo/a** seventh (**5**)
**ser** to be (**PA**); **~ alérgico/a (a)** to be allergic (to) (**9**)
**serpiente, la** snake (**11**)
**servilleta, la** napkin (**7**)
**servir (i)** to serve (**4**)
**sesenta** sixty (**1**)
**setecientos** seven hundred (**2**)
**setenta** seventy (**1**)
**sexto/a** sixth (**5**)
**si** if (**4**)
**Sí.** Yes. (**PA**)
**siempre** always (**3, 4**)
**siete** seven (**PA**)
**siglo, el** century (**3**)
**siguiente, el** following (**3**)
**silla, la** chair (**2**)
**sillón, el** armchair (**3**)
**simpático/a** nice (**1**)
**sin embargo** nevertheless (**2, 3, 6**)
**sin** without (**4, PB, 11**)
**sobre** on; on top (of ); over (**3, 4, 11**); **~ todo** above all (**5**)
**sofá, el** sofa (**3**)
**sol, el** sun (**PA**)
**solamente** only (**8**)
**solicitud, la** application (**2**)
**solo** alone (**9**)
**sombrero, el** hat (**8**)
**son** equals (**1**)
**sopa, la** soup (**7**)
**sorprendente** surprising (**5**)
**sorpresa, la** surprise (**8**)
**sospechoso/a** suspicious (**2**)
**sótano, el** basement (**3**)
**Soy...** I am . . . (**PA**)
**su/s** his, her, its, your, their (**1**)
**suave** smooth (**5**)
**subir (a)** to go up; to get on (**10**)
**subrayar** to underline (**7**)
**sucio/a** dirty (**3**)
**sudadera, la** sweatshirt (**8**)
**suelo, el** floor (**3**)
**suéter, el** sweater (**8**)
**sunami, el** tsunami (**11**)

**supermercado, el** supermarket (**4**)
**surgir** to emerge (**8**)
**suspiro, el** sigh (**11**)
**suyo/a/os/as** his, her/s, your/s (*for.*), their/s (**PB, 3, 10**)

## T

**tal vez** perhaps (**3**)
**taller mecánico, el** auto repair shop (**10**)
**también** too; also (**2**)
**tambor, el** drum (**5**)
**tamborista, el/la** drummer (**5**)
**tampoco** nor (**7**)
**tan** such (**2**)
**tan... como** as . . . as (**1**)
**tanque, el** gas tank (**10**)
**tanto** many (**2**); so much (**9**)
**tarde** late (**3**)
**tarea, la** homework (**2**)
**tarjeta, la: ~ de crédito** credit card (**7**); **~ de débito** debit card (**7**); **~ postal** postcard (**4, 10**)
**taxi, el** taxi (**10**)
**taza, la** cup (**7**)
**te** to/for you (**5, 8**)
**té, el (helado / caliente)** tea (iced / hot) (**7**)
**teatro, el** theater (**4**)
**techo, el** roof (**3**)
**tela, la** fabric (**8**)
**televisión, la** television (**2**)
**tema, el** topic; gist (**5**)
**temperatura, la** temperature (**PA**)
**templo, el** temple (**4**)
**temprano** early (**3**)
**tenedor, el** fork (**7**)
**tener** to have (**1**); **~ alergia (a)** to be allergic (to) (**9**); **~ ... años** to be . . . years old (**3**); **~ calor** to be hot (**3**); **~ cuidado** to be careful (**3**); **~ dolor de cabeza** to have a headache (**9**); **~ dolor de estómago** to have a stomachache (**9**); **~ dolor de espalda** to have a backache (**9**); **~ éxito** to be successful (**3**); **~ frío** to be cold (**3**); **~ ganas de + (infinitive)** to feel like + (verb) (**3**); **~ hambre** to be hungry (**3**); **~ (la/una) gripe** to have the flu (**9**); **~ miedo** to be afraid (**3**); **~ prisa** to be in a hurry (**3**); **~ que + (infinitive)** to have to + (verb) (**3**); **~ razón** to be right (**3**); **~ resfriado** to have a cold (**9**);

**~ sed** to be thirsty (**3**); **~ sueño** to be sleepy (**3**); **~ suerte** to be lucky (**3**); **~ tos** to have a cough (**9**); **~ (un) catarro** to have a cold (**9**); **~ un virus** to have a virus (**9**); **~ una infección** to have an infection (**9**); **~ vergüenza** to be embarrassed (**3**)
**tenis, los** (*pl.*) tennis shoes (**8**)
**tercer, el: ~ piso** fourth floor (**3**)
**tercero/a** third (**5**)
**terminar** to finish; to end (**2**)
**terremoto, el** earthquake (**5, 11**)
**tesoro, el** treasure (**10**)
**ti** you (**11**)
**tiburón, el** shark (**5**)
**tienda, la** store (**2**)
**tierra, la** land; soil (**11**)
**Tierra, la** Earth (**11**)
**tío/a, el/la** uncle/aunt (**1**)
**tíos, los** aunts and uncles (**1**)
**tirar** to throw (**9**)
**tiza, la** chalk (**2**)
**tocador, el** dresser (**3**)
**tocar** touch (**4**); **~** to play (a musical instrument) (**2, 5**)
**todavía** still (**4**)
**tomar** to take; to drink (**2**); **~ el sol** to sunbathe (**2**)
**tomate, el** tomato (**7**)
**tonto/a** silly; dumb (**1**)
**tormenta, la** storm (**11**)
**tornado, el** tornado (**11**)
**torneo, el** tournament (**4**)
**toro, el** bull (**11**)
**torre, la** tower (**3**)
**torta, la** cake (**7**)
**tos, la** cough (**9**)
**toser** to cough (**9**)
**tostada, la** toast (**7**)
**trabajador/a** hard-working (**1**)
**trabajar** to work (**2**); **~ como consejero/a** to work as a counselor (**4**); **~ como voluntario/a en la residencia de ancianos** to volunteer at a nursing home (**4**); **~ en política** to work in politics (**4**)
**trabajo en prácticas, el** internship (**8**)
**tradicional** traditional (**3**)
**traer** to bring (**3**)
**tráfico, el** traffic (**10**)
**tragedia, la** tragedy (**11**)
**trágico/a** tragic (**5**)
**traje, el** suit (**8**); outfit (**5**); **~ de baño** swimsuit; bathing suit (**8**)
**transitar** to enter/exit (**10**)

A34

**transporte, el** transportation (**10**)
**tratamiento médico, el** medical treatment (**9**)
**tratar de** to try to (**3**, **9**); to treat (**9**)
**trece** thirteen (**PA**)
**treinta** thirty (**PA**)
**tren, el** train (**10**)
**tres** three (**PA**)
**trescientos** three hundred (**2**)
**triste** sad (**2**)
**trompeta, la** trumpet (**5**)
**trompetista, el/la** trumpet player (**5**)
**tú** you (*fam.*) (**PA**)
**tu, tus** your (**1**)
**turnarse** to take turns (**3**)
**tuyo/a/os/as** yours (*fam.*) (**3**, **10**)

## U

**un/una/unos/unas** a, an, some (**1**)
**uno** one (**PA**)
**usar** to use (**2**, **4**, **PB**)
**uso adecuado, el** suitable use (**10**)
**usted/es** you (*for.*) (**PA**, **11**)
**útil** useful (**PA**)

## V

**vaca, la** cow (**11**)
**vacaciones, las** vacation (**10**)
**vaso, el** glass (**7**)
**Vaya(n) a la pizarra.** Go to the board. (**PA**)
**vehículo, el** vehicle (**10**)
**veinte** twenty (**PA**)
**venda, la** bandage (**9**)
**vendaje, el** bandage (**9**)
**vendar(se)** to bandage (oneself); to dress (a wound) (**9**)
**venir** to come (**3**)
**ventana, la** window (**2**)
**ver** to see (**3**); **~ la televisión** to watch television (**2**)
**verano, el** summer (**PA**)
**verbo, el** verb (**1**, **2**)
**verde** green (**3**)
**verdura, la** vegetable (**7**)
**vertedero, el** dump (**11**)
**vestido, el** dress (**8**)
**vestirse (e, i)** to get dressed (**8**)
**vez, la** time (**5**)
**viajar** to travel (**10**); **~ en canoa** to canoe (**4**)
**viaje, el** trip (**10**)
**viajero/a, el/la** traveler (**10**)
**vidrio, el** glass (**11**)
**viejo/a** old (**3**, **10**)
**viento, el** wind (**PA**)
**viernes, el** Friday (**PA**)
**vinagre, el** vinegar (**7**)

**vino, el** wine (**7**)
**visitar** to visit (**10**)
**vivir** to live (**2**)
**vivo/a** alive; living (**11**)
**volante, el** steering wheel (**10**)
**volar (o, ue)** to fly; to fly away (**10**)
**voluntariado, el** volunteerism (**4**)
**volver (ue)** to return (**4**); **~ loco/a** to drive him/her crazy (**12**)
**vosotros/as** you (*fam. pl. Spain*) (**PA**, **11**)
**votar** to vote (**11**)
**voto, el** vote (**11**)
**voz, la** voice (**5**)
**vuelo, el** flight (**10**)
**vuestro/a/os/as** your/s (*fam. pl. Spain*) (**1**, **10**)

## Y

**y: ¿~ tú?** And you? (*fam.*) (**PA**); **¿~ usted?** And you? (*for.*) (**PA**)
**ya** already (**4**); **~ no** no longer (**5**); **~ que** since (**1**)
**yo** I (**PA**)

## Z

**zapatillas, las** (*pl.*) slippers (**8**)
**zapatos, los** (*pl.*) shoes (**8**)

# Appendix 5

## English-Spanish Glossary

### A

a un/una/unos/unas (1)
ability la habilidad (5)
able to, to be poder (3)
about acerca de (11); sobre (4, 11)
above all sobre todo (5)
abroad el extranjero (10)
aburrida boring (5)
accompany, to acompañar (6)
according to según (3, 11)
account la cuenta (4)
acid rain la lluvia ácida (11)
acquainted with, to be conocer (3)
across from enfrente de (11)
act out, to realizar (7)
actor el actor (5)
actress la actriz (5)
ad el anuncio (3)
adjectives los adjetivos (1)
administration la administración (11)
advice el consejo (5)
afraid, to be tener miedo (3)
after después de (11)
afterward después (6)
agent el/la empresario/a (5)
agree, to estar de acuerdo (4)
air el aire (11); ~ conditioning el aire acondicionado (10)
airline la aerolínea (10)
airplane el avión (10)
airport el aeropuerto (10)
alarm clock el despertador (2)
alive vivo/a (11)
allergic (to), to be tener alergia (a) (9)
alone solo (9)
already ya (4)
also también (2)
altitude sickness el mal de altura (9)
aluminum el aluminio (11)
always siempre (3, 4)
American estadounidense (norteamericano/a) (PA)
among entre (11)
an un/una/unos/unas (1)
And you? ¿Y tú? (fam.) (PA); And you? ¿Y usted? (for.) (PA)
angry enojado/a (2)
animal animal (11)

animated animado/a (5)
another otro/a
answer, to contestar (2); ~. Conteste(n). (PA)
ant la hormiga (11)
antacid el antiácido (9)
antibiotic el antibiótico (9)
any algún; alguno/a/os/as (4)
anything algo (4)
apartment el apartamento (2)
appendix el apéndice (4)
apple la manzana (7)
application la solicitud (2)
appointment la cita (4)
approach, to acercar (8)
approved aprobado/a (10)
architecture la arquitectura (2)
arm el brazo (9)
armchair el sillón (3)
armoire el armario (3)
army el ejército (5)
around a eso de (7)
arrive, to llegar (2)
art el arte (2)
article el artículo (1); definite ~ el artículo definido (1); indefinite ~ el artículo indefinido (1)
articles of clothing las prendas (8)
artist el/la artista (5)
as . . . as tan... como (1)
ask (a question), to preguntar (2); to ~ for pedir (i) (4)
aspirin la aspirina (9)
assistant la ayudante (5)
at least por lo menos (3)
At what time . . . ? ¿A qué hora... ? (PA)
ATM el cajero automático (4)
attendant el/la empleado/a (12)
attic el altillo (3)
aunt la tía (1)
auto repair shop el taller mecánico (10)
average el promedio (7)
avoid, to evitar (9, 11)
awaken, to despertarse (e, ie) (8)
away, to go irse (8)

### B

back la espalda (9)
bad malo/a (1, 10)
baked al horno; cocido/a (7)
balcony el balcón (3)
ball la pelota (2)
ballpoint pen el bolígrafo (2)
banana la banana (7)
band el conjunto (5)
bandage (adhesive) la curita; el vendaje; la venda (9)
bandage (oneself ), to vendar(se) (9)
bank el banco (4)
bar el bar (4)
bargain, to regatear (7)
basement el sótano (3)
basket making la cestería (2)
bathe, to bañarse (8)
bathroom el baño (3)
bathtub la bañera (3)
be, to estar (2); ser (PA)
beach la playa (10)
beans los frijoles (pl.) (7); ~ stew la fabada (7)
bear el oso (11)
beat (heart), to latir (9)
beautiful bella (4)
because of por (11)
bed la cama (3)
bedroom el dormitorio (3)
bedspread la colcha (3)
beer la cerveza (7)
before ante (6); ~ (time/space) antes de (11)
begin, to comenzar (ie); empezar (ie) (4)
behave, to portarse (8)
behind detrás de (4, 11)
beige beige (3)
believe, to creer (2)
bellman el botones (10)
belong, to pertenecer (9)
belt el cinturón (8)
beside al lado (de) (3)
best el/la mejor (1, 4, 10)
better mejor (10); to get ~ mejorar(se) (9)
between entre (4, 11)
beverage la bebida (PB, 7)

bicycle la bicicleta (**10**)
bidet el bidet (**3**)
big grande (**1, 10**); **bigger** mayor
    (**10**); **biggest** el/la mayor (**10**)
bill la cuenta (**4**)
biology la biología (**2**)
bird el ave; el pájaro (**11**)
black negro (**2, 3**)
blanket la manta (**3**)
blood la sangre (**9**)
blouse la blusa (**8**)
blue azul (**3**)
boat el barco (**4, 10**)
body el cuerpo (**9**); ~ **weight** el peso
    corporal (**9**)
boiled cocido/a; hervido/a (**7**)
book el libro (**2**); ~**bag** la mochila
    (**2**); ~**case** el estante (**3**); ~**store**
    la librería (**2**)
boots las botas (*pl.*) (**8**)
bored (with *estar*) aburrido/a (**2**)
boring aburrido/a (**1**)
bother, to molestar (**8**)
bottle la botella (**11**)
box (*cardboard*) la caja (*de cartón*)
    (**11**)
boy el chico; el muchacho; **little**
    ~ el niño (**1**); ~**friend** el novio (**1**)
bread el pan (**7**)
break, to romper(se) (**9**)
breakfast el desayuno (**7**); **to have**
    ~ desayunar (**7**)
bring, to traer (**3**)
broken roto (**9**)
brother el hermano (**1**)
brown marrón (**3**)
brush, to (*one's hair, teeth*) cepillarse
    (*el pelo, los dientes*) (**8**)
budget el presupuesto (**8**)
building el edificio (**2**)
bull el toro (**11**)
burn, to quemar(se) (**9**)
bus el autobús (**10**); ~ **stop** la
    parada (**10**)
bush el arbusto (**7**)
business el negocio (**8**); ~ la
    administración de empresas (**2**);
    ~ / **shopping district** el centro
    comercial (**4**)
but pero (**2**)
butler el mayordomo (**10**)
butter la mantequilla (**7**)
buy, to comprar (**2**)
by por (**1, 11**)
Bye. Chao. (**PA**)

**C**

cabinet el armario (**3**)
café el café (**4**)
cafeteria la cafetería (**2**)
cake la torta (**7**)
calculator la calculadora (**2**)
called, to be llamarse (**8**)
campaign la campaña (**11**)
can la lata (**11**)
Canadian canadiense (**PA**)
candidate el/la candidato/a (**11**)
candy los dulces (**7**)
canoe, to viajar en canoa (**4**)
cap la gorra (**8**)
car el coche (**8, 10**)
care for cuidar (**3**)
careful cuidadoso/a (**5**); **to be**
    ~ tener cuidado (**3**)
carpet la alfombra (**3**)
carry, to llevar (**8**); **to ~ out** llevar a
    cabo (**11**)
castle el castillo (**3**)
casual informal (**8**)
cat el/la gato/a (**10, 11**)
cave la cueva (**11**)
CD/DVD player el reproductor de
    CD/DVD (**2**)
century el siglo (**3**)
cereal el cereal (**7**)
chain la cadena (**3**)
chair la silla (**2**)
chalk la tiza (**2**); ~**board** la
    pizarra (**2**)
change, to cambiar (**10**)
chapter el capítulo (**5**)
characteristic el rasgo (**1**)
charades, to play hacer mímica (**8**)
chase, to perseguir (i) (**4**)
cheap barato/a (**7**)
check in, to registrarse (en el hotel)
    (**10**); **to ~ out** irse del hotel (**10**)
checked de cuadros (**8**)
cheese el queso (**7**)
chef el/la cocinero/a (**4**)
chest el pecho (**9**)
chicken el pollo (**7**); la gallina (**11**)
children los hijos (**1**)
chili pepper el chile (**7**)
Chinese chino/a (**PA**)
chores los quehaceres (**3**)
church la iglesia (**4**)
circulate a petition, to circular una
    petición (**4**)
city la ciudad (**3, 4**)

classmate el/la compañero/a de
    clase (**2**)
Classroom instructions (*commands*)
    Mandatos para la clase (**PA**)
classroom la sala de clase (**2**)
clay barro (**2**)
clean limpio/a (**3**); **to ~** limpiar (**3**)
client el/la cliente/a (**7**)
clock el reloj (**2**)
Close your book/s. Cierre(n) el/los
    libros/s. (**PA**)
close, to cerrar (ie) (**4**)
closet el armario (**3**)
clothes la ropa (**3**)
clothing la ropa (**3, 8**)
cloud la nube (**PA**)
club el club (**4**)
clue la pista (**5, 7**)
coat el abrigo (**3**)
coffee el café (**7**)
cognate el cognado (**PA**)
cold el catarro; el resfriado (**9**)
cold, to be tener frío (**3**); **to have**
    **a ~** tener (un) catarro; tener
    resfriado (**9**)
color el color (**3**)
comb one's hair, to peinarse (**8**)
combat, to combatir (**11**)
come, to venir (**3**)
comfortable cómodo/a (**8**)
comforter la colcha (**3**)
comical cómico/a (**1**)
common endémico/a (**11**)
compact disk el disco compacto
    (el CD) (**2**)
composition la composición (**2**)
computer la computadora (**2**);
    ~ **science** la informática (**2**)
concern, to incumbir (**8**)
concert el concierto (**5**)
condiment el condimento (**7**)
congress el congreso (**11**)
contemporary contemporáneo/a
    (**3**)
content contento/a (**2**)
contest el concurso (**3**)
continue (*doing something*), **to**
    seguir (i) (**4**)
cook el/la cocinero/a (**7**)
cook, to cocinar (**3, 7**)
cookies las galletas (**7**)
corn el maíz (**7**)
correct, to corregir (**3, 10**)
cost, to costar (ue) (**4**)
cotton el algodón (**8**)

A37

**cough, to** toser (**9**); ~ la tos (**9**); ~ **syrup** el jarabe (**9**); **to have a ~** tener tos (**9**)
**country** el campo (**3**); ~ **club** el club de campo (**4**)
**countryside** el paisaje (**3**)
**course** el curso (**2**)
**court** la corte (**11**)
**courting** el cortejo (**7**)
**cousin** el/la primo/a (**1**)
**cover, to** cubrir (**8**)
**cow** la vaca (**11**)
**crackers** las galletas (**7**)
**create** crear (**4**)
**creative** creativo/a (**5**)
**credit card** la tarjeta de crédito (**7**)
**crime** la delincuencia (**11**)
**crop** la cosecha (**7**)
**cruise ship** el crucero (**5**)
**Cuban** cubano/a (**PA**)
**cup** la taza (**7**)
**cure, to** curar(se) (**9**)
**customer** el/la cliente/a (**7**)
**cut (oneself), to** cortar(se) (**9**)

## D

**dad** el papá (**1**)
**damage, to (do)** hacer daño (**11**)
**dance, to** bailar (**2**)
**danger** el peligro (**11**)
**dangerous** peligroso/a (**8**, **11**)
**daring** atrevido/a (**8**)
**dark** oscuro/a (**8**)
**daughter** la hija (**1**)
**day** el día (**PA**); **the ~ before yesterday** anteayer (**7**)
**dead** muerto/a (**11**)
**debit card** la tarjeta de débito (**7**)
**debt** (*foreign*) la deuda (*externa*) (**11**)
**defense** la defensa (**11**)
**defraud, to** estafar (**10**)
**delicate** fino/a (**5**)
**demanding** exigente (**9**)
**democracy** la democracia (**11**)
**demonstrate, to** demostrar (ue) (**4**)
**department store** el almacén (**4**)
**depressing** pésimo/a (**5**)
**deputy** el/la diputado/a (**11**)
**designer** el/la diseñador/a (**8**)
**desk** el escritorio (**2**)
**dessert** el postre (**7**)
**destination** el destino (**8**)
**destroy, to** destruir (**5**)
**destruction** la destrucción (**11**)
**dial, to** marcar (**9**)

**dictator** el/la dictador/a (**11**); **~ship** la dictadura (**11**)
**die, to** morir (ue) (**4**)
**difficult** difícil (**2**)
**dining room** el comedor (**3**)
**dinner** la cena (**7**); **to have ~** cenar (**7**)
**dirty** sucio/a (**3**)
**disappear, to** desaparecer (**5**)
**disappoint, to** desilusionar (**9**)
**disaster** el desastre (**11**)
**discuss, to** discutir (**PB**)
**dish** el plato (**7**); **~washer** el lavaplatos (**3**)
**distinguish, to** destacar (**7**)
**distract, to** distraer (**5**)
**divided by** dividido por (**1**)
**do, to** hacer (**3**)
**doctor** el/la doctor/a; el/la médico/a (**9**)
**documentary** el documental (**5**)
**dog** el perro (**3**, **11**)
**domesticated animals** los animales domésticos (**11**)
**donut** la dona (**10**)
**door** la puerta (**2**)
**dorm / dormitory** la residencia (**2**)
**double room** el cuarto doble (**10**)
**downtown** el centro (**4**)
**drama** dramático/a (**5**)
**drawing** el dibujo (**3**)
**dress** (*a wound*)**, to** vendar(se) (**9**)
**dress** el vestido (**8**)
**dresser** el tocador (**3**)
**drink, to** tomar (**2**); beber (**7**)
**drive, to** conducir (**7**, **10**); manejar (**8**); **to ~ him/her crazy** volver loco/a (**12**)
**driver's license** la licencia (*de conducir*) (**10**); **to get a ~** sacar la licencia (**10**)
**driving** la conducción (**10**)
**drum** el tambor (**5**)
**drummer** el/la baterista (**5**); el/la tamborista (**5**)
**drums** la batería (**5**)
**dry off, to** secarse (**8**)
**dumb** tonto/a (**1**)
**dump** el vertedero (**11**)
**during** durante (**PB**)
**dust, to** sacudir los muebles (**3**)
**duty** el deber (**4**)
**DVD** el DVD (**2**)
**dye, to** pintar (**9**)

## E

**each** cada (**3**)
**ear** la oreja (**9**); **ear** (*inner*) el oído (**9**)

**earlier than** más temprano que (**7**)
**early** temprano (**3**)
**Earth** la Tierra (**11**)
**earthquake** el terremoto (**5**, **11**)
**easy** fácil (**2**)
**eat, to** comer (**2**)
**ecology** la ecología (**11**)
**education** la pedagogía (**2**)
**egg** el huevo (**7**)
**eight hundred** ochocientos (**2**)
**eight** ocho (**PA**)
**eighteen** diez y ocho (**PA**)
**eighth** octavo/a (**5**)
**eighty** ochenta (**1**)
**either . . . or** o... o (**4**)
**eldest** el/la mayor (**10**)
**elect, to** elegir (**11**)
**elections** las elecciones (**11**)
**elegant** elegante (**8**)
**elephant** el elefante (**11**)
**eleven** once (**PA**)
**emanate, to** emanar (**11**)
**embarrassed, to be** tener vergüenza (**3**)
**emerge, to** surgir (**8**)
**emergency room** la sala de urgencias (**9**)
**emotions** emociones (**2**)
**enclose, to** encerrar (ie) (**4**)
**encompass, to** abarcar (**5**)
**end, to** acabar con (**4**); terminar (**2**)
**endangered** amenazada (**7**); **~ species** los animales en peligro de extinción (**11**)
**engine** el motor (**10**)
**English** inglés/inglesa (**PA**)
**Enjoy your meal!** ¡Buen provecho! (**7**)
**enjoy, to** disfrutar de (**4**); **to ~ oneself** divertirse (e, ie) (**8**)
**enter, to** entrar (**10**)
**enter/exit, to** transitar (**10**)
**entertain oneself, to** entretenerse (**8**)
**entrance** la entrada (**5**)
**entretenida** entertaining (**5**)
**environment** el medio ambiente (**11**)
**epic** épica (**5**)
**equals** son (**1**)
**eraser** el borrador (**2**)
**espadrilles** las alpargatas (**8**)
**essay** el ensayo (**2**)
**ever** jamás (**11**)
**evil** malvado/a (**10**)
**evolve, to** evolucionar (**5**)
**exam** el examen (**2**)
**exercise, to** hacer ejercicio (**2**)
**expensive** caro/a (**4**, **7**)

**experience, to** experimentar (11)
**expression** la expresión (**PA**)
**eye** el ojo (**9**)

**F**

**fabric** la tela (**8**)
**face** la cara (**9**)
**facing** enfrente de (**11**)
**factory** la fábrica (**8**)
**fall:** ~ el otoño (**PA**); **to ~ asleep** dormirse (o, ue) (**8**); **to ~ down** caer(se) (**9**)
**fame** la fama (**5**)
**family** la familia (**1**)
**fan** el/la aficionado/a (**5**)
**far from** lejos de (2, **11**)
**Farewells** Las despedidas (**PA**)
**farm** la finca; la granja (**11**)
**fascinate, to** fascinar (**8**)
**fashion** la moda (**8**); ~ **show** el desfile de moda (**8**)
**fat** gordo/a (**1**)
**father** el padre (**1**)
**feel, to** sentir (**PB**); sentirse (e, ie) (**8**)
**fever** la fiebre (**9**)
**fifteen** quince (**PA**)
**fifth** quinto/a (**5**)
**fifty** cincuenta (**1**)
**fight, to** luchar (**11**)
**fill, to** llenar (**10**)
**film** la película (**4**)
**finally** finalmente (**6**)
**find out, to** averiguar (**PB**, 4); enterar (8); enterarse (10)
**find, to** dar con (2); encontrar (ue) (**4**)
**Fine, thanks.** Bien, gracias. (**PA**)
**fine:** ~ fino/a (**5**); ~ la multa (**10**)
**finger** el dedo (de la mano) (**9**)
**finish, to** terminar (2); **to have just ~ed +** (*something*) acabar de + *infinitivo* (**9**)
**fire** el incendio (**11**)
**first** primer, primero/a (**5**)
**fish** el pez (*pl.*, los peces) (7, **11**)
**fit well / poorly, to** quedarle bien / mal (**8**)
**five** cinco (**PA**); ~ **hundred** quinientos (**2**)
**fix, to** arreglar (**3**)
**flight** el vuelo (**10**)
**flood** la inundación (**11**)
**floor** el piso (**3**); el suelo (**3**)
**flourishing** floreciente (**8**)
**flu** la gripe (**9**); **to have the ~** tener (la/una) gripe (**9**)

**fly** la mosca (**11**)
**fly, to** volar (o, ue); **to ~ away** volar (o, ue) (**10**)
**folk healer** el/la curandero/a (**4**)
**follow, to** seguir (i) (**4**)
**following** el siguiente (3)
**food** la comida (**7**)
**foot** el pie (8, **9**); **to go on ~** ir a pie (**10**)
**for** para (**PB**, 11); por (**11**)
**forest** el bosque (**11**)
**fork** el tenedor (**7**)
**formal** formal (**8**)
**forty** cuarenta (**1**)
**four** cuatro (**PA**); ~ **hundred** cuatrocientos (**2**); ~ **hundred thousand** cuatrocientos mil (3)
**fourteen** catorce (**PA**)
**fourth** cuarto/a (**5**); ~ **floor** el tercer piso (**3**)
**freeway** la autopista (**10**)
**French** francés/francesa (**PA**)
**french fries** las papas fritas (*pl.*) (**7**)
**fresh** fresco/a (**7**)
**Friday** el viernes (**PA**)
**fried** frito/a (**7**)
**friend** el/la amigo/a (**1**)
**frightened** asustado/a (**7**)
**frightening** aterredor (**9**)
**frog** la rana (**11**)
**From where?** ¿De dónde? (2)
**from:** ~ desde (**11**); ~ **time to time** a veces (**2**); ~ **about** de (**11**)
**front:** ~ **desk** la recepción (**10**); **in ~ (of)** enfrente (de) (**4**)
**fruit** las frutas (**7**)
**function, to** funcionar (**10**)
**funds** los fondos (**10**)
**funny** cómico/a (**1**)
**furnished** amueblado/a (**3**)
**furniture** los muebles (**3**); **piece of ~** el mueble (**3**)
**furthermore** además (2)

**G**

**garage** el garaje (**3**)
**garbage** la basura (**11**)
**garden** el jardín (**3**)
**gas:** ~ **station** la gasolinera (**10**); ~ **tank** el tanque (**10**)
**genre** el género (**5**)
**gentleman** el señor (Sr.) (**1**)
**German** alemán/alemana (**PA**)
**get: to ~** obtener (10); **to ~ dressed** vestirse (e, i) (**8**); **to ~ down** (*from*)

bajar (*de*) (**10**); **to ~** (*nervous*) ponerse (*nervioso/a*) (**8**); **to ~ off** (*of*) bajar (*de*) (**10**); **to ~ on** subir (a) (**10**); **to ~ ready** preparar (2), arreglarse (8); **to ~ the urge** entrar ganas (9); **to ~ together** reunirse (8); **to ~ up** levantarse (**8**)
**gift** el regalo (**8**)
**girl** la chica; la muchacha; **little ~** la niña (**1**); **~friend** la novia (**1**)
**gist** el tema (5)
**give, to** dar (**3**); **to ~ life** dar vida (5); **to ~ a concert** dar un concierto (5)
**glass** el vaso (**7**); el vidrio (**11**)
**global warming** el efecto invernadero (**11**)
**gloves** los guantes (**8**)
**go out, to** salir (**3**)
**Go to the board.** Vaya(n) a la pizarra. (**PA**)
**go: to ~** ir (**4**); **to ~ camping** ir de camping (**4**); **to ~ shopping** ir de compras (2); **to ~ to bed** acostarse (o, ue) (**8**); **to ~ up** subir (a) (**10**)
**Good afternoon.** Buenas tardes. (**PA**)
**good** bueno/a (**1, 10**); ~ **-bye.** Adiós. (**PA**); ~ **evening.** Buenas noches. (**PA**); ~ **morning.** Buenos días. (**PA**)
**government** el gobierno (**11**)
**governor** el/la gobernador/a (**11**)
**graduate, to** graduar (11)
**gram** el gramo (**7**)
**granddaughter** la nieta (**1**)
**grandfather** el abuelo (**1**)
**grandmother** la abuela (**1**)
**grandparents** los abuelos (**1**)
**grandson** el nieto
**gray** gris (**3**)
**green** verde (**3**)
**Greetings** Los saludos (**PA**)
**grilled** a la parrilla (**7**); asado/a (**7**)
**ground floor** la planta baja (**3**)
**group** el conjunto (**5**)
**grow, to** aumentar (11)
**guess, to** adivinar (**7**)
**guide** la guía (5)
**guilty** el/la culpable (**8**)
**guitar** la guitarra (**5**)
**guitarist** el/la guitarrista (**5**)
**gymnasium** el gimnasio (**2**)

**H**

**hair** el pelo (**9**)
**ham** el jamón (**7**)

**hamburger** la hamburguesa (7)
**hammock** la hamaca (11)
**hand** la mano (1, 9); **to ~ out food** repartir comidas (4)
**handsome** guapo
**hang up, to** colgar (7)
**happen, to** pasar (PB)
**happy** contento/a (2); feliz (2)
**hard: ~ -boiled** duro/a (7); **~ -working** trabajador/a (1)
**harm, to** hacer daño (11)
**hat** el sombrero (8)
**have, to** tener (1); **to ~ a... -ache** tener dolor de... (9); **to ~ a backache** tener dolor de espalda (9); **to ~ fun** divertirse (e, ie) (8); **to ~ a headache** tener dolor de cabeza (9); **to ~ just** acabar de (3); **to ~ lunch** almorzar (ue) (4); **to ~ a stomachache** tener dolor de estómago (9); **to ~ + (verb) to** tener que + (infinitive) (3)
**he** él (PA)
**head** la cabeza (9)
**headquarters** la sede (9)
**health** la salud (9); **~ insurance** seguro médico (9)
**healthy** sana (9); **to be ~** estar sano/a; saludable (9)
**heart** el corazón (9)
**heat** la calefacción (10)
**heaven** el cielo (11)
**heavy** pésimo/a (5)
**help, to** ayudar (3); **to ~ elderly people** ayudar a las personas mayores/los mayores (4)
**hen** la gallina (7, 11)
**her** ella (11)
**here** aquí (6)
**Hi!** ¡Hola! (PA)
**hide, to** esconder (8)
**high school** la escuela secundaria (9)
**highway** la autopista (10)
**hill** la loma (11)
**him** él (11)
**him/her, to/for** le (8)
**him/her/it** lo, la (5)
**his/her/its** su, sus (1)
**his/her/s/your/s** (for.) **/their/s** suyo/a/os/as (3, 10); suyo/a (PB)
**hole** el hoyo (11)
**holiday** el día festivo (7)
**home-made remedy** el remedio casero (7)
**homework** la tarea (2)
**honeymoon** la luna de miel (10)

**hope, to** esperar (2)
**horse** el caballo (11)
**hose** las medias (pl.) (8)
**hospital** el hospital (9)
**hot dog** el perro caliente (7)
**hot, to be** tener calor (3); **~** (temperature) caliente (7)
**hotel** el hotel (10); **to leave the ~** irse del hotel (10)
**house** la casa (3)
**housekeeper** el/la camarero/a (10)
**how: ~?** ¿Cómo? (2); **~ are you?** ¿Cómo está usted? (for.) (PA); **~ are you?** ¿Cómo estas? (fam.) (PA); **~ do you say . . . in Spanish?** ¿Cómo se dice... en españól? (PA); **~ many?** ¿Cuántos/as? (2); **~ much?** ¿Cuánto/a? (2); **~'s it going?** ¿Qué tal? (PA)
**hubbub** el bullicio (4)
**hug** el abrazo (PA)
**human body** el cuerpo humano (9)
**humble** humilde (3)
**hummingbird** el colibrí (11)
**hungry, to be** tener hambre (3)
**hurricane** el huracán (11)
**hurry, to be in a** tener prisa (3)
**hurt, to** dañar (11); doler (ue) (9); **to get ~** lastimar(se) (9)
**husband** el esposo (1)

## I

**I: ~** yo (PA); **~ am . . .** Soy... (PA); **~ don't know.** No lo sé. (PA); **~ don't understand.** No comprendo. (PA); **~ know.** Lo sé. (PA); **~ understand.** Comprendo. (PA); **~ would like to introduce you to . . .** Quiero presentarle a... (for.) (PA); **~ would like to introduce you to . . .** Quiero presentarte a... (fam.) (PA)
**ice cream** el helado (7)
**iced** helado/a (7)
**if** si (4)
**ill** enfermo/a (2)
**illness** la enfermedad (9)
**imaginative** imaginativo/a (5)
**important, to be** importar (8)
**impressive** impresionante (5)
**improve, to** mejorar(se) (9)
**in** en (11); **~ addition to** además de (7); **~ exchange** a cambio (4); **~ front of** delante de (11), en frente de (2); **~ order to** a fin de

(11); **~ order to** para (11); **~ the afternoon** de la tarde (PA); **~ the evening** de la noche (PA); **~ the morning** de la mañana (PA)
**infection, to have an** tener una infección (9)
**inflation** la inflación (11)
**influential** influyente (11)
**injury** la herida (9)
**insect** el insecto (11)
**inside of** dentro de (11)
**instead of** en vez de (8)
**intelligent** inteligente (1)
**interested in, to be** interesar (2)
**interesting** interesante (1)
**Internet café** el cibercafé (4)
**internship** el trabajo en prácticas (8)
**interview** la entrevista (3)
**intoxication** el embriaguez (10)
**introduce, to** presentar (3)
**Introductions** Las presentaciones (PA)
**involved** involucrado/a (11)
**it is necessary . . .** (you must . . . / one must/should . . .) hay que + infinitivo (5)
**it's: ~ a shame** es una lástima (11); **~ cold.** Hace frío. (PA); **~ cloudy.** Está nublado. (PA); **~ hot.** Hace calor. (PA); **~ necessary that** es necesario que (11); **~ raining.** Llueve. (PA); **~ sunny.** Hace sol. (PA); **~ windy.** Hace viento. (PA); **~ . . . o'clock.** Es la... / Son las... (PA)

## J

**jacket** la chaqueta (8)
**jam** la mermelada (7)
**Japanese** japonés/japonesa (PA)
**jazz** el jazz (5)
**jeans** los jeans (pl.) (8)
**jewel** la joya (9)
**joke** la broma (3, 8)
**journalism** el periodismo (2)
**judge** el/la juez/a (11)
**juice** el jugo (7)
**jungle** la selva, la selva tropical (11)
**jury** el juicio (11)
**Just fine.** Bastante bien. (PA)

## K

**keep, to** guardar (3)
**ketchup** la salsa de tomate (7)
**key** la llave (10)

A40

kill, to matar (11)
kind bondadoso/a (11)
king el rey (11)
kiss el beso (1); little ~ el besito (PA)
kitchen la cocina (3)
knapsack la mochila (2)
knife el cuchillo (7)
know, to saber (4)

**L**

laboratory el laboratorio (2)
lacking, to be hacer falta (8)
lady la señora (Sra.) (1)
lake el lago (5, 10, 11)
lamp la lámpara (3)
land la tierra (11)
languages los idiomas (pl.) (2)
large grande (1)
largest mayor (5)
last: to ~ durar (9, 11); ~ night
    anoche (7); ~ week la semana
    pasada (7); ~ weekend el fin de
    semana pasado (7); ~ year el año
    pasado (7)
late tarde (3)
later than más tarde que (7)
laugh, to reírse (4)
law el derecho (2); la ley (10, 11)
lazy perezoso/a (1)
learn, to aprender (2)
leather el cuero (8)
leave, to dejar (10); irse (8); salir (3)
left (of ), to the a la izquierda (de)
    (3, 11)
leg (of an animal) la pata (9); la
    pierna (9)
legend la leyenda (9)
lemon el limón (7)
lend, to prestar (8)
less . . . than menos + adjective/
    adverb/noun + que (10)
let's: ~ hope ojalá que (11); ~ see a
    ver (2)
lettuce la lechuga (7)
library la biblioteca (2)
lie la mentira (5, 7); to ~ mentir (ie)
    (4)
light a campfire, to hacer una
    hoguera (4)
light ligero (PB); ~ (colored) claro/a (8)
like very much, to encantar (8)
like, to gustar (PA)
like: ~ como (5); to feel ~ + (verb)
    tener ganas de + (infinitive) (3)
Likewise. Igualmente. (PA)

line (of people) la cola (10)
lion el león (11)
listen to music, to escuchar música (2)
Listen. Escuche(n). (PA)
literacy la alfabetazación (8)
literature la literatura (2)
little (a) (un) poco (1)
live, to vivir (2)
living room la sala (3)
living vivo/a (11)
loan to, to prestar (8)
locals los lugareños (4)
long largo/a (8)
look: to ~ at mirar (1); to ~ for
    buscar (4)
lose, to perder (ie) (4)
lost perdido/a (4)
loud fuerte (3)
love el amor (4); to ~ encantar (8);
    querer (3)
lucky, to be tener suerte (3)
luggage el equipaje (10)
lunch el almuerzo (7); to have
    ~ almorzar (ue) (7)
lyrics la letra (5)

**M**

magazine la revista (8)
mail a letter, to mandar una carta (4)
majors las especialidades (2)
make, to hacer (3); to ~ arts and
    crafts hacer artesanía (4); to ~ the
    bed hacer la cama (3)
mall el centro comercial (4)
man el hombre; el señor (Sr.) (1)
management el manejo (7)
manager el/la empresario/a (5)
many tanto/a (2)
map el mapa (2)
market el mercado (4)
marmalade la mermelada (7)
married casado/a (1)
match el acierto (11)
material el material (8)
mathematics las matemáticas (pl.) (2)
matter: ~ el asunto (6); to ~ importar
    (8)
mayonnaise la mayonesa (7)
mayor el alcalde/la alcaldesa (11)
me me (5); mí (11); to/for ~ me (8)
meal la comida (PB, 7)
meaning sentido (3)
meat la carne (7)
medical treatment el tratamiento
    médico (9)

medicine la medicina (2)
medium término medio (7)
meet, to reunirse (8)
melon el melón (7)
memento el recuerdo (3)
memory el recuerdo (7)
menu el menú (7)
mess el lío (9)
message el mensaje (3)
messy desordenado/a (3)
Mexican mexicano/a (PA)
microwave el microondas (3)
midnight la medianoche (PA)
mile la milla (PB)
milk la leche (7)
mine mío/a/os/as (10)
minus menos (1)
miss, to faltar (4)
Miss la señorita (Srta.) (1)
missing desaparecido/a (9)
mistaken, to be equivocarse (9)
mixed grill la parrillada (7)
mixture la mezcla (7)
model el/la modelo (8)
modern moderno/a (3)
mom la mamá (1)
monarchy la monarquía (11)
Monday el lunes (PA)
money el dinero (2)
month el mes (PA)
more . . . than más + adjective/adverb/
    noun + que (10)
mosquito el mosquito (11)
mother la madre (1)
motor el motor (10)
motorcycle la moto (1); la
    moto(cicleta) (10)
mountain la montaña (10, 11);
    ~ range la cordillera (11)
mountainous montañoso/a (4)
mouse el ratón (11)
mouth la boca (9)
movie la película (4, 5); action ~ una
    película de acción (5); science
    fiction ~ una película de ciencia
    ficción (5); war ~ una película de
    guerra (5); comedy ~ una película
    de humor (5); mystery ~ una
    película de misterio (5); romantic
    ~ una película romántica (5);
    horror ~ una película de terror
    (5); ~ theater el cine (4)
moving conmovedor/a;
    emocionante (5)
Mr. Sr. (1)
Mrs. Sra. (1)

A41

**much** tanto/a (**9**)
**museum** el museo (**4**)
**music** la música (**2, 5**); **classical ~** la música clásica (**5**); **folk ~** la música folklórica (**5**); **pop ~** la música popular (**5**); **rap ~** la música rap (**5**)
**musical** musical (**5**)
**musician** el/la músico/a (**5**)
**mustard** la mostaza (**7**)
**my** mi, mis (**1**)
**My name is . . .** Me llamo... (**PA**)

## N

**napkin** la servilleta (**7**)
**narrate, to** contar (**9**); narrar (**6**)
**narrow** estrecho/a (**8**)
**nationality** la nacionalidad (**PA**)
**natural resource** el recurso natural (**11**)
**nature** la naturaleza (**11**)
**nausea** la náusea (**9**)
**near** cerca de (**2, 7, 11**)
**neck** el cuello (**9**)
**need, to** hacer falta (**8**); necesitar (**2**)
**neither . . . nor** ni... ni (**4**)
**nervous** nervioso/a (**2**)
**never** jamás (**4**); nunca (**2, 3, 4**)
**nevertheless** sin embargo (**2, 3, 6**)
**new** nuevo/a (**3**)
**newspaper** el periódico (**11**)
**next to** al lado de (**11**)
**nice** simpático/a (**1**)
**Nice to meet you.** Mucho gusto. (**PA**)
**nickname** el apodo (**5**)
**Nigerian** nigeriano/a (**PA**)
**nightmare** la pesadilla (**8**)
**nine** nueve (**PA**); **~ hundred** novecientos (**2**)
**nineteen** diez y nueve (**PA**)
**ninety** noventa (**1**)
**ninth** noveno/a (**5**)
**no: ~ longer** ya no (**5**); **~. No.** (**PA**); **~ one** nadie (**4**)
**nobody** nadie (**4**)
**noise** el ruido (**PB, 3, 10**)
**none** ninguna (**3**); ningún (**4**); ninguno/a/os/as (**4**)
**noon** el mediodía (**PA**)
**nor** ni (**3**); tampoco (**7**)
**northeast** el noreste (**2**)
**nose** la nariz (**9**)
**not ever** (*emphatic*) jamás (**4**)
**notebook** el cuaderno (**2**)
**notes** los apuntes (*pl.*) (**2**)

**nothing** nada (**4**)
**now** ahora (**PB**)
**number** el número (**PA**)
**nurse** el/la enfermero/a (**9**)

## O

**object** el objeto (**3**)
**obligation** el deber (**4**)
**occur, to** ocurrir (**9**)
**ocean** el océano (**11**)
**offer** la oferta (**3**); **to ~** ofrecer (**2**)
**office** la oficina (**3**)
**often** a menudo (**2, 3**)
**oil** el aceite (**7**); **~ spill** el derrame de petróleo (**11**)
**oír** to hear (**3**)
**Okay.** Regular. (**PA**)
**old** antiguo/a (**3**); mayor (**1**); viejo/a (**3, 10**); **~er** mayor (**10**)
**on top** (*of*) encima (de), sobre (**3, 7, 11**)
**on: on** sobre (**3**); **~ hand** a mano (**10**)
**one** uno (**PA**); **~ hundred** cien (**1, 2**); **~ hundred million** cien millones (**3**); **~ hundred thousand** cien mil (**3**); **~ million** un millón (**3**); **~ thousand** mil (**2**)
**onion** la cebolla (**7**)
**only** solamente (**8**)
**Open your book to page . . .** Abra(n) el libro en la página... (**PA**)
**open, to** abrir (**2**)
**opening** el estreno (**5**)
**opera** la ópera (**5**)
**orange** anaranjado (**3**); **~** la naranja (**7**)
**orchestra** la orquesta (**5**)
**order, to** pedir (**7**)
**ordinal numbers** los números ordinales (**5**)
**organize, to** organizar (**4**)
**others** los demás (**4**)
**ought to** deber (**4**)
**our/s** nuestro/a/os/as (**1, 10**)
**outfit** el conjunto (**8**); el traje (**5**)
**outside** fuera (**7**); **~ of** (a)fuera de (**11**)
**outskirts** las afueras (**3**)
**over** sobre (**3, 11**); **~ there** (*and potentially not visible*) allá (**6**)
**overcoat** el abrigo (**8**)
**overhaul, to** revisar (**10**)
**own** propio/a (**6**)
**ozone layer** la capa de ozono (**11**)

## P

**package** el paquete (**10**)
**pain** el dolor (**9**)
**painted wooden animals** los alebrijes (**2**)
**painting** el cuadro (**3**)
**pajamas** el pijama (**8**)
**pants** los pantalones (*pl.*) (**8**)
**paper** el papel (**2**)
**parents** los padres (**1**)
**park** el parque (**4**)
**park, to** estacionar (**10**)
**parking** el estacionamiento (**10**)
**parrot** el loro (**11**)
**participate in a political campaign, to** participar en una campaña política (**4**)
**party** fiesta (**3**)
**passenger** el pasajero (**10**)
**passionate** apasionado/a (**5**)
**passport** el pasaporte (**10**)
**pastimes** los pasatiempos (**2**)
**pastry** el pastel (**7**)
**patient** paciente (**1**)
**pay, to** pagar (**7**)
**peace** la paz (**5**)
**pear** la pera (**7**)
**pedestrian** el peatón (**10**)
**pencil** el lápiz (**2**)
**people** la gente (**1**)
**pepper** la pimienta (**7**)
**percent** por ciento (**1**)
**perhaps** tal vez (**3**)
**personality** la personalidad (**1**)
**pet** la mascota (**10**); el animal doméstico (**11**)
**pharmacist** el/la farmacéutico/a (**9**)
**pharmacy** la farmacia (**9**)
**photo** la foto (**1**)
**physical** física (**1**); **~ exam** el examen físico (**9**)
**pianist** el/la pianista (**5**)
**piano** el piano (**5**)
**picture** el cuadro (**3, 5**)
**pie** el pastel (**7**)
**pig** el cerdo (**11**)
**pile** el montón (**7**)
**pill** la pastilla (**9**)
**pillow** la almohada (**3**)
**pink** rosado (**3**)
**place** el lugar (**2**)
**place, to** poner (**3**)
**planet** el planeta (**11**)
**plant, to** plantar (**11**)
**plastic** el plástico (**11**)

**plate** el plato (**7**)
**plateau (high)** el altiplano (9)
**platform** el programa (**11**)
**play, to** jugar (ue) (**4**); **to ~ an instrument** tocar un instrumento (**2, 5**); **to ~ basketball** jugar al básquetbol; **to ~ baseball** jugar al béisbol; **to ~ soccer** jugar al fútbol; **to ~ football** jugar al fútbol americano; **to ~ golf** jugar al golf; **to ~ tennis** jugar al tenis (**2**)
**Please.** Por favor. (**PA**)
**Pleased to meet you.** Encantado/Encantada. (**PA**)
**pleasure** el placer (**7**)
**plus** más (**1**)
**policeman** el policía (**10**)
**Polite expressions** Expresiones de cortesía (**PA**)
**political: ~ issues** las cuestiones políticas (**11**); **~ party** el partido político (**11**)
**politics** la política (**11**); **to get involved in ~** meterse en política (**11**)
**polka-dotted** de lunares (**8**)
**poll** la encuesta (**11**)
**pollute, to** contaminar (**11**)
**pollution** la contaminación (**11**)
**polyester** el poliéster (**8**)
**poncho** el rebozo (**8**)
**poor** pobre (**1**)
**pork** la carne de cerdo (**7**)
**post office** correos; la oficina de correos (**4**)
**postage stamp** el sello (**10**)
**postcard** la tarjeta postal (**4, 10**)
**posts** los cargos (**11**)
**potato chips** las papas fritas (*pl.*) (**7**)
**potato** la papa; la patata (**7**)
**poultry** las aves (**7**)
**practice, to** ensayar (**5**)
**prefer, to** preferir (ie) (**4**)
**pregnant** embarazada (**9**)
**preparation** preparativo (**5**)
**prepare, to** preparar (**2**); **to ~ a meal** preparar la comida (**3**)
**prescribe, to** recetar (**9**)
**prescription** la receta (**9**)
**presidency** la presidencia (**11**)
**president** el/la presidente/a (**11**)
**pretty** bonito/a, guapa (**1**)
**previous** anterior (**5**)
**print with a design or pattern** el/la estampado/a (**8**)
**professor** el/la profesor/a (**2**)
**proof** la prueba (**10**)

**propose, to** proponer (**5**)
**protect, to** proteger (**11**)
**proud** orgulloso/a (**4**)
**province** la provincia (**11**)
**psychology** la psicología (**2**)
**Puerto Rican** puertorriqueño/a (**PA**)
**pure** puro/a (**11**)
**purple** morado (**3**)
**purpose** el próposito (**7**)
**purse** el bolso (**8**)
**put away, to** guardar (**3**)
**put, to** poner (**3**)
**put: to ~ on** (*one's clothes*) ponerse (la ropa) (**8**); **to ~ on make up** maquillarse (**8**); **to ~ up a tent** montar una tienda de campaña (**4**)

## Q

**quality** la calidad (**11**)
**queen** la reina (**11**)
**Questions and answers** Preguntas y respuestas (**PA**)
**quiet, to keep** callarse (**8**)

## R

**rabbit** el conejo (**11**)
**radio** el/la radio (**2**)
**rain** la lluvia (**PA**); **~ forest** (*tropical*) la selva tropical (**11**)
**raincoat** el impermeable (**8**)
**rare** crudo/a; poco hecho/a (**7**)
**rat** la rata (**11**)
**raw** crudo/a (**7**)
**read, to** leer (**2**)
**Read.** Lea(n). (**PA**)
**Really well.** Muy bien. (**PA**)
**receive, to** recibir (**2**)
**recognize, to** reconocer (**8**)
**recommend, to** recomendar (ie) (**4**)
**record, to** grabar (**5**)
**recordings** las grabaciones (**5**)
**recycle, to** reciclar (**11**)
**red** rojo (**3**)
**reforest, to** reforestar (**11**)
**refrigerator** el refrigerador (**3**)
**regime** el regímen (**11**)
**region** la región (**11**)
**rehearse, to** ensayar (**5**)
**relatives** los parientes (**2**)
**release a CD, to** sacar un CD (**5**)
**release a movie, to** estrenar una película (**5**)
**remain, to** quedarse (**8**)

**remember, to** acordarse de (o, ue) (**8**); recordar (ue) (**4**)
**repeat, to** repetir (i) (**4**)
**Repeat.** Repita(n). (**PA**)
**report** el reportaje (**12**)
**representative** el/la diputado/a (**11**)
**request** el pedido (**9**)
**require, to** requerir (**11**)
**reservation** la reserva (**10**)
**reserve a table, to** reservar una mesa (**7**)
**resolve, to** resolver (o, ue) (**11**)
**respect, to** respetar (**5**)
**responsible** responsable (**1**)
**rest, to** descansar (**5**)
**restaurant** el restaurante (**4, 7**)
**return, to** regresar (**2**); volver (ue) (**4**); **to ~** (*an object*) devolver (ue) (**4**)
**reuse, to** reutilizar (**11**)
**review** la reseña (PB, 5)
**rhythm** el ritmo (**5**)
**rice** el arroz (**7**)
**rich** rico/a (**1**)
**riddle** el rompecabeza (**7**)
**ride: to ~ a bike** montar en bicicleta (**2**); **to ~ a horse** montar (a caballo) (**11**)
**right: to be ~** tener razón (**3**); **to the ~ (of )** a la derecha (de) (**3, 11**)
**ring** el anillo (**5**)
**risk** el riesgo (**9**)
**river** el río (**11**)
**roasted** asado/a (**7**)
**robe** la bata (**8**)
**rock** el rock (**5**)
**roof** el techo (**3**)
**room** el cuarto (**2, 3**); **~mate** el/la compañero/a de cuarto (**2**)
**rooster** el gallo (**7**)
**rough** áspero/a (**11**)
**roving** ambulante (**4**)
**row** la fila (**5**)
**rug** la alfombra (**3**)
**run, to** correr (**2**)

## S

**sad** triste (**2**)
**salad** la ensalada (**7**)
**salsa** la salsa (**5**)
**salt** la sal (**7**)
**sandals** las sandalias (*pl.*) (**8**)
**Saturday** el sábado (**PA**)
**save, to** salvar (**9**)
**say, to** decir (**3**)
**scare, to** asustar (**9**)

A43

**scarf** la bufanda (9)
**scary** espantoso/a (5)
**schedule** el horario (6); ~ (*of classes*) el horario (*de clases*) (2)
**science** las ciencias (*pl.*) (2)
**scream, to** gritar (8)
**screen** la pantalla (5)
**scuba diving** el buceo (4)
**seafood** los mariscos (7)
**seamstress** la costurera (8)
**season** la estación (**PA**)
**seasoning** el condimento (7)
**second** segundo/a (5); ~ **floor** el primer piso (3)
**security** la seguridad (2)
**see, to** ver (3)
**see:** ~ **you later.** Hasta luego. (**PA**); ~ **you soon.** Hasta pronto. (**PA**); ~ **you tomorrow.** Hasta mañana. (**PA**)
**seem, to** parecer (4)
**semester** el semestre (2)
**senate** el senado (11)
**senator** el/la senador/a (11)
**send a letter, to** mandar una carta (4)
**serve, to** servir (i) (4)
**set the table, to** poner la mesa (3)
**seven** siete (**PA**); ~ **hundred** setecientos (2)
**seventeen** diez y siete (**PA**)
**seventh** séptimo/a (5)
**seventy** setenta (1)
**shaman** el chamán (9)
**share, to** compartir (3, 5)
**shark** el tiburón (5)
**shave, to** afeitarse (8)
**she** ella (**PA**)
**sheet** la sábana (3)
**shirt** la camisa (8)
**shoes** los zapatos (*pl.*) (8)
**short** bajo/a (1); corto/a (8)
**shorts** los pantalones cortos (*pl.*) (8)
**shot** la inyección (9)
**should** deber (4)
**show, to** enseñar (2); mostrar (ue) (4); **to ~ a movie** presentar una película (5)
**shower** la ducha (3); **to ~** ducharse (8)
**shrimp** los camarones (*pl.*) (7)
**shrub** el arbusto (7)
**siblings** los hermanos (1)
**sick, to be** estar enfermo/a (2, 9); enfermar(se) (9)
**side** el lado (2)
**sigh** el suspiro (11)
**signature** la firma (4)

**silk** la seda (8)
**silly** tonto/a (1)
**similarity** la semejanza (6)
**since** ya que (1)
**singer** el/la cantante (5)
**single room** el cuarto individual (10)
**sink** el lavabo (3)
**sister** la hermana (1)
**sit down, to** sentarse (e, ie) (8)
**six** seis (**PA**); ~ **hundred** seiscientos (2)
**sixteen** diez y seis (**PA**)
**sixth** sexto/a (5)
**sixty** sesenta (1)
**skate, to** patinar (2)
**skill** la habilidad (5)
**skirt** la falda (8)
**sky** el cielo (11)
**sleep, to** dormir (ue) (4)
**sleepy, to be** tener sueño (3)
**slippers** las zapatillas (*pl.*) (8)
**slow** lento/a (3, 5)
**small** pequeño/a (1, 10); **smaller** menor (10); **smallest** el/la menor (10)
**smooth** suave (5)
**snack** la merienda (7); **to have a ~** merendar (7)
**snake** la serpiente (11)
**sneeze** el estornudo (9); **to ~** estornudar (9)
**snow** la nieve (**PA**)
**socks** los calcetines (*pl.*) (8)
**sofa** el sofá (3)
**soft drink** el refresco (7)
**soil** la tierra (11)
**solid-colored** liso/a (8)
**some** algún (4); alguno/a/os/as (3, 4); un/una/unos/unas (1)
**someone** alguien (4)
**something** algo (**PB**, 4)
**sometimes** a veces (2, 3, 4)
**son** el hijo (1)
**sore throat** el dolor de garganta (9)
**So-so.** Más o menos. (**PA**)
**soup** la sopa (7); ~ **spoon** la cuchara (7)
**source** la fuente (5, 9)
**sow, to** sembrar (e, ie) (11)
**spam** el correo basura (3)
**Spaniard** español/española (**PA**)
**Spanish-speaking** hispanohablante (3)
**speak, to** hablar (2)
**specialty of the house** la especialidad de la casa (7)
**speech** el discurso (11)
**spices** las especias (7)
**spicy** picante (7)

**spoonful** la cucharada (7)
**sports** los deportes (2)
**spring** la primavera (**PA**)
**stadium** el estadio (2)
**staircase** la escalera (3, 11)
**stand: to ~** pararse (10); **to ~ out** destacar (5); **to ~ up** levantarse (8)
**star** la estrella (5)
**start** el principio (8)
**state** el estado (9, 11)
**statehood** la estadidad (11)
**states** (*of being*) los estados (2)
**station** (*train, bus*) la estación (*de tren, de autobús*) (10)
**stay, to** quedarse (8, 11); **to ~ in bed** guardar cama (9)
**steak** el bistec (7)
**steering wheel** el volante (10)
**stepfather** el padrastro (1)
**stepmother** la madrastra (1)
**still** todavía (4)
**stirred up** alborotado/a (11)
**stockings** las medias (*pl.*) (8)
**stomach** el estómago (9)
**store** la tienda (2)
**storm** la tormenta (11)
**story** el piso (3)
**stove** la estufa (3)
**straighten up, to** arreglar (3)
**strange** extraño (4)
**street** la calle (3, 10)
**strike** la huelga (11); **to be on ~** estar en huelga (11)
**striped** de rayas (8)
**strong** fuerte (1)
**student** el/la estudiante (2); ~ **center/ union** el centro estudiantil (2)
**study, to** estudiar (2, 6)
**stupendous** estupendo/a (5)
**style** el estilo (8)
**subject** la materia (2)
**subway** el metro (10)
**successful, to be** tener éxito (3)
**such** tan (2)
**suddenly** de repente (**PB**)
**sugar** el azúcar (7)
**suit** el traje (5, 8); **bathing ~** el traje de baño (8)
**suitable use** el uso adecuado (10)
**suitcase** la maleta (10); **to pack a ~** arreglar/hacer la maleta (10)
**summarize, to** resumir (9)
**summer** el verano (**PA**); ~ **camp** el campamento de niños (4)
**sun** el sol (**PA**); **to ~bathe** tomar el sol (2)

A44

**Sunday** el domingo (**PA**)
**supermarket** el supermercado (**4**)
**support, to** apoyar (5, PB, **11**); **to ~ a candidate** apoyar a un/a candidato/a (**4**)
**surprise** la sorpresa (**8**)
**surprising** sorprendente (**5**)
**survey** la encuesta (**11**)
**suspenseful** de suspenso (**5**)
**suspicious** sospechoso/a (**2**)
**sweater** el suéter (**8**)
**sweatshirt** la sudadera (**8**)
**sweets** los dulces (**7**)
**swim, to** nadar (**2**); **~suit** traje de baño (**8**)

**T**

**table** la mesa (**2**)
**tablecloth** el mantel (**7**)
**tablespoon** la cuchara (**7**)
**tailor** el costurero (**8**)
**take turns, to** turnarse (**3**)
**take, to** tomar (**2**); llevar (**8**); **to ~ a nap** echar una siesta (**PB**); **to ~ a short trip** ir de excursión (**4**); **to ~ a walk** hacer una caminata (**4**); **to ~ care of** cuidar (**11**); **to ~ off** (*one's clothes*) quitarse (*la ropa*) (**8**); **to ~ out the garbage** sacar la basura (**3**); **to ~ someone to the doctor** llevar a alguien al médico (**4**)
**tall** alto/a (**1**)
**tax** el impuesto (**11**)
**taxi** el taxi (**10**)
**tea** (*iced/hot*) el té (*helado/caliente*) (**7**)
**teach, to** enseñar (**2**)
**team** el equipo (**2**)
**teaspoon** la cucharita (**7**)
**television** la televisión (**2**)
**tell, to** decir (**3**)
**temperature** la temperatura (**PA**)
**temple** el templo (**4**)
**ten** diez (**PA**)
**tennis shoes** los tenis (*pl.*) (**8**)
**tenth** décimo/a (**5**)
**Thank you.** Gracias. (**PA**)
**that, that one** (*way over there/not visible*) aquel/la; ese/a (**5**)
**that, those** (*way over there/not visible*); **those ones** aquellos/as (**5**)
**the** el/la/los/las (**1**); **~ check, please.** La cuenta, por favor. (**7**); **~ weather is bad.** Hace mal tiempo. (**PA**); **~ weather is nice.** Hace buen tiempo. (**PA**)

**theater** el teatro (**4**)
**their** su, sus (**1**)
**them** los, las (**5**); ellos/as (**11**); **to/for ~** les (**8**)
**theme park** el parque de atracciones (**10**)
**then** entonces, luego (**6**)
**there / over there** allí (4, **6**)
**there is / are** hay (**2**)
**these** estos/as (**5**)
**they** ellos/as (**PA**)
**thin** delgado/a (**1**)
**thing** la cosa (**3**)
**think, to** pensar (ie) (**4**)
**third** tercer, tercero/a (**5**); **~ floor** el segundo piso (**3**)
**thirsty, to be** tener sed (**3**)
**thirteen** trece (**PA**)
**thirty** treinta (**PA, 1**); **~ thousand** treinta mil (**3**)
**this** esto (**3**)
**this, this one** este/a (**5**)
**those over there; those ones** esos/as (3, **5**)
**threat** la amenaza (**8**)
**three** tres (**PA**); **~ hundred** trescientos (**2**)
**throat** la garganta (**9**)
**through** por (**11**)
**throw, to** tirar (**9**); **to ~ away** botar (**11**)
**Thursday** el jueves (**PA**)
**ticket** el boleto (8, **10**), la entrada (**5**); **free ~** la entrada gratis (**5**); **round-trip ~** el boleto de ida y vuelta (**10**)
**tie** la corbata (**8**)
**tight** estrecho/a (**8**)
**time** la hora (**PA**)
**time** la vez (**5**)
**times** por (**1**)
**tin work** hojalatería (**2**)
**tip** la propina (**7**)
**tire** la llanta (**10**)
**tired** cansado/a (**2**)
**to** a (**11**); **~ where?** ¿Adónde? (**2**)
**toast** la tostada (**7**)
**toe** el dedo (del pie) (**9**)
**toilet** el inodoro (**3**)
**tomato** el tomate (**7**)
**too** también (**2**)
**tooth** el diente (**9**)
**topic** el tema (**5**)
**tornado** el tornado (**11**)
**touch, to** tocar (**4**)
**tour** la gira (**5**); **to ~** hacer una gira (**5**)

**tournament** el torneo (**4**)
**tower** la torre (**3**)
**town** el pueblo (**4**); **~ square** la plaza (**4**)
**track and field** el atletismo (**2**)
**traditional** tradicional (**3**)
**traffic** el tráfico (**10**); **~ light** el semáforo (**10**); **~ ticket** la multa (**10**)
**tragedy** la tragedia (**11**)
**tragic** trágico/a (**5**)
**train** el tren (**10**)
**transportation** el transporte (**10**)
**travel, to** viajar (**10**); **~ agent** el/la agente de viajes (**10**); **~ agency** la agencia de viajes (6, **10**)
**traveler** el/la viajero/a (**10**)
**treasure** el tesoro (**10**)
**treat, to** tratar (**9**)
**tree** el árbol (**11**)
**trip** el viaje (**10**); **to go on a ~** ir de viaje (**10**)
**truck** el camión (**10**)
**true** cierto/a (**4**)
**trumpet** la trompeta (**5**); **~ player** el/la trompetista (**5**)
**trunk** el baúl (**10**)
**try on clothing, to** probarse (o, ue) la ropa (**8**)
**try to, to** tratar de (3, **9**)
**T-shirt** la camiseta (5, **8**)
**tsunami** el sunami (**11**)
**Tuesday** el martes (**PA**)
**tuna** el atún (**7**)
**turn: to ~** doblar (**10**); **to ~ in** entregar (**7**); **to ~ on** encender (**9**)
**turnover** (*meat*) la empanada (**7**)
**twelve** doce (**PA**)
**twenty** veinte (**PA**)
**two** dos (**PA**); **~ hundred** doscientos (**2**); **~ million** dos millones (**3**); **~ thousand** dos mil (**3**)

**U**

**ugly** feo/a (**1**)
**umbrella** el paraguas (**8**)
**uncle** el tío (**1**)
**uncomfortable** incómodo/a (**8**)
**under; underneath** debajo (de) (7, **11**)
**undercover** encubierto/a (**11**)
**underline, to** subrayar (**7**)
**understand, to** comprender (**2**); entender (ie) (**4**)
**underwear** la ropa interior (**8**)
**unemployment** el desempleo (**11**)

**A45**

**unpleasant** antipático/a (**1**)
**until** hasta (**11**)
**upset** nervioso/a (**2**)
**us** nos (**5**); nosotros/as (**11**); **to/for**
~ nos (**8**)
**use, to** usar (**PB, 2,** 4)
**useful** útil (**PA**)

## V

**vacation** las vacaciones (**10**); **to go**
**on** ~ ir de vacaciones (**10**)
**vacuum, to** pasar la aspiradora (**3**)
**vegetable** la verdura (**7**)
**vehicle** el vehículo (**10**)
**verb** el verbo (**1, 2**)
**very** muy (**1**)
**village** el pueblo (**4**)
**vinegar** el vinagre (**7**)
**virus, to have a** tener un virus (**9**)
**visit, to** visitar (**10**)
**voice** la voz (**5**)
**volunteer at a nursing home, to**
trabajar como voluntario/a en la
residencia de ancianos (**4**)
**volunteerism** el voluntariado (**4**)
**vote** el voto (**11**); **to** ~ votar (**11**)

## W

**waist** la cintura (**9**); **from the** ~ **up**
de la cintura para arriba (**9**)
**wait: to** ~ **for** esperar (**2**); **to** ~ **on**
atender (**9**)
**waiter** el camarero (**7**)
**waitress** la camarera (**7**)
**wake up, to** despertarse (e, ie) (**8**)
**walk, to** andar (**7**); caminar (**2**)
**wall** la pared (**2**)
**want, to** querer (**2, 3**)
**war** la guerra (**11**)
**warn, to** advertir (**8**)
**wash: to** ~ **dishes** lavar los platos (**3**);
**to** ~ **oneself** lavarse (**8**)
**waste, to** perder (ie) (**4**)
**watch** el reloj (**2**)
**watch television, to** ver la televisión (**2**)
**water** el agua; **fresh** ~ el agua dulce (**5**);
~ **(with ice)** el agua (con hielo) (**7**)

**waterfall** la cascada (**10**)
**we** nosotros/as (**PA**)
**weak** débil (**1**)
**wear, to** llevar (**8**)
**wedding** la boda (**4**)
**Wednesday** el miércoles (**PA**)
**week** la semana (**PA**)
**welfare** el bienestar (**11**)
**well: well cooked** bien hecho/a
(**7**); ~ **done** bien cocido/a (**7**);
~ **-being** el bienestar (**11**)
**west** el oeste (**2**)
**what** que (**3**)
**what?** ¿qué? (**3**); ~? ¿Cómo? (**PA**); ~?
¿Qué? (**2**); ~ **day is today?** ¿Qué
día es hoy? (**PA**); ~ **does it mean?**
¿Qué significa? (**PA**); ~ **is the gist**
**of . . . ?** ¿De qué se trata... ? (**8**);
~ **is this?** ¿Qué es esto? (**PA**); ~ **is**
**today's date?** ¿Cuál es la fecha
de hoy? (**PA**); ~ **is your name?**
¿Cómo se llama usted? (*for.*) (**PA**);
~ **is your name?** (*fam.*) ¿Cómo te
llamas? (**PA**); ~ **time is it?** ¿Qué
hora es? (**PA**); ~'**s the weather**
**like?** ¿Qué tiempo hace? (**PA**)
**whatever** cualquier (**8**)
**When?** ¿Cuándo? (**2**)
**Where?** ¿Dónde? (**2**)
**which** el cual (**11**); ~ **(one/s)?** ¿Cuál/
es? (**2**)
**while** mientras (**2**)
**whip, to** azotar (**11**)
**white** blanco (**3**)
**Who?** ¿Quién? (**PA, 2**); ¿Quiénes?
(*pl.*) (**2**)
**Why?** ¿Por qué? (**2**)
**wide** ancho/a (**7, 8**)
**wife** la esposa (**1**)
**wild animals** los animales salvajes (**11**)
**win, to** ganar (**6**)
**wind** el viento (**PA**)
**window** la ventana (**2**); **to** ~ **shop**
ojear las vitrinas (**8**)
**windshield** el parabrisas (**10**);
~**wiper** el limpiaparabrisas (**10**)
**wine** el vino (**7**)
**winter** el invierno (**PA**)

**with** con (**11**); ~ **me** conmigo (**9**);
~ **oneself** consigo (**11**); ~ **you**
contigo (**9**); ~**out** sin (**4, 11**)
**woman** la mujer (**1**); la señora (Sra.) (**1**)
**wool** la lana (**8**)
**word** la palabra (**PA**)
**work, to** funcionar (**10**), trabajar (**2**);
**to** ~ **as a counselor** trabajar como
consejero/a (**4**); **to** ~ **in politics**
trabajar en política (**4**)
**worried** preocupado/a (**2**)
**worry about, to** preocuparse (por) (**11**)
**worse** peor (**10**)
**worst** el/la peor (**4, 10**)
**wound** la herida (**9**)
**wrap, to** envolver (**7**)
**wrestling** la lucha libre (**2**)
**write, to** escribir (**2**)
**Write.** Escriba(n). (**PA**)

## Y

**yam** la batata (**7**)
**years old, to be . . .** tener... años (**3**)
**yellow** amarillo (**3**)
**Yes.** Sí. (**PA**)
**yesterday** ayer (**7**)
**you** te (**5**); ti (**11**); tú (*fam.*) (**PA**);
usted/es (*for.*) (**PA, 11**); vosotros/
as (*fam. pl. Spain*) (**PA, 11**); ~ **all**
os (**5**); ~ **all** los, las (**5**); **to/for** ~ te
(**8**); **to/for** ~ **all** os (**8**)
**young** joven (**1, 10**); ~ **man** el joven,
el señor (Sr.) (**1**); ~ **woman** la
joven, la señorita (Srta.) (**1**); ~**er**
menor (**10**); ~**est** el/la menor (**10**)
**your** (*for.*) su, sus (**1**); tu, tus (**1**);
vuestro/a/os/as (*fam. pl. Spain*) (**1, 10**)
**You're welcome.** De nada. (**PA**)
**yours** (*fam.*) tuyo/a/os/as (**3, 10**)
**yucca** la mandioca (**7**)

## Z

**zero** cero (**PA**)

# Credits

## Photo Credits

**p. 2:** Jack Hollingsworth/Photodisc/Thinkstock; **p. 4:** (l) Demetrio Carrasco/Dorling Kindersley; (c) Jupiterimages/Comstock/Thinkstock; (r) Digital Vision/Thinkstock; **p. 7:** (t) Stockbyte/Getty Images; (b) Comstock Images/Thinkstock; **p. 12:** Yuri Arcurs/Shutterstock; **p. 15:** Jupiterimages/Comstock/Thinkstock; **p. 16:** George Doyle/Stockbyte/Thinkstock; **p. 20:**(t) Stockbyte/Thinkstock; (1st row, left to right) Jupiterimages/Photos.com/Thinkstock; Jupiterimages/Comstock/Thinkstock; Pete Saloutos/Shutterstock; BananaStock/Thinkstock; (2nd row, left to right) James Woodson/Photodisc/Thinkstock; BananaStock/Thinkstock; Jupiterimages/Brand X Pictures/Thinkstock; BananaStock/Thinkstock; **p. 21:** Samot/Shutterstock; **p. 22:** (l) Medioimages/Photodisc/Thinkstock; (tr) David Kay/Shutterstock; (br) Eddie Gerald/Rough Guides/DK Images; **p. 26:** (t) Andi Berger/Shutterstock; (1st row, l) iofoto/Shutterstock; (1st row, c) Resnak/Shutterstock; (1st row, r) Brad Remy/Shutterstock; (2nd row, l) Jupiterimages/Comstock/Thinkstock; (2nd row, c) Brandon Seidel/Shutterstock; (2nd row, r) Saleeee/Shutterstock; (3rd row, l) Paul Yates/Shutterstock; (3rd row, c) olly/Shutterstock; **pp. 30–31:** Andresr/Shutterstock; **p. 35:** (t) monbibi/Shutterstock; (b) David Sacks/Lifesize/Thinkstock; **p. 45:** Rido/Shutterstock; **p. 46:** (t) Knotsmaster/Shutterstock; (b) Grigory Kubatyan/Shutterstock; **p. 50:** (l) Goodshoot/Thinkstock; (r) Comstock Images/Thinkstock; **p. 52:** (t) ImageryMajestic/Shutterstock; (c) Jeffery Allan Salter/Corbis SABA/Corbis Entertainment/Corbis; (cr) Aspen Photo/Shutterstock; (bl) Michael Moran/Dorling Kindersley; (bc) Samot/Shutterstock; **pp. 60–61:** Bill Perry/Shutterstock; **p. 64:** csp/Shutterstock; **p. 69:** Jack Hollingsworth/Photodisc/Thinkstock; **p. 72:** (tl) kaarsten/Shutterstock; (cr) Creatista/Shutterstock; **p. 73:** (l) Poprugin Aleksey/Shutterstock; (cl) John Foxx/Stockbyte/Thinkstock; (cr) Matthew Ward/Dorling Kindersley; (r) Comstock Images/Getty Images/Thinkstock; **p. 81:** (tl) Skylinephoto/Shutterstock; (tc) Stockbyte/Thinkstock; (tr) Jack Hollingsworth/Digital Vision/Thinkstock; (bl) Comstock/Thinkstock; (bc) Jupiterimages/Comstock/Thinkstock; (br) Donald Miralle/Lifesize/Thinkstock; **p. 82:** (1st row, l) Bikeriderlondon/Shutterstock; (1st row, c) Stockbyte/Thinkstock; (1st row, r) Stephen Mcsweeny/Shutterstock; (2nd row, l) BananaStock/Thinkstock; (2nd row, c) Digital Vision/Thinkstock; (2nd row, r) Stockbyte/Thinkstock; (3rd row, l) Poleze/Shutterstock; (3rd row, c) Maridav/Shutterstock; (3rd row, r) Daria Minaeva/Shutterstock; (4th row, l) Jupiterimages/Brand X Pictures/Thinkstock; **p. 83:** Stockbyte/Thinkstock; **p. 84:** John Gibson/AFP/Getty Images; **p. 86:** (t) Jack Hollingsworth/Photodisc/Thinkstock; (b) Jupiterimages/Comstock/Thinkstock; **p. 88:** (t) Jack Hollingsworth/Photodisc/Thinkstock; (cr) csp/Shutterstock; (b) csp/Shutterstock; **p. 89:** (t) Pixland/Thinkstock; (c) SoloHielo/Shutterstock; (b) Francesca Yorke/Dorling Kindersley; **pp. 96–97:** Audrey Heining-Boynton; **p. 100:** (tl) Audrey Heining-Boynton; (tc) Evok20/Shutterstock; (tr) gary yim/Shutterstock; (bl) javarman/Shutterstock; (bc) Jarno Gonzalez Zarraonandia/Shutterstock; (br) Audrey Heining-Boynton; **p. 104:** Mark Hayes/Shutterstock; **p. 105:** (t) Audrey Heining-Boynton; (b) Audrey Heining-Boynton; **p. 107:** HamsterMan/Shutterstock; **p. 111:** (1st row, l) Audrey Heining-Boynton; (1st row, c) Audrey Heining-Boynton; (1st row, r) Audrey Heining-Boynton; (2nd row, l) Audrey Heining-Boynton; (2nd row, c) Audrey Heining-Boynton; (2nd row, r) Audrey Heining-Boynton; (3rd row, l) Audrey Heining-Boynton; (3rd row, tc) Alberto Loyo/Shutterstock; (3rd row, bc) Audrey Heining-Boynton; (3rd row, r) Audrey Heining-Boynton; **p. 112:** Audrey Heining-Boynton; **p. 113:** Audrey Heining-Boynton; **p. 117:** (tl) Audrey Heining-Boynton; (tr) Natalia Belotelova/Shutterstock; (bl) Pres Panayotov/Shutterstock; (br) Audrey Heining-Boynton; **p. 119:** (t) Audrey Heining-Boynton; (b) Audrey Heining-Boynton; **p. 121:** Comstock/Thinkstock; **p. 122:** Photoroller/Shutterstock; **p. 124:** (t) Brand X Pictures/Thinkstock; (cr) Richard Wareham Fotografie/Alamy; (bl) Vinicius Tupinamba/Shutterstock; (br) imageZebra/Shutterstock; **p. 125:** (tl) Sillycoke/Shutterstock; (cl) Audrey Heining-Boynton; (cr) Joan Ramon Mendo Escoda/Shutterstock; (b) Audrey Heining-Boynton; **p. 126:** Pearson Education; **p. 128:** (l) Erin Baiano/Pearson Education/PH College; (c) Erin Baiano/Pearson Education/PH College; (r) Erin Baiano/Pearson Education/PH College; **pp. 132–133:** Grigory Kubatyan/Shutterstock; **p. 135:** (t) Peter Wilson/Dorling Kindersley; (bl) Stockbyte/Thinkstock; (br) olly/Shutterstock; **p. 136:** Suzanne Long/Shutterstock; **p. 137:** Jennifer Stone/Shutterstock; **p. 139:** Jupiterimages/Thinkstock; **p. 141:** Medioimages/Photodisc/Thinkstock; **p. 145:** ImageState Royalty Free/Alamy; **p. 146:** PhotoLibrary; **p. 148:** Jack Hollingsworth/Stockbyte/Thinkstock; **p. 151:** vadim kozlovsky/Shutterstock; **p. 153:** Pixland/Thinkstock; **p. 156:** Andresr/Shutterstock; **p. 157:** Pearson Education; **p. 158:** BananaStock/Thinkstock; **p. 161:** (t) Andresr/Shutterstock; (cl) Christopher Poe/Shutterstock; (cr) Dave Rock/Shutterstock; (b) John A. Anderson/Shutterstock; **p. 162:** (t) Jupiterimages/liquidlibrary/Thinkstock; (cl) Daniel Loncarevic/Shutterstock; (cr) Gugli/Dreamstime; (b) Mike Cohen/Shutterstock; **p. 163:** (t) iofoto/Shutterstock; (cl) rj lerich/Shutterstock; (bl) Yai/Shutterstock; (br) EpicStockMedia/Shutterstock; **p. 164:** Pearson Education; **p. 166:** (l, c, r) Pearson Education; **pp. 170–171:** AndrusV/Shutterstock; **p. 174:** (t) olly/Shutterstock; **p. 178:** (tr) JLC/ZOJ WENN Photos/Newscom; (bl) Miguel Campos/Shutterstock; (br) Helga Esteb/Shutterstock; **p. 186:** (tl) cinemafestival/Shutterstock; (cl) cinemafestival/Shutterstock; (bl) cinemafestival/Shutterstock; (br) DFree/Shutterstock; **p. 191:** (t) dwphotos/Shutterstock; (b) Dana Nalbandian/Shutterstock; **p. 192:** Pearson Education; **p. 193:** DeshaCAM/Shutterstock; **p. 195:** (t) Getty Images, Inc. – PhotoDisc; (cl) rj lerich/Shutterstock; (cr) rj lerich/Shutterstock; (b) Terry Honeycutt/Shutterstock; **p. 196:** (t) Kim Steele/Photodisc/Thinkstock; (cl) Sandra A. Dunlap/Shutterstock; (cr) Brandon Stein/Shutterstock; (b) Brand X Pictures/Thinkstock; **p. 197:** (t) Jack Hollingsworth/Photodisc/Thinkstock; (cl) Paul Katz/Photodisc/Thinkstock; (cr) Chris Howey/Shutterstock; (b) rj lerich/Shutterstock; **p. 198:** Pearson Education; **p. 200:** (l, c, r) Pearson Education; **p. 204:** (l) Michael Moran/Dorling Kindersley; (r) Vinicius Tupinamba/Shutterstock; **p. 205:** (l) Daniel Loncarevic/Shutterstock; (r) Brandon Stein/Shutterstock; **p. 207:** (tl) Jack Hollingsworth/Thinkstock; (tr) Creatas Images/Thinkstock; (b) Ryan McVay/Photodisc/Getty Images; **p. 208** (1st row, l) ImageryMajestic/Shutterstock; (1st row, lc) Jack Hollingsworth/Photodisc/Thinkstock; (1st row, rc) Brand X Pictures/Thinkstock; (1st row, r) Andresr/Shutterstock; (2nd row, l) Jupiterimages/liquidlibrary/Thinkstock; (2nd row, lc) iofoto/Shutterstock; (2nd row, c) Getty Images, Inc. – PhotoDisc;

**A47**

(2nd row, rc) Kim Steele/Photodisc/Thinkstock; (2nd row, r) Jack Hollingsworth/Photodisc/Thinkstock; **p. 211**: Ian Tragen/ Shutterstock; **p. 214**: Steve Mason/Getty Images; **p. 216**: Dwphotos/Shutterstock; **p. 219**: Frontpage/Shutterstock; **p. 220**: (all) Pearson Education; **p. 221**: (all) Pearson Education; **p. 222**: Santiago Cornejo/Shutterstock; **p. 223**: (bl) Joe Mercier/Shutterstock; (br) Aspen Photo/Shutterstock; **p. 224**: (t, 1st row, l) csp/Shutterstock; (t, 1st row, lc) Audrey Heining-Boynton; (t, 1st row, rc) John A. Anderson/ Shutterstock; (t, 1st row, r) Daniel Loncarevic/Shutterstock; (t, 2nd row, l) csp/Shutterstock; (t, 2nd row, lc) Audrey Heining-Boynton; (t, 2nd row, rc) Dave Rock/Shutterstock; (t, 2nd row, r) Mike Cohen/Shutterstock; (b, 1st row, l) rj lerich/Shutterstock; (b, 1st row, lc) Terry Honeycutt/Shutterstock; (b, 1st row, rc) Brandon Stein/Shutterstock; (b, 1st row, r) Paul Katz/Photodisc/Thinkstock; (b, 2nd row, l) EpicStockMedia/Shutterstock; (b, 2nd row, lc) rj lerich/Shutterstock; (b, 2nd row, rc) Brand X Pictures/Thinkstock; (b, 2nd row, r) rj lerich/Shutterstock; **pp. 226–227**: Andresr/Shutterstock; **p. 228**: (tl) Jack Hollingsworth/Photodisc/Thinkstock; (tr) Corbis; (bl) Julie Keen/Shutterstock; (br) Digital Vision./Digital Vision/Thinkstock; **p. 229**: Creatas/Jupiter Images; **p. 236**: (l) Ilja MaÅ¡Ãk/Shutterstock; (r) Pearson Education; **p. 238**: (l) Audrey Heining-Boynton; (r) russ witherington/Shutterstock; **p. 239**: (l) Audrey Heining-Boynton; (c) Pearson Education; (r) Audrey Heining-Boynton; **p. 240**: (l) Cheryl Casey/Shutterstock; (c) Giordano Aita/Shutterstock; (r) Michael Shake/Shutterstock; **p. 242**: Dean Mitchell/Shutterstock; **p. 243**: Jupiterimages/Thinkstock; **p. 246**: Creatas Images/Thinkstock; **p. 247**: Dario Sabljak/Shutterstock; **p. 248**: Barone Firenze/Shutterstock; **p. 250**: Marten Czamanske/Shutterstock; **p. 251**: Scott Leman/ Shutterstock; **p. 252**: (all) Pearson Education; **pp. 254–255**: Jupiterimages/Goodshoot/Thinkstock; **p. 261**: Digital Vision/Thinkstock; **p. 262**: (t) catman/Shutterstock; (1st row, l) C.J.White/Shutterstock; (1st row, c) Digital Vision/Thinkstock; (1st row, r) Yellowj/ Shutterstock; (2nd row, l) joingate/Shutterstock; (2nd row, c) Valentyn Volkov/Shutterstock; (2nd row, r) Michal Zajac/Shutterstock; **p. 264**: George Doyle/Thinkstock; **p. 267**: Yellowj/Shutterstock; **p. 270**: (t) Kiselev Andrey Valerevich/Shutterstock; (1st row, l) Valentyn Volkov/Shutterstock; (1st row, lc) Andrey Jitkov/Shutterstock; (1st row, rc) hfng/Shutterstock; (1st row, r) Robyn Mackenzie/Shutterstock; (2nd row, l) Shebeko/Shutterstock; (2nd row, lc) Denis Vrublevski/shutterstock; (2nd row, rc) epsilon_lyrae/Shutterstock; (2nd row, r) Ramon grosso dolarea/Shutterstock; **p. 271**: Audrey Heining-Boynton; **p. 279**: Comstock/Thinkstock; **p. 280**: Audrey Heining-Boynton; **p. 281**: Jupiterimages/Thinkstock; **p. 282**: (t) Deklofenak/Shutterstock; (b) Aleksey Kondratyuk/Shutterstock; **p. 284**: (t) Barbara Penoyar/Photodisc/Getty Images; (tr) Alexander Chaikin/Shutterstock; (l) Audrey Heining-Boynton; (br) Rhonda Klevansky/Getty Images; **p. 285**: (t) Andresr/Shutterstock; (c) iladm/Shutterstock; (bl) Pearson Learning Photo Studio; (br) Pixel1962/shutterstock; **p. 286**: Pearson Education; **p. 288**: (l, c, r) Pearson Education; **pp. 292–393**: Photos.com/Jupiterimages/Thinkstock; **p. 296**: (l) Suzanne Long/Shutterstock; (r) Joel Shawn/Shutterstock; **p. 297**: Brand X Pictures/Jupiterimages/Thinkstock; **p. 298**: Colin Sinclair/Dorling Kindersley; **p. 301**: Thomas Northcut/Photodisc/Thinkstock; **p. 304**: (t) NataliaYeromina/Shutterstock; (lc) Creatas/Thinkstock; (c) littleny/Shutterstock; (rc) Paul Sutherland/Digital Vision/Thinkstock; (b) Losevsky Pavel/Shutterstock; **p. 311**: (l) NataliaYeromina/ Shutterstock; (l, inset) Doug James/Shutterstock; (r) lev radin/Shutterstock; **p. 316**: jorisvo/Shutterstock; **p. 318**: Pictorial Press Ltd/ Alamy; **p. 319**: Linda Johnsonbaugh/Shutterstock; **p. 321**: Digital Vision/Thinkstock; **p. 322**: (t) lev radin/Shutterstock; (b) iofoto/ Shutterstock; **p. 324**: (t) Jack Hollingsworth/Thinkstock; (tl) Larry Lee Photography/Corbis; (c) Demetrio Carrasco/Dorling Kindersley; (bl) Dale Mitchell/Shutterstock; **p. 325**: (t) Hans Neleman/Getty Images; (tl) Brand X Pictures/Thinkstock; (c) Audrey Heining-Boynton; (bl) SF photo/Shutterstock; **p. 326**: Pearson Education; **p. 328**: (l, c, r) Pearson Education; **pp. 332–333**: Andresr/Shutterstock; **p. 336**: Stephen Schildbach/Getty Images; **p. 340**: AVAVA/Shutterstock; **p. 344**: Guido Amrein, Switzerland/Shutterstock; **p. 346**: Stockbyte/ Getty Images; **p. 351**: Galyna Andrushko/Shutterstock; **p. 352**: Regissercom/Shutterstock; **p. 355**: (t) Getty Images/Thinkstock; (b) BananaStock/Thinkstock; **p. 356**: TheThirdMan/Shutterstock; **p. 359**: Creatas/Jupiterimages/Thinkstock; **p. 360**: Pearson Education; **p. 361**: (t) Creatas Images/Thinkstock; (b) Andresr/Shutterstock; **p. 363**: (t) Maria Teijeiro/Photodisc/Thinkstock; (tl) Jarno Gonzalez Zarraonandia/Shutterstock.com; (c) terekhov igor/Shutterstock; (b) Maria Veras/Shutterstock; **p. 364**: (t) Andresr/Shutterstock; (l) gary yim/Shutterstock; (tc) Paul Clarke/Shutterstock; (bc) Jarno Gonzalez Zarraonandia/Shutterstock.com; **p. 365**: (t) Andresr/Shutterstock; (c) nouseforname/Shutterstock; (bl) Jacqueline Abromeit/Shutterstock; (br) Sofia/Shutterstock; **p. 366**: Pearson Education; **p. 368**: (l, c, r) Pearson Education; **pp. 372–373**: Bryan Busovicki/Shutterstock; **p. 377**: Andresr, 2010/used under license from www.Shutterstock.com; **p. 378**: Ramona Heim/Shutterstock; **p. 382**: (t) Creatas Images/Thinkstock; (b) Stockbyte/Thinkstock; **p. 385**: (t) Stockbyte/ Thinkstock; (b) gary yim/Shutterstock; **p. 386**: (t) Robert Kneschke/Shutterstock; (b) Noel Hendrickson/Thinkstock; **p. 387**: Thomas Northcut/Thinkstock; **p. 390**: John Foxx/Thinkstock; **p. 391**: (tl) Lysithee/Shutterstock; (r) Robert WrÃÂ³blewski/Shutterstock; (bl) Attila JANDI/Shutterstock; **p. 393**: Digital Vision/Thinkstock; **p. 398**: Andrey Yurlov/Shutterstock; **p. 399**: Stockbyte/Getty Images; **p. 400**: (t) Dmitriy Shironosov/Shutterstock; (b) nito/Shutterstock; **p. 402**: (t) Stockbyte/Getty Images; (l) gary yim/Shutterstock; (tc) max blain/Shutterstock; (bc) javarman/Shutterstock; **p. 403**: (t) Rido/Shutterstock; (l) Alexander Chaikin/Shutterstock; (tc) Audrey Heining-Boynton; (bc) Andriy Markov/Shutterstock; **p. 404**: Pearson Education; **p. 406**: (l, c, r) Pearson Education; **pp. 410–411**: James Thew/Shutterstock; **p. 413**: Pan Xunbin/Shutterstock; **p. 414**: (top to bottom) Ng Yin Jian/Shutterstock; Lucky Business/Shutterstock; marilyn barbone/Shutterstock; Denis Pepin/Shutterstock; Narcis Parfenti/Shutterstock; Hintau Aliaksei/Shutterstock; **p. 415**: kaarsten/ Shutterstock; **p. 419**: Colin D. Young/Shutterstock; **p. 424**: (t) Jupiterimages/Getty Images/Thinkstock; (b) George Doyle/Thinkstock; **p. 428**: stocklight,2009/Used under license from Shutterstock; **p. 429**: Jupiterimages/Thinkstock; **p. 433**: Jupiterimages/Thinkstock; **p. 434**: Jupiterimages/Thinkstock; **p. 437**: absolute/Shutterstock; **p. 438**: Jupiterimages/Thinkstock; **p. 439**: (t) Stephen Coburn/ Shutterstock; (b) George Doyle/Thinkstock; **p. 441**: (t) Riser/DreamPictures; (tl) Heidi Grassley/Dorling Kindersley; (bl) Jeff Whyte/ Shutterstock; (c) Paolo Pulga/Dorling Kindersley; **p. 442**: (t) Jupiterimages, Brand X Pictures/Thinkstock; (tl) Israel Pabon/Shutterstock; (bl) Lawrence Roberg/Shutterstock; (c) Joseph/Shutterstock; **p. 443**: (t) Blend Images/Shutterstock; (lc) rj lerich/Shutterstock; (rc) rj lerich/Shutterstock; (b) Demetrio Carrasco/Rough Guides/DK Images; **p. 444**: Pearson Education; **p. 446**: (l, c, r) Pearson Education; **p. 450**: (l) Larry Lee Photography/Corbis; (r) Dale Mitchell/Shutterstock; **p. 451**: (l) Galyna Andrushko/Shutterstock; (r) Salim October / Shutterstock; (b) Jupiterimages/Brand X Pictures/Thinkstock; (tr) Stockbyte/Thinkstock; **p. 453**: (tl) Jupiterimages/Brand X Pictures/Thinkstock; (tc) Blaj Gabriel/Shutterstock; (tr) Stockbyte/Thinkstock; (b) Catalin Petolea/Shutterstock; **p. 455**: Stockbyte/Thinkstock; **p. 456**: (t) Monkey Business Images/Shutterstock; (b) Phil Date/ Shutterstock; **p. 458**: (l) Comstock/Thinkstock; (c) photobank.ch/Shutterstock; (r) Horst Petzold/Shutterstock; **p. 459**: Tony Magdaraog/ Shutterstock; **p. 461**: (l) Cedric Weber/Shutterstock; (c) Galyna Andrushko/Shutterstock; (r) Comstock/Getty Images; **p. 462**: (t) George

A48

A53

A54

ESTADOS
UNIDOS

Mexicali

Tijuana

Nogales

Ciudad
Juárez

*Río Bravo del Norte*

*Río Grande*

*Golfo de California*

*Baja California*

SIERRA MADRE OCCIDENTAL

SIERRA MADRE ORIENTAL

Nuevo Laredo

Monterrey

MÉXICO

Guadalajara

Comala

México, D.F.
⊛

Taxco

Acapulco

Oaxaca

Veracruz

*Golfo de
México*

• Mérid

*Península
de
Yucatán*

Palenque

Tikal

Bel
BE

GUATEMALA

Quetzaltenango

Guatemala

*Volcán Izalco*

Sa
Salva

EL
SALVADOR

OCÉANO

PACÍFICO

| ⊛ | Capital |
| • | Otras ciudades |
| ▲ | Volcán |
| ∴ | Ruinas |

*Islas
Galápagos
(Ec.)*

# México, América Central y el Caribe